200 Years through 200 Stories

200 Years through 200 Stories

A Tennessee Bicentennial Collection

by
Anne Klebenow

TENNESSEE
200
Bicentennial Celebration
1796 - 1996

Copyright © 1996 by The University of Tennessee, Knoxville. All Rights Reserved.
Manufactured in the United States of America.
First Edition.

The paper in this book meets the minimum requirements of the American National Standard for Permanence of Paper for Printed Library Materials. ∞ The binding materials have been chosen for strength and durability.

Library of Congress Cataloging-in-Publication Data

Klebenow, Anne
    200 years through 200 stories : a Tennessee bicentennial collection / by Anne Klebenow.
        p.   cm.
    Includes bibliographical references and index.
    ISBN 0-9642219-6-9
    1. Tennessee—History—Anecdotes. 2. Tennessee—Biography—Anecdotes. I. Title.
F436.6.K58   1996   96-47663
                                            CIP

"Casey Jones, The Brave Engineer." Used by permission of Casey Jones Home and Railroad Museum, Jackson, Tennessee

"Tom Dooley." Words and Music Collected, Adapted and Arranged by Frank Warner, John A. Lomax and Alan Lomax. From the singing of Frank Proffitt. TRO © Copyright 1947 (Renewed) 1958 (Renewed) Ludlow Music, Inc., New York, NY. Used by Permission

Excerpts from Frontier Tales of Tennessee by Louise Littleton Davis, © 1976 used by permission of the publisher, Pelican Publishing Company, Inc.

Excerpts from More Tales of Tennessee by Louise Littleton Davis, © 1978 used by permission of the publisher, Pelican Publishing Company, Inc.

Excerpts from The Governors of Tennessee by Margaret I. Phillips, © 1978 used by permission of the publisher, Pelican Publishing Company, Inc.

Illustration credits appear before index

1 9 2 1 – 1 9 9 2

Dedicated to the memory of Alex Haley,
Pulitzer Prize-winning author of *Roots*

Contents

Bicentennial Message to the People of Tennessee

Governor Don Sundquist

History, as understood by most people, is the story of our past; but the dictionary defines it first and foremost as a tale or story. Tennessee's history, like this wonderful book Anne Klebenow has worked to compile, is a collection of stories, the real life stories of real people—not just the leaders of legend, but the pioneers and builders, the soldiers and craftsmen, the artists and writers who chronicled an age, the farmers, teachers, merchants, and all of the others whose recollections have been passed down to us by their children and grandchildren. Together they form a part of the tapestry of Tennessee, a part of the rich heritage we share and celebrate during our Bicentennial year, 1996.

Wilma Dykeman, our state historian, has remarked that "A sense of one's place and history makes distant places less strange and the past more pertinent to the present." For today's Tennesseans, on the cusp of a new century, there is much to draw upon in the example of our ancestors. In gaining an understanding and appreciation of their struggles and achievements, we gain a sense of our own possibilities and of the opportunities that lie hidden in the challenges before us.

It will fall to us to write our own stories, large or small, in the soil of Tennessee. This volume offers much to guide and inspire us along the way: the grit of the early pioneers; the noble heritage of the Cherokees, whose lands these once were; the courage and patriotism of the soldiers whose fervor won for Tennessee the designation "The Volunteer State"; the statesmen who shaped our government of laws; the enormous talents who influenced the larger world of music, literature, and the arts; and the countless "ordinary" citizens whose embrace of common effort for the common good proved anything but "ordinary."

This is a collection worthy of our state and its people as we celebrate two centuries of statehood and embark hopefully on our third.

Don Sundquist

Foreword

Lamar Alexander

"It helps to talk a story," my old friend Alex Haley used to say. We were rocking on the front porch of his farmhouse near Norris. It was one of those July evenings that must have reminded Alex of when he was a boy in Henning, sitting at the foot of the porch steps of his Grandpa Palmer's house listening to his grandma rock and tell stories of their African ancestors that later became the book of *Roots*. Alex used to say, with a twinkle in his eye, that his grandma, rocking on the porch telling those stories "could knock a lightning bug out of the air at 14 feet with an accurate stream of tobacco juice!"

There were lightning bugs in the air around the farmhouse in Norris as we talked on that night in 1989. We weren't just talking; we were actually having a conversation. Part of that conversation was about how infrequently anybody really takes time to converse anymore. We surmised that the absence of front porches from modern houses might have a lot to do with it.

Richard Marius was a part of our conversation that night. Richard likes to say he grew up in Dixie Lee Junc-tion, outside Knoxville. He is a wonderful writer. His job is teaching Harvard freshmen how to write. Ten years ago, when I was Governor, I persuaded Richard to come back to the University of Tennessee each summer to lead the Governor's School for Teachers of Writing. I had addressed his students that afternoon and had invited him to drive with me to Norris for supper and an evening with Alex. (Or perhaps Alex had done that. Alex was always inviting people to his farm. One time he was on the plane coming from Atlanta to Knoxville and invited literally an entire planeload of people to come to the farm for dinner! They, of course, all accepted.)

As the lightning bug danced and the evening cooled and you could feel the dew coming, we talked about Tennessee. Richard's father had come to Loudon County from Greece. I remembered meeting him in 1978. He was working in his yard when I passed him during my walk across Tennessee. My 7th-generation ancestor, John Alexander, had arrived in Limestone, in upper East Tennessee, at the time of the Revolu-tionary War. This was about 1783—before Tennessee became a state—when a stream of Scotch-Irish immigrants began arriving in our mountains looking for land and spoiling for a fight. John Alexander eventually came to live with his nephew, Francis Alexander Ramsey, the historian, and was buried in Knoxville.

Alex's 7th-generation ancestor was Kunta Kinte, who was captured by traders in the forests of Gambia while he was cutting wood for a drum. He was thrown into the hull of a ship, brought to Maryland, and sold as a slave. Stories of Kunta Kinte and Alex's other ancestors—Chicken George, his grandmother "Queen," his father Simon—have helped to fill libraries with Americans eager to discover their own roots.

Our family first met Alex in 1980. I can still see this friendly bear of a man cradling our newborn son, Will. Alex was at that moment the world's most celebrated writer, and I was governor of his home state. *Roots* had won the Pulitzer Prize and was being translated into 37 languages. The TV version had become the most watched miniseries in history.

The Reverend Jesse Jackson used to say that Alex made our grandparents superstars. I know that when I heard Alex tell his grandma's stories, I began to pester my oldest relatives to learn what my ancestors had been doing seven generations earlier. After hearing about his grandmother, my great-grandmother's snuffbox became a prize.

Alex also taught us that these superstars came from superplaces we often take for granted—our hometowns. Once, in 1987, Alex and I took a voyage together on a German freighter from San Diego to New Zealand. It was near Christmas 1987, and we were two of only eight passengers. Every night after dinner we would climb to the second deck to admire the stars. Alex would settle against the rail and talk about his grandmother, the slave named Queen, and Queen's father, an Alabama plantation owner of Irish descent. He would practice a phrase, then polish it, all the while judging my reaction to each serving.

Alex was talking that same way as we rocked on the porch of his farmhouse that night in 1989. He had bought that farm in Norris in the middle 1980's after I had introduced him to John Rice Irwin, the proprietor of the Museum of Appalachia. Alex and I had come to the Museum as a part of our Tennessee Homecoming '86, which was to be a celebration of all of the places in Tennessee we call home. Ironically, Alex—or so it seemed to me—was then hungry for his own

roots. He embraced our Homecoming as a way of getting his own feet back on the ground. He bought some land from John Rice and spent an enormous amount of time and money creating a place that he could call home. Living at the edge of the Smokies—so different from the cotton fields of Henning where he grew up—it wasn't long before he began telling new stories about pioneer men, strong-willed women. Those of us whose families had always lived in the mountains were enormously complimented when such a great man discovered such superstars in our midst.

That was what we were talking about that night in Norris, about a book of stories about Tennessee superstars, and the most important places in the world, the places we call home. Looking ahead to 1996, I had asked Alex to do a book for the Tennessee Bicentennial. As he talked through his ideas, it seemed that one good way to do the book would be to involve the gifted teachers of writing with whom Richard Marius worked each summer at the University of Tennessee. We had all marveled at the Homecoming '86 celebrations, which had produced hundreds of stories as Tennesseans rummaged through their memories, interviewed older relatives, considered the attributes of their hometowns and what made them so special.

If you will permit me one short commercial. The 1980s were a time of increasing turbulence in everyone's lives. We were turned upside down by this new time we call the telecommunications age. Tennesseans found ways to deal with this change on our own terms. We improved our standard of living and set our sights higher. *National Geographic* in 1986 even did a cover story entitled, "Rising, Shining Tennessee." Good roads and better schools helped. But I believe that homecomings reminding ourselves of what is most important to us—our values, principles and traditions—had more to do with it than anything else.

The night of talking on Alex's porch in the summer of 1989 ended too quickly—just as did Alex's life. In September of 1991, Alex and I and my son Will sweltered in 100-degree heat at the opening game of the University of Tennessee football season. Alex was breathing heavily, I noticed, perspiring more than even a slightly overweight, 70-year-old diabetic with an impossible schedule should.

A few months later, my wife, Honey, and I were in Memphis and then Henning listening as everyone talked about Alex. I once told Alex I hoped he would speak at my funeral, because it would sound so good. I did not want to speak at his. But, it came my turn, so I said, "He was God's storyteller. We loved him so much. We just used him up."

After the services, we proceeded to Grandpa Palmer's house and stood waiting by the porch. Early daffodils decorated the yard. Every now and then, we would hear the awkward winching noises of the contraption that lowered the mahogany casket—that eventually brought the gravestone etching into view, "Find the Good and Praise It." These were the words by which Alex Haley lived his life.

I believe Alex would be pleased with this book of Tennessee stories put together by his friend Anne Klebenow, Director of the Tennessee Bicentennial Folk History Project. He would hope that they would remind us to "Find the Good and Praise It." After all, these are stories about real superstars—our ancestors—and the most important places in the world, the places we call home.

Lamar Alexander was governor, president of the University of Tennessee,
and United States secretary of education.
Parts of this foreword were taken from Governor Alexander's
article in *Parade*, "Find the Good and Praise It," January 24, 1993.

Preface

*Let us read about everything and about all people; it is the
story line, the passing scene of history, we want to capture.*

—*Alex Haley (in conversation, 1986)*

There are many ways to tell the story of Tennessee's past and present. This work embraces an approach which author Alex Haley envisioned in 1986 after Governor Lamar Alexander asked him to produce a commemorative Bicentennial book at the University of Tennessee. Prior to Mr. Haley's untimely death in 1992, I had an association of six years as his editorial assistant and director of research before being asked to carry on the project and write the book.

It was Mr. Haley's special love of human-interest stories that led to the idea of writing an anecdotal history across Tennessee—of speaking to history from a human point of view. Mr. Haley had the ability to pick from within a historical time frame an incident or situation that spoke to the life and humanity of the period—to choose stories that say a great deal about time and place and people. We all sadly miss his way with words, but I hope this book has at least captured the spirit of his dream. The people on these pages are the kinds of people whom he would have enjoyed meeting; indeed, in a couple of instances, he did meet them.

Mr. Haley firmly believed that the anecdote, or human-interest story, was a key to enjoying history and to learning. Apparently many teachers of Tennessee history agree. In order to ignite their students' interest about Tennessee's past, a number of them have said that a book of stories would be helpful as a classroom tool—historically based tales in a volume that spotlights different types of people in dramatic moments. This work, *200 Years through 200 Stories: A Tennessee Bicentennial Collection,* which is dedicated to Alex Haley's memory and his passion for individual tales, should help kindle the interest not only of students but also of the average Tennessean, who perhaps will get a better feel for the history of our state. These stories, written to be both entertaining and enlightening, are a reminder to us all of the drama and wonder of history.

Mr. Haley was intrigued by a variety of personalities: the famous, the not-so-famous, and the infamous. He loved to hear about the various anecdotes as they were being collected for this book and began to think of them as a treasury—often calling them "nuggets" from Tennessee history. The book reflects his vision to get people thinking about Tennessee history and talking about Tennessee history. It is a sampling of human experiences in all decades and in all sections of the state—a stroll through Tennessee's bygone years via a collection of stories from the lives of two hundred selected personalities, along with their family, friends, acquaintances, and even a few enemies. These vignettes are small dramas, with leading players and frequent coplayers who are themselves compelling.

Most of the people you will meet on these pages were the strong, the fearless, the wise, the compassionate, the self-sacrificing, the hard-working and the thoughtful; indeed superheroes—the true pillars of society, who had to deal with the sneaky, the greedy, the thieving, the conniving, and the murderous. There are those who promoted life and improved it (the ones we enjoy talking about) and a sprinkling of those who would take from life and destroy it (the ones we enjoy best when true justice found them out). All of the people featured in this book were important to their time or represent a facet of Tennessee society and culture. Often their stories correspond to the major events of the era in which they lived, from the earliest pioneering days through the twentieth century. Some accounts highlight those who had a major impact on the future course of history; others simply tell us about a place and a time.

The state always has been a crossroads, with people and ideas moving into and out of its borders. Even before Tennessee's boundaries had been drawn, exciting personalities from other regions roamed the countryside influencing its social, political, military, and economic development. Many of these stories focus on those born and raised on Tennessee soil. Other stories involve those who were born elsewhere (like Tennessee's three United States presidents were) but who made Tennessee their home. Yet other stories center on those who journeyed here temporarily, either influencing the development of the state or being affected forever by their experiences in Tennessee.

The book is divided into four major time frames so that the reader can feel the progression of time but not be overwhelmed by it. Personalities and tales unfold in their respective eras in a chronological fashion. First there is the frontier period a few years before white settlement began on Indian homelands,

setting the stage for statehood and the early years. Next comes the Civil War, the great watershed of all American history, which affected Tennessee and Tennesseans as profoundly as any other state. It was not just another war—and its significance transcends its four-year duration. Because the Civil War is the defining event in southern history, and especially in Tennessee, it has been given enough space to cast light on its importance and its continuing fascination to the populace. With the end of that war, the Reconstruction-New South period follows, carrying the reader through the attempted rebuilding of shattered lives and communities and up to the doorstep of World War I. Finally, the twentieth century unveils a mixture of modern technological advances, major new entertainment forms, cultural and societal debates, and foreign wars to further shape the lives of everyday citizens.

Each time frame begins with a historical essay, giving an overview of pivotal events and trends that affected those who paraded across the stage of history. Dr. Wayne Moore, an archivist from the Tennessee State Library and Archives in Nashville, helped prepare these overview essays with the resources of the archives and his own years of knowledge as a Tennessee historian.

It was not possible to deal in depth with every subject or every person mentioned on these pages or to do justice to all facets of Tennessee history. The book is an attempt to strike a reasonable balance within the limitations of its two hundred selections. There are untold numbers of events and people that could not be mentioned in the space given, but they too await discovery by readers in search of exciting stories and personalities.

The information for these vignettes was collected as part of a multiyear effort established at the university. Originally, Mr. Haley intended to ask people statewide for family stories, planning to obtain such stories in a campaign through the news media. A series of taped interviews and research would follow. It soon became apparent that the resources needed to conduct this type of campaign, and the necessary follow-up with all individuals, were too immense. In addition, early publicity generated stories that did not touch on more than one or two historical events and did not portray the diversity of the state's culture and people. For this Bicentennial book, we wanted a variety of topics and personalities to span two hundred-plus years as part of the United States. Fortunately, the wealth of available written material provided the depth and breadth needed. Scholars and Tennessee history writers had been collecting valuable stories and information for years, but most of it had escaped the general reading public. It was to this body of material that we turned.

Before Mr. Haley died on February 10, 1992, he maintained a relentless worldwide schedule of speechmaking, often referring to the Bicentennial project in those speeches and reminding his listeners how important it is to preserve family stories. Although he did not personally oversee the research of this project, he maintained an active interest in it as University of Tennessee graduate students proceeded to obtain more than two thousand anecdotes by reading through primary and secondary sources which included books, magazines, newspapers, diaries, and quarterlies/journals. Occasionally the researchers and I were able to conduct personal interviews to obtain a story or add to an existing one. Only true accounts were collected (as true as history can remember in the lives of real people). There were no predetermined selections, except for presidents and vice presidents and others whose names are nationally known and forever associated with the state. Generally, a net was cast statewide to see whose names surfaced as historically significant to a time frame and place. Assigning each graduate student a section of the state guaranteed a balance of stories from border to border. The identities of a variety of personalities quickly unfolded. County historians and librarians across Tennessee periodically assisted in identifying some of the fascinating individuals prominent to their locales.

Entering all anecdotes into a computer database, I cataloged them according to parts of the state, the counties mentioned, time frame, general topic, and tone of the story (humorous, sad, informational). Because a main criterion was whether or not the reader would find the tales interesting, each sketch had to have a distinctive story line. Other criteria then entered the picture: historical significance, the era in which the story took place, plus a need-to-use basis (such as the need to add humor in the midst of more serious topics), and especially geographic location. Ultimately, I converted the anecdotes into more-fully developed stories, adding generalized information

from many other sources to establish a broad walk through the decades of Tennessee history.

A concerted effort was made to touch base in all Tennessee counties as well as to include men and women from different social classes and ethnic groups. The narratives were also designed to illuminate the evolving character of Tennessee's culture over the past two hundred years in such areas as education, agriculture, religion, medicine, art and literature, entertainment, business, the military, science and technology, sports, politics, and crime. But in the final analysis, each story had to be compelling.

Here then are some of the interesting stories that developed. Combined, they cover all parts of Tennessee. While these are not biographies, there is enough biographical information in each story to anchor main individuals in a reader's mind and answer basic questions that might arise about these lives. For those readers who prefer not to start at the beginning or for those who like their history in small doses, the book lends itself to unsystematic reading. Looking at the last page first or reading in spurts still has its rewards. Whether one is reading randomly or from cover to cover, the stories are unpredictable and often full of surprises. Collectively or individually, they serve as a springboard for further knowledge, revealing just enough history to stimulate the reader's desire to know even more about Tennessee and the people associated with its past. While extensive research has gone into this book, it is intended for pleasure reading and is not an academic text. Therefore, to avoid interrupting the flow of the stories with excessive documentation, citations for quotes are given in a separate "Notes" section at the end of the book. In order to point the reader toward additional information, a complete guide to the primary and secondary sources used for this book is also provided.

The number of vignettes chosen (two hundred) obviously is in honor of Tennessee's Bicentennial. I am grateful to the Tennessee Bicentennial Commission for selecting this work as an important contribution to the state's two hundredth birthday celebration by awarding it the official Bicentennial logo.

Acknowledgments

The road for such a vast project was paved with incredible dedication and enthusiasm from the University of Tennessee, which provided an equipped office; the service of graduate students and other technical assistance needed to help collect and assimilate information; and importantly, administrators who always had warm words of encouragement and a pat on the back. They never took their eyes off the valuable goal: giving the people of Tennessee a special product for the 1996 Bicentennial.

The first days of setting up the office and getting the project in motion were made easy with the help of Senior Vice President Homer Fisher, then-Chancellor Jack Reese, and Provost Hardy Liston. When Lamar Alexander later became president of the University of Tennessee, he continued to be as supportive as ever. As time went on, administrators changed, but the level of support and warmth did not. Equally dedicated to the Bicentennial and to the people of Tennessee was Governor Alexander's university successor, President Joe Johnson. President Johnson personally stayed tuned to the progress of the project and became involved in any way that might facilitate its completion. When Chancellor William Snyder learned that many teachers of state history were looking forward to the book, his spontaneous comment was, "That is wonderful, because we at the university are here to help secondary education all we can." His executive assistant, Marianne Woodside, became a champion of the project and remained so. My special thanks go also to Betsey Creekmore, the university's associate vice chancellor of space and facilities management, who has been an advocate of the book in many ways and whose own work on history projects is renowned and respected.

With these leaders, there were also those specializing in history at the University of Tennessee who understood that such an undertaking must be a "nice mix of traditional and intimate history." Such were the sentiments of Bruce Wheeler, a history professor who directed graduate students to this project, resulting in the hiring of dedicated people who labored part time in research and fact checking.

I am particularly indebted to archivist Wayne Moore at the Tennessee State Library and Archives, a specialist in Tennessee history, for his constant support and enthusiasm. He agreed to be a consultant to the book at a time when he was producing a section of state history for the legislative *Blue Book*, and he cheerfully read and reread the manuscript, offering many valuable suggestions.

Because Mr. Haley had heard about such things as "computer crashes," he worried somewhat about using a computer to store our information. But Stan Pinkleton, a computer professional with the University of Tennessee, put Mr. Haley's mind (and mine) at ease over lunch one day in Norris, Tennessee. He and the Office of Administrative Computing became allies against dreaded computer eccentricities.

One cannot praise highly enough the three major historical societies of Tennessee for the help they have provided. I truly appreciate their blanket permission to use information and quotes from any or all of their various publications. The East Tennessee Historical Society and West Tennessee Historical Society have a proud tradition of service. The Tennessee Historical Society itself, which makes its home in the War Memorial Building, Nashville, publishes the *Tennessee Historical Quarterly* and has a unique history of its own, dating to the early nineteenth century. Its vast collection is just as accessible to every citizen in Tennessee as it has been to this Bicentennial project.

At intervals during the writing process, there were volunteer readers who were extremely helpful. I took their reactions to the stories as a barometer of public taste and interest level. In this regard, I am especially grateful to both Mr. Pinkleton and his wife, Doris, a schoolteacher who tested some of the stories on her students—and with positive results; to Charles Moffat, a professor of history at Carson-Newman College, Jefferson City, Tennessee; to Wayne Cutler, director of the James K. Polk papers at the Tennessee Presidents' Trust, University of Tennessee Knoxville; to Walter Pulliam, Knoxville, member of the Tennessee Historical Commission and a noted author of regional historical works; and to Sally Bullard in the University of Tennessee's computer and administrative systems, Knoxville.

Even with such caring and sensitive people reading the stories, making the final selections was difficult, because each personality from times past seemed like a newfound friend.

Helping me find these "newfound friends" were the wonderful part-time graduate students and research technicians, all of whom I consider friends as well. The university provided three such assistants at any one time. Some were able to work only one semester, others remained longer. (They are listed here according to length of time.) Helping in the stages of library and archival research were John Walter, Walter Lynn Bates, Laura A. Owings Demko, William E. Buchanan, Steven M. Wilson, Connie Lee Lester, Elizabeth Clare "Beth" Henson Tudan, Jennifer E. Brooks, Patricia Brake Howard, William G. "Jerry" McCaskill Jr., Louis Burklow, and William Todd Groce. Those who helped in continual fact checking and proofreading were Beth Vanlandingham, Leonard Butts, Randy L. Moore, Joe L. Rosson, Kathy Byrd, Rhetta A. Russell, and J. Anthony Brown.

I want to extend my heartfelt appreciation to Tennessee's Bicentennial governor, Don Sundquist, for writing a special message to the people of Tennessee, and to the former governor, Lamar Alexander, for writing the foreword.

Tennessee Bicentennial Commission members deserve accolades from all Tennesseans for the work they have done to commemorate this milestone year in Tennessee history. They are Martha Ingram, chairperson; Steve Adams, Joan Ashe, Andy Bennett, Johnny Cash, Irby Cooper, Riley Darnell, former Governor Winfield Dunn, Jim Epps, Amon Carter Evans, Joe Fowlkes, John P. Franklin Sr., Pam Garrett, H. Carey Hanlin, Thelma Harper, Joyce Hassell, Douglas Henry, Alfred D. Hill, John M. Jones Sr., Keith Jordan, Kay Leibowitz, Richard Lewis, Mary Jane McWherter, Jimmy Naifeh, Bill Peeler, Mary Pruitt, Jeanette Rudy, William Snodgrass, Tennessee State Historian Wilma Dykeman, Jesse H. Turner Jr., Virginia "Miss Jenny" Vaughan, Bill Whitson, Lieutenant Governor John Wilder, and Marcelle Wilder. Spearheading work with the commission was the staff of the nonprofit Tennessee 200, Inc., where Kelly L. Tolson was executive director.

My special personal gratitude also goes to the following people: Carolyn Brackett and J. Bucy at Tennessee 200, Inc., Nashville; Ann Toplovich, executive director of the Tennessee Historical Society, and Susan Gordon, the society's managing editor of the *Tennessee Historical Quarterly*, Nashville; Kent Whitworth, executive director of the East Tennessee Historical Society, Knoxville; Douglas W. Cupples, president, West Tennessee Historical Society through the Oral History Research Department, University of Memphis; Stephen D. Cox, Tennessee State Museum, Nashville; Beth Howse, Fisk University Special Collections, Nashville; Norma Myers, director of the Archives of Appalachia, in addition to archives librarian Georgia Greer and archives public-service director Ned Irwin, East Tennessee State University, Johnson City; University of Tennessee librarian Felicia Felder-Hoehne and to all other librarians throughout Tennessee who were (and are) always eager to help locate the events and people of history; Larry Daughtrey, *The Tennessean*, Nashville; author Thelma Present, Knoxville; Ralph Perrey, assistant to Governor Don Sundquist, Nashville; Sherry Smith, Judy Dooley, and Monica Bennett, all of whom (joyfully, thank goodness) helped facilitate paperwork at the University of Tennessee; and to my mother, Eileen Klebenow, whose encouragement was never-ending and whose preservation of our own family history in upper East Tennessee was an inspiration.

And finally to Alex Haley himself. I believe the best legacy to his memory would be for all of us to preserve the experiences of our elders or other family members. By conducting taped or written interviews and recording the never-ending story of Tennessee, we can leave a priceless gift to our families, to our communities—to all of those who come after us.

Anne Klebenow
1996

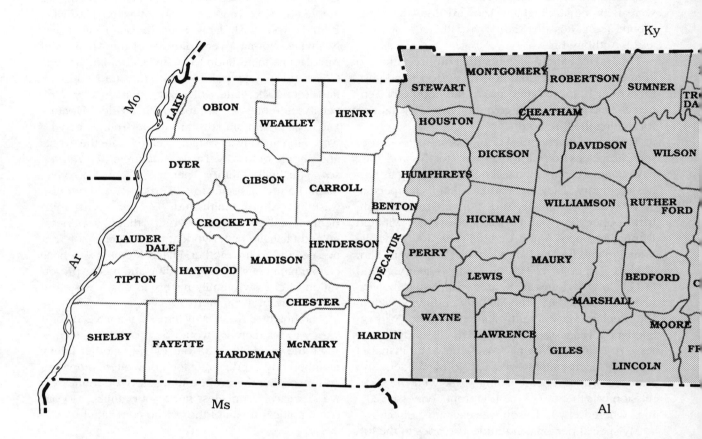

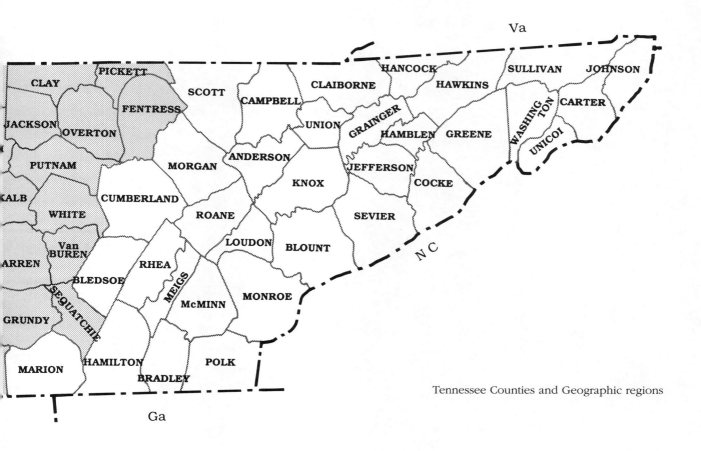

Tennessee Counties and Geographic regions

Va

NC

Ga

Section One

Frontier to Secession

Historical Background
Frontier to Secession

Broad rivers, unlimited forests, rolling grasslands, fertile soil, and a vast array of wildlife lured the early pioneers away from the original thirteen colonies to pursue the incredible natural wonders of the Tennessee country. Beginning in the 1750s and 1760s, the rich land beckoned irresistibly, first to traders and hunters and then to farmers. Upper East Tennessee, in fact, became America's first postcolonial frontier. It was a natural avenue for westward migration from the time of the very first homestead, believed to have been established in 1769.

The future state stretched five hundred miles from the border of the original colonies to the Mississippi River—a perfect east-west path. Restless immigrants—who came primarily from Virginia, North Carolina, and South Carolina—did not stay long in one place, but continued to seek new frontiers of unbroken land and, in some cases, distance from the injustices they had experienced in older colonies. Tennessee eventually became the seedbed for the settlement of many other states.

But the craving for this majestic region caused people to move where there was resentment and ultimate danger. Steeped in centuries of their own culture, several native Indian tribes inhabited or hunted this vast place which would become Tennessee. On East Tennessee soil lived the Cherokee, whose Tanasi village reportedly gave the state its name. The Chickasaw owned and hunted West Tennessee and kept their claims there until 1818—perhaps living only on the edge of the tract, a bluff overlooking the Mississippi River which would become Memphis. Between the Chickasaw in the West and the Cherokee in the East lay a far-reaching hunting ground, which many tribes claimed and occasionally fought over. Venturing into this area (future Middle Tennessee and Kentucky) on seasonal hunting excursions were tribes who lived in other regions of the Southeast, such as the Creek in northern Alabama territory and the Choctaws in Mississippi territory. The confrontations between these tribes were so severe that one leading Cherokee rebel warned white settlers that they were getting into "a dark and bloody ground."

English and German traders had originally trekked over the mountains to barter with the natives for animal skins. The eagerness of white people to settle this territory increased with every trip over the Allegheny and Appalachian Mountains by Long Hunters. These men, roaming a year or more at a time hunting wild game, returned to their homes with tales of the lush wilderness and the bounty of its wildlife.

Next came the Scots-Irish, the hardy backcountry families who were accustomed to living on the western fringe of the nation's original colonies. Ever since the end of the French and Indian War in 1763, these settlers had felt secure enough to leave the relative safety of their older colonies and look for new homes in the Tennessee country. They often brought second- or third-generation African descendants with them as slaves.

These European, African, and Indian cultures came together in the Tennessee wilderness and blended into something new and distinctly American. From their different backgrounds, each group fell under the influence of the others—and all of them were molded by the forces of nature.

Land companies, which employed Long Hunters to guide surveying teams, laid the groundwork for future settlement. The earliest pioneers, who made their homes in upper East Tennessee, became known as the Overmountain Men. They took up the ways of the early Cherokees, quickly learning the hunting and other woodsman skills that were necessary for survival. But as the newcomers' ranks swelled and their system of farming spread, the Indians began to adopt some of the settlers' ways. The tribes, who once had lived in harmony with the wilderness, began to welcome the blankets, guns, farm animals, whiskey, and other items that the traders brought to them. Although the trappings of civilization seemed to make their lives better, the new conveniences came at a high price. The Indians gave up many skills that had made them self-sufficient; they also began to relinquish their rich culture, their land, their health, and often their lives.

Settlers moved so aggressively into the ancient lands of powerful tribes that outbreaks of violence were inevitable. These tribes each had a formidable warrior class, long accustomed to driving intruders from their domain. Such intruders had included earlier Europeans who came directly from England,

Spain, and France and tried to occupy the land. When the Americans came, many natives were willing at first to share their homeland and hunting grounds, but as the number of pioneers grew, the Indians began fiercely to resist any further encroachment. One of the defining characteristics of early Tennessee was a long period of Indian warfare. The region probably suffered longer than any of the settled states, as hostilities plagued the countryside from 1756 through 1814. This constant conflict shaped many attitudes, often unforgiving, in men like Andrew Jackson.

The American Revolution, between 1775 and 1781, was also part of the continuing fight to gain access to the back country of future Tennessee. The British, in keeping with old agreements between England and native tribes, had denied the colonists the right to settle on Indian homelands. Tennessee, however, was a frontier ready to happen. When the British threatened upper East Tennessee, the Overmountain Men of that region took up arms and gave America one of its first major victories of the Revolution, in the 1780 Battle of Kings Mountain (South Carolina). Ultimately, England's defeat in that war broke a major barrier to westward settlement. New settlers poured into the Tennessee territory. Since future Tennessee was then the western half of North Carolina, many people received North Carolina land grants for wartime service.

In 1790, the federal government designated this region as the Territory of the United States South of the River Ohio, with William Blount as territorial governor and superintendent of Indian affairs (the region's title was shortened to the "Southwest Territory"). Indian dangers, however, had not been eliminated. For a while, the Indians held the upper hand, and white settlers ventured westward only at considerable peril. Those who tried to establish a foothold deep within Tennessee were frequently ambushed and robbed by Indian warriors, some of whom traveled great distances from their own villages to conduct raids. After 1794, the pioneer-militia force in what would soon become Tennessee began to outweigh the tribal forces.

In 1796, the lands over which natives and pioneers had fought for decades became the sixteenth state in the union. A convention of delegates (mostly East Tennesseans) met in downtown Knoxville to draft a state constitution. Hammering out the details, they soon asked Congress for admission to the union. Upon congressional approval, President George Washington declared Tennessee a state on June 1, 1796. Knoxville became the state's first capital and remained so for nearly a quarter of a century.

Tennessee's varied landscape and mobile people in time produced three distinct societies. The isolated, small mountain-and-valley communities of East Tennessee, which had been settled first, remained a place for small, independent farmers. Fueled by a lust for even richer soil and the bluegrass area, many restless pioneers, some bringing slaves with them, carved out the family farms of Middle Tennessee. A quarter-century after the state was founded, West Tennessee was finally opened for settlement. A rush of homesteading there led to larger slaveholding plantations. Because of the cultural and geographic diversity of these three sections, representatives often clashed with one another, establishing an uneasy coexistence within the confines of a single state government.

By the time of the last Indian war (the Creek War, from 1812 to 1814), the natives were heavily outnumbered, outgunned, and effectively subdued. However, the problems of land rights had to be resolved before the young state could grow. Relations between the invading settlers and the Indians consisted primarily of endless negotiations over access to and ownership of the land. Controversy sprang from every treaty, every land purchase by the United States. In 1838, President Andrew Jackson engineered the Cherokees' removal from their ancient homeland to Oklahoma. This journey became known as the Trail of Tears. Ultimately, the tragedy of the Indians in Tennessee was that they either lived or hunted in territory that lay in the path of United States expansion.

Early Tennesseans' search for ever-better land dominated both their politics and economic prospects. Buying and selling land was the principal business of the area—and, in some places, the only business. The quest for fresh, undisturbed lands shaped an expansionist outlook which evolved into a philosophy of Manifest Destiny—the idea that Americans had a divine right to spread out across the continent. This campaign theme won the presidency for Tennessean James K. Polk.

Tennesseans figured prominently in the young nation's political leadership and the manifestation of democratic ideas. Perhaps because of the great distance from the nation's "civilized" settlements in the original colonies, early Tennesseans were the first

Americans to live under an elected government created by their own hands. Removed from the reach of authority, the independent pioneers continuously experimented with self-government. They created the Watauga Association (predating the Declaration of Independence), which guided East Tennessee; the Cumberland Compact of Middle Tennessee; and the State of Franklin, which attempted in vain to break away from North Carolina and become the nation's fourteenth state.

Formidable frontier leaders such as John Sevier, James Robertson, Andrew Jackson, Sam Houston, David Crockett, and many others had a monumental impact not only on Tennessee but also on the surrounding territories and the nation. As the United States expanded beyond its original thirteen colonies, Tennessee supplied leadership that helped to create a vibrant western democracy. In addition to sending Jackson and Polk to the White House, frontier Tennessee also sent numerous influential statesmen to Congress and to European courts to serve as ambassadors. Tennesseans became speakers of the United States House of Representatives, presidential cabinet officials, and territorial governors in newly developing areas. Foremost among them was Andrew Jackson, an imposing figure whose political party transformed American politics and whose policies and actions revolutionized the presidency. The Jacksonian era dominated the nation for two decades. Early nineteenth-century Americans defined their politics according to where they stood on Jackson, and even his opponents claimed to be the true Jacksonian Democrats.

Tennessee was an essential arena in the winning of the Old Southwest—that region bounded by the Mississippi and Ohio rivers, the Gulf of Mexico, and the Appalachian Mountains. The struggle for the entire southern frontier was won (or lost, as in the case of the native Indian tribes) largely in Tennessee.

From statehood to the Civil War, Tennessee loomed as large as any state in national affairs, leading not only on the battlefields and in the halls of power but also in economic achievement. The state led the nation in the production of key farm commodities and served as the breadbasket for the Deep South. Because a flood of settlers kept a steady pace across Tennessee with the opening of former Indian lands, the population by 1840 ranked fourth among all states. Nashville and Memphis especially developed into important commercial centers for the river-borne trade, and, later, for national railroad traffic.

Tennessee's contributions to the nation were as remarkable in the military realm as in the political. Beginning with the 1780 Battle of Kings Mountain, which helped turn the tide of the Revolutionary War, Tennessee soldiers became central to major American conflicts. During the War of 1812, Tennessee commanders leading their volunteer forces drove belligerent Creek Indians, the British, and the Spanish from the nation's southern borders. Jackson's surprising 1815 victory at New Orleans secured American control of the Mississippi River and the Louisiana Purchase. His campaigns against the southern tribes opened up Alabama, Mississippi, Florida, and West Tennessee. The colonization of Texas was accomplished in large part by Tennesseans; it culminated in the Texas Revolution, in which David Crockett and Sam Houston fought their way into immortality, Crockett at the Alamo and Houston at San Jacinto.

President Polk crowned the era of territorial expansion by going to war with Mexico, a conflict that resulted in the annexation of what would be one-fourth of the continental United States. The zealous enlistment of Tennesseans to fight in both the War of 1812 and the 1846 Mexican War earned for Tennessee its nickname, "the Volunteer State." Seen in this light, the pivotal role played by Tennesseans in the upcoming Civil War would be the continuation of a long and illustrious fighting tradition. The state's powerful militia would form the nucleus of one of the Confederacy's two greatest armies.

Tennessee's progress from a rough-hewn, embattled frontier to the capital of Jacksonian democracy spanned the coming-of-age years of America itself. Tennesseans loved to tell stories about the state's early history, from the earliest homesteaders' struggle for survival through the golden age of Tennessee politics and military prowess. These stories depict larger-than-life personalities as well as lesser-known players in Tennessee's life: men and women, warriors and peacemakers, hunters and farmers, preachers and outlaws, statesmen and tribesmen. Here are some of those stories, tales as rich and varied as the land itself.

Historical background essay written in collaboration with Dr. Wayne Moore, archivist, Tennessee State Library and Archives.

1

Little Carpenter (Attakullakulla)

Finding More Foes Than Friends
for the Cherokee Nation

In September 1730, seven Cherokees were sitting in their guest quarters in London, England, reeling in disbelief at a British document they had naively signed. The youngest and smallest member of the group was Attakullakulla, the Little Carpenter. He and his comrades had earlier placed their marks on what they thought were simply "Articles of Friendship and Commerce" between England and the Cherokee nation. But another truth surfaced when the Cherokees ordered their interpreter to translate the document in the privacy of their room on Kingstreet. The treaty, they learned, also gave King George II sovereignty over all Cherokee land.

Quickly calling a council meeting among themselves, the Cherokees debated what to do. To nullify any such claim, they first thought about killing the messenger (their interpreter) and then the traveling spokesman (their oldest member) who had made a speech affirming the treaty. Finally deciding against such a severe strategy, the group elected to return home and leave the matter to tribal elders.

The document was eventually declared invalid, but Little Carpenter learned much from the experience. He became more seasoned in the art of negotiations. Even his name would take on new meaning with the Cherokees, who soon learned that he was a carpenter of diplomacy, for "he could make every joint and notch in a controversy fit smoothly." He made his reputation in trying to achieve more lucrative trade agreements with colonists and in negotiating peace with the British who, along with the French, had invaded North America. To prove his loyalty to England, Little Carpenter often led raiding parties against the French or their allies.

Born sometime after 1700 on Sevier's Island in the French Broad River, Little Carpenter grew up in the Overhill towns located along the banks of the Little Tennessee and Hiwassee rivers. Despite being from a family of robust men, he was described in *Bartram's Travels* as "remarkably small, and slender and [of]

delicate frame." From his youth, he was a respected member of the Cherokee nation.

The 1730 trip to England, highlighted by the pomp and grandeur of the king's court, was the first time any member of the Cherokee nation had visited that country. The Cherokees had traveled there with Sir Alexander Cuming, an English explorer known for his fanciful reports of the New World and the Indians who lived there. He once attended a tribal counsel, talked the Cherokees into paying homage to King George, and bestowed the title "Emperor" on the chief Moytoy. Cuming's account of trips across the Appalachians marked the first use of the word "Tennessee," which he applied to a major Cherokee town in the future Monroe County. Intent on bolstering his credibility with the king for converting loyal new subjects, Cuming invited prominent Cherokees to England to verify his stories about the Overhill country which would later become East Tennessee. He also hoped that the natives would pay homage to the king in person.

Throughout London, the Cherokees created a sensation. They were immortalized in a group painting ordered by an English duke, treated to royal dinners, taken to the theater, and shown sights of interest. These included a "fashionable spa," a trip into Saint James Park, and a viewing of the Crown Jewels of England. When invited to watch a ceremonial knighthood, the Cherokees were given the royal privilege of kissing King George's hand. Then they were given garments laced with gold.

Little Carpenter was so shy when the curious stared at him that he chose to go incognito to public places. As reported years later in the August 1762 issue of *The Court Magazine,* his disguise also allowed him to better observe the British people: "'They are welcome,' said he to the interpreter, 'to look upon me as a strange creature. They see but one, and in return they give me an opportunity to look upon thousands.'" Having learned some English, Little Carpenter in embarking "took . . . the last person's hand that met his, which happened to be an old Fisher Woman's; when wringing it hard, with tears in his eyes, he repeated . . . 'I tank you, I tank you, I tank you all.'"

Upon his return to the Overhill Cherokee villages, he soon rose to the rank of tribal leader and, in 1736, refused to join the French in their war against the British in North America. Captured in 1740 by the French,

Little Carpenter became familiar with their ways during his eight years as a well-treated prisoner.

When Little Carpenter gained greater power among his people, he sought to break the monopoly of trade enjoyed by South Carolinians who cheated the Cherokees, to preserve the independence of the Cherokee nation and to keep peace with what he realized was the overwhelming presence and power of the English colonists. To do so, he walked a diplomatic tightrope, always dallying with groups that despised one another and frequently reversing his position, sometimes causing all sides to consider him self-serving. But his main goal was to obtain the best deal he could for the Cherokee nation.

In 1756, Little Carpenter convinced the British to build Fort Loudoun on the Tennessee River (about thirty miles from the future Knoxville) in order to protect Cherokee women and children from pro-French Indian tribes. It was here that the first English-speaking people—soldiers, traders, and their families—actually lived in Tennessee.

At the same time, Little Carpenter's tribal rival, the war chief Oconostota, decided to join the French in making war on the British. The result was a bloody wave of violence across the southern frontier. The two chiefs, who on the trip to England had been comrades, faced each other on opposite sides of the wall at Fort Loudoun. Oconostota's five-month siege of the fort was successful, and many of the surrendering British (to whom Little Carpenter had smuggled food) were later killed en route to the East Coast by renegade Indians.

Removed from power during this 1761 siege, Little Carpenter helped surviving prisoners return to pro-British forces in the East and tried to end the war. For his efforts, he received numerous British gifts, which he proudly displayed to show that the English were the real friends of the Cherokees. Meanwhile, Oconostota received nothing from the French but an army commission and an officer's sword. After Oconostota's warfare caused the British to destroy fifteen Cherokee towns, Little Carpenter managed to arrange a peace treaty, and his nation returned him to power. As the tribe's peacemaker, he worked with the still-powerful Oconostota in future dealings with British colonists.

By 1772, a crisis was looming. White settlers continued to invade Cherokee land, forcing Little Carpenter to choose a plan of action. Because the only viable alternative seemed to be to lease the land, he helped negotiate a land lease to the upper East Tennessee pioneers of the Watauga Association, but he did so unhappily. According to speculations by some historians, Little Carpenter may have believed he could avoid trouble by leasing land that settlers probably would take anyway. The same reasoning possibly led him in 1775 to assist in a massive land sale of twenty million acres, giving over the greater part of present-day Middle Tennessee and Kentucky to the North Carolina land speculator Richard Henderson (the Transylvania Purchase). The door was now open wide to the western frontier.

From the time he reassumed power, Little Carpenter kept the peace on behalf of the Cherokees for at least twenty years until his death, which is believed to have been in 1780. Two things would eventually dismantle this truce that Little Carpenter had painstakingly built. The first was the rebellion of his own son, Dragging Canoe, who did battle with a new wave of settlers invading Cherokee land. The second was a full-scale war—the American Revolution—which pitted England and her Indian allies against the colonists.

2

Nancy Ward
(Nan-ye-hi)

The Beloved Woman of the Cherokees

When warring Cherokee factions in East Tennessee captured white settler Lydia Bean in 1776 and were ready to burn her at the stake, Nancy Ward stepped to the execution mound and cut her loose. Nancy, born Nan-ye-hi, declared that as long as she was the Beloved Woman of the Cherokee, no other woman would be burned alive. This was not the first or last time that the Cherokees' most powerful woman would save the lives of many first settlers in Tennessee.

Lydia Bean was the wife of William Bean, a well-known gunsmith and Tennessee's first (documented) permanent white settler. The Beans lived along the Watauga River at the mouth of Boone's Creek. Lydia, who reportedly had not responded to the warning of an impending Indian attack, was captured in her home.

Her neighbors, meanwhile, had rushed to the safety of the nearest stockade, Fort Watauga. Located in up-

Nancy Ward, a friend to the early settlers.

After her rescue, Lydia traveled as Nancy's guest to Chota and demonstrated many white customs, including the making of butter and cheese. Nancy later purchased cows, which she called "white man's buffalo," and introduced dairying to her people.

Described as a majestic woman of courage and kindness who became legendary in trying to promote harmony, Nancy had been a heroic figure to her people since a 1755 battle with another tribe. At that time, she grabbed the rifle of her fatally shot husband, Kingfisher, and took up the fight. Having accompanied him to the Battle of Taliwa near Canton, Georgia, Nancy lay "behind a log, chewing lead bullets" to make his weapon even deadlier. Suddenly she saw her husband fall. Her instantaneous bravery in the onslaught inspired her tribesmen, who won a victory and proclaimed her Aqi-qa-u-e, meaning "Beloved Woman of the Cherokee," an official tribal title. Tribal members believed that the Great Being spoke to them through the Beloved Woman, and Nancy thus assumed a place on the Council of Chiefs, serving as head of the Women's Council. She was greatly influenced by her uncle, the peace-loving Chief Attakullakulla ("Little Carpenter"). She also shared his dilemma in obtaining the best deals with colonists while also appeasing British and French soldiers, and the dilemma caused a misunderstanding with some Cherokees about her motives.

In the late 1750s, she married frontier trader Bryant Ward. From this union she became Nancy Ward and gave birth to a daughter. Her husband stayed with the Cherokees for several years but later returned to his own family in South Carolina, where Nancy would later visit him.

The Revolutionary War brought new problems to the frontier during late 1780 through the summer of 1781. Nancy again warned the East Tennesseans of a major Indian attack planned for Watauga. This assault was prompted by the British, who had made allies among the Cherokees. Upon hearing the warning, Fort Watauga's John Sevier and his Overmountain Men, already battling the British on other fronts, rushed to "intercept" the raiding party and destroyed many Cherokee towns in the process, including Nancy's beloved Chota.

She afterwards joined her brethren in a peace-treaty session, the first time in Cherokee history that a woman had been involved in treaty negotiations. Nancy Ward acted as the chief spokesperson and declared:

per East Tennessee at present-day Elizabethton, the fort was a refuge for homesteaders in the outlying areas during Indian assaults. Giving the call to arms around the countryside was Isaac Thomas, also a captive of the Indians until set free by Nancy Ward so that he might give advance warning to the fort and surrounding cabins. Pioneers then fought off a two-week siege by Dragging Canoe, Nancy's first cousin, and his many tribal supporters.

The state's first white settlers had been putting down roots on Cherokee homeland across the East Tennessee region. The invasion included an area near the Cherokee capital at Chota (or Chote), which was located on the Little Tennessee River in present-day Loudon County. To stop the pioneers, Dragging Canoe was willing to spill blood, despite the willingness of Nancy and other peace-loving Cherokees to lease portions of ancient tribal lands to prevent ill will. Dragging Canoe continued to torment the settlers with his private war, rallying his makeshift band of warriors called "Chickamaugans," who were renegades from many tribal nations. Setting up strongholds near Chattanooga on Chickamauga Creek, Dragging Canoe welcomed into his fold rebellious Cherokees, Creeks, British sympathizers, and any others who desired to wage war against the colonists.

You know that women are always looked upon as nothing; but we are your mothers; you are our sons. OUR CRY IS ALL FOR PEACE; let it continue. This peace must last forever. Let your women's sons be ours; our sons be yours. Let your women hear our words.

Nancy Ward and the Cherokees rebuilt Chota, and when she reached middle age there, she settled into a quieter life away from politics. She lived inconspicuously for thirty years, bestowing her love on grandchildren and homeless orphans. (Her son and daughter by Kingfisher had married white settlers; her daughter by Ward was the wife of a federal Indian agent, General Joseph Martin, one of the original Overmountain Men of upper East Tennessee.)

As white migration increased, the Cherokees continued to be as accommodating as possible while also retaining their sovereignty. The United States, meanwhile, "officially" continued to forbid white settlement on Indian lands, as in the case of Scots-Irish immigrant William Stewart, who settled with his family on Looney's Creek in future Marion County. After living peacefully in the Cherokees' shadow for many years, the Stewarts were forcibly removed in 1811 by United States soldiers who burned their house and destroyed their crops. The family simply journeyed north along the Sequatchie Valley to lands already relinquished by the Cherokees, becoming some of the earliest settlers of Bledsoe (future Sequatchie) County.

In 1819, the Cherokee nation, against Nancy Ward's advice, ceded to the settlers even more land, including Chota. Nancy, now nearing eighty, was forced to move. She relocated to present-day Polk County near Benton, where she died a year or two later.

Even the drama of Nancy Ward's last moments passed into history. Writer Ben Harris McClary claimed:

> When she died, so her great-grandson reported in sworn testimony, a light rose from her body, fluttered like a bird around the room, and finally flew out the door. It was watched by the startled people in attendance until it disappeared, moving in the direction of Chote. Thus Nancy Ward passed from life into legend.

3

William Cocke

*An American—And a Tennessean—
In the Making*

William Cocke laughed at suggestions that he could throw a knife from a hundred paces and slice the leaf off a tree. "I don't reckon I could throw a knife accurately more than seventy to eighty paces," he surmised.

Cocke may have set limits on his accomplishments, but some friends did not. They considered him the ultimate frontiersman. Many peers called him "the Daniel Boone of the Cumberland." Cocke's friends, however, called Boone "the Bill Cocke of Kentucky." The two knew each other well. Cocke came to the Holston Valley in 1774 and helped Boone found the colony of Transylvania in modern Kentucky. A year later, Cocke served in the House of Delegates for Transylvania.

Utterly self-sufficient, Cocke lived alone in a homemade cabin in the upper East Tennessee woods, shot wild game, cooked his own meals, and wore clothing and moccasins he fashioned from animal skins. In 1778, Cocke served simultaneously in the legislatures of both North Carolina and his native Virginia, trying to represent the Watauga Settlement, the upper East Tennessee territory being claimed by both states.

Prior to the American Revolution, England's Lord Dunmore, royal governor of colonial Virginia, offered Cocke any rank except commander in chief if he would lead British forces against the American colonies. Cocke's reply was terse. He was quoted as saying that "the King did not have enough money to buy him, the cause of the Colonies was just, and that he would devote his life to it."

Once the fighting began, the American cause seemed lost. Morale was low, and so was recruiting. The British, however, were recruiting great numbers of Loyalists from within the colonies. The British also encouraged Indian tribes to attack inland settlements while British forces moved toward them from the East Coast, hemming in the settlers from all sides.

Although he could have been a leading militia general for Great Britain, Cocke contented himself with being a regular soldier and quickly joined his neighboring mountaineers—thereafter called "the Overmountain Men." In October 1780, the direction for Tennesseans became clear when England's Colonel Patrick Ferguson, leader of Britain's North Carolina forces, sent a warning through Tennessee's hillsides that he intended to attack and burn all settlements unless the locals swore allegiance to the king.

Preparing for combat, the area's patriots gathered at Sycamore Shoals (present Elizabethton) near the Watauga River. They placed themselves under the command of John Sevier of Washington County and Isaac Shelby of Sullivan County. Word spread to neighboring states that mountaineer help was needed to fight the British. Rather than wait for Ferguson to arrive at their homes, the Overmountain Men decided to meet the enemy en route.

At Kings Mountain (South Carolina) the likelihood of a British victory turned quickly into a royal retreat out of the Carolinas. In an assault that lasted just an hour, the mountaineers triumphed and Ferguson lay dead. Kings Mountain, the first significant loosening of England's grip on the South, began a series of British battle losses that led to England's surrender to General George Washington at Yorktown. Thomas Jefferson called Kings Mountain the turning point of the American Revolution. East Tennessee's commanders in that effort later became heads of state: Sevier and Shelby became the first governors of Tennessee and Kentucky, respectively. (Shelby's father, Evan Shelby, owned land upon which the city of Bristol would be established.)

Cocke's life changed dramatically again in 1780, when, at age thirty-six, he began to study law. He passed the bar two years later and became one of the frontier's most prominent political orators. After the Revolution, Cocke stirred his neighbors with a new talk of freedom, claiming they were being taxed without representation by their mother state of North Carolina. Indeed, they had just fought a war over the same issue. His convictions led him out of the backwoods and into the political limelight.

In 1784, in defiance of the North Carolina government, he helped establish the State of Franklin, named in honor of Benjamin Franklin and located in upper East Tennessee. Many of Cocke's neighbors believed, as he did, that they needed to claim their independence from North Carolina. The mother state was so financially weakened from the Revolution that it was unable to offer them a court system, military protection against Indians, or any basic services of government except tax collection. Since North Carolina (temporarily at least) had ceded the Tennessee country to the young federal government, there was also a legal question about Carolina authority.

Some neighbors, however, maintained loyalty to North Carolina's side in the issue, much to the dismay of Cocke and his friend Sevier. Frustrating the State of Franklin's attempts to attain statehood was Colonel John Tipton, a prominent Washington County farmer and Revolutionary War veteran who once served in the Virginia House of Burgesses. He gathered a group of followers, including Sheriff Jonathon Pugh, and set up a parallel government in Washington County on behalf of North Carolina. When Tipton seized Sevier's slaves in 1788 to satisfy a North Carolina court judgment, the controversy over statehood turned into a battle. Sevier-led Franklinites attacked Tipton's farm near Johnson City, and a three-day siege ensued. Two of Tipton's men were killed, and Sheriff Pugh later died from his wounds. After retreating eventually to Jonesborough, Sevier learned that two of his sons had been captured. Tipton threatened to hang the young men but eventually set them free.

Having won the so-called Battle of Franklin, Tiptonites settled into an uneasy coexistence with their fellow settlers, because there was a dual government on the frontier. Cocke was resolute that only one of those governments would prevail. After helping to draft the State of Franklin Constitution, Cocke spoke for statehood before the newly created United States Congress. His neighbors then elected him to serve as a congressman from Franklin, but the gesture was in vain. The State of Franklin failed by one congressional vote to become the newest member of the United States.

Years later, Cocke remembered how the first attempt at statehood was born:

> No one wrote pamphlets urging our people to form their own government . . . and no one bothered to make speeches. We held meetings only when we thought the Indians might attack, and no one could afford the waste of hours spent in the saddle, riding through unmarked woods just to hear what he already believed. It was enough that we were being treated unfairly. We stood together because it never crossed our minds to do otherwise.

In 1790 when the territory came permanently under federal control, Cocke, living in Hawkins County, found himself on the same side as Tipton: each being named to the Southwest Territory legislature. With a new attempt at statehood in the making, both men remained on the same side of the issue.

When in 1796 the state of Tennessee came into being, Cocke helped frame the Tennessee Constitution. He and William Blount became the state's first United States senators. A year later, a section of upper East Tennessee was named Cocke County in his honor. Along with Blount, Sevier, Archibald Roane, Joseph Anderson, and David Campbell, Cocke became one of the original trustees of Blount College, the future University of Tennessee. After serving twelve years in the Senate, Cocke became a circuit court judge. Like many other early judges, he received his share of criticism and did not remain in office long. Although removed from his position by the state senate, Cocke soon ran for the state legislature and won.

At the age of sixty-six, and still possessing the fire for a good fight against England, Cocke enlisted in the War of 1812's volunteer army under General Andrew Jackson. Jackson later recommended him as Federal Chickasaw Indian agent in Mississippi, where he died in 1828 at the age of eighty.

Cocke's accomplishments were unprecedented, according to the Tennessee General Assembly: "Senator Cocke's record as a public official has probably never been equaled, having represented Transylvania, Virginia, North Carolina, the State of Franklin, the Southwest Territory, Tennessee, and Mississippi in legislative bodies." His last home, the state of Mississippi, built a memorial in his honor.

Once a man of few words, William Cocke became known as the premier orator of his day. "The defense of freedom," he often explained, "has made me articulate."

4

Samuel Doak

Strengthening Souls and Shaping Minds
on the Frontier

Before upper East Tennessee's fighting settlers helped turn the tide of the American Revolutionary War, they turned an ear to the Reverend Samuel Doak, a Presbyterian who sought any opportunity to influence the events taking shape around him. He was the frontier's leading minister-educator.

In October 1780, Doak accepted the invitation of militia leader John Sevier to address a stopgap army of farmers and hunters, who lived over the mountain from North Carolina, as they were preparing to engage England's superior forces in combat. Doak's sermon was typically fiery, closing with the Bible quotation: "Help us as good soldiers to wield the Sword of the Lord and of Gideon." Again and again, the troops repeated "the Sword of the Lord and of Gideon!" adopting it as their battle cry. In their grueling march from Washington County (present-day Carter County), the men rallied other mountain settlers like themselves from neighboring counties in Virginia and North Carolina to achieve what few expected, a complete victory at Kings Mountain.

Doak's knack for spurring others to arms may have exceeded his own ability to carry the fight. Once in Washington County, a messenger rushed into his church with news that Indians were attacking the McGhee place, two miles south. Parishioners were quickly on their feet, but Doak silenced them, then spent ten minutes praying for divine assistance. By the time Doak and his congregation arrived at the site of the attack, the Indians were gone. The unappreciative McGhee noted that if the pastor had spent some of the time riding that he had spent praying, the family's goods, including its only horse, might have been saved.

Doak was not above some verbal sparring either. Another tale describes the theological disagreement of Doak and Dr. Hezekiah Balch (well-known minister of the First Presbyterian Church at Greeneville and Doak's former classmate at Princeton) over theological tenets known as Hopkinsianism. This dispute became so heated that the two temporarily became virtual enemies. One day when "they unavoidably came face to face on the narrow boardwalk in Greeneville," one of the disputants (history does not reveal which one) said, "I will not make way for the devil." To which the other promptly stepped aside and responded: "I will!"

The outspoken, sometimes eccentric Samuel Doak had been a towering figure in East Tennessee since his arrival about 1779 on his old "flea-bitten gray" horse. A native Virginian, Doak was impressed with the pioneers he met cutting timber in the woods of Washington County. After agreeing to an impromptu horseback sermon, he decided to settle among them and anchor his family in future East Tennessee. Showing considerable physical strength in using his solid and stocky build, Doak joined a group of fellow Scots-Irish Presbyterians to construct Salem Church, one of the state's first churches. (Historians generally agree that the first permanent minister was living nearby on Boone's Creek: the Baptist Tidence Lane, whose six sons fought at Kings Mountain. He had built a church in 1779 on Buffalo Ridge.)

Doak soon built a log-cabin school, credited with being the "first real institution of learning in the Mississippi Valley." The schoolhouse was on Little Limestone Creek a few miles south of Jonesborough, a town that would be known as the nation's first planned community west of the mountains. The school received a 1783 charter from the mother state of North Carolina, becoming Martin Academy and finally Washington College. In 1795, Doak saddled the same faithful, old gray horse, rode to Philadelphia, Pennsylvania, and returned with saddlebags filled with books, thus beginning a respectable library at the school. It would become the key location for classical learning, a training ground for young men hoping to become doctors, lawyers, or ministers.

During the early nineteenth century, Doak became the first prominent preacher to deliver sermons characterized by a physical expression called "the jerks." Because the jerks were a religious phenomena prevalent during this period of the Great Revival, thousands often attended a camp meeting to partake in such religious zeal. One witness in Jonesborough described how the jerks shook Pastor Doak:

> Often it would seize him in the pulpit with so much severity that a spectator might fear it would dislocate his neck and joints. He would laugh, stand and halloo at the top of his voice, finally leap from the pulpit and run to the woods, screaming like a mad man. When the exercise was over he would return to the church calm and rational as ever.

After his first wife died, Doak married Margaretta McEwen, one of the frontier heroines of an Indian siege in 1785. At the time, she was living in Houston Station, six miles from present-day Maryville and along Nine Mile Creek. Indians were systematically attacking numerous isolated forts throughout what would become Knox and Blount counties. This early settle-

ment (one of the most important in Blount County) would have disappeared that day without rapid fire from its sharpshooters, reputedly the best in the area.

The outnumbered settlers had a secret weapon in Margaretta, who was determined to insure the swiftness with which the men could fire their rifles. "Give me the bullet molds," she yelled. "We can surely mold the bullets while you men do the fighting." Soon, she was bent over the flagstone hearth, melting lead and pouring it into molds, then quickly distributing freshly made bullets. Within moments, a bullet fired by the enemy struck a nearby wall, ricocheted, then settled near Margaretta's feet. She quickly snatched up the flattened projectile, melted it into a new bullet, and handed it to the nearest fighter, with the comment: "Here is a ball run out of the Indians' lead. Send it back to them as quickly as possible. It is their own; let them have it and welcome."

Pioneer life was safer for her after her marriage to Doak. In his later years, he remained a vigorous leader. At sixty-nine, he helped the Presbyterian Church to found Tusculum College in Greeneville, where he moved in 1818 to become the school's first president. When he died in 1830, Doak had a reputation as "the Apostle of Learning and Religion in the West."

5
John Sevier

*Creating a Free
and Very Independent Government*

Called one of the most imposing and handsomest men on the East Tennessee frontier, early leader John Sevier swept Catherine "Bonnie Kate" Sherrill from her feet, and away from death, in 1776's major Indian attack at Fort Watauga.

The fort's women, caught unaware while milking cows in the fields, had fled toward home. By the time Catherine reached the fort, the gates were already closed. But Sevier reached over the spiked walls, yelled "Jump, my Bonnie Kate, jump!" and pulled her to safety. Catherine reportedly recalled the dramatic moment by saying "I would gladly fall into the peril of the Indians if I could fall into the arms of John Sevier." Years later, Catherine would marry the man who saved her, and the quote would become a part of family lore.

John Sevier. Winning battles came naturally.

The rest of Tennessee's first settlers, who built small frontier stations or forts along the Holston, Watauga, and Nolichucky rivers of upper East Tennessee, saw Sevier as a man who knew how to fight and win and how to build and govern. In this new country, America's most isolated settlement, Sevier claimed victory after victory in Indian battles and in political elections within the government that he helped to create. For more than twenty-five years before Tennessee statehood, the man who would become Tennessee's first governor made a good impression on most people whom he met or fought to protect.

A natural political leader, Sevier (a native Virginian) helped originate and frame what future President Theodore Roosevelt considered the nation's first declaration of independence among "the first men of American birth to establish a free and independent community on the continent." A result of this activity was a written constitution: the Watauga Association's "Articles of Association." The year was 1772. This document, which was not preserved, became the model of government for the original settlers in upper East

Tennessee years before the nation made its own move toward independence and self-government.

An engineer and well-known surveyor, Sevier also helped to build Fort Watauga, Tennessee's first settlement, located near present-day Elizabethton. During this time, Sevier was married to the former Sarah Hawkins, by whom he fathered ten children (she died in 1778). Homesteaders within a two hundred-mile radius depended on Fort Watauga's protective walls when Indian or British troubles brewed.

But it was Sevier's leadership in the American Revolution that made him famous on the frontier. In 1780, he helped organize upper East Tennesseans, encouraging neighboring settlements to join the cause against England and then calling for a rendezvous at his home base, Sycamore Shoals. Sevier and the soon-to-be famous Overmountain Men endured a punishing trip across rough, mountainous terrain, stopping awhile atop Roan Mountain, and then proceeding (the last day in drenching rain) before finally confronting and defeating the enemy at Kings Mountain, South Carolina.

As militia leader, Sevier won all of his thirty-five battles against the Indians and/or the British, prompting Roosevelt to call him the "greatest Indian fighter of them all." Yet Sevier was so generous with his enemy that he once hosted thirty-five Indians in his home for a week after capturing them in battle. The Cherokees reportedly held considerable respect for him.

Sevier's popularity carried him quickly to two governorships: in 1784, on behalf of the ill-fated State of Franklin; and, in 1796, as Tennessee's first governor (serving six terms, 1796-1801 and 1803-1809). Because of these early heroics and leadership, Sevier County was named in his honor in 1794 and he became a founding trustee of several early colleges—among them the future University of Tennessee, then called Blount College.

With the birth of the state, however, emerged a feud so intense and so longstanding that Tennessee was split accordingly. The conflict arose between Sevier and the state's first congressman, the young Andrew Jackson. Sevier, by now an elder statesman as well as political master of Tennessee, saw Jackson, twenty-two years younger, as a challenge to his sole authority. The two warred with each other for more than nineteen years, and some historians claimed that permanent political sectionalism in Tennessee was one result.

As Jackson traveled to Congress in 1796, he learned of a massive land fraud scheme in North Carolina in which Sevier was implicated. He reported it to anyone who would listen. When North Carolina requested extradition of the suspects, Governor Sevier refused to go.

Angry letters passed between Sevier and Jackson, and their feud spilled over into a contest for a later appointment as general of the Tennessee militia. When Sevier could not succeed himself as governor in 1801, he set his sight upon this title—the other most powerful position in the state. Jackson sought the post with equal relish, but Sevier doubted Jackson's abilities, believing him *"a poor pitifull petty fogging Lawyer."*

Militia officers, who chose their own leaders, were evenly divided over the two men. The situation forced Tennessee's second governor, Archibald Roane, to cast a tie-breaking vote. Roane selected Jackson, who had tipped the scales in his favor by revealing letters suggesting Sevier's involvement in the land-fraud case. Sevier's supporters in the state legislature, hoping to dilute Jackson's power, managed to split the state militia into a Middle Tennessee wing headed by Jackson and an East Tennessee wing headed by Sevier's designee, William Cocke.

In October 1803, when Sevier and Jackson passed each other in front of the Knox County Courthouse, their feud escalated into a "showdown." Sevier, who now lived near Knoxville, made the first verbal attack. Their political shouting match digressed into personal insults after Jackson said that his services to Tennessee were worthy of acknowledgment. "Services?" shouted Sevier. "I know of no great service you have rendered the country, except taking a trip to Natchez with another man's wife." The reference was to Rachel Donelson Jackson, who once took a trip to Mississippi in the company of Jackson, as both believed that she was divorced at the time. Sevier's insult provoked Jackson to violent response: "Great God! do you mention *her* sacred name?" Pistols were drawn and shots fired. One bystander was grazed by a bullet, but friends separated the two men before the incident provoked a riot.

Jackson quickly dashed off a challenge to Sevier to meet him in a duel. Sevier did not answer immediately but eventually agreed. Since dueling was illegal in Tennessee, Sevier insisted that they meet outside of "the sacred soil of Tennessee." Jackson arrived at the appointed time and place in what was still Indian territory near Roane County, but Sevier did not appear.

After waiting days, Jackson decided to return to Knoxville. En route, he came upon Sevier near Kingston. Although each grabbed for a pistol, they soon holstered their weapons and resorted to trading insults. Jackson then strode toward Sevier with a cane in striking position. Sevier drew his sword and, in so doing, caused his horse to bolt and run, carrying his guns away in a saddlebag. When Jackson drew his gun, Sevier took cover behind a tree. Standing near, Sevier's son then leveled a pistol at Jackson.

Finally realizing the absurdity of the situation, the would-be combatants agreed to go home. They rode to Knoxville (together) but no closer to reconciliation. Sevier continued to wage a war of words through the newspaper, and the populace seemed to favor the former governor against a man with a combative reputation.

Apparently Sevier thought their feud had spread all the way to heaven. On the night of January 10, 1804, at Marble Springs, the governor had "a curious dream." His father, Valentine Sevier, who lived 120 miles away, appeared in the dream and described life in heaven. The father appeared "descending in the air" riding "in one of the finest rigged vessels I had ever seen," wrote Sevier. During the dream's conversation, the father told his son that despite the peace and friendship in heaven, there was much talk about the ongoing feud with Jackson and the need for John Sevier to "act a prudent part." Sevier then wrote: "I began to think I was dreaming and immediately awakened." Four days later, Sevier received notification of the death of his father, who, in fact, had been dead the night of his son's dream.

Nonetheless, the feud continued more than a decade longer, ending only with Sevier's death. In 1815 President James Madison assigned him to a surveying trip between Georgia and the Creek Indian nation. Sevier, seventy, died of a fever along with twenty of his soldiers. Meanwhile, the people of Tennessee, unaware of his death, reelected him to the United States House of Representatives.

Years later, in Washington, D.C., statues of John Sevier and Andrew Jackson were placed in close proximity, so that even in death the two unfriendly giants of early Tennessee history were unable to escape each other's shadows.

Thomas Sharpe Spencer cooking over a fire at the entrance to his hollow-tree home, as depicted in a 1930 history book.

6

Thomas Sharpe Spencer

The Long Hunter Putting Down Roots

During a late eighteenth-century militia muster in Middle Tennessee, four hundred-pound Thomas Sharpe Spencer gingerly lifted an enraged Bob Shaw, a rather large fellow himself, and tossed him over a fence ten rails high. Shaw, who had punched Spencer in the face because the big man had interrupted a fist-fight Shaw was promoting, got up from the ground and steadied his stance. According to legend, Shaw dusted himself off, looked Spencer square in the eye, and stated, "Mr. Spencer, if you will be kind enough to pitch my horse over, I will be riding."

Spencer once discussed his herculean strength in conversation with his friend William Hall, a recorder of early Tennessee history, as well as a keen Indian fighter and community leader (who would become Tennessee's seventh governor). Hall wrote: "Spencer told me—that knowing his own strength, he was really afraid to strike a man in anger, for fear he would kill him!"

Called Middle Tennessee's first permanent white settler, Spencer was actually a wanderer: one of the many famous Long Hunters who spent months (sometimes a year or more) seeking wild game in the forested depths of Tennessee and Kentucky. He arrived about 1776, perhaps from Virginia, and wherever he wandered in the wilderness, he carried the nickname "Big Foot."

This mythical handle was given to Spencer in 1778 after an Illinois hunter saw his huge footprints in the snow and imagined that some wilderness giant was on the prowl. The hunter had found refuge in a cabin often used by French trader Timothy DeMonbreun, one of the earliest Europeans to trade with the Indians at the area's major salt lick, appropriately called French Lick. While still imagining that a giant was lurking in the dense forest, the Illinois hunter next heard a commotion, created by Spencer and his companion John Holliday (or Holladay) as they pursued a wounded buffalo. The nervous, nameless hunter became so frightened at the surrounding clamor and uproar that he bolted into the woods, swam the Cumberland River, and did not stop until he reached a group of traders, some two hundred miles north of Spencer's tracks.

Spencer and Holliday parted company that same winter, with Holliday (fearful of Indians) returning to Virginia and Spencer taking up residence in a tree. The hollow sycamore log, two stories high and nine feet in diameter was not only Spencer's winter dwelling but also the lookout from which he watched Indian hunting parties pass. The tree was located at Bledsoe's Lick in the future Sumner County, and Spencer's residence there made the spot famous. (Fifty years later, the A. R. Wynne family built Wynnewood Inn and natural-springs resort at that locale and changed the area's name to Castalian Springs.)

When Spencer made improvements on nearby land, planted crops, and later obtained permanent land claims, he earned his title as the first permanent settler in the region. Soon he was joined by nearly seventy other hunters who wanted to build cabins. In 1779, Spencer decided to homestead near the French Lick, where a heavy immigration of East Tennesseans would arrive to construct the town of Nashville and dozens of surrounding "stations" and forts, collectively called the Cumberland Settlements.

Joining their ranks, Spencer fulfilled military obligations and court duty, but he still preferred to hunt alone, only occasionally allowing a companion. He inspired famous stories that grew in proportion to his many bloody engagements with Indians. In one episode, when his camp was attacked, Spencer used his great strength to grab and carry his mortally wounded fellow hunter with one hand, while using the other hand to tote their guns. In order to take the man for a proper burial, he loped off into the wilderness. Amazed at his size, Indians kept "a respectful distance," wrote Hall, "enabling him . . . to get clear . . . unmolested," and arrive safely in Nashville.

Not all Indians held him in such respect. The end came for Thomas Sharpe Spencer in 1794 on the Cumberland Plateau. While returning with traveling companions from a trip to Virginia, where he had collected an inheritance of one thousand dollars in gold, Spencer was shot from ambush. His killer was the Chickamaugan renegade-assassin Doublehead, who had also murdered many other leading settlers, among them John Rice, the original proprietor of the land where Memphis stands, and three nephews of John Sevier. Now adding Spencer to his list of victims, Doublehead made off with Spencer's saddlebags and money. The frontiersman was buried on the trail near where he was killed, at the border of Cumberland and Van Buren counties, the latter of which would name its county seat "Spencer."

7

Anne Robertson Cockrill

Riding the River: An Adventure to Settle Middle Tennessee

In the winter of 1779 to 1780, the raft *Adventure* led a fleet of thirty flatboats carrying mostly East Tennessee women and children to the unsettled wilderness that would become Middle Tennessee. A select group of the men, led by Captain James Robertson, had already gone overland with their farm animals to begin building Fort Nashborough at the French Lick.

Robertson's younger sister, Anne (or Ann), was among those who left Fort Patrick Henry on the Holston River (at present-day Kingsport). They merged with a new set of boats at the Clinch River and expected that their journey to Middle Tennessee would last a few weeks. The river-borne travelers, however, fought

Indians and endured harsh elements in a nightmarish voyage that was not completed for months.

But Anne Robertson was accustomed to a fight for survival. Three years earlier, her heroics saved most of the pioneers when Indians attacked one of their main settlements, Fort Watauga at Elizabethton. During that attack, she poured boiling water down the fort's walls and onto the unsuspecting Indians who were using the walls as a shield from gunfire. The invaders fled the scene quickly, and the state's earliest settlers were able to keep their foothold in the East Tennessee mountains.

Long Hunters then brought tales of the rich soil in the Cumberland area. Many pioneers packed their belongings to settle further west. To reach French Lick via the river meant a circuitous route: first negotiating the Tennessee River, then making connections with the Ohio River, and finally traveling the Cumberland River. At the helm of the *Adventure* was another early settlement leader, Captain John Donelson, whose large family was aboard, including his daughter Rachel, the future wife of Andrew Jackson.

Their journey was plagued with boats sinking and running aground, bad weather, rough water, and dangers from the native population along the route. Indians who lived near Muscle Shoals, Alabama, assaulted the flotilla at every turn. Despite the troubles, Anne Robertson gathered all the children each morning and conducted makeshift classes. She used a sandbox instead of a blackboard, and on Sundays she taught Bible lessons and hymns.

Her finest hour, according to family narration, began after the Stuart family (occupying the last boat in the flotilla) was killed by renegade Chickamaugans at the bluffs near Chattanooga. Because the boat had been lagging behind with a case of smallpox aboard, the Stuarts were easy victims. As it happened, so were their attackers—who, having scalped the Stuarts and taken prisoners as well, contracted the fast-spreading disease and passed it along to their own families.

Several days later, the rest of the flotilla became stalled in the tormenting currents at Muscle Shoals. Indian women began lining the shore, holding aloft their pathetic, dying babies who had quickly fallen victim to the white man's scourge. Facing the likelihood of contracting the disease herself, Anne left her raft, tore bandages from clean petticoats, and showed the grieving mothers which herbs would heal the sores on their children's bodies. Despite Anne's best efforts, this outbreak of smallpox became so widespread that it decimated some southern tribes. Later historians claimed that smallpox actually prevented the warring tribes from wiping out the fledgling Tennessee colonies around Nashville in their first years of existence.

When the Donelson flotilla finally reached its destination, Anne continued to teach the settlers' children, earning her place in history as the first teacher in Middle Tennessee. She was also one of a few women given a land grant for Revolutionary War service against the British and their Indian allies (her land parcels were in downtown Nashville).

Anne Robertson married John Cockrill and began a famous Middle Tennessee lineage which would contribute greatly to the advancement of both Tennessee and American agriculture. From their huge area farms, these descendants, among them their son Mark Robertson Cockrill and grandson Mark Sterling Cockrill, would earn immense national respect for their world-renowned stock-breeding farms and their business integrity.

Anne Robertson Cockrill died in 1821 at the age of sixty-four.

8

Hugh Rogan

Fending Off Fears (and a Few Tears)
on the Frontier

At least one frontier marriage was as strong as the man about whom legends were told. Hugh Rogan left his heart in Ireland, made his mark in the Middle Tennessee country, and rediscovered his wife after two decades of separation.

Rogan, an Irish Catholic immigrant who arrived in America in 1775, was a strong, simple pioneer and a man who customarily helped others. Forced to leave his wife and child in Ireland's County Donegal because he had been fighting alongside the "Irish Defenders" against the British, Rogan decided to build a homestead in America and then send for his family. Moving to North Carolina, he discovered the rich lands of Middle Tennessee in 1779 when he joined a surveying party to help determine the boundary between North Carolina and Virginia (this would become the northern

boundary of Tennessee/Kentucky). He and the others, including General Daniel Smith, camped for some time along Goose Creek near present-day Hartsville.

In 1780, Rogan made the river journey with Captain John Donelson's party from upper East Tennessee to settle Fort Nashborough, where James Robertson and his men had already arrived by overland passage and had begun to build cabins. Rogan also joined these early pioneers in signing the Cumberland Compact, the region's governing document. He received a land allotment of 640 acres near the present site of Vanderbilt University but decided to trade it for money, horses, and nearby farmland in future Sumner County, not far from the area where he once camped. Rogan took the money and horses and set out to retrieve his family from Ireland. Headed for the coast of North Carolina, he encountered his brother-in-law, Daniel Carlin, who happened to have wives in both Ireland and America. Desperate to hide his bigamy and prevent Rogan from returning to their homeland, Carlin claimed that Rogan's own wife had remarried. Heartbroken, Rogan made his way back to the Cumberland Settlements and started life anew.

By virtue of his many Indian encounters, Rogan became a fearless figure who had "an affinity for Indian fights and hardly ever missed one in his vicinity," recounts historian Hugh Walker, who points out that Rogan's exploits became the stuff of bedtime stories told to children on the Tennessee frontier.

Such tales always included the adventurous night in 1788 when he helped militia Colonel Anthony Bledsoe, a former Long Hunter who was mortally wounded in an Indian attack (Bledsoe County would be named for him). In Bledsoe's small fort besieged by raiders, the dying man wanted to write a final will bequeathing to his seven daughters an inheritance of land. Night had fallen. There was no fire in the fireplace and not enough moonlight spilling through the cabin's split logs to provide Bledsoe with the light he needed.

Rogan somehow slipped through the surrounding war party to the nearby cabin of an elderly widow named Shaver, whom the Indians avoided, believing that she was a witch. Rogan obtained lit coals from the widow and slipped back to Bledsoe's Fort, located near modern Castalian Springs. He was just in time to provide the dying colonel with the light he required to write his will. Rogan believed simply that a man's last wish should always be granted.

Rogan did not have his own fondest wish granted until seven years later in 1795 when he unexpectedly received a letter from Ireland. Hand-delivered by a nephew recently arrived in America, the letter said: "Deliver to your uncle if alive and on the continent of America." In an impassioned plea, Nancy Rogan reminded her husband that she still waited for him. Rogan packed immediately, journeyed east, and caught a ship to Ireland.

Upon hearing that he had landed at an Irish port, Nancy asked, "What does he look like?"

The answer came back: "He is an old man wearing a tall hat."

"That's not my Hughie," she countered. "My Hughie is a young man."

Indeed it was Hughie, and he in turn found that his infant son, Bernard, was now a man of twenty-two. Gathering his family, Rogan returned to America, then to Tennessee and to the homestead he had built in Sumner County. Making a new life on their farm, Rogana, the couple soon became parents of another child. Hugh Rogan lived another seventeen years, dying in 1813 at the age of sixty-six. He was buried on the farm.

9

James Robertson

Staying Power in Frontier Nashville

Nashville would have been an abortive attempt at settlement but for the fighting spirit of James Robertson, who kept the first Middle Tennessee settlers from bolting in the face of hardship and brutal Indian attacks.

Robertson had already helped settle upper East Tennessee after he built a family cabin on the Watauga in 1771. In 1779, he and a small group arrived in Middle Tennessee to investigate the Cumberland River area's rich soil and plant a crop of corn for a larger body of settlers, notably women and children who would come by river in the fall.

Fort Nashborough was born, and a struggle to establish a permanent community also began. These first pioneers were confronted by harsh winter weather and an even harsher enemy, the many native Indian tribes who treasured their ancient hunting grounds throughout Middle Tennessee and Kentucky. After being demoralized by the weather and attacked by the Indi-

ans, the settlers were about to agree that they had no place there. One of their leaders, John Donelson, eventually left with his family and moved to Kentucky. Robertson, however, stood his cold-winter ground and inspired other stout-hearted pioneers to do the same. He called on them to "fight it out here." Most were persuaded. "He had an elevation of soul that enabled him to take upon himself the burden of the whole community," claims an early twentieth-century history book by John Trotwood Moore and Austin P. Foster of the man they called the "Father of Tennessee."

Robertson's burdens grew by the day. The settlers were running low on corn and gunpowder. Game was scarce in the Cumberland Settlements because the Indians had intentionally driven animals away from the area, hoping to starve the pioneers and force them to leave. When the settlers refused to give in, the natives began their attacks. One of their many victims was David Hood, who was shot and scalped by the Chickasaws journeying from West Tennessee in January 1781 to assist in driving out the white intruders.

Hood's encounter with the enemy began while he was trying to travel between stations. Suddenly, three bullets hit him, and he fell to the ground. A Chickasaw began to remove Hood's scalp, sawing tirelessly with a dull knife, then trying to yank off the hair. Hood withstood the torture without flinching or groaning, hoping the Indian would presume him dead. Finally the Indian had his prize, and "After scalping him, he stamped upon him to dislocate his neck, and left him for dead."

Hood was far from dead, however, and he got up and began to walk to the nearest fort, the Bluff (or Nashborough). He topped a bank, only to confront the same band of Indians, pointing and laughing at his pitiful condition. Hood ran back, as best he could, took two more bullet wounds, and finally fainted in some brushwood. Shortly, several men from Bluff Station found Hood and carried him home. Thinking him dead or dying, they placed him in an outbuilding. The Chickasaw attacked a nearby station that night, and, while the men assisted their neighbors, the pathetic Hood lay unattended and forgotten.

The next morning, Robertson, after a night of fighting (and a brief moment of celebration over the birth of his son Felix Robertson, the "first white child born in Nashville") set out to find Hood. At the outbuilding, the resilient Hood reportedly said to him: "Not dead yet, and I believe I would get well if I had half a chance."

With a technique he had learned in upper East Tennessee from a French surgeon who taught him how to save a scalp, Robertson began to operate. He used a pegging awl (which resembles an ice pick) to perforate the exposed skull and assist new skin growth. The resulting "granulation" would then form a covering over naked areas, keeping the bone from dying and exposing the brain. The procedure was used widely on the frontier, and every station had at least one person who could perform this operation. Many scalped individuals lived for years, and Hood reportedly lived to a ripe old age.

After this attack on Hood, Robertson met with the Chickasaw chief and made a private agreement which cemented a friendly alliance between the Chickasaws of West Tennessee and the Cumberland Settlements. This 1781 alliance, however, did not end the settlers' trouble with other tribes. There were still the Chickamaugans near Chattanooga, who made constant raids throughout East and Middle Tennessee. A few months later, one such raid revealed the courage of Robertson's wife, Charlotte.

Fort Nashborough's men had left the stockade's protection to work in the fields. They had planted their first crop near the stockade, but spring rains had destroyed the effort. This time, they were working fields further away. The women and children were alone, protected only by the bloodhounds at the fort. The dogs generally could detect the presence of Indians within a two-mile radius, and because they howled and whined all morning, Charlotte Robertson became increasingly anxious.

She took up a vigil in the fort's lookout. A movement in the forest caught her attention. In the distance, she saw an Indian triumphantly brandishing a scalp. She knew instantly that the scalp belonged to her son, Jonathan, who had gone alone into the forest to hunt. She called for a horse and a gun, bundled up her infant, Felix, and rode off to warn the men, while the remaining women barricaded themselves inside the fort.

The men quickly made their way to the stockade but found no enemy in sight. Suddenly, they spotted Indians in the distance and ran toward the Cumberland River—and into a trap. The fort's men were surrounded by hundreds of Chickamaugans, and there was no path home. Charlotte Robertson was again at her lookout. Taking in the desperate situation, she

ordered the dogs to be turned loose—causing the enemy to flee in all directions and giving the men time to retreat home. Thanks to such a quick response, the settlers won the Battle of the Bluffs, one of the major assaults on the infant Cumberland Settlements.

Five settlers were dead, two or three were wounded, and Jonathan Robertson was still missing. His mother led the search of nearby woods. Scalped and left for dead, the youth had been trying to crawl home. Charlotte found the boy and nursed him back to health, most likely using the same surgical technique her husband had learned.

By 1782, many disheartened local families were ready to abandon the Cumberland Settlements until James Robertson's leadership changed their outlook. Two years later, their centrally fortified station, the Bluff, received a new name—"Nashville."

In 1790, the Tennessee country became a federal territory, and President George Washington named Robertson militia general of the middle district. In 1794, Robertson ordered a major attack on the renegade Chickamaugans' home base across the Georgia border. A collection of men from throughout East and Middle Tennessee banded together and won the battle at Nickajack, making the frontier nearly free of armed conflict between the two sides.

In 1796, when Tennessee became the sixteenth state, Robertson County was created along the Tennessee-Kentucky border in honor of a key figure in the self-governing structure of both East Tennessee (the Watauga Association Compact) and Middle Tennessee (the Cumberland Compact).

Robertson lived until 1814, dying at the age of seventy-two among the friendly Chickasaws as their Indian agent. His son Felix Robertson would become one of Middle Tennessee's leading physicians. A later descendant, Benjamin Franklin Cheatham, would become a leading Confederate general.

10
Joseph Brown

Captured and Condemned—
And a Boy's Prayer to Heaven

The old Indian woman pleaded with tribal men to kill the captured boy immediately. He would bring trouble some day, said the prophetess who predicted

The French woman, Mrs. Tom Tunbridge, challenges an Indian ally, insisting that the boy Joseph Brown (left) be executed away from her cabin.

The Joseph Brown saga was one of the most frequently told of all pioneering adventures in homes throughout early Tennessee because he *did* fulfill the old woman's prophesy.

The youth's tale began with his family's migration from North Carolina. His father, Colonel James Brown, was a Revolutionary War veteran who took advantage of North Carolina's offer to compensate its soldiers with an abundance of western land since the state treasury was empty. During the winter of 1786-87, the elder Brown built a boat for the journey to the spot he had chosen on the Cumberland about five miles from the future Nashville. On May 4, 1787, he began his voyage, leaving one of the original East Tennessee settlements (at Kingsport) with his wife, two grown sons, the teenaged Joseph, a younger son, George, and three daughters. In addition, five other white men and several slaves were aboard.

Five days into their venture, the Browns passed a Cherokee village on the lower Tennessee. A canoe of seemingly friendly Indians, led by their headman Cutleotoy, hailed the boat. Colonel Brown permitted them on board. When the Indians disembarked, they sent runners downriver to Nickajack and Running Water villages with orders for warriors to stop the boat and attack it. These villages, located across the Tennessee border into Georgia, were part of the Five Lower Towns of the rebellious Chickamauga tribe.

An English-speaking tribesman of mixed blood, John Vann, led a party of forty militant companions to the Browns' location. Under the pretense of trading, Vann asked to board the boat. But when hordes came on board, the colonel protested. He was killed immediately, his boat taken to Nickajack, and his family and slaves doled out among the various renegade tribes.

A group of Creeks took Mrs. Brown, her three daughters, and son George, to their towns on the Coosa and Tallapoosa rivers. A Nickajack of mixed blood claimed Joseph. While he was being led away, the youth heard distant gunshots, later learning that his older brothers and the other men had been killed.

Joseph Brown was now the prisoner of a trading-post family within the Chickamaugan camp. That family included his Nickajack captor's mother (a woman of French descent who had lived with the Chickamaugans since being captured in her own childhood) and her husband, Tom Tunbridge (a British army deserter and the trading-post operator). After Joseph arrived

in 1787 that he would be a grown man bringing death and destruction upon her people.

Fifteen-year-old Joseph Brown, a prisoner of renegade tribes near present-day Chattanooga, prepared for his execution. He later wrote a description of the scene:

> I fell on my knees again and tried to pray, and beg the Lord for the sake of Jesus to have mercy on my poor soul, expecting every moment the tomahawk to sink into my brains; and after I had prayed, possibly five or ten minutes, I remembered the mercy and favor the Lord showed to Stephen when he was stoned—that he was enabled to see the Heavens opened, and the dear Savior sitting on the right hand of God; and involuntarily opened my eyes! Looking up, as they were gathered all around me, I happened to discover one of them smile; whereupon, casting my eyes around, I saw the countenances of all changed from ferocity to mildness, which was the first gleam of hope I had.

at the Tunbridges', the old Cherokee prophetess suddenly appeared, angry that the youth had not also been killed. Because she foretold the boy's ultimate role in the destruction of their villages, her son Cutleotoy burst into the cabin with plans to kill him.

"I was within six feet of the door," Joseph told in a later narrative on his life, "but the old French woman begged him not to kill me in the cabin." With one hand, Cutleotoy grabbed the youth and jerked him out of the door. Other executioners were waiting. "I saw that there were ten of them surrounding it," Joseph added. "Some of them had their tomahawks in their hands, others had knives drawn and guns cocked, all ready to dash me into Eternity."

Mrs. Tunbridge tried to intervene again, this time begging Cutleotoy not to kill the boy in front of her cabin "nor on the road where she carried water!" Joseph continued: "She begged them to take me up on the mountain where the wolves would eat me up!"

Not until Joseph sank to his knees and offered up his prayer did Cutleotoy realize this killing might not be wise. The youth's death could bring retaliation and perhaps the killing of Cutleotoy's own prisoner from the Brown boat. Without understanding what had happened, Joseph saw his salvation as an answer to his prayers.

He was forced to live among his captors for nearly two years. In 1789, Joseph Brown regained his freedom in a prisoner exchange when General John Sevier brought Cherokee prisoners on one of his many expeditions and negotiated the release of American captives. Eventually, the other Brown family members who had not been killed were reunited. They all returned temporarily to South Carolina.

In late 1790, apparently undeterred by their previous harrowing experience, the surviving Browns headed again for the Cumberland Settlements and began farming there on their land grant. Joseph became a post rider between the middle settlements and Knoxville. During these journeys, he was a frequent target of Indian attacks, narrowly escaping death more than once.

Seven years after the old Indian woman's prediction, the white man came again to Nickajack. As she envisioned, Joseph Brown led the way, guiding hundreds of men who had banded together from East Tennessee, Middle Tennessee, and parts of central Kentucky. Under the leadership of Major James Ore, they traveled through thick forests to stamp out this In-

dian stronghold in Georgia territory. It was from here that most of the violence against the settlers seemed to originate, and where Spaniards encouraged and paid for Indian uprisings. The military campaign against Nickajack in 1794 more or less ended Indian raids against the settlers.

Brown, later homesteading with his wife and family on his father's land grant at the Duck River, became the first white settler in present-day Maury County. In 1807, he built the county seat, becoming one of the first county commissioners. Before he died in 1868, Brown also became one of the most important sources of information for historians who relied upon his descriptions of the settlers' frontier life and the culture that existed within various Indian nations.

11
William Blount
George Washington's Man in the New Southwest Territory

William Blount was elated in 1790 when told that he had been appointed federal governor of the Southwest Territory. His wife, however, was not. Although Blount saw this as an opportunity to establish a government for the pioneers and to have a national political career, his wife, Mary, dreaded leaving her stately house, her longstanding social friendships, and the cultural advantages of coastal North Carolina. Although moving into a rough wilderness had no appeal for Mrs. William Blount, her husband possessed more than a million acres in the wilderness that would someday be Tennessee, and it too needed attention.

Blount owed the honor of being Tennessee's only territorial governor to his friend George Washington. The two had met in Philadelphia at the 1787 Constitutional Convention of the United States. Washington was impressed with the delegate from North Carolina, and when a federal territory was created, now-President Washington remembered Blount. By placing him over a vast land which would later be divided into states, the president was virtually guaranteeing Blount's coveted path to national prominence.

Mary Blount maintained her refined life in North Carolina while her husband rode into the future East Tennessee and set up the territory's first capital at Rocky Mount, which was the home of William Cobb near

William Blount refused to be tried for treason.

giving dignity to the rugged and independent town. Mary Blount managed to be gracious and welcoming to all. The people loved her, and she grew to love the Tennessee territory. At Blount Mansion "the door stood open to visitors from far and near." When nearby Blount County was created in 1795, its county seat of Maryville was named for her (as was Grainger County, in honor of her maiden name).

Territorial Governor William Blount was an educated and cultured man, and frontier settlers who had dotted Tennessee with a series of log structures did not know if a refined stranger could be trusted to govern their lives. Blount won them over with his fair-mindedness. Among his great achievements on behalf of the pioneers was a successful land negotiation with the Cherokees. In the 1791 Treaty of the Holston, the Indian nation accepted one thousand dollars and other favors to relinquish East Tennessee, where land claims had been disputed since the pioneers first took up residence. Blount, moreover, accepted the realities of the settlers' lives, although he did not try to live a frontier life himself. He did not interfere in 1794 when, without federal approval, the pioneer militia raided renegade Indian strongholds at Nickajack near Chattanooga.

Blount was determined to achieve his greatest goal—a seat in the United States Senate. To do so, he had to turn the surrounding wilderness into a new state. He completed the task in six years; and in 1796 he became Tennessee's first senator, along with backwoodsman-turned-statesman William Cocke.

But Blount enjoyed the Senate only briefly. He soon returned to Knoxville with treason charges in his wake. Blount, however, enjoyed enough popularity among his Tennessee constituents that they refused to let such charges shake their faith in the man. Nor would his constituents allow an outsider—in this case the United States Senate—take him to trial.

Blount's problems began in the summer of 1797 when a letter he had written to a friend found its way into the hands of President John Adams. The letter spoke of a plan to seize New Orleans and other land from Spain and give it to Great Britain, rather than allow it to become French territory. The plan was considered treasonous because Spain was an ally of the United States.

Blount had hatched the plot along with Knoxville innkeeper John Chisholm in hopes of placing the

Piney Flats. Blount had reassured his wife that he would build her the finest house the frontier had ever seen. He would build it in a new town which he would help to create further west at James White's Fort. It was named "Knoxville" in honor of United States Secretary of War Henry Knox. Philadelphia surveyor Charles McClung laid out the town under Blount's watchful eye. Soon thereafter, Blount encouraged a young Massachusetts printer, George Roulstone, to settle in Knoxville; his creation, *The Knoxville Gazette*, appeared as Tennessee's first newspaper (its first issue was printed in the Hawkins County town, Rogersville).

While Blount Mansion was being built, onlookers watched in amazement. Materials such as paneling and shingled roofing arrived from North Carolina for the two-story clapboard structure. When the window-panes were installed, "the Indians looked at it and saw what they had most likely never seen before, a house with many glass eyes." The stately house subsequently became the center of social and political life,

Mississippi River in the hands of a nation that might be friendly to Americans, and more specifically, to Tennesseans. Blount could profit because he owned massive acreage in West Tennessee near the Mississippi. But if France obtained New Orleans, Blount believed the Mississippi would close to American navigation and trade. River commerce vital to Tennessee's economic well-being would be crushed as well.

Blount was expelled from the Senate, and while the Congress at Philadelphia adjourned for the summer, a committee investigated the matter. Charges of impeachment were read against Blount in February 1798. The following summer, the Senate's sergeant at arms was dispatched to East Tennessee to arrest and transport Blount to the nation's capital to stand trial.

When the arresting officer, James Mathers, arrived in Knoxville, he found the populace surprisingly cordial, and the Blount family even more so. Mathers was wined and dined for several days and even welcomed at Blount Mansion, where Mary shone as a gracious hostess. Met by warm greetings at every turn, Mathers postponed announcement of his purpose in Knoxville, although no one doubted his intentions. When he finally revealed to Blount why he had come, the former senator remarked casually that he had no desire or intention to go to Philadelphia at this time. Mathers tried to organize a posse to remove Blount forcibly, but Knoxvillians, having supported their senator throughout the incident, declined to cooperate.

Realizing that he had no recourse but to return to Congress empty-handed, Mathers set out on his journey. Knoxvillians surprised him again when many of them accompanied him to the edge of town and showed every courtesy. Bowing to him, they bid him farewell with these parting words: "We beg to assure you, sir, that William Blount cannot be taken from Tennessee." According to historian Octavia Zollicoffer Bond, "This goes to prove that there are times when the will of the people who are governed is superior to the government itself."

Mathers returned home, the United States Senate withdrew its charges of treason, and William Blount turned his attention to his new duties in the Tennessee legislature, where he became Speaker of the Tennessee Senate. He died two years later, in 1800, at the age of fifty-one. After her husband's death, Mary Blount did not consider moving back to North Carolina. She remained a Tennessean until her own death two years later.

12
Hugh Lawson White
Forts and Fighting; Learning and Leading

Although he felled many trees on the East Tennessee frontier and took up arms to protect homesteaders against Indian attacks, one son of Knoxville founder James White was considered rather "bookish." In 1786, Hugh Lawson White helped to erect the stockade which came to be known as James White's Fort and later the site of Knoxville. But the boy was drawn to intellectual pursuits. Fortunately for him, two pioneers arrived in the settlement with the credentials to help him: Presbyterian minister Samuel Carrick from Virginia and Dartmouth College graduate Archibald Roane from Pennsylvania.

At the age of fifteen, White found himself living in the Carrick household, five miles from White's Fort, under the tutelage of both Carrick and Roane. They gave him an excellent education in the classical languages, math, ancient history, philosophy, physics, and astronomy. Carrick later founded the First Presbyterian Church in Knoxville and became first president of Blount College, named for Territorial Governor William Blount (it later would become the University of Tennessee). Roane, a lawyer and eventually a district judge in Knoxville, became Tennessee's second governor and the inspiration for Roane County.

In the short interval between completing his education by Carrick and Roane and assuming the leading role he would play in Tennessee government and business, the refined White gained a considerable reputation (which he despised) in a major Indian war. In September 1793, frontiersmen all across the Southwest Territory swore revenge on the Indian terrorist Doublehead, whose renegades slaughtered settlers (despite their surrender) at Cavett's Station, a small fort west of Knoxville. Acting Territorial Governor Daniel Smith ordered General John Sevier into action with the militia. They invaded and destroyed Cherokee and Creek towns in what would become Sevier's last and most famous Indian expedition. At the final Battle of Etowah (Rome, Georgia) in October 1793, nineteen-year-old White sealed a victory when he killed the Creek leader, whose forces quickly gave up the fight. Appalled that he had taken a life, White later refused to cooperate with noted frontier historian and family friend J. G. M. Ramsey, who sought to glamorize him with the other early Indian fighters in the popular nineteenth-century book *Annals of Tennessee.*

White busied himself instead with public service, setting the stage for a patchwork career in which he would journey from one professional calling to another. A year later, he became private secretary to Governor Blount. After studying law in Pennsylvania and opening a Knoxville law practice around 1796, young White immediately established a friendship with fellow attorney Andrew Jackson. Their relationship became strong and long-lasting, but future politics would fracture their alliance.

Thanks to the White family gristmill on First Creek, Knoxville was becoming a center for commerce. The patriarch James White set the stage for other water-powered industries, including spinning mills, a paper mill, and an iron foundry. His son, meanwhile, would soon play a role in stabilizing the frontier's economy.

At twenty-eight, young Hugh Lawson White was a judge of the Superior Court, the highest judicial body in the state. He left the bench in 1807 to become a state senator, then United States district attorney in 1809. By 1812, when White became the first president of the Bank of the State of Tennessee, Knoxville's economy was depending less and less on the practice of bartering. For the next fifteen years, White supervised the bank (without pay), and it was the only Tennessee bank to survive "all the financial storms of that tempestuous period." Even in the banking community, White could not escape his role as a tough frontiersman. A back-breaking, dangerous horseback journey to the East Coast was necessary to obtain needed plates, engravings, and other equipment for the bank's printing capabilities. Meeting the challenge, White rode east. Procuring and then protecting the essential bank equipment against land pirates, he returned home with the "first machinery of the first Bank of Tennessee."

Honest, humane, dignified, dependable, White was rapidly becoming as popular in Tennessee as the nation's war hero and populist politician, Jackson himself. In subsequent years, White returned twice more to the state senate, receiving every Knox County vote but one in the 1817 election. In 1819, he became one of only three men in the nation chosen to handle America's treaty claims after Spain ceded Florida to the United States.

In sudden failing health and realizing that he could not withstand the rigors of that job, White retired to his farm to begin a regimen of rest and exercise. (The pioneering White family reportedly was prone to some type of degenerative disease). He seemed to effect his cure quite by accident. One winter morning, his daily walk brought him to an icy stream, which he attempted to cross by walking a log. He slipped and fell into the frigid water. His clothes froze instantly to his body and remained a block of ice until he reached home. As his overall health steadily improved, he credited the turnaround to his immersion in the icy creek.

White's health held out for years to come, enabling him to make a bid for the United States presidency in 1836. He was no longer in the same camp with his longtime friend and fellow Democrat from the early East Tennessee frontier, the outgoing president, Andrew Jackson. Though always fond of Jackson, White could not agree on such issues as the concept of political patronage or a harsh attitude toward the removal of the Cherokees from their homeland. Nor could he agree that the president should have as much power as Jackson intended. The election pitted White against Jackson's designee, the unpopular northerner, Martin Van Buren of New York. Although White lost the election, he carried Tennessee (even Jackson's Hermitage district) and signaled massive damage to the Jacksonian political machine. Jackson's power in Tennessee was nearing its end and creating (out of Jackson's own party) the Whig Party in Tennessee.

White, one of the founders of this anti-Jackson coalition, died in 1840 at the age of sixty-seven. He missed seeing the Whigs come to political power in the decade that followed.

13
Elve Bowie

Pistol Packin': A Local Sheriff's Dilemma

When Elve Bowie's husband, Rezin, was arrested in 1795 for killing a squatter who refused to move, she seemed resigned to the Sumner County sheriff's decision to put her Rezin behind bars, at least for a while.

The sheriff was not keen on arresting a man like Rezin Bowie. He was a respected settler at Elliott Springs, a Revolutionary War hero who bore scars from his duty with Francis Marion ("the Swamp Fox") and other early fighting men. Bowie had built a small five-hundred-acre plantation with six slaves brought from Georgia. He was hardly a wealthy man, but he was secure enough, having produced cotton, corn, and tobacco on the land which he had been given by the government as compensation for his war duty. He also operated a small lumber mill at Elliott Springs.

The sheriff explained almost apologetically to both Bowies that, in this matter, he needed to give credibility to his role as a law enforcer.

Bowie went along with him willingly. After three days had passed, however, Elve Bowie thought the sheriff had given enough credibility to his role. Her husband, after all, was an independent man who made independent and fair decisions. He had warned the squatter many times about trespassing, and, according to the law, was justified in killing an intruder encroaching on his domain.

Elve Bowie, who was pregnant, rode in a buckboard to the small log jail. She was annoyed but presented herself in a most ladylike fashion. Could she see the prisoner? The sheriff was more than happy to accommodate her. Ushered into the cell, she stayed only five minutes before calling for the sheriff's return. "Mr. Sheriff," she declared, "I have decided to take my husband home. All this foolishness has gone far enough." Two drawn pistols—one held by each of the Bowies—made her point. The sheriff agreed, and, with a sheepish grin, stepped aside and watched them go. He believed that on the frontier an upstanding citizen like Rezin Bowie should be allowed to stand up for his rights.

Shortly after the 1795 episode, Elve Bowie gave birth to her eighth child and named him James. The growing Bowie family decided to move seven years later, at which time the couple gathered their large brood and left Middle Tennessee for Louisiana. Two of their sons, James and older brother Rezin Jr. (born at Elliott Springs in 1793), would lead a life of constant adventure and, in time, engrave their names in American history. In Louisiana, the Bowie sons became known as "those wild Bowies" for such antics as riding alligators in the swamps of lower Louisiana and lassoing wild bulls and killing them with a knife.

In 1836, Jim Bowie joined Tennessean David Crockett as one of the heroes who died defending the Alamo during Texas's fight for independence from Mexico. Older brother Rezin Pleasants Bowie Jr. added luster to the family name with his famous Bowie knife.

14

Solomon Massengale

Pillory Post Justice

Losing his ear was not nearly so traumatic for Solomon Massengale as the prospect of losing his reputation.

In the late eighteenth century, justice on the frontier was swift and often crude. A convicted lawbreaker might have the first letter of his offense branded on his cheek (*T* for theft, *M* for manslaughter, etc.). Or he might be whipped. Or he might lose an ear.

Ear cropping became so common during this era that any person who entered a town with part or all of an ear missing, even if the loss was suffered in a noble pursuit, immediately aroused the suspicion of the townfolk. When Massengale (or Massengill), missing his right ear, arrived in Jonesborough along the Great Stage Road, he was worried that he might be considered untrustworthy. He therefore petitioned the East Tennessee court for a certificate of character, as follows (spellings are given as recorded):

> Jordan Roach made oath that he was in company with Solomon Massengill in South Carolina at which place they both were in an action against the Brittish at Blackstocks under Command of General Sumpter and that in said action he had just reasons to believe that said Massengill had his right year cutt off by a Brittish Dragoon, and the same is ordered to be recorded.

Thus wearing his injury as a hero of the Revolutionary War, Massengale settled into a life of respect in the upper East Tennessee mountains. Home was the Watauga Settlements, where his father, Henry Massengale Sr., was one of Tennessee's first settlers and the owner of considerable property along the Watauga River and Boone's Creek.

Originally from North Carolina, the Massengales had moved to Watauga in 1769, the same year as the territory's first recorded permanent white settler, William Bean, owner of the adjacent plantation. In 1777, the elder Massengale became sheriff of the Washington District (created that year by an act of North Carolina) and also built one of the region's first churches. He and each of his three sons then fought in the Revolutionary War.

Solomon Massengale, like his father, participated in the development of the Watauga Settlements. When the area became part of a federal territory in 1790, Territorial Governor William Blount appointed him an ensign in the Washington County, North Carolina, militia. Blount, a family friend, was then residing near present-day Johnson City. He set up the first territorial government in the house where he was staying: Rocky Mount, the home of Solomon Massengale's father-in-law, William Cobb (Massengale was married to Tabitha Cobb).

In 1796, when Washington County was absorbed into the newly created state of Tennessee, Massengale became a member of the first county court, helping select Jonesborough as the county seat.

The laws of the frontier did not change, however. In 1799, the Washington County Court sentenced one perjurer to be nailed by the ears to the pillory post and left there for an hour. After his time had ended, his ears were to be cut off and left on the pillory until sundown—a reminder to others of the wages of sin.

15
Daniel Smith

Commanding All about Him—Except the Women in His Life

One summer day in 1797, sixteen-year-old Mary Smith (called "Polly"), the apple of her father's eye, sat at home listening to the romantic yearnings of her heart and dreaming about her escape in a few hours into the arms of Samuel Donelson. His father was the late John Donelson, cofounder of Nashville; hers was General Daniel Smith, one of the most prominent men on the early Middle Tennessee frontier.

A doting father by all accounts, General Smith had great plans for Polly, including an education at a boarding school in Philadelphia, where she could mix "with girls of her own class." But Polly was in love with Donelson, and her mother, Sarah, reluctantly agreed that she had "all the education she needs to make her a good wife and mother."

Having found Donelson courting Polly and seeing a gold ring on her finger, Smith determined to send her away immediately. But he could not act fast enough. That night, Donelson and his best friend, law partner, and brother-in-law, Andrew Jackson, came for Polly. The two placed a sapling ladder under her window,

and down Polly climbed, leaping into her lover's arms and riding off with Jackson and a third accomplice to Jackson's house. A clergyman was standing ready.

The next day, Jackson called on General Smith hoping to secure the father's blessing for the new couple. "Tell her," thundered the grieving Smith, "to forget that she has a father and a mother, and we shall forget that we ever had a daughter. Tell Sam Donelson to keep out of my way, and as for you, Andrew Jackson, keep out of my way also."

Some people claimed that Smith was the only man whom Jackson ever feared. In a political irony, when Jackson resigned his United States Senate seat a year later, Smith succeeded him. Soon thereafter, Smith County came into being, yet another tribute in a long list of honors and accolades that were filling Smith's life.

A Revolutionary War hero, Smith produced the first Tennessee map (giving Tennessee's northern border its shape) and helped settle Middle Tennessee after his 1783 arrival. He also guided new settlers there. In 1790, President George Washington appointed him secretary of the Southwest Territory, the far-reaching frontier that included present Tennessee. Upon Tennessee's statehood, Daniel Smith became the first militia general. He was also admired by Washington's rival, Thomas Jefferson, who claimed in writing that Smith was one of the best surveyors in the nation, and added: "For intelligence, well cultivated talents, for integrity and usefulness, in soundness of judgement, in the practice of virtue and in shunning vice, he was equalled by few men, and in the purity of motive excelled by none."

The Smith homestead in Sumner County was a 3,140-acre farm, featuring the house called "Rock Castle," the first frontier dwelling built of stone. National and regional politicians, literary figures, and cultural-minded leaders often visited and were surprised to find a civilized outpost in the wilderness. The Smith library contained books in English, Spanish, French, and German.

But the house would take on a somber mood after Polly left. Smith boarded up the window from which she eloped, cut down the maple tree that had helped her escape, and forbade her name to be spoken in the house. Polly never returned.

Ten years later, Smith's house servant, who had been Polly's "mammy," begged to go to her and care for her three children. Smith consented. Later, Samuel Donelson died from pneumonia, having fallen ill on a wintertime visit to the home of his sister and brother-in-law, Rachel and Andrew Jackson. On his deathbed, Donelson solicited a promise that Jackson would become guardian of his small sons—two of whom were named Andrew Jackson Donelson and Daniel Smith Donelson.

Jackson kept his word. He and Rachel took the children into their home when Polly Donelson remarried. He guided his namesake through West Point, into law school, and toward a political career. General Smith, who had apparently forgiven Jackson for his part in the elopement, wrote Jackson many times in appreciation of his assistance to Polly and the boys.

Andrew Jackson Donelson grew up to marry a cousin, Emily Donelson. She was especially dear to Andrew Jackson, who would face his 1829 presidency in deep despair due to Rachel's death. President Jackson thereupon asked twenty-one-year-old Emily to be hostess of the White House. It was a role that Emily Donelson would not relinquish in her lifetime; she died seven years later. Her husband, serving as the president's secretary, continued in politics, married again, and later became the vice presidential candidate on the unsuccessful 1856 ticket with Millard Fillmore.

16
The Harpe Brothers
The Frontier's Worst Nightmare

In terms of sheer carnage, the most feared outlaws of the late eighteenth century were the Harpe brothers. No respecters of persons, they vented their bloodthirsty rage on men, women, and children of every race and occupation.

The Harpes, Micajah and Wiley, called "Big Harpe" and "Little Harpe," arrived about 1797 from Georgia (or so they said) and settled along Beaver Creek in Knox County. They married girls from surrounding communities and, for about a year, were peaceful farmers who seemed outwardly neighborly. The Harpes' friendliness, however, quickly evaporated.

First there were a few thefts of their neighbors' farm animals. When Knoxvillian Edward Tiel lost some of his prize horses, he and several friends gave chase, suspecting the Harpes. The entire countryside being covered in deep grass and pea vine, Tiel and his companions were able to follow a perfect path of hoof prints. Tracks left in the lush undergrowth led all the way to the Cumberland Mountains, where the Harpes were apprehended and the horses rescued. However, the brothers escaped Tiel's custody and began their life on the run.

Shortly thereafter, wholesale plundering and murder came naturally. Having crossed back across the Clinch River to Copper Ridge, the Harpes came across a Knox County youth named Coffey who was headed for a grist mill. For no apparent reason, they killed him. That murder was followed quickly by another—a Hawkins County man named Johnson, who encountered the Harpes two miles from Knoxville. He was shot in the head. The Harpes then extended their inhuman deeds to the Cumberland Plateau and into Kentucky. In 1842, historian J. W. M. Breazeale described, in *Life As It Was,* the Harpes' full impact on the infant state of Tennessee:

> The whole community was now in a state of consternation and alarm; companies were raised, scouts kept continually out and rewards offered for the apprehension of these murderous and marauding wretches; in consequence of which they were compelled to seek shelter in a more wild and uninhabited region; and they, therefore, fled, taking their women with them, to the mountains, along the line between Tennessee and Kentucky; occasionally breaking into the settlements . . . and committing the most awful, horrible and bloody murders.

Often their victims were innocents whose only transgression was being in the wrong place at the wrong time (that being anywhere the Harpes were at any given time). The brothers even victimized members of their own family. To cover their tracks, the Harpes would often use grisly methods. Johnson, for instance, was split open, his chest cavity filled with stones, then dumped into the river (a method imitated by later criminal types on the frontier).

Although they lived for a time across the Kentucky border, the Harpes returned to Tennessee, committing one of their last regional murders near Kingston. But Roane County settlers formed a manhunt to find them, and the brothers fled again across the state border.

The Harpes were caught in Kentucky a few times by citizen posses but always managed to escape or, according to one account, bribe their way out of jail. However, the frontier system of justice would not let them get away. Two men who lost family members to the Harpes would bring them down.

Their last joint criminal venture was in 1801. While hiding in Kentucky, they killed the wife and infant child of former Knox County resident Moses Stegall. After an eight-mile chase on horseback, a small group of outraged citizens overtook Micajah. The grief-stricken Stegall meted out his brand of punishment, avenging his family's murder by decapitating the outlaw on the spot. Micajah's comment when his own knife was being raked across the back of his neck revealed his character. With a fiendish and contemptuous expression, he looked Stegall in the eye: "You are a d——d rough butcher, but cut on and be d——d."

Big Harpe's severed head was displayed (either atop a pole or in the fork of a tree) at a crossroads in Union County, Kentucky, where it remained for some time as a reminder of the horror he had wrought. The crossroads area was named Harpe's Head and the street passing through it Harpe's Head Road.

Tennessee historians later began to theorize about the true origin of the naming of the Harpeth River, which flows just south of Nashville. Some believed the river came by its name from the Harpe brothers, who terrorized the area. Others seemed to think there is little evidence available to establish the true source of the Harpeth River's name and hoped that the likes of the Harpes are not associated—especially since early documents in 1784, years before the brothers appeared, were already using a similar name, "Harpath."

Three years after Micajah's death, Wiley was captured and executed—a victim of his own greed. He was identified in Natchez while trying to claim a bounty by turning in the severed head of a fellow gang member. The man who ended Wiley's days was Nashvillian John Stump. He was among the Tennessee troops being sent by the United States into newly acquired Louisiana. En route through Natchez, Stump recognized the face of his brother's killer; and, fulfilling his long-held hopes, Stump pointed out Wiley to authorities, bringing an end to the horrible Harpes.

17
Garner McConnico
Booming Voice for Christianity

Garner McConnico, whose voice was as strong as his faith.

His voice was "like a trumpet." Not even the roaring, rain-swollen Harpeth River, which neither man nor beast could cross one day in the late 1790s, could drown out the sounds of Garner McConnico, one of the most famous Baptist preachers in the Cumberland region.

Unable to reach his followers on the opposite riverbank, McConnico planted his feet along the Harpeth, and, according to a witness, "raised his voice a little above its usual pitch and preached a fine sermon, every word of which was distinctly heard, notwithstanding the distance and the dashing of the swollen stream against its banks." Being able to pitch his voice across a river was but one talent that McConnico brought to early Middle Tennessee. Other witnesses claimed that he also could (and did) cast out devils.

That he developed such a dramatic reputation seemed unlikely for a man who was actually fleeing from the Lord when he left his native Virginia in 1795.

Accompanied by his bride, McConnico had a case of western fever and simply sought a better life near Nashville, as well as a respite from the call to preach. Settling in Williamson County at Franklin, McConnico found that he could resist his calling no longer. About 1797, while tracking a stray farm horse, he encountered Elder Dillahunty, a Baptist minister who soon learned of McConnico's indecision about being a preacher. Dillahunty literally dragged him into the pulpit.

In 1800, McConnico built the Big Harpeth Church and became the key organizer of the Cumberland Association, of which Big Harpeth was the most renowned member church. When the Great Revival (or the Second Great Awakening) began about the same time, a religious expression surfaced called "the jerks," sudden fits of convulsive dancing, falling, or running engaged in by some Christians who claimed these spasms were divinely inspired. Although McConnico did not like them, the jerks were widespread. So, too, was the concept of a camp meeting—an interdenominational "camping out" for several days. This gathering of Christians featured sermonizing, singing, and socializing. A single meeting could attract thousands of worshipers. (Smith County's Methodist minister John McGee reportedly was the "father of camp meetings in America.") The Baptists were reluctant partners with the Methodists and Presbyterians at such camp sessions, but all three major denominations were so successful that their frontier memberships mushroomed overnight.

McConnico refused to condone the jerks in his own Great Revival sermons. When one of his parishioners suffered a case of the jerks in one meeting, McConnico paused briefly, then issued an order: "In the name of the Lord, I command all unclean spirits to leave this place." The worshiper ceased his convulsions, calmed down, then returned to his seat, causing reports to circulate that preacher McConnico had cast out another devil.

Most early Baptist ministers were farmer-preachers, and McConnico was no exception. In addition to his home church and many evangelical services, he also found time to help begin numerous regional churches. In 1806 during his frequent travels to Dickson County, he helped organize the Turnbull Creek Church, where slaves were brought into membership. (Generally, they were only allowed to worship in a separate section of the congregation.)

Although McConnico helped to start at least seven other churches, he remained the only pastor of Big Harpeth Church. He stayed with Big Harpeth for thirty-three years until his death in 1833 at the age of sixty-two.

18
Margaret Russell Ramsey
The Molding of Great Men

Bereaved and pregnant: that is how Margaret Russell's husbands left her. Three times she was married. Three times she was widowed. Each time she bore her grief, and then she bore her late husband a son.

Her first husband was James Cowan, whom she met and married in her hometown, Dandridge. The couple had just moved to Knoxville, where Cowan planned to open a store in 1801. He then died of a fever in June of that year. Six months later, the widow gave birth to a son, James H. Cowan, a future Knoxville mayor and merchant.

Within the year, she married her second husband, Thomas Humes, who gave her four sons over their fourteen-year marriage (one of whom, named for his father, became an 1830s newspaper editor, an Episcopal clergyman, then president of East Tennessee University and its successor, the University of Tennessee). Her husband died in 1816. A few months later, Margaret Humes gave birth to their fifth son, Andrew, who became a member of the Knoxville Board of Mayors and Aldermen and donated a building in Knoxville for his brother's church, St. John's Protestant Episcopal.

Her third husband was widower Francis Alexander Ramsey, the father of grown children (among them physician and state historian Dr. J. G. M. Ramsey, who later said that he often sought his stepmother's wise counsel). Francis Ramsey was one of the first Knoxville settlers. After marrying Margaret in 1820, he became a prominent local banker and died the same year, of malarial fever. Five months later, Margaret Ramsey gave birth to his son, Francis A. Ramsey, who would become a physician like his half-brother and would help to establish the East Tennessee Medical Society, the Confederate military hospitals, and the first civilian hospital in Knoxville.

Although pursued by many suitors after the demise of her third husband, Margaret Ramsey did not marry again. She did, however, see each of her sons to adulthood and prominence before her death in 1854 at the age of seventy-seven. Her tombstone in Knoxville spoke to the contributions she had made as a mother and as a member of the community. Upon it is written: "A Mother in Israel," a title reserved for those who were leaders in civic, church, and charitable contributions to the betterment of their pioneer neighbors.

19
Louis Philippe

French Royalty Roving the Tennessee Country

In the mid-nineteenth century, the king of France, Louis Philippe, would often ask American visitors, "Do you still sleep three in a bed in Tennessee?" The king, in recalling his nearly four-year sojourn in America between 1796 and 1800, remembered with amusement his Tennessee nighttime lodgings. His journal of that trip became one of the more unusual and famous accounts of a European traveler who described what life was like on the Tennessee frontier.

Louis Philippe, then the Duc d'Orleans, was an exile from France's political wars. He became "that earnest tourist" after landing in Philadelphia in October 1796. Louis Philippe heard President George Washington's farewell address and later visited the president's home, Mount Vernon, where Washington encouraged him to embark on a journey across America, as it existed then. President Washington planned each detail of the expedition.

Equipped with Washington's map, Louis Philippe pursued a frontier itinerary bringing him into the new state of Tennessee. In Louis Philippe's company were his two brothers, the devoted servant Baudoin, and an unnamed dog (all of them exiles from France). For the most part, they found the inland country to be uninhabited.

Arriving April 30, 1797, in Knoxville—a growing metropolis of one hundred houses—Louis Philippe was attacked by bedbugs while staying at Chisholm's Tavern. Billed in newspaper ads as a "house of entertainment," Chisholm's had offered reasonable rates: one shilling for breakfast and supper, one shilling and a six-pence for dinner, plus whiskey at six-pence per half pint and wine for one dollar a quart. No price was given for hog lard, the popular home remedy for

bedbugs. Although Louis Philippe greased his body with it, he found no relief from the itching. According to local accounts, he rushed outside screaming and jumped into the Tennessee River.

From Knoxville—where Louis Philippe also was the guest of the former Territorial Governor William Blount—the royal party made its way through Maryville, an outpost on the border of the Cherokee nation. Taken by the beauty of the area, they continued to Tellico Plains, desiring to visit a Cherokee village. At the Tellico Block House, a small fort operated by Indian agents, Louis Philippe bought a turkey, a pig, and a gallon of strawberries from the Cherokees.

While in the area, he fell from his horse and treated himself with the medical technique known as "bleeding." According to one source, Louis Philippe's success in treating his wounds prompted the Cherokees to ask him to give medical care to an important chief. This too was a success. As a reward, Louis Philippe received the honor (which had never been given to another white man) of sleeping in the chief's quarters, and "more than that," wrote a later historian, "upon the family mat, and in the place of highest honor—between the grandmother and the grandaunt, the most venerable of the squaws." Despite good-natured joking from his two brothers, Louis Philippe spent the night thus, for fear of offending his hosts.

The Frenchmen remained as guests of the Cherokees and observed their culture, which was of particular interest to Louis Philippe. Impressed with the Cherokees' skill at playing ball games, he offered them two barrels of brandy if they would stage a contest for his viewing. The resulting match involved six hundred players using hands, feet, and lacrosse sticks to drive a deerskin ball through a goal. (The area where they staged their games became known as Ball Play.)

The next morning, Louis Philippe and his party decamped for Nashville, the limit of civilization on their journey (they would then turn north). The route to Nashville was little more than a narrow path, and there were no settlers for a hundred miles. At one point, the Frenchmen lived on smoked bear grease and corn until they got to Castalian Springs, near Gallatin, and had their first taste of coffee in some time.

Arriving in Nashville on May 10, 1797, Louis Philippe cheerfully anticipated comforts not found in the wilderness. But Nashville was still small, with only eighty houses. When he and his group stopped at Captain

Jesse Maxwell's (whose place became the location of the future Maxwell House Hotel), they discovered that because court was in session and overnight accommodations were overrun with guests, they had to sleep three to a bed.

20
"Granny" White

Best Inn and Tavern between Here and There

Lucinda "Granny" White operated an early nineteenth-century inn near Nashville, where travelers could find "the best brandy, best pancakes and cleanest beds of any tavern on the road." Granny's inn was one of the most popular between Louisville and New Orleans and the first stagecoach stop out of Nashville on the road to New Orleans. United States Senator Thomas Hart Benton (the former Tennessean who became a national political figure in Missouri and inspired the naming of West Tennessee's Benton County) loved to tell Granny White stories to Congress in the 1820s every time he encouraged land grants for the worthy poor. Granny's was an inspiring frontier rags-to-riches story.

The most popular version is Benton's, describing how North Carolina courts took custody of sixty-year-old Granny White's orphaned grandchildren (some said children), claiming she was too poor to care for them. She loaded the youngsters, a slave, and her few worldly possessions in an ox cart, and escaped to Tennessee, slowly traveling several hundred miles through Indian territory and across mountains. She could only move a few miles each day because she was too poor to buy feed for the ox and had to let it graze along the way.

Granny had an eye for business locales. She broke up her journey periodically to work. Each time she relocated, she set up stands to sell ginger cakes. Purchases from passing wagon trains helped business boom. Granny made her first stop between Knoxville and Kingston, then stopped again in Rhea County. While selling ginger cakes from a stand near Piney Creek, she realized the potential market for tar, which travelers needed to lubricate their wheels and hubs. Piney Creek, as the name implies, had plenty of the pine trees needed to make tar. She dug an earth pit and proceeded to burn the pine and extract the tar. Once

again, her business prospered; she soon sold it to the Haney family, who established an important inn on the site and became prosperous at her location.

Granny finally settled in Nashville and there bought what appeared to be unpromising land. It was located in a gap with steep hills on either side. She farmed the land anyway (some claimed she staked her pumpkins to keep them from rolling down the hill). She also built a frame house and began to take in travelers, since she was near the Natchez Trace and just outside of Nashville on the road going south.

The odd configuration of her rooms at the inn gave rise to much confusion. When Granny expanded her accommodations, she did so haphazardly, merely adding rooms to one another without building connecting hallways, thereby creating a mazelike effect. Dwellers, who could reach their rooms only by going through someone else's, generally relied on Granny to escort them to the correct location. According to some accounts, one guest became lost and fired a shot to be found. The innkeeper counted heads each morning at breakfast to make certain all the guests had found their way out.

Granny's legend lived on in Senator Benton's stories for the *Congressional Record*, but historians' efforts to find out who she really was have produced conflicting versions of her life. One version stated she was the widow of an early Middle Tennessee pioneer, Zechariah White, killed in a 1781 Indian raid known as the Battle of the Bluffs. Since her husband left a land grant, Granny's fortunes may not have been so bleak. Another version claimed she was unable to pay the surveyor's cost to obtain possession. Court records showed she purchased many acres from a Wolsey Warrington in 1803 and that her family and her slave helped build a house. According to other reports, Granny had children already living in Nashville when she began her famous journey.

Granny White died in 1816. Later generations became familiar with her name by way of famous Granny White Pike—heading south from Nashville and pointing toward New Orleans. As for Benton, he later would fall out of favor in his namesake county over the issues of states' rights and slavery. Benton Countians, however, liked the name of their county and sought another Benton (popular local farmer and War of 1812 veteran David Benton) for the honor of having the county named after him instead.

21
Meriwether Lewis

Mystery Killing on the Natchez Trace

One October night in 1809, celebrated American explorer Meriwether Lewis, suffering from a gunshot wound to the head, begged his servants to kill him, mumbling, "I am no coward; but I am so strong, so hard to die!"

When he succumbed to his wounds two hours later in a Middle Tennessee wayside inn, his death created one of the great unsolved mysteries along the old outlaw-ridden Natchez Trace, a five hundred-mile wilderness path that cut across the state from a point near Nashville and dipped into northwestern Alabama and then Mississippi. This overland route was an ancient animal and Indian pathway, sometimes called the Nashville Road. But in the early nineteenth century it became a path of murder and robbery. Returning flatboatmen who had sold their goods in major ports like Natchez (Mississippi) or New Orleans walked the trail, heading home to cabins in Tennessee and beyond. These men, carrying their profits, were easy prey for bandits and killers waiting in the tall canebrakes and heavy brush of virtually uninhabited territory that bordered the road. Lewis's death became the most famous of those that occurred routinely along the Trace.

Lewis's friend and mentor, President Thomas Jefferson, eventually ruled the death a suicide. But conflicting accounts and reports suggest Lewis likely was murdered, either by a random attack, as so often happened on the Trace, or from an assassination ordered by political rivals of Jefferson's. A Tennessee inquest only confused the matter, and Tennesseans joined the speculation in earnest as Lewis was buried near Grinder's Stand, where he had died.

Two years later, renowned naturalist Alexander Wilson, who greatly admired Lewis, was on a bird-study tour of the Trace and visited the grave. He later wrote: "He lies buried by the common path with a few loose rails thrown over his grave. I gave Grinder money to put up a post fence around it, to shelter it from the hogs, and from the wolves."

Lewis, who had once been Jefferson's secretary, had returned to the president's side in 1806, fresh from the successful Lewis and Clark expedition to the Pacific Northwest and the mapping of the Louisiana Territory. This adventure had captured the imagination of the American public, and Lewis and fellow explorer William Clark were welcomed back in the East as national heroes.

As a reward in 1808, Jefferson appointed the somewhat emotionally unstable, hot-tempered Lewis to succeed controversial General James Wilkinson as governor of upper Louisiana Territory. Lewis was told to report immediately to the territorial headquarters in St. Louis to replace Wilkinson, who had fallen from favor partly because of an entanglement in land deals and other profiteering in the St. Louis area.

Adding to what would become a political quagmire for Lewis, another controversial man, Frederick Bates, was acting governor. Later revealing that he also had prospered while serving as an official of the federal territory, Bates had wavering political loyalties to Jefferson. Bates quickly made known his disdain for Lewis, accusing him of being "spoiled by 'elegant praises.'" He also noticed that Lewis occasionally drank to excess and seemed overly concerned about his health. Despite the criticism, Lewis apparently did a better job governing than Wilkinson, creating a militia, codifying laws, and negotiating with nearby tribes. Yet Lewis was soon troubled by United States War Department clerks who began to challenge each voucher for his office expenditures (Bates is said to have given "extra twists" to the problem).

Lewis decided to return to Washington to clear up the matter. Intending to travel by way of the Mississippi River and then the open sea, he changed his mind when he learned that the United States and Great Britain were nearing war. Lewis now feared that he might lose his critical paperwork plus his accounts from the Lewis and Clark expedition, which he also carried. Arriving at Fort Pickering near present-day Memphis, Lewis decided to go overland through Chickasaw country. Since he had once been the commander of Fort Pickering, Lewis was familiar with the Tennessee countryside as well as the friendly Chickasaw and their language.

Arriving on the Natchez Trace with two servants (one of whom was a Cajun derelict he had hired on the St. Louis docks) and United States Chickasaw agent Major James Neely, Lewis proceeded slowly over difficult terrain. On October 10, thunderstorms and torrential rains caused their skittish pack horses to run away, carrying with them Lewis's papers in saddle-bags. Neely gave chase, the servants temporarily lagged behind, and Lewis began walking to the nearest over-night stand or inn.

The stand, located at the edge of Chickasaw land in United States territory, was owned by Robert E. Grinder, who happened not to be home. But Lewis secured a room from the nervous Mrs. Grinder. She allowed the servants to stay in the barn, a hundred yards away. That night Lewis acted strangely, accord-ing to later accounts by Mrs. Grinder when the natu-ralist Alexander Wilson interviewed her. Alternating between moments of agitation and composure, Lewis was drinking and taking a white powder from a canis-ter; then he began talking to himself.

After dinner, Mrs. Grinder shut herself and her chil-dren into the kitchen. Lewis retired to his room, where she said that he paced the floor "like a lawyer." Dur-ing the night, she heard a pistol shot from his room and something fall to the floor. A voice cried, "O Lord!" There was a second shot, and Lewis came to her locked door, calling out, "O, Madam! give me some water and heal my wounds!"

Mrs. Grinder did not open the door, although she could see (through the unchinked logs) Lewis stum-bling around the yard and scraping an empty water bucket in a futile search for water. She offered no aid until two hours later, at sunrise, when she sent for Lewis's servants. They found him still alive with a piece of his forehead blown away and begging for death. He died in his room as the sun topped the trees in the clearing. From Wilson's notes, Lewis appears to have been shot through the side and then finished off by an assailant with a bullet to the head.

At the time of Lewis's passage, the Natchez Trace was also known for the violence occasionally done to travelers by unscrupulous innkeepers. Some fron-tier hosts were known to have robbed and murdered their guests, then buried the evidence nearby. A local coroner's jury met and seriously considered the pos-sibility that Grinder may have returned and killed Lewis. Reports surfaced that the jurors believed Grinder guilty, but because they feared him, did nothing.

Some people suggested that the Cajun servant who accompanied Lewis was involved, since Lewis's watch later surfaced in New Orleans. Others believed that Lewis was the victim of a political conspiracy that be-gan with Wilkinson and Bates. (The latter continued to undermine Lewis's achievements as governor, and he grew rich in St. Louis during three later appoint-ments as acting governor.)

While former President Jefferson, in 1813, seemed to think that Lewis committed suicide, many Tennes-seans insisted that he was murdered. During the on-going controversy, the Middle Tennessee area where the explorer lost his life became Lewis County in 1843. His burial site at the old Grinder's Stand then received a state of Tennessee monument in 1849-50. The monument, however, only added to the continu-ing mystery, acknowledging the possibility of suicide but also stating: "It seems more probable that he died at the hands of an assassin."

As for the Natchez Trace, its history of robbing and killing ended when steamboats began to ply the Mis-sissippi River, giving Tennesseans and other travelers a safer and faster way of journeying home.

22

Daniel Buchanan

A Bear of a Man in the Wilderness

Houston County's manliest of men around 1810 was two-fisted, fleet-footed, quick-witted Daniel Buchanan. Considered without equal either in strength or valor on the Middle Tennessee frontier, he could build any-thing without any other man's help. Buchanan is said to have erected an entire split-rail fence: cutting the forest timber, shouldering the massive cut logs to the site, and assembling the final product with more muscle than anyone could imagine, in what was then Stewart County. But what absolutely bewildered his friends was the day Buchanan single-handedly car-ried a bear carcass from the woods—or what was left of the bear.

The night before, Buchanan had been forced by dark-ness into making camp. As he slept, the bear attacked. Seizing a burning stick from his campfire, he "thrust it down the bear's throat," and the real fight began.

A Houston County history by Iris Hopkins McClain explains: "In the struggle that followed he beat the life out of the bear with his fists and feet. The next day when the bear carcass was stripped of its hide, it was discovered that nearly all the ribs were broken and the flesh had been beaten into a jelly. Buchanan was scarcely scratched." He had, as she notes, "no match in the settlement."

Since Houston County was not founded until 1871, all of its frontier history is tied to its parent counties: Montgomery, Stewart, Dickson, and Humphreys. From Dickson County, one of Buchanan's direct descendants would be the multiterm Tennessee governor, Frank Clement, who held office in 1953-59 and again in 1964-67.

Buchanan, meanwhile, soon crossed the nearby Tennessee River and built one of the first homesteads in West Tennessee (present-day Benton County). When the region was finally relinquished by the Chickasaw in 1818, Buchanan filed one of the first West Tennessee land claims, remaining with his family along the banks of Big Sandy River.

23

Tecumseh

A Seething Warrior's Response to Invasion

If one person justified Tennessee settlers' fears of Indian uprisings, it was the magnetic Shawnee chief Tecumseh. He journeyed into their midst from the Midwest in 1811, exhorting various local tribes to join him in a war to stop settlers from grabbing ancient Indian lands. With Tennesseans at the center of the storm, he eventually persuaded the Creeks to join a confederacy that would tear apart the southern frontier.

This was not Tecumseh's first experience shaping events in the region. In his youth, he and one of his brothers were among a group of Shawnees who traveled across the future Tennessee. They made extended journeys, much like the white Long Hunters who came from North Carolina, Virginia, and other settled states to hunt the plentiful wildlife on Indian hunting grounds. These hunting ventures were a rite of passage for young warriors. But Tecumseh reached adulthood in the Tennessee countryside in 1788, fighting settlers and mourning the death of his brother. Both men had possessed a hatred from childhood against white invaders who had burned their villages and killed their father and other family members.

The day his brother was killed, Tecumseh and his fellow hunters had been part of a Cherokee raid on the Cumberland Settlements. When the Cherokees quit the fight and his brother lay dead, Tecumseh led

the remaining Shawnees against the Montgomery family on Drake Creek in Sumner County, killing the men and making captives of the women and children. For the next two years, Tecumseh journeyed throughout the region carving a path of destruction alongside the Cherokees and Creeks. (They also made assaults in Kentucky territory and future Alabama and Florida.) Stories began to circulate within the tribes that Tecumseh was someone special, perhaps peculiarly special. He could, for instance, hear and see things that eluded others, especially at night when he seemed to sleep with one eye open. After he accurately predicted at least three surprise nighttime attacks by whites, Tecumseh assumed luminary stature.

With his anger continuously aimed at the white settlers' unrelenting expansion, Tecumseh began to plan a major war that would include every known tribe. When he came again to the South in 1811, he visited local tribes (the Choctaws, Chickasaws, and Creeks), preaching a message of unity and a plan to divide and conquer foreign invaders. Part of his strategy was the foretelling of events as predicted by yet another brother, the Prophet.

If Tecumseh could get the tribes to unite in a confederacy, he would enlist Spanish and British aid against the United States. With divine help, he claimed, the combined tribes would defeat American intruders—and next the Spanish and British as well. Tecumseh repeated the Prophet's words: "When the white men approach your towns the earth shall open and swallow them up." Tecumseh's message was severe: "Burn their dwellings—destroy their stock—slay their wives and children, that the very breed may perish." He declared with force: "War now! War always! War on the living! War on the dead! Dig their very bones from their graves. The red man's land must give no shelter to a white man's bones!"

The Choctaws refused to participate because of their longstanding animosity with the Creeks. Unhappy with the news, Tecumseh uttered a curse. He proclaimed that his fiery arm would appear in the sky (meaning that he was on the warpath). He also promised to stamp his foot and cause the earth to shake. By the end of 1811, the tribes witnessed both a comet and the beginning of an earthquake so massive that its shock waves continued until spring of 1812. These events seemed to verify Tecumseh's power.

While Tecumseh may have learned of the comet from British officers, the great earthquake of 1812 was one of history's great coincidences. Sometimes called the New Madrid earthquake, it caused the Mississippi River to flow backwards. Consequently, a sinkhole in present-day West Tennessee filled with the Mississippi's overflowing waters and became Reelfoot Lake.

Because of his charisma and predictions, Tecumseh had been able to stir a faction of his Creek relatives, who plunged their own tribe into civil war on the issue of white expansion. The earthquake was a signal to these militants to pillage pioneer homes and kill the settlers. Tecumseh had given the warriors what were reported to be supernaturally endowed sticks, painted red—the color of war and blood. In 1813, Red Sticks destroyed the inhabitants at Fort Mims, Alabama, and in so doing, set the frontier into a frenzy. Among the fort's slaughtered residents were many Tennesseans, prompting Tennessee Governor Willie Blount (half-brother of Territorial Governor William Blount) to send his militia across state lines.

The result was the Creek War, which also came to be known as the Tennessee War. Taking full responsibility, Governor Blount took action without federal approval and personally financed the military when he encouraged influential friends into cosigning three hundred thousand dollars in loans. Answering the call to arms, General Andrew Jackson and the Tennessee militia carried out this war. Having already displayed an outpouring of manpower for the accompanying War of 1812, the militia set the stage in Tennessee for the nickname of "the Volunteer State." Jackson destroyed the Red Sticks in a victory celebrated throughout America as part of the larger war against the British and their Indian allies.

Before 1813 had ended, Tecumseh had lost his life fighting with the British on other fronts. Surprisingly, he was considered a great man among Americans. The last notable symbol of Indian resistance in the East, he became a mythical figure admired by people for his valor. Many in Tennessee, as in other parts of the nation, felt inspired to name their sons "Tecumseh." One namesake, born in 1820, became an even more terrifying scourge to the South. Union General William Tecumseh Sherman began life as Tecumseh Sherman, but at the age of six, "William" was added at the request of a Catholic priest who would not baptize him without a Christian name.

24
Andrew Jackson

The Strength behind the Age of Jackson

Andrew Jackson as portrayed in an 1845 rendering.

On May 30, 1806, the major general of the Tennessee militia, thirty-nine-year-old Andrew Jackson, reeled from the impact of a bullet that entered his chest, fractured his ribs, ripped his chest muscles, and lodged close to his heart, where it would remain throughout his life. Standing on the dueling grounds of Kentucky, Jackson staggered with blood pouring from beneath his long overcoat, filling his boots.

He had prepared for the moment by donning an oversized coat so that his opponent, Nashville attorney Charles Dickinson, might misjudge the exact location of his heart. Dickinson, who could not believe he had failed to kill Jackson, yelled out: "Great God! Have I missed him?"

Then the critically wounded Jackson took aim. His pistol failed to fire. He took aim again and this time delivered a fatal shot into Dickinson's bowels. Jackson then made his way to Buttermilk Springs to rest and finally to a nearby tavern where he had spent the previous night. After he crossed the border back into Tennessee, Jackson was bedridden for more than a month. A pulmonary abscess formed, plaguing him with violent coughing attacks that also persisted throughout his life.

Many say that the argument with Dickinson was over a horse race, which would be conceivable for Jackson, whose fiery passion for racing also led him into part ownership of the famed Clover Bottom track in Davidson County. But others claim an insulting remark about Mrs. Rachel Jackson gave rise to the duel. The Jacksons had been fending off rumors of bigamy for more than a decade—and would continue to do so throughout Jackson's political career.

Although he is remembered as a strong, fierce Indian fighter, war hero, and the first populist president of the United States, Andrew Jackson lived the second half of his seventy-eight years in intense pain. His tendency to resolve conflicts physically nearly cost him his reputation as well as his life. The duel with the well-liked Dickinson might have eroded Jackson's early political luster in Tennessee had it not been for his heroics in the War of 1812 and the Creek War that accompanied it.

Jackson first arrived in what is now upper East Tennessee in 1788. He was a backwoods North Carolina lawyer appointed to be a public prosecutor in that state's western district, which would eventually comprise the state of Tennessee. Jackson hoped to find fame and fortune on the Carolina frontier. Leading a race horse (he engaged in races along the way) and a collection of hunting dogs, Jackson settled briefly in Jonesborough, waiting until enough travelers banded together for a safe wilderness journey to Nashville. While in Jonesborough, he obtained a license to practice law.

Mostly by virtue of his friendship with the federal territory's governor, William Blount, Jackson managed to become a member of the state's 1796 constitutional convention. He immediately became Tennessee's first congressman, then a United States senator, and soon a judge of the state's infant superior court—all within the first five years of statehood. But his hotheaded approach to argument soon became well known be-

cause of his intense feud with Tennessee Governor John Sevier, whom he also challenged to a duel.

During the War of 1812's early campaigns, Jackson earned his famous nickname "Old Hickory" when, according to the most popular account, he led home stranded militiamen who were freezing, hungry, and ill as the result of a long winter expedition to Natchez in February 1813. He was as tough as the toughest substance they knew: the hickory tree. Willing to share his men's suffering, Jackson gave up his horse to the sick and walked most of the distance home, sharing his meager ration of hickory nuts and acorns with his troops. Since Congress aborted the Natchez trip and refused to pay for it, Jackson used his own money and raw stubbornness to get his soldiers back to Tennessee. There, the troops waited to become actively involved in the war's battles.

During that wait, Jackson sustained his next serious injury. In keeping with his penchant for a good fight in defense of honor, Jackson agreed to be the second to one of his officers, William Carroll (a future six-term governor), in a duel with another soldier, Jesse Benton. No one was seriously injured, but a later Nashville tavern melee with Jesse and his brother, Thomas Hart Benton, left Jackson near death with a wound from Jesse's gun. Because of the fight, both Bentons left the state. (Thomas Hart Benton became famous as a United States senator from Missouri, and a grandnephew of the same name would become a famous American artist.) For weeks, Jackson lay convalescing from the brawl. With a gun at his side, he refused to have his arm amputated. He carried this bullet for most of his life.

In the fall of 1813, a pale and weakened General Jackson was summoned from this sickbed. Governor Willie Blount (pronounced "Wylie") asked him to lead volunteers against the Creek Indians who had slaughtered more than 250 inhabitants at Fort Mims, Alabama. With only one good arm, Jackson pulled himself out of bed for the expedition, which was financed by Tennessee and was Jackson's first major test as a battle commander. The enemy was a faction of young Creeks, the so-called Red Sticks, who hoped to repulse white immigration on Indian land. Members of the older Creek generation were long accustomed to whites and favored good relations; they would help Jackson in what would become known as the Creek War. The campaign started well but bloodily with a massacre of the enemy by Tennesseans at the Red Stick village of Tallushatchee. David Crockett, a scout for the expedition, observed, "We shot them like dogs."

The soldiers brought back to Jackson's camp eighty-four women and children captives. One of the children was a ten-month-old infant torn from the clutches of his dead Creek mother on the battlefield. When Indian women were asked to care for him, their only comment was, "No, all his relations are dead, kill him, too!" This response triggered something in Jackson, as he was orphaned during the Revolutionary War. He had the boy taken to his tent. His injured arm now in a sling, Jackson dissolved some brown sugar in water and coaxed the baby to drink. He then sent the infant temporarily to Maria Pope in Huntsville. She named the baby Lyncoya and took care of him with Jackson's financial support.

In subsequent battles, Jackson effectively fought both the Creeks and his own troops, who mutinied against him over short rations and long enlistments. In a series of confrontations, Jackson pitted his will against that of starving and exhausted men whose enlistment time had ended. He either blocked their path himself— once holding a musket propped across his horse's neck with his one good arm and threatening to shoot any man who crossed him—or he ordered his artillery to fire into the ranks. His belief that these men were guilty of desertion became an ongoing argument that would wage for years and become an issue in his presidential campaign (as did his placing of one soldier before the firing squad for insubordination).

Jackson's ultimate victory over the Creeks, who were British allies, led to a military reputation and recognition in Washington, D.C. He smashed through Creek defenses at the decisive and historic Battle of Horseshoe Bend on March 27, 1814. The United States government was so impressed with his militia leadership that he was immediately commissioned a United States Army general. In a grim foreshadowing of things to come (the Cherokees' removal on the Trail of Tears, which he encouraged), Jackson required that the remaining Creeks remove themselves to a new homeland so that they no longer would be close to British and Spanish influence. The Creeks relinquished millions of acres to the United States, opening up most of the Deep South for white settlement.

At the end of the Creek campaign, Jackson sent Lyncoya to live at the Hermitage as his ward and as a playmate for his other adopted son, Andrew Jackson Jr. Lyncoya enjoyed all the advantages of being a planter's son, including an education. Jackson gave explicit instructions on how the boy should be treated and wrote Rachel that "he may have been given to me for some valuable purpose." Although raised completely in a white society and regarded as a true son of Jackson, Lyncoya was known to paint his face and once fashioned a bow in the style of the Indians, which surprised the family because he had little contact with people of his own race.

Jackson next escalated his national heroic image by expelling the British from the Gulf of Mexico at Mobile, Alabama, and Pensacola, Florida. When he destroyed superior British forces in December 1815 during the War of 1812's Battle of New Orleans, Jackson became an American hero without equal—winning the war's only major American land victory. His success also ended British control of the Mississippi River and the Gulf.

Against the odds, Jackson and his Tennesseans had beaten the best of Great Britain. The casualties were lopsided, causing only six United States losses in the thrashing of a veteran British force. Aiding Jackson's contingent were free black troops, who were promised 160 acres of land each, plus regular pay, rations, clothing, and a $124 bonus; the coastal pirates; friendly Indians; and almost anyone else Jackson could recruit for the victory, including the man who provided cotton bales for a wall of protection. That man, Sam Denton, later settled near Sparta, Tennessee.

While enjoying this popularity, Jackson welcomed the arrival of his wife, Rachel, for whom he had sent prior to battle when he was especially ill. During one of the many social occasions they attended, one local French observer was struck by the seemingly mismatched General and Mrs. Jackson, who wanted to demonstrate for New Orleans sophisticates how the young people of Tennessee danced in the old days. The observer wrote:

> To see these two figures, the General, a long, haggard man, with limbs like a skeleton, and Madame la Generale, a short, fat dumpling, bobbing opposite each other like half-drunken Indians, to the wild melody of *"Possum up de Gum Tree,"* and endeavoring to make a spring into the air, was very remarkable, and far more edifying a spectacle than any European ballet could possibly have furnished.

Jackson was not so popular in other areas of New Orleans, because he had imposed martial law on the city. One Creole woman was especially unhappy when she was cajoled to prepare a feast for "a great General," only to be greeted by a sickly Jackson who had little appetite for her rich food which he could not digest. Indignant at having put forth so much effort, she remarked, "and now I find that all my labor is thrown away upon an ugly, old Kaintuck-flatboatman!"

Despite his health problems, Jackson became increasingly admired for his exploits. Wanting to capture East Florida for the United States, he conducted an 1818 raid into Spanish Florida, forcing the Seminoles farther into that territory. Jackson claimed to have had authorization from President James Monroe, but a congressional investigation claimed otherwise. Still, the general continued as the people's hero. His efforts quickened the Spanish sale of Florida a year later, and, in 1821, Jackson became military governor of the Florida Territory.

In 1822, Jackson's ill health forced him to take stock of his life. He complained to Colonel James Gadsden that his sons' education had been neglected. "Justice to them require my attention when I have health to give it," he said. While Jackson hoped to enroll Lyncoya in West Point, he knew that political opponents would not allow it. Lyncoya said he preferred the saddler's trade (Jackson had the same aspiration as a boy). In 1827, the youth was apprenticed to a saddler in Nashville. But Lyncoya soon became so ill that he returned home, permanently. Some historians believe he contracted tuberculosis. Rachel nursed Lyncoya but in vain. In the summer of 1828, Jackson was away campaigning for the presidency when Lyncoya died at age sixteen.

Despite Jackson's haggard appearance and physical ills, it was his wife who first succumbed to the strenuous life they shared. Though not always aware of the charges of bigamy and adultery which swirled around her, Rachel knew enough to dread the notion that her husband might one day become president of the United States. The stature of being in the White House could only renew the gossip of their earliest wilderness days when Rachel—having been notified incorrectly that she was already divorced—traveled with Jackson to Natchez and later married him. The easy-to-anger Jackson would forever challenge to a duel any man who assaulted Rachel's character.

Jackson had some idea of Rachel's hardship in the political arena. Following her husband's election to the

presidency in the fall of 1828, Rachel dealt poorly with the strain of moving to Washington, D.C. At one point she stated she would "rather be a doorkeeper in the house of God than to live in that palace at Washington."

When Rachel made a tiring trip into Nashville to purchase clothes for the inauguration, she stopped at the office of a newspaper publisher (to whom she was related) and sent word for her coach to come. While waiting, she came across some campaign literature defending both Jacksons, and, for the first time, Rachel realized the intensity of the attacks against their reputations. The propaganda and Lyncoya's death were too much for her, and Rachel experienced an emotional breakdown. After a rapid decline in health, she died just before Christmas of 1828, never to serve as First Lady of the United States. Her death followed Lyncoya's by six months.

Andrew Jackson, the nation's seventh president, arrived in Washington a grieving man. On behalf of the common people for whom he had campaigned, Jackson struggled against what he called the "monied aristocracy" of his day. Even after his 1845 death, the force of his personality influenced future presidents (his protégés Martin Van Buren and James K. Polk) so completely that historians would refer to that period of American history as the Age of Jackson.

25
John Overton/John Overton Jr.

Waiting for the Land Rush:
Buying Future Memphis

John Overton got a bargain in 1794 when he spent five hundred dollars for five thousand acres at Chickasaw Bluffs on the Mississippi River. The land, part of vast land grants given out by the North Carolina government following the Revolutionary War, actually belonged to the Chickasaws. Overton bought the John Rice land grant and hoped he could develop it someday. When in 1818 the Chickasaws were compelled to relinquish their claims to all of West Tennessee, Overton was poised to become a wealthy man. In 1819, recognizing the potential of the site for a great city, he laid out the streets of Memphis and began selling lots, earning the title "the Father of Memphis" and a tidy sum in the process.

Overton had been in Tennessee since 1789, when he arrived from a Kentucky law practice and made his home in Nashville. Andrew Jackson arrived at the same time, and the two became lifelong friends. They shared space in a law office, living accommodations at the block house of the widow Mrs. John Donelson, and mutual interests in land and politics. Jackson bought part ownership in the Memphis property, which he resold as he needed money.

Overton's rise to prominence began with land purchases in Davidson County, upon which he built in 1792 his popular inn and home, Traveller's Rest. Overton's impact on the state was considerable. He was elected to the Tennessee Superior Court in 1804, serving until 1809. Two years later he served on the Tennessee Supreme Court (1811-1816). As a jurist, he was not, by all accounts, a brilliant man but excelled in common sense. He was particularly suited by temperament and self-education to deal with cases involving land disputes. Overton was generally regarded as eminently honest and practical, and his knowledge translated into power. He helped shape Tennessee land laws when he prepared the 1813 book *Tennessee Reports,* a compilation of some of Tennessee's first law precedents. The book was a guideline for attorneys who previously found their only advice from printed cases originating either in England or in the North Carolina courts.

From 1820 to 1824, Overton busied himself with Jackson's unsuccessful presidential campaign. Undaunted by Jackson's failure, he remained campaign manager and helped put his law partner into the White House in 1828.

Despite the fact that Overton did not marry until he was fifty-four, one history book claims "one of the largest and strongest families in Tennessee is descended from John Overton. It is connected with leading families in all parts of the state, and is especially strong at Nashville, Memphis and Knoxville." His wife was the daughter of Knoxville's founder, James White.

John Overton Jr., thirteen years old when his father died, inherited his father's good business sense and expanded the family's fortune by supervising the development of Memphis as well as other investments. The son was known throughout Tennessee for his compassion toward the less fortunate and his willingness to help any honest person who came to him for assistance.

On the eve of the Civil War, the younger Overton was among the wealthiest men in Tennessee, having helped build Memphis into a thriving metropolis. According to a eulogist, he was opposed to secession, but when Tennessee joined the Confederacy, John Overton Jr. cast his lot with his fellow citizens and plunged himself and his fortune into the service of the Southern cause. It was during the war that he became known affectionately as "the Colonel." When hostilities ended, his fortune was gone, but he set out to restore it—both for his sake and for the sake of his fellow Tennesseans.

Overton's generosity and warmth may be best illustrated by an incident that occurred during the Reconstruction era. Among his many interests was a Chattanooga bank, which he served as president. The bank was destroyed during the war, but at war's end, Overton personally located many of the poor depositors hardest hit by the bank's demise and repaid them out of his own pocket.

Such acts of kindness became routine for Overton, whose reputation as a man of honor spread throughout the South. Just how widespread it was became evident during an 1866 visit to the White House. He wanted the government to return his property seized by Federal officers during the war; he also wanted compensation for its use. This, he knew, would be a difficult task, especially for the fellow Tennessean sitting in the Oval Office. President Andrew Johnson ranked the former Confederate high on his list of enemies. In fact, while serving as the military governor of Tennessee, Johnson tried to have him arrested.

Overton's welcome at the White House was hardly warm. Author and friend, the Reverend J. H. McNeilly, recalled the confrontation in these words:

> the President went directly to Colonel Overton, and began to vent his personal resentment, abusing him with great coarseness of expression, finally with an oath calling him an aristocrat and oppressor of the poor. A distinguished Presbyterian minister of Mississippi, the Rev. Dr. Lyon . . . stepped forward and said: "Mr. President, you are mistaken in your man. While I have not met him before in person, yet I know that he is recognized all over the South as the friend of every one in need. He is no aristocrat in the sense in which you use the word. He holds himself above no man, however poor, if he be honest.

Overton's steady reply was, "Of course you can put me in prison and hang me, too, as you threaten. I am in your power. But you cannot frighten me from claiming my rights, or bring me to the level of one who insults those who can not help themselves."

Overton eventually obtained his land and received compensation for the use of his property, although the sum he received fell far short of what he believed to be fair.

His wife, in honor of whom he built the luxurious Maxwell House Hotel in Nashville, never relinquished her love for the Confederacy. Her one wish was to die before all the old Confederate soldiers were gone, so that she could be buried by their hands. After her husband's death 1898, Harriet Maxwell Overton died a few months later. Her body was wrapped in a Confederate flag and laid to rest by Confederate veterans.

26
Elihu Embree
Raising a Voice against Slavery

Only a year after Tennessee had become a state, East Tennessean Thomas Embree addressed an open letter to the state's inhabitants calling for "a gradual abolition of slavery of every kind." Unable to stir the masses to action, Embree left his home in Washington County in 1800 and headed for slave-free Ohio. His teenaged son, Elihu, decided not to follow. While abolition was not his major concern at the time, Elihu Embree was destined to raise an even bigger noise against slavery nineteen years later, when, at Jonesborough in 1819-20, he published the nation's first abolitionist newspaper.

The younger Embree was born in Washington County in 1782. His Quaker father owned a successful iron manufacturing company, which Elihu and his brother Elijah continued to operate after their father's departure from Tennessee. The brothers, in fact, became wealthy.

When he married, Elihu Embree only grudgingly allowed his wife to bring her slaves into the household. Having readopted his father's Quaker persuasions, Embree joined the Methodist's Manumission Society of Tennessee, active on antislavery issues from its headquarters in Jefferson County. In 1817, the society sent the Tennessee legislature two "Memorials on Slavery," asking for the state to pass certain specifics. Among them was a request to prevent slaveowners from breaking up slave family units. To do otherwise, the soci-

ety claimed, was "to trample on the divine," reported historian Robert H. White, who discovered the papers. Another called for a ban on importing slaves into Tennessee. The legislature, however, failed to consider the society's concerns.

In 1819, the society and Embree formed a partnership to produce a weekly newspaper, *The Manumission Intelligencer,* which Embree filled with antislavery articles. A year later, he began his own historic and popular national monthly, *The Emancipator,* first issued in April 1820. Both publications have been credited as the nation's first to be written entirely for the abolition of slavery.

Months after *The Emancipator* began, however, Elihu Embree, thirty-eight, died of a fever, leaving the antislavery fight to others. Embree's will directed that his estate free all of his slaves and establish a fund to educate their children. Every dollar after the first ten thousand dollars in his estate was to be used to help abolish slavery.

Shortly after Embree's death, East Tennessee became the printing site for yet another abolitionist newspaper. Ohio's Benjamin Lundy, seeking good printing presses (which the Methodists had), relocated to Greeneville and printed *The Genius of Universal Emancipation* between 1822 and 1824. Lundy then moved to Baltimore and joined forces with fellow abolitionist William Lloyd Garrison, who helped continue the publication for another fourteen years and brought the entire nation into the controversy with his growing fame on the issue. Garrison's prominent publication, *The Liberator,* made him America's leading spokesperson in the movement against slavery.

27
Montgomery Bell
Calling Forth the South's Mighty Industrial Power

It took a man as hardheaded and hardhearted as Montgomery Bell to outlast the rock at the Narrows of the Harpeth River, where, around 1820, he carved a tunnel between two portions of the river and through the center of a mountain. In so doing, he actually harnessed the Harpeth River. Bell accomplished this feat, in what was then Dickson County, within one year, but only by working his slaves seven days a week as many hours as they could endure. One of the nation's first major industrialists, Bell believed that this tunnel, through which the Harpeth River would rush, could then generate twice the water power for one of his largest iron furnaces.

Bell had come to Dickson (the future Cheatham) County about 1800 for the sole purpose of making money. He had migrated from his native Pennsylvania and worked in Kentucky, where he was a hatter and assisted his widowed sister and her children. He did well for the entire family and paid for each child's education, an advantage he had not had himself. When Bell arrived in Middle Tennessee, Dickson County was so large that it made up a sizable portion of the entire region. By purchasing an iron foundry in 1804 from original settler James Robertson and expanding it along the Highland Rim west of Nashville, Bell became the dominant iron maker in early Tennessee and in the South.

His famous Cumberland Iron Furnace supposedly made all of the cannonballs that Americans used at the Battle of New Orleans in 1815. Bell, in fact, became wealthy making war materials for the United States government by virtue of a contract he negotiated just before the War of 1812. His local empire was made up of slaves (more than three hundred, making him one of the largest slaveowners in Dickson County), considerable land (thousands of acres in Middle Tennessee), and numerous iron furnaces and forges in Dickson and the surrounding counties which were rich in iron ore. After Bell's success in iron manufacturing, others joined the rush to exploit the hills for ore, but no one matched his level of profit.

Bell did not triumph in the iron industry by being nice. He had a reputation not only for driving his slaves to the breaking point (in addition to carving tunnels, the slaves mined the ore and operated the furnaces and forges), but also for avoiding payment of any debt and stretching the limits of the law wherever possible. As the result of his tendency to ignore bills, Bell had many lawsuits brought against him, including one from a widow who had cut and delivered a cord of firewood to him. After he refused to pay her, she won a court judgment of $114.40.

Persistent rumors also spread that Bell had fathered numerous illegitimate children by black and white women alike. He never married and counted few friends.

Late in life, his heart softened somewhat. In 1853, Bell offered to free any of his slaves who agreed to relocate in Liberia. For those who wanted to leave, Bell agreed to pay transportation and provide temporary support, according to historian Robert Ewing Corlew. About ninety of his three hundred slaves accepted the offer, and, en route to freedom, one of them made this request of the ship's captain: "Do write a most loving letter to my old master, and tell him how much we love him, and will never stop thanking the Lord for his goodness to us."

In another late-life act of generosity, Bell made certain that Middle Tennesseans had Montgomery Bell Academy, which he founded to give boys who could not support themselves the education that he had never received. Despite the softening of Montgomery Bell's heart, he remained a friendless man, who died in 1855 at the age of eighty-six. According to accounts, Bell's wealth did not prevent him from dying alone in his elegant homestead with snow blowing across his bed through a broken window.

28

John Christmas McLemore

The Land and More Land—
On Now to West Tennessee

The "barren grass" at Christmasville, one of the earliest West Tennessee towns, grew significantly taller than people or their horses. So tall was this variety of grass that frontier settlers trained their dogs to track children lost in it.

The village's remoteness also forced boatmen, whose only "highways" were the waterways they traveled, to train their own dogs for specialized duty: walking the riverbanks ahead of them, their collars containing a list of available items for sale. By the time boatmen floated along the Obion River's South Fork branch toward Christmasville's site, customers were already waiting on the riverbanks to buy the cleverly advertised wares.

The community itself was founded by a man who understood the value of such faraway places, who more than anyone else turned newly opened West Tennessee into one of America's most sought after frontiers. He was John Christmas McLemore.

McLemore, who endured the twin nightmares of dense wilderness travel and chaos over frontier land titles, had been buying and selling much of West Tennessee since the region left Indian hands in 1818. Some estimates claimed that his real estate possessions were in excess of three hundred thousand acres. Christmasville sits somewhere in the northeast corner of Carroll County, but its exact location (it has moved three times) has been difficult to determine. The original location existed before statehood as an outpost for land surveyors who wandered into the Chickasaw country in 1785. It was located on a bluff about a half-mile north of the South Fork. Thirty-three years later, General Andrew Jackson, on behalf of the United States, was able to negotiate the entire West Tennessee area out of Chickasaw hands. As a result, the hamlet began to attract a few settlers.

Flourishing briefly, Christmasville waned as the rest of West Tennessee grew considerably under McLemore, who was perhaps the leading 1820s land dealer there. McLemore also inspired the nearby Carroll County town of McLemoresville and founded numerous other Tennessee towns as he wandered the region putting land into the hands of migrating pioneers.

Born in North Carolina in 1790, he moved to Nashville in 1806 and married into the Donelson clan, becoming an in-law of Andrew Jackson and later a business associate (McLemore married Elizabeth Donelson, a niece of Rachel Donelson Jackson). Providing such services for Jackson as researching land titles and helping to buy land at a profit, McLemore was considered one of Jackson's closest friends in Nashville for thirty years and a great helpmate in Jackson's United States presidential races.

McLemore's secret to buying and selling West Tennessee was simple—he relentlessly pursued copies of every land title that came from North Carolina. But he did so "at great expense and trouble," according to one of his partners, Memucan Hunt Howard. McLemore made it convenient for anyone with a land claim in the former Chickasaw territory to finalize that ownership with a title. His company often collected fees from land-grant owners who needed someone to locate, survey, and register their claims. Most land-warrant holders, however, lived great distances away (or they died) and never ventured into such a vast wilderness as this to claim their property. As a result, McLemore and his partners, who also included Sugars McLemore and Samuel Dickens, were able to amass hundreds of thousands of acres at fairly cheap prices. Memucan

Hunt Howard said that he personally had traveled and camped in the region's woods "nearly all the time" for four years. Fascinated with the Chickasaws, he wondered why they never lived in West Tennessee; their reply was that "it leaked too much." Howard agreed: "For a time after I first went there I thought it rained, hailed, thundered and lightened with more wind that [sic] I had known elsewhere."

Although most of the early history of Christmasville was never recorded, John Christmas McLemore kept a title to its thousand acres (which included the town site) after it was commissioned by the Tennessee legislature in 1823. While he encouraged settlement there, McLemore was unwilling to release deeds to either residents or businesses for nearly ten years—at which time, in 1832, he purchased Jackson's part ownership in Memphis and departed for the Mississippi River area.

During this time, McLemore and Jackson endured the only real misunderstanding of their long friendship when a major scandal hit Jackson's presidency. The source of the problem was fellow Tennessean and United States Secretary of War John Eaton, whom McLemore considered a growing political liability to the president. Eaton (whose home was in Franklin) and his wife, Peggy, were being ostracized by Washington, D.C., society because of their adulterous love affair before their marriage to each other. Having been accused of similar behavior, Jackson was sympathetic to the Eatons. While he stubbornly befriended the couple, Jackson found little support from McLemore and the Donelson family. Even the White House hostess, Emily Donelson, shunned the Eatons. By early 1832, however, McLemore's loyalty to Jackson was more important than his concern over the famous Peggy Eaton affair. At Jackson's request, he began to take the lead in urging the entire family to accept Peggy Eaton socially.

For the most part, McLemore and Jackson hardly saw each other during the 1830s. While Jackson ran the nation from Washington, McLemore was engrossed in his many West Tennessee land pursuits, especially Memphis. He spent the rest of his life in that city and died there in 1864.

The many small towns McLemore established kept their place on the Tennessee map, although Christmasville grew obscure with the passing years and ultimately lost its post office. Twentieth-century residents tried persistently, but in vain, to resurrect the post office for no other reason than to allow the novelty of mailing their holiday cards with a Christmasville postmark. While postal officials refused, claiming they could make no money from such a venture, Christmasville's most devoted citizens seemed astonished that love for their hometown was not reason enough.

29

Marcus Brutus Winchester

A Mayor's Mixed Marriage and Memphis's Mixed Reactions

If the story behind his frontier marriage was true, then Marcus Brutus Winchester's reputation as a man of honor was especially true in the realm of romance. In 1826, he was a respected man, well-liked by the first Memphis settlers, whom he served as the town's first mayor and one of its earliest general-store owners. Nonetheless, Winchester's reputation began to suffer in a rugged wilderness society that refused to accept his marriage to a "honey-skinned" woman of mixed blood.

The only published source regarding the love affair was written by a contemporary, the "father of Memphis history," James D. Davis, accused by some modern historians of occasionally getting his facts wrong. No one, however, disagreed that something about Winchester's marriage caused the mayor's problems.

The story began when Winchester reportedly agreed to take care of his friend Thomas Hart Benton's former mistress, Mary. Realizing that his political future might be jeopardized by a relationship with a woman of mixed-race descent, Benton placed Mary in the kindly Winchester's care, then left town and courted the national political scene, eventually becoming famous as a United States senator from Missouri.

Winchester fell in love with Mary and determined to marry her. Since Tennessee did not sanction mixed marriages, the couple went to New Orleans for the ceremony. His social difficulties with his new wife actually began as a smear campaign among the con artists, gamblers, and thieves who drank their evenings away in Old Bell Tavern and who relished the opportunity to bring down an honest community leader. Among those less-than-admirable tavern types was the notorious Madison County thief John A. Murrell, who disliked

Winchester's skill in spotting a counterfeit bill at a mere glance. Murrell specialized in "homemade money," which he could never cash in Winchester's store.

One person who could have capitalized on Winchester's troubles but instead befriended him was his business rival, Isaac Rawlings. Rawlings was an old Indian trader who, along with a handful of other veterans from the War of 1812, had been living on the Mississippi Bluffs since that war's end. His was the area's first store. Preferring to barter for goods, Rawlings avoided money altogether and attracted as clients the old squatters and nearby Indians. In contrast, Winchester usually attracted new settlers bringing currency to do business (they also depended on his wise counsel in business decisions and his ability to spot counterfeit money). Despite their competition, Rawlings offered Winchester his sympathy. Perhaps Rawlings could be generous because his own mistress was a woman of color (he had a son by her, to whom he willed his estate). Although such love affairs were not uncommon on the frontier, Rawlings reminded Winchester how socially unacceptable a subsequent marriage could be.

At risk was Winchester's undisputed leadership in the community, which he had held since 1818 when General Andrew Jackson forced the Chickasaws into a treaty relinquishing West Tennessee. With Jackson, Winchester had helped get supplies for the Indians during negotiations. He then rode to the Fourth Chickasaw Bluff, the chosen site for a new city. A man of good manners, a courtly bearing, and integrity, Winchester was sent by Middle Tennessee businessmen who held title to most of the region. Among them was his father, General James Winchester, a veteran of the American Revolutionary War and the War of 1812, who lived near Castalian Springs. The elder Winchester, as one of the cofounders of Memphis, reportedly gave the city its name. He had bought into its ownership with General Jackson and the majority partner, John Overton of Nashville. To protect their interests and oversee Memphis's development, the proprietors trusted young Winchester. He opened a store there in 1819, oversaw the laying out of city streets according to Overton's specifications, and became Memphis's first mayor when the town was chartered in 1826.

Local political conflict began to develop when Rawlings was equally intent upon fighting for the interests of poor squatters who had carved out a life there—years before any other white men appeared.

Mayor Winchester, on the other hand, faithfully represented the interests of the land's absentee owners, who, by 1826, also included West Tennessee's leading land speculator, John Christmas McLemore.

Mary Winchester tried her best to gain the respect of the community by feeding the hungry, helping the injured, and sharing with the needy. But the couple and the eight children they had were never able to overcome the social stigma of a racially mixed marriage. Despondent, Winchester turned to strong drink, eventually becoming an alcoholic. Then in 1840, Mary abandoned her family for reasons unknown. Perhaps the disapproval of the citizenry and the Winchester family as well as her husband's drinking defeated Mary. Or perhaps, as one version suggested, she did not leave at all but simply died.

Two years later, Winchester remarried. But he apparently never regained his social standing, he lost his latest job as postmaster, and he was unable to pay for his children's education with the town's only schoolmaster, Eugene Magevney. Despite family wealth and his father's having once given him more than four hundred acres of downtown Memphis, Winchester wrote to a friend in 1851: "I must have bread for my family and I must have the means of educating my children when and where they can reap the advantages of it."

Memphians took pity on him and elected Winchester to the state legislature in 1851. He died in 1856, apparently still dogged by his decision to marry for love.

David Crockett, in his autobiography, remembered becoming friends with Winchester after being rescued from a flatboat accident near Memphis. During their many conversations, Winchester urged him to seek a congressional seat. Crockett described Winchester simply as the kind of friend whom "I never can forget as long as I am able to go ahead at any thing. . . ."

30

John Bell

Now Appearing:
The Soon-to-Be Famous Bell Witch

John Bell's houseguest was so maddening that she was credited with having caused his death in 1820 and attracting the fascination of every neighbor within miles,

John Bell lies on his deathbed as family and friends use a cat to test a mysterious potion found at Bell's bedside.

and eventually people throughout Tennessee. Even General Andrew Jackson could not stay away from her.

The Bell farm was located in Robertson County, and "the Bell Witch," as she came to be known in one of the most enduring and famous ghost stories in Tennessee history, appeared to each member of the Bell family. However, she singled out the patriarch, John Bell, for her disdain and her most painful tricks.

Bell's daughter Elizabeth ("Betsy") was the first to receive the spirit's attention. At first she saw a strange woman walking in the orchard on the Bell's thousand-acre farm outside of Adams, a small Middle Tennessee town near the Tennessee-Kentucky border. Several more sightings were followed by a variety of tricks. Bedcovers were pulled from sleeping family members, and Betsy and a brother, Richard Williams Bell, were subjected to painful hair-pulling episodes. John Bell developed a strange illness that left his tongue swollen and jaw muscles affected, making speech and swallowing difficult.

Neighbors were invited to spend the night to help solve the mystery. After losing their bedcovers and experiencing other antics, visitors described the spirit as an intelligent being. When they tried to communicate, asking questions that required numerical answers, the spirit rapped out correct responses. The ghost soon progressed to whistles and indistinct sounds, then made her first intelligent comment one night when Richard Williams Bell asked her who she was and what she wanted. She uttered: "I am a Spirit; I was once very happy, but have been disturbed."

The day before he died, John Bell and a son were walking to the hog pens when the spirit played another of her tricks, grabbing Bell's shoes from his feet and later striking the old man in the face. When the attack ended, Bell was helped to the house and into bed. The next day, he was found unconscious. Attempts to revive him failed. Bottles of medicine in the cupboard were gone, and in their place had appeared "a dark bottle containing a brown fluid which none of us had ever seen before," recalled John Bell Jr.

The spirit called out: "He will never get up. I did it." She boasted that she had given her victim a dose from the vial, which caused his death. When the doctor arrived, he could not identify the medicine and suggested it be tested on a cat. The cat went into convulsions and died within a few hours.

While stories abound of the witch's torment of Bell, it was also noted that she loved Mrs. Bell and numerous farmers in the community, all of whom she helped in varying ways. Slaves' recollections, reported by descendant Charles Bailey Bell, claimed that the witch gave accurate weather reports to the community and friendly hints to farmers regarding the proper time for haying and other planting or harvesting activities. Visitors to the Bell home listened to the witch describe the activities of their family members during their absence. They found these reports to be accurate. When Mrs. John Bell became ill one day, the witch overheard her say that she liked fruit, especially grapes; suddenly some grapes fell onto her bedside table.

After hearing repeated tales of the Bell Witch, General Andrew Jackson arranged a visit with his entourage. When Jackson neared the gates of the Bell farm and prepared to camp with his men outside the house, "the driver could not make his horses budge the wagon. . . . The general examined the wagon and said there was no reason why the horses could not pull it; the driver again tried them without success."

The general shouted: "It is the witch!" A voice called from the roadside, "They can go on now, General!"

Neither Jackson nor his men could see anyone.

In the group that night was a man who claimed to be a witch tamer, and he was confident that no witch would appear while he was present. Other members of the party boasted that this fellow had the witch bluffed. He claimed his pistol was loaded with a silver bullet; he merely needed opportunity to try it.

John Bell Jr. remembered the story well. He recalled that when the impatient fellow dared the witch out,

suddenly the braggart jumped from his chair, grabbed the seat of his trousers and shouted, "Boys, I am being stuck by a thousand pins." A voice spoke out, "I am in front of you; shoot." The man drew his pistol and tried to shoot, but it would not fire. Then the voice cried, "It's my night for fun." Soon there was heard repeated slapping of the man's jaws, and he yelled, "It is pulling my nose off." Making a break for the door, which flew open, he jumped out, running with all his speed toward the wagon, yelling every step, while the voice kept giving him all sorts of advice.

Jackson roared with laughter and exclaimed that he had never seen or heard anything so funny or mysterious. He wanted to stay a week. Again, the voice said: "'There is another fraud in your party, General; I'll get him tomorrow night. It is getting late. Go to bed.'"

While Andrew Jackson would have remained, his men would not. By noon, they were already twelve miles away in Springfield, and the other fraud (whoever he was) went with them.

31
Betsy Walker Howard

Staking a Claim on the King of England's Land

In 1821, the widow Betsy Walker Howard accomplished what no one else in the Howard family had been able to do in two hundred years. She laid claim to land originally bestowed in the king of England's court in 1629. Although still grieving over her husband's death, the widow Howard struggled through the Middle Tennessee wilderness to collect her husband's birthright—four thousand acres located along the Tennessee River in Perry County.

The original owner of this land was his ancestor, the Englishman Thomas Arundel Howard, who had purchased the acreage from an official in the king's court. That man, Sir Robert Heath, had been granted what was considered a vast tract in North America for having helped King Charles I out of financial troubles. The king's land, named "Carolana" for himself, was a rather speculative venture intended as a royal colony and reportedly stretching from the Atlantic to the Pacific Ocean. Sir Robert, given the power to raise taxes and form an army there, hoped to make a personal profit by selling parcels to prominent friends. The Howards of England (whose lineage included Lord Leofric, husband of Lady Godiva) were among those friends close to the royal government.

The Howard title passed from one generation to another in England, Virginia, Maryland, and North Carolina. In 1784, Revolutionary War veteran Benjamin Howard showed the title to American authorities. They honored it with the four thousand acres in North Carolina's western district. Decades passed, and the land warrant again lay dormant. In 1819, Howard's son Benjamin Howard II scouted the territory, which, by then, was in the hands of the young state of Tennessee. This Howard went back to North Carolina to gather his family but died suddenly.

His widow was eager to follow her husband's frontier trail and settle the family upon its ages-old inheritance. She left North Carolina with her eleven children and her brother's wagon convoy, keeping her heart fixed on the four thousand waiting acres. After enduring the long and grueling journey, Betsy Walker Howard and her family arrived at the mouth of Cypress Creek and there began to build homesteads and the nucleus of a community which would remain in the Howard family for more generations to come.

With their arrival, she had placed her land claim into the hands of her son James Walker Howard. He took the claim to Nashville, where the state land assessor converted it into a Tennessee land grant signed in 1821 by Governor Joseph McMinn. The family farmed the land and also became postmasters at the town of Pope.

Upon building a river landing, James Howard formed a partnership with his uncle, Robert Walker, to operate Walker & Howard general store, overlooking the river. The store prospered through the nineteenth century and had the distinction of hosting a political rally held by Congressman David Crockett in 1831. Whiskey flowed freely, and the event was best remembered by Crockett's failure to pay the $3.50 bill for the liquor consumed. Although everyone drank whiskey on this occasion, the drink was on store shelves primarily to be used as medicine, some of it transported there via the Tennessee River system on

which Perry County would always depend (whiskey was also distilled in caves along the river).

The Howards of Tennessee continued to pass along their inheritance to successive generations. As undisputed head of the clan, James Walker Howard bought out his brothers in 1839 and became sole owner of the land. He died in 1863. Direct descendants continued to run the store (until a flood destroyed it in 1897) and farm the land, some of which was given in plots to freed slaves who were living on the farm. Other acreage was given to area churches and schools.

By the 1950s, descendants were still farming what was left of the original king's grant, among them rural mail carrier Benjamin Richard Howard II and his son, educator Benjamin Richard Howard III. After 1979, the land was passed to Benjamin Richard Howard IV and James Deere Howard, also educators, who refused to give up the farm.

As the years passed, TVA came into ownership of some of the property, and the state of Tennessee created Mousetail Landing Rustic State Park in honor of an early river landing nearby. The landing was once near a tannery. Mice dwelled among the green hides, and when a Civil War fire destroyed the tannery, thousands of mice frantically exited the scene, giving rise to the folklore name, Mousetail Landing. A sizable portion of the surrounding lands, however, from the original royal grant along the banks of the Tennessee River, still remained in the hands of the Howard family, as had been the case since 1629—a legacy that came to fruition when Betsy Walker Howard set her sights on the unknown wilderness.

32

Sequoyah

An Alphabet for the Cherokee Nation

Sequoyah's greatest dream, to make the Cherokee people literate, ultimately hinged on the performance of a little girl. Although he had finally developed a Cherokee alphabet, Sequoyah knew that his task was not finished. He still had to encourage his brethren to adopt it, and he succeeded in this quest in 1821. With skeptical tribal leaders looking on,

Sequoyah, whose English name was George Gist (or Guess).

Sequoyah wrote a message in his newly devised language. When his little daughter read it and answered it, tribal leaders were so astonished that they enthusiastically approved the syllabary. After almost thirteen years of work, Sequoyah had triumphed in doing what no one else in the history of mankind had ever accomplished: He single-handedly devised, in its entirety, an alphabet and syllabary.

Born in an area that became present-day Monroe County, Sequoyah was the child of an Indian mother and a Fort Loudoun white soldier—Nathaniel Gist, a direct descendant of England's Lord Protector Oliver Cromwell. The boy, who was born with a club foot, was fascinated at an early age by the white man's "talking leaves" (printed pages), despite the fact that he could not read them. White missionaries had been trying for years to transcribe the Cherokee language into written form, but they had been unsuccessful.

In 1809, Sequoyah set out to succeed where they had failed. Many people would ridicule him over the next twelve years, but the quiet and devoted man persisted. His tireless effort finally completed, he had devised an eighty-six-letter syllabary, each symbol representing a syllable of the Cherokee language. Most of the symbols were English, Greek, and Hebrew letters—some of which Sequoyah turned to his own use by incorporating them sideways or upside down.

Sequoyah was interrupted by two major events during the creation of his alphabet: He fought under General Andrew Jackson in the Creek War (1814), using his English name, George Gist (or Guess); and he temporarily left Tennessee in 1818 to join tribal leader Chief John Jolley, who recruited him and thousands of other Cherokees to move to Arkansas. When Sequoyah finished his alphabet, he traveled home to share it with the Eastern Cherokees.

What his alphabet meant to the Cherokee people may be summarized best by missionary Samuel A. Worcester in a letter to his superiors in New England:

> Young Cherokees travel a great distance to be instructed in this easy method of writing and reading. In three days they are able to commence letter-writing and return home to their villages prepared to teach others. It is the opinion of some of the missionaries that if the Bible were translated and printed according to the plan here described, hundreds of adult Cherokees who will never know English, would be able to read it in a single month.

As hoped, a Cherokee translation of the New Testament was available by 1825. By 1828, the tribe began publishing the *Cherokee Phoenix,* a bilingual newspaper which carried each item twice, once in Cherokee and once in English.

In the 1820s, the United States exchanged the Indian land in Arkansas for land in future Oklahoma, and Sequoyah moved again. There, he played a role in assimilating the thousands of Cherokee refugees forced in the 1838 Trail of Tears from their homes in and around East Tennessee. He died in 1843 seeking the whereabouts of other Cherokees in Mexico.

33
Return Jonathan Meigs

A Guardian Agent:
Safeguarding the Cherokee People

His name was Jonathan Meigs, and his curse was a maiden who refused repeatedly to be his wife. "Nay, Jonathan," she would say. "I respect thee much, but I cannot marry thee."

In the early eighteenth century, on what was to be his last visit to her Middletown, Connecticut, home, Jonathan was slowly mounting his horse when the young lady relented and beckoned him to stop. "Return, Jonathan! Return Jonathan!" she shouted. These words were so sweet to his ears that he would name their future son Return Jonathan Meigs.

The story may or may not be true, but this much is certain: Return Jonathan Meigs, the Tennessee frontier's leading Cherokee Indian agent for more than twenty years, was born in Connecticut in 1740. During the Revolutionary War, Meigs served with distinction and earned the rank of colonel. In honor of his brilliance leading the 1777 Sag Harbor expedition against the British, he also gained the gift of a sword from Congress. In 1801, President Thomas Jefferson appointed him Cherokee agent and an agent of the War Department in Tennessee. He proved to be perfectly suited to both roles.

Meigs possessed a genuine concern for the Cherokee people, and his warmth toward them earned their trust. When the Holston Treaty of 1791 stipulated that the United States government would encourage the Cherokees to become settled farmers by giving them "useful implements of husbandry," Meigs became their advisor on farming and made certain they received their plows and various other farm equipment. He also arranged for artisans to settle in Cherokee land to provide farm and domestic implements and teach their crafts to young tribal members.

One of Meigs's chief duties was to distribute the annual United States annuities owed to the Cherokees in compensation for their land. Payments were a combination of money and goods. The Cherokees, however, complained to Meigs about the type of goods that typically were paid to them and which had little practical value. Meigs's list of impractical items included "Fine muslin, Tamboured [embroidered] muslin, Silk Stockings, Ostrich Feathers, Gold & Silver lace, fine dimity, Earrings, Cambrick, Diaper & Damask Table Cloths, Morocco Shoes, & one Sett of Officers Canteens complete." Meigs wrote the government for articles "that are really usefull for them in their circumstances." The Cherokees, he realized, were willing and eager to become a part of the farming community; they needed and asked for a range of goods from brass kettles to blankets, fur hats, thread, broadcloth, ribbon, needles, and "1 Gross of Scizzars."

Meigs had a difficult job protecting both the Cherokees from the whites who tried to victimize them and the white settlers from Cherokee criminals such as James Vann. White authorities were known to respond to the attacks of any Cherokee by punishing the whole tribe, sometimes as an excuse to gain land. When United States negotiations were held to purchase the ancient tribal lands, Meigs made valiant attempts on behalf of the Cherokees to obtain fair payments from the government.

In bringing law to the frontier, Meigs helped get rid of unauthorized white squatters. One of his letters in 1806 explained the problem:

> Under some pretext they enter on the Indian lands disturb the peace & quiet of the Indians; then teaze the Government to purchase the land, which raises the price, & embarrasses the Government in effecting purchases—If they are moved they complain of hardship, while at the same time they are the sole cause of all they suffer.

In 1817, Meigs set about transforming the Cherokee nation's political structure. He successfully suggested that the Cherokee move from a tribal organization to a republican system, thus placing the Cherokees even closer to English-speaking civilization's way of living and hoping that the two societies could live in harmony.

But his final act of kindness toward the Cherokee people cost him his life. On a brisk night about 1823, the eighty-two-year-old Meigs slept on a cold floor in order that an aged chief could use his comfortable quarters. Meigs contracted pneumonia and died shortly thereafter.

The state of Tennessee honored its old agent when Meigs County came into being in 1836. Meigs's tireless efforts to civilize the Cherokee nation, however, were not enough to avoid what came to be known as the Trail of Tears. In 1838, the United States drove the Cherokees from Tennessee in this bloody march to Oklahoma. The irony of Meigs's efforts to mold the Cherokee into successful, prosperous farmers (many of whom owned plantations and even slaves) was that the envious white farmers coveted the Indians' lands even more.

34
Lawrence Effler

*Mustering the Militia—
For One Reason or Another*

Greasy Cove's Lawrence (or Lorance) Effler fell to embarrassing defeat in a good-natured fistfight with a fellow East Tennessean in 1824. The two challengers were members of neighboring militia-mustering camps, where a good fight was welcome entertainment.

Fistfights and wrestling matches were commonplace during all nineteenth century mustering camps, especially at the famous Greasy Cove (present-day Erwin in Unicoi County), where mountaineers made themselves battle-ready in case of Indian attack or a call to war. Sometimes these bouts proved to be one-sided, as was the case in Effler's first meeting with one particular challenger, a local doctor. Humiliated in defeat before his family and friends, Effler swore revenge.

When he got a rematch at the next mustering, he proved too slick for his opponent. (Effler's militiamen were called "the Moccasin Gang," and the doctor belonged to the "Cherokees.") Effler slipped away from their gathering long enough to cover his body with a thick coating of bear grease. Then donning an old shirt that would be easily torn, he squared off with the doctor a second time.

Effler's tattered old shirt was quickly ripped away, exposing his grease-covered torso. Try as he might, the doctor simply could not get a decent grip on his foe. The fight concluded with Effler sitting astride his larger combatant, who in futility yelled "Enough!"

One of Effler's descendants, author Roxie Masters, later wrote that her ancestor might have taken certain advantages (referring to the only restrictions imposed on a good fight—eye-gouging and biting): "After the fight, a part of the doctor's ear lobe was missing. They could find no proof that it had been bitten off. Many years later, our grandmother told us that she had once heard her father telling an old friend that he had filed his teeth before going to the Cherokee Muster."

A French immigrant, Effler knew how to fight other battles as well. He was a veteran of the War of 1812, having gone to war as a substitute for another man who wanted to escape military duty. The other man, however, received full military benefits, including forty acres given as salary. Pension fraud flourished on the frontier, because those who hired military replacements often claimed full honors and compensations while those who fought in their place generally could not prove their own entitlement. Although Effler's claim to a land grant was rejected, he succeeded in getting a small pension after his regiment commander backed his story.

The pension was a considerable assistance to him, since Effler lived to be ninety-one. At the time of his death in 1886, Effler was still living in Unicoi County near the old Greasy Cove mustering grounds.

35
Sterling C. Robertson

*On to Texas Territory—More Land,
More Dreams, More Schemes*

Sterling C. Robertson's portrait, painted during his lifetime, reveals the wavy hair that spared him a branding.

When land-hungry Texan Stephen F. Austin tried to grab a huge portion of central Texas belonging to Tennesseans, Nashville's Sterling C. Robertson threatened to cook and eat the conniving land speculator. The land in question was particularly valuable—

reportedly the size of the entire state of Tennessee. Austin was allowed to keep his life, however, and Robertson's Colony, which became home to a stream of Tennesseans, rose to prominence in the history of Texas settlement.

The seeds of conflict between the two men were planted years earlier, at Nashville in 1822, when Robertson helped to form the Texas Association. Made up of Tennesseans and Kentuckians, the group planned to colonize Texas territory then being claimed by Mexico. Robertson, a veteran of the War of 1812, was the nephew of Nashville founder James Robertson, who once declared, "We are the advance guard of civilization; our way is across the continent."

The "advance guard," as it involved Tennesseans, picked Texas to settle. This decision came after Middle Tennessean Nelson Patteson's son wandered the region and returned home to Giles County with glowing reports. Sterling C. Robertson, who owned a farm in Giles County, helped spread the word about this new frontier. Among the spellbound listeners were his Nashville cousins, Dr. Felix Robertson, who became president of the Texas Association, and George Childress, who would write the Texas Declaration of Independence and suggest a lone star as the Texas symbol.

Other friends became leaders in the movement also: Andrew Erwin from Coffee County and Robert Leftwich, a Kentuckian who had moved to Nashville. These two men were chosen to negotiate with the new Mexican government which had overthrown Spanish control. The Mexicans agreed to the colonization of "Coahuila y Texas" through land agents, or "empresarios," who promised to bring families in units of one hundred or more. One such empresario was Austin, who in 1821 chose an area of rich, river bottom lands. In 1825, the Mexican government finally accepted the Tennessee petition to colonize nearby on equally rich land.

But a twist of fate kept Texas Association members from their rightful holdings. The title of empresario, and along with it eight million acres northeast of Austin's colony, went to Leftwich and not the association. Flabbergasted that Leftwich's name was on their grant, Texas Association members quickly paid him ten thousand dollars plus other privileges to relinquish sovereignty of the land.

A survey party of thirty Tennesseans, led by Dr. Felix Robertson and James Overton (chairman of the board), immediately set out for the Texas territory. They planned to divide the eight million acres among association stockholders who, in turn, would recruit settlers. *The Nashville Republican* reported that a great crowd gathered on the banks of the Cumberland River to say farewell to these prominent Tennesseans, who set sail with "the successive peals of artillery" reverberating across the countryside. In letters home, many of the surveyors compared the Little River, which ran into the Brazos, to the Cumberland River. (Nearly ten years later, the town of Nashville, Texas, was established on that site.)

In recruiting settlers, few Association members had better luck than Sterling C. Robertson, who traveled throughout several states extolling the virtues of Texas soil. In 1829 his early recruiting success was nearly undone by his violent nature when he stabbed to death Nashville's Edward Randolph. Convicted of manslaughter (a hanging offense), Robertson escaped the hangman's noose by invoking Benefit of Clergy, an English law that dated back centuries. Still in effect in nineteenth-century America, the law gave exemption from capital punishment, but only once. The exemption was available to anyone who could read the biblical passage in Psalms: "Have mercy upon me, O God, according to thy lovingkindness: according unto the multitude of thy tender mercies blot out my transgressions."

The court accepted Robertson's plea but ruled he would, in keeping with the same law, be branded upon the hand with the letter *M* so that he could not invoke Benefit of Clergy a second time at a later date. However, the "young ladies of Nashville" were smitten by the dashing Robertson, a spiffy dresser with flashing gray eyes and wavy hair. When the women appealed to Governor William Carroll, the branding was canceled. But the accused did serve nine months in jail for the killing. Robertson may have been the last Tennessean awarded Benefit of Clergy as a defense. Six days after his conviction in December 1829, the Tennessee legislature passed a new criminal law effectively ending whippings and brandings in favor of jail time in the soon-to-be-opened state penitentiary in Nashville.

During his appeal on the jail sentence, Robertson continued his work for the Texas Association. Traveling to Texas to expedite negotiations for a colony, he was unaware that Austin viewed Tennesseans as competitors. Robertson asked him to intercede with Mexican authorities on behalf of Tennessee, and Austin promised to do so. But when Robertson returned home to deal with his personal problems, Austin secured Tennessee's land for himself and his cohorts. Infuriated by this betrayal, Robertson filed suit in Mexico against Austin, then traveled to Texas to hunt him down.

When the two came face to face in an apparent showdown, Robertson tried every method he knew to prompt a duel. But Austin would not fight. Turning in frustration to leave the scene, Robertson was reported to have said "that if he [Austin] wasn't such a coward that he would cut him up in mince meat, broil him over a slow fire and eat him."

In Mexican courts, Robertson was victorious against Austin. The Tennessee triumph came in 1834 when Mexico awarded Robertson the massive land holding thereafter known as Robertson's Colony. Its early settlers included former Tennessean Jesse Benton, who once shot Andrew Jackson during a tavern brawl. In 1836, Benton became one of the first to organize a regiment of Texas Rangers.

By this time, Robertson was responsible for bringing six hundred families into the region, nearly half of them transported at his own expense. A widower with a young son, he decided to settle there, building a home at Nashville, Texas.

Robertson signed the Texas Declaration of Independence and the Constitution of the Republic of Texas. In the spring of 1836, he commanded a company in the Texas Revolution. Later named major in command of the militia of Texas, Robertson was credited with being second only to Austin in bringing families to the central Texas region. But because of previous dealings by Austin and his friends (parceling out land grants before Robertson could regain the colony), mid-Texas land titles for many Tennesseans were in contention for years to come.

In 1842, Robertson caught pneumonia after trying to cross a rain-swollen river and died at the age of fifty-seven. At that time, he had been residing in the place named in his honor, Robertson County, Texas.

36

John C. Barnes

Discovering Chickasaw Honor
with Moses, the Mule

John C. Barnes, Tipton County's first pioneer blacksmith, was an enterprising businessman who quickly recognized an early 1820s need: livestock to cultivate farmland in newly opened West Tennessee. Toward this end, he sought the great Moses.

Observing that settlers did not bring more than the basic items to begin their homesteads, Barnes hoped to install a "jack" (jackass) at his Fisher Creek smithy for the purpose of hiring it out to stud. Lacking the six hundred to eight hundred dollars needed to buy a suitable animal, Barnes decided to rent one. He negotiated a one-year agreement on the most famous frontier jack, Moses, owned by General Jacob Tipton of Covington. Tipton was already a leading citizen whose late father of the same name inspired the naming of Tipton County in 1823 (having been killed in a 1791 attack against Indians in the Northwest Territory). General Tipton was more than glad to assist his neighbors.

Barnes tacked up handbills on the schoolhouse, the meeting house, and other public places. The handbill announced: "General Tipton's celebrated Jack, 'Moses,' fifteen and a half hands high, would keep his headquarters for the season at Barnes blacksmith shop."

Settlers, prepared to pay their stud fees, rushed to view Moses. Barnes seemed about to achieve his goals, not only to help West Tennessee farmers along the Mississippi River but also to make his own healthy profit. Then bad fortune struck. After returning home on his wedding day, Barnes learned that Moses had escaped and fled into the wilderness along the Hatchie River. A frantic search proved futile.

The area was filled with creatures of prey, among them wolves, panthers, bears, and wildcats. Although the Chickasaws, the land's original owners, were in the area on a seasonal hunting expedition, they were such an honorable tribe that Barnes never considered they had anything to do with Moses's disappearance. He assumed that Moses had drowned in a river overflow.

When the lease on Moses expired a year later, Barnes had to face General Tipton with the truth of the prized jack's disappearance. The two agreed on suitable compensation, and the matter was forgotten.

Afterwards, a shocking discovery sent Barnes directly to the Chickasaws, whose integrity he counted upon. He had met a trader who had just purchased a novelty fur from the Chickasaw trading post, which could be reached by following the Hatchie River to Bolivar in nearby Hardeman County. The hide, complete with head, ears, and eye holes, was none other than Moses. The trader agreed to give the hide to Barnes, who rolled it up and put it away at his home. The next fall, when the Chickasaws returned for their seasonal hunt, Barnes proposed a shooting match between the settlers and the Chickasaws. The winner would receive a rare pelt.

When a Chickasaw competitor won the event and demanded his prize, Barnes unveiled Moses's hide. The winner immediately recognized it and began to brag that he had originally killed the animal. Apparently the Chickasaws, who were encouraged to hunt beasts of prey, had thought Moses to be a strange new breed. But when Barnes explained the extraordinary value of Moses and the considerable monetary loss to his business, the Chickasaws, true to their honorable reputation, agreed to make good on the loss, giving Barnes thirty-five ponies as compensation for the "murdered" Moses.

The story of John C. Barnes and Moses became part of written history when a contemporary, Joseph S. Williams, retold the tale in his 1873 history of West Tennessee. Williams's father, hoping to improve his own livestock, was the one who encouraged Barnes to rent the animal from Tipton.

37
Frances "Fanny" Wright
An Experiment to Free All Slaves

In the fall of 1825, Frances "Fanny" Wright, a wealthy, intellectual, and majestic Scots woman, whom one friend called "the most interesting woman in Europe," guided her horse through the West Tennessee wilderness trying to reach the tiny backwoods village of Memphis, then hardly more than a trading post. She was carrying twelve thousand dollars of her own money and a dream to solve America's slavery problem. Her plan was to begin a colony where she would teach slaves to become self-reliant and then set them free.

Fanny Wright had the support of the nation's leading politicians, whom she had charmed after arriving in America as secretary and biographer (and lover, by most accounts) of the Marquis de LaFayette, the aging French hero who had helped America during the Revolutionary War. Thirty-year-old Fanny had a hypnotizing effect on most people, with the exception of LaFayette's family, who resented that she and her sister were living in LaFayette's French chateau. Tall, commanding, well-educated, and outspoken, Fanny was driven by her compassion toward those less fortunate. She influenced people with a richly "coarse" voice, a driving personality, and her practical approach to problems.

The sixty-eight-year-old LaFayette, whom President James Monroe had invited to travel America and receive the accolades of its people, was not with his companion on her journey deep into West Tennessee. He was, however, a visitor months earlier to Nashville, where his arrival sparked several of that city's major social events (banquets and the like). Merchants temporarily closed all shops for the planned festivities, and a parading band followed LaFayette through town.

Fanny's escort, instead, was one of LaFayette's friends, a fellow emancipationist from Illinois. The territory into which they rode was not long removed from Chickasaw possession; only forests and untamed rivers welcomed them. Memphis, not yet incorporated, had a few hundred settlers. Securing three hundred acres on the nearby Wolf River (present-day Germantown) at a locale Andrew Jackson suggested, Fanny Wright began her colony. She called it "Nashoba," the Chickasaw word for "wolf."

Fanny planned next to purchase several slaves and teach them practical skills with which to earn their way in life. From an earlier trip to the United States in 1818, she understood that states were economically dependent on slave labor and hoped her reform would create a humane solution without financial loss. She then wrote a book, *Views on Society and Manners in America*. LaFayette shared her views against slavery, as did many American leaders such as Presidents Monroe and Jefferson, both apologetic slaveowners.

Nashoba settlement, Fanny Wright believed, could be self-sustaining and even money-making. The profits would be used to buy more slaves and ultimately free them. After training the slaves for five years, she planned to resettle them in Africa. Her initial purchase of three hundred acres eventually grew to two thousand. Fanny first purchased eight slaves in Nashville (five men, three women) and then hired workers to help her carve Nashoba out of the dense forests. She made frequent trips into Memphis, where she was often seen strolling the dusty paths in a man's hat and talking to herself.

The Nashoba task was greater than Fanny expected, and her health failed. Although she had hired a few supervisors and farm trainers, she and her sister Camilla worked the fields alongside their new charges. Both women were unaccustomed to the stress of hard labor. When Fanny returned to Europe in May 1827 to regain her vigor, her sister proved incapable of running the colony. Even when Fanny hastily returned from Europe, the problems at Nashoba continued: labor idleness, arguments among workers, and illness, real or imagined. Whippings also had become part of the punishment for various transgressions.

Fanny had been back at Nashoba less than two months when her sister left for the North with her own health problems. Preparing slaves for freedom was forgotten; preparing Nashoba for dissolution was the greater concern. But before the colony could die of natural causes, scandal struck. In 1827 Scottish-born colony supervisor James Richardson wrote publicly that he was an atheist who was living at Nashoba with a black woman. Then he departed. This story quickly spread across the nation, sparking tales of Nashoba as a place where free love and equality of the races were encouraged. Public condemnation followed.

Within five years after her arrival in West Tennessee, Fanny Wright found herself putting thirteen former slaves and their eighteen children on a flatboat to New Orleans. The trainees boarded a ship that took them to freedom in Haiti. Thus ended the first of several utopian colonies that ultimately formed in Tennessee.

Nashoba colony was abandoned, but it was not forgotten. In 1830, Fanny married and gave birth to a daughter. That daughter, after Fanny's death at fifty-seven (in 1852), traveled to Tennessee to explore her inherited property, and decided to keep it. After many visits to Germantown and a failed attempt to develop Nashoba into a resort, Fanny Wright's daughter moved her own family there permanently in 1873. She lived in the old manor house until her own death in 1903.

38
Sam Houston

*A Romantic's Bumpy Political Trail:
Tennessee to Texas*

Sam Houston was passionate about the epic poem
the *Iliad* and its warrior heroes.

In 1813 Sam Houston was watching a recruiting parade in downtown Maryville (the East Tennessee community where he had migrated from Virginia with his widowed mother and eight siblings) when he became seduced by the drum beat of military life, and with it the chance to become a real hero. Twenty-year-old Houston reportedly ran into the street and snatched a silver dollar from the drumhead, the customary act for young men who wanted to enlist as the parade passed.

In the army he became Ensign Houston, immediately on his way to the Creek War in Alabama. He was the second man over the ramparts at the decisive Battle of Horseshoe Bend, following an officer who had been instantly killed. Houston took an arrow in the groin, but despite the grave injury, he continued to fight, using his sword like one possessed. In desperation, he yelled at a nearby officer to pull the arrow from his body, but the man failed in his first attempt. Wild with pain, Houston threatened the soldier with death if the arrow was not removed. In response, the fellow braced himself, got a good grip on the arrow, and gave a mighty tug, leaving a wound that would never heal.

Sam Houston, who had passionately studied the war heroics in a translation of Homer's *Iliad,* was not finished with the battle. After a surgeon plugged the gaping hole, the seriously injured Houston was resting by a tree when his commander, General Andrew Jackson, rode by and ordered him to retire from the fight. In the best tradition of the ancient Greek heroes he had studied, Houston leaped into action. He later took two rifle balls to his right shoulder and arm and fell into a ravine; his compatriots left him for dead. How Houston survived is a mystery and a miracle. But when he finally returned home to Blount County, he was in such bad shape that his mother did not recognize him until she looked into his eyes.

Horseshoe Bend might have finished Houston's career forever, but instead it earned him the attention and friendship of General Jackson, who knew a hero when he saw one.

Houston's earlier life had not been one of over-achievement—except that it is claimed he had memorized Pope's version of the *Iliad* and developed a sense of heroic fantasy from its pages. Prior to that, he was a mediocre student and a rather rebellious one, as evidenced when he asked his teacher to instruct him in Greek and Latin so that he could read the classics in original form. The refusal was not well received: Houston bolted from the classroom, determined that he would never recite a lesson again. He ran away to his friends, the nearby Cherokee Indians. Chief John Jolley virtually adopted the boy and gave him an Indian name which meant "the Raven."

When Houston's brothers finally came for him, he was lying under a tree on Chief Jolley's idyllic island on the Tennessee River, and true to his passion, he was still reading his favorite book. Houston explained his errant behavior, claiming that he "liked the wild liberty of the Red men, better than the tyranny of his own brothers, and if he could not study Latin in the Academy, he could, at least, read a translation from the Greek in the woods, and read it in peace."

Once back in Maryville, however, Houston taught school for a year. He needed the money to pay off debts he had accumulated on buying trips into town for personal clothing and gifts for his Indian friends.

For his learned mind and solid discipline, he quickly became the most sought-after teacher within miles. When he left town with his silver dollar in hand to join the 1813 Creek War, Houston marched toward a bright future. With Jackson's patronage, he would also shine in a few political battles.

Sam Houston's rise through politics was rapid. After his beginning as an attorney in Lebanon, he became an Indian agent, Nashville district attorney, adjutant general of the Tennessee militia, and in 1823 a congressman.

Despite Houston's flair for physical combat, the traditional duel which was then so fashionable among southern gentlemen never appealed to him. Only once did he participate in such fights, which were illegal in Tennessee. Even then, in the 1820s and as a United States congressman, he tried to avoid the matter until pushed by caustic remarks from a second. Newspaper reports of the day added fuel to the argument, and his close friend Jackson gave Houston pointers on dueling during practice sessions at the Hermitage. He taught Houston to grip a bullet between his teeth to better steady his aim while firing. Houston won his duel, but he averted future dueling opportunities at least once a year. Standing tall at six feet, six inches, he always refused with a prepared response: "Tell him I won't fight him, for I never fight downhill."

In 1829 at the age of thirty-five, Sam Houston became the dashing bachelor governor of Tennessee. Throughout his political career, he was known for his remarkable, even flamboyant, wardrobe. People often commented about the swashbuckling figure he cut in "plum-colored coat, tight breeches, [and] colorful waistcoats," or how he campaigned for governor in his ruffled shirts, silk trousers, beaded red sash, and for good measure, silver buckled shoes. A popular governor of the state, Houston seemed to enjoy his stature as a recognized military hero and important governmental figure. But supporters worried that his bachelor status could damage future political progress. Almost on cue, Houston fell in love.

The object of his affection was Eliza Allen, the blond, blue-eyed, teenaged daughter of longtime Gallatin acquaintance John Allen. Allen was a wealthy man who viewed the much sought-after governor as a perfect social match for his daughter. Eliza reportedly had known Houston since her childhood, but they met as "man and woman" at a Lebanon dance. The courting began immediately, and just months later, on January 22, 1829, the two were married by candlelight at the bride's Sumner County estate, Allendale. Recent widower and now-President Andrew Jackson gave the couple his blessing and a silver tea service which had belonged to his late wife Rachel.

That marital trouble was already brewing became evident after the wedding dinner, when the bride reportedly collapsed into the arms of her black mammy and began to sob tears of despair. Within three months the marriage was over. Eliza Houston went home to her family, and Sam Houston prepared to resign the governorship of Tennessee.

The couple parted for reasons that neither they nor their families ever revealed. Rumors ran rampant at the time, but the mystery remains. One Nashville historian/writer, Louise L. Davis, was shown a letter written by an Allen family friend which suggests that Houston was insanely jealous and had questioned his wife's virginity before their marriage and her faithfulness afterwards. Some reports, quoting Eliza, said that Houston was a "demented man" who demanded that she lock herself in her room during the day (even on visits to her family's home) until his return. She also was disgusted by Houston's old war wound to the groin which had never healed.

Houston did try to win her back, and even made a trip to Gallatin to plead his case. His wife's aunt, who was present at the meeting, remembered, "He knelt before her and with tears streaming down his face implored forgiveness . . . and insisted with all his dramatic force that she return to Nashville with him." She refused, and in the days to come, the people of Gallatin expressed their displeasure at the governor's perceived treatment of Eliza by burning him in effigy. Houston, seeing both his marriage and his career in ruin, resigned as governor on April 16, 1829.

In a historic irony, the man who succeeded him as governor was an old friend, William Hall, also from Eliza Houston's hometown of Gallatin. When Hall finished the term of office, the citizens of Gallatin named him chairman of a committee to investigate whether or not Houston had tainted his wife's good character. This course of events became maddening to Houston, who wrote a letter of outrage to Hall but refused to condemn him personally.

Houston again responded to adversity and his natural wanderlust by seeking out his good friends, the Cherokees. He trailed Chief John Jolley to Arkansas, where a portion of the Cherokee nation had moved. Once there, he was often seen sitting under a tree, drunk, crying, and clutching a leather bag that contained the engagement ring he had given his bride. In time, he found his usual happiness in the wilderness with the Cherokees, then took a Cherokee woman as his wife—despite his continuing marriage to Eliza, who refused for several years to consider a socially unacceptable divorce. The divorce finally came, however, around 1838. Houston eventually remarried and fathered eight children. Eliza married again also, to a Middle Tennessee doctor, and began her own family.

Sam Houston remained four years with the Cherokees. Then in 1833, he left for Texas and immortality. He began his life there as a military leader in the successful fight against Mexico to obtain Texas independence. The struggle ended in 1836 when Houston led a force that destroyed the Mexican army. He also captured its leader, Santa Anna, whose soldiers had killed all within the Alamo. (More of the defenders inside this church mission had been from Tennessee than from any other state.) In confronting the powerful Santa Anna, Houston again displayed his battlefield daring, despite being wounded and having two horses shot from under him. In a pivotal moment, he sought inspiration to help his outnumbered Texas troops and gave the rallying cry, "Remember the Alamo!" which historians would later repeat and Tennesseans, as well as Texans, would never forget.

Houston became president of the Republic of Texas in 1836 and pushed Texas toward statehood in 1845, serving the new state as both a United States senator and governor (the latter from 1859 to 1861).

Houston then suddenly resigned as governor a second time. Based on his personal conviction, he refused to support the Confederacy, although Texas sentiment was demanding secession and his own sons were enlisting in the Confederate army. Ever the individualist, Houston enjoyed visiting his sons in the local Confederate camp, where he was a popular and welcomed visitor.

Before his death during the Civil War at the age of seventy, the towering Tennessee-Texas giant was aware of his immortal heroic image—not unlike those he once studied in the *Iliad*. He had lived long enough to enjoy the many honors attached to his name, including the creation of Houston, Texas.

39
Mary Hayes Gloster

A Long Ride to Get a Church

The only known photograph of Mary Hayes Gloster, who fortified herself on her journey with a jug of peach brandy.

By 1832, an old Indian trading post in West Tennessee had been transformed into the town of LaGrange, a riverport haven with charm enough to entice the more sophisticated settlers from Virginia and North Carolina. LaGrange, in fact, had a social, cultural, and educational atmosphere quite beyond anything that could be found in the rough frontier river town of Memphis fifty miles away. It had everything that fifty-two-year-old Mary Hayes Gloster was seeking, except a church.

The widow Gloster was descended from the nation's founders dating to the seventeenth century in Virginia. Coming from Warrenton, North Carolina, after her physician husband died, Mary arrived in 1827 with her children and their families. Settling in LaGrange, they found 240 people, a few stores, and two taverns, but no church. Believing that LaGrange could hold more religion, Mary pondered the situation until she finally took off on an overland journey. Her horseback ride in 1832 to get the town an Episcopal church was no small feat. With a jug of peach brandy slung over her saddle and a grandchild cradled in one arm, Mary headed for Franklin, two hundred miles away, accompanied by the servant of her son-in-law, John Anderson. A later regional church historian would write: "The grandchild's presence would protect her from any advances by males and the brandy would ward off chills and fever!"

Arriving in Franklin, the widow Gloster sought a sympathetic ear. She pleaded with a priest, her godson, James H. Otey, later the first Episcopal bishop of Tennessee. Otey petitioned church superiors on behalf of the little town, and in due time, Dr. Thomas Wright of North Carolina arrived to establish a church in LaGrange as well as numerous other parishes in the rugged western part of the state. Mary Gloster's efforts, in fact, resulted in five churches throughout the region. The LaGrange church was organized in 1833 in her home, followed later by a permanent structure built on land that she donated. Her slaves hewed the timber and made the bricks with which it was constructed, finally completing in 1842 the oldest Episcopal church in West Tennessee.

What Mary did not realize was that her church would be built twice, and the second time it would serve a congregation in Illinois.

That occurrence came about after other newcomers, the Cossitt family from New York, fell in love with LaGrange. The Cossitts joined the local fever to build stately antebellum mansions which would become a hallmark of the town's continuing charm. When one of those family members, Frank Cossitt, later moved to Illinois, he despaired at having left LaGrange. Rather than mourn, Cossitt duplicated the entire town just as it existed in Tennessee. He constructed LaGrange, Illinois. It was a replica of every street, every public building, and Mary Gloster's beloved Episcopal church, which was also named Immanuel.

Cossitt left behind a mansion, Tiara, which, along with his brother's Cossitt's Castle and LaGrange's other imposing homes, would later became a favorite retreat for Union generals who established a Union outpost there during the Civil War. Among those generals in temporary residence was Ulysses S. Grant, who sent for his wife to share a vacation in LaGrange. Immanuel Episcopal Church, which bore a plaque in memory of the 1854 death of Mary Gloster, was turned into a Union hospital and its pews ripped out to make coffins for Union soldiers.

40
David Crockett

Backwoods Political Hero
Courting National Celebrity

David Crockett. A rare charcoal rendering, circa 1835,
a year before his death.

In 1833, Congressman David Crockett stood up in the audience of a Washington, D.C., theater, grinned proudly, and then exchanged bows with the star of one of America's most popular plays, *The Lion of the West.* The play featured as its main character Nimrod Wildfire—an Indian-fighting frontiersman whose jovial spirit, sure-fire aim as a hunter, ability to spin tall tales, and plain-spokenness as a champion of the common people made him a national fictional hero. The audience went wild when Crockett—a mythical figure himself—appeared. He accepted the gleeful applause as a real-life version of Nimrod Wildfire.

Crockett and the play's star both possessed a flair for publicity and had planned this moment. Each profited from the occasion. The play became even more popular with the appearance of the colorful Crockett, and Crockett became even more famous as the backwoods embodiment of Wildfire. Crockett's tall tales about himself (his Indian-fighting days and his hunting excursions back home in Tennessee) mixed well with his good-humored frankness in politics to make him a nationwide legend.

That Crockett had traded his renowned bear-hunting excursions in Tennessee for the political wilderness of Washington also fascinated the populace. After years in state and national politics, nearly always speaking for the ordinary yeoman farmer, Crockett was so popular with voters that he seemed poised to remain in Washington, at least in his own mind.

But in 1835, two years after his grand moment in the theater, Crockett lost his bid for a fourth congressional term, blaming a coalition that included President Andrew Jackson, Tennessee Governor William Carroll, and the Union Bank of Jackson, Tennessee. The bank reportedly paid twenty-five dollars per vote to anyone who cast their ballot for his opponent. Crockett grumbled that twenty-five dollars was "a pretty good price for a vote, and in ordinary times a round dozen might be got for that money."

The most ironic twist was that Crockett, who was a master of political trickery, felt victimized by dirty politics. Crockett practiced his art primarily in West Tennessee, where his political office and his gigantic reputation as a hunter gave nineteenth-century America one of its most celebrated personalities. While stumping Madison County in his unsuccessful 1835 reelection bid to Congress, Crockett took lodging at the home of a wealthy local farmer. The farmer also provided lodging for rival candidate Adam Huntsman, whose service in the Creek War had left him with a wooden leg, a handicap Crockett did not hesitate to exploit. Once the rest of the household was asleep, Crockett walked down the hall, using a chair to simulate the sound of a wooden leg. He knocked on the door of the farmer's daughter, then disappeared quickly to his room. Moments later the furious host burst into Huntsman's room, and the candidate had a difficult time maintaining his innocence. Although Crockett lost the election, he had once again shown that he was a colorful, mischievous rascal of a politician. He loved to embarrass opponents with the practical jokes that marked his nearly twenty years in politics.

Born in 1786 in Greene County near Limestone, David Crockett (no evidence suggests that he used the nickname "Davy") lived in all three sections of Tennessee. Later Crockett authorities such as Michael A. Lofaro consider Crockett a true Tennessean, spending as he did twenty-five years in East Tennessee, ten in Middle Tennessee, and the last fifteen in West Tennessee.

Living most of his childhood at Morristown in Hamblen County, David began his wanderings early. His father, who owned a local tavern, was often in debt and frequently hired out the boy to pay off obligations, once in Virginia. At the age of thirteen, David ran away in a dispute over skipping school and ended up in Baltimore. But he returned home to Morristown three years later to help pay seventy-six dollars that his father owed. When the family moved to nearby Jefferson City, he met his first wife, Polly, and spent five years toiling on a rented farm with little success.

Around 1811, Middle Tennessee lured Crockett, and he began a steady move across counties along the Tennessee-Alabama border. He joined the Lincoln County militia, then relocated to Franklin County, where he became an Indian scout for General Andrew Jackson during the 1813 Creek War. After Polly died in 1815, Crockett married a widow, Elizabeth Patton. (Each brought two children to the union, then they had three more together.)

Crockett next became enamored with Lawrence County, settling on Shoal Creek. He was becoming well known and well liked. Here in 1821, he capitalized on his down-home style and stature as an Indian-fighting hero to launch his political career from Lawrenceburg. Taking his seat in the Tennessee legislature representing Lawrence and Hickman counties, he learned that winning the respect of his colleagues at Murfreesboro (then the legislative seat) would not be easy. He was dubbed "the gentleman from the cane," and Crockett's rugged frontier nature often faced ridicule by his more elegantly dressed political equals. He was routinely lampooned by James C. Mitchell, who often wore ruffled shirts. Crockett, tiring of the insults, avenged himself one day by pinning ruffles on his rough-hewn leather shirt. When he rose to address the legislature, the ensuing laughter forced the humiliated Mitchell to vacate the chamber.

Crockett's greatest skill was his ability to excite people's imaginations. Among his great loves were tall tales. He could spin yarns that were as entertaining as they were outlandish, many centering around his prowess as a hunter.

In the early 1820s, one man familiar with Crockett's growing fame as a bear hunter happened to corner him at a tavern in Jackson. Crockett was now enchanted with West Tennessee and living in Weakley County at the junction of the South Fork and Rutherford's Fork of the Obion River; he traveled to Jackson to trade furs and other goods.

A fellow asked Crockett if he could tell by the scratches on a tree how tall a bear was and by its tracks whether it was male or female. Mockingly, Crockett answered that his smallest son could make these judgments.

The fellow persisted in what became an annoying interrogation, asking Crockett about other critters in the wild. "I understand the country down your way is alive with alligators," he prodded. "I suppose you often hunt them. It must be pretty dangerous work."

Crockett's imagination seized on this new tack:

Sometimes they get atop our cabin, and once they knocked the chimney level with the roof and tore off all the bark and shingles. But I don't hunt 'em. I throw out a rope and snare 'em. Last spring I caught one thirty-seven feet long, and tamed him. In summer he comes up beside the cabin and we use him for a bench.

Drawing a huge bear tooth from his buckskin bag, Crockett informed the fellow that bears make better pets than alligators—and they also make good candidates for Congress. Crockett said, "My little boy brought a cub home in his pocket one day, and we tamed him. He's a big bear now and sits at the table like a man. We call him Death Hug, and I shouldn't wonder if he was smart enough to travel some day, and maybe go to Congress."

Several in the tavern suggested that Crockett run for Congress, or at least again for the state legislature. "I like hunting too well to get into such things again," he retorted. But Crockett soon learned that others had entered his name in the state-legislative campaign. He carried his good humor to a victory, now representing a vast West Tennessee terrain: Carroll, Henderson, Humphreys, Madison, and Perry counties. In 1823, he helped form Gibson County, where he later lived.

In 1825, when Crockett finally ran for Congress, he was defeated by only two votes. Returning to the Obion River and the life of a bear-hunting frontiersman whose nearest neighbor was seven miles away, he also engaged in the making of staves (part of a barrel). This was a popular pursuit among early settlers, but Crockett nearly lost his life trying to float a cargo down the nearby Mississippi River in 1826.

Later that year, his skills in wilderness survival were put to the test on a winter hunting trip. The expedition followed the path of Reelfoot Lake, which had been created by the earthquake of 1812. While pursuing bear, Crockett's party was caught in another quake, and he feared the temblor "might swallow us up like the big fish did Jonah." Startled hunters were "rocked about like we had been in a cradle," claimed Crockett, who trailed a bear until it fell into one of the earth's cracks. He tripped over fallen trees and in crevices caused by the earthquake but lunged at the bear with a knife and killed him in a hole four feet deep. The group was able to collect forty bears in four weeks, although the freezing weather was nearly too much to overcome. In the spring, Crockett said he "took a notion to hunt a little more." Adding to the winter haul, he claimed that he took down 105 bears in about eight months.

His path finally led to Congress in 1827, and Crockett became a maverick who voted his convictions, no matter whom he insulted; but he did heed the wishes of his constituents as well. He was not offended when a Tennessee voter criticized him for free spending in Washington. Crockett admitted he had made a mistake and afterwards refused to support routine charity bills. It was against the Constitution, he said, and would risk the finances of the nation. But the most curious slant to his years in Washington was his break with the president of the United States: his fellow Tennessean and former wartime commander Andrew Jackson, who also ascended the political ladder by appealing to common men as one of their own. Crockett openly opposed Jackson's policy to remove the Cherokees from their ancestral lands and fought for the rights of West Tennessee squatters who had built homesteads long before land grants were issued (even proposing a bill to make land ownership easier for poor farmers).

The opposition party to Jackson, recognizing a celebrity, lured Crockett into their ranks and helped turn his backwoods mystique into a national legend. The Whigs then published Crockett's *Autobiography,* a popular book full of his humorous tales, frontier wisdom, and barbs at Jackson. The party also sent Crockett on a festive northern tour in 1834 and published other books in his name.

In the end, Crockett could not sustain his magic in a growing power struggle with Jackson. When Crockett lost reelection to Congress in 1835, he also lost his temper. The public was not accustomed to a humorless David Crockett, who chastised his constituents for allowing him to be "knocked down and dragged out" in an unfair fight. His departing words were a proclamation, after the wooden-legged Adam Huntsman had won: "Since you have chosen to elect a man with a timber toe to succeed me, you may all go to hell, and I will go to Texas."

Convinced that the odds were stacked heavily against him in Tennessee politics, he left his home state, never expecting to encounter even steeper odds at his next destination: a little Texas church mission, the Alamo. The circumstances surrounding Crockett's 1836 death at the Alamo while helping to gain Texas independence remain a topic of debate. One version asserts that he was not killed in battle against the Mexican army, but captured and executed after vainly attempting to bargain for his release. Whatever the manner of his death, Crockett filled his life with adventure, public service, humor, and an array of self-created myths that lived after him in his zigzag path across Tennessee and across the nation.

Throughout his fifty years, Crockett remained committed to his motto: "Be always sure you're right—then go ahead!" He left behind a son who would take up one of his battles for the poor. John Wesley Crockett succeeded Adam Huntsman in Congress and championed his father's land bill, which won passage in modified form in 1841.

In 1871, after many attempts, West Tennessee honored the late David Crockett with the formation of Crockett County, followed by the naming of the county seat "Alamo." In 1872, a theatrical play about him began a twenty-two-year run in the United States and England and ended only when its cowriter and star, Frank Mayo, died in 1896. The play, called *Davy Crockett; Or, Be Sure You're Right, Then Go Ahead,* propelled the Crockett legend into the twentieth century. Davy, as the public now called him, became the heroic subject of silent films, modern motion pictures, and a Walt Disney television series that initiated a Crockett craze among American youngsters in 1955.

41
Elizabeth "Bettsey" Hill
The Memory of a Slave's Best Friend

No one in Clay County can remember the details of a woman who founded a remote community around 1830 for the protection of the slaves that she brought there. Whoever she was and whatever her personal life, this much seems certain: She was a white woman (probably wealthy), and she created Tennessee's only settlement for freed blacks (perhaps the South's only continuing rural black community).

Legend claims that her name was Hill and that she transplanted the slaves from either Virginia or North Carolina. Some people believed that the slaves were her children by a black lover; others stated that she simply transported the slaves from her family plantation to freedom in Tennessee.

Upon her arrival along the Tennessee-Kentucky border, this woman purchased four hundred acres of timberland around the Obed River (in what was then Overton County), freed her slaves, gave them the land and then vanished. Although she disappeared from the pages of history, her legacy lived on.

An easier person for history to record was one of those newly freed slaves (or "children" as the case may be), Elizabeth "Bettsey" Hill, called affectionately "Bettsey Mamie." Her own family made up the "most significant ancestors" in this historic upper Cumberland Plateau community, located on hilly terrain and flanked by two major rivers. One elderly Free Hills resident once stated assuredly about Bettsey Mamie: "She's the mother of 'em all."

Little is known of her personal life, except that she was a grown woman by the Civil War. But historians have been able to document the community's early existence by her very presence. One writer claims that Bettsey Mamie fell in love with a slave and purchased her future husband "out of bondage and made a down payment on him, but before the final payment was made, the Negroes were set free during the Civil War and the remaining payments were cancelled."

Her new husband took her surname, Hill, as his own. They had at least seven children, whom they raised on one hundred acres which she apparently owned. (History has lost track of Bettsey Hill's siblings.)

The community's name of Free Hills was full of double meanings, perhaps originating from the many freed blacks named Hill. The land that they acquired was free; their benefactor was a woman named Hill; and the terrain on which the slaves settled was hilly. The easiest access was by fording one of the surrounding waterways, either the Obed (Obey) River or the Cumberland River. One Clay Countian pointedly noted, "It's practically an island." Nearby, on another side, is Dale Hollow Lake.

During the Civil War, this isolated settlement, which is located about eight miles from the county seat at Celina, attracted many runaway slaves. Upon the abolition of slavery, numbers of Middle Tennessee blacks either departed for the city, settled at Free Hills, or began their own black communities (most of which sprang up during the Reconstruction era when large communities of newly freed slaves banded together).

Although most black communities eventually disappeared, the residents of Free Hills remained together, continuing as the state's oldest black community and numbering several hundred at its peak. They kept alive their common heritage and gained strength from their Wednesday night prayer meetings. Surviving all social and economic adversity, the community coexisted peacefully with its all-white Clay County neighbors generation after generation.

There would be times during the early 1990s when some Clay Countians worried that a bleak job market might destroy the population base of Free Hills. In 1993, a Celina High School football player from Free Hills declared that (like others before him) he might move to the city to attend college, but he would return to the homeplace, where the population was falling below one hundred. "I'll come back," he explained. "As soon as we move away, others will be coming back. We know we have something special here: our history. Our family ties are strong."

42
Chief John Ross

Holding onto the Homeland;
Holding Off the Intruder

John Ross, lifetime friend of the Cherokees, chief of the
Eastern Cherokees and, from 1838, chief of the
United Cherokee Nation.

In November 1835, Cherokee Chief John Ross was sitting in jail, but he was charged with no crime.

The arrest, made in Tennessee by the Georgia Guard, was not an official act. Perhaps it was a delaying tactic by the state of Georgia so that Ross would be unable to attend a critical Cherokee-United States conference. At stake was possession of the Eastern Cherokee Nation's ancient tribal homeland—coveted by the white settlers who had been whittling away at the land for years.

Ross had always crusaded for the Cherokees to retain their native territory, which prior to the arrival of the oncoming settlers had stretched over the equivalent of several states. Now the fight was nearing its end.

That Ross would be taken as a hostage could not have astonished him. He and his family already had

been left homeless when the state of Georgia confiscated their stately house, considerable land, and a ferry. The property (along with that of other Cherokees) was distributed in a lottery to Georgia citizens. The Ross family fled to Tennessee, finding refuge in a two-room log cabin in present-day Bradley County. Here too was the capital of the Cherokee nation.

When the Georgia Guard burst into his new dwelling, Ross was visiting with a houseguest, John Howard Payne, an eminent American playwright, poet, and writer of the popular song "Home Sweet Home." For good measure, the Georgia Guard arrested Payne also. Both men were taken to Spring Place, Georgia, and confined in a small building for two weeks.

Although he was only one-eighth Cherokee, John Ross had spent most of his life in the service of the tribal nation. He was born in 1790 in present-day Alabama (then Georgia) to a father who was Scottish and a mother who was one-quarter Cherokee. Raised according to the traditions of the Cherokees, the boy was educated by white tutors near his childhood home, the base of Lookout Mountain (and in Tennessee schools at Maryville and Kingston). Ross barely spoke the Cherokee language, but his great orations in English were an asset in dealing with the United States government throughout the early nineteenth century. Some historians attest that he was also the "Father of Chattanooga," because the city first carried the name Ross's Landing. In his youth, Ross reportedly operated a local ferry and had a trading business on the river.

Ross became a Cherokee spokesman in 1809 when United States Indian agent Return Jonathan Meigs sent him across the Arkansas River on a mission to the Western Cherokees. Ross later led a Cherokee regiment and fought for General Andrew Jackson in the 1814 Creek War. Continuing as a Cherokee aide, Ross helped establish democracy within the Cherokee Nation, became chief of the Eastern Band of the Cherokees, and finally chief of the entire Cherokee Nation.

One of the reasons the Cherokees held Ross in such high esteem was that he, unlike others, could not be bribed with money or favors to forsake the best interests of the Cherokee people. In 1823, a Creek chief, William McIntosh (who was half white and related by marriage to the governor of Georgia), tried to lure Ross into arranging the sale of the Cherokee homeland to land-hungry Georgia.

Ross, holding a letter from McIntosh promising money for this deed, went before the Cherokee National Council, where he revealed the traitor, McIntosh, who was in attendance. "A traitor in all nations is looked upon as more despicable than the meanest reptile that crawls the earth. . . . I would rather live as poor as the worm that inhabits the earth," Ross declared, "than to gain all the world's wealth, and have my reputation tarnished by the acceptance of a bribe." He then revealed: "It has become my painful duty to inform you that a gross contempt is offered to my character, as well as to the members of the general council. The letter I hold in my hand will speak for itself, but fortunately, the author of it has mistaken our character and sense of honor."

Despite this setback with the Cherokees, McIntosh went on with his own plans to assist Georgia. Two years later, he signed a treaty relinquishing all Creek land east of the Mississippi to the United States.

With Ross standing firm, all attempts to grab the Cherokee nation were fruitless for more than a decade. Ross remained a barrier to the state of Georgia and to the United States government.

He had a clear vision of what it would take for the Cherokees to survive in the United States and coexist with the white intruders, who were gaining one foothold after another. The Cherokees, he insisted, should adopt a constitution (tailored after the United States Constitution), establish a code of written laws, and claim sovereignty over their ancient lands. This they did in 1827.

Named chief of the Eastern Band of the Cherokees, Ross echoed Indian agent Meigs in encouraging the Cherokees to adopt some of the daily living methods of their white neighbors in order to prove that the Cherokees were legitimate settlers. Perhaps, Ross thought, the Cherokee Nation could even become a separate American state. The Cherokees responded by building houses, becoming farmers, and accepting Christianity.

The plan might have worked, except that gold was discovered on Cherokee land in Georgia in 1829. As a result, the state of Georgia was even more determined to drive the Cherokee people from their homes. Even Tennessee Congressman David Crockett was unable to help the Cherokee nation, although he tried. Taking a jab at Georgia, Crockett offered a brand of his famous frontier tough talk when he "poked cutting sarcasm at the whole idea of removal of the

Cherokee by introducing a bill calling for the removal of the white residents of East Tennessee to the West, 'lest they impede the territorial designs and sovereignty of the state of Georgia.'"

The Cherokees also sought help from the United States Supreme Court to stop Georgia and to gain clear title to their homeland. Their first attempt was unsuccessful. But when the state of Georgia arrested Christian missionaries who refused to leave the Cherokee nation, the Supreme Court took issue with Georgia's attempt to violate Cherokee sovereignty. In a new case, *Worcester v. Georgia,* the court ruled that Georgia state law could not be imposed upon the Cherokee nation and that the prisoners must be released. A defiant President Andrew Jackson said of the chief justice of the Supreme Court: "John Marshall has rendered his decision; now let him enforce it."

Ignoring the Supreme Court, the state of Georgia was slow to release its prisoners and quick to annex all Cherokee land within its borders. A state lottery became Georgia's useful tool, giving white men any land (mostly farms) from which the Cherokees could be removed. Chief John Ross happened to be in Washington, D.C., on one of his many lobbying trips when his own home was seized. The only Cherokees spared were those like Major Ridge, who agreed to assist Georgia and the United States government.

In contrast to the Georgians, many East Tennessee settlers (especially those in McMinn County, where the Cherokees had a strong tradition) sided with their Indian neighbors. These homesteaders opposed the government's interference with a peaceful and settled Indian nation. A portion of the tribe, nonetheless, voluntarily left for the West immediately, while others remained and became part of the emerging white culture.

Soon after his release as a hostage of the Georgia Guard in 1835, Ross took yet another delegation to Washington, D.C., hoping his people could retain even a small portion of their homeland. His pleas fell on deaf ears. During his absence, a hurried Cherokee-United States conference proceeded at a great cost to the natives. The meeting took place at the old Cherokee capital of New Echota, Georgia, even though the Cherokee legislature did not agree to it. Most of the nearly sixteen thousand members of the Cherokee Nation were unaware that a few within their ranks would seal the fate of all.

Leading a small dissident group, Major Ridge and his cohorts signed a treaty selling to the United States all of the Cherokee nation east of the Mississippi River for five million dollars. Ross immediately tried to protest United States acceptance of a treaty which the Cherokee nation did not approve. He rushed again to the Capitol. But President Andrew Jackson said he no longer recognized a Cherokee government. The United States Senate quickly approved the minority treaty, and the margin was one vote. Defeated, the Cherokees now had two years to vacate their ancient lands and relocate in Oklahoma.

Counting those who died in concentration camps awaiting their exile, an estimated four thousand Cherokees perished during the relocation that would go down in history as the Trail of Tears. This number constituted roughly one fourth of the tribe. Casualties included Ross's wife, Quatie. According to one account, she gave her only blanket to a sick child, then developed a fatal case of pneumonia from riding thinly clad through the severe 1838 winter sleet and snowstorm.

From the Trail of Tears until his own death in 1866 at the age of seventy-six, John Ross officiated as chief of the United Cherokee Nation, during which time he led a divided tribe through the Civil War and even switched sides. Both the North and South had Cherokee soldiers. While Ross retained respect among his people by fighting for their land, both Major Ridge and the Creek William McIntosh suffered disgrace and death by execution, as did Ridge's principle helpers, his son John Ridge and nephew Elias Boudinot. Each, branded as a traitor, was executed by his own people for having violated tribal blood laws in relinquishing their ancient homelands.

43

John G. Burnett

Tragedies along the Trail of Tears

When John G. Burnett of Sullivan County looked back over the course of his life in memoirs for his eightieth birthday (he died three years later in 1893), the incident that stood out most vividly in his mind was his role in the Trail of Tears. In his twenties at the time, Burnett was a private in the United States Army who helped escort a group of Cherokees to their new lands west of the Mississippi and watched hundreds die from hunger and exposure during the winter trek.

Burnett was a product of the tough East Tennessee frontier. Born in 1810 at King Iron Works near present-day Kingsport, he spent his youth roaming the wilderness, hunting and fishing much like his Cherokee neighbors. In 1829, Burnett rescued a Cherokee from certain death and after returning him to his tribe, stayed among them for a while. "[I] remained so long," he remembered, "that I was given up for lost." During his stay with the Cherokees, Burnett became, by his own reckoning, "an expert rifleman, a fairly good archer, and a good trapper." He learned to respect his new friends, to appreciate their customs and manners, and to value the Cherokee as a separate nation, distinguished and honorable.

Several years later he was in the army, and his fluency in the Cherokee language became useful to a United States government intent upon removing the Cherokees from their homeland. Burnett was sent into the Smoky Mountains as an interpreter and aide. He watched as thousands of men, women, and children were taken by surprise in their homes and herded at gunpoint into stockades to await removal. Looking back on it, Burnett called this "the blackest chapter on the pages of American history."

Burnett's memoirs discussed briefly his version of the real origin of the Trail of Tears: "In the year 1828, a little Indian boy living on Ward Creek had sold a Gold nugget to a white trader, and that nugget sealed the doom of the Cherokees." When the white man learned that gold existed on the Cherokees' ancestral lands (between northern Georgia and East Tennessee) a series of widespread dishonorable and tragic events would result, he claimed. Burnett explained to his own children: "Future generations will read and condemn the act and I do hope posterity will remember that private soldiers like myself . . . had to execute the orders of our superiors. We had no choice in the matter."

Burnett described a moment when the soldiers herded the Cherokee people into groups:

In another home was a frail mother, apparently a widow, and three small children, one just a baby. When told that she must go, the mother gathered the children at her feet, prayed an humble prayer in her native tongue, patted the old family dog on the head, told the faithful creature good bye and with her baby strapped on her back and leading a child with each hand started to her exile, but the task was too great for that frail mother, a stroke of heart failure relieved her sufferings. She sunk and died with her baby on her back and her other children clinging to her hands.

Chief Junaluska who had saved President Jackson's life at the battle of the Horseshoe witnessed this scene, the tears gushed down his cheeks, and lifting his cap he turned his face toward the Heavens and said, "Oh my God, if I had known at the battle of the Horseshoe what I know today, American history would have been differently written."

A band of Cherokees, however, managed to escape into the Smoky Mountains and became the ancestors of the Qualla Cherokees. Junaluska's wife and brothers were among those to lose their lives on the march. Years later, the aging Junaluska left Oklahoma and walked home to the Smoky Mountains. He spent the rest of his days there among tribesmen who, having escaped the migration, were citizens of North Carolina. The state of North Carolina recognized Junaluska and granted him land, money, and citizenship in honor of his earlier service to the United States. He lived to be nearly one hundred.

Burnett considered himself a true friend of the Cherokees. "I made the long journey to the west with the Cherokees and did all that a Private soldier could do to alleviate their sufferings," he said. "When on guard duty at night I have many times walked my beat in my blouse in order that some sick child might have the warmth of my overcoat."

He also watched the wife of Chief John Ross die and then helped bury her body by the roadside. As the tragedies mounted during the march, Burnett's greatest personal victory came when he intervened to stop a white teamster named Ben McDonal from using a bullwhip to goad an elderly Cherokee man into a wagon. Burnett reached for the hatchet handle he kept in his belt from his hunting days. McDonal, he recalled triumphantly, "was carried unconscious from the scene."

44
Stephen Foreman
A Cherokee's Last Lament

His tombstone is engraved with the words, "He Labored with the Cherokees and Walked with God."

Stephen Foreman, a man who was caught between two cultures, was one of the most unlikely of the Indian "prisoners" the United States Army herded into an 1838 concentration camp in Bradley County. A Princeton graduate, Foreman was a Presbyterian missionary to the Cherokees in Tennessee. He was a kindly, unassuming man who went quietly with his pregnant wife and two small children to await the forced march to the West. The articulate Foreman probably could have spent his life in the white community and done well there. He chose, instead, to go with his people and work on their behalf in their new lands in Oklahoma.

Born in 1807, Foreman was the son of a Scottish father and a Cherokee mother. Heeding his father's advice to get an education, Foreman, who was raised a Cherokee, was passionate in the pursuit of knowledge. It was apparently common in mixed homes for the boys to learn English and the girls to speak Cherokee. One account says that Foreman was reluctant to embrace the Cherokee language until he became convinced that it would help him convert his own people to Christianity. At the urging of white missionaries, he studied in Virginia at the Union Theological Seminary and then completed his Princeton degree in just two years.

Foreman returned to Tennessee in 1833 to marry, begin a family, and build his home, which he called "Pleasant Hill," located near Candy's Creek Mission and the town of Cleveland. He began to preach the gospel among his people, but his life was soon caught up in the dislocation caused by the United States government's Indian removal policy. Chief John Ross asked that he lead one of the tribal detachments to the West. Foreman's group of 938, mostly Christians, left in October and endured the bitter winter's march. In his group, nineteen babies were born and more than forty people died.

For the white populace along the way, Foreman effectively used the pulpit to expose the true impact of the Cherokee removal. One man who accompanied the tribe was Henry Parker, who remembered how

Foreman preached to numerous Tennessee communities which were eager to hear him, occasionally riding several miles to reach his impromptu congregations. Said Parker: "Four miles the other side of Nashville he preached, and at the close of his sermon, when he came to speak of the cruelties and wrongs the Indians had suffered, I think every individual was in tears and many sobbed aloud."

In Oklahoma, Foreman became involved in Cherokee politics in an effort to reunite his divided people. He became a member of the tribal supreme court and also executive counselor for the tribe. Since the Cherokees carried their printing press from Tennessee, they were able to continue publication of the *Phoenix,* for which Foreman became associate editor. He helped translate the New Testament and most of the Old Testament from Greek to Cherokee.

He never gave up his faith in education, Christianity, and American culture. Before dying in 1881 at the age of seventy-four, Foreman succeeded in founding a Presbyterian church in the western lands and establishing a school system for the Cherokees. He was called the first superintendent of education west of the Mississippi River.

All of his own surviving children received extensive education, many in eastern colleges. Foreman's advice to his many children, according to one of his daughters, was reminiscent of his own father's directive to him: "Get a good education. That is one thing that cannot be taken from you."

45

John A. Murrell

The "Great Western Land Pirate"
Stirring Up the Slavery Issue

Madison County's seemingly charming outlaw, the "Great Western Land Pirate," John A. Murrell, presented to the world at large an attractive appearance and a convincing personality. He was a slave stealer and counterfeiter, but few people knew whether he was really a master criminal or merely a petty thief. As a thief, Murrell persuaded slaves to leave their plantations, promising to sell them and steal them back several times, then divide the profits and set them free. This ploy generally worked well for Murrell, but not so well for the slaves. He abandoned many without giving them their share of the spoils and may have killed others to cover his tracks.

Because so many tales surround his life, few people have been able to separate fact from fiction. He inched his way into passages by Mark Twain, who believed that escapades by later outlaw Jesse James were tame compared to John A. Murrell's. Twain wrote that Murrell was a "stately old time criminal, with his sermons, his meditated insurrections and city-captures, and his majestic following of ten hundred men, sworn to do his evil will!"

Even Murrell's parentage has been a curious guessing game in his life story. Was he the son of a minister, as many claimed, or was his father a farmer? Did his mother teach her boys, all of whom turned bad, how to steal, cheat, and lie? Murrell, in fact, did credit his mother with teaching him the necessary skills of a good thief. But he was caught so often stealing horses that law enforcement agents finally branded *HT* on his thumb to warn everyone that he was a horse thief.

Born in 1806, Murrell was raised primarily in Williamson County. He later moved to West Tennessee and Madison County, where he lived with his wife and children in Denmark and created an image of "genteel manners" with his "fine beaver hat and an elegant 'Bolivar' coat." It was from Denmark that the outlaw operated his supposedly large-scale gang and spread terror throughout many states (notably western Mississippi). He exercised such power that sheriffs and judges everywhere lived in fear. A favorite Murrell ploy involved posing as a Methodist minister; while he held his listeners spellbound, his accomplices stole their horses.

His undoing did not come from a law officer, but from citizen Virgil Stewart, whose stories helped create the Murrell legend. Stewart portrayed him not as a rascal, who loved to steal horses and slaves and did counterfeiting in his spare time, but as a murderer with a multistate gang called the "Mystic Clan of the Confederacy." In all of these criminal endeavors, Murrell was rather unsuccessful, or so his Madison County neighbors believed. If he had been the leader of a major criminal organization, surely he would not have been destitute most of his life. Nor would he have been caught by law officials so many times, beginning with the rampages of his wild youth in the 1820s.

Whatever the truth, Murrell had an impact on the South during his lifetime and helped nurture fear in the hearts of southerners toward slaves. This fact became apparent when whites panicked in the wake of his planned "slave insurrection" of major southern states on Christmas Day, 1835. Murrell's scheme was simple. While each town dealt with its insurrection, he and his men would move quickly to rob the communities.

The insurrection never took place, because John A. Murrell found himself in jail. Rumors of a slave insurrection, however, sent incredible terror into the hearts of Deep South plantation owners, who were aware of the recent Nat Turner slave rebellion in Virginia. A number of plantation owners, realizing they were outnumbered by the slaves, placed their wives and children under guard. Others tortured their slaves in an attempt to get information about the possible insurrection. In some locations, beatings, whippings, and hangings became commonplace. Eleven men died in one Mississippi county from the panic. And in an ironic twist, many of those beaten and hanged were white men suspected of complicity in the upcoming insurrection.

For Murrell, the beginning of the end came a year earlier, in 1834, when he stole slaves in Jackson belonging to the Reverend John Henning. Virgil Stewart, a friend of the preacher, took it upon himself to infiltrate the Clan of the Confederacy and eventually capture Murrell. This done, Stewart appeared as the main witness in a trial before Judge Joshua Haskell of Jackson. Portraying Murrell as the most notorious outlaw of the time, Stewart supposedly unveiled numerous tall tales. Following the trial, the tales were released in a pamphlet by one Augustus Q. Walton (most likely Stewart).

While credible enough to get Murrell convicted, the witness did not bring about a conviction for murder. Onlookers began to believe that Stewart was actually a member of the Murrell gang who had fallen from grace and sought revenge on his leader. Murrell, who was adept at character assassination, apparently planted the idea that Stewart was a criminal. Eventually Stewart was asked to leave town.

The Great Western Land Pirate spent the next ten years in a Nashville prison. Upon his release in 1844, Murrell journeyed to East Tennessee and, settling in Pikeville, became a Bledsoe County blacksmith. But freedom would not last long. He died of tuberculosis the same year.

46
John A. Gardner
Boiling Political Pot:
No United States Senators for Tennessee

In 1841, when freshman State Senator John A. Gardner rose to speak in the Tennessee Senate, he gave an oration that tested the endurance of his listeners. Before he finished, Gardner had spoken for seven hours.

But the lengthy filibuster pleased Gardner's fellow Jacksonian Democrats, as well as the party leader, the elder statesman and former president, Andrew Jackson. Proving a flair for the game of politics that day, Gardner had become involved in a political happening that would never be repeated in Tennessee.

His speech was directed toward an unusual occurrence: Both United States Senate seats from Tennessee were vacant. By tradition, both state houses would meet in unison to vote on replacements. But Gardner and his comrades were staging a showdown with the opposition party, the Whigs, which had been founded to oppose Jackson and his political machine.

Each side held control over a state house, although Gardner's Democrats were not enjoying their majority in the state senate, of only one vote. Sparta's colorful Democrat Sam Turney was enough of an individualist to break ranks. Turney remained in the fold, however, and the standoff with the Whigs was permanent. While Democrats might have welcomed a compromise (perhaps each side electing one senator), no compromise was forthcoming from the stubborn Whigs, and the state of Tennessee had no United States senators for the next two years.

Gardner's role in this stalemate placed him among those Democrats thereafter called the "Immortal Thirteen"; opposing Whigs carried the name of the "Twelve Destructives." From his home, the Hermitage, Jackson spoke well of the Immortal Thirteen, claiming that they had guarded "the fundamental principles of our Republican system."

Always eager to promote the former president, Gardner did not stop at a filibuster to assist Jackson. He also proposed a state senate bill in December 1841 asking that the entire region of West Tennessee be given to the United States as a separate state called "Jacksoniana," a resolution that was defeated fourteen to nine.

The two men had been friends since 1828 when Jackson won his first presidential election, and Gardner was then the eighteen-year-old publisher of a Paris newspaper, the *West Tennessean,* a propaganda organ for the new president. Gardner eventually moved to Dresden and began a law career; he later published yet another partisan newspaper called the *Jacksonian.*

Originally from Robertson County, Gardner (along with his six brothers and two sisters) was among the first settlers of Weakley County. In 1840, Gardner purchased a farm that eventually grew to seventy-five hundred acres, making him one of the largest landowners in this area of West Tennessee. It was from here that he won his seat in the state senate.

In the 1843 elections, the opposing Whigs continued to overpower Democrats statewide, this time sweeping the legislature and winning the governor's chair against Jackson's protégé James K. Polk. One of the Whigs' first legislative bills dealt with vacant United States Senate seats: Now it was official that two empty seats must be filled by an assembly of both state houses.

Despite the growing political muscle of the Whig Party in Tennessee, Gardner was able to win reelection through 1847, thereafter deciding to become a railroad man. In 1852, he helped found the Nashville & Northwestern Railroad (it became the Louisville and Nashville, or L & N). Gardner also offered the railroad right-of-way passage through his farm, which was located in northern Weakley County near the Tennessee-Kentucky border. When the tracks were built in 1856, Gardner's Station was a natural outgrowth. Its town founder also built the area's first flour mill operated by steam and ran mercantile businesses.

With access to the railroad, the Gardner community prospered. Despite the interruptions of the Civil War, the community became the principle trade center between Dresden and Union City during the late 1860s. A windfall of good fortune seemed assured when, in 1872, another railroad, the Mississippi Central, surveyed the area and recommended Gardner as the perfect site for a proposed northern route between Jackson, Tennessee, and Cairo, Illinois (the so-called Cairo Extension).

But unforeseen competition emerged three miles away on the estate of the late William Martin. Martin's sons cut a deal with the railroad, and, repeating what John A. Gardner himself had once done, the Martins gave free passage rights through their land. The deal put the Gardner community out of the picture. When the Mississippi Central moved its route, most businesses in the town of Gardner moved with it. Together, they helped to build a major rail junction and town which became Martin, Tennessee.

As for John A. Gardner, he entered politics again, serving in the Tennessee House of Representatives between 1879 and 1881; he then moved to Texas in 1887 to spend his remaining years. He died in 1892.

47

George C. Furber

*Mexican War Mix: Volunteers,
Gators, and Guerrillas*

When the volunteers from Tennessee, many of whom had never fought a battle, marched off to the Mexican War in 1846, they encountered a strange semitropical land as hostile as the Mexican army. Germantown attorney George C. Furber left Shelby County as part of the astonishing turnout of Tennesseans heeding the call to war, or as he said, "to take up the sword and carbine, exchanging the office for the camp."

Nearly thirty thousand Tennesseans had volunteered to fill the United States War Department's request for twenty-eight hundred men, and the nickname "Volunteer State" was forever attached to Tennessee. Furber was a private in West Tennessee's "Eagle Guards," or Company G of the Tennessee Regiment of Cavalry, which had more than nine hundred men.

That Furber never lost his initial enthusiasm for the camaraderie of soldiering is apparent in his wartime journal and history of the war, *The Twelve Month Volunteer.* Nonetheless, he and his fellow Tennesseans soon realized that getting to their destination in Mexico was more than a camping trip. Furber and his comrades had gotten no further than Little Rock, Arkansas, when they were forced to discipline one of their own for stealing a horse to replace his dead mount. The ritual of drumming a man out of the militia nearly fell short of its goal because the regiment had no drummers. The officers in charge, explained Furber, decided that drumming could mean "noise made upon any instrument whatever." The men took up mess pans, camp kettles, brick-bats, and even large bones from a nearby slaughterhouse to send the fellow on his embarrassed way. Under armed guard with buglers behind, he was forced to walk a gauntlet of his fellow soldiers who "joined in the concert" of deafening clatter "accompanied by groans, hisses, squeals and yells."

Although Furber's regiment was well provisioned, the opportunity to bathe became scarcer as the men entered Texas. Deciding to wash in the nearest deep river, they discovered that they had to share the space. An intruder became apparent, wrote Furber, when the men saw "the rusty head of a large alligator emerging from the turbid water." He added: "There being no such 'varmints' in Tennessee, most of the men had never seen one before, and the view of his ugly phiz was enough for them."

As the Tennessee troops neared Mexico, problems began to mount: poor water, no pay, and wagons carrying tents and food bogged down indefinitely in mud holes (necessitating eighty boat trips to transfer the men and equipment across a small river). To worsen matters, the semitropical climate offered up a storm that was like a hurricane. It left the volunteers caked in mud, the roads impassable, and the rivers uncrossable. The men weathered the situation by becoming insensible to the cold torrents with the help of liquor. According to Furber, "all were so cold and wet, and exhausted, that the liquor did not operate quickly; . . . it was to them, rest, supper, and shelter; . . . every body was drunk, last night;—as I heard the Colonel say this morning that out of the thousand men, teamsters, and all, in the regiment, there were *eleven* hundred intoxicated."

As his regiment finally saw its way clear to travel in Mexico, Furber began to hear about the heroics of other Tennesseans already there. Many of them, in order to get into the war after Tennessee's quota was met, had enlisted in neighboring states. They had played a critical role at the Battle at Monterey, the heavily fortified city surrounded by the Sierra Madre Mountains. A Mexican general there, trying to rally his men, had ridiculed the American force, made up mostly of volunteers from Tennessee and Mississippi who had joined about twenty-five hundred regular-army troops. Dismissing the volunteers as "adventurers, without valor or discipline," the Mexican general

was astonished when the Americans heroically tore into the city. Furber described volunteer regiments "pouring over its walls in the face of five pieces of artillery, throwing a shower of grape and canister into their ranks. . . . He [the Mexican general] then compared their fighting to that of devils."

Excited about the prospects of playing an equally important part in the Mexican War, Furber's troops drilled relentlessly. Their destination was the port city of Veracruz, a major target in the 1847 United States invasion deep into Mexico. The regiment had spent more than three months in covering more than fourteen hundred miles after leaving Tennessee. Now, as they were finally en route by way of the Gulf of Mexico to Veracruz, yet another storm caught the men. Most became "dizzy and bewildered" in a squall that wrecked several ships and drowned a number of soldiers, sailors, and horses by the time of their landing.

Other Tennessee units were already engaged in a battle below that city's walls. The Second Tennessee under General Gideon Pillow "found themselves on the top [of a hill] in full view, and within a short range, of the city walls and batteries; they planted their flag, and in answer to their three loud cheers, they received the first fire of the Mexican batteries."

What was thought to be the "impregnable fortress" of Veracruz fell to the Tennesseans and other American forces in only five days. Furber and his comrades spent most of their time hauling the mortars and great guns from one place to another, since the fight at hand was an artillery duel. Near the end of the engagement, however, a force of Mexican lancers did attempt an attack, and a group of Tennesseans were sent to meet the threat. Furber wrote:

> The enemy retreated, run, broke, *vamosed*—the lancers going at full speed up the road, and the infantry taking the thick chapparal in every direction. Some were overtaken and killed; and we pushed on in a trot after the main body of lancers. . . . After four miles' chase, we were halted by General Patterson, who seemed to be in his right element, and extremely pleased with the spirit and conduct of the troops. He took off his hat, as he rode by us, after the pursuit was done, and carried away by enthusiasm, raised himself in his stirrups, and, as he swung his hat around, called out, *"Hurray for Tennessee!"*

When the bombardment was over on March 26, 1847, Veracruz was in ruins, and the Tennesseans, Furber among them, marched triumphantly alongside the smaller regular army into the city. In May, General Winfield Scott ordered the twelve-month volunteers home before the yearly onslaught of the deadly sickness known as "vomito" could descend upon the region and upon the battered Tennessee cavalry regiment. Before heading back to Tennessee, the regiment casually toured parts of Mexico.

By September, the Mexican War was progressing toward its conclusion. Remaining Tennessee volunteers helped to capture a string of cities and played a critical role in the final Battle of Chapultepec, causing the fall of Mexico City. Two leaders in decisive Mexican War battles who lived to return home were immediately elected (in succession) to be Tennessee governors. William Trousdale, "the War Horse of Sumner County," was wounded commanding two infantry regiments against Chapultepec in Mexico City's final fall. He was made a general for his bravery and was elected governor after arriving back in Tennessee; he also inspired the naming of Trousdale County. William Bowen Campbell led the so-called Bloody First Tennessee regiment under Trousdale in pivotal battles throughout the war, including the critical Battle of Monterey, in which the Bloody First was the breakthrough unit and suffered the heaviest casualties. Campbell succeeded Trousdale in the governor's chair.

Reflecting on his own cavalry regiment, Furber was both elated and sad in later writings:

> each experienced a feeling of pride upon reflection that he had nobly served his country for one year of his life. But with our joy a feeling of sadness was mingled, when we thought of the many brave spirits that a year before had gone out with us, who now returned not—fallen in the ranks before the enemy, or sunk beneath the baneful effects of a sickly climate.

48

James K. Polk

Manifest Destiny of the Soul

Of the many lifetime battles that faced James K. Polk, a president who completed each of his major

James K. Polk, the nation's first "dark horse" president, accomplished his goals as chief executive.

campaign goals within one term of office, few weighed more heavily in 1848 than one that began at his birth and waged privately in his last years: a battle for his soul. This conflict came to a conclusion at the end of his presidency—on his deathbed.

Polk had never belonged to a church. He had always disliked organized religion and had been aware of a controversy that his father, Sam, and grandfather, Ezekiel, had waged with the Presbyterian church of Mecklenburg County, North Carolina. In 1796, shortly after James Knox Polk's birth, Polk's father became so angry during his infant son's baptism ceremony that he whisked him away. The elder Polk's fury stemmed from the minister's request that he first make a profession of his own faith. Having come all the way to the church primarily to appease his extremely religious wife, Sam Polk refused, exiting the scene and carrying his unchristened baby with him.

Shortly thereafter, the Polks moved to Tennessee's middle country and settled in the future Maury County. Their inspiration to expand their horizons and make such a move in 1802 came from the rebellious family patriarch, Ezekiel Polk, who had spent years opposing British rule in America and also the organized church as he knew it. Ezekiel, an American Revolution veteran, had been involved in the nation's earliest freedom talk when he helped draft the Mecklenburg Declaration—often said to be the opening act of the revolution, one year before the Declaration of Independence. In Tennessee, Ezekiel even composed his own epitaph reflecting his continued distaste for foreign rule and the church, attitudes that he passed along to his grandson, the future President Polk. Referring to himself, Ezekiel proclaimed in his epitaph:

He can foresee, (and for foreseeing He equals
most of men in being,)
That church and state will join their power,
And misery on this country shower;
The Methodists with their camp bawling;
Will be the cause of this down falling;
An error not destin'd to see
He wails for poor posterity,
First fruits and tenths are odious things,
And so are Bishops, Tithes and Kings.

In Maury County, James K. Polk developed into one of the state's most famous citizens, entering politics at an early age. While trying to build a political base, Polk had no trouble attracting voters in West Tennessee's Hardeman County. He always found a large voting block of relatives there because Ezekiel Polk helped to settle the county in 1823. Ezekiel reportedly fathered 24 children, who, in turn, produced roughly 92 of their own children and 307 grandchildren. During this time, Polk family members became land speculators.

Deeply wounded by the family's baptism controversy and raised with a Presbyterian education, young Polk was developing into a shy individual. Particularly fond of politics, however, Polk used his straitlaced upbringing as an asset. Included in his "rigid" pursuit of political fame was the calculated, hurried courtship of Rutherford County's Sarah Childress, who was recommended to him by Andrew Jackson. Jackson's brand of politics was always favorable to Polk, and so now was Jackson's advice on romance. According to historians, Polk asked his mentor how to be successful in politics; Jackson advised that Polk should become a married man. The choice was obvious, observed Jackson: "The one who will never give

you trouble. Her wealth, family, education, health, and appearance are all superior. You know her well."

Polk immediately sought Sarah's hand, and months later, on January 1, 1824, the two were married. He became a member of the United States House of Representatives in 1825 and remained until 1839, during which time he served four years as Speaker of the House. The Polks hardly saw each other for the first two years of their marriage, but nothing upset Sarah, as Polk would discover when she was at his side during heated political campaigns. She portrayed the calm, loving wife who became a popular social hostess to her husband's political circle.

One 1834 incident, however, brought Sarah Polk into direct conflict with her husband on the issue of banks and paper money. Like President Jackson, Congressman Polk disliked both. En route to Washington, D.C., Polk discovered, when stopping for a night's lodging, that he did not have enough money in his pocket. Sarah, forced to open their trunks, found the necessary coins, then began a lecture on the inconvenience of metal coins: "Don't you see how troublesome it is to carry around gold and silver? This is enough to show you how useful banks are."

Polk retorted: "Sarah, you've turned your politics then, but all I want now is that money!"

He later related this story with considerable embellishment to his stagecoach traveling companions, and they were so amused that their boisterous laughter rang out for several minutes, although several of the men happened to share Sarah Polk's opinion about the usefulness of banks.

After becoming Tennessee's governor in 1839, Polk made two subsequent attempts to return to the governorship, but he failed. Undeterred, he set his sight on a bigger goal: the United States presidential ticket. "Who is James K. Polk?" asked his fellow Democrats in 1844 while pondering their options for a presidential nominee. He was the so-called dark-horse candidate, a virtual has-been in Tennessee politics. However, because of his party's discontent with the other candidates, Polk became the nominee, and in a strong election (although failing to carry Tennessee), he became the eleventh president of the United States.

Polk was the youngest president to that date and the nation's first dark-horse candidate to reach the White House. Dubbed "Young Hickory" because of his unyielding loyalty to Jackson and his policies, especially territorial expansion, Polk caused the annexation of more than a quarter of the continental United States. His platform was Manifest Destiny, extolling the divine right to pursue land across the continent. Polk defended the annexation of Texas (a major issue of his campaign) and acquired the American Southwest through the Mexican War, which has been called "Mr. Polk's War."

Polk's presidency also produced one of the more notable conveniences of the nineteenth century: the postage stamp. During his presidential campaign, opponents had regularly sent volumes of mail, forcing the candidate to pay for delivery, as was customary for any recipient of mail. When elected, Polk appointed his good friend from Montgomery County, Cave Johnson, to be the United States postmaster general. Johnson immediately resolved the problem by working with the New York postmaster in introducing the stamp and, thereby, placing all postage costs on the sender.

Touted by historian Earl Irvin West as "undoubtedly the nation's strongest President between Jackson and Lincoln," Polk had other considerable achievements in addition to expanding the United States to the Pacific Ocean. Among them were the establishment of the United States Naval Academy, the creation of the United States Department of the Interior, and the founding of the Smithsonian Institution. He fulfilled all of his major campaign promises, the first president to do so.

During his four years in the White House, Polk's religious routine was to accompany the devout Sarah to her Presbyterian church on Sunday mornings; he attended the Methodist meetings on Sunday evenings. President Polk's attraction to Methodism had been haunting him for years, ever since a congressional reelection campaign when he attended a Methodist camp meeting. The camp meeting was a favorite place to socialize and politic, "religion's answer to the political barbecue," claims historian West. Polk was moved profoundly that day by the words and emotions of the circuit-riding Reverend John B. McFerrin from Rutherford County. Polk thereafter found some way to attend a Methodist service, either for politics or for the benefit of his soul.

In 1845, Polk's true religious conversion seemed at hand when he reached his fiftieth birthday. A pensive Polk later wrote in his diary:

It awakened the reflection that I had lived fifty years, and that before fifty years more would expire, I would be sleeping with the generations which have gone before me. I thought of the vanity of this world's honors, how little they would profit me a century hence, and that it was time for me to be "putting my House in order."

The president first put the nation's house in order. Four years later, he kept the most unusual of his campaign promises: to be a one-term president. Refusing to seek reelection and proud that he had fulfilled all of his other campaign pledges, Polk returned home to Tennessee. He immediately realized he was in failing health (from cholera) and sent for Reverend McFerrin, who baptized the president and gave him communion. Polk's elderly mother and other family members were in attendance, as was a Presbyterian minister (to whom the president admitted that he had always held respect for many ministers of that faith). Polk told his brother that his heart was in Methodism, which he had planned to join, "but in the hurry and business of life and the political affairs of the country, I postponed it till now."

One day later, James Knox Polk was dead. He was fifty-four. Reverend McFerrin presided at the funeral. In honor of his friendship with Polk, he preached the identical sermon that had captured the president's heart and soul sixteen years earlier during the Methodist camp meeting.

49

Loyd Ford Sr.

A White Man and His "Black Children's" Inheritance

In the early nineteenth century, Loyd Ford Sr. referred to the three men and two women who tended his 112-acre Washington County farm as his "black children," and they may have been. Whether or not they were his offspring (eventually a major court issue) Ford's slaves were closer to him than were his seven legitimate sons—none of whom, as adults, chose to remain on the family farm and help their father. The situation resulted in a controversial will, a bitter family dispute, and a Tennessee Supreme Court ruling.

Ford's fondness for his slaves led him in 1840 to have a neighbor, Robert Hale, draw up a will granting them eventual freedom and possession of the farm. Two years later, he returned to Hale's home an unhappy man. Under the influence of alcohol and angry sons (Loyd Ford Jr. had threatened to kill him), Ford asked that the will be destroyed. Sarah Hale instead retrieved another document, "an old school article," and gave it to Ford. Though illiterate, Ford recognized that this was not his will. With a shake of his head and a laugh, he gave the phony document to the Hales with instructions to "put it in the fire and burn it, maybe it will satisfy them."

This ploy did not fool Ford's sons. They sent an emissary to try to buy the will from Mrs. Hale. She refused, then hid it in loose planks above her bed.

When Ford died in 1843, the court battle began. Tennessee law allowed county courts to decide whether or not freed slaves could remain in the community or had to leave the state (a law that changed many times during this era). A Washington County court, showing no desire for the slaves to leave, ordered a jury trial concerning the contested will. The "black children," meanwhile, had to meet certain requirements before they could appear in court. They had to find a white person, called a "next friend," who was willing to initiate a civil suit on their behalf. Phoebe Stuart (otherwise unidentified) agreed to fill this post, and on December 4, 1843, she began proceedings before the Washington County Circuit Court—*Ford v. Ford*.

Attorneys representing the sons tried to establish that their father was insane, that the Hales were untrustworthy, and that the will was a forgery. Attorneys for the slaves countered by introducing evidence that Ford's "black children" were precisely that—his natural offspring.

The Washington County jury upheld the will. The Ford sons appealed, citing errors in the circuit court proceedings. The matter went to the three-man Tennessee Supreme Court. Here, Justice Nathan Green dismissed the argument that the slaves were not "proper parties" to be involved in legal proceedings. Green's pronouncement was eloquent in its clarity and its simplicity:

> A slave is not in the condition of a horse or an ox . . . he is made in the image of the Creator. He has mental capabilities, and an immortal principle in his nature, that constitute him equal to his owner

but for the accidental position in which fortune has placed him . . . the laws under which he is held as a slave have not and cannot extinguish his high-born nature nor deprive him of many rights which are inherent in man.

Although the Tennessee Supreme Court agreed with the Washington County verdict, it conceded that errors had been made in the case. There was no choice but to order a retrial. Ford's white heirs asked for a change of venue to Johnson County, but Johnson Countians also upheld the original will. Looking a second time at the case, the state Supreme Court that same year, 1850, again backed an East Tennessee lower court in favor of the slaves.

Loyd Ford's "black children" took possession of the farm he willed to them . . . many years, four hearings, and one change of venue later.

50
Matthew Fontaine Maury
The Landlocked "Pathfinder of the Seas"

In 1814, eight-year-old Matthew Fontaine Maury could not envision his future worldwide acclaim as the first American to chart the oceans and to know more about the sea than any other sailor or admiral before him. While his childhood home in Middle Tennessee was some distance from the ocean, Williamson County was not too far for tales of ocean adventure.

When older brother John, a United States naval midshipman missing for more than two years, suddenly appeared in Franklin and brought tales of overseas intrigue, young Matthew was spellbound. The boy begged to hear the story time and again of how his then fifteen-year-old brother had disappeared on a South Sea island. With a handful of fellow sailors, John had been assigned to gather sandalwood for two months. He was stranded, however, for a year and a half and became involved in an intertribal conflict in which five shipmates were killed by cannibals and served up as long pig. John and one other survivor managed to make friends with the main tribe and, to protect themselves from the cannibals, built a tree house with a retractable rope ladder. From their lofty position, the men could also scan the horizon for ships. Their long vigil ended in 1814 when another ship, the USS *Essex,* sailed into bay. Finally en route home, John learned that while he had fought cannibals, America had fought the War of 1812, and his ship had been bottled up in a Chinese port.

Immediately upon landing in America, John sought out his family. The Maurys had moved from Virginia three years earlier, in 1811, to be near relatives at Franklin, Tennessee. The town was founded by a cousin, Abram Maury, who already enjoyed prominence as a Tennessee surveyor, speculator, and legislator, and for whom adjacent Maury County was named. In general, the Maury family had always played a key role in its surroundings: Maury forebears had included advisors to French kings, thriving land owners, business leaders, clergy, and an influential teacher of Thomas Jefferson. When Jefferson became president of the United States, he gave John Maury his midshipman's appointment.

In 1813, while struggling on a Tennessee farm, the Maurys managed to send their youngest children to school. Matthew's fascination with science and mathematics, however, began when he noticed some inexplicable *x's* and *o's* scrawled on the soles of a pair of shoes made by a Franklin cobbler. When Matthew asked the cobbler about the markings, he was introduced to algebra by the shoemaker, who customarily carved out problems and equations with his awl while working on rough leather. "My earliest recollections of ambition in science are connected with the aspiration to emulate that man in mathematics," Matthew Fontaine Maury later recalled.

Also enthralled with his brother's seafaring life, Matthew knew that inland Tennessee could never hold him. When, in 1824, John died of yellow fever in the West Indies, eighteen-year-old Matthew decided to leave home and head for the East Coast, disobeying his grieving father's wishes that he become a doctor and avoid the navy. The elder Maury refused to help his son or to say good-bye. Hoping to carry on his brother's legacy, Matthew received a midshipman's assignment through Tennessee Congressman Sam Houston and then rode to Washington, D.C., on a borrowed horse.

That he would become famous for his contributions to the lives of seafarers was an accident. In 1839, while visiting his ailing father in Franklin, Maury was seriously injured in a stagecoach accident that impaired his ability to walk. Because he could never again

Matthew Fontaine Maury, one of America's greatest forgotten scientists.

command a ship, Maury became bound to a desk and there created a more enduring legacy than his brother. Soon becoming known as "the Pathfinder of the Seas," Matthew Fontaine Maury is credited with single-handedly inventing the modern science of oceanography (he wrote a textbook in 1855) and helping to lay the foundation of weather forecasting (on which modern meteorology would be based). He also was the early guiding force of the United States Naval Observatory and urged the creation of a naval academy.

Maury had a passion for amassing facts. He wrote letters to all ships' captains and asked them to record specific information as they journeyed around the globe. Among these captains were whalers, hundreds of whom worldwide believed that Maury's work was critical and agreed to record whale behavior: the type of whale they encountered and its location; the temperature of the ocean location; and, if the whale was killed, its stomach contents. Believing that whales were the secret to uncovering many ocean mysteries, Maury assessed one fact at a time until he pieced together a portrait of the ocean paths.

"The sea is the highway of the world," wrote Maury, who was always bewildered that navy men navigated the oceans without systematic direction or design.

American ships, he believed, could not find their way home without the help of a British almanac.

In revolutionizing modern sailing with his ocean charts and weather forecasts, Maury altered forever the manner in which mankind dealt with the ocean. His books were the first to create and combine relevant data that allowed navigators to dispense with massive shipboard libraries in order to chart their path. By pinpointing the quickest routes and best means of sailing, Maury saved millions of dollars annually in the cost of world commerce and acquired international attention. Kings, emperors, and even the czar of Russia gave Maury their highest awards and honors; nation after nation considered him to be one of the greatest scientists in history.

In 1853, Maury theorized that whales traveled underneath the North Pole and wrote, "It is another link in the chain of circumstantial evidence going to prove the existence of the Northwest Passage." Later explorers proved him right, and Admiral Richard Byrd's trip to the South Pole in 1927 was influenced, he admitted, by the theories Maury worked out in the 1860s. Ever humble, Maury once characterized his work by stating simply, "I set out with no theory, and I have none to build up. . . . I set out with the view of collecting facts."

During the 1850s, he was consulted about the construction of the transatlantic telegraph. He is credited with discovering the undersea plateau that made the laying of the first cable possible. Although appointed a United States Navy commander by the president, Maury relinquished the post when the Civil War began and gave his allegiance to the Confederacy. As a result, several jealous naval officers worked to discredit some of his books and theories and attempted to erase his name from United States naval history.

Matthew Fontaine Maury was a man displaced by the war. He journeyed to England in 1862 seeking that nation's help for the Confederacy and also conducted research on electric mines. When the end of the war was announced, he was on his way to Cuba. By virtue of being out of the country, Maury was ineligible for a United States pardon for his wartime activities. He went to Mexico for a while, working with that nation's emperor, and then traveled back to England, where his wife and children joined him in 1866. Although Maury was penniless, European scientists helped him financially. He finally returned to the United States in 1868.

Welcomed by former Confederate General Robert E. Lee, Maury began a professorship with the Virginia Military Institute. When he died in 1873, the sixty-seven-year-old Maury was memorialized at his funeral service with the flag of Tennessee displayed just as prominently as that of Virginia. He was buried in Richmond between the tombs of two United States presidents: James Monroe and John Tyler.

Maury's name remained a symbol of greatness in other nations and in the state of Virginia, which, in 1916, recognized Maury Day throughout its school system. But for most of the United States, Matthew Fontaine Maury's name had been erased so completely by wartime foes in the United States Navy that it was also omitted from American history books.

51

Henry Downing

Storybook Fanfare:
A New Steamer and a Dashing Captain

The fog was so heavy over Memphis on Christmas Eve 1842 that few buildings were visible along Front Row. Memphians had lit timbers throughout the waterfront to better guide Mississippi River pilots. More than one hundred people, including the mayor, had gathered waiting for one particular riverboat captain to appear. Whenever a new steamboat was making its maiden voyage, there was considerable excitement in the populace, and most always a major celebration.

The air this night was damp and cold, but despite the chill, no one was leaving the pier. They were expecting Henry Downing, the handsome young captain who was bringing in the long-awaited showpiece of the Mississippi River, the *Edwin Hickman*, a steamboat rumored to be "the finest that had so far ever been sent down the Ohio or the Mississippi Rivers," boasted the Memphis *Commercial Appeal*. The newly built vessel was named for the mayor, who planned to show it off to his friends on this night and perhaps promote romance between one of them and the bachelor Downing.

Cheers erupted when the crowd finally spotted the elegant steamboat cutting its way through the dense fog. The steamer had been built under the watchful eye of Captain Downing exclusively for the city of

Memphis and her trade route to New Orleans. During the boat's construction near Pittsburgh, Pennsylvania, Downing had supervised the design and manufacture of every feature, including the faultless woodcrafted interior. He was now going to host a reception and tour for the proud throng of waiting Memphians, each hoping to inspect every piece of machinery and every regal cabin on the vessel. Those lining up to see the new steamer included other river pilots, anxious to view the very best.

After docking amidst the resounding ovation, Downing welcomed his eager guests aboard. Following the tour, Downing gave a grand dinner for the mayor and nearly thirty of the mayor's friends. The guests included distinguished Memphis businessman W. B. Morriss and his daughter, Sallie. Mayor Hickman introduced his friend's daughter to Downing with the encouragement: "may you and Miss Sallie become the best of friends—I hope you do."

Late in the evening, glasses were raised high with toasts for the new vessel and her captain's good fortune. As the captain bade good-bye to Sallie, he lifted her hand to his lips and asked the pleasure of seeing her again. Soon they became inseparable and announced plans for their wedding, one year and one day after their introduction.

When that day arrived in 1843, Downing pulled the *Edwin Hickman* into dock after his customary journey from New Orleans. It was Christmas Day. Wedding bells rang out from a church on Market Street. The captain came ashore where a horse-drawn carriage waited to whisk him to the wedding site. Captain Charlie Van Dusen of the steamer *Somerville* offered a few words of congratulations: "Good luck, Captain Downing, and may your—"

Before Van Dusen could finish the sentence, the groom-to-be uttered a quick thanks and yelled back, "Come over to the wedding dinner tonight, on my boat!"

There would be no wedding dinner, however. Nor would there be a wedding. While Downing was en route, a small piece of paper blew into the path of his high-spirited horses. The horses whirled. The carriage overturned, and Downing was killed instantly, mere moments before he was to make his wedding vows.

52

Anna Chavannes

Finding a Mountain Home for the Swiss Immigrant

In 1848, Anna Chavannes, a self-described woman of abiding religious faith, left her native Switzerland forever, and trusted in the unknown. Leaving behind religious persecution and political upheaval, she and her husband, the Reverend Adrien Chavannes, set sail for America; they were joined by their friends, the Sterchi and Gouffon families, all French-speaking Swiss.

Anna Chavannes was the daughter of the wealthy Francillion family; her husband was a minister-farmer who was related to the Swiss Christian reformer, Alexander Chavannes. Carrying with them a strong family unit and a sense of community, they would form and hold together a major Swiss colony in Tennessee.

Docking in New York City, the immigrants were lured by the glowing promises of the East Tennessee Colonization Company. Land agents were issuing pamphlets designed to entice German and Swiss settlers, urging them to homestead Morgan and Scott counties as well as adjacent Fentress and Cumberland counties. High on the list of recommended destinations was the town of Wartburg, which had been settled by the German-Swiss in honor of Wartburg Castle, a stronghold for the Lutheran Church located in an east German province.

Based on enthusiastic land-agent reports about Wartburg, Tennessee, colonists expected to find fertile farmland. The company that promised them as much was a shipping firm founded in 1844 at Antwerp, Belgium. The Chavanneses, however, decided to visit Wartburg before signing their names to land contracts. With the Gouffons, they embarked on a thirteen-day journey while the Sterchis remained in New York.

The travelers went by steamer to Charleston, South Carolina, then by creaking train along narrow passes and deep gorges to Dalton, Georgia, and finally by wagon along rough and bumpy roads to Chattanooga. Writing in her journal at Chattanooga, Anna praised southern hospitality but could not help criticizing what she saw of American women:

Everybody goes on horseback, the women, the children; and they rarely go on foot. We see pretty equipages, and some pretty homes; but what struck me was that, in the middle of a great deal of luxury, you did not see one garden in order. Fine ladies, in dresses of flowing white muslin, holding by the hand well-dressed children who have neither shoes nor stockings. You see handsome covers on your bed, but with big holes in them; men with fine clothes, but torn; broken shoes through which you see the stockings. I think the American women do not do anything at all. They pass the day fanning themselves.

After getting passage on a rickety steamboat, the group arrived in Kingston, "which pleased us very much," according to Anna's diary. "It is a charming place. I had, for a while, the idea of staying there, and to let Adrien go alone to Wartburg; but we did not find a house where I could do housekeeping."

When they reached the end of their journey, the Chavanneses and Gouffons were disappointed, finding only timberland and two or three houses in the midst of the hilly, forested terrain. Anna wrote various comments:

The director of the colony received us in the best way possible, but we did not hide from him our astonishment, and the little probability that we would stay here. . . . There are some charming views; very good air; it is altogether mountainous. . . . We wish to allow ourselves to be led by the Saviour, Who has helped us until this time, and Who, I am very sure, will not desert us now.

The group remained for two months, getting through the heat of summer by renting a newly built house in which they would try to make the best of a bad situation. Under that roof were all in the Chavannes family (plus two youths who accompanied them from Switzerland), the Gouffons, and another man who was a friend. Anna described their lifestyle:

As we are at a very intelligent man's house, who built his house all alone, who has a workbench and all his tools, we began by asking him to give us two planks placed at two angles, in which we put some straw, and there, our beds are made. The

next day we bought 6 planks, with which our David, who is very handy, made us a big table, 2 planks smoothly planed, nailed together, with 4 feet; then 2 benches, some stools; and there we are; settled like princes.

Despite her original disillusionment, Anna was able "to congratulate myself every day for having come here." She added: "We have found an English doctor who gives English lessons to our boys 4 times a week. One cannot imagine how many difficulties one encounters if one does not know the language."

Eventually joined by the Sterchis, the families relocated. Journeying eastward, they found their ideal location in North Knoxville. There, Reverend Chavannes purchased a 275-acre farm in an area called "Grassy Valley"—the nucleus of an emerging Swiss colony of importance to the region. The Swiss called it "La prairie," a place so lush that a twentieth-century Swiss researcher, David Babelay, describes reports that "animals could be tracked in the tall grass almost as easily as if it had been snow." (Babelay would help compile and edit various diaries, journals, and letters of many early Swiss in East Tennessee).

As pillars of the Knoxville Swiss community, the Chavanneses assisted dozens of future Swiss settlers who soon found their way there. (By 1850, the Swiss were the "largest European ethnic group in Knox County.") Thanks to Anna's family resources, Adrien routinely loaned money and goods to his compatriots, and boarded many of them until they could afford their own homes. During 1849, as many as twenty-eight people lived in the Chavannes house at one time. Among them was the family of Alfred Buffat, who was nine at the time. He recalled years later: "In a very short time Mr. Chavannes had acquired considerable knowledge of the laws and customs of the country. The Swiss would often go to him for advice."

In loaning money, Chavannes had low interest rates and a lengthy repayment period. "When any of the Swiss lacked any of the necessary appliances to do their work, they borrowed from Mr. Chavannes or went to his farm to do their work," added Buffat, who became the founder in 1861 of Buffat Mill and, in 1904, was elected Knox County trustee. (Many other Swiss immigrants would also build major Knoxville businesses.)

Equally as generous, Anna Chavannes once told Buffat's father to help himself to her supply of oats, saying, "Brother, be sure to heap the half bushel well, this is the way that oats are measured in this country." When he tried to pay, she refused his offer.

Adrien Chavannes, who had long suffered from ill health, died in 1855. When Anna died in 1891 at the age of eighty-one, Alfred Buffat wrote this eulogy:

> Her whole life was full of good works, all done for the sake of her Lord, yet when at the age of 81 years and on the day before her death, she took my hand in hers and in her usual earnest way she told me that she would be with her Savior soon and that she was glad to go, yet she regretted that she had done so little to honor Him throughout her life.

From the time of the Chavanneses' arrival in 1848 until 1913, at least one Swiss family settled each year in Knoxville, all of them following other family members or escaping European religious persecution. Many of the Swiss youth fought in the Civil War, generally favoring the Confederacy. After the war, one German-speaking Swiss immigrant and a future Knoxville mayor, Peter Staub, helped found yet another Swiss colony, this one in 1868 along the Cumberland Plateau. Located in Grundy County, it became the timberland community of Gruetli. (Gruetli had its share of disappointed colonists who also thought they were buying farmland. Staub helped to calm the situation with a peace offering when he purchased expensive musical instruments for his brethren. They survived the hard times by pulling together as a community around their Swiss culture. The immigrants joined in song, formed a brass band, and held concerts, religious services, and other community-oriented activities in a different home each week. Staub would return to his home in Knoxville where he was elected mayor twice, in 1874 and in 1881.)

Among the Chavannes descendants who became well-known were a grandson, Edward Terry Sanford, who became a United States Supreme Court justice in 1923; and Edward L. Chavannes, who became mayor of Knoxville in 1946.

53

Francis Joseph Campbell

*Leaving a Slave State Behind;
Casting the Light Within*

Francis Joseph Campbell, blinded in a frontier childhood accident, gave hope to thousands.

In 1835 when he was three years old, Francis Joseph Campbell ran into a thorn bush while he was playing with other children at his Middle Tennessee home near Winchester. The bush punctured an eye and destroyed its vision; the other eye became infected, resulting in his complete blindness. Either a local school teacher or a relative taught Francis the alphabet by carving letters on a cedar shingle so that the boy could feel (and learn) each one.

Although his overprotective father considered blindness an overwhelming handicap, Francis developed a passion to prove him wrong. The Reverend

James Campbell was a Cumberland Presbyterian minister and often away from home. During one of Reverend Campbell's many absences, Francis decided to chop six cords of firewood, by himself, leaving his father a reminder of an independence that would bring fame years later and on another continent.

Eventually the boy was able to leave Franklin County and attend the Tennessee School for the Blind in Nashville. For the first time, Francis heard the sound of a musical instrument. At the age of twelve, he attempted to learn music as a way to support himself. Despite his best efforts, however, he could not carry a tune, even by humming. His teacher dropped him from the class, doubtful that he could ever learn music.

Undaunted, Francis convinced a friend to give him each day's lessons. Soon, he had learned how to play the piano, and, in three months, he could play as well as anyone else in the school. By the age of eighteen, the once rejected student was a music instructor at the same school.

During this time, Campbell was affected by America's argument over slavery. Announcing that he could not morally support such a practice, he left Tennessee. In 1858, he settled in Boston, remaining eleven years as resident superintendent and musical director of an institute for the blind.

Suffering poor health, Campbell began to travel and eventually visited England. At a London social gathering, he met a wealthy, blind Englishman who mentioned that visually impaired persons in England could not make a living even by tuning pianos, which Campbell had been teaching since his earliest days in Tennessee. Once again, the challenges of life lured him, and Campbell settled permanently in London. In 1872, he joined forces with the wealthy Englishman and the Duke of Westminister to establish the Royal Normal College and Academy of Music for the Blind. The school became a stepping-stone to Campbell's prominence throughout England as that nation's leading educator of individuals with visual impairments.

In 1880, Campbell astonished the populace of Great Britain when he went mountain climbing with family and friends and successfully tackled the Alpine peaks. Having been an avid mountain climber in his Tennessee youth, Campbell became "the first blind man who ever made a successful ascent of Mont Blanc." So many people questioned how he triumphed in this accomplishment that he wrote to the *London Times* with an explanation. In published letters, Campbell said that the greatest factor was being in good condition, the specifics of which may also have shocked his audience. "Skating, swimming, rowing, riding have all contributed their share to this end," he wrote.

In the climb itself, Campbell explained how his son remained particularly close: "I took my place on the rope in the ordinary way, except that the distance between my son and myself was only a few feet. This enabled me to follow his footsteps closely."

So fascinated was the editor of the *London Times* that he wrote a tribute to Campbell in the same issue, consuming "almost two columns to editorialize on the letters from Campbell and his unique feat."

But it was Campbell's unrelenting assistance to the blind that gained him the most attention. In 1909, the seventy-seven-year-old Tennessean eclipsed even his own expectations when the king of England, Edward VII, knighted him Sir Francis Campbell.

54
William Walker
"Gray-Eyed Man of Destiny"—
His Latin American Slave Republic

In 1853, Nashville native William Walker led an expedition to establish colonies in Mexican provinces, hoping to have them annexed by the United States. With forty-five men, he landed in Baja California, captured the peninsula, and declared it a republic. His men immediately elected him president of the new government, and Walker annexed neighboring Sonora without setting foot in the area.

The plan ultimately failed when Mexican forces bloodily expelled the American "filibusters," a term applied to United States mercenaries who sought to take over foreign territories. As the most prominent of these filibusters, Walker was intent upon expanding the South's economic base by setting up slave-holding republics. According to poet Joaquin Miller, who served with Walker in one of his later campaigns, there was a gallant attitude in the conqueror. Miller was quoted as saying: "On entering a town, he as a rule issued a proclamation making death the penalty for insulting a woman, for theft, or for entering a church save as a Christian should."

William Walker's piercing eyes swayed many followers.

As a soldier of fortune, Walker was one of the most feared international revolutionaries. Once he took action to alter Central America's history, he was called the "gray-eyed man of destiny." He stood five feet, six inches, and weighed little more than one hundred pounds.

Born in 1824 to a prosperous family, Walker spent his Nashville childhood as a freckled, unathletic type dodging nicknames such as "Missy" and "Honey" given him by playmates. He was described as a strange child. But at the age of fourteen, he graduated summa cum laude from the prestigious University of Nashville. Fending off his father's desire for him to become a minister, Walker studied extensively at the world's finest medical colleges and became, at the age of nineteen, arguably the youngest physician in Tennessee. Some believe that he might have been the youngest physician in the United States. He gave up medicine when he could not save the one person he adored above all others—his gravely ill mother.

Walker next turned to law, practicing in New Orleans and becoming one of the city's best attorneys. Despite his success in this career, Walker altered his

life's course once again and determined to become a newspaperman. He was named an editor of the *New Orleans Daily Crescent* and managed to anger and alienate most local readers with his editorials. Encouraged by the great love of his life, a local deaf woman named Ellen Galt Martin, Walker wrote scathing editorials attacking slavery and advocating voting and property rights for women (one of the first Southern writers to do so), as well as making other comments and criticisms that many readers found disagreeable. In 1849, Ellen died from yellow fever shortly before her wedding to Walker. He was devastated. When his editorial attacks focused on New Orleans, he lost his position with the newspaper and disappeared for ten months.

Walker surfaced in San Francisco in 1850. His clothes were shabby, and his skin was leathery at the age of twenty-six. Becoming a journalist again, Walker crusaded against crime and supported vigilante committees. He also fought three duels, being wounded in two.

In 1853, while leading the band of military adventurers to colonize the Mexican provinces of Baja California and Sonora, Walker quickly gained his international notoriety. After Mexican forces expelled him as president of the republic, Walker returned to California. In many parts of the city of San Francisco and throughout the South, he was pronounced a hero.

William Walker next turned his attention to civil war in Nicaragua, a decision that would lead to his ultimate downfall. In 1854, he signed a contract with a Nicaraguan rebel leader to help oust Nicaragua's government. Walker received financial assistance from Cornelius Vanderbilt, one of the wealthiest of United States businessmen, who owned most of a trans-Nicaraguan railroad.

As soon as he became commander of the Nicaraguan army and then president of Nicaragua, Walker discovered that winning a Central American revolution was easier than governing. He met opposition at every turn, and his presidency was short-lived. His problems began when the United States revoked its recognition of his government. Other Central American nations formed an alliance to overthrow him, and Vanderbilt became furious when he heard that Walker had tried to block Vanderbilt's attempts to build a canal linking the Atlantic and Pacific oceans via Nicaragua. Vanderbilt hired a man for twenty thousand dollars to "get rid of Walker."

Walker's only real support came from the Southern planters who wanted to build plantations and eagerly applied for Nicaraguan land grants. In 1856, Walker revoked the nation's Emancipation Proclamation, prompting one Southern newspaperman to write: "In the name of the white race, he now offers Nicaragua to you and your slaves at a time when you have not a friend on the face of the earth."

Aid and approval poured to Walker from portions of the South and from San Francisco, but it was not enough to keep him in power. Central America's alliance defeated Walker and his army, which was already decimated by a cholera outbreak. Walker himself surrendered to a United States naval commander who took him to a tumultuous welcome in New Orleans. Many Southern men volunteered to join Walker in an attempt to reclaim the country. Two subsequent expeditions failed. On the third attempt, Walker decided to use Honduras as a base of operations. Instead, the British captured him, turning Walker over to Honduran officials, who executed him before a firing squad in September 1860.

55
John Clemens
His Beloved Tennessee Land—
Never the Twain Shall Meet

When John Clemens uprooted his Middle Tennessee family in 1835, he resettled in Missouri and returned to his former home mostly in his thoughts and in the stories he told to his many children. His fascination with the Upper Cumberland Plateau was especially appealing to his sons.

Clemens, who migrated from Virginia and Kentucky, had been among Fentress County's first office holders. He was county court clerk, attorney general, the architect for the county courthouse and jail, and a practicing attorney (one of only two lawyers) in Jamestown, the community he had helped to build ten years earlier. He was also one of Fentress County's major landowners, owning somewhere between seventy-five and one hundred thousand acres. As his family had grown, so had Clemens's eagerness for more land.

Clemens spent so much money buying land as an inheritance for his four offspring that he jeopardized the family's daily existence. He had tried farming

along the Wolf River and working as the postmaster of nearby Pall Mall until he simply left the state. His wife was pregnant when he uprooted the family to Missouri.

The son, Samuel, born a few months after their arrival, would know as much as anyone about Jamestown and the surrounding area his father called "The Knobs." John Clemens died in 1847 at the age of forty-nine, but not before he had revisited, one more time, his great passion in life: his vast land in Tennessee. Because he died young, Clemens never knew how much impact the land would have on Samuel, who was then eleven. Eventually pursuing a writing career, Samuel created a fictionalized treatment of his father's world in Middle Tennessee, and because he liked to dabble in satire, he changed the names of the community and its characters. He also changed his own name—to Mark Twain. His first novel, *The Gilded Age,* written in 1873, offered a less-than-sterling assessment of the backcountry as it existed in Tennessee and in Missouri. What became apparent to future historians was the resemblance not only between Jamestown and the fictional Obedstown but also between the novel's character Si Hawkins and Twain's father.

Twain probably never visited Jamestown (which named an avenue and a park after him), although he never forgot his father's plea to hold onto their Tennessee land. The oldest Clemens brother, Orion, born at Gainesboro, visited the area many times on behalf of the family's holdings. But Twain was a river man, busy piloting steamers on the Mississippi River and often making port in Memphis.

He later told the story of his younger brother, Henry, and the tragic events at Memphis in the summer of 1858. The brothers were then working on the same steamer, Henry as a clerk and Twain as an apprenticed river pilot. One night, while docked in St. Louis awaiting the regular departure to Memphis, Twain said that he dreamed about a metal coffin sitting on two chairs and bearing the body of Henry. On Henry's chest lay a bouquet of white flowers with one crimson flower in the center. The image was so real that Twain awoke, dressed, and walked a block before realizing that he had only dreamed the tragic scene. He mentioned nothing to Henry.

Soon after the nightmare, Twain was suddenly assigned to another boat headed for Greenville, Mississippi. There, he received the grim news that Henry's steamer, the *Pennsylvania,* had exploded near Memphis. The death count was high, and those badly burned were in critical condition. Twain rushed to Memphis and to his brother's bedside. The youth died six days later. Overcome by grief and exhaustion, Twain was taken in by a Memphis family.

Henry's body was placed in an unpainted wooden coffin for burial, as were all the dead, but the women of Memphis were so taken with his sweet and innocent looks that they took up a collection of sixty dollars to purchase a metal casket, exactly like the one Twain had seen in his dream. The casket was placed on two chairs, as the dream had also revealed. Only the flowers were missing. But when Twain paid his last respects, an elderly woman entered the room carrying a bouquet of white flowers with a single red rose in the center. She placed the bouquet on Henry's chest, thus finalizing all the elements of Twain's dream. Despite the devastating loss of his young brother and three hundred other lives in the disaster, Twain said gratefully in a letter to his sister: "But may God bless Memphis, the noblest city on the face of the earth!"

With the passing decades, Mark Twain encouraged Orion to sell their Tennessee land, according to University of Tennessee English professor and writer Allison Ensor. Believing that their father was right about its great fortune, however, Orion actually rejected two hundred thousand dollars from a buyer who wanted to cultivate a vineyard there. Holding out for even greater money, Orion ended up disappointed. Eventually, the land brought less than ten thousand dollars when the majority was sold in parcels during the 1870s and 1880s. Some portions remained in the family into the twentieth century, when all of it was finally sold. The most money that John Clemens's land ever generated was in his son's profits from *The Gilded Age.*

56
William B. Isler/
Margaret Clark Griffis

One Plantation Lifestyle—One Tutor's Viewpoint

Tiptonville's William B. Isler spent the fall of 1857 searching nationwide for a refined young woman to tutor his children. The one he found, nineteen-year-old Margaret Clark Griffis, was not only a young woman with impeccable credentials but also one whose later letters and diary entries provided her own insights into the pre-Civil War South.

Ladies of breeding, particularly those from Philadelphia, Pennsylvania, were highly prized as tutors in the antebellum plantation period. Described as someone of considerable "social, intellectual, economic and religious personal heritage" from that city, Margaret seemed perfectly suited to the needs of the Isler family's five children as well as the offspring of neighboring planters in Obion County (an area that became Lake County several years later).

The daughter of a once-wealthy Philadelphia coal family, Margaret decided to find employment following the economic panic of 1857 which eroded her family fortune and brought near poverty. She made her way in December to the Mississippi River area and then to the eleven-hundred-acre Tiptonville plantation owned by Isler's mother-in-law, the widow Elizabeth E. Meriwether.

For the following ten months, Margaret tutored Isler's children, studied languages and the Bible, played music, sewed, enjoyed horseback rides, and socialized with family and friends during the evenings and weekends. She then recorded her insights (generally complimentary) of plantation life from the perspective of a Northern girl fascinated by Southern ways. The Islers' lifestyle and those of their Tiptonville neighbors were included in many of Margaret's letters home. Mirroring what she saw and offering her own thoughts, some of those comments are included below:

A Typical School Day on the Plantation

We began our school to-day and it lasted from nine until 12 o'clock, the children are very intelligent. . . . My time is my own after 12 o'clock. We generally take a walk after school. . . . I have been talking to them the students on city life and city ways and they seem to like to hear it very much.

The Mississippi River

The river is very high and in a great many places it has overflowed the banks, ruining many plantations and causing loss and ruin to hundreds of families, who have been robbed of their all by the waters. It is dreadful to hear of the destitution and utter ruin which millions of dollars will not repair.

A Plantation Barbeque (Summer 1858)

. . . On Monday which you know was celebrated in stead of Sunday for the Fourth, I was invited to a dinner party at Mrs. Neville's, who lives on the next plantation. We were all dressed and started about 11 o'clock and soon got there, the house is very large and has a drawing room and parlor one side, dining room and sitting room on the other, the carpet was removed from the sitting room and the dancing was to be there, the fiddlers came early and the floor was filled from 12 o'clock until late night or rather the next morning. The tables were set out in a grove near the house and the dinner was splendid.

. . . The Southern ladies all use paint and chalk [on their faces] and think nothing of it at all. They are much more matured than the Northerners, and marry very early, at fifteen and sixteen, they think twenty is quite old.

A Religious Camp-Ground Meeting

(Margaret was accustomed to attending church in Philadelphia on a daily basis and all day each Sunday.)

The singing was very strange to me and the sermon still stranger, the preacher was a very ignorant man and never in my whole life did I ever hear such an odd jumbling of words, it was impossible to understand his meaning, the concluding prayer was the only thing I could listen to with any pleasure or comfort.

A View of Slavery

(Based only on her perceptions at the Isler place and neighboring plantations, Margaret wrote her comments after watching a party which Mrs. Meriwether had given for her slaves. Admitting that everything she saw in the South was new to her, Margaret seemed impressed with the guarantees of room and board, without realizing the oppressive and demeaning nature of the institution of slavery.)

I just wish some of our abolitionist folks could see what we have often read of but never seen in all its truth, . . . I never saw a field hand whipped yet and as to a hard master they are few and far between. I think they have a very easy life and sometimes almost envy their careless happiness, with no care for the future, a good home, plenty to eat and wear. . . .

Southern Life versus Life in the North

The Southerners seem so free from the stiff formality of the Northerners, they welcome a stranger with kindness and one feels at home in their midst very soon.

. . . After dinner we all went to a show on a flat boat which stopped at the landing, a miserable daub called a panorama and a leopard and Australian bear formed the chief attractions. Such things are common on the Mississippi and seem very strange to me, every thing is so different from the North.

An overwhelming sentiment in Margaret's diary, however, was her loneliness. "I feel an intense longing to see Mother and those I dearly love. I am weary of being among strangers, I want home, although all are so kind and I really love them, there is no place like home. . . ."

William B. Isler asked Margaret to remain beyond her contract expiration in October 1858, but she declined because she was so homesick for Philadelphia and her family. In the protective style of a Southern gentleman, Isler escorted her on the train through Illinois, Indiana, Ohio, and Pennsylvania until she reached her home. Margaret never saw him again.

Three years later, when the Civil War commenced, Isler became a captain in the Confederate "Madrid Bend Guards," mostly men from Lake County who organized as E Company, Fifteenth Infantry. He was soon killed in one of the war's earliest battles in the western theater, the Battle of Belmont, fought in November 1861 at a small steamboat landing on the Kentucky-Missouri border. The battle was also the first wartime engagement for Union General Ulysses S. Grant, who claimed an indecisive victory. Margaret Griffis's only return to the South came twice between 1859 and 1861, to tutor children in Virginia.

57

Mark Robertson Cockrill

*"Wool King of the World"—
But Is There a War Coming?*

While other farmers in the early nineteenth century scrambled to make cotton king, Mark Robertson Cockrill surveyed his own land and those of his neighbors and thought prospects looked grim. Because he realized the limitations of continuously planting cotton, he soon visualized something that would alter the future of Tennessee agriculture, and the nation's. Cockrill knew a basic truth: cotton could ruin the earth, but wool could save it.

Cockrill's rise in prominence to "wool king of the world" began in 1815. When he sold his share of his father's Nashville estate to buy sheep, his neighbors and friends were aghast at his reckless behavior. But Cockrill chose the best sheep he could find, the famous Merino breed originally from Spain. In the decades that followed, his breeding techniques and obsessive, scientific record-keeping brought forth finer sheep than American farms had produced or most farms in the world had seen. Basic also to Cockrill's thinking was the truth (gained by observation) that manure restored the soil depleted by constant cotton planting. He began to develop and share a diversified knowledge of the interactions among animals, crops, the soil, and climate—subjects on which he would spend a lifetime, placing him in the forefront of the world's agriculturists.

Born in 1788 at Nashville, Cockrill was a son of original Middle Tennessee founders John Cockrill and Anne Robertson Cockrill (the first teacher in the region). Young Cockrill spent his youth as a surveyor and was responsible for marking most of Maury County, including the town of Columbia. At first, his farming opinions were not well received, especially after he sold his inherited land to buy thirteen Merino sheep, a decision many neighbors thought foolish. Family descendants, such as Mrs. Albert Ewing III, have preserved Cockrill's later writings, in which he observed:

> Some of the oldest and most respectable men of my acquaintance treated my project with derision, and even went so far as to say that I had fooled away my land and would never again be the owner of such another tract. . . . In this great matter of producing the golden fleece, I was acting in opposition to the opinions of experienced men and had to go it "solitary and alone."

In 1828, he moved temporarily to Mississippi to grow cotton, but Cockrill also took his sheep. By breeding these animals year-round in the warmth of the Deep South, Cockrill produced healthier sheep, and they produced a longer, superior wool. He relocated in 1833 to Kentucky, this time herding his sheep more than six hundred miles over rough terrain and proving, he said, the breed's durability. Cockrill decided to test his animals and, in 1835, competed against the nation's preeminent sheep breeder. Kentucky's renowned United States Senator Henry Clay, whose northern sheep were unaccustomed to losing the blue ribbon, was no match for Cockrill. To Clay's chagrin, Cockrill's animals won, and the exuberant Tennessean inscribed the trophy "Clay's defeat."

Cockrill, however, wanted to get back to Nashville's bluegrass area and the mild Tennessee winters. Selling his Mississippi plantation for $210,000 in cash, he moved his one thousand sheep to a farm five miles from the city and began to gain a national reputation and immense wealth. His system of farming was direct and simple; in order to restore the land, he often sowed only clover and bluegrass or oats, explaining that a farmer "feeds the soil by feeding his stock on it."

Through his many published articles and his annual auctions of purebred animals sold to buyers from throughout the United States, Cockrill was able to advance agriculture worldwide. In a nation that often depended on fine goods from Europe, he was proud that American clothing was being made from American wool.

Cockrill's knowledge of his own sheep recalled biblical images of the "good shepherd." He could return a stray lamb, from a herd of thousands, to its rightful mother. While once instructing his son Mark Sterling Cockrill to bring a sick sheep to the house for special care, Cockrill gave a detailed description of the invalid animal. When Mark Sterling returned, a disappointed father said he had the wrong sheep and cited a dozen details that marked the correct one.

In 1851, Cockrill achieved European recognition and became the acknowledged "wool king" after displaying his wares at England's Crystal Palace, the cultural showcase of Queen Victoria's empire, and reportedly the first "international or world's fair." There, Cockrill received a medal for having the finest wool of its class in the world, even defeating the Spanish, who had originally bred the coveted Merino. One Nashville newspaper described Cockrill's wool "as fine as silk, and almost as gossamer as a spider's web."

In 1854, Mark Robertson Cockrill became the first Tennessean to receive a medal from the state legislature. The honor recognized his "unrivaled" contributions to agriculture and gave him a place in the Tennessee Agricultural Hall of Fame. He is also credited with introducing shorthorn cattle to Tennessee. Throughout the 1850s, Cockrill improved every animal breed on his five-thousand-acre plantation, which was bounded by either the Cumberland River or a stone fence. The estate featured 120 acres of corn, 300 acres of oats, 100 acres of wheat, about 100 slaves, and 3,000 animals (2,300 in sheep).

Then, in 1860, Cockrill predicted that a civil war would end in devastation for the South, something he had also prophesied twenty years earlier. Now seventy-two, he called forth his three sons and asked each, "Is there going to be a war?"

His eldest, Ben, theorized, "No, people will keep their heads; this is only a lot of talk."

The second son, Jim, claimed, "No, no war, but if they start anything we will whip them."

The youngest son, Mark Sterling, simply did not know.

Cockrill was disappointed: "You haven't been observing what is happening; we will have a war; we will lose it; the slaves will be free and the South will have nothing, nothing but land. I'm going to buy land."

Cockrill consolidated his property. He bought twelve small neighboring Davidson County farms, which became known as Cockrill Bend (where, decades later, the state's main prison would be located). He divided his new holdings into separate tracts for his children. To his daughter, Jane Cockrill Watkins, the patriarch deeded Tulip Grove, the plantation neighboring the late Andrew Jackson's Hermitage. Another daughter, Henrietta Cockrill Ewing, received the "homeplace," Stock Farm. All of his slaves who had trades (such as brick making or carpentry) were

freed, enabling them to provide for their families. All others were kept at the farm for their protection.

Cockrill, one of the largest landowners in Tennessee, was correct about the effects of the Civil War. He and his great farm were also among its earliest victims. Union soldiers tore down his fences and slaughtered many of his prize sheep. Without fences, the common sheep from surrounding areas mingled freely with his surviving Merinos and destroyed the purity of their bloodlines. According to one family member, federal troops destroyed "in one night" all that Cockrill had accomplished in his lifetime. Gone were both Tennessee's sheep industry and the diversity of Tennessee agriculture that was showcased here.

When the aging Cockrill complained, Union officials arrested and imprisoned him. He became sickly and finally agreed to a bond not to fight for the South. But he refused to take an oath of allegiance, because his son Mark Sterling was in the Confederate army.

By war's end in 1865, most of what Cockrill had remaining was the land. He never regained his health after his imprisonment. In 1872 Cockrill died while living at the home of Mark Sterling Cockrill, who in his own years as a dominant Nashville personality, became a major philanthropist and promoter of church and education.

But Mark Robertson Cockrill's priceless land did not remain idle. It had been left in the capable hands of his heirs, who returned to the level of greatness the fine stock of sheep, horses, and shorthorn cattle their father had introduced to the state of Tennessee, and in some cases, to the world. Descendants also added to the state's great agricultural base with continuing improvements in farming techniques.

Section Two

Civil War

Historical Background
Tennessee: The Civil War

There was an illness in the land, and it had not been treated by the framers of the United States Constitution. When the nation entered the second half of the nineteenth century, the problem of slavery could no longer be ignored, postponed, or compromised. Slavery was confronted and the question resolved. A portion of the nation practiced slavery, while the remainder reviled it; the two could no longer coexist within a single national government. Southerners grew defensive in the face of repeated Northern attacks on their way of life, partly because slave-grown cotton had become so profitable during the prosperous 1850s. By 1861, with the value of slave property at an all-time high, the South was even less willing to consider abolishing its "peculiar institution."

That Tennessee would play a major role in the great war to come was no mystery. Geographically, Tennessee extended half the distance from the Mississippi River to the Atlantic Ocean—a long border zone between North and South. Major navigable waterways, railroads, and roadways crossed and crisscrossed the state, and it was an important source of agricultural produce, factory goods, money, and human resources.

When South Carolina stood its ground by seceding from the United States following President Abraham Lincoln's election and shots were fired at Fort Sumter on April 12, 1861, the die was cast for war. Tennessee, however, had not made up its mind. The state's first secession vote, back in February, had kept Tennessee in the Union. When President Lincoln threatened to invade the South and called for volunteers to coerce the seceded states back into the fold, sentiment in Tennessee swung abruptly against the Union. A second vote on secession came on June 8, 1861. One of the main forces nudging and pushing Tennessee into the Confederacy was the secessionist Governor Isham G. Harris. According to reports, he stationed armed state militiamen at the polling places with instructions to intimidate and turn away Union supporters. After the second ballot, Tennessee joined the Confederacy—the last state to leave the Union.

The governor had already mobilized the state militia, and, in violation of Tennessee law and its constitution, entered into a military league with the Confederate States of America. This militia would form the nucleus of the Army of Tennessee, the principal Confederate army in the western theater of the war. Most of Tennessee's soldiers, consequently, served in a largely home-grown force and had the distinction, like Robert E. Lee's Virginians, of fighting on their home soil against an invasion of their state.

While Governor Harris, of Tullahoma, remained Tennessee's staunchest advocate of secession, another man—in the East Tennessee mountains—emerged as an equally powerful voice for the Union. When the state voted to secede, United States Senator Andrew Johnson of Greeneville called for a convention in his hometown to consider the question. The Greeneville convention was attended by delegates who believed in the preservation of the Union—loyal East Tennessee counties as steadfast in their cause as any of the secessionists who dominated in Middle and West Tennessee. The convention concluded with a petition to the Tennessee legislature to secede from Tennessee and form a separate state which would remain loyal to the United States. Legislators never seriously considered the petition. But the document signaled a potential source of trouble for the new Confederacy, which sent an army into East Tennessee to contain and control this "rebellion within a rebellion." East Tennessee was the only area in the nation to be placed under martial law by the Confederacy.

Tennessee presented a unique microcosm of the conflict that tore apart the nation. Here was classic civil war, breaking up the traditional bonds of society and pitting one element against another. While the Civil War was often termed the "war of brother against brother," the phrase was less true for those from the North (few, if any, soldiers in most Northern states had brothers in the Deep South). But Tennessee experienced all the evils of such a war: divided families, bushwhacking, guerrilla warfare, summary executions, and incidents of a near-total breakdown of civil order. Not only regions of the state, but also counties, towns, and families were divided in their loyalties. In Knoxville, Confederate and Union recruiters signed up enlistees within a stone's throw of each other.

Ironically, the pro-Confederate sections of the state were invaded and occupied early in the war by Union troops, while Unionist East Tennessee chafed for two years under Confederate military rule (some East Tennessee locales chafed the remainder of the war under East Tennessee Confederates fighting against local Unionists). Military occupation offered many opportunities for settling blood feuds, vendettas, and scores of all sorts. With most of the soldiers away, bands of armed men (little more than bandits) roamed the countryside, preying on the weak and defenseless. The "home front" in Tennessee was often little safer than the military front.

Tennessee experienced what amounted to total war between 1861 and 1865: involving civilians as well as soldiers, slaves as well as slaveowners, women as well as men. With troops stationed throughout much of the state, civilians were subjected to all the demands and excesses of military occupation. Soldiers on both sides took anything of value that could be carried off or eaten. Tennessee served as the breadbasket and foraging ground for both armies, and undisciplined troops caused more destruction and loss of property than actual combat. Vindictive leaders were determined to make the hostile Tennessee citizenry feel the lash and sting of war—in the words of one, "to make treason odious."

Warfare was also total in its geographic scope. From one end of the state to the other, dozens of battles and hundreds of lesser skirmishes were fought—more, in fact, than any other state except Virginia. As a divided border state, Tennessee sent large numbers of men (and a few women) to fight on both sides of the Civil War. A sizable part of Tennessee's male population signed up—187,000 Confederates and 51,000 Union soldiers. The state also furnished one of the largest contingents of black troops: 20,133 served in Federal units, comprising 40 percent of all Tennessee Union recruits.

In Tennessee—which was center stage for the war's western theater—Union forces achieved some of their earliest wartime successes. The state contained two parallel flowing rivers—the Tennessee and the Cumberland—which pointed like twin invasion routes into the heartland of the Upper South. The Confederate defense line ran across northern Tennessee, anchored by two forts—Fort Henry on the Tennessee and, twelve miles away, Fort Donelson on the Cumberland River. The Union high command quickly recognized these weak points, and in February 1862, forces under General Ulysses S. Grant took the forts. Inept Confederate leadership contributed to the capture of these forts and the surrender of twelve thousand soldiers, the cream of the Confederacy's western volunteers.

Now the entire Middle Tennessee region was open to Federal invasion. The Rebels (and Governor Isham G. Harris's government) fled Nashville. With the fall of Nashville and Middle Tennessee, the South lost one of its main manufacturing centers, tons of badly needed supplies, and a rich farm region.

Two months later, in the first large-scale battle of the war, opposing armies of roughly equal size collided in the woods near tiny Shiloh Chapel in Hardin County. The battle continued to wage on the west bank of the Tennessee River. One of the early deaths was the western theater's Confederate commanding general, Albert Sidney Johnston. Bloody as the two-day Battle of Shiloh was (one out of every four who went into battle was killed, wounded, or captured), it settled nothing. The savagery of Shiloh gave a preview of how costly this war would be. Shiloh had more casualties than all previous United States wars combined. It horrified the nation—on both sides. After this battle, Grant said he "gave up all idea of saving the Union except by complete conquest." The Confederate retreat from Shiloh left West Tennessee open to Federal occupation.

Memphis fell easily after a brief naval battle on June 6, 1862. Women and children eventually would share the brunt of enemy occupation. For the remainder of the war, both Memphis and Nashville were used as a troop headquarters and supply depots for Union operations. Now, just one year after Tennessee's secession, only the pro-Union part of the state in East Tennessee was still held by the Confederacy.

Just before New Year's Day of 1863, the Confederate Army of Tennessee, commanded now by the irascible Braxton Bragg, tried once again to break the invader's hold on Middle Tennessee. The Confederates smashed into Union forces in a dawn attack along Stones River in Murfreesboro. In two days of fighting, the armies lost a total of 25,000 soldiers, making the Battle of Stones River bloodier than Fredericksburg (Virginia) or Antietam (Maryland) earlier that year. With many fewer troops involved, the "butcher's bill" for Stones River was greater than all but the largest battles in the East—a fact that suggests something of the ferocity of the fighting in Tennessee. While both

sides claimed victory at Murfreesboro, the South's army fell back under General Bragg, and the North solidified its grip on Middle Tennessee.

The Army of Tennessee's next large battle was fought at Chickamauga Creek just across the state line in northern Georgia. On September 19-20, 1863, Chickamauga became the war's bloodiest battle yet in the West—a sprawling, chaotic struggle that one general likened to "guerrilla warfare on a grand scale." Combined casualties of more than 34,000 were exceeded only by the three-day slaughter at Gettysburg (Pennsylvania). The Army of Tennessee won a great tactical victory at the Battle of Chickamauga, but at a frightful cost (18,454 casualties out of 50,000 troops), and again its commander Bragg failed to follow up his success. The shattered Union army, under General William Rosecrans, retreated to the nearby railroad center of Chattanooga; the Confederate army occupied the heights above the city.

One month later, General Grant was on the scene as chief commander of Union forces in the western department. At the same time, Confederate General James Longstreet attempted to seize Knoxville and staged a bloody assault on Fort Sanders, which failed. East Tennessee, therefore, remained in Union hands.

With reinforcements, Grant routed the Confederates from Missionary Ridge and Lookout Mountain and cleared the way for a Union invasion of the Deep South. It would be nearly a year before the Army of Tennessee returned to its home state, as it struggled in vain to prevent the fall of Atlanta in the summer of 1864 and Union General William Tecumseh Sherman's subsequent march through Georgia.

When the Rebel army did return to Tennessee, it was under the command of General John Bell Hood. He planned what would be the Confederacy's last big offensive. On November 30, 1864, at Franklin, an entrenched Union army waited under Hood's old West Point classmate General John Schofield. The Army of Tennessee met disaster. Hood, like other combative Southern generals, had made his reputation leading successful frontal assaults against Union positions, and he intended to repeat this success at Franklin. Against the advice of his leading generals, Hood gave the reckless order to assault an entrenched enemy behind strong defenses, an order that virtually destroyed the Army of Tennessee. The heavy Confederate casualty rate once suffered in two days of fighting at Shiloh was now equaled in just five hours at Franklin. Regiment after regiment hurled itself in a futile assault against the well-protected Union breastworks.

When the carnage was over, Schofield continued his march to Nashville to join Union General George Thomas and his fifty thousand troops. Hood rashly followed with what was left of his army and engaged this superior enemy in the hills outside of Nashville. The Confederate lines were overrun on December 16, 1864, and only the rear-guard heroics of the Confederacy's General Nathan Bedford Forrest prevented total annihilation of the Army of Tennessee. As the disabled and exhausted remnants of Hood's army retreated toward Alabama, the Civil War in Tennessee came to a close. The Civil War itself would end in four months with the Confederacy's surrender.

The wreckage of the Army of Tennessee at Shiloh, Chickamauga, Franklin, and Nashville meant that a whole generation of young men was lost or disabled, resulting in an unusually high percentage of unmarried women in the years to come. Even the final surrender could not end the death toll of Tennessee men of both sides. A postwar accident involving the steamboat *Sultana* claimed the lives of many more. Holding five times its 376-passenger capacity, the *Sultana* was carrying paroled Union prisoners from several states when it sank outside of Memphis in April 1865. A contingent from East Tennessee (most of the Third Tennessee Cavalry, U.S.A.) was all but wiped out when the boat went under in America's "greatest marine disaster" (second only to the *Titanic* in being the world's greatest maritime disaster, claims James Cornell in *The Great International Disaster Book*).

While the major cities would recover from the war and soon profit from industrialization, large plantations and small farms alike reverted to wasteland. Prewar economic gains were erased, and Tennessee farm production and property values would not regain their 1860 levels until 1900. But the end of the war guaranteed freedom for 275,000 Tennesseans who had been enslaved four years earlier. Many had earned their freedom by military service in the cause of the Union.

Veterans of both sides lived with their wounds and the memories of their service for the rest of their lives. Whether soldier or civilian, each Tennessean who lived through the Civil War had his or her own story to tell. Here are some of those stories.

Historical background essay written in collaboration with Dr. Wayne Moore, archivist, Tennessee State Library and Archives.

58
Peter Turney

Rallying the South's First Tennessee Troops

When Tennessee's first secession vote in early 1861 kept the state in the Union, the people of Franklin County knew what their course of action would be: secede from Tennessee and become annexed to nearby Alabama. The outspoken young Winchester attorney, Peter Turney, led the petition drive.

While legislators argued a second time over the course of action, Turney organized Tennessee's first fighting regiment for the Confederacy. Recruits also rushed in from several adjacent Middle Tennessee counties to swell the muster rolls. Turney then readied his men for the journey to the battlefronts of Virginia, where the regiment would spend the war under General Robert E. Lee. One of the few Tennessee units to go east, the First (Turney's) Tennessee Infantry would finally surrender with Lee at Appomattox (final reports estimated that only thirty-eight of the original nine hundred to one thousand men in the First Tennessee answered the final roll call).

Just as Turney and his men were about to depart, a runner dashed across the Winchester town square and handed him a note from his aunt, Annie Finch, who was quite excited about the course of history being shaped in Franklin County. Aunt Annie's note read: "Peter—march your men here before you go to war with them. I want to sing them a song." Turney chuckled to himself and promptly ordered his men to march out Tullahoma Road to her house. The volunteer fighting force gladly obliged; carriages of local citizens followed.

Aunt Annie was ready at her "old colonial house among the pines." Her platform was two boxes with a chair perched on top. When Turney came into view, the apparently aged woman appeared unsteady: "Peter, you had better come and help me up—and then you had better hold me, too; I might fall." He climbed onto the platform and put his arm around her. She cleared her throat and began to sing in her best voice: "Hail Columbia, happy land. Hail ye heroes, heaven born band." That was that. "That's all I know, Peter," she confessed. He smiled and helped her from the platform. The volunteer soldiers "cheered madly." She kissed him good-bye, and he gave the command to march.

Although Tennessee had yet to secede from the United States, the First Tennessee Infantry reached Virginia to engage in the fight to the finish. Action with the enemy was constant.

Leading his men on the battlefield, Colonel Turney treasured and depended upon his horse, Tom. Their special bond saved both Turney and Confederate forces on a day in December 1862 that history remembers as the Battle of Fredericksburg (Virginia). Leading a charge, Turney took a bullet through his mouth and fell helpless to the ground. The bullet had "passed through his throat, taking half his tongue" and "lodged in the left side of his neck." The Confederates fell back, and the riderless Tom followed. Suddenly, as Union troops advanced, Tom whirled around, neighed loudly, and returned at full gallop to his unconscious master. His devotion inspired the retreating Confederates to rally and claim ultimate victory.

Four of Turney's men were killed by an exploding shell as they attempted to carry his limp body to safety. The order was given to take no more risks to save Turney. Captain Sam Estill, a hometown friend from Company C's "Mountain Boys," defied the order and crawled under heavy fire to reach him. Estill rolled Turney over to prevent him from choking to death, then managed to remove him from the field.

Turney could barely talk for a year. In the course of time he regained sufficient strength to rejoin the Confederate troops. In early 1863, he was given a command in Lake City, Florida, where his wife and children also relocated.

During the Turney family's absence, Union General William Rosecrans led a Federal army into Franklin County and gave orders to burn the family's homeplace near Cowan. When Union soldiers approached the house, a beloved house slave, "Aunt Sally" Turney, who had helped raise Peter from infancy, answered the door.

"Who lives here?" demanded a Union soldier of Aunt Sally. She confirmed quickly and proudly that this was Colonel Turney's house and that he had gone South to fight the Yankees.

The officer wanted to know how many men were in the Turney family. Aunt Sally answered that there were just three, all in the army, and her old mistress had wished that she had thirty sons—"and all of 'em fighting de Yankees." Aunt Sally's grit notwithstanding (she lived to be 120), Union soldiers burned Turney's Tennessee homeplace that day.

Following the war, the Turney family returned to Winchester, where Turney reopened his law office and began to rebuild the family's meager resources. But he suffered ill health from his war wound, prompting action from his wife, Hannah. Because the slug was lodged near his jugular vein, numerous surgeons had refused to operate, fearing the consequences of such a delicate procedure. Turney's continued suffering, however, prompted his wife to announce that she would remove the bullet herself. The family doctor (Hannah's brother) finally relented, claiming he could not stand to see Turney die at the hands of his own wife. The operation was a success, and the patient lived to be seventy-six. He led a normal and noteworthy life, becoming chief justice of the Tennessee Supreme Court.

In 1893, Turney also became the twenty-seventh governor of Tennessee. Hannah Turney, however, did not live to see her husband's gubernatorial success. She had died five years earlier.

59
Andrew Johnson
Struggling to Save the Union

In June 1861, United States Senator Andrew Johnson fled Tennessee in a buggy accompanied by a bodyguard. En route back to friendlier territory in Washington, D.C., Johnson dodged bullets from ambush in several attempts to kill him. As the South's most recognizable Unionist and speechmaker against secession, Johnson knew that his life was in danger because the Confederacy reviled him as a traitor to the Southern cause.

He had spent the previous month in East Tennessee making speeches against secession with his good friend Congressman Thomas A. R. Nelson of Jonesborough. Although the region was predominately pro-Union, pockets of pro-South supporters were especially strong in Washington, Sullivan, and Hawkins counties. In Washington County, these supporters were furious at the Johnson-Nelson rhetoric. Believing that President Abraham Lincoln had hired the two, Southern sympathizers harassed both men and shouted down Johnson by yelling "Traitor!" The speechmakers finally gave up and sought refuge in

Andrew Johnson bore the burden of a nation in turmoil.

Nelson's Jonesborough home. Mutual friend W. H. Crouch later wrote about the mood in town, principally against Johnson. Observed Crouch, "you never saw such a time. Men on horses ripping up and down the streets, screaming upon the top of their voices 'You Damned Traitor, You Damned Traitor!'"

Since Lincoln's recent 1860 presidential election, several Southern states had left the Union. With each withdrawal, senators quit their posts in Washington and headed home. Johnson did not. Although a slaveholder, he was the only one of twenty-two Southern senators who remained in Congress.

Despite his stand against secession, Johnson happened to agree with the South's criticisms of Lincoln. Johnson had once declared, "I voted against him; I spoke against him; I spent money to defeat him; but still I love my country." Because he and Lincoln shared a reverence for the Constitution, Johnson made a thundering pro-Union speech when he addressed the United States Senate in late December 1860:

I intend to stand by the Constitution as it is, insisting upon a compliance with all its guaranties. I intend to stand by it as the sheet-anchor of the Government; and I trust and hope, though it seems to be now in the very vortex of ruin . . . that it will be preserved, and will remain a beacon to guide, and an example to be imitated by all the nations of the earth. . . . I intend to cling to it as the ship-wrecked mariner clings to the last plank, when the night and the tempest close around him. It is the last hope of human freedom.

Not only was he a hero in the North with such passionate pro-Union oratory, Johnson may also have inspired as many as one hundred thousand Southern men to join the Union army. After Union troops began to seize control in Tennessee, Lincoln rewarded Johnson by making him the military governor of the state in 1862 and his vice-presidential running-mate in 1864. That Johnson would soon become, upon Lincoln's assassination, the president of the United States was quite a climb from his uneducated, poverty-stricken youth.

In September 1826, when he first arrived in Greeneville from North Carolina, Johnson was a bedraggled youth of seventeen. He was leading a small cart, in which his mother rode; other family members walked alongside. Johnson asked for a recommendation on a camp site from a local girl, Eliza McCardle, a native of neighboring Washington County. She seemed entranced by this newcomer. Her friends teased her about her attraction to the stranger. "He's all right," Eliza quipped, indicating that she might make him her "beau" someday. Eight months later, she made good on her comments when she married Johnson, who opened a tailor's shop to earn his way in life.

While the bride did not have a sizable dowry, she brought to the marriage, in addition to love and companionship, something equally important: the determination to teach her husband how to write. Johnson had learned to read by painstakingly memorizing the appearance of different words but could not write and had trouble reading large words. His wife constantly read aloud to him while he worked, and this routine gave Johnson many ideas, a vocabulary, and a style which led to his fine oratorical skills. The future United States president began to take pride in the fact that he had never attended school. He believed that

personal experience and good mental deduction were the only tools needed to increase knowledge.

As a "a man of the people and the people's man," Johnson won every major political office that was within his grasp—ascending from town alderman to mayor of Greeneville, to the Tennessee legislature, to the United States House of Representatives, and twice to the governorship of Tennessee (1853-57 and 1862-65). During his rise through the ranks, he showed courage and conviction in dealing with political enemies. After his barely successful 1853 gubernatorial campaign, for instance, a sign was posted in Nashville announcing that Johnson was to be "shot on sight." When friends wanted to escort him as bodyguards, the new Governor Johnson responded: "No, gentlemen, if I am to be shot at, I want no man to be in the way of the bullet." With that, he walked alone to the state Capitol, as was his habit every day.

On April 14, 1865, Vice President Andrew Johnson—a man who preferred not to socialize or to attend public events—turned down tickets to the theater in Washington, D.C. Wishing to stay home and read something instructive, Johnson gave up an evening at Ford's Theater where *Our American Cousin* was playing. Hours later, the assassination of President Lincoln at the theater catapulted the Tennessean into the job of rebuilding the United States after the Civil War.

Like Lincoln, now-President Johnson believed in a true reconciliation with the defeated South, but he would have to battle Congress on behalf of that principle. A showdown with Congress's dominant Reconstruction radicals was inevitable. The opposition had stripped Johnson's presidency of any real authority—and drew the line when the president tried to terminate, without congressional approval, a cabinet member who had proven disloyal to him. And so it was that on February 22, 1868, the president prepared to face impeachment proceedings brought by the United States House of Representatives.

Ironically, Johnson's honesty made his predicament dangerous. Johnson had enlisted longtime advisor Jeremiah Sullivan Black as a legal counsel, but Black was more interested in a business deal that he wanted the president to protect. Black had been hired by a Baltimore firm seeking claims to exploit mineral deposits on a tiny Caribbean island. The president ruled against the firm's claims and personally relayed his decision to Black. A few days after being chosen the president's legal counsel, Black tried to force Johnson to reverse his decision. If Johnson refused, Black was prepared to resign as the president's attorney, creating the appearance that his client was guilty. President Johnson stood firm. "I will suffer this right arm to be cut off," he replied, "before I will sign any such paper." Black resigned, and the impeachment commenced with a cloud of suspicion hanging over the president.

Even the Tennessee governor, former wartime ally William G. "Parson" Brownlow (now a Reconstruction radical), lobbied for Johnson's ouster from office. There were few political friends, but one did rise to the occasion in an effort to save Johnson: The ever-loyal Thomas A. R. Nelson arrived from Knoxville to become one of the president's counsel and contributed immense oratory skills as a preeminent Tennessee attorney. In the end, Congress fell one vote short of convicting the president.

Later portraits of Johnson show a man with an uninviting grimace. Perhaps because he suffered from a condition called "the gravel" (a name given for either kidney stones or gall stones), persistent and excruciating pain heightened his grim countenance. Apparently Johnson did not allow children to see this side of his demeanor, as evidenced by a little boy's remembrance when he lunched once at the White House and described the president's "dazzling, tender, beautiful smile." On another occasion, a girl at the White House Easter-egg roll—a tradition started by Johnson—recalled how "his face beamed and his eyes smiled with the greatest affection."

Six years after leaving the White House, where he and his family (one of the largest ever in residence) had "left behind a reputation for spotless behavior," Andrew Johnson was again elected to the United States Senate—the only ex-president to reenter that congressional body. He died the same year, 1875, at the age of sixty-seven. Eliza Johnson, who had been ill for years, followed six months later.

60
Lucy Holcombe Pickens
The "Queen of the Confederacy"

Lucy Holcombe Pickens, the only woman featured on Civil War currency.

While family economic woes in 1852 forced her to leave her native LaGrange, eighteen-year-old Lucy Holcombe Pickens proudly carried with her a Southern bearing and charm. It would distinguish the rest of her life—elevating her in the Civil War to the title "Queen of the Confederacy."

Lucy's parents, who had lived in Fayette County since moving from Virginia in the early years of the century, had hoped to start over in the young state of Texas, a favorite mecca for many Tennesseans in recent years. Lucy soon became engaged and was devastated when her fiancé was killed in an expedition to free Cuba from Spain. In her grief, Lucy agreed to accompany her mother to a Virginia resort—and there met the man she would marry, South Carolina's wealthy Francis W. Pickens, a secession leader and former congressman.

The two wed in 1858 shortly before Pickens became the United States minister to Russia, a position Lucy urged him to accept. She was candid with Pickens that she married him because he could pay off her family's debts and secure her future as well. Nonetheless, Pickens adored his wife and doted on her; to the outside world, they were extremely happy. During their subsequent residence in Russia, the couple became close friends with Czar Alexander II and his wife, who loaned the Winter Palace for the birth of the Pickenses' daughter and only child. The baby also became the godchild of the Czar and Czarina, who lavished the family with expensive gifts and many honors throughout a two-year stay. Keeping a diary, Lucy continually corresponded with Tennessee friends about life in Russia. Some of her letters were published in the *Memphis Eagle and Enquirer*.

In 1860, when South Carolina prepared to secede from the Union, Francis Pickens immediately returned home to become the state's wartime governor. He guided South Carolina out of the Union and ordered the firing at Fort Sumter, the dramatic incident which ignited the Civil War.

A governor's wife at twenty-six, Lucy entertained many distinguished guests who visited the Pickens plantation. Such people became her admirers and broadcast her many virtues, which included a welcoming spirit, innate kindness to all, intelligence on the day's events, a diplomatic bearing, and religious piety. Because of Lucy Holcombe Pickens's fine example of Southern womanhood, one of the Civil War's first fighting regiments called itself "The Holcombe Legion" in her honor. Lucy sold the jewels given to her by the Czar and Czarina in order to help equip the troops. After listening to Lucy give them a stirring talk, seven regiments fired an infantry salute in farewell to her.

One year later, Lucy, by now the most "widely known and popular woman of the South," was honored with her likeness on the Confederate one-dollar note. Her picture, reproduced from a marble bust done in Rome, was later placed on Confederate hundred-dollar notes. Affectionately known as the "Queen of the Confederacy," Lucy Holcombe Pickens, who lived until 1899, was the only woman to be honored on wartime currency or on any American banknote.

61
Radford Gatlin
A Secessionist's Plight

Radford Gatlin was not well liked by the general populace in Sevier County, and he stood conspicuously alone in dissent during the election to determine whether Tennessee should remain in the Union. Gatlin, according to local lore, was the only one of the county's 1,303 registered voters to vote for secession and to cast his lot with the Confederacy.

Originally from North Carolina, Gatlin was a merchant and sometime preacher. When he and his wife moved to the area from neighboring Jefferson County, Gatlin built a store, filling it with the best goods he could find in nearby Sevierville. Since there were no wagon roads, he transported those goods on his shoulder, building what became a popular mountain store at White Oak Flats.

Gatlin reportedly owned a slave woman, which in itself was enough to lead Sevier Countians to despise him. Neither did an overbearing manner endear him to the locals. In 1857, both Gatlin and his wife were indicted for assault and battery upon their neighbor, Thomas Ogle Sr. Various other incidents followed, with Gatlin at the center of each controversy. Enemies burned down his barn, assaulted him, and even barred Gatlin from preaching in the New Hampshire Baptist Gatlinites Church, which he had founded.

Being an outspoken secessionist proved to be the last straw. In the middle of the night sometime in 1860 or 1861, masked men beat Gatlin severely and ordered him to leave the community. He immediately took flight. Gatlin actively joined the Confederate cause at his next destination, Strawberry Plains, where he opened a school. When that community was overrun by Union troops in 1863, he next fled to Atlanta.

Gatlin never returned to Sevier County. In a sense, however, he never left. His name lingered in daily life, despite the animosity against him. The post office that existed in his store bore his name, changing forever the name of the White Oak Flats settlement—to Gatlinburg.

62
Daniel Ellis

The First Hostilities:
A Bridge Burner's Dream Comes True

Daniel Ellis believed in the dream of the Union's ultimate victory but readily admitted, "As a general thing, I do not believe in dreams." He would change his mind in November 1861.

The Carter County native was a wagon maker by trade. Then he decided to join a force of East Tennessee civilians hoping to hinder Confederate troops by burning a Holston River bridge. These men and other area bridge burners preceded the first real outbreak of the war's violence in Tennessee.

Ellis's target was a Bluff City bridge located in adjacent Sullivan County. Here, Southern sympathy and Confederate activity were particularly strong.

"Orders had been received from the government of the United States," Ellis later wrote, "to burn all the bridges, and to destroy the railroad from Chattanooga on up the country as far as it possibly could be done." President Abraham Lincoln had sanctioned the burning after meeting with Rogersville preacher William Blount Carter, who helped design the plan. Carter himself was originally from Carter County (named for his pioneering grandfather), a county that stood tenaciously for the Union. The strategy of destroying key East Tennessee railroad bridges was intended to cripple Confederate supply lines while Union troops simultaneously invaded from Kentucky to rescue the region's loyalists.

President Lincoln determined to hold as many Tennesseans as possible for the Union and certainly to protect Unionist East Tennessee—not only a Federal stronghold but also a place where Lincoln once had relatives. (His late uncle, Isaac Lincoln, had been a Carter County farmer living along the Watauga River at Elizabethton and a major landowner in the town itself.)

The Carter Countians, faced with growing Confederate troop strength and harassment, had transformed themselves into citizen soldiers for self-protection. Numbering in the hundreds, they were joined by hundreds more from neighboring Johnson County. Their leaders were Daniel Stover, son-in-law of future President Andrew Johnson, and James Grayson, an influential farmer in Johnson County.

When Bluff City's bridge was destroyed, the perpetrators returned home to the Elizabethton area, having done their part to impede Confederates in the region. Word came, however, that the Confederates were receiving reinforcements at Carter's Depot in Piney Flats and planned to kill any Union-sympathizing Carter Countian who stood in their way.

"This was sad news indeed for our little party of undrilled mountaineers, who had been suddenly collected together to resist the tyranny of rebel desperadoes," Ellis later wrote in his postwar autobiography. The bridge burners learned that two of their released prisoners—despite promises otherwise—had identified them to Confederate authorities. A manhunt began.

Ellis and some of his comrades quickly moved to various hiding places at Doe River Cove six miles above Elizabethton. The Confederate enemy under Colonel Danville Leadbetter ("A more bloodthirsty and infamous scoundrel," said Ellis, "never set his foot upon the soil of East Tennessee") raided the area. Some bridge burners fell to capture (and prison) and others managed to find refuge. Ellis found his in a clump of trees near his home. Suddenly, he spotted a number of men walking down the road. He assumed his group had reunited. "Entertaining as I did this very erroneous impression," continued Ellis in his memoirs, "I left my place of concealment, and went down to them, when, to my utter surprise, I found myself in the hands of the rebels."

Identified as one of the hated bridge burners, Ellis prepared to die after a Confederate officer stepped forward and declared to him angrily, "You shall not live two minutes." But recalling his dream of the night before, in which he saw a large company of armed men and went out to meet them, Ellis thought seriously about his next move. In the dream, he remembered, "I became frightened, and suddenly turned and ran away with all possible speed, . . . when they attempted to shoot me their guns would not fire."

Now facing the same scene in real life, Ellis waited until the commanding officer stepped away, then asked permission to get water from a nearby log house. Without waiting for a reply, Ellis began running, leaped a fence, and ran toward a cedar thicket some two hundred yards distant. As he would later recall: "Some bawled out at the top of their voices, 'Shoot that man running!' but that only served to impart strength to my legs."

Then, by a miracle, every Confederate rifle malfunctioned. "Surely at this time I was a special object of the care of divine Providence, for not a single gun fired which was aimed at me, and I reached the desired cedar thicket in perfect safety," Ellis wrote. His enemy spent several minutes vainly scouring the thicket, all the while uttering "oaths which were enough to raise the hair on a Christian man's head."

When the Confederates finally departed, Ellis had a newfound perspective: "I must here acknowledge that the dream which I had the night previous to my capture had a decided agency in saving my life, . . . I have not, since my escape, been such a total disbeliever in dreams."

As to the cedar thicket, Ellis felt most poetic, since it "saved one poor, unprepared soul from being suddenly expelled from its tenement of clay, and violently precipitated upon the great ocean of eternity." In part, his poem begged: "Oh, woodman, let me beseech you to spare that *cedar thicket;* touch not a single bush in its umbrageous pride; let it stand forever. . . ."

The bridge-burning movement of 1861 did not last long, because the Union did not make a quick invasion to save East Tennessee loyalists. As a result, the loyalists, dubbed "Lincolnites," were left without protection. A reign of fear settled into East Tennessee. Those who took part in bridge burnings and those merely suspected of the deed had few places to hide from Confederates. Many were hanged immediately.

The lucky Daniel Ellis—one of the more noted bridge burners—later became a professional guide, or pilot, in East Tennessee's Underground Railroad, leading Unionists to the safety of Kentucky. He often took a route through the mountains of Sullivan County when Confederate troops had control of Cumberland Gap. (It would be a year before the first successful Union cavalry strike, and the man leading the charge would be Reverend Carter's brother, Samuel Powhatan Carter, a naval officer given a presidential appointment as an army brigadier general. His critical raid into the Tri-Cities area of Bristol, Johnson City, and present-day Kingsport would bring some relief to the loyalists.)

Ellis, who now made his living as a guide, claimed to have "taken thousands of refugees, prisoners and a few negroes, through the mountains into the Federal lines," proudly boasting that he "never lost a man." He made ten trips between 1862 and 1863. When local Confederates kept a strong hold on several upper East Tennessee counties, he guided seven more parties from Elizabethton to Union-controlled Knoxville from 1863 to 1865. He lived to be eighty, dying in 1908.

63
Benjamin Franklin Cheatham

An Early Border Battle—
And the Real Exchange That Follows

Benjamin Franklin Cheatham before
his uniform lost its buttons.

Several days after the late-1861 battle at the tiny Missouri-Kentucky steamboat landing of Belmont, Confederate General Benjamin Franklin Cheatham and Union leader Ulysses S. Grant (two former comrades in arms) exchanged prisoners—then they exchanged champagne toasts.

Cheatham, a Nashville native, was the former major general of the Tennessee militia. He and his opposing general, Grant, were friends of longstanding, having served together in the Mexican War under Zachary Taylor. This early Civil War battle along the Mississippi River (very near the northwest tip of Tennessee) renewed their association. Both sides claimed victory: Grant said he prevented Confederates from reinforcing troops entering Missouri, while Cheatham claimed to have driven Grant "back upriver."

Once they had concluded their official business, Grant invited Cheatham for refreshments in his boat saloon, where the two bemoaned the toll of war. Both were hard-drinking men (excessive drinking and rumors of excessive drinking plagued both men throughout their careers), so it was no surprise that the alcohol flowed. Cheatham was finally persuaded by his own boat captain to depart.

Several concluding toasts were made, after which Grant requested a souvenir to commemorate the event. Cheatham agreed, and Grant promptly cut a button from the Confederate commander's coat, leaving a "silver half dollar"-sized hole in the material. Cheatham, apparently too groggy to care, invited members of Grant's staff to have a button as well, and, amid mutual hilarity, Union officers quickly reduced his coat to a tattered garment.

Cheatham, a grandson of Nashville-founder James Robertson, continued as one of the leading Confederate generals—commanding Tennessee divisions in the most fierce battles of the entire war and remaining a favorite of his men. Known on the battlefield as a brilliant and unrelenting fighter, Cheatham never asked his men to fight any harder than he was willing to do. He was also careful to guarantee the safety of his soldiers, if at all possible. One 1899 military history claims, "There was no name in the army of Tennessee more familiar to the soldiers than that of [General Benjamin Franklin] Cheatham."

One year after Belmont had given Tennesseans their first taste of a Civil War battle came the monumental Battle of Stones River at Murfreesboro. Cheatham had three horses shot from under him, but his division was one of four that successfully sent the Union in retreat three or four miles, causing enemy forces to double back toward their own center. A Confederate victory was not to be, however. When he later lost huge numbers of his troops in a suicidal assault ordered by the commanding general, Braxton Bragg, Cheatham vowed never to serve under Bragg again. In retaliation, Bragg accused Cheatham of being drunk that day.

Never able to have the same camaraderie with his own commander that he shared with his enemy, Grant, Cheatham was not alone in his dislike of Bragg, who also argued constantly with his other generals. The arguments ended only with Bragg's later resignation when he failed to follow up the victory at the Battle of Chickamauga outside of Chattanooga. By allowing the Union army to rest and receive fresh troops for a counterattack, the Confederates were put on the run. Cheatham and his men fought a good fight, however, holding off advancing Federals at Missionary Ridge when the Confederate center broke.

In the Battle of Kennesaw Mountain near Atlanta (he led a division composed entirely of Tennessee regiments), Cheatham joined General Patrick Cleburne in inflicting far heavier casualties on the Federals than any other Confederate units. Cheatham soon advanced in rank to corps commander, leading his troops back into Tennessee and continuing in the midst of devastating combat until the last battle.

After the war, Cheatham married and settled into a life of farming, which he left in 1872 to run unsuccessfully for Congress. Now-President Ulysses S. Grant offered his old friend a civil-service job, but Cheatham declined. He instead became a superintendent of Tennessee state prisons for four years and then a Nashville postmaster until his 1886 death.

64
Reed (a Slave)
Search for Peace of Mind with a Name That Never Changes

Slaves lived close to God and "God lived close to them," one Middle Tennessee slave would claim. He was identified only as "Reed" in a slave narrative which he later provided for Nashville's Fisk University. He explained:

A Negro has got no name. My father was a Ransom and he had a uncle named Hankin. If you belonged to Mr. Jones and he sell you to Mr. Johnson, consequently you go by the name of your owner. Now, whar you got a name? We are wearing the name of our marster [master]. I was first a Hale then my father was sold and then I was named Reed.

Slave survival in every area of life, Reed related, was often a case of outwitting the plantation owners and overseers. On some plantations, slaves were forbidden to conduct religious ceremony and told that slaves have no souls. But Reed described a ritual which became commonplace on many plantations prohibiting the opportunity to pray and sing to God:

> but God Almighty let them have it, for they would take an old kettle and turn it up before the door with the mouth of it facing the folks, and that would hold the voices inside. All the noise would go into that kettle. They could shout and sing all they wanted to and the noise wouldn't go outside.

Although never whipped or beaten on the Sumner County plantation where he lived, Reed saw an older sister beaten mercilessly for breaking a clock. To avoid such punishment, he noted, some slaves ran away—not to another place, for they had no idea of what lay beyond the plantation—but to the nearby woods. There they lived with the help of plantation slaves until they died or were captured. During the Civil War, some slaves made their way to Union forces who often returned them to the plantation, which the soldiers then plundered.

As a child whose own family consisted of his parents and "five or six children," Reed recalled having no meat to eat at night, only buttermilk, and the rest of the time a great deal of "pot-likker" (the juice of cooked greens) into which he crumbled cornbread. "I love it till today." Another staple included the peelings of sweet potatoes used to make a kind of coffee. To get salt, slaves scraped the dirt in the spot above which "Marster" hung his salted pork. The dirt was then boiled with water to extract the salt.

What little education he and other slaves received came from the white children who, he said, would "come out and teach them sometimes when the old folks wasn't looking." Still a child at the end of the war, Reed got a job for fifty cents a day. Considering himself a native of Hartsville, he apparently lived in different locations. He eventually received some formal education and wandered as a preacher throughout Middle Tennessee after the war. Reed eventually settled in Nashville and continued as a preacher.

65

Julia Marcum

A Stairway Fight to the Death

Sixteen-year-old Julia Marcum's tenacity cost her an eye but gained her a Civil War pension.

Her father, Hiram, was a prominent officer in the pro-Union Scott County Home Guards. Future historians noted how Scott County, almost exclusively pro-Union, had given the "highest proportionate vote" against secession over any other county in Tennessee. When word came that Tennessee was no longer in the Union, the people of Scott County immediately voted to secede from Tennessee. The county became the Independent State of Scott after a special meeting in which one farmer vowed: "If the [expletive deleted] State has a right to secede from the Union, Scott County has a right to secede from the State." Further evidence of the county's overwhelming pro-Union sentiment is the fact that it produced 560 soldiers, 541 of whom joined Federal forces.

Late one night in September 1861, a band of Confederates decided to destroy the Marcums' East Tennessee home, located along Buffalo Creek nearly four miles from Huntsville. Approaching the farmhouse about two o'clock in the morning, the Rebels were looking for Hiram Marcum, who was hiding in the barn. The intruders could be heard threatening to burn the house to the ground. Julia Marcum rushed upstairs to fetch a large candle so that the rest of her family could huddle downstairs by candlelight. She also carried an ax with her.

A two hundred-pound Confederate broke through the front door, followed the girl up the stairs, and threatened to kill her. A life-and-death struggle ensued on the dimly lit stairway. Julia turned and hit him several times in the chest with the ax. He fired his rifle. A bullet severed one of her fingers, and, when she kept hacking at him, the Confederate ran his bayonet into her forehead, putting out one eye. Her father arrived on the scene and fired a shot. Sources differ on whether or not Marcum's shot hit its mark, but Julia had so weakened the Confederate that he was easily killed.

The Confederates who were camped nearby got word of the man's death and sent some of their men for his body. After one of their doctors treated Julia's wounds, the soldiers departed from the farm without further molesting the family.

Two years later, however, other Confederates did burn the Marcum home. During this confrontation, a bullet grazed Julia's hair and killed a cousin. The family fled to Casey County, Kentucky, and remained until the end of the war (Hiram Marcum, while subsequently serving in the Union army, died of smallpox). Julia eventually moved back to East Tennessee and taught school until her wounds made a career impossible. When the United States government awarded her a military pension in 1885, she said the thirty-five-dollar monthly stipend was "plenty to live on," and proved it by surviving to the age of ninety-two. At her death, she was residing in Williamsburg, Kentucky, and was given full military honors at her funeral.

Regarding Scott County's status as an "independent state," records give no indication that the county ever rejoined Tennessee, according to one regional historian in 1972. As a result, some twentieth-century Scott Countians jokingly wondered about the status of two native sons who were in Congress together one century after the Civil War: Congressman John Duncan Sr., a Republican who would spend twenty-four years in the House of Representatives, and United States Senator Howard Baker Jr., the first Republican elected to the Senate from Tennessee by a popular vote and later the chief of staff for President Ronald Reagan. Could these two, asked historian Esther Sharp Sanderson, have been "men without a county?"

66
Champ Ferguson

Sounding the Alarm:
A Terrorist Loose on the Plateau

In late 1861, Champ Ferguson walked up to the bedside of his first wartime victim—a fellow trying to recover from a case of measles—and put a fatal bullet into him in front of the man's wife and infant son. A month later, Ferguson confronted his second victim. This one begged for his life and professed that he had taken care of Ferguson as a child. Ferguson gunned him down anyway.

What both men had in common was that they were Union Home Guards who had trained at Kentucky's Camp Dick Robinson. Ferguson had decided to kill any man who was trained there. He seemed to have his reasons, which have given rise to many theories surrounding one of the most feared Civil War terrorists on the Cumberland Plateau. Ferguson eventually killed any Yankee who crossed his path. He became one of the behind-the-lines bushwhackers who preyed on civilians left defenseless by the wartime conscription of men in every community.

Born in Kentucky and raised in the Cumberland Mountains along the Kentucky-Tennessee border, Champ Ferguson settled in Calfkiller Valley near Sparta with his second wife and their daughter. He was tried for murder in Fentress County before the Civil War. According to the story told at war's outbreak, an incident involving his family started Ferguson on a trail of mayhem. His crimes and list of victims—the robbed, mutilated, or murdered—created horror and panic throughout the region.

There are several explanations for Ferguson's entry into violence. Some sources claim that passing Union soldiers forced their way into the Ferguson home while he was away. Twelve men, whom he discovered had all trained at Camp Dick Robinson, reportedly forced his wife and daughter to strip off their clothes and parade down the street before Union troops. Another source believed Martha Ferguson also was raped, stating, "They said that a whole bunch of men took her over, mistreated her. Some people thought it maybe affected his mind. He went crazy. Was a fanatic on killing people."

In becoming the most famous vigilante of the era, Ferguson tracked down and killed the twelve Union soldiers who had violated his family and declared war on anyone else who could be called "Yankee." As time progressed, terrorists on the Plateau (and there were many) failed to distinguish between North and South; they all became self-serving in their pillaging, and so did Ferguson.

On the South's behalf, however, he offered a cavalry force, formed in early 1862 from Fentress and surrounding counties (no muster rolls were kept). Often called a "marauding band," the company sometimes mixed with legitimate Confederate units, including those of John Hunt Morgan in action near Celina in July 1862. As Middle Tennessee skirmishes multiplied, other Confederate officers began to mention the reinforcement they received from Ferguson and his men. Union officers, taking a different view, simply described his troops as murderous outlaws. Ferguson roamed free, terrorizing Fentress, White, Overton, Clay, and Scott counties.

But the United States Army caught up with Champ Ferguson. After the war, on October 20, 1865, he was arrested and then tried by a Nashville military court for the murder of fifty-three people. Ferguson claimed the number was much higher. One of those who testified against him was none other than his nemesis, Fentress County's Tinker Dave Beaty, a wartime vigilante guilty of similar crimes on behalf of the North. Beaty's own plundering apparently was "forgotten," and many other wartime guerrillas also received pardons for their murders, thefts, and other villainous acts.

Ferguson did have a high-ranking defender in former Confederate General Joseph Wheeler, who claimed that Ferguson was once attached to his command and deserved to be treated as a prisoner of war. But Ferguson was convicted and sentenced to death. He asked that his body be returned to White County for burial in Calfkiller Valley. His wife, Martha, and daughter, Ann, made the long trip home in a wagon with his body in a cherry casket, but they soon left the county and were never heard from again.

Even in death, Ferguson excited imaginations, because citizens everywhere believed that he was still alive. Perhaps the disappearance of his wife and daughter gave validity to these rumors, which persisted for years. Several accounts state that Union soldiers, out of deep respect for their foe and realizing that other terrorists had been pardoned, arranged his escape the day of the hanging. Soldiers may have surrounded the scaffold to conceal a hangman's knot purposely tied loosely around Ferguson's neck. According to this version, Ferguson dropped harmlessly through the scaffold's trap door to a waiting casket, where he remained well hidden. His wife and daughter then drove him to safety in Oklahoma. Subsequently, there were numerous "Champ Ferguson sightings" in Oklahoma and Missouri after the war.

More than one hundred years later, Cumberland Plateau residents continued to discuss Champ Ferguson as if he had been around only the day before. (Tinker Dave Beaty was treated with equal relish by Middle Tennessee Civil War enthusiasts.) Twentieth-century historian William L. Montell balances the Champ Ferguson reputation with this observation: "Ferguson was described by his enemies as a thief, a counterfeiter, a robber, a murderer, and a man of blood, and by his defenders as Morgan's pathfinder, an exemplary citizen, and a respected family man. Feelings in the area today are still divided along these lines."

67
Nathaniel Cheairs

Deploring a Southern Surrender:
The Loss of Middle Tennessee

Nathaniel Cheairs, defiant in the face of defeat.

Despite the fact that Nathaniel Cheairs was known throughout Middle Tennessee for his gracious and warm manner, he would not be intimidated by anyone—be it his father, Nathaniel Cheairs Sr., or an enemy officer, most notably Union General Ulysses S. Grant or the infamous Union raider Fielding Hurst.

Cheairs, the youngest of eleven children in a family that dated back two centuries to Maryland, was born in 1818 at Spring Hill. His father was one of Maury County's major landowners. In 1840, Cheairs knew that his father opposed his marriage to Susan

McKissack, the daughter of another prominent family. Nothing about his intended was objectionable, except her first name. But because five previous generations of Cheairs heirs named Nathaniel had taken wives named Sarah, a tradition was being threatened. The Cheairs patriarch tried to bribe his stubborn son with five thousand dollars to call off the engagement and find a woman named Sarah. But this sixth Nathaniel was deeply in love. One fall day in 1841, he turned his back on his father and made Susan McKissack his wife. After the marriage, the couple remained in Spring Hill, home to the Cheairs family since 1811. The two shared a classic Southern plantation life with their several children at Rippo Villa (or Rippavilla), built over a four-year period in the early 1850s as a showplace of hospitality.

When the Civil War approached, Cheairs was against secession but decided not to fight his neighbors. Forming a company from Maury County for the Confederacy, he was soon a major in the Third Tennessee Infantry Regiment, made up of men from several Middle Tennessee counties. He was assigned to Fort Donelson, strategically located near the Tennessee-Kentucky border in Stewart County.

On February 15, 1862, after engaging the enemy there, Major Cheairs and his comrades felt confident of a victory when the Union retired from the field. Cheairs and his Third Tennessee were then sent to nearby Dover to await special orders. Cheairs was stunned when superior officers selected him to deliver Fort Donelson's flag of surrender to the Union. His first reaction was to explode: "Surrender? After whipping Grant? I can't believe it!"

Resentfully, Cheairs led the truce party across Federal lines at daybreak on February 16. Union generals were as surprised as Cheairs at this turn of events. Union General Charles F. Smith actually asked the approaching Confederates the nature of their business. A deflated Cheairs was immediately escorted to Grant's headquarters, where the commander quickly produced written terms demanding an unconditional surrender.

When Grant asked him about the number of troops Confederates had in battle the previous day, Cheairs did not know. "General," he said, "you have asked me a question I can't answer. If I said any number, it would be guesswork."

Grant persisted: "Well, I would like to know your best idea of the number."

Replied Cheairs: "My best impression is that we did not have exceeding seven or eight thousand."

Grant retorted: "I did not ask you for a falsehood, sir."

Cheairs jumped up, threw off his coat, and thundered back at Grant, "Sir, you are commander-in-chief of the Federal forces, and I suppose I am your prisoner, but my father taught me to take the lie from no man. If you will take off your shoulder strap. . . ."

Uncharacteristically, Grant backed away and apologized to his prisoner: "Oh, Major, I did not mean to insult you, Sir."

Cheairs later wrote that he reluctantly accepted Grant's apology, claiming he told Grant to be mindful of his future language. He also described the surrender of Fort Donelson as "the most disgraceful, unnecessary and uncalled-for surrender that occurred during the four years of war." Lack of a unified command and miscommunication led to the surrender, much to the shock of the entire South. When the Confederates failed to exploit their opportunities after repulsing Union gunboats and forcing a gap in Union land forces, Grant was aggressive and quick to surround them.

The surrender was also criticized by Confederate General Nathan Bedford Forrest, who escaped the fort with seven hundred of his own men. Because the enemy was nowhere in sight, he rode away without firing a shot. Escaping also, with more than fifteen hundred troops, were two of the fort's commanders, Gideon Pillow from Williamson County and John Floyd of Virginia. Only Kentucky General Simon Bolivar Buckner was left in command, and he surrendered the fort and nearly thirteen thousand men—perhaps the largest number of prisoners taken in one engagement during the entire war.

The surrender gave the Union army its first major victory in Tennessee and led to the immediate fall of Nashville and Middle Tennessee, setting up a Union route into the Deep South. Grant, only marginally known, was now acclaimed in Northern newspapers. President Abraham Lincoln immediately promoted him to major general, making Grant second in command in the western theater.

Cheairs was imprisoned briefly in Massachusetts. After being released in August 1862 in an officer exchange, he went home to what was left of his plantation. Life on the family homefront, however, was not without serious personal problems. Cheairs's sister-in-law, Jessie McKissack Peters, was involved in a romantic scandal with Mississippi's "darkly handsome" General Earl Van Dorn, who had arrived in Spring Hill as commander of a Middle Tennessee Confederate cavalry operation. Jessie's husband, George B. Peters, was a local physician, businessman, editor, and politician who decided on the night of May 7, 1863, to walk over to Ferguson Hall where the general had set up headquarters. Peters slipped up behind Van Dorn working at a desk and fired a bullet into the general's brain. The doctor fled into Union-occupied Nashville (later moving to Memphis with Jessie), and the murder of Van Dorn became national news.

Cheairs remained on his own plantation until early 1863. When General Nathan Bedford Forrest and his men camped on the estate, Cheairs reentered the war as a volunteer to Forrest and to General Joseph E. Johnston. In March 1864, Cheairs was assigned to purchase army supplies in Union-occupied West Tennessee. In that pursuit, he discovered that being a Mason would save his life.

Although Cheairs and two others were in civilian clothes as they attempted to buy cattle, their activities caused suspicion. Accused of spying, the three were apprehended by Union Captain Albert Cook, whose commanding officer was the unsavory West Tennessean, Colonel Fielding Hurst. Living up to his reputation for harshness, Hurst convened a drumhead court-martial, convicted the three of spying, and sentenced them to death by a firing squad.

Awaiting his execution, Cheairs learned that Captain Cook's uncle was the town marshal of Columbia and an acquaintance. Cheairs also discovered that the captain and the infamous Hurst were fellow Masons. Once Hurst understood this, he remitted Cheairs's death sentence but insisted the others be shot.

Cheairs then took the biggest gamble of his life. "Colonel Hurst, I am responsible for them. Unless you revoke the sentence passed on them, I must and will respectfully refuse your clemency for myself. Let their fate be my fate."

Extending his hand to Cheairs, Hurst relented on all three men. The prisoners were subsequently shipped to Memphis, where Cheairs and one of his comrades were sent to a prisoner-of-war camp and the third, a civilian, was paroled.

Cheairs was exchanged for yet a second time after the November 30, 1864, Battle of Franklin. Months later when the war ended, local Reconstruction officials indicted him for treason to the United States. Fleeing to Washington, D.C., Cheairs sought protection from President Andrew Johnson. The president, Cheairs later said, issued a full "pardon of all my Confederate sins."

The fully pardoned Nathaniel Cheairs lived to be ninety-six, dying in 1914 at a daughter's home in Texas. But his body was returned to Columbia and placed beside that of his wife, Susan, at Rose Hill Cemetery.

68
William Driver

Bringing "Old Glory" Out of Hiding

Retired sea captain William Driver had lived in Nashville since giving up his career in 1837 after the death of his wife. Only thirty-four at the time, Driver had three young children to raise and wanted to be in Tennessee near his brothers and their families. His had been a distinguished seafaring life, but renowned as Driver might have been, "Glory" was ahead.

The captain's passion for his huge American flag inspired a nation torn by the Civil War and in need of a rallying symbol. It was the same flag that had flown over his ship in earlier days.

Early nineteenth-century Nashvillians were accustomed to seeing the flag displayed every holiday and every election day—draped from a rope that connected an upstairs window to a tree across the street. But most Americans came to know Driver's flag by the name he had given it during his days at sea: "Old Glory." The name stuck, and Americans everywhere adopted it.

Born in Massachusetts in 1803, Driver had been on ships his entire life, serving as a cabin boy at fourteen and master mariner by twenty-one. The captain's first meeting with fame came when he transported refugee descendants of the famous mutineers of the *Bounty*. In 1831, he returned them to Pitcairn Island from Tahiti, where they had lived a year since being rescued by the British from starvation at Pitcairn. Captain Driver considered this adventure the high point of his life—until the Civil War.

Driver, who had remarried and had nine more children, watched as three sons joined the Confederate army, while he stood by—in solid allegiance to the

Union. As the war progressed, he became worried for his flag's safety. Hiding the flag by sewing it into a quilt, Driver took up pen and paper, continuously writing editors in the North about "Old Glory." As his fame spread, he earned his own nickname: "Old Glory Driver."

When Nashville fell to the Union on February 16, 1862, Driver's flag, brought from safekeeping, was raised over the Capitol. The joys of such a victory, however, could not relieve a father's despair over losing a son killed during one of the war's battles.

More than a year later, Union officials named Driver to a special claims board, where he reviewed damages inflicted by the occupational Union army upon the citizens of Nashville and the surrounding area. (Claims were so numerous, the five-man board had to meet nearly every weekday for a year and a half.) In September 1863, Driver was selected as the main speaker for a mass meeting to reestablish civilian control in Davidson County, and to ask Military Governor Andrew Johnson to begin the process for legislative elections in Tennessee once again. Soon chosen to be a Nashville city councilman, Driver also urged the reopening of public schools and worked to help the destitute.

In 1886, upon the captain's death in Nashville at the age of eighty-three, the United States Congress granted permission for an American flag to be flown twenty-four hours a day at his gravesite in Old City Cemetery.

69
Elizabeth Avery Meriwether

Refugees of War—Women and Children First!

Union General Ulysses S. Grant, commander of the occupation forces in Memphis in 1862, was impressed enough with Elizabeth Avery Meriwether to allow her to go home.

Elizabeth, the wife of a Confederate officer, had appealed to the general after Irish squatters set up a tent saloon on her lawn. Serving liquor to Union soldiers camped nearby, the squatters forcibly drove her away at knifepoint in order to take up residence in her house. Even some of Grant's soldiers disapproved of the turn of events. Grant himself did not have many words to say. Without mentioning to her what his decision would be, he wrote a message and placed it in Elizabeth's hands. She had instructions to deliver it

Elizabeth Avery Meriwether knew no fear when confronting enemy commanders.

to one of his men. Outside of Grant's office, Elizabeth and a concerned neighbor read it aloud: "To the Provost Marshal: See that Mrs. Minor Meriwether is protected in her home. U.S. GRANT."

Grant's Memphis successor, however, was not as accommodating to Elizabeth. When she met with General William Tecumseh Sherman in late 1862, Elizabeth was on a different mission. She was now trying to retrieve her livelihood, she later said in her autobiography. "I learned to my consternation that Gen. Sherman had confiscated my rents and that thence forth my tenants would have to pay their rent to the Provost Marshal." She assumed that this was a mistake—that Sherman thought the property belonged to her husband. With her deeds in hand, she had a personal audience with this new enemy general.

Sherman, ignoring the papers, "and looking me over coldly, demanded, 'Why did you let your husband go into the rebel army?'" Elizabeth tried to tell Sherman that she could not stop her husband.

"Did you try?" he asked.

"Yes, I did," she responded.

Of the persistent bantering on the subject, Elizabeth would later write: "'General Sherman,' I said as calmly as I was able to speak under the circumstances, 'by all the laws you men have made, and by all the religions you men do teach, we women have been brought up to obey our husbands, not to rule them. I had no power to keep my husband out of the army.'"

Ignoring her pleas that she and her children had no other way to live, Sherman was emphatic: "I won't give you back your property as long as your husband is in the rebel army."

Her husband, Major Minor Meriwether, was a civil engineering genius who had gained regional fame for constructing a railroad tunnel between Nashville and Chattanooga. In the Confederate army, he continued in his profession as a supervisor over engineers. While the family had servants, he and Elizabeth were both against slavery and had freed their slaves long before the war. However, they were not against secession and threw their lot with the Confederacy.

Sherman would soon issue an order to banish the wives of ten Confederate officers with each Confederate attack upon Union gunboats on the Mississippi River. Learning that she was near the top of the list, Elizabeth appealed again, explaining that she was pregnant. But Sherman declared: "I am not interested in rebel wives or rebel brats." He ordered her banished from Memphis—or the choice of imprisonment. When she began her exile, she was eight months pregnant with her third son, Lee.

Though barely standing five feet, two inches tall, Elizabeth Avery Meriwether was sturdy and resilient. She was a daughter of Hardeman County, born in 1824 near Bolivar and moving to Memphis at eleven. After the death of both parents, she became a schoolteacher along with her sisters; at the same time, her brother William "Tom" Tecumseh Avery entered law and then congressional politics to help the family finances. In the political arena, Elizabeth was an effective campaigner. Although she was not beautiful, she had pleasant looks and a forceful personality, and she knew how to use them.

Major Meriwether realized that he had left behind a wife who could take care of herself. She was once threatened for speaking against slavery, but Elizabeth never allowed fear to consume her. She had always

been independent. And when she married, it was with the mutual understanding that the couple would share equally, would never go into debt, and that she would be a businesswoman who held property in her own name.

Wandering the South as a refugee of war, Elizabeth Meriwether employed that same self-sufficient spirit in order to survive. The odds were against her. Banished Memphians were not allowed to take with them firearms, medicine, or gray cloth that could be used for the Confederacy. Beginning her exodus virtually empty-handed, she was stopped and searched for illegal contraband. Elizabeth quickly bribed an inspector in order to keep a pistol for safety. Stopping at a friend's estate, she found only smoldering rubble and a tearful family slave, who explained that the Yankees had burned the house and killed the owner.

Eventually finding refuge in Alabama, Elizabeth explained decades later in *Recollections of My 92 Years: 1824-1916* that her exile from Tennessee and the devastation she witnessed created a hatred for William Tecumseh Sherman which she nurtured for more than fifty years. During her pilgrimage into the Deep South, she and her children faced near starvation and spent many days and nights scavenging for food. Due to her strong will—combined with her natural writing talent—she was able to provide food and shelter for her children. In Selma, Alabama, she won five hundred dollars from the *Daily Mississippian* for the best story involving war experiences.

While the first postwar months found the Meriwether family reunited and rebuilding their lives together, Elizabeth pursued one more audience with a commanding officer. Hoping to retrieve the rental property that Sherman had taken, she journeyed to Washington, D.C., to meet with President Andrew Johnson. While the president only recently had issued a pardon to her brother, he was in no mood to meet her request.

The cause, however, took new life with the help of a friend in the church, Ann Kesterson, known among Union soldiers for her charity work. Due to Elizabeth's previous stand against slavery, Ann was able to intervene with the Memphis military commander, who gladly renewed all property rights.

When the Meriwethers moved into one of their city dwellings on Union Street, they became neighbors with some of the Confederacy's leading figures, including

General Nathan Bedford Forrest. Tennessee's ousted secession governor, Isham G. Harris, was a visitor about whom Elizabeth wrote in her memoirs: "Gov. Harris had long been our friend; we were glad to help him." Without describing the nature of that help, she said of him:

> when the Yankees captured Nashville, Gov. Harris escaped, taking with him a large sum of money belonging to the State School fund—just how much money he took I do not know, but it ran into the hundreds of thousands of dollars. For four years Gov. Harris kept that money safely, carrying it from place to place as the Yankee invasion of the South progressed; and when the war ended, he brought every dollar back to Nashville and turned it over to the State Treasury. He was as poor as a church mouse; not one cent of his own did he have.

The exiled Tennessee governor was not the only one in need of help. When Minor Meriwether managed to collect four thousand dollars from a debtor in Kentucky in order to pay bills, he and Elizabeth took on many new responsibilities. She wrote:

> During the first year or two after Lee's surrender hardly a day passed but some poor Confederate soldier came to our door for help; they were ragged, shoeless, moneyless. Some wanted help to get on to their former homes in distant states. . . . Others were wounded and could not work. Every soldier who came out of that dreadful war unhurt felt it his sacred duty to help those who were less fortunate, and so it was that a considerable part of that four thousand dollars . . . went for charity.

The house on Union Street was soon used for a meeting at which Minor Meriwether and Nathan Bedford Forrest, along with Matthew Galloway of the *Memphis Daily Appeal,* agreed that the recent formation of the Ku Klux Klan was the best way to protect Southern property from overtaxation by Northern carpetbaggers and to have some voice in the election process. Since Confederate veterans were prohibited from voting and carpetbaggers were being elected by freed blacks, the KKK would try to scare blacks away from the polls. Unknown to Elizabeth, the men's parlor conversations were the beginning of a local KKK.

Fully confident that ex-Confederate males would eventually regain the right to vote, Elizabeth Meriwether seemed more interested in voting rights for women. That interest would become a passion. By 1872, she

was making history as the first Tennessee woman to fight for women's suffrage and the first to speak from a public platform. Often described as "the chief representative of liberal thought in Tennessee," she also published her own newspaper, *The Tablet,* specifically to encourage women's voting rights.

In the 1876 presidential election, Elizabeth applied for the privilege of voting and rented a theater to give a well-attended public lecture about women's suffrage. To avoid national publicity, election officials issued her a special voting permit. With mixed pride and disappointment, Elizabeth grumbled that her ballot probably had been removed before being counted. She later joined prominent suffrage activists, including Susan B. Anthony, for a nationwide speaking tour.

Throughout the decade, Elizabeth Meriwether also fought for equal pay on behalf of women teachers in Memphis. In this battle, her husband was again her equal partner, this time in 1879 as a Memphis delegate to the National Suffragists Convention.

With whatever time she could muster, Elizabeth added novelist to her list of achievements, writing romantic books about the South with a feminist slant. Her first novel, *Master of Red Leaf,* published in England in 1872, eventually gained widespread favorable reviews despite her defense of secession. (Having also penned popular histories and a play, she was ninety when she wrote her last novel, *The Sowing of the Swords.*)

St. Louis was home after 1883 due to reports that the devastating yellow fever might return to Memphis. Nonetheless, Elizabeth Meriwether continued to be an inspiration to West Tennessee's suffrage movement and the Progressive Reform movement. After the death in 1910 of her husband of sixty years, she resided with her son Lee, now an attorney and railroad president. In the foreword to his mother's lively autobiography, published in 1958 by the Tennessee Historical Commission, Lee Meriwether closed with the following words:

> In 1916 both the Republican and the Democratic party promised to support an amendment to the Constitution forbidding withholding the ballot from women because of their sex. When my mother read this "plank" in the platforms of the two major political parties she said: "Lee, my work is done. I am content now to face the setting sun and fall asleep as the night comes on."

A few months later, as a clock stops ticking, so stopped the beating of my mother's heart—no pain, no illness, no attempt to cling to life. One moment she was discussing the topic of the day; the next moment she closed her eyes and silently slipped into the vast ocean of yesteryears.

In her death I lost not only a mother; I lost the intellectual companionship of a woman who was the peer of any woman I have known in all my 95 years.

Because of her lasting impact on American society, Elizabeth Avery Meriwether was commemorated in the 1920s with a postage stamp bearing her likeness.

70
Fielding Hurst

Carrying a Torch to His Hometown

While serving as the leader of Union troops stationed in predominately Confederate West Tennessee, Colonel Fielding Hurst decided to burn most of his hometown of Purdy.

Hurst's feelings toward his neighbors had changed dramatically, considering that he had once been a respected man in McNairy County, a surveyor who first arrived with his wife in 1833 from East Tennessee's Claiborne County. Members of his extended family soon followed and joined Hurst in buying vast acreage. Over time, the large, close-knit clan owned much of the county, and with it, most of the area's few slaves and control over numerous county roads.

When Tennessee voted on secession in June 1861, the balloting in Purdy was not secret. In a voice vote, Hurst stood against the majority of his neighbors by announcing that he was against secession. Further riling the local populace with a pro-Union speech, fifty-one-year-old Hurst was arrested, chained, and taken to Nashville, where he "laid on the cold stone floors of the penitentiary" for several weeks. Returning home, Hurst was determined to help the Union army—offering both his services and that of his family as scouts and spies. It was said the Hurst family knew "every pig path" in the area. Neighbors dubbed their property the "Hurst Nation," a long and narrow section of McNairy County spreading into present-day Chester County.

The strongest pockets of Unionism in lower West Tennessee existed either within the Hurst Nation or

in portions of neighboring Henderson and Decatur counties, where Asa "Black Hawk" Hays, a friend of President Abraham Lincoln, was stumping the countryside (at the president's request) to build Union support. Because Black Hawk Hays had hundreds of relatives in both of those counties, he had little trouble making converts. For the most part, Confederate West Tennessee held few admirers of Lincoln and had a name for all Unionists: "Lincoln Black Republicans."

By March 1862, Fielding Hurst was busy mustering local Union troops (including twenty-three family members) for Tennessee's new military governor, Andrew Johnson, a Lincoln appointee. Hurst and his followers, assigned to Union General Grenville M. Dodge, displayed little if any respect for military rules. The men routinely dispersed each evening for reconnaissance (and raiding) and rejoined Dodge's troops the next morning. This prompted the general to remark, "If I got into a fight I hoped it would be about noon so I could have the services of his regiment."

After the April 1862 Battle of Shiloh in Hardin County, the Union established martial law in much of West Tennessee and Hurst's men reportedly committed numerous atrocities against Confederate-sympathizing civilians. One West Tennessean said that these "Tories" proved to be "the meanest and cruelest class we had to deal with. They scrupled less at murder and all sorts of outrages, most of them being the very scum of the country."

Hurst's men, nonetheless, were mustered as a United States cavalry unit (the Sixth Tennessee Cavalry, U.S.A.) so that Governor Johnson could control Tennessee with state forces, who were then assigned to the Union army. Even as a regiment, Colonel Hurst's men often disappeared to conduct private raids. The citizenry accused them of robbery, rape, and murder—or any crime, in fact, that occurred in the area.

Denying many of the charges, Hurst and his troops were blamed for the looting, pillaging, and burning of Jackson in the summer of 1863. Mrs. A. A. Newman accused them of wrecking her millinery shop and stealing hats, strapping them to the heads of their horses as they rode out of town. She eventually convinced Union leaders to make Hurst's men reimburse her $5,139.25 in store damages.

A few months later, when Hurst was assigned to his hometown, Purdy, and ordered to destroy enemies of the United States in the surrounding region, he saw an opportunity for revenge on those who had jailed him. Hurst ordered the town torched. According to one regional historian, he "played the role of Nero in Purdy, even singing songs and praying while the church was burning."

Returning to Jackson in February 1864, Hurst demanded repayment of the $5,139.25 his men had been forced to pay in damages from their previous visit. Otherwise, he vowed, his men would burn Jackson also. Townspeople raised the money in the allotted five days, but Hurst burned fourteen buildings anyway.

Hurst's greatest enemy, Confederate General Nathan Bedford Forrest, sent a message to Union authorities under a flag of truce, demanding restitution to the people of Jackson. Forrest also demanded the surrender of Hurst "and the officers and men of his command guilty of these murders, to be dealt with by the C.S. authorities as their offenses require." The Union command ignored Forrest. While Hurst's regiment continued raiding West Tennessee in the summer of 1864, Forrest declared Hurst an outlaw, claiming that the regiment and its leader were "a disgrace to the Federal army, to the state and to humanity." Forrest's later order to raid nearby Fort Pillow, near Henning, was a partial retaliation for Hurst's plundering.

The many crimes of which Hurst was accused did bring punishment to his family. A nephew was captured by Confederate troops, tied to a tree, and shot between the eyes. Finding Hurst's aging mother bedridden, the Confederates snatched the sheets from beneath her, sending her tumbling to the floor and breaking her hip. Hurst's men, in their own retaliation, captured six Confederates (all former neighbors) and killed one for every mile they traveled, burying them "as mile posts."

When the war was over, Hurst was given a seat in the Tennessee State Senate by Reconstruction-era Governor William G. "Parson" Brownlow, who afterwards appointed him judge for the twelfth judicial circuit. With little legal training, Hurst had to rely on Judge Elijah Walker's advice. Later appointed to command a Grand Army of the Republic post, Hurst resigned when a misuse of funds, reportedly by his deputies, left him liable for security bonds and forced him to sell much of his land.

Hurst died in 1882 at the age of sixty-nine, heavily in debt and a broken man. His neighbors openly celebrated, riding their horses over his gravesite, and, in their contempt, spitting on the grave. Nearly a century later, their offspring continued to harbor ill will, refusing the highway marker at Purdy intended to designate the site of the Unionist Hurst Nation. The marker thus was placed at nearby Bethel Springs.

71
Leonidas Polk
The Confederacy's "Fighting Bishop": A Symbol at Shiloh

When "Follow your Granny!" became his war cry at Shiloh, Confederate General Leonidas Polk became the idol of his troops.

The former Episcopal bishop had strapped on a sword of war in 1861 and insisted that his duty was now with the Confederate States of America. Polk's men meant no compliment when they nicknamed him "Granny" because of his ministerial background. He knew what they called him and threw it back at them in April 1862 after the Battle of Shiloh had commenced near the Tennessee River in Hardin County.

In a diary, Private Thomas Jefferson "T. J." Walker of West Tennessee recalled when their corps commander saved one critical moment:

> suddenly there came riding down in front of our lines, as magnificent a specimen of noble, courageous manhood, mounted on his magnificent roan charger, I then thought and still think, as I have ever seen. With his sword unsheathed and with fire flashing from his eyes, he pointed toward our retreating and broken lines. He rode in front of us with the Federal line in pursuit. Then wheeling his horse as he reached the center of our regiment and raising himself in his stirrups and shouting, "Follow your Granny!", he led the charge. . . .
>
> From that moment, his corps loved and worshipped him until his deplored death and still revere him as few heroic commanders have been loved and worshipped in the world's history.

The Battle of Shiloh, which took place around Pittsburg Landing, became America's bloodiest battle to that time and took the life of the Confederacy's western-theater commander (and Polk's good friend), Albert Sidney Johnston of Texas. Polk, who had recommended Johnston to Confederate President Jefferson Davis, personally led four charges. Confederate artillery fire—reportedly the largest concentration of artillery yet discharged in North America—became so intense against the Federal stronghold called "Hornet's Nest" that a rabbit raced from the woods near the battlefield, sprinted across three hundred yards of clearing, and cuddled up alongside an Iowa soldier—less afraid of humans than the mighty roar of the cannons.

The first day held numerous assaults, withdrawals, and fresh assaults by the Confederates against the Federal center, which finally broke. Securing overnight reinforcements, however, the Federals virtually owned the next day, at which time both sides simply ended the battle by consent.

Leonidas Polk had come to the war well prepared in military training because he was a graduate of West Point. Born in North Carolina and a distant cousin of the late President James K. Polk, he settled on a Middle Tennessee plantation in 1833, with his three brothers and their families. Located near Columbia, this five-thousand-acre Maury County plantation was called "Rattle and Snap," in honor of the dice game in which their father won the property from the North Carolina governor. The land was then carved into separate plantations for the Polk sons.

On his own tract, Polk built a plantation church, St. John's Episcopal, and held services for both white and black families. He also served as rector of St. Peter's Church in Columbia. But in 1838, Polk became the first missionary bishop of the Southwest, in charge of the Indian territory as well as Alabama, Arkansas, Texas, and Mississippi. Three years later, he became the Bishop of Louisiana. Polk created churches wherever he went, including thirty-five congregations made up of slaves (he, too, was a slaveholder, his wife having inherited a great number of slaves).

In 1857, Polk's burning desire to see a regional Episcopal college led him to hold several church meetings to establish the University of the South. His companion in that effort was James H. Otey, bishop of Tennessee. With endorsements from both men, the town of Sewanee in Franklin County became the chosen site of the school. Polk loved the entire Cumberland Plateau area and often stayed at John Armfield's Beersheba Springs resort. By the time of the Civil War, Polk had finalized a fund-raising tour to finance the University of the South, had already begun the build-

ing of a campus and selection of a faculty, and had returned temporarily to his neglected diocese. His wife and five daughters remained at their cottage in Sewanee built for them by Armfield.

Bishop Polk incorrectly believed that the war would sweep past Sewanee and that his family would avoid the conflict. During his absence in April 1861, a fireball flew through the window of his home and that of Bishop Stephen Elliott's family, burning both structures to the ground. A longtime Polk house servant, Altimore, pulled Mrs. Polk and her daughters from the burning structure. Elliott, the bishop of Georgia, was a Polk assistant at the University of the South; neither he nor his family were home at the time of the fire. In his fury that defenseless women were attacked ("The spirit of hell was never more exhibited," he proclaimed), Polk became even more resolved to put on a military uniform. President Davis, his former West Point classmate, personally awarded him a commission of major general.

Soon nicknamed "the Fighting Bishop," Polk immediately began construction of forts that would protect the Mississippi River, locating them at Memphis, Island Number Ten, New Madrid, Fort Pillow, and Columbus, Kentucky. In October 1862, he was promoted to lieutenant general after a strong showing by his corps in battles from Belmont (Missouri) to Shiloh to Perryville (Kentucky). After Albert Sidney Johnston's death, he was often second in command to the new western-theater commander, Braxton Bragg, whose battle orders he often criticized. When victories kept slipping through Confederate hands, Polk recommended that Bragg be replaced. Bragg relieved him of command at the Battle of Chickamauga in late 1863, but Polk was reinstated by President Davis.

The Fighting Bishop met his death in June 1864 at Georgia's Pine Mountain. On that day, the Confederates were well entrenched trying to defend Atlanta from their position near Marietta. Union General William Tecumseh Sherman, frustrated and furious at the situation, was reviewing his own forces when he looked through his field glasses and spotted three high-ranking Confederate generals atop the nearby mountain. He ordered his cannoneer to fire at them. Polk, fifty-eight, was standing near the crest of the hill with his "arms folded," apparently taking one last look when a cannonball went through his chest. His fellow generals, unhurt, were amazed at the sudden cannon fire which seemed directed at their comrade. Sherman afterwards denied knowing that the bishop-general was among the officers.

72
William G. "Parson" Brownlow

The Union's "Fighting Parson"
Taking His Show on the Road

William G. "Parson" Brownlow's controversial Capitol portrait.

Northerners during the Civil War danced the "Parson Brownlow Quickstep" and relished every word of his quickly penned-for-profit life story, which sold more than one hundred thousand copies midway through the war. Meanwhile, untold numbers of Southerners spent much of their time dodging the "Fighting Parson's" spite and venom, aimed at anyone who disagreed with him about anything.

William G. "Parson" Brownlow was many things in his life: circuit-riding preacher, controversial newspaper editor, staunch Union supporter from Knoxville, and powerful Reconstruction governor of Tennessee. And in all these things he was often hated—much to his satisfaction.

He knew how to find the most blazing and impassioned words that would irritate people. Brownlow claimed his "exuberance and redundancy of language was justly considered one, among the many other *winning* ways I have, to make folks hate me." He created commotion wherever he went, and it seemed his supreme talent was for getting a rise out of people. On any given day, on any given subject, Brownlow had to have the last word.

Even his wife was swayed by the force of his personality. Asked in later years why she married him, Eliza O'Brien Brownlow of Sullivan County explained: "I was influenced by my respect for his talent; and besides he was so earnest, persistent and eloquent in his wooing, there was no resisting him."

She was the daughter of a merchant and iron manufacturer near present-day Kingsport. Parson Brownlow said of her: "I never courted but one woman and her I married." He saved his kindness, his generosity, and his gentle ways for his wife and children and close friends, as well as for his neighbors and the orphaned or widowed who were in need.

Born in Virginia, where he was orphaned at eleven, Brownlow came to Tennessee in 1828 at the age of twenty-three. Beginning his career as a Methodist revival preacher, the Fighting Parson became a newspaper owner in order to spread his religious and political messages. As editor of the *Whig,* first published in Elizabethton and then for ten successful years in Jonesborough, Brownlow declared open war on editors of other religious publications and fostered a visible hatred of all Baptists, Presbyterians, and Catholics. The feeling seemed mutual.

He so hated Kingsport's Presbyterian editor Frederick A. Ross that he published a Jonesborough magazine for two years just to attack Ross and to defend Methodism's John Wesley. A Jonesborough newspaper rival, Dr. Thomas A. Anderson, became a target for whom Brownlow had these words: "This is the name of the last and we presume most filthy of the Editors of that dirty sheet, *The Tennessee Sentinel.*" (The paper was owned by another Brownlow enemy,

Washington County attorney Landon Carter Haynes, who shot him in the leg during a street fight between the two. Haynes, a talented orator called the "Cicero of the South," was from a prominent Carter County family, later becoming one of two Tennessee senators in the Confederate Congress—again on the opposite side of Brownlow.)

Another religious editor, Baptist elder J. R. Graves of the *Tennessee Baptist*, put Brownlow "into high gear" with the 1856 publication, *The Great Iron Wheel*, which attacked Methodists and touted Baptists. In rebuttal, Brownlow tore into a personal attack on Graves with *The Great Iron Wheel Examined, or Its False Spokes Extracted*.

Despite the force of these attacks, the public took delight in the battles. So entertaining were the church participants that modern historian James C. Kelly likened their interdenominational donnybrooks to "wrestling matches or cockfighting," perhaps filling "a need now met by allegiance to sporting teams."

When Brownlow transplanted the *Whig* to Knoxville in 1849, the town shuddered at his arrival. Many people ignored Brownlow's spiteful words, but fascination with his anger, his articulate manner, and his latest battle made the *Whig* an irresistible product. Although shut down for a while during the war, the newspaper became East Tennessee's most popular publication, leaving readers eager to read what would be written next. Throughout the war, Brownlow used the paper to broadcast his staunch pro-Union stand, although he personally defended slavery, despised abolitionists, and reviled President Abraham Lincoln.

In Knoxville, Confederates temporarily jailed the parson, accusing him of conspiring to burn five East Tennessee railroad bridges. Brownlow had surrendered after hiding in the mountains of Sevier and Blount counties with a two-thousand-dollar reward on his head. In a curt message to the Confederacy's attorney general, Brownlow declared: "If you will help me in this, I will do more for your Confederacy than the devil himself, for I will leave it."

He received quick passage to Nashville, now controlled by Union-occupation forces. Theatrical as always, Brownlow stood on his carriage and shouted toward all curious bystanders, mostly Yankee soldiers: "Glory to God in the highest, and on earth peace, good will toward all men, except a few hellborn and hell-bound rebels in Knoxville."

Later that day, he held a public reunion with another enemy, Military Governor Andrew Johnson, who once defeated him in a congressional election (when Johnson later was elected governor, Brownlow declared in Nashville, "I therefore pronounce your Governor, here upon his own dunghill, an UNMITIGATED LIAR AND CALUMINATOR, and a VILLAINOUS COWARD"). Now in the same philosophical camp, the two "rushed into each other's arms, and wept like children." Brownlow was happy to see that Johnson felt "all the malice and venom requisite for the times."

In the spring of 1862, the Fighting Parson, accompanied by his daughter Susan, embarked on a Northern lecture tour—and he was a sensation. He delivered speeches filled with his customary vengeance and made a handsome profit doing so, claiming he would use the money to resurrect the *Whig*. He fired the hearts of Northerners in every state he visited, and after he spoke, a Union recruiter was prepared to sign any man ready to fight those Southerners. Riding a crest of fame and stellar popularity, Brownlow accepted a ten-thousand-dollar offer to write his biography and took but a few weeks to complete what was an immediate bestseller. It spurred several pamphlet biographies as well as the popular dance, "The Parson Brownlow Quickstep."

In Hartford, Connecticut, workers in the Colt factory presented Brownlow with a revolver and holster. In a blazing speech that followed, he called for a manhunt to seek out the Hartford secessionists and ride them out of town on a rail. The Parson was so pleased with himself that he resurrected this thought in every town he visited. Cheers and a passionate dislike of Confederates grew with his every fiery word.

When his adopted hometown, Knoxville, returned to Union hands in the fall of 1863, Brownlow made his way back and reintroduced his brand of journalism under a new name: *Brownlow's Knoxville Whig and Rebel Ventilator*. Again in the business of outraging his fellow Tennesseans, Brownlow continued to enjoy attention. He delighted in walking the streets, knowing people would rush to their windows to see if this were the day he would be shot dead.

An irony of the war—certainly for one so unforgiving as Brownlow—occurred during Knoxville's Battle of Fort Sanders on November 29, 1863. The battle, a spin-off of the Chickamauga-Chattanooga campaign, was fought in frigid temperatures, to the horror of Confederates hoping to recapture the city. Although the Union was hidden atop hilly earthworks and protected by deep ditches with icy walls, one wounded Confederate managed access to the fortress just before being captured. The prisoner, Lieutenant Colonel Alfred Gaines O'Brien of Mississippi, would not admit that he had a sister in Knoxville who might treat his wounds (the hospital being full). When they learned otherwise, Unionists sent for her. Rushing to his side, she was escorted by her faithful husband—William G. "Parson" Brownlow. The Brownlows subsequently removed the prisoner to their home, and Eliza nursed him back to health.

Many Tennesseans' worst nightmare came true when Brownlow became their governor in a wartime election in late 1864. That election did not involve the entire populace, because Confederates were not allowed to vote. Ruling with an iron hand and forming special police forces garrisoned in Memphis, Nashville, and Chattanooga, Brownlow did not make life easy for his former wartime foes. In addition to his natural desire to impose vengeance upon enemies, he also controlled every local election. Such harsh repression led to underground resistance. Brownlow's Reconstruction policy—which spared his cherished Knoxville—contributed ultimately to the rise of the Ku Klux Klan.

Once during Brownlow's reign, a group of schoolgirls visited him at the State Capitol. Now in his sixties, his health had deteriorated, he was decidedly shriveled, and any speaking he did was in a whisper. One little girl remarked to her school friend: "Anna, is that the Egyptian mummy you were going to see?"

Anna replied: "Oh, no, that is our Military Governor."

"Military indeed. . . . I am sure he could not shoot off a popgun. I am almost certain he is not a real man at all."

Tennesseans would hurl other direct insults Brownlow's way, even decades after his 1877 death at the age of seventy-two. One traditional tale claims that Tennessee legislators spit tobacco juice on his portrait in the Capitol. There were numerous failed attempts to remove the portrait, but it did come down in the 1980s. It was put back up but removed yet again, showing that Brownlow would not cease being controversial.

Toward the end of his tumultuous life—perhaps during his brief stint in the United States Senate after resigning the governor's chair—the consistent Brownlow penned a few thoughts about his time on earth, concluding, "had I my life to live over, I would pursue the same course I have pursued, ONLY MORE SO."

73

"Josey" Towson Ellis

Petticoats and Pianos: The Only Place to Hide

Josephine "Josey" Towson Ellis demonstrated that a petticoat could cover a Confederate soldier as well as a uniform could, and probably better if the need arose.

"Miss Josey," as she was called, who was a member of a large Middle Tennessee land-owning family, often provided aid for Confederate troops after the Union overran present-day Trousdale County in 1862 and occupied her hometown, Hartsville. Despite her Southern sympathies, she also offered hospitality to Federal soldiers camped nearby and invited Union officers to her parties (she was an accomplished pianist). Her friendship with the Union actually provided a means to secure Confederate supplies. If a Confederate needed a particular item, such as shoes, she petitioned Federal officers, claiming that she sought the item for her household or her slave.

One evening, while Miss Josey entertained friends and a visiting Confederate soldier, there was a knock at the door. Seated at the piano, she motioned for the Confederate to hide in the only secure location available—beneath her large hoop skirt, which was well disguised by the piano.

When several Union soldiers entered the room in search of the man, Miss Josey graciously invited them to search her home, while she kept her place at the piano. Their fruitless search completed, the soldiers departed, soon followed by the relieved Confederate, who quickly rejoined his troop elsewhere in Middle Tennessee.

Josey Ellis was a woman of appreciable means, by virtue of her father, Jacob, who was a leading citizen in Hartsville, and her husband, Captain H. C. Ellis, who was then serving with the Ninth Tennessee Cavalry under Confederate General John Hunt Morgan. Morgan, in fact, routed the Union soldiers at Hartsville in a later attack on December 7, 1862. The success was short-lived, because a new Union force soon re-occupied the town. Captain Ellis was later captured with Morgan on a famous raid into Ohio.

After the war, Ellis became a Hartsville banker and businessman. He also owned a large farm on the Cumberland River, where his accomplishments in agriculture gave the place a reputation as one of the best farms in Middle Tennessee. Upon his death in 1903, his wife spent her final days residing either at the family homeplace or the old Maxwell Hotel in Nashville during the hotel's peak as a prominent place of social activity.

Josey Ellis was as generous with her money as she was with her hospitality and her petticoat, donating large sums to charitable causes until her death in 1912.

74
William Giles Harding
*Protecting a Plantation
and a Horse-Racing Tradition*

Abolitionists might not have thought much of William Giles Harding, but his slaves thought the world of him. The Harding home was Nashville's Belle Meade, the nation's first and most famous thoroughbred-breeding nursery and plantation, where caring respect abounded among Harding and the 136 slaves whom he knew personally.

Though in his fifties and too old to fight in the Civil War, Harding was active as a member of the state's military board and helped to finance the Confederacy with five hundred thousand dollars of his own money. When Federal troops descended on the farm in April 1862 with orders from Military Governor Andrew Johnson to arrest Harding, the slaves prepared to resist the intruders. But Harding motioned for the servants not to interfere.

During his subsequent six-month imprisonment in Michigan, the servants offered their hard-earned gold pieces to Harding's wife, Elizabeth, in hopes of helping buy back their master's freedom, according to family historian W. Ridley Wills II. That Belle Meade's slave population could earn and keep their own income was part of a lifestyle that did not go unnoticed by one abolitionist leader, United States Senator

Charles Sumner, who, during a visit years earlier, had expected to find barbaric conditions and intense cruelty. After touring the grounds in 1855, he reportedly said, "if this is a fair type of Southern slavery, I shall have greatly to modify many of my preconceived views of it." Of Belle Meade, Harding felt compelled to confess: "I fear that this cannot be taken as an average specimen."

Elizabeth Harding was equally known for her ability to take care of Belle Meade. She was the daughter of former Nashville mayor Randal McGavock, who built the Franklin mansion Carnton, her childhood home. During her husband's imprisonment, she was able to run Belle Meade with the aid of two overseers and her faithful housemaid, Susanna Carter. In addition to caring for the needs of her own family, including an invalid sister, Elizabeth often went to the slave quarters to tend the sick; if her efforts failed, she sent for her family doctor.

Belle Meade survived a steady confiscation of food and crops and the drafting of its male servant population each Monday to build Union defenses in Nashville. Slaves remained in their status of bondage, and soldiers returned them to the plantation on weekends.

Susanna Carter, although illiterate, sent letters to Harding. She managed the letter-writing task by securing a scribe for the "consideration of certain glasses of peach cordial, blackberry wine and other 'knick knacks.'"

In August 1862, she dictated the following to Harding:

You said in your letter to me that I could pretty near always find some idle fingers to write for me. In this you were partly right and partly wrong; there are idle fingers in abundance but it is hard for me to make them industrious. I have at length engaged Mars. Randal Ewing as my amanuensis and he has most kindly offered to do all my writing for me.

Harding was finally released from prison after his wife appealed to Military Governor Johnson, saying that she alone could not prohibit the plunder by Union soldiers who held no mercy for the servants and their homes. She claimed that when the servants "fly to me for protection, their houses are entered and robbed."

With the help of his wife's persistent lobbying and a fair-sized bond of twenty thousand dollars, Harding returned home. Belle Meade's cheering slaves met him a mile from the city and asked him to leave his carriage. They lifted Harding to their shoulders and carried him to the cabin of "Uncle Bob" Green, the plantation's horse trainer who had been wounded by Union troops ransacking the farm during a midnight raid. His knowledge of thoroughbreds and their care made him as well known to the horse industry as was Belle Meade itself.

Born on the plantation in 1829, Green had offered to accompany Harding to prison, but failing that, tried to protect the farm. Elizabeth Harding wrote that he was shot "without the least provocation." Green proudly displayed his war wound to Harding, who was overcome with emotion. Moments later, the servants carried Harding home.

Harding also had lived his entire life at Belle Meade, the frontier home of his parents, which dated to the 1780s and was one of the original Cumberland Settlements (Dunham's Station). "Giles," as he was called, managed the plantation beginning in 1840, so that his father, John Harding, could personally develop and manage out-of-state plantations. Young Harding elevated Belle Meade to prominence in agriculture as well as in horse breeding. He held strict principles regarding his servants, whom he never called "slaves." Like his father, Harding toiled in the fields side by side with the workers. He would not sell any of them, separate families, or entrust them completely to overseers.

At war's end, most of Belle Meade's servants took advantage of their new freedom and left to seek education and other benefits. Some, preferring to remain associated with Belle Meade, lived nearby and earned their living working for Harding. Susanna Carter so loved her plantation life that she could not imagine how others preferred freedom and its anxieties in obtaining food and shelter.

Although the estate had been a thoroughbred-breeding farm of national significance since 1816, its worldwide stature came after the war. Harding's son-in-law, former Confederate General William H. Jackson, took over Belle Meade's great stables, and the general's wife, Selene, became plantation hostess after her mother's death in 1867 at the age of forty-eight (the patriarch John Harding, ninety, also died that year).

During these postwar days, the celebrated Bob Green helped produce several great horses in Belle Meade's consistently superior stables. America's leading horse-racing enthusiasts and dealers converged on the plantation's annual thoroughbred sales. Iroquois and Bonnie Scotland especially enjoyed great prestige in the 1870s and 1880s. Iroquois was the only American horse, until 1954, to win the English Derby. When news of his 1881 win reached New York City, Wall Street suspended business. Bonnie Scotland's strong bloodline, meanwhile, would produce Secretariat, a Triple Crown winner one hundred years later.

Horse breeding aside, Harding also raced his own steeds and "had won more purses with his own horses than any man then living" in the nation. Some of Harding's fellow church members pointed out the contradiction of a Christian supporting the horse-racing industry. Harding was defensive on this issue. Evil raised its head, he argued, not in horse racing but in the gambling associated with it. A true lover of the track, Harding supposedly never bet on a race.

When he approached his final days, Harding routinely enjoyed visits from former servants or their family members. One of these, Henry Harding, brought tears to the old man's eyes when he confided, "You have been the truest friend to me and my race I have ever known."

When William Giles Harding died in 1886, his faithful friend and horse-breeding genius Bob Green served as pallbearer, just as he had done for Harding's father (and would do for Harding's daughter Selene at her death in 1892). Remaining as housemaid, Susanna Carter lived out her long life on the plantation with her own family.

Green witnessed the sale of Belle Meade at public auction in 1904, when it was purchased by Jacob McGavock Dickinson, a family friend and distant cousin of Elizabeth Harding's. Two years after the auction, Green died. The new owner buried him near the Hardings, thus completing the lengthy chapter of the great estate's original occupants.

75

Lu Mayberry

A House Slave Outwitting the System

As a result of spending her childhood in slavery without her mother and after watching her two brothers die of illness, Lu Mayberry used her resourceful personality to get ahead in a white man's plantation world. She considered herself one of the lucky ones. Her best reward would come on a rainy February morning three years after the end of the Civil War, when she would answer a knock at her door.

In the 1930 slave narratives collected by Nashville's Fisk University, Lu told how she came face to face with her mother, Ada, whom she failed to recognize after twenty-one years of slavery-enforced separation. Standing beside her mother was one of Lu's half-brothers. Only when Ada displayed an old facial whip scar did Lu remember the mother who was sold away to a Mississippi plantation after running away and disappearing for a year. Lu was six at the time.

Now with a husband and two children of her own, Lu invited her mother to join their Williamson County household. "She stayed with us a long time, and she died right here in this house," Lu would recall on her eighty-ninth birthday interview.

Lu Mayberry said she had spent her earliest childhood on the Morrison plantation near Franklin. At the age of eleven, she was sold to Tom Ellison, who had married one of the Morrison daughters, "Miss Janie." Moving with the young couple to the state she called "old Sip" (Mississippi), Lu became a house slave and caregiver to the Ellison children, living a life that she considered luxurious—wearing calico dresses and underwear and walking barefoot across soft carpets in the mansion.

When Miss Janie died years later, Lu returned with the family to Tennessee. They all lived together on the old Williamson County plantation, where she took care of Tom Ellison and the children. Without the protection once given her by her mistress, Lu suffered the jealousy of fellow house slaves. When she felt particularly mistreated, she approached the Ellison children, who adored her, and threatened to leave. "I'm going to the Yankees," she would announce. The children reported this turn of events to their father and threatened to go with her. Ellison apparently responded by seeing to Lu's happiness.

In return, Lu protected the children from their father whenever Ellison thought his offspring needed a spanking. She usually intervened by poking successfully at his conscience: "You just let these chillen alone. Miss Janie . . . said you was gonna marry some other woman and be mean to her chillen." Ellison begged Lu not to mention such a thought. She regu-

larly replied: "Yes, I is too; I'm gonna tell you every time you hit one of these chillen."

Despite the freedom she would possess after the war, Lu chose to remain in the Ellison household. She left only after marrying Kay Mayberry in a ceremony officiated by Ellison. Ironically—considering her role as protector of the Ellison children—Lu told the Fisk interviewer that she was in the process of spanking one of her own children when her mother suddenly appeared on that rainy day in 1868.

76
Nathan Bedford Forrest

A Confederate Counterattack: "First with the Most"

Nathan Bedford Forrest, the "Wizard of the Saddle."

His mother called him Bedford; his men called him "Sir"; admirers dubbed him "the Wizard of the Saddle"; his foes (and they were many) swore at "that devil Forrest."

The Confederacy's General Robert E. Lee reportedly proclaimed this western cavalry commander as the "greatest general" of the South; the Union's General

William Tecumseh Sherman said straightforwardly that he was "the most remarkable man our Civil War produced on either side."

Even fifty years after the Civil War, in 1914, a United States Army officer from Tennessee encountered the military reputation of Confederate General Nathan Bedford Forrest of Bedford (future Marshall) County, Tennessee. The American officer was Granville Sevier, who was in a London, England, book shop when an Englishman remarked that he was looking for a certain Forrest biography. In the course of conversation, the Englishman was excited when he learned that Sevier had known Forrest as a friend and frequent visitor in his childhood home. A discussion of Forrest's campaigns then ensued. The Briton was Sir Douglass Haig, the successful World War I commander of the British Expeditionary Forces in France. He had just returned victorious from the first Battle of Ypres (Belgium). When Sevier asked him why a Confederate general would be so well known, Haig explained: "Officers of our British cavalry service study his campaigns and his methods. We regard him as one of the greatest, if not the greatest, of English-speaking commanders of mounted troops."

In subsequent wars and in peacetime, military officers continued to study his tactics. Even the German general staff planning for its blitzkrieg of Europe during World War II analyzed Forrest's strategies.

With little military training, Forrest, a native of Chapel Hill, was the only soldier to rise from the rank of private to lieutenant general in the Civil War, and possibly in any war. He was the Confederacy's greatest tactician, using daring and maneuvering to achieve success in battle. Tennessee historian John Trotwood Moore estimated that Forrest captured at least thirty-one thousand Union troops during his career.

The more desperate the Confederacy's fight, the more daring were Forrest's military tactics. He brought to warfare a flair for total secrecy combined with the element of surprise from a concentrated force. "First with the most," it was said of him. He also had the ability to inspire what one writer described as "the incalculable value of that imponderable, the fighting heart of the soldier."

Forrest's greatest military victory, at Brice's Crossroads, Mississippi, ironically became one of the Confederacy's greatest strategic defeats. In the spring of 1864, Sherman was heavily employed in the campaign to take Atlanta—not only an important military objective but also critical to President Abraham Lincoln's reelection at a time when opposition in the North was gaining strength against the president and the war effort. Sherman was moving one hundred thousand men and thirty-five thousand animals through North Georgia, and their supply by Tennessee railroad was critical. Worried about an attack by Forrest, Sherman gave the order to his new commander at Memphis to "keep Forrest occupied," and prevent him from inflicting damage on this portion of the Union army.

Forrest confronted the Memphis Union expedition at Brice's Crossroads, a remote area near Tupelo, Mississippi, where he was outnumbered two to one. The master of deception, Forrest deployed his men in the scrub-filled and wooded area in order to create the illusion of a much larger force. As elements of his force penetrated through and around the Union army, he created a panic that soon became a rout and resulted in an overwhelming victory. When Forrest counted his spoils at Brice's Crossroads, he had acquired 18 cannons, 176 wagons, 5,000 small arms, 300,000 rounds of ammunition and more than 1,600 prisoners. Union losses were 2,600 compared to less than 500 for the Confederates. Despite Forrest's incredible success, however, Union General Samuel D. Sturgis had inflicted a great strategic defeat on the Confederacy: He had, in fact, "occupied" Forrest.

One of the more bizarre incidents of the war occurred months later in October 1864 at Johnsonville, Tennessee. Here, Forrest became not only a cavalry leader but also a naval commander. Johnsonville was a large supply-transfer point on the Tennessee River and therefore a strategic prize. Supplies for the Union were carried by steamboat from the North, unloaded at the Middle Tennessee town, and transported by rail to the large Union supply depot at Nashville. On October 28, 1864, Forrest led his force to the west bank of the Tennessee River below Johnsonville and trained his artillery on the routes used by Union supply ships. Forrest quickly captured two Union vessels and attempted to establish his own navy. From both water and land, he fought against Union gunboats for several days and finally shelled the great supply depot of Johnsonville itself. The depot commander ordered supplies burned rather than let them fall into Rebel hands. Forrest's losses in this raid were two killed and nine wounded—his enemy's losses were four gunboats, fourteen transports, twenty barges, twenty-six pieces of artillery, and 6.7 million dollars worth of property.

In the last major offensive of the Confederacy—the blood bath that was the Franklin-Nashville campaign in November and December of 1864—Forrest so denounced General John Bell Hood's battle strategy that he nearly came to blows with him. In the end, Hood's strategy (as Forrest feared) all but destroyed the great Army of Tennessee. Its survivors—on foot—tried to escape southward from Nashville in a bitter cold made more miserable without supplies, artillery, and even without shoes in many cases. Only Forrest and his troops, acting as rear guard and throwing themselves between the Confederate vanquished and the oncoming Union victors, saved the lives of those left.

The military renown of Nathan Bedford Forrest was but one side of the persona he left history. Most people who knew him, or knew of him, either loved or hated him.

His capacity to take command could be traced to his sixteenth year, at which time his father died and left him head of a family that included ten brothers and sisters. The family had moved from their longtime homestead in Marshall County to Mississippi. Forrest labored daily in the fields and nightly making buckskin clothing, shoes, and caps for his younger brothers.

One Sunday morning in 1844, the twenty-three-year-old Forrest was riding near his Hernando, Mississippi, home when he suddenly noticed a carriage up to its axle in mud and two women in distress—one of them the prettiest woman he had ever seen. Nearby, sitting atop their horses were two men watching in idle curiosity.

The neatly dressed Forrest waded into the morass and carried each woman to safety, then moved back to the carriage and put his shoulder to the wheel. With considerable effort, he loosened the carriage and turned to the watching men. With carefully chosen words, he advised both that if they were to stay much longer, each might fall victim to a thrashing. They departed.

The rescued women, mother and daughter, were appropriately thankful and ready to depart when Forrest asked the pleasure of calling on them in the future. The daughter, Mary Montgomery, became Mrs. Nathan Bedford Forrest a year later in April 1845, and spent a lifetime as the object of his intense affection and respect—some say even worship.

In 1851, with the encouragement of his uncle who had taught him the mercantile business—including slave trading—Forrest became a part of the Memphis business world. He became rich in the slave trade, and in 1859 discontinued both his Memphis businesses and his position as a Memphis alderman to devote time to his Mississippi farms. But on June 14, 1861, he was in Memphis again, this time to enlist in the Confederate army, the stepping-stone to national and international attention that lasted beyond his wartime exploits.

Even the postwar period had its moments of surprise and even more controversy for Forrest. After he returned to his Mississippi plantation in 1865 to develop his crops and restore his fortune, he developed strong friendships with former enemies. Several former Union officers rented from Forrest and shared his crops; others testified before congressional committees on his behalf or tried to obtain presidential pardons for him regarding his wartime activities.

One day, his war-horse King Philip (given him as a gift from the women of Columbus, Georgia, after Forrest saved their homes from raiders) became agitated when he saw a local military unit in Union uniforms riding onto the farm. The riders hoped to catch a glimpse of the famous general. The horse rushed the interlopers with teeth bared and front hoofs kicking toward them. When some of the confused soldiers struck back at the animal, Forrest's elderly black servant, Jerry, intervened and attacked the men with his bare hands. Both man and animal might have been hurt in the proceedings had not Forrest appeared from the house and restored order. The Federal officer in charge reportedly said: "General, now I can account for your success. Your negroes fight for you, and your horses fight for you."

Not all of Forrest's black workers, however, were as eager to fight for him. Some remembered his controversial West Tennessee raid at Fort Pillow near Henning, where 250 black Unionists were among the massacred in a fort of 600 defenders. Forrest later claimed that he offered a surrender that was accepted by the white soldiers but turned down by the blacks. He further claimed that many of the deaths had resulted as a retaliation for Union plundering under Colonel Fielding Hurst, a West Tennessean hated by local Confederate civilians (several of Hurst's men were in the fort). A Union doctor at Fort Pillow testified that Forrest and his officers rode up after the massacre and had trouble bringing order to their out-of-control men, but many historians lay the blame on Forrest's leadership.

After the war, Forrest invited even more fury when he killed one of his black plantation workers in a scuffle. The rest of the farm's two hundred workers (who were also members of the local militia) converged on the house in battle formation. The unarmed Forrest, with his wife standing near, gave a command to halt, order arms, and to disperse—which they agreed to do. Then they awaited the general's trial. He was taken before a black judge in a Reconstruction government. Testimony revealed that Forrest had heard a woman screaming in the black quarters, rushed to her aid, and, in self-defense, killed the husband who was attempting to beat her to death with a piece of stove wood. With the help of the woman he had rescued, Forrest was cleared.

In 1867, Forrest stepped into postwar notoriety after he became aware of the underground activities of his former chief of artillery, Williamson County's John Watson Morton, now a Nashville businessman. Morton belonged to a movement opposing the Reconstruction edict that denied former Confederate males the rights to vote and to bear arms. The men who belonged to this movement had learned the usefulness of scare tactics aimed at the black voters who were gaining a measure of political power. Using a name and costumed appearance created a year earlier by a group of Pulaski college students (who intended merely to amuse themselves as a fraternal group), the evolving Ku Klux Klan caught Forrest's attention. He traveled to Nashville to see Morton. In their meeting on a Nashville street, Forrest said, "John, I hear this Kuklux Klan is organized in Nashville, and I know you are in it. I want to join."

That day, Forrest was officially admitted as a Klan member, reportedly becoming the first Grand Wizard. By 1870, however, the Klan was ready to fold. Radical Reconstruction was ending, and the oppression of former Confederates was beginning to ease. The KKK was receiving bad publicity nationwide, and the threat of government action against the group weighed heavily on the minds of its members. Forrest issued an order which, according to various sources, either disbanded the Klan or suspended its activities. (A new KKK made its resurgence after 1915.)

Forrest's life of unending action finally came to a close at the age of fifty-six. His health had been weakened from wounds in a Confederate retreat from Hardin County's Battle of Shiloh and in engagements at Tupelo. He also took falls from at least fifteen horses shot from under him during heavy fighting. The battered Forrest, however, died in 1877 from a common wartime ailment, a chronic dysentery from which he had been suffering for years.

77
Sam R. Watkins
Chronicles of an Everyday Soldier

Sam R. Watkins, who saw tragedy, humor, and compassion.

Columbia native Sam R. Watkins became one of the most respected chroniclers of the Civil War, but even his reporting skills failed him when he tried to relate the horror he witnessed one winter's night in 1862 at Hampshire Crossing, Virginia.

Watkins was then a private (later a corporal) in the "Maury Grays," part of the Confederacy's First Tennessee Regiment. The Grays were to relieve Arkansas and Georgia regiments stationed at the stream, St. John's Run. When they reached their destination, however, they found a terrifying sight. In unbelievably frigid cold, they discovered eleven soldiers frozen as if in suspended animation. Each had frozen to death at his post of duty. Two of the men, still standing, had held onto their guns. Watkins later recalled the corpses being "as hard as the icicles that hung from their hands and faces and clothing."

Watkins was so shaken that when he recounted his war recollections twenty years later as a series for his hometown newspaper, the *Columbia Herald*, he found that the St. John's Run incident still haunted him. "I cannot tell the facts as I desire to," he said. "In fact, my hand trembles so, and my feelings are so overcome, that it is hard for me to write at all."

Watkins's memoirs were written in 1881-82. The work was later published, and two thousand copies were quickly purchased. In 1900 another two thousand copies of the rare book were issued in a reprint edition by the *Chattanooga Times*, and again they quickly sold out. The book was called *"Co. Aytch": Maury Grays First Tennessee Regiment, or a Side Show of the Big Show*. Many historians consider Watkins's accounts one of the best offered by a common soldier about the Civil War. He was thorough in his descriptions of everyday life, its horrors and humor, its dullness and excitement, its inefficiencies and moments of success.

Many of his recollections were painful. One involved a friend and comrade injured in the fierce fighting at Perryville, Kentucky, in October 1862:

I helped bring off our wounded that night. We worked the whole night. The next morning about daylight a wounded comrade, Sam Campbell, complained of being cold, and asked me to lie down beside him. I did so, and was soon asleep; when I awoke the poor fellow was stiff and cold in death. His spirit had flown to its home beyond the skies.

On the retreat from Kentucky, military necessity required that Watkins and his comrades set fire to a large number of army stores in order to deny them to the Federals. The Maury Grays drew three days' rations from provisions and, much to their regret, de-

stroyed the rest. The immense waste was not lost on Watkins, who mourned the fact that he helped destroy enough goods to supply the South for a year. Assuming that supplies would be issued when the army stopped for the night, Watkins and his friends continued their retreat.

We supposed our general and commissaries knew what they were doing, and at night we would again draw rations, but we didn't.

The Yankee cavalry are worrying our rear guards. There is danger of an attack at any moment. No soldier is allowed to break ranks.

We thought, well surely we will draw rations tonight. But we didn't. We are marching for Cumberland Gap; the country has long ago been made desolate by the alternate occupation of both armies. There are no provisions in the country.

The Battle of Shiloh (April 6-7, 1862, around Pittsburg Landing in Hardin County) was the first major conflict for the Maury Grays on their home soil. Of Shiloh, Watkins wrote with as much humor as could be mixed with tragedy about "a big, fat colonel," wounded and rallying the First Tennessee with "Give 'em goss, boys . . . Give 'em Hail Columbia!" Watkins asked the colonel where he was wounded; the officer thundered his response: "My son, I am wounded in the arm, in the leg, in the head, in the body, and in another place which I have a delicacy in mentioning."

In a separate moment that Sunday on the first day of battle, a Confederate courier rode ahead of his men before the last attack, aboard a "captured" mule. One of Watkins's friends exclaimed: "Just look at that brave man, charging right in the jaws of death."

The courier, yelling back, corrected him: "It arn't me, boys, it's this blarsted old mule. Whoa! Whoa!"

Watkins's writings provided keen insights into the effects of war—on the body and the mind. "The soldier," he wrote, "may at one moment be in good spirits, laughing and talking. The wing of the death angel touches him. He knows that his time has come. It is but a question of time with him then. He knows that his days are numbered. I cannot explain it."

He recounted the story of Bob Stout. En route to Chattanooga in September 1863, the Maury Grays stopped for the night outside Chickamauga. Three days of provisions were rationed to each soldier, but his friend Stout, who appeared "woe-begone," somberly declined his rations. Asked if he felt ill, Stout shocked his fellow Confederates by answering: "No . . . Boys, my days are numbered, my time has come. In three days from today, I will be lying right yonder on that hillside a corpse. Ah, you may laugh; my time has come."

He began to distribute his belongings among various companions, asking that a silver watch and twenty-dollar gold piece be sent to his father. Two days later, the regiment engaged the Union at the Battle of Chickamauga. Two hours of close, intense fighting ended when Confederate General Nathan Bedford Forrest ordered a retreat. Crashing artillery shells overhead seemed to Watkins "the very incarnation of death itself."

Finally, Watkins and Stout stopped. Watkins looked toward his friend and exclaimed happily: "Bob, you wern't killed, as you expected." Stout turned as if to speak, but, before he could answer, fate fulfilled his premonition. An enemy cannonball struck Stout near the waist. "His spirit had flown before his body struck the ground," wrote Watkins, who added, "Farewell, friend; we will meet over yonder."

When the Confederate army wintered at Dalton, Georgia, during the early months of 1864, many soldiers experienced a renewed sense of religious fervor. Some attended divine services each day. One nighttime service was particularly symbolic to Watkins when the Reverend J. G. Bolton, chaplain of the Fiftieth Tennessee Regiment, led services as usual. A long bench stood at the front of assembled men for the purpose of "calling up mourners." During this service, ten men kneeled at the mourners' bench in fervent prayer. The bench was situated beneath a tree which a few days earlier had caught fire and smoldered and burned during routine street cleaning. On this night, no one noticed that the smoldering continued. In Watkins's words:

> Ten of them were kneeling at this mourner's bench, pouring out their souls in prayer to God, asking Him for the forgiveness of their sins, and for the salvation of their souls, for Jesus Christ their Redeemer's sake, when the burning tree, without any warning, fell with a crash right across the ten mourners, crushing and killing them instantly. God had heard their prayers. Their souls had been carried to heaven.

That the tragedy of war could also produce heartfelt friendship with the enemy became the centerpiece of another Watkins story. On duty at Palmetto, Georgia, where the new Confederate army commander, General John Bell Hood, headquartered in the fall of 1864, Watkins often traveled to enemy outposts for a chat. His side trips were enjoyable as long as "some popinjay of a tacky officer" did not appear. Friendships between soldiers of North and South were not uncommon, and Watkins enjoyed friendship wherever he found it.

He joined his Yankee acquaintances for breakfast one morning. While thus engaged, he happened to look down the road and dishearteningly noticed approaching Union infantry. He did not run, for reasons he could not explain. The approaching soldiers were black, led by what appeared to be a white captain, who announced he would relieve the outposts. While he talked, the captain also noticed Watkins.

"What is this Rebel doing here?" he demanded to know.

One of Watkins's Union friends tried to speak in his favor, hoping to prevent a capture, but the more the fellow talked, the angrier his captain became. Watkins remembered the captain's intense anger: "He started toward me two or three times. He was starting, I could see by the flush of his face, to take hold of me, anyhow."

While Watkins's Union friends "tried to protest, and said a few cuss words," the captain peered at them in apparent hostility. Watkins seized the moment to try his escape. He cocked and pointed his gun toward the captain, who was too fearful to turn his head and command his troops to take action. "The cavalry motioned their hands at me, as much as to say, 'Run, Johnny, run.'"

Watkins wrote that he "ran like a quarter-horse. I never saw or heard any more of the captain of the blacks or his guard afterward."

Sam R. Watkins fought in every battle in which the Confederacy's Army of Tennessee participated and finally surrendered with the war-torn fighting force in 1865 to Union General William Tecumseh Sherman. After the war, Watkins returned home to Columbia, where he married his sweetheart, Virginia "Jennie" Mayes. Watkins was sixty-two when he died in 1901.

78
Charlotte Gailor

A Wife's Search for News from the Battlefront

Shortly after her Confederate husband was killed October 8, 1862, at the Battle of Perryville, Kentucky, Charlotte Gailor made a weary journey from her Memphis home to the battle site. She was dismayed that she could find neither details of the death nor her husband's body. Confederates had already retreated from the area under General Braxton Bragg. The battle itself, after an early possibility for the South's victory, left the Confederacy in a bad situation. It had failed to clinch the pivotal victory that might have lured legions of Kentuckians into the Confederate army.

Charlotte's despair immediately deepened when her young daughter, Hattie, became ill and died. Her son, Thomas Frank Gailor, would later write, "The doctor was sent for; but the pickets refused to let him come to the house at night; and my sister died in my mother's arms."

In a grief-stricken pursuit of information about her husband, Charlotte had few clues. Her first real hope came about six months later when a friend from Jackson, Mississippi, paid a visit. That friend, a Mrs. Dudley, was en route home with the body of a slain brother from the Perryville battlefield. She asked Charlotte to accompany her through Union lines to Jackson.

In Mississippi, where Confederate forces had withdrawn, Charlotte Gailor thought she might learn the details of her husband's last day, perhaps from his regiment. The night before her departure (this time with seven-year-old Thomas Frank in tow) she received yet another visitor—who happened to be a Confederate spy. Having heard of her pending journey, he asked her to smuggle papers of vital importance for his commander, General Nathan Bedford Forrest. Charlotte hid the papers in her bosom. Thomas Frank, meanwhile, had his clothing stuffed with letters from neighbors for delivery to their loved ones on the battlefield. "The most important of them were sewn into the lining of my jacket, which was buttoned up to my throat, and I remember that I felt like a mummy, hardly able to move," he recalled years later in his memoirs, *Some Memories.*

The next day, when asked by a Union general to take the "iron-clad" Union oath (not to assist a Confederate, even one close to death), Charlotte Gailor flatly refused. Asked to sign a "parole of honor," she again declined.

"My word is as good as my oath," she said. "Why can't you let me go, I cannot fight, neither can my little boy; and then you will be giving the poor Confederacy two more mouths to feed." The general scribbled a pass and hurled it at her feet. Retrieving it from the floor, she snapped: "I am almost as much obliged as I would be, if you had acted politely." Then she strode from the room.

"We met General Forrest and his Staff some miles further on and mother gave him that precious report, which may have helped him when he made his raid on Memphis," wrote Thomas Frank Gailor of the raid which Forrest would not conduct until August 1864, a year later. The Union army's control of Memphis suffered from the smuggling activities of Southern women, whose favorite hiding place was generally their oversized skirts. The reluctance of Federal troops to search women aided numerous smuggling operations. (Union soldiers, however, overcame their shyness about checking beneath the petticoat of one woman, who stepped out of her carriage with great difficulty. Beneath her oversized girdle were tied a dozen pairs of boots, each containing supplies of great value to the Confederate cause.)

Charlotte Gailor's continued search for information about her husband proved fruitless in Mississippi. She followed the Confederate army throughout the state and then back to Tennessee. Her trail put her on a Chattanooga-bound train crowded with Confederate soldiers. The train held even more suspense for the mother-son duo, as her son later described:

Maj. Martin Walt, a friend of ours, was on the train, and just as we were approaching the tunnel, near Sewanee, he brought a satchel to my mother, saying:

"We are about to enter a long tunnel and there are no lights. This satchel is full of money for the soldiers, who are to be paid in Chattanooga. There are rough people on this train, and they may attack me in the tunnel. Please keep the satchel and hold it tight until we get out of the darkness."

. . . when we moved into the dark tunnel mother said to me:

"Tom, quick; someone is trying to take this satchel away from me."

I reached over and felt a hand pulling at the satchel and I bit into it with all the might of my strong young teeth. The hand was hurriedly withdrawn.

When we emerged from the darkness of the tunnel we saw a woman in the seat in front of us nursing her hand.

Eventually, the details of Major Frank M. Gailor's death did become known to his family. As Charlotte would learn, he had been killed as he knelt to offer water to a fallen comrade who had urged him to leave the field. Alabama Captain L. A. McClung, the wounded soldier he had aided, quoted Major Gailor's last words: "I will never desert a friend in your condition." McClung related the story before dying himself ten days after the battle.

Her search over, Charlotte Gailor returned to Memphis. Another visitor suddenly appeared on her doorstep—an unidentified young woman, later exposed as a Confederate spy, who brought Major Gailor's sword and spurs. The woman happened to be in Kentucky when the major's effects were delivered to army headquarters. Since she was headed toward Memphis, the woman strapped the items around her waist under a hoopskirt to prevent their being commandeered en route.

Delighted to receive her husband's effects, Charlotte mentioned the kind gesture to several neighbors, one of whom betrayed to Federal authorities the whereabouts of the sword, which was soon confiscated.

When Charlotte marched to the office of Union General Cadwallader C. Washburn, he insisted that she had five minutes to state her business. In less than one minute, she declared: "You have taken away my husband's sword. I cannot use it, neither can my little boy. Please give it back to me. If you were to be killed tomorrow, you would like your wife to have your sword."

The general relented, admitting: "Of course you can have that sword. And I am glad to find a woman who can say what she wants in few words."

As for Thomas Frank Gailor, the carrier of contraband letters, he grew up to become the Protestant Episcopal church's third bishop of Tennessee, a position he held for forty-two years. From being a rector of the Church of the Messiah in Pulaski in 1879, Gailor went into education. He began a lifetime association in 1882 with the University of the South in Sewanee, from professor and chaplain to chancellor—a posi-

tion he held from 1908 until his death in 1935. He was also the first president (1919) of the National Council of the Episcopal Church in America. Gaining an international reputation, Bishop Gailor often preached at London's Westminster Abbey at the request of King Edward VII and King George V. His favorite saying, frequently repeated in sermons, was: "Don't be afraid, only believe."

79
John Hunt Morgan
"Thunderbolt of the Confederacy"
—In Love and War

General and Mrs. John Hunt Morgan on their wedding day.

In his romantic pursuit of Murfreesboro's Martha "Mattie" Ready, Confederate cavalry leader John Hunt Morgan of Kentucky was determined to present her (and her sister for good measure) with an extraordinary gift. Rather than flowers, Morgan planned to deliver a captured Union general to her door. He settled for thirty-eight Union prisoners instead.

Mattie was the twenty-one-year-old daughter of a prominent Middle Tennessee family. Her father, attorney Charles Ready, had been a congressman from 1853 to 1859. While residing in Washington, Mattie had become a stylish society girl and a trendsetter, popularizing the 1850s' vogue of combing a neat curl in the middle of her forehead. Back home in Rutherford County during the Civil War, she patiently held out some hope of marrying the man of her dreams. She had turned down numerous suitors in Washington, including a congressman from Illinois.

She finally found her true love in Morgan, the "Thunderbolt of the Confederacy." He was known for his guerrilla-warfare expeditions behind Union lines destroying railroad and communication lines. The couple's first meeting was in the spring of 1862 when her father invited the already famous Morgan to dinner. The elder Ready sent advance word home: "Tell Mattie that Captain Morgan is a widower and a little sad. I want her to sing for him."

Morgan was entranced with the songs—and with his young hostess. On a later day, he would appear in front of her father's house at the head of a twenty-six-member cavalry unit. Vowing he would capture a Union general and bring him to the Readys' house, Morgan set off on his mission. He also hoped that his prisoner would be worthy of an exchange for captured Confederate General Simon Bolivar Buckner, one of the officers who made the controversial decision to surrender Fort Donelson (and Middle Tennessee as a result).

Departing the Ready home March 7, 1862, and arriving six miles southeast of Nashville, Morgan and his men donned Union overcoats and proceeded to capture every Yankee soldier in the vicinity. The Confederates, however, did not find any high-ranking officers. Morgan, sending the prisoners with his command in different directions, moved alone to Nashville. He came upon a Union outpost commanded by a lieutenant. Posing as a Yankee colonel, Morgan denounced the lieutenant for not properly running his post and arrested the whole group for dereliction of duty. Only after Morgan had disarmed the soldiers and moved them toward Confederate lines did the confused Yankees realize they had been duped.

Morgan's troops, meanwhile, had confronted a larger group of Union cavalry and lost most of their prisoners. Unable to find a general, the undaunted Morgan still returned to Murfreesboro and the Ready house with thirty-eight prisoners in tow.

The wedding between Morgan and Mattie Ready took place in Murfreesboro on December 14, 1862, barely two weeks prior to the major battle for that town, the Battle of Stones River. The couple's nighttime ceremony was one of the great social events of Murfreesboro and of the Army of Tennessee. It is said to have been "a scene from the romance novels come to life. . . . [Mattie] was a beautiful Southern belle in her elegant lace gown and bridal veil; John stood handsome and proud in his new general's uniform." Even the Confederacy's president, Jefferson Davis, made a quick appearance earlier in the day to sign Morgan's official promotion to brigadier general. The vows were given by the Confederacy's "Fighting Bishop," General Leonidas Polk, and in attendance were Generals Braxton Bragg, William Hardee, Benjamin Franklin Cheatham, and John C. Breckinridge (the latter a former United States vice president and an 1860 presidential candidate against Lincoln).

In one of history's not uncommon coincidences, on this same night an unknown Arkansas infantry sergeant, Andrew J. Campbell, was enduring the cold night in camp north of town. An Irish immigrant, Campbell had been drafted into the Confederate army but, when pressed into action, realized his sympathies lay with the Union. In a twist of fate that would bring Morgan's famous escapades to an end, Campbell and the Thunderbolt of the Confederacy would soon cross paths more than one hundred miles east in the small town of Greeneville.

But settling now with his bride in Murfreesboro and calling Tennessee "their state," Morgan became interested in religion. He also began to consider that being with his wife was more important than conducting the business of war—going so far as to promise her that his days of raiding would soon end. Morgan's career, moreover, began to decline following his victorious Christmas Raid into Kentucky days after the wedding. (That raid forced the Union to divert thousands of soldiers from the Battle of Stones River in order to chase Morgan.)

Having gained a reputation for protecting his men by using a calculating approach with the enemy, Morgan soon developed a reputation for throwing his troops recklessly into battle so that he could return quickly to Mattie. Historians continue to argue whether the marriage may have caused Morgan to lose his effectiveness as a raider. He and his men also carried a reputation for robbing and looting after the Kentucky raid. Reportedly, they robbed banks, civilians, and prisoners of war. Morgan was later captured during his great raid into Ohio, where he was imprisoned until he escaped in November 1863.

More than a year and a half after the noted marriage, a Greeneville boy, thirteen-year-old James Leahy (or Leady), decided to seek out Union forces at Bulls Gap, sixteen miles from his East Tennessee home. Angry because Confederate soldiers had taken his corn crop, the boy wanted revenge and told Union General Alvan C. Gillem the exact whereabouts of Southern troops.

Attacking Confederate outposts near Mosheim the next morning, on September 4, 1864, Gillem and his men turned toward Greeneville, where Morgan was resting comfortably in the family home of Mrs. Catharine D. Williams, widow of a wealthy physician. Morgan and his men had just completed a fifty-six-mile ride in the rain from Bristol to Greeneville and had hoped to surprise Gillem at Bulls Gap.

Roused from a deep sleep by Mrs. Williams's cries, Morgan soon realized the town was under attack. Pulling on his uniform pants and still in his nightshirt, Morgan rushed to ask, "Where are they?" Mrs. Williams's reply was: "Everywhere!"

Running from the house with several of his staff officers, Morgan hid briefly under the porch of St. James Episcopal Church. Reporting the seriousness of the situation to him, Major Charles Albert Withers begged Morgan to return to the house and wait for their own troops. "It's no use," Morgan replied. "The boys can not get here in time. The Yankees will never take me prisoner again."

While one of his staff officers managed to escape and the rest were captured, Morgan headed for the Williams garden, determined not to surrender. He had promised his wife as much and had repeated that promise in his last telegram to her the day before.

During his escape attempt, he was chased by two Union soldiers across the Williams's grounds. Then, in the "twist of fate" brought full circle, Morgan was spotted by his former soldier Andrew J. Campbell, now a private in the Union army. Campbell, ordering him to halt, fired when Morgan continued in the opposite direction. Campbell's fatal shot "pierced Morgan's heart six inches below the chin. Morgan threw up his hands, gasped 'Oh God!' and fell forward into the mud."

Not until two of Morgan's captured officers were asked to identify the body did the Union realize that it had killed General John Hunt Morgan. A number of other ironies surrounded Morgan's death. After the rainy march, for instance, Morgan had ordered his troops to discharge their weapons in case their ammunition had been dampened by rain. When the enemy attacked that morning, Morgan's staff assumed that the gunfire they heard was in response to their commander's orders. Furthermore, a Williams family member, Jacob Rumbough, had warned Morgan to sleep with his troops rather than in a private home, but Morgan had ignored the advice.

In death, Morgan traveled nearly as much as he would have in leading his men in battle. Reports surfaced that Union troops celebrated Morgan's death by parading his body through the streets of Greeneville. They took the body from town, and confronting Confederate soldiers, placed it on a blanket beside the road while a skirmish ensued. Afterward, Morgan's remains were transferred back to the Williams house where his staff officers and the Williams family prepared the body for burial.

Morgan's body then was carried to three different funeral services and burial sites. The first funeral was for the benefit of his men at Abington, Virginia, where he had a headquarters. Morgan was placed in a vault for a week. He was taken afterwards to Richmond, Virginia, where he lay in state at the Capitol for grieving Southerners. The next day, while proceeding to a nearby cemetery, the funeral cortege had to stop while soldiers in the procession quelled a Federal attack near Richmond. Upon their return, the soldiers placed Morgan in yet another burial vault. But Morgan's travels did not end there. After the war in 1868, his family and admirers had Morgan's body returned to his native Lexington, Kentucky, for "interment in the Bluegrass country out of which he had marched to fame seven years earlier."

Mattie Morgan was unable to attend the Richmond burial because she was pregnant with the couple's child. When she bore a daughter, Mattie named her Johnnie in her husband's honor. Eventually Mattie remarried, to Lebanon's Judge James Williamson, and had more children. She died at the age of forty-six in 1887; Johnnie died a year later of typhoid fever at the age of twenty-three, shortly after her marriage to an Alabama minister.

80
Spencer Talley

*Surviving Hell's Half Acre
at the Battle of Stones River*

As Christmas 1862 neared, so did the origin of "Hell's Half Acre," a plot of ground near Murfreesboro that became death's door for the Confederate Army of Tennessee.

Confederate Captain Spencer Talley, from nearby Wilson County, had approached the holidays with a festive heart despite the events of the Civil War. He was within reach of home for the first time in months because the huge Army of Tennessee had chosen Murfreesboro for its winter quarters. The Confederacy's leaders immediately began a series of parties and celebrations, including the marriage of one of its leading generals, John Hunt Morgan, to Murfreesboro's Martha "Mattie" Ready.

Since the Middle Tennessee country was home to so many Confederate soldiers, untold numbers of relatives and friends in neighboring counties kept up a steady stream of visits into the army camps that dotted Rutherford County. All the while, Rebel pickets kept a close watch on the road to Nashville, where the Union's Army of the Cumberland was encamped. With winter weather threatening, Captain Talley was assigned a journey into the countryside to seek supplies. He went home, knowing that his mother would help. Indeed, Mrs. Talley had made her sons "a goodly supply of heavy jeans and wool socks," and her neighbors had contributed clothing and food for the soldiers.

The day after Christmas, the Army of Tennessee staged a ball in the new Rutherford County Courthouse for its highest-ranking officers. Talley was thrilled when his commanding officer, Colonel P. D. Cunningham, chose not to attend and offered his uniform to Talley, who had fantasized about attending a gala for generals and colonels only. But his fantasy was cut short when news that Union movements had

been spotted toward town broke up the gathering. Officers bolted in every direction to prepare for the coming battle. Talley returned his borrowed uniform and joined the troops in position west of Murfreesboro along Stones River. The enemy, moving southeast from Nashville, lumbered into position. Both armies, realizing during the night that a battle was imminent, waited for daylight.

As was customary, the respective regimental bands serenaded their troops—the Union bands playing such tunes as "Yankee Doodle" and "Hail Columbia," while the Confederate bands rendered such songs as "Dixie" and "The Bonnie Blue Flag."

Because of the proximity of the two camps, each side could hear every note played by its rival band, a situation which prompted a battle of the bands. This musical duel continued until an unidentified Union band struck a stirring rendition of "Home, Sweet Home," a mournful tune immediately picked up by a Confederate band. Soon, all of the bands from both armies had joined the effort, filling the wintry evening air with sentiments of home.

W. J. Worsham, a Knoxville native (who would return home at war's end and become a pharmacist) was a fife player and head musician in the Confederacy's Nineteenth Tennessee Infantry Regiment. Worsham recalled the incident in his later regimental memoirs: "After our bands had ceased playing, we could hear the sweet refrain as it died away on the cool frosty air on the Federal side." Worsham noted the irony in the playing of "Home, Sweet Home" on the eve of the devastating Battle of Stones River, in which more than twenty thousand soldiers would be killed, wounded, or captured. "Who knows what stimulus this 'Home, Sweet Home' gave each one the next morning in battle," he wrote. "And as the minnie balls and grape sounded the early reveille next morning, each thought it was for home and country."

Perhaps the strains of "Home, Sweet Home" most effectively inspired the Confederates, who launched a surprise morning attack. They were at first victorious, because, caught unprepared, Union forces suffered heavy losses and withdrew. The tide was turned when the Union concentrated its cannons in a clump of trees which Rutherford Countians called "Round Forest" but which the soldiers renamed Hell's Half Acre. The cannon fire cut down one Confederate regiment after another.

In the second day of fighting, January 2, 1863, Talley was wounded in the Union's artillery blast. Unable to "tell whether the ball had lodged in me or passed through," Talley said, he began crawling toward safety. Suddenly, he saw his colonel's uniform—this time shredded and bloodstained, because P. D. Cunningham was dead. Talley managed to make his way back to the Murfreesboro courthouse, by now converted into a hospital. There, he would see Cunningham's body again. Talley later wrote:

> When his body was brought to the Hospital my heart was full of sorrow, and regardless of my wound I secured a vessel of water and washed his blood stained face, and hands. The coat which I had worn a few nights before to the grand ball & festival was now spotted & saturated with his life's blood. I removed the stains from his coat as best I could with the cold water and a rag, combed his unkempt hair & whiskers and laid his body with many others in the Court House at Murfreesboro.

Historians claim that Stones River effectively split open the Confederacy in the Southeast, allowing a Union line to develop toward Chattanooga and Atlanta. The spoils included strategic rail lines and immense supplies. Murfreesboro, meanwhile, became one gigantic hospital when the Confederacy's commander, General Braxton Bragg, ordered a retreat and abandoned thousands of wounded.

Talley was able to survive the war and return home to Lebanon. The father of five children, he became a schoolteacher and farmer. He lived until 1920.

81
Adelicia Hayes Acklen

*Fortune at Stake: Manipulating Men
from Both North and South*

In 1863, Nashville's Adelicia Hayes Acklen plotted and charmed her way into a million-dollar fortune by playing both Confederate and Union soldiers to her advantage.

Her second husband having died of apparent pneumonia on their Louisiana plantation, Adelicia learned that their cotton crop was in jeopardy of being burned by retreating Confederates under General Leonidas Polk to keep it out of Union hands. With a female cousin, she headed for Louisiana in a daring eight-month adventure. According to one version, Adelicia Acklen conducted "some of the cleverest scheming of the war." Crossing battle lines, she and her cousin secured the Confederacy's permission to move the cotton to the river. While Rebel soldiers agreed to guard more than two thousand of her cotton bales, Adelicia engaged Yankee soldiers to help transport the cotton to Union-held New Orleans.

The ruse worked because she convinced each side that the cotton's sale would help its cause. A ship transported the goods to Liverpool, England, and the widow Acklen collected nearly a million dollars in gold—a deal that made her one of America's wealthiest women.

In the life of Adelicia Hayes Acklen, however, wealth and social status were mixed with personal tragedy. Born in 1817, she was one of seven children of a prosperous Nashville lawyer, Oliver Bliss Hayes. A distant cousin of future President Rutherford B. Hayes, Adelicia was educated at the Nashville Female Academy and there saw the Marquis de LaFayette, who addressed her class during his 1820s' American tour. This event possibly sparked her urge to travel overseas, which she would do in grand style both before and after the Civil War. She was engaged to marry at seventeen, but her betrothed, Harvard-educated lawyer Alfonso Gibbs, died that year of typhoid fever. She refused further romantic involvement—a commitment that lasted five years.

In 1838, Adelicia thought again about romance. She agreed to a cousin's suggestion that they visit Fairvue Estate in Gallatin—the home of Middle Tennessee's wealthiest and most eligible bachelor. Isaac Franklin was known as a leading slaveowner whose wealth was tied to the slave trade. He personally worked more than six hundred slaves on his plantations in three states (Tennessee, Louisiana, and Texas). Adelicia's visit, however, was a disappointment: While the home was lovely, the owner was absent.

As she signed the house register under the clever eye of an elderly black butler, she mentioned her disappointment at missing the proprietor. "It don't make no difference ma'am," the butler drawled knowingly. "You couldn't have caught him." When Franklin did return home, he did not fail to notice Adelicia's frank message scrawled in the register: "I like this house. I'd like to meet the owner."

Within a year, the two were married. Adelicia was twenty-one, and Isaac was fifty. The couple remained happily married for seven years until his death in Louisiana after a short illness. Afterward, his body was brought home to Tennessee reportedly preserved in three barrels of whiskey.

But the young widow's tragedies were not over: Six weeks later, the couple's two eldest daughters died of croup and bronchitis. Reeling from despair, she was forced into litigation (which took years) because her husband's will stipulated separate legacies for his daughters and other endowments for local institutions. She successfully fought for the legacies of her daughters and became probably the wealthiest woman in the South—owning more than eight thousand acres in Louisiana, more than ten thousand acres in Texas, the two-thousand-acre Fairvue in Tennessee, and many other assets.

Adelicia's second marriage, three years later in 1849, was to Joseph A. S. Acklen, prominent Huntsville lawyer, Mexican War colonel, and grandson of the founder of Huntsville, John Hunt. Their romance was avidly followed in Nashville newspapers, becoming the talk of the town. Together, the Acklens built the stately Belmont Mansion, a stylized Italian villa that became the center of Nashville's social scene after 1850 and one of the South's most elegant homes. One of the couple's sons, William Hayes Ackland (he changed the spelling of his surname), wrote interesting accounts of his mother . Whenever Adelicia held her annual ball at Belmont, remembered Ackland, "My mother always consulted an almanac before sending out cards of invitation so that the evening selected should be the evening when the moon was full in order that her guests might wander through the gardens by its light."

Adelicia Acklen generally spared no expense for either Belmont's house or grounds. A conservatory, bear house, and zoo were also added, and the grounds were open to the public on most days.

For more than a decade, the family divided its activities between Nashville and a winter home in Angola, Louisiana. The Acklens established a tradition of fine entertaining and Southern hospitality. But the happiness was broken in 1855 by the deaths of three children, including the last child from Adelicia's first marriage (she had ten children in all).

During the Civil War, the Acklens relied on the kindness of President James K. Polk's widow, who stored silver and other valuable possessions in danger of being taken by advancing Union troops. Since she was protected as the widow of a president, Mrs. Polk provided this favor for several of her friends. Meanwhile, the Acklens donated as much as thirty thousand dollars to the Confederate war effort, and Adelicia worked in area hospitals. When the Union advanced into Middle Tennessee after the February 1862 fall of Fort Donelson, she encouraged her husband to escape to their Louisiana home, where pneumonia took his life in September 1863. Because Belmont was occupied by invading Federals, it remained safe from destruction.

After her successful plot that generated a fortune in cotton sales, Adelicia Acklen traveled in Europe with her surviving children. She was received in England at the court of Queen Victoria and in France at the court of Emperor Napoleon III. In Paris, the highest ranks of French society toasted her as a living example of the aristocratic Southern style surviving the war.

Returning to Nashville in late 1866, Adelicia married a third time, to Dr. William Arthur Cheatham, a cousin of Confederate General Benjamin Franklin Cheatham. After an elaborate ten-thousand-dollar wedding, Adelicia's fortunes seemed to reverse during the course of a long-term Southern depression. She later became estranged from her husband and sold Belmont. The mansion would become an exclusive girls' school: first Belmont Junior College (1890-1912) and then Ward-Belmont (1912-1951), Belmont College, and finally Belmont University.

Living with a daughter, Adelicia built a new home in Washington, D.C., along Pennsylvania Avenue. After developing pneumonia during an 1887 furniture-buying trip to New York, she died at the age of seventy. She was buried in the Acklen Mausoleum in Nashville's Mt. Olivet Cemetery under the shadow of a white-marble statue of "Peri," a fallen angel, which she once had transported from Italy to Tennessee.

82
Henry Watterson

Words Fired in Anger:
The Rebel Newspaper on the Run

Newspaperman Henry Watterson once set up his printing presses in the face of advancing Union forces, and, as a consequence, was forced to abandon the editorial type he had prepared which cursed Northern troops. Reading the type, Northern artillery battery members promptly fed the material into a cannon barrel and shot it at Watterson's retreating wagon. Although no one was harmed, Watterson loved to recall this incident as the only time he ever had his words fired back at him.

The son of Bedford County's Congressman Harvey Watterson, Watterson was born in 1840 in Washington, D.C. He spent his earliest years shuttling with his politician father between the United States capital and Bedford County. During his childhood, he overcame partial blindness from scarlet fever and learned to scan written works quickly in order to save his eyes. Later, as a congressional page, Watterson became particularly fond of an aging and bald congressman who offered his time to recommend books from the Library of Congress. Watterson later recalled the death of his friendly mentor—former President John Quincy Adams—in the midst of a congressional session.

When the Civil War erupted in 1861, Watterson was a twenty-one-year-old journalist in the nation's capital, having stood beside Abraham Lincoln during the president's first inaugural address. Several months later when his home state seceded from the Union, Watterson wanted to be identified as a Tennessean. Despite his opposition to secession, he returned to Tennessee and joined the Confederate army.

During much of the war, Watterson served on the staffs of various Confederate leaders, including ousted Tennessee Governor Isham G. Harris, and Generals Leonidas Polk, Nathan Bedford Forrest, John Bell Hood, and Joseph E. Johnston. While General Braxton Bragg commanded the Army of Tennessee, Watterson edited the popular Southern propaganda newspaper, *Rebel*, which catered to members of the Confederate army. He and the paper were always on the run, along with the Tennessee seat of government. (Those who led the state into secession were in exile with

The obstinate Confederate journalist Henry Watterson.

the Confederacy, never able to control enough territory to reestablish the government; the archives and treasury were also packed up and moved regularly.)

Watterson used the *Rebel* to entertain the South's readers, to feed disinformation to any Northerners who found copies, and to criticize Bragg's generalship. Angered, Bragg forced Watterson to resign by threatening to restrict the paper's distribution in Southern army camps. Unaware that Watterson had quit, the Union army later captured the presses in Selma, Alabama. Publishing one final issue, the Union attacked Watterson in print, broke up the presses, and dumped the equipment in a river.

When the war ended, Watterson resumed his civilian career in journalism and married Rebecca Ewing, the daughter of former Tennessee Congressman Andrew Ewing. At Nashville, Watterson briefly operated the *Republican Banner* until his fame as an editor spread to Kentucky. He accepted an offer to be editor of the *Louisville Journal*, which he later consolidated with another paper to form the *Louisville Courier-Journal*.

In addition to being an owner of the Louisville paper, the former Confederate wrote his way into journalism history. Over the course of the next fifty years at the helm of the *Courier-Journal*, he became one of the most influential and most quoted Southern editors of his time, and a champion of the New South.

In 1917, the nationally prominent Watterson received the Pulitzer Prize for his editorials in support of America's entry into World War I—a crowning achievement in a life that had always been associated with the nation's issues. Prior to his death in 1921, Watterson carried the distinction of having met every president of the United States from his friend Adams to Franklin D. Roosevelt, with the one exception of William Henry Harrison.

83
Lucy Virginia French

Witnessing the Erosion of the Old South

In the summer of 1863, McMinnville's Lucy Virginia Smith French visited nearby Beersheba Springs resort, hoping to remain long enough to work on her writing and escape the strife of bad health and strains on her marriage. The resort, known as the "queen of the hill country in Tennessee," also seemed the best place to escape the Civil War, since McMinnville was occupied by Federal forces. What Lucy found at this noted Grundy County resort was even greater strife, because the war inevitably ended all genteel life in Tennessee.

For nearly thirty years, people had been coming to Beersheba Springs for relaxation and health benefits. Writers especially found inspiration there, among them Mary Murfree, who came from nearby Rutherford County and spent fifteen summers there. (She would use the resort as a model in her famous novels and short stories of the late nineteenth century under the pen name Charles Egbert Craddock.)

The retreat had been founded in 1834 when McMinnville merchant John Cain built a few log cabins near a big iron springs and named the site for his wife, Beersheba. When the iron-rich springs were found to possess medicinal qualities, establishment of a resort soon followed. Beersheba Springs' turning point came in 1854, when John Armfield, one of the South's

Lucy Virginia French found no refuge from invading troops.

biggest slave dealers, bought out several of the landowners, sold lots to wealthy Southerners, built fine cottages, and then constructed his showpiece, a four-hundred-room hotel which indulged guests with a French chef and a band from New Orleans.

Lucy French's husband, John Hopkins French, a wealthy Warren County landowner and horse breeder, encouraged her prolonged visit there (which lasted a year) to take advantage of the healing powers of the spring waters and the hospitality offered by the resort owners, the Armfields. A former literary editor for the *Southern Homestead* and the *Georgia Literary and Temperance Crusader*, Lucy was glad to get away.

After her first few weeks at the resort, which resulted in improving health, she was joined by her entire family and some house servants. Both the Frenchs and the Armfields, all staunch Confederate sympathizers, finally relented to Federal demands and took the dreaded oath of allegiance to the United States on July 25, 1863. The couples were thereafter prohibited from providing hospitality to Confederate troops.

A day later, Beersheba Springs was invaded by "bushwackers" and renegades who ransacked the place. According to Lucy French, the sixty-six-year-old Armfield, "seeing that the place was going," invited his servants to help themselves quickly to any and all belongings in the nearest cottages.

In her diary, Lucy produced what historian Herschel Gower calls a major insight into the Middle Tennessee invasion and "one of the most dramatic recordings of a Tennessee family's domestic tribulations" during the war. Stored in a family trunk, the diary was discovered in 1939 by Lucy's granddaughter, Mrs. Fred Frazier. Excerpts from a few of the diary entries, edited by Gower, revealed her reaction to the conflict and her particular disdain for President Abraham Lincoln. In the first episode, Union Colonel John T. Wilder and his cavalry, the Seventeenth Indiana, had arrived at Beersheba Springs.

July 29, 1863

We had been at home perhaps an hour when in dashed a company of Yankees, Wilder's Cavalry, and we were environed by the "blues" once more. Darlin' went out immediately—hunted up the Col. [Wilder] and brought him in, and the consequence was we were not "run over" as much as we would have been. . . .

Neither did they trouble the kitchen much—but amused themselves with running about that Heaven forsaken Hotel—where they broke into everything—outhouses, kitchens, bowling saloons, etc. I suppose they would have rung all the bells in the establishment had not all the bells been pulled down and carried off both from the Hotel and cottages. They amused themselves by pulling down chandeliers in the dining room, throwing ink bottles against the wall in the office—setting up bottles of wine upon the long Piazza and rolling nine-pin balls at them—using the bottles for pins (the Piazza floor was crimsoned with claret,) cutting the green cloth from the elegant billiard tables, one of which they broke to pieces, and divers other capers of like calibre such as distinguish the Yankees wherever they go.

Despite a general disgust with Yankees, the Armfields were actually glad to see that one of their former servants was riding with them, having returned to get his family. Lucy described the moment:

Letha, one of Mrs. A's negro women, had a husband who went to the Yanks last summer—he came with this band, for his family, and they all went off—the wife and 8 children, 3 other boys also went. He had one wagon. . . . Letha seemed to me bewildered and not well pleased—she bid no one good bye. It was amusing to see the Yanks move off—one carried one negro baby behind him and one before him—Letha had about 6 babies. Before they left Mrs. Armfield said to the officers who dined here that she was under great obligations to them for taking off the negroes—"Oh!" he replied, "you must not say that, *we* are not taking them—we don't want them." "Very well, you have afforded them an opportunity to leave, and I am greatly obliged to you, they were of no profit to us—only a dead expense, and it is a happy riddance." He said it was unfortunate for them that they should leave such a home as this, as they had no place to keep them, and one half of the children would die before the year was out. Doubtless this was *once* when he told the truth. After dinner they all moved down the mountains—we ladies stood on the rock, and wished—that Forrest might get them!

(Lucy was here referring to Confederate General Nathan Bedford Forrest. She used several names for her husband. On "good days," she called him "Darlin." On other days he was known as the "Colonel." Much of the time, however, he was simply "Mr. F.")

August 12, 1863

On Sunday last when I wrote in my journal I was sufficiently lowspirited to have satisfied the very Prince of the Blue Devils himself [Lincoln]. I was so low down as to persuade myself I didn't care one jot for the Confederacy or anybody in it—which was a dreadful pass for *me* to come to.

In the midst of this "blue" mood, Lucy spotted approaching riders, whom she happily recognized as Confederates. Their leader was Chattanooga's Captain George W. Carter, and his sons were riding with him. Having led various Confederate groups, Carter gained fame as a mounted scout. These new visitors demanded food of Armfield, who apparently was none too happy that the captain was raiding his corncribs of what little had been left by the Yankees. The rations, however, were prayerfully appreciated. Lucy wrote about the more leisurely Confederate visit:

While the Capt. was at supper, I threw a dark mantle over my light muslin dress, and went out in the garden with Darlin' to see the men at their bivouac. We went softly along the walk—they were under the locust trees, between us there was the paling, and a row of raspberry bushes—so they could not see us—but we could both see and hear them. We did not wish them to know we were there—they were chatting cheerfully, like a band of brothers, and eating the rations Bob was bringing out in a huge tin pan. I saw William Carter down on his knees before the pan.

Longing to go home to McMinnville "after frost" in October 1863, Lucy was preparing to take some of Armfield's housekeeping articles, assuming that the Yankees had destroyed or carried off her own household goods. McMinnville, meanwhile, was hit with "scarlet fever and flu almost epidemic."

The French family finally returned home in July 1864, reestablishing their lives at the rundown family estate, Forest Home. Despite her long sojourn at Beersheba Springs, Lucy Virginia Smith French's health did not afford her a long life. She died at age fifty-six in 1881.

84
William B. Stokes

*From Slaveholder to Union General
to Reconstruction Radical*

That the "Bald Eagle of DeKalb"—as William B. Stokes was called—would be loyal to the Confederacy seemed a natural conclusion in Middle Tennessee. Stokes was a slaveholding, antebellum congressman—someone who simply loved being a Southerner. People recognized him by his receding hairline and his patriotic speeches (hence his nickname). When he volunteered to fight against anyone who would invade the South, Stokes's allegiance to the Confederate States of America was not questioned. He then raised a company of Confederate soldiers, sealing what appeared to be his undying fidelity to the South. Perhaps that is why his Confederate neighbors in and around DeKalb County in 1862 were astounded to see "Bald Billy" (which some called him) riding into their midst as a Union colonel for the United States.

Ultimately, Stokes would be promoted to the rank of general and become, after the war, a prominent radical Reconstructionist who held little regard for ex-Confederates. By switching his loyalty, Stokes insured a lifetime of hatred from pro-Southerners. (Unionists, of course, loved him.) There were few clues that he would be such a "scalawag," the term reserved for Southerners regarded as traitors to their own region.

Born in 1814, Stokes had always typified the good life of Tennessee landed gentry. Carrying a reputation as a "gentleman gambler," he enjoyed betting on steamboat races and horse races, the latter being such a passion that he built a track in front of his house near Alexandria and kept a stable of thoroughbreds. The sport gave him yet another nickname, "Ariel," also the name of his most famous racehorse, so fast that track owners had to bar the animal from racing. Not to be outdone, Stokes began painting Ariel black and passed him off as a different horse, winning even more races before the trick was revealed. Legend credits him with having introduced the ringer in Tennessee horse circles (a horse that races under false pretenses).

Stokes was born to wealth as the son of a North Carolina landowner and then acquired even more wealth through his marriage, in 1832, to Parilee Overall, the daughter of one of the wealthiest landowners in DeKalb County. Over the course of the following years, Stokes became the leading slaveholder in the county.

A flashy dresser who sported a gold cane and charming, gentlemanly manners, he was a welcome guest at Southern dinner tables and lavish dances, and a frequent one whenever he campaigned for political office. Throughout the 1850s, Stokes was a favorite stump orator, who was rewarded with victories as a state representative, state senator, and finally congressman. He drew huge crowds by the very mention of his name.

As with many in the South shortly before the Civil War, Stokes was torn between his desire to remain in the Union and his belief in states' rights. His sudden anger with President Abraham Lincoln had pushed him over the edge toward states' rights, initially causing Stokes to join the Confederacy. That reaction was caused both by Lincoln's ordered defense of Fort Sumter (South Carolina), which pushed the nation into war, and the president's call for troops to overrun the South's seceded states. Stokes wrote a letter to a friend that was published May 16, 1861, in the *Republican Banner*. Outlining his rebellious position in no uncertain terms, Stokes reported that he had enrolled his name as a volunteer against an invasion on Tennessee soil. Then, addressing the issue of states' rights, he called for:

> [the] right of revolution, and the right to resist the oppression of the Federal government, and to throw off their allegiance to the same when that oppression becomes intolerable. . . .
>
> The South ought to be a unit during the war by all means. . . . I claim to have done my duty in trying to heal our difficulties and restore peace. That having failed, I shall now march forward in the discharge of my duty in resisting Lincoln.

The day after he wrote that letter, Stokes had an abrupt change of heart. The catalyst was a legislative referendum on secession being placed before the voters of Tennessee. Stokes knew that the populace was now favoring the Confederacy, and he did not want Tennessee to leave the Union after all. Realizing that emotions toward secession were flowing through DeKalb County as well, Stokes simply campaigned for Tennessee to remain neutral. He also disbanded the Confederate force he had mustered.

On the heels of the secession announcement, Stokes retired to his farm. In July 1862, he surfaced as a major wartime figure when Military Governor Andrew Johnson, a trusted friend, awarded him a colonel's commission. Stokes now helped raise the Union army's Fifth Tennessee Cavalry Regiment.

Because his men came from different areas of Tennessee and some parts of Alabama, Stokes had trouble from the start with discipline, even among his officers. His regiment, known both as the Bloody Fifth and Stokes Cavalry, rarely saw action as a complete unit, usually because there were never enough men in camp at one time. One of the commanding generals over the regiment, Robert H. Milroy, later said, "Officers and men absent themselves without authority whenever they take a notion to visit their homes." The regiment, therefore, usually operated in small groups in Middle Tennessee—engaging in skirmishes and trying to rout Southern guerrillas from Putnam County (the center of terrorist activity) and from Overton and Jackson counties.

In February 1864, one Putnam County skirmish ended in a tragedy that would haunt Stokes for years. From his Sparta headquarters in neighboring White County, he ordered about eighty men to scour the countryside for enemy guerrillas. Because of a leak in intelligence, news spread that Union troops had been dispatched to the surrounding area. When Stokes's men rode along Calfkiller Creek, enemy decoys lured them to Dug Hill Road. An assembly of Confederate soldiers, guerrillas, and other pro-Confederacy locals waited in hiding. In the ensuing ambush, all Union soldiers were either killed or routed.

The fight brought to the stage one of the most feared Southern terrorists, Champ Ferguson, who was then helping the Confederate Eighth Regiment under John M. Hughes, George Carter, and W. S. Bledsoe in what became known as the battle of the Calfkiller (or the battle of Dug Hill). When Stokes sent wagons for his slain troops, forty-one were found shot in the head; they were laid side by side in an old store in Sparta. Stokes subsequently found himself with two more nicknames: "the dung-hill chicken" and "the buzzard of the Calf-Killer." One month later, however, his remaining troops cleared the area of most guerrilla trouble.

When Stokes was promoted to brigadier general two years after the war for "gallant and meritorious services during the war," many Southerners were angry. That anger evolved into fury when Stokes, elected to Congress in 1865, voted as a radical Reconstructionist. He continued to inflame the citizenry after entering the 1869 governor's race against acting Governor DeWitt Clinton Senter (Governor William "Parson" Brownlow had gone to the United States Senate and chosen Stokes as a candidate against Senter). In that race, Stokes rejected the concept of voting rights for ex-Confederates. In contrast, Governor Senter lifted restrictions at the polls against all former Confederates. When Stokes refused to give way on the issue, he threw away his only chance to be governor. Senter was elected by a large margin.

In 1870, Stokes returned in Congress, but not for long. That same year, a Tennessee constitutional convention sealed voting rights for former Confederates, settling the issue at last. When Stokes faced reelection in 1871, he had an uphill battle. Because he had pushed for congressional legislation designed to punish the South, Stokes was sent into permanent retirement by the voters. But later historians explained how the politics of Stokes (and men like him) kept Tennessee from suffering the severe military reconstruction of other seceded states—in addition to assuring passage of the Fifteenth Amendment, which gave voting protection to all black Americans.

Returning home to DeKalb County from his controversial but historic congressional service, Stokes practiced law until his death in 1897. He was then eighty-three and still unable to escape the title of a scalawag. For years after Stokes's death, many picnic revelers dropped spoonfuls of ice cream on his grave to cool the tongue of the man they considered a hellbound radical.

85
Sam Davis

Youthful Martyr of the Confederacy

The only known photograph of young Confederate hero Sam Davis.

Twenty-one-year-old Sam Davis of Smyrna stood on the scaffold November 27, 1863, refusing a deal by Union General Grenville M. Dodge which would spare his life. The general persisted in the offer—an

exchange of Davis's life for the name of the spy for whom Davis was carrying information about Union movements in Tennessee. "I pleaded with and urged him with all the power I possessed to give me some chance to save his life, for I had discovered he was a most admirable young fellow," Dodge later admitted.

When the hangman was about to place a rope around his neck, Davis was asked if it would not have been better to trade life for admission of the traitor's name. Davis replied with indignation: "Do you suppose I would betray a friend? No, sir; I would die a thousand times first!"

Davis's reply became the basis of a famous story which resurfaced in 1894 when a student at Peabody College spoke about his father, who had been a soldier with Davis. When excerpts of the Davis speech were printed in the *Confederate Veteran* magazine, letters poured in from people who had known Davis or had served with him. Efforts began in 1895 to erect a memorial in his honor. In 1909, a statue of Sam Davis was placed upon the Capitol grounds in Nashville, and by 1930, the Davis estate in Rutherford County had been purchased by the state and turned into a historic site depicting antebellum plantation life.

Davis, who never confessed to being a spy, served Confederate General Braxton Bragg in a unit called the Coleman Scouts, a special company formed to discover the plans of Dodge's army as it moved sixteen thousand soldiers from Corinth, Mississippi, to Pulaski, Tennessee. The Scouts were under the command of Captain Henry B. Shaw, who posed as an itinerant herbal doctor so that he could travel behind Union lines. The information he collected, sources say, was transmitted by the Scouts to Bragg's headquarters.

On the day he was captured, Davis was carrying several dispatches, but a certain letter, which Davis testified was given to him by Captain E. Coleman (actually Shaw), was the evidence that condemned him to death. Written by someone in the Union army, the letter contained information about Dodge's headquarters, the location of his main force, and accounts of the orders Dodge had issued.

At his court martial by Dodge, Davis claimed he had no idea what information the letter contained, saying that he was carrying it as a favor to Coleman. A three-man tribunal condemned Davis to hang. That evening, Davis is said to have written the following in a letter to his mother: "Oh how painful it is to write to you. I have got to die tomorrow morning—to be hung by the federals. Mother do not grieve for me. I must bid you good bye forever more—Mother I do not hate to die. Give my love to all."

In a postscript, Davis added that his remains could be located in Pulaski. "I will leave some things too with the hotel keeper for you," he continued in a special note to his father, who was given directions that "Pulaski is in Giles Co., Tenn., South of Columbia."

Davis's calm in the face of execution was also observed by the soldiers charged with carrying out his hanging:

> He displayed great firmness, glancing casually at his coffin as it was taken from the wagon. Turning to Capt. Armstrong, he inquired how long he had to live, and was told that he had just fifteen minutes. He then remarked: "The boys will have to fight the rest of the battles without me."
>
> Capt. Armstrong said: "I am sorry to be compelled to perform this painful duty."
>
> The prisoner replied with a smile: "It does not hurt me, Captain. I am innocent and I am prepared to die; so do not think hard of it.

No one has been able to confirm exactly who Davis died to protect that day. There are indications that it could have been Shaw (ironically in the same jail), or a Yankee captain, or a black porter in Dodge's office. One person who did know (but never told) was Davis's black servant Coleman Davis Smith, captured with him and released after the execution. He claimed "the person who gave the papers stood 'in ten feet of him' at the time of the execution yet 'gave no sign.'"

Smith had been close to Davis since their childhoods. Interviewed in 1926, Smith explained that he had been purchased in Virginia and "given to Sam as a play fellow." The two also worked at each other's side, he said, "plowing and hoeing . . . until the war." (Smith's parents were also farm workers.) "My young master . . . was always good and kind to me. When he ate I ate. When he slept I slept," Smith related.

As wartime scouts together, the two burned a Yankee wagon train carrying Union supplies and ammunition. When Davis later faced death, Smith begged him to tell the Yankees what they wanted to know. After the hanging, Smith returned home with some trepidation: "I was afraid to go home without my master; [but] they at home were glad to see me."

Smith, however, remained afraid of the Yankees.

For the sixty years that followed, he believed that he might be arrested by Federal troops and hanged for his participation in the Coleman Scouts. In 1920, Smith did not apply when former Tennessee Confederate blacks were given the right to receive a state pension for Civil War service. Six years later, while being interviewed about the war in his Memphis home, he was told that he had nothing to fear from the United States government. In 1927, the eighty-four-year-old Smith finally received his first pension payment.

86
Perez Dickinson

Working on the Underground Railroad

While Perez Dickinson's nieces sewed, passersby could not guess what secrets lay beneath their feet. In the early 1860s, Dickinson's nieces often could be found seated on the front porch of their uncle's Knoxville mansion, serenely involved in needlework while simultaneously covering up one of the larger runaway slave operations in Tennessee, as clandestine escapes took place every day in the cellar.

Dickinson was a Massachusetts-born merchant and a popular man in Knoxville. He founded the *Knoxville Times* twenty years before the Civil War to advance his antislavery message in opposition to other Knoxville papers. An abolitionist who nonetheless remained in the South, he built a tunnel connecting his downtown home to a cave that led to the edge of the Tennessee River. Dickinson routinely hid runaway slaves in his cellar by day and aided their escape through the cave at night.

A generous man who enjoyed the company of family and friends, Dickinson had built the home on Main Street for large gatherings. For a time, only he and his mother lived there, but the bachelor decided in 1845 to return to Boston and marry Susan Penniman. In Knoxville, the couple lived in the city house, but they also wanted a summer home where Susan could enjoy and share with others acres of flowers, luxurious lawns, and huge trees. While the Dickinsons planned their special place, they anticipated the birth of their first child.

Dickinson's happy married life, however, came to an end when his wife and baby died within twenty-four hours of the birth. Going on with his life, Dickinson used the house (with his mother as hostess) to extend hospitality to his friends and family members. The house stayed crowded with numerous nieces, nephews, and the New England cousins—many of whom stayed months, as was customary during the nineteenth century. One of the visiting cousins was the reclusive poet Emily Dickinson, who found the East Tennessee countryside inspirational.

When Perez Dickinson's sisters also died in the 1840s, his house became home to their young daughters, who grew up to manage his household affairs and play an important role in his Underground Railroad. Many of Dickinson's Civil War activities remain a mysterious part of his life, so secretive was he about certain plans. Historians are unclear about the route from his cellars that he connected to Knoxville's underground caverns. Runaway slaves reportedly would travel cavern pathways to the river, where another channel—perhaps one under the Tennessee River, according to legend—could take slaves to a cave beneath Cherokee Bluff. There they awaited passage to freedom in the North.

At the height of the Civil War, Dickinson moved his family to New York and there remained until it was safe to return home in 1863 when Knoxville was in Union hands. His cellars remained active in harboring ex-slaves hiding from the emerging Ku Klux Klan.

In 1864, to help revitalize Knoxville's economy, Dickinson joined Governor William G. "Parson" Brownlow and others to establish the First National Bank. During his tenure as bank president, all stockholders received their dividends in gold. Dickinson subsequently became one of Knoxville's leading businessmen, along with his business partner and brother-in-law, James H. Cowan, and helped organize the Board of Trade, which evolved into the Chamber of Commerce.

In 1865, Dickinson at last built the dream home he had planned for his wife—on a hill overlooking an island near the Tennessee River. He called it "Island Home," a showplace which hosted numerous overnight guests in the subsequent years, although its owner never spent a night there. Immaculate lawns, winding walkways, and the tree-lined entrance became favorite features for guests, just as Susan Dickinson had planned. The estate, which became one of the most popular entertainment meccas in Knoxville for citizens and civic and church groups, eventually became the campus of the Tennessee School for the Deaf.

During the 1880s, another important aspect of Dickinson's life was Island Home's fine animal stock and its progressive agricultural development, managed by a Swiss overseer. One year, Knoxvillians looked forward to seeing one of Island Home's biggest hits—Dickinson's prize hog, a prodigious porker which was reputed to weigh in excess of one thousand pounds. During a livestock parade along Gay Street in downtown Knoxville, the huge swine occupied a place of honor. But city streets were not paved, and the hog labored mightily on its journey. Finding an enticing mudhole at a main intersection, the animal paused to wallow before resuming the march. The exertion of the journey proved too much: The hog rose unsteadily, then, according to one historian, "in the sight of hundreds of spectators, he turned on his bulging side, and died!"

The New Englander Perez Dickinson, even in his later years, remained a true Tennessean, always interested in the city and state. At the age of seventy-six, he helped raise funds for the removal of the body of Tennessee's first governor, John Sevier, from Alabama and its reburial in Knoxville. Dickinson rode the train to Alabama to help accompany Sevier's body and took part in the ceremony honoring a Sevier monument at the Knox County Courthouse.

Dickinson himself died in 1901 at the age of eighty-eight and was buried in Old Gray Cemetery.

87
Hanson Caruthers
A Black Union Soldier Slips Home

Sometime in the summer of 1863, sixteen-year-old slave Hanson Caruthers was shucking corn on a Middle Tennessee plantation, still brooding over being struck by his master. As he explained, "Marster would shake my ears, but he seldom would hit me." Then Caruthers heard the music of a military band. It was the Union army advancing through Middle Tennessee. Despite his master's apology and plea to stay on the farm, Caruthers and fellow slaves quickly flocked to the oncoming Bluecoats and offered their services.

Born near Franklin, Caruthers lost his parents in his early childhood. When he grew older, the boy was hired out to other farms. Later suffering a near-fatal illness, he was given over to his young mistress's care. She was told that if he survived, she could keep him.

She cared for him twenty-four hours a day until he recovered, and the two became friends. Despite this close tie to her, Caruthers yearned for freedom and was willing to fight for it.

Joining the advancing Union soldiers, Caruthers first worked as a contraband laborer on Union fortifications in Rutherford County near Murfreesboro. Since slaves were impressed by the Union army and used for hard labor (later as soldiers), Caruthers then marched with his new comrades to Nashville to help in the construction of Fort Negley. Little did he know that this fort would be decisive in his future and in the future of Union-held Nashville.

Caruthers said he and his fellow former slaves were soon given the chance to become actual soldiers rather than mere laborers for the Union army. In the fall of 1863, he mustered into a newly created Tennessee black unit: Company F of the Twelfth United States Colored Troops. They received military training in Tullahoma, at the southern border of Coffee County. According to Caruthers: "This was the biggest thing that ever happened in my life. I felt like a man with a uniform on and a gun in my hand."

Caruthers himself was not a model soldier, he admitted, but was perhaps typical of those volunteers who received minimal training before bearing arms. He got along well with his white captain, who seemed to show him preferential treatment. Such was the case when Caruthers was arrested one day for leaving camp near Nashville. During a disciplinary hearing that the captain conducted, Caruthers explained that he was visiting the farm of a Squire Henderson, for whom he had done a favor shortly after joining the army. Because Caruthers had delivered medicine to his wife, Henderson promised him apples anytime he could return to the farm. "I was hungry and I thought it wouldn't mean any harm if I went and got a little snack to eat and some fruit," Caruthers explained. "This is my first wrong. Can't you be a little light on me?" Although a harsher treatment usually accompanied desertion, the captain simply placed him on a work party to dig up stumps.

The moment of glory for Caruthers came in late 1864. "I was in the Battle for Nashville, when we whipped old Hood." The black troops relied on the defenses of Fort Negley to protect them during the siege. On the first day of battle, December 15, 1864, Caruthers and his comrades streamed out of their defensive positions and pushed the Confederates back, breaking the siege. The next morning, the Twelfth United States Colored Infantry participated in bloody assaults on Overton's Hill. These attacks were unsuccessful and left one-fourth of the black soldiers wounded or dying on the battlefield. Despite the stinging defeat during this portion of the fight, the attack on Overton's Hill has since been remembered as one in which "the troops exhibited a courage and steadiness that challenged the admiration of all who witnessed the charge." Afterward, the Union army routed the Confederate Army of Tennessee, which began a retreat back to Franklin and finally into Alabama.

Because of his captain's friendship, Caruthers was allowed to go on leave when most soldiers were required to remain in camp. Caruthers soon found himself on the plantation near Franklin where he had spent most of his life:

> I went to see my mistress on my furlough, and she was glad to see me. She said, "You remember when you were sick and I had to bring you to the house and nurse you?" and I told her, "Yes'm, I remember." And she said, "And now you are fighting me!" I said, "No'm, I ain't fighting you, I'm fighting to get free."

Hanson Caruthers told his story to Fisk University interviewers from Nashville who were collecting slave narratives during the late 1920s and early 1930s.

88
Thomas Nixon Van Dyke
A Civilian's Distress and Arrest

Thomas Nixon Van Dyke felt so strongly about the South's cause that he vowed not to shave his face until the Confederacy prevailed. His friends later recalled that the Athens attorney and former chancery court judge kept his word. His whiskers grew so long that they finally had to be flung backward across his shoulders. No one could recall that he ever shaved again.

The sixty-one-year-old Van Dyke's stubborn protest was grounded in agony: three sons killed in the war, the rest of his family banished from Tennessee, and his own kidnapping and imprisonment in Ohio for more than a year without any charges being brought against him.

Born in 1803, Van Dyke was the son of East Tennessee pioneers: Penelope Smith Campbell Van Dyke, a native of Roane County near Kingston, and United States Army Captain Thomas James Van Dyke, who was stationed near her home at Southwest Point Garrison. The captain, from a prominent Delaware family, was later a surgeon during the War of 1812 and died in Alabama; Van Dyke was still a boy when his mother also died there. Sent north to live with relatives, he received a classical education and earned a law degree. After a brief stint as a clerk for the Alabama state legislature, Van Dyke returned to his native Tennessee in 1833. He married Eliza Ann Deaderick and became involved in banking and railroads. Before the war, Van Dyke was also the chancery court judge in adjacent Bradley County.

Due to his prominence in lower East Tennessee, the Confederate sympathizer made an easy target for invading troops. The family home, Prospect Hill, located about a mile from Athens, was first raided in the middle of the night in January 1864. Union soldiers roused Van Dyke from his sleep and carried him away immediately to nearby Calhoun. There, he awaited transfer to a Columbus, Ohio, prison and learned why he had been abducted. Union leaders hoped to exchange him for another McMinn County citizen imprisoned by the Confederacy. Such arrests throughout East Tennessee—the collecting of "citizen prisoners" for future exchanges—were becoming commonplace by both sides.

Still in Calhoun a week later, Van Dyke made a written appeal to the Confederacy's President Jefferson Davis, explaining that two other McMinn Countians, John L. Bridges and Alfred Swafford, were also kidnapped from their homes the same night. Collectively, they were being held as hostages for Jesse B. Blackburn, who was in a Confederate prison on charges of helping Union bushwhackers. Van Dyke related that many local friends thought Blackburn was innocent.

"If these are the facts, surely Mr. Blackburn ought not to have been arrested or molested in any way," Van Dyke wrote. "I trust, therefore, you will have this matter inquired into, so that justice may be done to all parties." Van Dyke, however, heard nothing and suffered imprisonment for the next fourteen months.

In the summer of 1864, Union soldiers swarmed over the Van Dyke home again, this time to arrest his wife, three daughters, a three-year-old son, and his wife's niece. Banished from Tennessee, the women and children were carried north across the Ohio River. Taking up residence in the mansion was Union General William Tecumseh Sherman. Occupying the region during the early winter months of 1864, Sherman developed such an affection for Athens that he decided not to torch the town (a fate that would soon befall Georgia towns along his famous March to the Sea).

Van Dyke's whereabouts became known to Confederate General John C. Vaughn of Sweetwater, who deplored the taking of civilian prisoners and made a pact with Union officials in late 1864 to release all such persons, many of them elderly or infirm. Vaughn, now in charge of East Tennessee forces since the killing of General John Hunt Morgan, was angry that the agreement was not honored. He then sent a warning dated February 20, 1865, to Union General L. S. Trowbridge, provost marshal of the Department of East Tennessee, which stated, in part:

> Unpleasant as the duty may be, and as much at variance as it is with the spirit and intentions animating your predecessor and myself in our interview and agreement at New Market, I am reluctantly compelled, in consequence of the disregard of that agreement on the part of the Federal authorities in persisting in the arrest and confinement of citizens, to resort to this mode of retaliation. . . . I will continue to arrest man for man one Union citizen for every Southern man arrested on your side.

The threat did not help Van Dyke and his family. They remained separated until relatives, petitioning President Andrew Johnson, were able to obtain Van Dyke's release at war's end in March 1865. Making his way to Wisconsin, Van Dyke found his family and moved near relatives in Quincy, Illinois. Despite success as a midwestern attorney, Van Dyke soon returned home to Athens. He became a judge and special appointee to the state of Tennessee—and attracted considerable attention in the following years for his growing—and growing—beard.

Van Dyke lived to be eighty-eight. When he died in 1891, he was buried in the Van Dyke cemetery in Athens. His wife lived another four years.

89

Montgomery "Gum" Hopkins

Saluting His Brother—The Enemy

After shooting the horse from beneath a Confederate soldier during a brief skirmish, Union sharpshooter Montgomery "Gum" Hopkins of Cocke County received a salute from his fallen enemy. Closer inspection revealed that the downed Confederate was his brother, Jacob Hopkins, whose command had been roaming the East Tennessee mountains near their home. At Jacob's insistence, Gum remained only briefly at his brother's side but offered his horse to aid Jacob's escape.

Gum began walking down Chestnut Mountain to hide from the enemy. Hours later, Jacob's fallen horse (addled from a scalp wound) showed signs of life, slowly got up, and began roaming the mountainside. The animal soon came across Gum. After a lengthy wait for the possibility of reuniting with Jacob, Gum finally rode away—the brothers having swapped horses in a strange afternoon of good fortune for both.

The "Fighting Hopkins Brothers," as they were called in Cocke County, numbered far more than Gum and Jacob. Twelve sons had been born to Benjamin Parker Hopkins and Ruth Tinker, originally from Jonesborough. Three served in the Confederacy and seven served in the Union. One Union son, Abraham, was killed in December 1863 in another brief skirmish in Cocke County. Remaining at home were a deaf-mute son, a twelve-year-old boy, and a younger sister. The Hopkins brothers all departed the area after the war, and accounts claim that each of the twelve brothers died in a different state.

90

Amy Elizabeth Higgason

No Woman Can Be Safe at Home

Sometimes the sweetest notes are the ones that are not played. Amy Elizabeth Higgason discovered as much when she and other war-weary Fayette County women gathered for an old-fashioned party at Frogmore, the family's Somerville estate established in 1829 by Amy's late husband, Dr. Josiah Higgason.

Inexplicably, the piano malfunctioned during the party, according to family accounts. The resulting silence dampened festivities, but allowed the partiers to hear the distant approach of Union soldiers. Quickly, the women hid their Confederate garb and weaponry—items that if discovered by the enemy would have resulted in the burning of the house. Moments later, Union troops arrived and conducted a lengthy but futile search. Soon after their departure, the piano mysteriously was able to be played again.

Frogmore survived the enemy's intrusion again the next morning when Amy Elizabeth Higgason, who was alone with her four young daughters, decided to open a trunk sent to her by a Confederate relative. In the process, she was startled by the presence of an unannounced Union officer, who walked up behind her, looked over her shoulder, and grabbed a Confederate pistol from the trunk. "I guess you know what this means," he reminded her. And then he motioned for his men to burn the house.

In desperation, she grabbed her late husband's Masonic symbol, held it up, and begged, "Does this mean anything to you?" Nodding in acknowledgment, he said simply: "It means everything to me." With the abruptness of his previous order, the officer stopped his men from torching the home and placed a guard at the door to protect the family. Frogmore endured the rest of the war, and Amy Elizabeth continued to live in the home until her death in 1899 at the age of eighty-seven.

Such endurance by the old mansion became part of a family history recounted in 1987 by two of her great-granddaughters, Lucy Anne Claxton and Polly Claxton of Somerville. The Claxton sisters also recalled a tale involving their aunt Liza Shaw, a longtime spinster who prior to the war had finally married a Northerner named Blake. Hearing that Federal troops had arrived in Somerville, Blake dutifully hid his wife's silver, but did not divulge its hiding place. He feared that Liza's honest nature might crumble under enemy interrogation, thus revealing the silver's location.

When the Federals invaded his house, Blake informed them that he was a fellow Northerner and that his home should not be violated. The intruding soldiers merely displayed contempt that a man of the North would choose to live among Southerners, and as they forced their way into the house, encouraged their horses to wander among its rooms. This so distressed the nervous Blake that he became ill and died in his sleep that night.

Since his wife had not been informed of the silver's whereabouts, the valuables were lost forever, despite a concerted family search conducted over many years. The Claxton sisters, when they finished telling the "lost silver" tale, conceded that they did not remember Blake's first name. This did not disturb them greatly, however. He was, they whispered, "after all, a Yankee."

91
George W. Gordon
Confederacy's Winter Retreat:
A Snowball's Chance in Georgia

He distinguished himself in numerous major battles, but gained his greatest recognition, he said, for a minor one—fought not with minié balls but with snowballs. "The famous snowball battle" was recounted by Civil War Confederate veterans with considerable relish, and Giles County's General George W. Gordon recalled how he was drafted into leading a charge of Tennessee troops against their Georgia counterparts.

In January 1864, the Confederate army was in winter quarters in Dalton, Georgia, having been driven out of the Chattanooga area by a heavily reinforced Union army. Gordon said one of the happier moments of that winter was when boyish soldiers (untold numbers were still teenagers) watched the falling snow in below-zero temperatures and broke into the biggest snowball battle on record. More than five thousand Rebels engaged in playful warfare which began within companies and camps and eventually involved states. The Tennesseans challenged the Georgians, and several thousand men were embroiled for more than two hours.

Those soldiers who protected their magazines— piles of snowballs "as high as a man's head all along the line and prepared beforehand"—were able to force "assaulting columns" into a retreat. Finally, the weary ceased their action, "rested upon their arms" . . . and quickly began making more snowballs. An even bigger assault was obviously at hand.

Gordon, then a colonel for the Eleventh Infantry, had been an onlooker. The Tennesseans sent a messenger to him, begging that he mount his horse and command them in battle. Meanwhile, the hillsides and housetops were filling with hundreds of spectators from the vicinity.

Gordon, years later, wrote a description of the scene at the request of General A. J. Vaughan, whose postwar memoirs immortalized the record of the Thirteenth Regiment, Tennessee Infantry. Part of Gordon's account is as follows:

With a shout that signaled victory, and an impetuosity that seemed irresistible, we dashed upon the brave Georgians, and for a few minutes the struggle was fierce and furious, desperate and doubtful. The air was white with whizzing and bursting balls; men were tripped up, knocked down, covered with snow, or run over. The writer was struck with at least a hundred balls, and his horse by as many more. The momentum of the charging column was too great, however, to be successfully resisted, more especially so when it outflanked both wings of the enemy, which soon gave way. The center then being flanked, and at the same time being sorely pressed in front, also gave way, and his entire army fled in great confusion. The rout on the field was now complete, and the enemy was not only driven therefrom, but through his own camp and into the woods beyond. The object of the campaign (victory) being now accomplished, I ordered the pursuit to cease and the men to return to their camps. As they did so, however, some of them stopped in the deserted camps of the Georgians and plundered their mess chests, which had been well filled by supplies from their friends at home. When I heard of this, and reproved it as not being a legitimate object of the campaign, the reply and defense were in that questionable old maxim, "All is fair in love and war."

. . . The writer never afterward passed or met the Georgia Division, that its men did not greet him with shouts, often with "Three cheers for the Snowball Colonel!" . . . This "snowball battle" seems to have made a deep and indelible impression on all the soldiers who took part in, or who witnessed it; for one of the first questions I am often asked by old soldiers whom I have not seen since the close of the war, is: "General, do you remember the snowball battle at Dalton, Ga.?"

. . . I suppose the writer can say, without being charged with vanity, that he won more "reputation" . . . than in all the other battles in which he participated during the war.

The "snowball colonel," who would soon become one of the Confederacy's younger generals, was captured at year's end during the Battle of Franklin.

Spending the remaining months of the war in a Union prison, he finally returned home to Middle Tennessee and became an attorney. In 1885, President Grover Cleveland appointed him to the Department of the Interior as an Indian agent. Upon later moving to Memphis, Gordon became superintendent of public schools, and in 1908, a United States congressman. Prior to his death in 1911, he devoted his time to the welfare of Confederate veterans.

92
A. J. Vaughan

A Mobile Battlefront: Retreating toward Atlanta

Confederate General A. J. Vaughan, who began the war as leader of the "Dixie Rifles," or the Thirteenth Regiment of Tennessee Infantry, recollected rather jokingly in later regimental memoirs just how he lost his leg during the Civil War: He was so drunk at the time of the amputation that he had no recollection of exactly when or where someone had removed it.

In July 1864, Vaughan was ordering his men to entrench near Marietta, Georgia. The general decided to take his lunch break under a shade tree near the rear of his line. Although no direct fighting was underway, both sides were exchanging artillery fire. As he lit his pipe after lunch, "a shell from the enemy's battery came whizzing through the air over my line and exploded just as it struck my foot and the ground, tearing off my foot and making a hole almost large enough to bury me," Vaughan recounted. He experienced very little pain or loss of blood, but he was immediately sedated with morphine and placed in a wagon bound for the field hospital.

News of Vaughan's injuries preceded him, and Generals Benjamin Franklin Cheatham, William Hardee, and Joseph E. Johnston each stopped his progress, sympathized with him, and, noticing his pale appearance, offered him a drink of whiskey or brandy.

Upon encountering Cheatham, Vaughan mentioned, "I then began to feel pretty good." After a stop with Hardee, Vaughan said that he "continued to feel better." After downing a "big drink" of apple brandy handed him by Johnston, Vaughan claimed he "knew nothing until I awoke on the platform in Atlanta at sunrise the next morning. . . . Thus I lost my leg, and I have never seen it since."

A. J. Vaughan became a casualty on his lunch break.

Vaughan's greatest period of suffering actually began during his recovery from the amputation, which he said was done incorrectly by someone other than field surgeon R. W. Mitchell, who was performing his duties elsewhere.

A Virginia native, Vaughan was a graduate of the Virginia Military Institute. Prior to the war, he had become a Mississippi planter who actually held Unionist views. His allegiance changed quickly when Virginia and its neighboring states seceded. He raised a company for the Confederacy, but Mississippi was unable to equip the troops. So Vaughan headed for West Tennessee, settling at Moscow and enlisting troops in Fayette County.

The high regard Vaughan's men had for their leader was illustrated by their determination to raise three thousand dollars to buy him a fine horse late in the war. They declined outside contributions, choosing instead to raise the entire sum within the regiment. Vaughan wrote:

These few men, drawing eleven dollars per month, with their uniforms in rags, and living on half rations, agreed to buy the horse, . . . I have lived to forget many things, but never will pass from my heart the gratitude I felt that day when my war-worn soldiers in their ragged gray gathered around me to show their love and confidence. If nothing else, that act alone makes dear to my heart every soldier of the Thirteenth Tennessee Regiment.

The horse—which he described as "a magnificent Gray Eagle," secured from a Dr. Yandell of Louisville, Kentucky—was named Chickamauga, in honor of the battle at which Vaughan was promoted to brigadier general in the field. Assuming his rank upon the death of Tennessee's General Preston Smith of Giles County, Vaughan led the brigade through all subsequent combat, seeing it through the Atlanta campaign until the loss of his leg. (Succeeding Vaughan as brigade commander was the Tennessean George W. Gordon.)

After the war, Vaughan temporarily became a Mississippi farmer again. In 1873, he moved to Memphis, where he became what one historian called the city's "favorite son" in the postwar period. Vaughan spent most of his life as proprietor of a mercantile house, became a clerk of the criminal court in Shelby County, and involved himself in the Grange movement on behalf of area farmers. Until his 1899 death in Indiana at age sixty-nine, Vaughan also headed the Tennessee chapter of the United Confederate Veterans.

93
Harriet Leonora Straw Whiteside

A Ladylike Hellion at Chattanooga

Although she lost her husband and a fortune in assets during the Civil War, Harriet Leonora Straw Whiteside never lost her determination. She eventually managed to earn an even bigger fortune along with a reputation as one of the shrewdest businesswomen in Tennessee. Along the way, she made many enemies. One legal opponent, however, said of Harriet: "She brought to her assistance the highest degree of culture, education, polish, refinement, and never forgot that she was a lady."

Her story of prominence and wealth began with her marriage in 1844 to one of Chattanooga's pio-neers, James A. Whiteside, an attorney, landowner, and father of five motherless children. He was forty when he fell in love with nineteen-year-old Harriet, piano teacher to one of his children. Harriet, a Virginia native who trained as a governess, was equally accomplished on the flute and guitar and by all accounts had a fine singing voice.

By the outbreak of war, she was thirty-four and the mother of her own eight (surviving) children by Whiteside. He was fifty-eight and one of the city's most respected businessmen—owning the most scenic part of Lookout Mountain and the Lookout Mountain Hotel, each utilized by both armies during the Civil War. But James Whiteside became sick following a journey to the Virginia battlefields, where he had gone to retrieve a son fallen ill in General Robert E. Lee's army. Unable to overcome his exhaustion from the trip, the elder Whiteside died in November 1861. Not only did he leave property and a statewide enterprise in railroad interests and coal mines, he left great debts and a young widow ready to make good on those debts. She was also ready to stand her ground against the rampages of war.

During the siege of Chattanooga and the Union's occupation of that city in late 1863, Harriet Whiteside was able to buy food at the commissary by giving overnight board to a few Union officers. When a Union lieutenant sent a soldier to take possession of her rosewood piano, however, she became less than hospitable. The lieutenant came in person, and she informed him that she had ax-wielding daughters stationed at each end of the piano with instructions to destroy it should he set foot inside the home.

Such acts of defiance led Union General William Tecumseh Sherman to order her deported in the spring of 1864. Given just twenty-four hours' notice, Harriet sold all of her possessions, including her furniture, which brought $3,000, and her late husband's extensive law library, for a mere $150 to a Union officer. She and her children were hauled away in a cattle car. After two weeks in a stockade prison at Louisville, Kentucky, they were released with help from a Union friend in East Tennessee who pleaded with Federal authorities.

The family spent the next year in Springfield, Ohio, where the widow rented a house. Upon President Abraham Lincoln's assassination in April 1865, a mob roamed the streets of Springfield threatening to set fire to any house not draped in mourning—and Harriet Whiteside's was the only one. Fearing for her children's safety, she finally removed her black underskirt and had it draped across the front of her dwelling.

In the fall of 1865, months after the war finally ended, Harriet returned to Chattanooga from her forced exile, but it was an expensive homecoming. She had to pay twenty thousand dollars as evidence that she would keep an oath of allegiance given two years earlier. Then she discovered Federal officers occupying her home. Allowed to stay, she and her children were confined to a single room. But the resourceful mother conceived a scheme to reclaim her house when one of her children contracted chicken pox. She convinced the doctor to post a sign that read "smallpox." Occupying Federals quickly scattered, and the house fell solely to the family.

Harriet remarried in the 1870s, taking as her second husband a newcomer to the area, Varney A. Gaskill, a lawyer known for his eloquence as a public speaker and his good looks. Gaskill successfully defended his wife against a charge of renting her home for use as a "bawdy house." She was back in court shortly thereafter in a case over access rights to Lookout Mountain, a controversy that would last decades. Harriet controlled the only road leading to the mountaintop and demanded a toll of every traveler. The *Chattanooga Times* referred to this request as "extortion," and a stock company began planning a second road. Harriet responded in May 1879 by filing a lawsuit to protect her monopoly. Gaskill again represented his wife but lost the case, and soon thereafter lost his wife. Harriet was awarded a divorce two months later.

The new road cost her considerable income. Harriet recouped part of her losses by charging twenty-five cents per person to see the panorama from the Point, which she still owned. She also sold to the Owen Livery Company, for five thousand dollars annually, exclusive rights to transport visitors on her old road (its customers got a free view from the Point). To prevent encroachment, she built a fence around the Point and posted shotgun-wielding guards to protect it. Harriet eventually fought all efforts to open the area to any traveler not using her road. Once during this battle of the roads, she was cited for contempt of court for failing to adhere strictly to a judge's ruling.

Throughout her many battles, Harriet Whiteside was often misunderstood. But perhaps few knew her as well as Tomlinson Fort, the prominent attorney who argued cases against her for thirty years. Fort, writing a tribute to her for the *Confederate Veteran*, also declared:

> The fight in every instance was forced on her by the situation; and she made it, not only for the property involved, but to protect the reputation of her husband, insisting that, but for the loss of papers and burning of public records, no lawsuit ever could have arisen. She was much misunderstood because none except lawyers can appreciate exactly why . . . she would so prolong litigation.

Harriet sold her property on Lookout Mountain in March 1887. Her troubles, however, took a dangerous turn. In 1890, someone with murder in mind laced her sipping wine and her custard with huge doses of arsenic. Without tasting either, she sent both as gifts to a sick grandchild. The poison was found when others in the youth's household became ill after sampling the goods. When the authorities were contacted, the *Chattanooga Times* proclaimed the new crisis as "The Poisoning Sensation." The headline added: "Mrs. Whiteside unable to guess who the culprit is."

Harriet, however, continued targeting Lookout Mountain's profitable tourist trade. She would finance construction of an incline railroad up the side of the mountain. The particularly difficult engineering feat helped make a national name for one of its Chattanooga designers, Josephus Conn Guild (later a driving force and builder for one of the first hydroelectric dams ever built on a navigable waterway). The steep, mile-long railway up Lookout Mountain that Guild designed with Lynn White became a national historic site. As to the mountaintop, the fight over public access finally came to a halt when the United States bought the Point for the Chickamauga-Chattanooga National Military Park.

Harriet Whiteside fought to protect her various financial interests until her death in 1903 at the age of seventy-nine. Author Kay Baker Gaston noted her passing with these words: "Harriet Whiteside breathed her last at her home on College Street. Some Chattanoogans might have breathed a corresponding sigh of relief, seeing an end to the controversy that had surrounded her for over forty years."

94
J. G. M. Ramsey

*A Confederate Sympathizer's History
Goes Up in Smoke*

When a Unionist torched the Knoxville home of one of Tennessee's first historians, Dr. J. G. M. Ramsey, much of the early history of Tennessee went up in flames. The year was 1863.

Gone were manuscripts, original documents, and letters from the state's early leaders. As Ramsey would later write, "I had the honor of a correspondence with the elite and distinguished every where whether in church or state—with A. Jackson, Calhoun, Polk, . . . all railroad presidents—the scientific generally—Democratic leaders and editors everywhere." Among the papers were unpublished biographies obtained in personal interviews with Tennessee's pioneers—those who gave birth to the state and shaped the destiny of the nation. The fire also consumed a massive library of more than four thousand volumes: medical books, history, and literature collected from throughout Europe and America. Ramsey considered it the best library "in the western states." With his home gone and enemies all around, he went into self-exile. Ramsey was sixty-six at the time.

Although the arsonist was never identified, Ramsey held one man responsible, the man whom he believed contracted the torching—fellow Knoxvillian William G. "Parson" Brownlow, the Unionist newspaperman and an outspoken antagonist of the Confederate Ramsey. The arson, Ramsey claimed, was done out of "low revenge and private and personal hate."

Ramsey's family—originally from Mecklenburg, North Carolina—included Tennessee's earliest pioneers. His surveyor father, Francis Alexander Ramsey, was an official with the old State of Franklin while living at Little Limestone Creek in Washington County, North Carolina (now Tennessee). After moving in 1792 to the new town of Knoxville, the elder Ramsey became a court clerk within the federal Southwest Territory. He was among those leaders who contributed early official documents to the Ramsey collection.

J. G. M. Ramsey described himself as one of Tennessee's first native sons. Born in 1797 at Knoxville, he also helped mold much of the state's early history.

In business, the arts, church, and politics, Ramsey was a force. In addition to being an eminent Knoxville physician (from 1820) and a state historian, he was the manager of several farms, a Presbyterian elder, poet, register of deeds, contributor to magazines, president of banks (a state director of at least six banks and a state banking commissioner), trustee of three colleges, canal commissioner, school commissioner, postmaster, and a major railroad financier (considered one of the most important figures in the development of the railroad in Tennessee). His mansion, called "Mecklenburg," was located outside of Knoxville at the confluence of the Holston and French Broad Rivers. He operated a sawmill and a ferry there.

Among Ramsey's great achievements was the popular 1853 history *Annals of Tennessee* featuring the state's founding citizens, most of whom were friends or acquaintances. When the Civil War began, he was working at home on the second volume of Tennessee history, using his massive collection of original material. He was also looking forward to retirement.

Professing allegiance to the Confederacy within the heart of Unionist East Tennessee, Ramsey became one of the South's leading war-treasury agents, collecting funds and paying them out. By his estimates, he disbursed "more than forty-two million dollars for the Confederate States Government." All five of his sons were in the Confederate army. (His youngest, eighteen, was killed on a Virginia battlefield, and another, General James Crozier Ramsey, became a prisoner of war.) Of his six daughters, two died during the war years. His wife and a daughter (who was banished from Knoxville for refusing to walk under a United States flag) became refugees with whom he later reunited in Bristol, Virginia. During his own war travels as a treasury agent, Ramsey tended to the Confederate wounded on one battlefield after another. Escaping the Union path, he ultimately went to Charlotte, North Carolina, where he remained and gathered most of his scattered family around him. At war's end, the sixty-eight-year-old Ramsey had to make a living once more. Borrowing a horse and a doctor's bag, he resumed his work as a physician.

While he was making a new start in North Carolina, his son General James Crozier Ramsey died suddenly in Knoxville. "Some of the circumstances lead to the suspicion of poison. The judgement of the Great Day will reveal it all," said a grieving father, who was then writing an autobiography, *Dr. J. G. M. Ramsey: Autobiography and Letters*. Part of the book relied upon his memory regarding some papers and manuscripts lost in the fire; the rest recounted his family's experiences during the Civil War. Ramsey finally returned to Knoxville in 1872 when he was seventy-five; he lived to be eighty-seven.

95
Milton Mallicoat

A Prison Camp Miracle Springing Forth

When East Tennessean Milton Mallicoat saw water burst forth from dry ground, he was certain that what he had witnessed as a prisoner of war was a miracle.

Mallicoat, from Campbell County, was among the tens of thousands of Union soldiers held captive in Georgia at the Confederacy's infamous Andersonville Prison, an open-air stockade built in early 1864. That summer, thirty-three thousand men were heaped into the unsheltered area which covered twenty-six acres. Only makeshift overhangs from the prisoners' own supplies of blankets or tents dotted the landscape. Often one hundred men died each day from the heat, malnutrition, and disease.

Mallicoat and fellow prisoners pleaded daily for more than their tiny water allotment. A stream ran along the side of the stockade, but Confederates restricted its use—either because of the dysentery that was rampant or in an attempt to force prisoners to reveal the whereabouts of the main Union army. When guards ignored their pleas for water, the prisoners made their requests directly to God. Forming prayer groups, the soldiers prayed nightly, although some among their number "scoffed."

One evening, the stillness of the stockade was broken by the sound of a prisoner yelling, "Water!" Water indeed had appeared, bubbling forth from the ground in the center of the stockade. Prisoners scrambled to drink their fill. Some cried. Some screamed. Some gave thanks. All drank, and drank, and drank. The supply seemed inexhaustible.

Much later, after returning home to his wife and children in Campbell County, Mallicoat related the incident to a friend. The fellow explained that hard clay at the center of the stockade probably had been packed over a tributary of the nearby spring. Mallicoat,

with "a faraway look" in his eye, countered: "It was the Lord's work, young man. It was the Lord's work."

Despite suffering from common wartime illnesses of kidney failure and chronic diarrhea, Mallicoat lived to be eighty-three. He died in 1927.

96
David Nelson Rees

One United Front:
A Confederate-Union Romance

Loyalty to the cause of either the Union or the Confederacy took a back seat to love in the case of David Nelson Rees and Anna Margaret "Ann" Johnson—who held opposing allegiances.

They met late in the war, in the closing weeks of August 1864. Rees was riding with the Confederacy's General John Hunt Morgan, who sent Rees's battalion into the small East Tennessee mountain town of Elizabethton, Ann's lifelong home. She was the daughter of Thomas C. and Nancy Tipton Johnson, who were Union sympathizers.

When Rees stepped onto the front porch of the Johnson house, it was a Sunday morning. He was struck by the tranquillity of the upper East Tennessee area—as if there were no war. Adding to that feeling was the hospitality of the Johnson family, all of whom should have been his enemies. But the elder Johnson had declared that his home, known as the Tipton-Johnson house, was open to both Union and Confederate soldiers. Some military men, as a result, began calling the place "Fort Johnson." Both sides felt equally at home.

Rees's later family memoirs would recall Ann Johnson as "a beautiful young lady, faultlessly dressed, who had started to church." There was an immediate attraction.

A former schoolteacher from Cynthiana, Kentucky, Rees knew about divided loyalties among family and friends. When he joined the Confederate army after the firing on Fort Sumter (South Carolina), his schoolteacher sister raised the Confederate flag over their schoolhouse, irritating most of their cousins, who favored the Union.

Rees thereafter saw the worst of war. He spent his first year's duty on the Virginia battlefront under General Stonewall Jackson in the fiercest fighting of the first Battle of Bull Run in July 1861. Rees was nearby when Jackson was given his famous nickname, "Stonewall." Of his role in that historic moment, Rees wrote in his family memoirs:

> Gen. Bee had said to Gen. Bartow, "See Jackson standing like a Stonewall, let us rally on the Virginians." About that time they both were shot and killed. Jackson said to his men, "we must sweep the field with the bayonets and when you charge, yell like devils." That celebrated rebel yell. Everything there was completely routed. . . . I and a squad of soldiers put up a wooden marker where General Bee and Bartow were killed on the Bull Run Battlefield near the old Henry House, close to where Stonewall gave his famous orders that won the battle.

Although Rees's enlistment ended soon, he returned home to Kentucky, reenlisted, and eventually joined Morgan's cavalry, fighting with Co. "A" Jessee's Battalion Mounted Riflemen of Kentucky, which became the Confederacy's Sixth Battalion. The force headed for Tennessee. Rees fought at Chickamauga, where the unit was sent under General Joseph Wheeler, and in Knoxville at the Battle of Fort Sanders prior to his assignment at Elizabethton, the county seat of Carter County.

A commissary sergeant, he described that first day when he approached the Tipton-Johnson house. Johnson's father-in-law greeted him on the porch:

> I hitched my horse and walked onto the porch where Major Abe Tipton was sitting there and after a few words invited me and a few others to go out into the orchard where there was plenty of good eating apples. . . .
>
> All was peaceful and quiet and there was such bountiful crops that it reminded me of the Biblical description of the land of Canaan, a land flowing with milk and honey.

The elderly Tipton, crippled from fighting under Andrew Jackson in the War of 1812, had served as the local militia leader, sheriff, and state senator. His grandfather was Revolutionary War veteran Colonel John Tipton, who, in his own attempt to remain loyal to an existing government (the mother state of North Carolina), had been a key figure in defeating the upstart State of Franklin eighty years earlier.

Working out of the Tipton-Johnson house as a temporary paymaster to his men, Rees had many occasions to enjoy the family's company—and Ann Johnson's. "She was bright, quick and good company, and I learned she was a good cook; could spin and weave and I thought would make a splendid housewife," he said in his memoirs. The couple began taking long horseback rides together along the banks of the Doe and the Watauga rivers. "She seemed at home in the saddle," Rees added, "and was a crack shot with a pistol and was not afraid to use one if occasion required it." But his battalion did not remain in the area more than a couple of weeks. The troops moved toward Greeneville and joined General Morgan. Days later, Morgan was slain trying to flee from Union forces converging on the town. Many of his troops managed to escape the surprise attack. Among them was Rees, who headed back to Elizabethton, now overrun with the enemy. Fearing his capture, Ann Johnson hid Rees on the family farm until he could get away. He returned to Morgan's headquarters in Abington, Virginia, where the general's body had been taken under a flag of truce; he was able to visit the commander's grave before the body was removed for two more funerals.

Rees and Ann managed to correspond, then decided to marry on December 13, 1864. When the Confederacy surrendered months later, he was serving with another unit in Bland County, Virginia. Rees journeyed to Nashville, took the oath of allegiance to the United States, and decided to settle permanently in his wife's East Tennessee mountains. Building a house outside of Johnson City at Watauga, he became one of that community's first merchants, a schoolteacher, and a prominent regional columnist, writing for several newspapers in Tennessee and Kentucky.

Rees, whose descendants changed the spelling of the family name to "Reese," lived to be ninety-one; he died in 1931, and was among the last surviving Confederate soldiers in Tennessee. Of the couple's ten children, only four grew to maturity. Two of those became prominent in other parts of the nation: Thomas Tipton Reese was instrumental in the early development of Palm Beach, Florida, where he was the second mayor and leading bank president; and George Alvin Reese made his fortune as president of a major Chicago tool company.

That such a staunch Confederate, who rode with one of the South's feared fighting units, "Morgan's Men," would marry a woman whose sympathies lay with the

Union was not a mystery. Apparently he was a Rebel without a steadfast cause, as this excerpt from his family memoirs seems to suggest: "I expect I served under more commanders of infantry and cavalry than any other soldier in the Confederate army, but I was all wrong. Gen. Washington said the Union must and shall be preserved in his Palladium of our liberties."

97
Thomas Jefferson "T. J." Walker
Surviving Atlanta with a Sweetheart's Shield

A Union bullet would have claimed Thomas Jefferson "T. J." Walker's heart—if Betsy Elizabeth Sweet had not claimed it first. Both were natives of Haywood County in the heart of West Tennessee.

Private Walker (T. J. to those who knew him) was among the Confederate troops engaged against Union General William Tecumseh Sherman's forces during the siege of Atlanta in late summer of 1864. When Walker arrived at the covered pit that served as a mess hall, he was struck in the chest by a Union minié ball. The blow would have been fatal, except that it hit a leather case from Betsy—actually an elaborate sewing kit. Most soldiers carried a sewing kit to mend their clothes, and it was usually in "our side shirt pocket next to our hearts," explained Walker in his memoirs. Since Betsy had saved his life, Walker later gratefully packaged the shattered case with the near-fatal minié ball and sent them home to her with the following note: "You have been the means of saving my life and if I ever get through this cruel war you will have to say 'Yes' or 'No.'" She said yes.

Walker's close call may have impressed Betsy, but it gained him no popularity with his fellow Confederates. They were having dinner when the force of the minié ball sent him sailing through the mess hall door and into their midst. One soldier was heard to grumble: "Confound the luck! Why couldn't that damned Yankee bullet have struck him before he entered the door so that he wouldn't have fallen on the table and ruined our dinner!"

The other woman in T. J. Walker's life was his widowed mother, who, he later said, had denied herself "many comforts in order that her boy might acquire a classical education and be prepared for the duties and trials of life." An only child, Walker was a senior in college when he left home on April 23, 1861, to join the Confederacy's Ninth Tennessee Infantry Regiment. He would always remember his mother's parting words, "My son, I would rather hear that you had been killed than to hear that you had acted the coward." Roughly a thousand young men made up the Confederacy's Ninth Tennessee, only forty of whom answered its final roll call. Walker was among the survivors, although he was wounded five times during his forty-seven months of active duty.

The Ninth Tennessee also participated in one of the more unwarranted battles of the war, which occurred during the Atlanta campaign. One evening at New Hope Church, Georgia, both sides were at rest when a swarm of lightning bugs lit up the pitch-dark sky near the Union encampment. The Confederates, mistaking the flickering lights for musket fire from their counterparts, opened fire. Union soldiers retaliated, and guns roared for several hours. Once the cause of the false alarm was discovered, the futile engagement was dubbed "The Lightning Bug Battle."

Early in the war, soldiers might be seen exchanging gunfire one minute and pleasantries the next. Walker recalled one of his own such experiences in 1862 when the two enemy armies were facing each other on opposite sides of the Tennessee River:

> Often times a truce would be agreed to between the pickets during the changing of the guards. They would lay down their guns and holler across the river, "Hello Johnny Reb," or "Hello, Yank!, let's have a friendly chat and trade a little." The reply would come back, "All right!"
>
> Some bar or log in the middle of the river would be selected, and they would meet by swimming from both sides to the designated place. There they would carry on a friendly conversation and exchange knives for tobacco and sugar for coffee. Then they would again swim back to their respective posts and holler out, "Get to cover," for if either side showed his head a bullet would whizz and very frequently it would hit the mark. I mention this to show that there wasn't animosity between the true soldiery on either side.

Walker's most heartrending moment came during the Battle of Shiloh in April 1862, during which the Army of Tennessee's commanding General, Albert

Sidney Johnston, was killed, and Walker was left wounded on the field. "Oh! How my young boyish heart sank within me! Our General dead. What will become of the Army?" Walker was carried from the Hardin County battlefield and laid near a little stream. His despair continued, as he explained:

> While water was being procured for me, I turned my weary head to get a new position and my eye fell upon the prettiest face of a boy I think I have ever seen. He was a little golden headed wounded Yankee drummer boy lying there dying. . . . When water was brought he was lifted up and water placed to his parched lips. He fell back and with his last breath said, "Oh! Mother!" That scene still lingers in my memory although many years have passed. . . . From that day, the last bitterness that rankled in my breast for the rank and file of the Federal soldier departed never to return.

When he made his way home to West Tennessee after the war, Walker immediately went to his own mother, and they moved to Dyer County along the Mississippi River. Like his late father, Walker decided to become a doctor. He began the study of medicine and saved enough money to travel to Louisville and to enter the university there. Graduating in 1867, he returned to Dyersburg to begin his medical practice. T. J. Walker and Betsy Sweet were married in 1868. He died in 1920 at the age of seventy-eight.

98
Virginia "Miss Ginger" Moon

A Woman Spy Loose in the North

In a matter of seconds, Virginia "Miss Ginger" Moon, on a steamboat that was ready to depart from Ohio to her hometown of Memphis, grabbed a critical Confederate dispatch from her bosom, soaked it in a pitcher of water, and ate the document in three bites.

Only moments before, Ginger had used a gun to force a Union officer from her stateroom. As she swallowed the last bite of the secret document, he returned to arrest both Ginger and her mother, who was accompanying her daughter home. The young woman was defiantly proud as she was being escorted off the boat and to her incarceration. Northern

headlines on April 4, 1863, dramatically publicized the arrests of women "Secesh" (secessionist) spies.

But Ginger Moon knew that she had connections in high—and very near—places. General Ambrose Burnside, the local Union commander, was notified immediately of the arrests. Burnside treated the women like old family friends of bygone years—for indeed they were.

Among the South's most daring and colorful spies, the Moon women were descendants of an aristocratic Virginia family. Ginger and her mother made their home in Memphis near Ginger's brother and her uncle, owner of a mercantile business. With a dramatic style that in another half-century would allow her to make a living in silent films, nineteen-year-old Ginger could flirt and intimidate her way into and out of nearly impossible situations. Joining Ginger in her cleverness and in her mission to save the South was her older sister, Lottie Moon Clark, a master of disguises. Both sisters were good friends of Confederate President Jefferson Davis, who perhaps was their advisor as well.

Lottie operated as a Confederate spy out of Ohio, where her husband was a judge and a Southern sympathizer. In Lottie's frequent travels, she once disguised herself as an English invalid and managed a ride in President Abraham Lincoln's carriage. Lincoln was appalled when he later became aware of the ruse, and the United States secretary of war ordered a ten-thousand-dollar reward for the female spy "dead or alive."

Ginger, while temporarily attending an Ohio female academy, openly resented the school's pro-Union attitudes. She asked to be sent to her mother in Memphis, and the college refused. She then shot out every star on the flag waving over the campus, and was soon on her way home to Mother.

On a later trip into Ohio, Ginger Moon again outraged local Unionists. Walking into a popular dry goods store, she slipped a diamond ring from her finger and scratched on the front window, "Hurrah for Jeff Davis."

She was it seems a natural choice for a spy mission, despising the Federals as she did. The document that she swallowed aboard the steamboat was evidence that an economic-alliance agreement had been reached between the South and the Northwest—a scheme that some pro-South advocates believed could mean a Confederate victory. The heart of the alliance would be a nationwide group of businessmen, farmers, and politicians organized under the banner of the Knights of the Golden Circle. Ginger Moon was one of the group's primary messengers.

After her steamboat arrest (she was betrayed by a visitor in Lottie's home), Ginger asked for a meeting with commander Burnside. She did not know what to expect. She only knew that her best chance at survival was in the hands of this man whom she had known since her earliest childhood. Burnside, who was once engaged to Lottie, had often visited the Moon home and bounced young Ginger on his knee. She, in turn, nicknamed him "Buttons." Lottie, after walking down the aisle with Buttons, abruptly changed her mind, refused to marry him, and walked out of the church.

Her younger sister now waited in the general's outer office, and when the door opened, she walked toward the commander. With outstretched arms, Burnside exclaimed: "My child, why have you done this? Why have you tried to go South without coming to me for a pass?"

Ginger admitted, "I have a little honor. I could not have asked you for a pass and have carried what I did."

Burnside did not pursue her obvious meaning. He merely inquired: "What did they find?"

The general tried the case himself. He immediately sought avenues of parole and ruled that letters to family and friends (all fifty of them) did not constitute Rebel dispatches. Burnside also encouraged his officers to entertain the young woman prisoner. Her arresting officer asked her to dinner; another young officer on Burnside's staff asked to accompany her to the theater.

Soon, sister Lottie, disguised in her usual costume of an English invalid, appeared at the general's office to seek official passage out of the city (perhaps to obtain help in rescuing Ginger and their mother). Burnside was not fooled. After a moment of pretense in which he conversed casually, the general made his third and final arrest of the Moon women. In so doing, he also confessed to Lottie: "You may have forgotten me, but I have not forgotten the many happy hours I spent with you in Oxford."

Burnside never made public the arrest of this woman spy nor his jailing of her in a fine Cincinnati hotel. All three women actually became a sore trial for him. Ginger and her mother repeatedly turned down parole offers with terms they thought disagreeable. After many revisions, they agreed to modified versions which allowed all to return home.

The women's activities continued, although Lottie and her husband moved to New York to escape notoriety. Ginger returned to her home in Memphis, and stories of her escapades continued to circulate. Tales abounded that she could be seen "galloping through Union lines to carry information and medicines." She was arrested again but found some way to get out of trouble, although she spent several months in prison.

"Miss Ginger" Moon's life of high drama continued far beyond the war. She ran an exclusive Memphis boarding house, where she also welcomed the homeless and took care of several children. Her heroics reappeared during the 1870s' yellow fever epidemics (in which she lost a brother and a sister), when she nursed sick and dying Memphians.

By the age of seventy-five, the former Civil War spy was in California, knocking on Hollywood's door and soon playing character roles in silent movies. She appeared with Theda Bara, Douglas Fairbanks (in the original *Robin Hood*), Pola Negri, and other movie notables of the day. At a casting interview, she was asked if she thought she could really act. Her reply seemed almost autobiographical: "I am seventy-five years old, and I have played all the parts."

In 1925, while living with an adopted daughter in New York City's Greenwich Village, Ginger Moon died at eighty-one. Her body was taken to Memphis's Elmwood Cemetery and placed in an unmarked grave.

99
The Offield Brothers

Five Brothers Toiling in Sickness and in Health

They were from pioneering East Tennessee families that had settled in the Holston Valley. Joseph and Elizabeth Bolling Offield had made a good life on a five-hundred-acre homestead near Bristol, where they raised a large family. Among the children were six sons, five of whom left home to serve the Confederacy. But only one would return.

The brothers wrote letters during their trials away from home, and because the letters revealed different handwriting and varying degrees of expression, some may have been the product of fellow soldiers taking dictation from the Offields. The letters eventually were edited and reproduced with only slight modification by Leona Taylor Aiken, a member of the Watauga Association of Genealogists. She noted how the letters reveal the degree of literacy among Civil War soldiers. Two of John Offield's letters, both written from the site of a Confederate victory at Fairfax Courthouse, Virginia, were filled with confidence:

June the 28 1861

Dear father[:] it is with great Pleasure that i . . . let you know that i am well . . . I have found our Company . . . wee reached Winchester the 27 about midnight . . . the Company has had a little scrimage[.] they run the Yankees from newcreek Dept [Depot] and taken too [two] cannons and Bernt the railrode Bridge up and [took] aright smart of other plunder and lost narry man[.] we taken there [their] flag also.

Apparently John dictated the letter, because whoever penned it twice misspelled the family name. Another letter—written to his brother Joseph, who was eventually killed in the war—was a reminder about the *real* war:

August 25, 1861

we hav[e] had a heap of sikness . . . Jo if you cant cum to our company i dont want you to join . . . times is teribel hard. We have bred un meat and met and bred; and crackers and coffey ur giten cerce [scarce] and we dont think the[y] will git any . . . til we whirp [whip] the yankeys and git ther purvisien [provisions]. . . .

In a separate note:

you no [know] nothing aBout Warr til you git in wher the men lie on the ground[;] you cold walk on them fir an hunderd yards . . . I leveld my old muskit at one. . . . But I dont no whether I kild him ur not. . . . I promised to Bring you a scalp and that Cap is as ni[gh] it as things gits[.]

The following letter, from Tullahoma, Tennessee, arrived from James Offield to his brother William, the oldest of the Offield brothers:

Apr 21st 1862

Dear Brother: . . . myself & John are both well. . . . Bill you don't know how glad I was when I heard

the unexpected news that you had got home for we had all given you up as dead[.] Bill I would be glad if you could stay at home awhile some 2 or 3 weeks, but Lt. Carrier talked to the Col. about getting you a furlough & and he said that it was impossible to get it & perhaps you had better come as soon as you can for the orders are verry strict & there might be some danger in staying too long. When you come I want you to bring me 2 shirts & 1 pair of socks & the same amount for John . . . we want you to get the money at home & bring us a pretty good supply of tobacco for we cant get any here that is worth anything & we have to pay 1.50 cts per plug for that[.]

James, who had "the Rheumatism," according to brother Joseph, was soon taken prisoner and died ten months later in a Union prison camp near Murfreesboro. Word of his death was relayed to his parents in a letter from H. R. Jobe. An excerpt follows:

June the 4th 1863

Dear Sir—Having just learned of the fate of your son Ja's [James], I decern [discern] it a duty I owe to his relatives to inform them concerning him, & therefore embrace this opportunity & devote it to that purpose. We received by flag of truce this morning a report of all the members of our Regiment who died in the Yankee Hospital at Murfreesboro while prisoners & I am sorry to say that your son James' name appears on that list, he died on the 9th day of February 1863. . . .

Nearly eighteen months later, John Offield was wounded near Marietta, Georgia, in the defense of Atlanta. He died eleven days later on July 3. His brother Joseph tried to find consoling words in a letter home, excerpted here:

Aug 19th '64

My Dear Father, Mother & Sister: . . .

I was with John untill he died[.] he was wounded 22 of June[;] Died 3rd July [after having] lived 11 days[.] He was sensible of his death all the time—saw [saying] he new [knew] that he wants [to] die and that he was willing to go for he was agoing to rest[;] he did not seem to suffer much untill the last[;] he was up 3 minutes before he died[.]

Another letter, from William, this time to their mother only, further discussed John's death:

I was truly glad to here that he was prepard to meet his God in Peace[.] I no he is far better off that [than] we ar[.] you wanted to no how he was beried[;] Jo sayd he had good cloth[e]s and a verry good coffin and was put away verry decent[.] tell Georg to stay at home as long as he can and then go to cavalry[.] I dont want him to come here[.] . . . If I never meet you no more in this life I want you to meet me in Heaven[.] I will close[.] Wm Offield.

William also wrote of the physical hardships he suffered. Because of unclean food and rampant infections, disease struck untold numbers of soldiers, including William, who wrote August 23, 1864, from Atlanta that illness had caused his blindness:

August 23rd '64

Dear Companion and Friends: . . . I want to come home[.] I has been so blind on there [their] marches that they hav had to leed me after night[.] I think they ought to do something for me[.] I think I ought to go to the Hospital or bee discharged[.] I dont think Im any use to the government[.]

While William's mood suggested that either his death or total disability might be imminent, he would, in fact, be the lone survivor among the five Offield brothers who had marched to war. The final brother to die was Washington Offield, who, although he was officially too young to serve in the army, ran away from home and lost his life fighting for the Confederacy. His twin, George, took heed from William's letters and remained at home with their parents and four sisters.

William Offield would spend the remainder of his life in Sullivan County. After the death of his wife, Mary, in 1892, he lived until 1914, dying at the age of eighty-two.

100
David Glasgow Farragut

The Battle at Sea—and "Full Speed Ahead"

At the age of thirteen, David Glasgow Farragut was in the War of 1812 aboard the USS *Essex*—and not far removed from the Tennessee frontier. Born in 1801 near Knoxville, he had been a midshipman in the United States Navy since the age of nine. When seamen serving two British ships overpowered the *Essex* and began

David Glasgow Farragut, America's first admiral.

to board the fallen vessel, a youthful member of the British navy scooped up the *Essex*'s pet pig, Murphy, and proclaimed, "A prize! Ho, Boys! A fine grunter."

Aware that personal property was not considered a prize, Midshipman Farragut shouted out, "I claim that animal as my own." To this his British counterpart responded: "Ah, but you are my prisoner, and your pig also."

Humiliated and furious, young Farragut latched onto the pig, and a tug of war ensued. As English sailors and their American prisoners crowded around to watch the tussle, one of the former shouted: "Go it my little Yankee! If you can thrash Shorty, you shall have your pig."

Abandoning the tug of war, the boys set aside the pig and engaged in a fistfight, "landing slug after slug with Murphy squealing excitedly on the sidelines."

The Briton was game, but David won handily, and he managed to salvage a small victory in the midst of the larger humiliation, noting that he "took Master Murphy under my arm, feeling that I had, in some degree, wiped out the disgrace of our defeat."

Farragut would display the same grit in the face of defeat during the Civil War, becoming the Union's greatest naval commander. After capturing New Orleans for the Union in one of the war's most pivotal battles, Farragut also succeeded at the Battle of Mobile Bay, where his fleet had lapsed into confusion after a lead ship was sunk by Confederate torpedoes (mines) in August 1864.

To rally his men, Farragut shouted: "Damn the torpedoes—Full speed ahead!" Ordering his ship into the lead position and proceeding up the channel, Farragut maneuvered through the mines, dodged the enemy's ramming efforts with their own vessels, and absorbed a furious onslaught of firepower from sea and shore alike before claiming victory. His rallying cry became one of the most famous and most quoted in American history; and his Civil War heroics prompted the United States in 1866 to establish the navy's rank of admiral expressly for him.

Farragut came from a long line of fighting men, the most illustrious being Don Pedro Feragut who, in 1229, helped expel the Moors from a Mediterranean island off the coast of Spain. Five hundred years later, George Farragut, father of the future Admiral Farragut, took to the sea from his native Spain and fought in the service of Russia against the Turks. After this episode, the elder Farragut set sail in 1775 toward New Orleans, where he took up the American cause in the Revolutionary War. In the 1790s, he settled in the Tennessee country. But George Farragut was not born to the frontier farming life, and Tennessee was too far from the sea. In 1807, he moved his family to New Orleans, where, by a strange chain of events, his son would follow a path to greatness.

While fishing on Lake Pontchartrain, George Farragut spotted a boat in which he found naval Captain David Porter exhausted from sunstroke. Farragut took the old captain home where, despite devoted care, Porter passed away. George's wife, Elizabeth, died of yellow fever at the same time, and she and the captain were both buried on the same day.

As events unfolded, the Farraguts learned that Porter was the father of the younger Captain David Porter, soon elevated to commodore and placed in charge of the New Orleans naval station. Hearing stories of the kindness shown his father by the Farraguts, he visited the family and offered to adopt one of the now-motherless children.

David Farragut would recall years later:

I, being inspired by his uniform and that of my brother William, who had received an appointment in the navy some time before, promptly said I would go. . . . Thus commenced my acquaintance with the celebrated Commodore David Porter, of the United States Navy, and I am happy to have it in my power to say, with feelings of the warmest gratitude, that he was ever to me all that he promised, my "friend and guardian."

Historian Samuel C. Williams considered this visit the beginning of "a series of coincidences that are without parallel in the history of the American Navy." Because of Commodore Porter, Farragut not only entered the United States Navy before he was ten (thus joining Porter on the *Essex*), but also the commodore's grandson, David D. Porter, became a protégé of Farragut and succeeded him as the navy's second full admiral.

Farragut's exploits were so extraordinary that he won acclaim from one of the nation's great writers, Oliver Wendell Holmes, who composed a poem in Farragut's honor:

I give the name that fits him best—
Ay, better than his own—
The Sea King of the Sovereign West.
Who made his mast a throne.

Although he traveled the world over and lived in different places prior to his death in 1870 at age sixty-nine, Farragut had but one home: On the navy rolls, he always remained a man from Tennessee. His birthplace outside of Knoxville became the town of Farragut.

101
Father Abram Ryan
The "Poet-Priest of the Confederacy"

A favorite story among the girls at St. Cecilia's Academy in Nashville involved the "the poet-priest of the Confederacy," Father Abram Ryan, who related the original version of this tale while visiting Nashville about 1862.

Catholic priests, when necessary, ministered to both Union and Confederate armies. In New Orleans, the Union's Major General Benjamin Butler, a New

Father Abram Ryan eulogized the Southern cause.

Ryan, born in 1839 to Irish immigrants on the Virginia coast, was inspired early in life to both the priesthood and the music of poetry, which he composed throughout his life. His poems were more spontaneous than artistic, and the feelings expressed in his "poems of personal life" and in his "public poems" dealing with the Civil War echoed common ideas and attitudes, making him one of the most popular of Southern poets. His published works passed through many editions.

Having lost a brother who served in the Confederate army, he finally reconciled himself with the Union in 1878. He was so impressed by the North's charitable response to the devastation of Memphis during its third yellow fever epidemic that, in 1883, he helped Northern charities by making a lecture tour on their behalf. But Father Ryan was getting noticeably tired. He lived only to the age of forty-seven, dying in 1886 in a Franciscan monastery in Louisville, Kentucky.

102
Mary Elizabeth McDonald
In Pursuit of an All-Woman Troop

Union General J. B. Steedman peered in surprise at the Confederate prisoners brought before him in April 1865. Peering back was the group's leader, Captain Mary Elizabeth McDonald—and her all-woman troop from Rhea County.

Steedman, from Ohio, was post commander during the Federal occupation of Chattanooga, where the Union established a major supply base for its operations in the Deep South. Reports of Confederate activity from area Home Guard units were arriving daily at his office. When news of a Rhea County mounted troop also reached Chattanooga, local authorities became even more concerned. Prodded by local Union sympathizer John P. Walker, they ordered an arrest of the offenders.

Union soldiers, however, discovered that the enemy looked more like homemakers than Home Guards. The women, having formed into a mounted troop, had given themselves military ranks and a name— the Rhea County Spartans. According to reports, they assisted struggling Confederate families, principally widows and orphans. Other sources claimed that the Spartans went into the field to provide clothing and

Englander who commanded occupation forces there, summoned Father Ryan. Answering the general's call immediately, Father Ryan sat before Butler, who said he understood that Abram Ryan would not minister to or bury Union soldiers. Father Ryan corrected him: "General, you have been misinformed. I would like to bury the last one of you."

After the Confederacy's surrender, Father Ryan pastored small missions in the South, including one in Knoxville on Summit Hill (site of the future Immaculate Conception Catholic Church), where he wrote what church members described as a requiem to the Lost Cause. In part of the Knoxville poem, "The Conquered Banner," he implored his reader:

Take that Banner down! 'tis tattered;
Broken is its staff and shattered;
And the valiant hosts are scattered
    Over whom it floated high.
Oh! 'tis hard for us to fold it;
Hard to think there's none to hold it;
Hard that those who once unrolled it
    Now must furl it with a sigh.

supplies to Confederate soldiers who were their relatives and friends. In a later letter, Mary Elizabeth McDonald stated that her troop was organized in the summer of 1862 and often met secretly in the town of Washington, usually in a local church.

Most of the female captives ranged in age from their teens to their twenties and were the offspring of prominent Rhea and Hamilton County families. Mary Elizabeth (later married to J. E. Sawyers) was, according to the 1860 census, one of eight children of major landowner Bryan R. McDonald, who also had other family members in the group.

Ordered to make an arrest, Hamilton County Federal officers Lieutenant W. B. Gothard and Captain Thomas Walker of the Sixth Mounted Infantry did their duty. They then marched the prisoners to the river and transported them by riverboat to Chattanooga. Marching them through the mud of city streets to local Union headquarters, the officers stopped first at the provost marshal, then proceeded to General Steedman. The thunderstruck general, upon hearing a full account of their activities, instantly released the prisoners and congratulated them on their efforts to help destitute Confederate families. Steedman, who hoped to recommend similar efforts for Union families, ordered his men to escort the women safely home.

The other identified members of the Spartans included Caroline McDonald, first lieutenant; Ann Paine, second lieutenant; Rhodie Thomison, third lieutenant; Jane Keith, first sergeant; Rachel Howell, second sergeant; Sallie Mitchell, third sergeant; Minerva Tucker, fourth sergeant; and Privates Mary Paine, Mary Keith, Mary Crawford, Sidney McDonald, Jennie Hoyal, Ann Gillespie, Barbara Allen, Jane Locke, Margaret Sykes, Martha Bell, Mary Robinson, Josephine Allen, Mary Ann McDonald, Sarah Rudd, Kate Dunwoody, Kate Hoyal, Martha Early, Tennessee Thomison, Louisa McDonald, and Maggie Keith.

One report claimed that Rhea County's female Home Guard began an effort which evolved into the "Confederate Memorial Association and the Daughters of the Confederacy."

103
George King

*The Enforcer: Law and Order
in the Countryside*

George King confronted murderers and thieves.

With the breakdown of law and order on the homefront during the Civil War, civilians in West Tennessee pleaded for protection against marauding bands of raiders. Any man who brought justice during the absence of civil authority could expect cheers wherever he rode and sometimes an unusual offer of reward. Such was the experience of Confederate Captain George King.

One day in 1864 he decided to visit the widow and children of a man whose murder he had avenged. The widow, excited to meet King, immediately sought a suitable gift and wished that she had a good horse to offer. King disclosed in later memoirs: "I told her . . . that a present from her to me would not bring back her husband to her. She said she knew that, but that she felt like that she wanted to do something for me."

During this exchange, one of the widow's daughters offered an alternative: "Mother give him one of us girls."

The suggestion startled King and prompted a round of laughter from one of his lieutenants, who explained that King was married. Declining the proposal of marriage as graciously as he could, King was about to depart when "the girls and old woman fell to begging me to stay and let them fix something for me to eat, and I thanked her and left her a gazing after me and wishing me to live forever."

King was a native of Gibson County, located in the heart of the regional lawlessness he fought. He had formed King's Scouts in late 1863. The Home Guard consisted of about forty men trying to defend Gibson and neighboring Dyer County from bushwhackers, thieves, and vandals who preyed on defenseless women, children, and the remaining male population that was either too old or too young to fight. Although West Tennessee was technically under Union occupation, few Union troops were available to patrol the countryside, leaving the citizenry open to acts of violence.

Fearful of being called a marauder himself, King quickly joined the Confederate army. At the urging of both Union and Confederate sympathizers, the Confederate government assigned King and his men to continue their home-guard duties as before. This arrangement was agreeable to local Union commanders, who gave King the freedom to cross their lines in the pursuit of outlaws.

King's efforts were successful, and he recounted his exploits after the war in a book-length manuscript which was never published. Only loose and disconnected pages were left for such regional historians as Frederick M. Culp to pore over and assimilate.

King's aim, the writings revealed, was to "write for the rising generation to take warning and never steal and to show what had become of thieves heretofore." Showing no mercy even toward childhood friends from Gibson County, King resolved to track down and bring to punishment all scoundrels.

One of his first captives was a thief who had married into the family of King's wife. The thief appealed for his freedom on the basis of family relations, but King's only acknowledgment was to offer to kill him "quicker" out of respect. When the prisoner tried to escape, King's men shot him eight times. This was the first time King had seen a man killed, and the sight of blood forced him to leave the scene. But it did not deter him from his mission.

In another incident, King's men tracked down a Confederate deserter named Johnson, who, in the company of a Union deserter, robbed area citizens. Johnson also appealed for his life—on behalf of his mother. But King showed little mercy: "I told him that he was not a caring for his Mother or he would have been with her when he was with that Yankee a robbing."

As the war progressed, King furthered his zeal for justice by tracking two of his own childhood friends who were brothers, one of whom was killed during the chase. Having stolen horses from a local farm, the surviving thief asked to keep his spoils, explaining that he needed an artificial leg. His captor was moved but not swayed. King returned the horses to their rightful owner, then raised enough money to buy his prisoner an artificial limb.

Another boyhood friend was not so lucky and proved to be King's most formidable foe. G. W. Hobbs, a Confederate deserter turned horse thief, began to display a sudden wealth of fancy clothes and fine horses. King began watching Hobbs closely. Quickly proving that Hobbs plundered his neighbors, King arrested him.

The prisoner escaped, only to be arrested again. He escaped yet again in a scenario played out several times until King tracked Hobbs to a local dance. Confronted, Hobbs bolted for the door and raced into a nearby field, where King gunned him down. The death of this childhood friend did not disturb King, who noted that after such an intensive chase he "hollared with joy" when he saw that Hobbs "was no more."

King gained a reputation for his resolve to protect civilians and his frequent executions of Civil War outlaws and guerrillas. After tracking down a man named Atterbury, who with an accomplice had killed two boys named Stone, King ignored the killer's prayers and ordered him before a firing squad. Shots rang out—but to no avail: The man was still alive. King ordered his men to shoot again, but the prisoner continued to live. After twenty-five rounds had been fired into the seemingly indestructible Atterbury, King departed the scene. When he returned the next day to find that Atterbury finally had succumbed, King observed that the killer's sins had been so severe that they were not easily removed.

King's Scouts were so welcome in the small towns

they visited that local residents often treated them to festive outpourings. King said Dyer Countians threw a party for his men anytime they were in the area ("After I had driven all of the desperadoes, thieves, pick pockets and murderers out of Dyer County"). He added:

> (Because) the Company had formed with such a marvelous character the ladies were not afraid of them like they were others. I went to Dyer County several times after I relieved them of such a heavy burden. The citizens acted to me like I was their kindred. I will say Dyer County paid more respects to me than any other except Gibson, my home County.

King surrendered his post at war's end in May 1865. He insisted on the same parole that occupying Union forces had given to other Confederate soldiers rather than the less-restrictive oath of allegiance administered to civilians. King's life, however, came to a mysterious end in 1876 when he was killed by unknown assailants near the Gibson-Weakley County line in the Walnut Grove community. Later speculations focused on his death as possible revenge from war-time enemies.

104
George L. Knox
The Emancipated Heart

Like most ex-slaves, George L. Knox never forgot the treatment he received from his former master. When an opportunity for payback arose in the 1880s, he would reciprocate—kindness for kindness.

Born in 1841, Knox began his life on a Middle Tennessee plantation, but at age five he was sent to the auction block when his Wilson County master died. Taken to Statesville, the boy was purchased by his late master's children, who determined to keep the child and his siblings together. At Statesville, according to Knox's later memoirs, "the Negro-traders gathered from every part of the country to buy slaves to take further South and sell."

The new master, never identified in Knox's memoirs, had no need for a slave and proved to be a gentle and considerate man. Referred to merely as "Young Master," he was believed to be R. A. Knox, who hired out George L. Knox and once turned down sixteen hundred dollars in gold for him; he protected Knox

from beatings and removed him from any job that Knox disliked.

Despite a deep appreciation for his master's acts of goodwill, Knox longed for freedom. During the Civil War, he and his brother escaped with a group of slaves and placed themselves in the hands of nearby Union soldiers. Assigned to a work detail at Murfreesboro, Knox found his new surroundings no improvement over his old life. "Our masters had been telling us all the time that the Yankees wanted to get us and sell us in Cuba as slaves," Knox wrote. He added:

> I overheard a couple of Yankees saying, "There is a big fellow up there . . . that we could get $2,000 for in Cuba." . . . Tired, and in the midst of strangers, all new faces to us, I began to reflect. I said to my brother in a low tone as I passed him, "this is hell isn't it." He said, "it is."

The brother soon died from one of the many camp illnesses, leaving Knox without any relations other than a sister, whom he would not see for another twenty years.

Making himself useful as a "cook, nurse, servant, messenger, and teamster" with Indiana troops, Knox worked for a Union captain who was wounded during the 1863 battles at Chattanooga and who died in his arms. Knox then worked for another captain, who, during a furlough in 1864, took him to Indiana.

Knox discovered that racial prejudices also existed in the North, but he decided to remain in Indiana and pursue barbering—one of the few lines of work in which black men could prosper or attain community stature. He became a successful apprentice barber, eventually saving enough money to own his own shop. Knox also learned to read and write with the help of several people, including his wife, some houseguests who were schoolteachers, and an Englishman who taught Knox's Sunday School class.

Devotion to hard work and a kindly disposition became great assets for Knox, who made many friends and attracted powerful white clients—most of them business leaders and politicians, including future President of the United States Benjamin Harrison. By the late 1880s, Knox was a wealthy man, owning many barbershops. As the years passed, he gained a reputation as a successful church leader, popular newspaper publisher who supported Harrison's presidential elections, and a Republican political leader whose power crossed color lines. In addition to President Harrison, Knox counted among his friends the national black leader Booker T. Washington.

Knox's weekly newspaper, *Indianapolis Freeman*, in 1894-95, published the events of his early life and his Civil War experiences. By now, he was called the "preeminent black Republican in Indiana."

In his recollections, Knox told of his travels during the late 1880s back to his native Tennessee, where his onetime master, now seventy-six, was in a desolate condition. Overwhelmed by memories, Knox made him a promise:

> Do you remember at your father's sale your sister bought my sister and brother and you bought me? I have gone north and have been blessed. That act was bread cast upon the water to be gathered many days after. As long as I have one dollar, half of it is yours.

True to his word, he provided financial support for the rest of "Young Master's" life. During subsequent visits to Tennessee, Knox also found his long-lost sister, now in poor health, whom he took home to Indiana.

Knox lived to be eighty-six. At his death in 1927, both the white and black press called him the "dean of Negro publishers" and honored a man who was never bitter. Knox's philosophy of life had been printed on the masthead of his paper: "If a newspaper does not take a cheerful, hopeful and constructive view of things, it is not a healthful force in the community. This paper exists to render service to society. It will not become rabid, yellow or truculent."

105
"Carrie" McGavock

*Carnage and Compassion
from the Battle of Franklin*

Carnton Mansion, the most elegant estate in all of Williamson County after its construction in 1826, was noted for its thoroughbred horses and its elite guest list. Presidents had stood on the veranda to take tea and discuss politics with their friend and host, former Nashville mayor Randal McGavock. (the McGavocks were considered by some people to be the wealthiest family in Nashville during the late eighteenth and early nineteenth centuries.) After serving as mayor, McGavock retired to build this showplace of early Tennessee wealth, to spend time with his family, and to entertain. Such scenes were ancient history when Randal McGavock's daughter-in-law, "Carrie," opened Carnton's doors on the night of November 30, 1864, and invited in the Confederacy's wounded and dying from its last campaign in Tennessee.

The carnage began with a decision by the Confederate commander, General John Bell Hood, to chase recklessly after Union troops under General John M. Schofield, an old West Point classmate. At the time, Hood was suffering from previous battle wounds and had to be strapped to his horse. One arm flopped at his side from wounds received at the Battle of Gettysburg (Pennsylvania), and one leg was amputated above the knee after the Battle of Chickamauga. Reports circulated that he was on heavy doses of laudanum, a mixture of opium and pure alcohol.

Angered that Schofield had slipped by him in the night at Spring Hill and entrenched at Franklin, Hood was quick to follow. He then ordered the Army of Tennessee into a frontal assault across open ground against well-protected enemy artillery. The attack, which began at dusk and continued into the night, annihilated one Confederate regiment and division after another. It became an "individual's war" of hand-to-hand combat between the survivors and their assailants.

The Franklin homestead of F. B. Carter was at the center of the action. Twenty-two of his family members and friends hovered in the basement until the last blow could be heard above. His son, Captain Tod Carter, was among the Confederates mortally wounded during the assault. The elderly father and his daughters found the young soldier only two hundred yards away and carried him home to die.

As temperatures dipped considerably that night following the bloody and perhaps needless Battle of Franklin, Carnton Mansion was turned into a hospital. A concerned General Nathan Bedford Forrest, who had been opposed to the Confederate attack at Franklin which claimed six thousand of his brethren in less than five hours, visited the home during and after the battle.

Carrie McGavock asked only that one bedroom be left so that her children could be separated from the events of the evening. The front upstairs bedroom, a former nursery, became an operating room. According to accounts, "the amputated limbs were dropped out of the window," and the wood floors were soaked with blood. Small footprints—stained into the floor—became permanent. Perhaps they belonged to Carrie, who assisted the wounded throughout the night. She was described as an "angel of mercy" by the hundreds of Rebel soldiers who managed to get into Carnton. Carrie also took care of Clarksville's General William Quarles when his wounds forced him into a two-month convalescence at the estate. (He was later captured and imprisoned by the Union until the war's end.)

In a letter dated January 14, 1865, William Dudley Gale told his wife about Carrie McGavock and that fateful night:

> Every room was filled, every bed had two bleeding fellows, every spare space, niche and corner, under the stairs, in the hall, everywhere but one room for her family. And when the noble house could hold no more, the yard was appropriated until the wounded and dead filled that, and all were not yet provided for. Our doctors were dificient [sic] in bandages, and she. . . . began by giving her old linen, then her towels and napkins, then her sheets and tablecloths, and then her husband's shirts and her own undergarments.

The compassionate Caroline "Carrie" McGavock was from Louisiana but had Tennessee ancestry; she was the granddaughter of Nashville's preeminent frontier attorney and national politician Felix Grundy. She was also a second cousin of her husband, John McGavock. After their marriage in 1848, the couple moved to Carnton's one thousand acres. When McGavock inherited the farm in 1854, he added a special touch to the house: a grand veranda at the back in remembrance of the "cool porches of her plantation home in Louisiana." Carrie added a different touch altogether by inviting orphans from a New Orleans asylum to become her household servants. This gave her the opportunity to educate them, provide religious training, and find homes and employment for each.

Carrie McGavock kept alive the tradition of entertaining amid grand gardens. From the back of the house, a boxwood-edged walkway led to the garden, which seemed identical to that at Andrew Jackson's Hermitage. And so it was: Carrie McGavock's mother-in-law was a close friend of Rachel Jackson, who

helped in the garden's design and assisted in the planting stages. In those days long past, Presidents Jackson and Polk were frequent visitors, as were many other famous Tennesseans of the 1830s and 1840s, including Grundy, who was the United States attorney general in President Martin Van Buren's administration. They often gathered in "McGavock's Grove," now filled with the casualties of the Battle of Franklin.

History would remember Carrie's grand veranda long after her death in 1905 at the age of seventy-six (John McGavock had died twelve years earlier). Their historic site eventually would be advertised as the place where four of six slain Confederate generals lay in flag-draped coffins. Two of the generals were Tennesseans.

General John Adams, thirty-nine, a former West Point graduate from Giles County, was mortally wounded when he spurred his white charger to the top of a Union entrenchment and took nine bullets to his body. He was lifted from beneath his fallen horse and taken to Union surgeons, who tried in vain to save him. Adams noticed that many of his enemy were sad that such a gallant man was dying. In his last breath, he reminded them that it was the duty of a soldier to die for his country.

General Otho French Strahl, thirty-three, a resident of Dyer County, had moved to Tennessee from Ohio in 1855 to study law under Judge John W. Harris in Fayette County, then moved to Dyersburg to practice law. The morning of the battle, Strahl felt a compulsion to give his horse to his friend Charles Todd Quintard, a Connecticut native who had settled in Tennessee and had become a popular Confederate chaplain and occasional regimental surgeon. During the day's disastrous frontal assault, Strahl's brigade became trapped underneath Union breastworks. Urging his men on, Strahl helped load rifles and passed them forward to troops firing over the hostile parapet. Strahl took a bullet in his neck and crawled to Colonel Fountain Stafford to surrender command. Strahl was shot a second time. A moment later, another burst killed Strahl, Stafford, and several others.

The other two generals on Carnton's porch were Patrick R. Cleburne, an Irish-born and Arkansas-affiliated commander, who favored the freeing of slaves in order to encourage black men to fight for the South and who died leading his men on foot toward the Union center; and Hiram B. Granbury, a Mississippi attorney recently moved to Texas, who died with Cleburne in that same charge. (The body of General States Rights Gist of South Carolina was taken elsewhere.)

Another Tennessee general was mortally wounded at Franklin but died later. General John Carpenter Carter, who had made Tennessee his home after leaving Georgia, was a onetime faculty member of Cumberland University Law School in Lebanon. He had married the daughter of the school's founder, Judge Abraham Caruthers, later becoming a Memphis attorney. His injury also came in a charge of enemy breastworks.

In the days following, the McGavocks made another contribution to Civil War history when they asked that deceased Confederates be brought from the nearby Franklin battleground. McGavock donated two acres adjoining the family's cemetery to serve as the final resting place for 1,481 fallen Rebels. As the bodies were prepared for burial, Carrie McGavock wrote down their names and whatever other information had been sewn into their coats. Each was buried with some identifying marker. The cemetery became the nation's only privately owned and maintained Civil War cemetery.

106
Edmund W. Rucker

The Last Stand over Crossed Swords:
The Battle of Nashville

The Confederacy's last major offensive, which ended at Nashville on the night of December 16, 1864, was fought in an icy total darkness. Soldiers could not distinguish one another in the battering, freezing rain except by the light of exploding shells and burning wagons and underbrush. A dogfight was all that opposing forces could wage in this final moment, which ended all hope of a Confederate States of America. The Battle of Nashville became one of the war's most decisive Union victories.

Outnumbered, ill-equipped, hungry, and cold, Southern soldiers were no match for the overwhelmingly superior Union forces waiting at the state capital. In their retreat, scores of the vanquished Confederate infantrymen were shoeless, leaving bloodied footprints in the frozen mud during a chaotic escape. Confederate Colonel Edmund W. Rucker, a native of Murfreesboro and the grandson of a War of 1812 com-

mander, General James Winchester, made a crucial decision. He and his Twelfth Tennessee Cavalry were part of General Nathan Bedford Forrest's troops helping to hold Granny White Pike at all costs. Their action was a sudden rear-guard defense to save what was left of the Army of Tennessee.

Rucker ordered his brigade to build a barricade of logs and brush across the pike. Thousands of oncoming Union soldiers responded by charging in classic cavalry fashion—sabers drawn and using their new Spencer repeating rifles to full effect. Mere hundreds of Rebels were fierce in their defiance. Their barricade stand did what it had to do: buy time for the Confederacy's retreating infantry to pass through Brentwood toward Franklin.

Rucker was a half-mile away trying to position an artillery unit, but he returned quickly to the fight. A horseman approached him. Unable to see through the darkness and icy rain, Rucker moved out to meet the rider, whom he believed to be one of his own men from the Twelfth (Confederate) Tennessee. The unknown horsemen yelled out that he was Colonel George Spalding of the Twelfth Tennessee *Federal* Cavalry.

Grabbing for Spalding's bridle, Rucker yelled back, "You are my prisoner. I am Colonel Ed Rucker of the Twelfth Tennessee *Rebel* Cavalry."

Spalding countered, "Not by a damned sight," spurred his horse and bolted away.

One of Spalding's men, Captain Joseph C. Boyer, rushed to the scene and engaged Rucker in a spirited, mounted saber duel. In the numbing cold, Boyer wrested Rucker's saber from his grasp but in the same instant lost his own saber to Rucker. The dramatic duel on horseback continued, each man using the weapon of his foe until a stray shot struck Rucker's saber arm, and he fell. Taken prisoner, Rucker was carried to a Nashville hospital, where his arm was amputated. His saber became a souvenir for Colonel Spalding.

By the end of the war months later, Rucker had been promoted to the rank of general. He was healthy enough to resume the career of civil engineer which he had begun in Memphis before the war. Returning there, Rucker helped to build a forty-mile stretch of the Memphis and Little Rock Railroad. He soon became superintendent of the Selma, Marion and Memphis Railroad, owned by his former cavalry commander Forrest. Assuming his duties in Birmingham, Alabama, Rucker became prominent in numerous other Birmingham manufacturing interests as well. Even after Forrest had resigned as president of the financially troubled railroad in 1874, Rucker was retained as president. He and his family remained in Birmingham.

Rucker's sword, meanwhile, went north with Spalding, who also was promoted to general. A native of Scotland, Spalding made his home in Michigan. Eventually he would become a congressman.

Twenty-five years after the wild night-fight in snow and sleet at the barricade and his dramatic horseback saber duel during the Confederacy's last big battle, Rucker was honored at a public ceremony for his wartime service. As part of that 1889 ceremony, he received a special gift: In a gesture of reconciliation, George Spalding returned his saber.

Rucker lived to the age of eighty-eight; he died in 1924 in Birmingham.

Section Three

Reconstruction

New South to World War 1

Historical Background

Reconstruction

New South to World War 1

Tennessee's ordeal of conflict did not cease with the end of the Civil War's military hostilities, but continued during the postwar period known as Reconstruction. The war's legacy of political bitterness endured for years after the Confederate surrender, as rival camps of conservatives and radicals sought to use politics to punish their enemies and bar them from participating in the political system. This political warfare was only slightly less violent emotionally than the military struggle.

The state suffered considerable devastation—both human and physical—as a result of the war. Farm wealth and agricultural production plummeted, but perhaps the greatest loss of all was in human resources. Thousands of young men of marriageable age had died in combat and from disease and wounds. Freeing the slaves added to an already acute labor shortage, and agriculture languished for want of hands to work the fields. Emancipation and the war's human losses led to a booster campaign by the state of Tennessee to attract skilled immigrants from Europe to make up the shortfall.

From the end of the war in 1865 until 1869, Tennessee came under the rule of the unpopular, even tyrannical, regime of Governor William G. "Parson" Brownlow. Although a strong Union man, he personally believed in slavery. Brownlow's faction of radical Unionists wished to break utterly the political and social standing of those Tennesseans who had supported the Confederacy, especially former slaveholders. Such policies were not popular among the vast majority of white citizens, so Brownlow in 1867 forced the Tennessee General Assembly to give the vote to black freedmen in order to bolster his support at the polls.

Tennessee became the first state to endorse black suffrage—a full two years before Congress did so by passing the Fifteenth Amendment—and the only one of the seceded states to abolish slavery by its own act. Obnoxious as the Brownlow regime was to many of the state's citizens, its ascendancy during Reconstruction meant that Tennessee would be the only state to escape the harsh military rule inflicted on the South by a radical Congress seeking punitive measures for a defeated South. Brownlow's eagerness to bow to Congress's demands also ensured that Tennessee was the first state to rejoin the Union.

Such an unpopular and undemocratic government as Brownlow's soon called forth the agents of its own demise. Robbed of their political voice and driven underground by the governor and his militia, ex-Confederates organized into bizarre and secretive groups to express their opposition to the radicals. One such shadowy vigilante organization was the Ku Klux Klan, which intimidated Brownlow supporters and kept freedmen in a subordinate position throughout the countryside. The Klan flourished primarily because the radicals excluded ex-Confederates from the normal channels of political activity. Hence, when Brownlow left Tennessee in 1869 to become a United States senator, the Klan formally disbanded. The man who succeeded him as governor, DeWitt Clinton Senter, quickly used his office to restore voting rights for ex-Confederates and to put an end to radical Reconstruction in Tennessee. By 1870, a new state constitution, reflecting the changes wrought by Reconstruction, was ratified. Black men retained voting privileges, but most could not afford the poll tax that all voters were now required to pay.

While much of the countryside was devastated by war, pillage, or neglect, Tennessee's cities emerged from the carnage relatively intact and even prosperous. Memphis, Nashville, Chattanooga, Knoxville, and a host of smaller towns had been collection points for troops and supplies, and city merchants had been able to flourish on the trade of thousands of regularly paid soldiers. Overcrowding during the 1870s was, in fact, a contributing factor to the crisis of the deadly yellow fever in Memphis. The city was ravaged by three separate outbreaks of the mosquito-borne disease between 1871 and 1879. All who could flee did.

Tennessee cities experienced a large increase in their black population during this time, as many freedmen left the plantations or fled the rural areas where the Klan's violence could be felt. Such refugees often congregated near military posts in so-called contraband camps, which formed the nuclei of later black communities. The Freedmen's Bureau set up scores of black public schools, and newly established colleges, such as Fisk in Nashville, provided the first higher education available to freedmen.

Other black schools, like Knoxville College, were founded by church groups. The formation of urban black enclaves made possible the growth of a black professional and business class. Since economic self-sufficiency was one of the main objectives of freedmen, many former slaves rose from the chaos of war to become successful leaders and entrepreneurs in Tennessee.

The migration of large numbers of black citizens into Tennessee's fast-growing cities had two results: It created the tightly knit communities that produced successful civic leaders, and it drew whites and blacks into a close but uneasy coexistence. Black Tennesseans built on their newfound legal gains after the war and were active politically well into the 1880s. With the restoration of the old Democratic Party rule, however, a reaction set in against the moves that had been made toward racial equality. Statutory discrimination, commonly referred to as "Jim Crow," went hand in hand with a restricted political role for black Tennesseans.

The state of Tennessee, in addition to setting up immigration offices to woo skilled immigrant labor, encouraged Northerners to come back as investors, not invaders. Starved as it was for hard dollars, Tennessee (for the most part) welcomed the relocation of Northern businessmen, many of whom had served in Tennessee during the war. Contrary to the mythical "carpetbagger" image, they brought much-needed capital and the entrepreneurial ability to help develop Tennessee's abundant natural resources. Combining goodwill and deep pockets, these transplanted Yankees played a major role in reviving Tennessee's prostrate economy after the Civil War and in bringing the state into the industrial age. The heroes of late nineteenth-century Tennessee were not the military and political figures of an earlier time, but individuals who achieved success rebuilding commerce and industry.

Because the new commercial age had its share of outlaws who preyed on railroads and the wealthy scions of the New South, violence was a continuing occurrence in postbellum Tennessee. And while the formal custom of dueling had fallen into disuse, that did not stop men of wealth and position from occasionally settling their differences by killing one another in street shoot-outs.

Although Tennessee would remain an agrarian state until well into the twentieth century, the New

South that rose from the ashes of the Civil War was based primarily on railroads, mines, and industry. Railroads reached into the coal and iron fields of the Cumberland Plateau and linked Tennessee cities with growing industrial centers such as Atlanta and Cincinnati. Northern capitalists showed a keen interest in developing the rich coal seams of East Tennessee. Chattanooga rapidly grew into one of the South's premier industrial cities. Knoxville became a strong textile-manufacturing locale and home to major iron and marble industries, emerging as the South's third-largest wholesale center for goods. Nashville became a center of flour milling, meat packing, and other agricultural processing. Memphis developed into a major inland port and the foremost supplier of hardwood flooring and cottonseed oil. Despite almost ceasing to exist as a functioning city due to yellow fever and even losing its city charter, Memphis became a bustling metropolis of one hundred thousand by 1900.

The whole state underwent a rebirth in the decades following the war. The Tennessee Centennial Exposition, held at Nashville in 1897, commemorated the state's recovery from near oblivion. Said Governor Robert Love Taylor, "Some of them who saw our ruined country 30 years ago will certainly appreciate the fact that we have wrought miracles."

With industrial towns and immigrant colonies surfacing, some people were searching for a new vision of the ideal community. This breed of settler frequently chose Tennessee as a destination. Because of its inexpensive land and great natural beauty, the state was a haven for utopian colonies, land-company settlements, and recreation spas.

Times were generally bleak for Tennessee farmers, although Middle Tennessee horse breeders were able to perfect the first great Tennessee Walking Horse. The economic position of small and tenant farmers was becoming more precarious with each passing decade. Tennessee's once vibrant and diversified farm economy, devastated by the war, was now increasingly dependent upon cash crops such as cotton, tobacco, and peanuts. Because of steamboats and the reemergence of the railroads, farmers were able to transport their goods more easily. Sharecropping spread rapidly across areas where cash crops were cultivated. Sharecroppers, who usually had to pay half of their profits in rent, were nearly always in debt and typically were the poorest class of farmers.

Aware of their declining status during the 1880s, Tennessee farmers began to organize. In a series of political movements, farmers' organizations such as the Agricultural Wheel and Farmer's Alliance enrolled more than one hundred thousand members to create (briefly) a powerful grassroots agrarian force. The Alliancemen in 1892 elected a governor (John Price Buchanan of Williamson County), affiliated with the national Populist Party, and for a time looked as if they might mount a serious challenge to the traditional two-party system in Tennessee. The Democratic Party absorbed the Alliance movement, however, and farmers sank back into the political oblivion that reflected their declining economic fortunes.

As the twentieth century dawned, cultural rather than economic issues dominated the political dialogue in Tennessee. Liquor prohibition, women's suffrage, religion, and education came to the fore of often-heated political debate. Such problems reflected the tensions of a largely agrarian society with one foot already planted in the modern, industrial age—unsure of which direction to go. Tennessee, consequently, became a battleground where the forces of modernism clashed with older traditions. To outsiders during the early twentieth century, many of the conflicts that troubled Tennessee appeared to result from the clash of city versus country values: Religious advocates tried to resist the intellectual and scientific innovations coming from the cities.

The state became an important arena in the struggle over the use of liquor. Distilling whiskey and other spirits was an old and accomplished craft in Tennessee, one that had continued despite various law enforcement agencies' efforts to stamp it out. Temperance—the movement to limit the consumption of alcohol—had, by 1900, become a moral and political crusade to prohibit liquor altogether. Originally a woman's issue and therefore couched in nonpolitical terms, prohibition in 1908 turned into the central issue in statewide politics. In the wake of that year's bitter gubernatorial contest, the loser and a champion of prohibition, Edward W. Carmack, was killed in a gun battle by supporters of the "wet" governor, and the cause gained a martyr. Prohibition also gained the momentum it needed to be enacted by the Tennessee General Assembly. Although the law was now in place, it was not enforced in some places, like Memphis and Nashville. Tennessee would remain nominally "dry" for nearly a quarter of a century—from 1909 until the repeal of national Prohibition in 1933.

Tennessee also played a pivotal role in the campaign for women's voting rights. Like temperance, women's suffrage was an issue that had roots in the late nineteenth century, although the Tennessee Equal Suffrage Association was not organized until 1906. Despite the middle-class character and moderate tactics of the Tennessee suffragists, they faced a determined (and largely female) opposition. Universal voting rights for women finally came in 1920, when Tennessee became the pivotal thirty-sixth state to ratify the Nineteenth Amendment.

The First World War marked a watershed in Tennessee history, virtually drawing a boundary between two eras. Economically, the war gave a boost to industrialization in the cities and to migration off the farms. Some young men had traded their places on the farm for the arena of politics. Culturally, the impact of large numbers of young men and women from rural counties moving cityward is hard to overesti-mate. Farm prices and industrial wages alike rose during World War I, and Tennessee farmers enjoyed their last period of growing prosperity for the next two decades. On the military front, Tennessee contributed its usual full complement of personnel to the nation's war effort. About one hundred thousand Tennesseans volunteered or were drafted into the armed forces, and a large proportion of those served with the American Expeditionary Force in Europe. Four thousand Tennessee soldiers perished in combat.

The period between a civil war at home to a world war on another continent meant a search for new identities, or a struggle for daily survival and the rebuilding of a state and a nation. Some of the people who brought a transforming spirit to Tennessee, or who themselves were transformed, are depicted in the following stories.

Historical background essay written in collaboration with Dr. Wayne Moore, archivist, Tennessee State Library and Archives.

107
Thomas Burr Fisher

Loving Arms for the Returning Veteran

In May 1865, Marshall County's Thomas Burr Fisher was overcome with emotion upon the surrender of his commander, Confederate General Nathan Bedford Forrest, whose troops were in Alabama when he made the announcement. While some Rebels spoke of starting guerrilla activity against Federal forces, Forrest set the stage for total peace. During his farewell address to his troops, he stated: "Reason dictates and humanity demands that no more blood be shed. . . . You have been good soldiers, you can be good citizens."

Tearfully laying down their arms, reported Fisher in his later memoirs, the troops headed home in military formation until they crossed the Tennessee River. Then they began to spread out in the direction of their respective farms and households. Fisher was riding with his four brothers, all of whom had served in either the Fourth or Eleventh Tennessee Cavalry under Forrest. Accompanying them were a few comrades also from Marshall County. One brother, too sick to continue, stopped for a day's rest. Nearing their home at Cave Spring, a small community between Farmington and Verona, the arriving Fisher brothers were embarrassed at how they looked. Fisher described the moment:

Our hearts were beating faster, the nearer we came to the old familiar scenes. We had not thought of it before, but when we came in sight of old Rock Creek camp ground, we saw the congregation just coming out of the large shelter under which the service was held, and we remembered it was the annual May meeting at which hundreds of people gathered every year. Then came the self-consciousness of our faded, ragged appearance, and we would have dodged the multitude if we could, but the glad heartiness of their greetings soon made us feel they were not thinking of our clothes but of us.

One more mile brought us to our old home and all of its familiar scenes and memories. And so the war was ended, and after all the marching and fighting and suffering we were at home—no more startling bugle calls—no more sanguinary battles—no more burials on distant fields in lonely graves. Life was to start anew, and we were so fortunate. Five brothers—and all returned without loss of limb!

The most poignant memories for twenty-one-year-old Fisher were of growing up within sight of the focal point of the community, Cave Spring school and church, institutions that would shape his future life. "Here my life began to unfold and to appropriate what was offered from without. When I reached the age of five years, I insisted on going to school. My four brothers and two sisters were going, why shouldn't I go?" By his own account, he "always loved books and study," and his only regret in joining the Confederate army was that it forced him to neglect his education.

Unlike thousands of returning veterans after the Civil War who left the state to build a life in more prosperous areas, Fisher decided that his Tennessee home was the only place to pursue dreams that the war had interrupted. He remembered the struggles of his great-grandfather, a German immigrant and Revolutionary War veteran wounded at Kings Mountain, one of the first settlers in what was then Bedford County who had labored to homestead lower Middle Tennessee.

Fisher was also influenced by his family's strong attachment to the Methodist Church. His father, blacksmith and wagon maker John Fisher, made certain that each child was active in the church. Most of the children were either named after biblical figures or Methodist leaders. Thomas's middle name, Burr, was after the Reverend William Burr, a member of the Tennessee Conference of the Methodist Episcopal Church, South. "The first time I ever met him was in October 1862," wrote Fisher of his Civil War days. "I was standing picket on the Nashville turnpike seven miles from Murfreesboro, when he and Rev. Larry Bryant came along on their way to Conference."

Upon settling down again at war's end, Fisher began teaching at the Cave Spring school. He realized that his own limited education was forcing him to "work harder than I ever did to keep ahead" of his students. His brother Monroe, also a schoolteacher, soon decided to advance his education and made the same suggestion to Thomas. The school Monroe wanted to attend was an academy at Lily Hill operated by former Confederate captain James J. Finney. So it was that two Civil War veterans found themselves walking five miles round-trip daily to school, as if they were children again. The greater surprise was that others in the school were veterans also. Wrote Thomas: "There were many grown up young men and young ladies . . . for the war had closed the doors of this school house and the teacher and many of his pupils had been in the Confederate Army."

While learning Greek and Latin, Fisher joined the weekly debating society organized by the area's most prominent citizens as a form of intellectual entertainment. But his tutor, Captain Finney, had greater ambitions for him. A graduate of Murfreesboro's Union College, Finney secretly arranged admission and a deferral of tuition for his penniless student. Fisher was able to obtain his room and board in the home of an elderly couple, the W. A. Ransoms, who treated him as a son. In 1869, he fulfilled his educational dream when he and his friend Will Campbell were the only two members of a graduating class. Although Fisher briefly returned to his farm and also continued to teach intermittently throughout his entire life, he discovered his true calling within the Methodist Church.

In the fifty-one years that followed, Fisher roamed Middle Tennessee as one of the region's most prominent Methodist preachers, ministering in small towns where he was assigned, generally near Nashville. In 1905, while pastoring the Arlington Church in Williamson County and its surrounding district, he was also the chaplain for Central State Asylum at Nashville. Among the inmates was General Thomas Benton Smith, once the youngest general in the Confederate army. Smith, a West Point graduate from Rutherford County, had finally given way to a dementia probably caused while surrendering at the Battle of Nashville. Fisher said that the general "was standing with other prisoners, when a cowardly Federal officer galloped up and struck him on the head with his saber," leaving a gaping wound that exposed the brain.

Although he had been in the asylum nearly thirty years (since 1876, when his mother died), Smith knew many sane moments. He once told the pastor, "I venture to say you don't preach to a better behaved and more attentive audience any where than we are, if we are lunatics." Fisher agreed, and said of his congregation at the asylum, "I found them very attentive, noticing the slightest mistake, and sometimes a smile would spread over the faces of all at the same instant. . . . They enjoyed the worship, especially the singing, in which they loved to join, and they listened more attentively than the ordinary congregation."

The Reverend Thomas Burr Fisher, along with his wife and children, witnessed the transformation of a war-ravaged area into the New South period. His memoirs, "Life on the Common Level," written between 1915 and 1920, provided what has been called a sensitive look at Middle Tennessee life during this transitional period.

Fisher and many others like him had turned to education and religion to make the long climb back to a productive life. His work in communities throughout the region continued until his death in 1922.

108
Thomas Stowers
A Divided Homefront:
One Brother's Exile into History

When one discharged Union soldier rushed home to his family at the end of the Civil War, only ill feelings greeted him. Thomas Stowers had run away at fifteen, driven by a desire to join his older brother in the Confederate army. During that pursuit, Union troops grabbed the teenager and conscripted him into their ranks, and there he remained. After he returned home to the Nashville area in 1865, Stowers discovered that his brother was unforgiving of his wartime service. Stowers later described their reunion. The brother, chopping wood at the time, warned him: "You can stay for supper, but you better be gone by sundown. I left a leg in the war and won't have you staying here."

Stowers was soon on his way, traveling east away from Davidson County. Perhaps his sister, Margaret Lucinda Robertson of Baxter, would feel more kindly toward him. Indeed, she was glad to take him into her home. But the area around Putnam County had also been predominately Confederate. Occasions of bitterness toward Union soldiers eventually became a problem.

In 1874, Stowers decided to leave Middle Tennessee; then he enlisted in the United States Army. Stowers was assigned to the Seventh Cavalry under the new command of General George Armstrong Custer, who had gained fame during the Civil War as a Union cavalry leader. Now on western patrol duty, Custer awaited fresh troops to fight Sioux Indians in the Great Plains of Montana.

In June 1876, General Custer led his men on a three-pronged operation near Little Big Horn, aimed at punishing the elusive Sioux for leaving their government reservation. Historian Wayne Wells discovered different accounts about Stowers. According to one source, Thomas Stowers pulled out of line to adjust his stirrup and, for falling out of line, he and his company were sent to the rear of the column, where the pack mules were located. Another source within the Stowers family claims that he actually was arrested and detained for being inebriated the previous night, but Wells discounts this.

Probably with some regret, Stowers watched his comrades ride off to do battle without him. He never saw many of them again. Custer and five of his companies found more Sioux than expected (along with a force of Cheyenne) at Little Big Horn that day. Of the 210 United States soldiers who entered the valley, none survived. (Another 53 troops were killed in related action on a bluff a few miles away.)

In later years, ill health forced Stowers into a military home in Ohio, but he managed the journey each summer to visit his sister at Baxter. In 1931, Stowers returned permanently there to live with the family. Totally deaf (perhaps from artillery fire during the Civil War), Stowers spent most of his time reading from his large collection of books and sharing them with area children, a practice he maintained until his death in 1933 at the age of eighty-four. His tombstone at Oddfellows Cemetery in Baxter, while recognizing his service with General Custer, misleadingly names Stowers "the sole survivor" of the Battle of Little Big Horn.

109
James W. M. Grayson/Tom Dula

Mountain Man on the Run
and Folk Song to Be Sung

Because he stopped by the Johnson County farm of James W. M. Grayson in 1866, long enough to earn a pair of boots that did not fit, Tom Dula wound up in a noose that did.

Dula became immortalized through folk tales and eventually a folk song recorded more than sixty years later. The song would fall quickly into obscurity before springing to life in 1958 as a major part of the folk music revival throughout America.

A Confederate veteran, Dula had returned from the Civil War to learn that his North Carolina fiancée, Laurie Foster, was engaged to another. Torn and tormented, he reportedly murdered her, made a clumsy attempt to bury her body in a nearby forest, and fled

across the state border to the mountains of upper East Tennessee. Dula then made his brief but ill-fated visit to the farm of Grayson, a Union veteran (and later Tennessee legislator) who lived at Trade.

Under an alias, Dula worked for Grayson until he could buy a pair of boots, then he disappeared. When a North Carolina posse soon appeared at the farm, Grayson and law enforcement officials realized that the fugitive and the farm worker were one and the same. Grayson joined the manhunt and personally arrested Dula on the other side of the county near Pandora. In no position to resist, the prisoner was soaking his feet in a creek because his new boots had caused him such pain.

Dula, whom Grayson returned to North Carolina for trial, was later convicted of murder and hanged May 1, 1868, in Statesville. In the subsequent retelling of these events, his captor was also immortalized in verse (Grayson lived until 1900).

Sixty-one years after the hanging, Grayson's nephew, renowned blind fiddler Gillam Bannom Grayson, recorded a song for Victor Records in Memphis based on his uncle's encounter with Tom Dula, whose name became altered somewhat in translations. Considered one of the most important fiddlers of his time, the younger Grayson was killed in a car accident one year after the 1929 recording of "The Ballad of Tom Dooley," which echoed:

This time tomorrow
Reckon where I'll be
If it hadn't been for Grayson
I'd a-been in Tennessee.©

The tune fell into obscurity for three decades, though another Johnson Countian, Frank Proffitt of Laurel Bloomery, taught it to a folk song collector who re-recorded it for Electra Records in 1952. Proffitt, who also became famous in folk music circles, was a leading source of information in constant attempts to preserve regional folk music. The ballad became a nationwide hit in 1958, in its third recorded version, performed by the Kingston Trio, which consisted of two Hawaiians and a Californian. Its haunting refrain sounded the following lament:

Hang down your head, Tom Dooley,
Hang down your head and cry,
Hang down your head, Tom Dooley,
Poor boy, you're bound to die.©

110
Jack Daniel

Postwar Whiskey and Taxes:
The First Registered Distillery

Jack Daniel cultivated a gentlemanly appearance
throughout his life.

He was a young fellow, Jasper "Jack" Newton Daniel of Lynchburg, and a keen student—not of books, but of the art of making whiskey. And the whiskey he learned to make was the best most people around Lincoln County had ever tasted.

His mentor was Dan Call. They had met in 1853 when Call was riding through the county looking for someone to run errands. Then seventeen, Call had just moved to the area with his young family, having inherited a large farm nearby, a general store, and a mountain whiskey operation. He was also performing the duties of a lay preacher and sometime elder for the local Lutheran church. Call was considered the busiest fellow and largest landowner in Lincoln County.

Jack was eager to begin work. Although only seven at the time, he was fairly independent. His mother was dead, and since his father's remarriage, Jack had been living with his neighbors, the Felix Waggoner family. He soon made a home with the Call family, getting his early schooling from Call's wife and learning how to run a store, to operate a farm, and (to his delight) how to make sour-mash whiskey in the hills.

Call's slaves instructed him, particularly master-distiller Nearest Green. The slaves became the boy's friends, and Green introduced him to the method of whiskey-making called the "Old Lincoln County Process." It involved filtering or mellowing true sour-mash whiskey through a thick layer of finely ground sugar-maple charcoal. Jack was such a hard worker on the Call place that on his eighth birthday, Call raised his wages to five dollars per month and encouraged him to save all he could. He soon made Jack a business partner.

Call, however, began to buckle emotionally under constant criticism from his fellow Lutherans about his distillery and the sale of whiskey in his store. Jack, a Primitive or "foot washin'" Baptist, escaped the heavy church pressures brought to bear on his senior partner, whose choice was simple: either give up the whiskey business or give up the church. As history now attests, Dan Call gave up more than a whiskey business in 1859 to his thirteen-year-old friend and partner; he relinquished a budding Tennessee tradition. The story of Jack Daniel has been made a familiar one around Lynchburg, Tennessee, through the pen of regional writer Ben A. Green.

Whether or not Jack Daniel needed advice about purchasing the whiskey stills (Call advanced him the credit), local accounts claim he sought out his old friend Felix Waggoner. "One of your troubles right now is your conscience," Waggoner reportedly said. "You like Dan Call and Mary Jane Call a lot—and what they have decided to do about putting whiskey out of their lives has been eating on you. You wonder if the Lord is trying to tell you to get out of the whiskey-making business too. . . .

"In a lot of ways, whiskey is like wind and water, like fire and food," Waggoner continued. "Wind can blow you away or just cool you off. Water can drown you or quench your thirst. Fire can burn you up or keep you warm. Food can kill you or keep you alive. Whiskey can hurt you or help you. It depends on how you use it."

In 1866, the beginning of the oldest registered distillery in the United States got underway. Because the post-Civil War federal government was beginning to enforce registration of whiskey-making operations and the collection of whiskey taxes, Daniel did not try to avoid the restrictions. He met with United States government officials and agreed to abide by the new rules. Jack Daniel Distillery, awarded registration Number 1, used the process handed down by the slaves in the hills who soon became its employees. Former head distiller Nearest Green, however, chose to help returning war veteran Dan Call get back into production on the farm.

Having relocated in Lynchburg to be nearer the railroads of Tullahoma and the pure water of a cave spring, Daniel purchased the "Hollow" where the whiskey was being produced and 220 acres that lay around it. The area would become part of Moore County in a few years.

Upon his twenty-first birthday in 1867, Jack Daniel celebrated by simply "disappearing" for a few days. He went to Tullahoma. When he came back, he started dressing like a country gentleman of means, an image that he would carry the rest of his life. He was wearing fancy new clothes consisting of a knee-length frock coat, silk shirt, silk vest, flamboyant bow tie, and rakish planter's hat. Part of this new romantic image also included tales of his several deeds of heroism as a child.

All Daniel needed now was national recognition. His company did well without much advertising, but, in 1904, the World's Fair in St. Louis was offering a gold medal for the best whiskey in the world. Nervously, Daniel entered. He shipped two cases of his best Old No. 7 to St. Louis and then followed it on the L & N Railroad. At a city hotel, he could overhear prominent whiskey manufacturers speculating as to who he was. One onlooker offered, "I've heard that little guy is from Tennessee. Probably up here to find out how real good liquor is supposed to be handled."

Full of apprehension, Daniel attended the judging. The judges' room had twenty-four tables, each holding an entry and some of them belonging to the most famous and prestigious whiskey makers in the world. Hours after extensive tastings, the announcement was made: "Gentlemen, the judges have decided that the Gold Medal for making the finest whiskey in the world goes to Jack Daniel Distillery of Lynchburg, not Virginia, but Lynchburg, Tennessee."

Returning home a World's Fair winner, Daniel and the town of Lynchburg became a team. As a community leader, Jack Daniel was a walking donation of money to good causes and people around him. He is credited with helping finance nearly every church in Moore County. His big home often had opulent displays of food, which he loved to share with the community, especially for religious gatherings. Beginning in 1890, Daniel's traditional May Day dinner fed everyone from the church. Long tables were set up from noon until five in the evening with ample portions of ham, chicken, and beef for the more than three hundred people who attended. While he did not formally join the Primitive Baptist Church until 1907, Daniel loved to ride by the church at the end of Sunday service and, according to tradition, shout: "Hey Elder Webster, you've talked long enough. Turn loose your congregation and come with me for dinner." The custom lasted about fifteen years and ended only when Daniel began to suffer ill health.

In time, he placed his product in square bottles. Daniel liked his bottles that way, and folks called him a "Square Shooter" as a result. No one called his whiskey "bourbon"; it was simply "Tennessee Whiskey," which in 1941 became a unique and separate classification by the federal government.

Daniel, who never married, died in 1911 suffering from gangrene which had settled in an old foot injury (incurred six years earlier when, in anger, he had kicked the safe in his office). Suffering from ill health, he had already handed down the distillery to a favorite nephew, Lem Motlow, who never deviated from the great tradition that Dan Call had encouraged in the seven-year-old boy he hired.

111
Julius Eckhardt Raht
Mining Away the Landscape

Julius Eckhardt Raht, according to some theories, arrived in East Tennessee as a penniless twenty-eight-year-old German immigrant and departed as the richest man in the state. In the course of his climb to prosperity at Ducktown, located near the Tennessee-Georgia border, a small corner of the Polk County landscape was transformed from a green wilderness into a barren wasteland, which someday would be visible on satellite imagery as nothing more than a vast brown patch created in the feverish pursuit of copper.

Raht came to town in 1854, having already followed the mining industry path in such states as Missouri and Wisconsin. Some Tennesseans believed that although he was poor, Raht was not simply a miner looking for work. A New York mining company had entrusted some of its investments to him and perhaps sent him to Tennessee. Raht was armed with a letter of recommendation from the New York company, passable English, a solid knowledge of chemistry and mineralogy from an education at two European universities, and an incredible capacity for hard work. With these assets, he began to amass a fortune. Within a few months, "Captain Raht" had earned a promotion to mine captain, and he was on his way.

Before he established his life firmly in the region, however, he returned to his homeland in Europe. There, Raht married the daughter of French Protestants, after which he brought his bride to America for a new life free of religious and political persecution.

At Ducktown's Union Consolidated Mining Company, Raht made $125 a month. But his ambitions were greater, and he was soon operating a store to sell goods to the other miners. His business thrived, and he invested store profits in livestock and real estate throughout Polk County.

His real job was still with the mine, and by the time he was thirty-four, Raht was chief of operations for all of the mines and smelting works in Ducktown. On his initiative, he built complementary business enterprises. Raht obtained the right to operate company stores and keep all profits. He invested this money in mule teams, which he then leased to the mining company for hauling copper out of Ducktown. Raht also stocked the mining stores with grain grown on his own land and dairy products produced by his own cows.

Eight years after Raht had arrived, he estimated his net worth at more than one hundred thousand dollars. As he said rather modestly some years later, "I couldn't help to make money, receiving salary from three different companies, having store privileges, and the selling of copper at a high commission."

The Civil War almost proved to be Raht's undoing. He managed to avoid conscription into the Confederate army because the South needed copper. According to some estimates, Raht and his fellow Ducktown

miners provided 90 percent of the Confederacy's copper supply. But when the Confederacy also needed his services as a soldier, he hired a substitute. Union troops then began to descend into lower East Tennessee, and Raht decided to leave. He headed north with his family and took forty mules, which he sold to a Union general to secure safe passage.

After the war, Raht returned to Ducktown and rebuilt his fortune. By 1869, he owned three of the mines in Ducktown, and by 1875, he owned seven thousand acres of the best land in Polk County. True to his nature, when he died in 1879, Raht was laboring away in a business meeting. He was fifty-three.

What he left behind was a net worth, by his own meticulous and conservative reckoning, of six hundred thousand dollars. But the land around Ducktown did not prosper as well as Raht had. Because the smelting process required tremendous quantities of lumber, the entire forest within fifty square miles was sacrificed. What vegetation the clear-cutting did not claim was devastated by corrosive sulfur-dioxide gas, a by-product of the smelting process.

Decade after decade of soil erosion would take a toll. By the 1920s, the area around Ducktown resembled a pockmarked moonscape. However, reforestation in the 1930s by miners and the newly formed Tennessee Valley Authority (TVA) began to restore part of the greenery once prevalent around Ducktown. Even as the trees were making a comeback, people in Ducktown still referred to an era of their history as "Raht's time."

112
Thomas Green Ryman
"Steamboatin' Tom" Running the River— And a Famous Tabernacle

In the late nineteenth century, Thomas Green Ryman sought an empire in the steamboat industry, but he finished his life building a landmark to the music industry.

In the summer of 1867 this twenty-six-year-old Nashville fisherman rode a raft downriver to New Orleans hoping to buy his first steamboat. With his mother's help, Ryman had saved three thousand dollars, which she sewed into his coat lining prior to the journey. The oldest of five children, Ryman was the sole support of his mother, sisters, and young brothers. The grandson of early nineteenth-century German immigrants, he was tenacious, personable, and good-hearted, and perhaps vulnerable. Sarah Ryman told her son not to remove the jacket for any reason until he paid for his steamer. Despite sweltering heat, Ryman heeded his mother's advice and sweated out the trip. He was rewarded with the purchase of the *Alpha*, a small but well-built secondhand steamer that had been used as a transport packet during the Civil War. The vessel would bring Ryman consistent income. He subsequently would become such a success and so well-known along the length of the Cumberland River that a poor fisherman would write to him and ask permission to fish in *his* (Ryman's) river.

Born in 1841 at Nashville, Ryman developed his love and knowledge of the river early in life. At seventeen, he could be found along the Tennessee River at Chattanooga in a commercial-fishing partnership with his father, John. Assisting them was an eleven-year-old Chattanoogan, James Tyner. During the winters, the three also made money by manufacturing ice, accomplished by filling flatboats with enough water to freeze in the shade.

After the outbreak of the Civil War, Ryman left Chattanooga and made his way alone. He followed the river's path to Decatur, the seat of Meigs County, and there prospered with his own fishing business. The needs created by war then took him to a series of Confederate outposts where he sold his fish to army troops. That route included Fort Henry on the Tennessee River near the Kentucky border; then Fort Donelson a few miles away on the Cumberland River; and finally back to Nashville. Arrested and imprisoned by Union forces occupying the state capital, Ryman was released days later by Military Governor Andrew Johnson. Showing his gratitude, Ryman delivered the best fish available to the governor's house.

When his father died during the last year of the war, Ryman resettled permanently in Nashville, building up his fishing business and setting his sights on steamboating. In 1869, after a profitable beginning, the *Alpha* hosted Ryman's honeymoon cruise when he married Mary Elizabeth Baugh from Franklin, one of his sister's classmates at a local Episcopal school. Inviting thirty-five of their family and friends, the couple hosted a week-long cruise up the Mississippi to the Ohio River. On the return trip, the group encountered a rival boat and entered into an informal race. At one point, the two steamers touched, and a passenger jumped from one boat to the other during their frolicking. Lavishly entertaining his guests, Ryman showered on his friends the kind of generosity for which he would become renowned. Displaying her own brand of hospitality, Elizabeth became the *Alpha's* official hostess.

When Ryman could afford to custom-build his own steamboat four years later, he moved his family temporarily to Evansville, Indiana, so that he could supervise construction of the *Eddyville*. Returning to Nashville, Ryman and his old friend James Tyner renewed their association and became lasting partners. Tyner, who had been a drummer boy in the Confederacy, also knew how to pilot a boat. Becoming the *Eddyville's* captain, he carried cargo between Nashville and Paducah, Kentucky.

In the years following, Ryman Steamboat Lines operated the Cumberland River's finest and largest fleet of more than thirty boats, many of which were jointly owned with Tyner. So much freight was transported on Ryman steamers that a portion of the Nashville warehouse district was built to house the volume of goods. In small Tennessee river towns, daily life changed rapidly for farmers and loggers now able to transport their goods quickly to market and to receive manufactured products from other cities. In addition, raftsmen who floated logs to Nashville no longer had to walk home.

Known for his attention to every detail of his steamboating business and for his quick decisions, Ryman built a large frame house on Rutledge Hill overlooking the river. From here he could keep track (even from home) of the comings and goings of his steamers. In the 1870s, atop this towering position, Ryman fought off attempts by the railroads to steal steamboating business. He offered special rates and deals for commercial shippers, including free warehouse storage of their goods, and named his steamboats for businessmen who shipped goods on his fleet.

In 1885, Ryman made another decision which would alter his life and that of the people of Nashville: He decided to attend a tent revival. Having been born into a devoutly religious family which prayed twice a day, Ryman was especially receptive that night to the preachings of famous evangelist Sam Jones. During the revival, Ryman was converted. Determining now that alcohol was an evil to society, he also decided to quit serving liquor on his boats. A tale surfaced that Ryman marched to the river and personally threw overboard all the whiskey bottles within reach. This gesture may have been his desire, but, in reality, he waited for the expiration of contracts with bar owners who serviced the boats. Ryman's decision was costly. He lost immense income both from his percentage of alcohol profits and from the loss of passengers who preferred to travel aboard a steamer equipped with a bar.

In his spiritual transformation, Ryman resolved to build an interdenominational tabernacle where all Nashvillians could hear the word of God. He purchased a downtown lot, donated twenty thousand dollars, and raised the balance of needed money with a series of fund drives featuring famous lecturers and concerts. The building was constructed in stages as one fund-raising drive ended and another began. By 1892, the tabernacle neared completion, and Ryman made it clear that the building would not be named for him. Nor would it be used for politics, but only by those, he said, who have a respect for God. When the new Union Gospel Tabernacle was not holding religious services, therefore, it was a center for cultural events. In the years following, Nashvillians had occasion to attend a concert there by the New York Metropolitan Opera Company and a speech by the nation's foremost black educator and leader, Booker T. Washington, among many other scheduled events.

Ryman next opened a religious mission adjacent to his office and hired a permanent minister who could offer spiritual assistance to steamboating men. For neighborhoods without a church, Ryman built a "Gospel Wagon" to travel the streets offering sermons and religious music from a choir and organist.

Stories abounded of Ryman's generosity, which often manifested itself toward Nashville's poor. One winter, he learned that many suffered in the cold without any fuel for heat. Ryman had stored so much coal at the previous summer's low prices that he felt he could share with the city. When he asked his groundskeeper to spread the word that anyone with a tote sack could have a free bag of coal, hundreds came. By nightfall, Ryman's cellar was empty. His own family might have been without coal had his wife not filled a bucket earlier in the day.

When Ryman died in 1904 at sixty-three, his funeral became a testament to his life. It was held on Christmas Day at the tabernacle, and the holiday did not prevent throngs of Nashvillians from attending his service. Both the elite and the many poor people Ryman had helped were present. Evangelist Jones presided but kept his words to a minimum, he said, for the man he knew as a simple Christian who never wanted glory.

Later in the same year, the tabernacle was renamed Ryman Auditorium, despite its builder's refusal to have such an honor during his lifetime. In 1943, the Ryman building and its near-perfect acoustics became a landmark in the country-music industry—the best-known home of the internationally famous Grand Ole Opry.

113
Abraham Jobe
Circuit-Riding Doctor—And Other Chores

When Dr. Abraham Jobe rode through Elizabethton one day in 1873, he heard a bystander say, "There goes Dr. Jobe to kill Kite." If what Jobe's fellow East Tennessee surgeons (twenty-five in all) had said was true, Kite would soon be dead.

Johnson Countian Ham Kite suffered from a mammoth, nonmalignant tumor on his neck, "fully half as large as his head," according to Jobe's autobiography. It was a deformity which hampered Kite's breathing (he slept sitting upright to avoid suffocation). In consulting the other doctors, Kite learned that the growth overlapped major arteries. Each physician predicted that surgery would almost certainly cause Kite's death. But Jobe was willing to try the operation, staking his reputation on the outcome. "I never suffered so much uneasiness about all the operations I ever performed as I did about Kites," he would write.

Because of the Kite family history of consumption, chloroform could not be used to mask the pain. The surgery would be long as well as painful, and performed in the open air in front of an audience. The entire community gathered in front of Kite's home to watch, although people began to move some distance away when the surgery began.

Jobe was familiar with cancerous and noncancerous growths. He believed cancer was incurable. He often investigated clinics and doctors that claimed to cure cancer and denounced them as frauds. If Kite's tumor had been cancerous, Jobe would have refused to operate. Kite's family fully expected him to die. His brother had said farewell the previous day. Kite's wife and two-year-old daughter cried for Jobe not to kill their loved one. Jobe then had to convince two volunteers from the crowd to hold Kite during the operation. Finally, the doctor calmed his own nerves so that he could hold his instruments steady.

Although Jobe described the operation in his 1893 autobiography as "difficult, dangerous, and bloody," the patient survived. Twenty years later, when Jobe recorded the incident in writing, Kite was still healthy.

But Jobe was more than a surgeon. In his memoirs of a half-century, he detailed his adventures not only as a doctor, but also as a mercantile salesman, fugitive Unionist, Reconstruction businessman, and Federal Indian agent.

Born near Elizabethton in 1817, Jobe grew up in Cades Cove after his parents moved to Blount County. His maternal grandfather was Colonel John Tipton, an early Watauga settler who opposed formation of the ill-fated State of Franklin, which separated upper East Tennessee from the mother state of North Carolina. As a teenager, Jobe lived among Cherokees and Creeks in Georgia and Alabama. Later, he traded with the Cherokees and was a guest of Chief John Ross immediately before Ross's arrest in Tennessee by the Georgia Guard (Jobe was a temporary member of the Georgia militia). Jobe also worked as a store owner before financial failure persuaded him to try the medical profession in 1841.

He learned medicine in the common fashion, reading under the guidance of a physician. Jobe's mentor was popular Jonesborough physician Dr. Samuel B. Cunningham, with whom he rode to witness various operations. Though Tennessee law prohibited the dissection of cadavers, the unpopular law was not enforced. Jobe's dissections, many of which were conducted on hanged criminals, were occasionally watched by the local judge and numerous attorneys.

When Jobe got his own medical practice as a circuit-riding doctor, it required mountainous horse treks across several counties in East Tennessee and North Carolina. Along his route, citizens had never known a doctor's services or a doctor's bill. Jobe supplemented his income with business ventures and a farm which his wife managed. He owned slaves but was a loyalist to the Union when the Civil War began. During one harrowing period, Jobe was a fugitive

from Confederate authorities and lived for several weeks under the floorboards of his Elizabethton home. He eventually had to flee Tennessee.

When the nation entered its postwar period of Reconstruction, President Andrew Johnson appointed Jobe federal postmaster to rebuild mail service in the Carolinas. In 1868, his experience with the Creeks and Cherokees earned Jobe leadership of a federal mission to the Chippewas of Minnesota. But he also continued his medical practice. Returning eventually to Carter County, he became Andrew Johnson's family physician. Jobe watched over the former president, who was living at a daughter's home, until Johnson's death from a stroke in 1875.

In his memoirs, published as the *Autobiography of Dr. Abraham Jobe of Elizabethton, Tennessee*, Jobe detailed life from 1849 into the twentieth century and presented numerous medical theories and case studies. His final entry was penned in 1905 when he was eighty-eight years old and spending his twilight years at a daughter's Elizabethton home.

114
Ella Sheppard Moore
Uplifting a Black College with Gospel Song

In 1871, with Nashville's Fisk University headed for economic oblivion, Ella Sheppard Moore and eight other students agreed that the best way to raise funds was to raise their voices in song.

Their hastily organized chorus, lacking money or even a name, set out for a tour of the North under the direction of the college's treasurer/singer, George White, who made this trip without the endorsement of university leaders. The singers, either former slaves or the children of slaves, were aged fifteen to twenty-five.

After an uninspiring start, the singers dropped their classical repertoire of singing popular white music to unenthusiastic audiences and returned to their musical roots—black spirituals and old slave songs. Their decision to emphasize black traditional music gave birth to the Fisk Jubilee Singers, who gained international fame and appeared in the world's great palaces before kings, queens, and ambassadors. (A famous painting at Fisk depicts all original Jubilee singers as they sat for Queen Victoria's palace artist in London.) Audiences cheered loudly and screamed for encores.

Ella Sheppard Moore (fourth from left, at piano) with the famous Fisk Jubilee Singers.

That the singers would be such a rousing success was inconceivable to Fisk officials in 1871. They were simply upset to lose Ella Sheppard to the tour group. She was the school's music teacher and its first black staff member; her popularity was so great that officials feared that her loss from the classroom would cause a student protest.

Born in 1851, Ella was a native Nashvillian. Her father, Simon, had worked tirelessly for the $1,800 needed to buy his freedom from his master. He earned an additional $350 for the child Ella's freedom. Simon also negotiated a promise to buy Ella's mother, but the promise was never honored. When her mother was sold to Mississippi planters, Ella remained with her father, who began a small Nashville business. Knowing that he would never see his wife again, Simon remarried and immediately labored even longer hours to purchase his new wife's freedom. The price was $1,300.

When the nation's economy slipped into a depression in 1857, Simon Sheppard's business failed. Fearing seizure of his wife and daughter as property to satisfy business debts, he escaped with them to Cincinnati.

In Ohio, Ella studied music at her father's urging. After Simon's death in 1866, his destitute daughter taught piano lessons to support herself and her stepmother. A prominent Cincinnati musician took the girl under his tutelage, but only if she promised to accept lessons in secret. As his only black student, Ella slipped through back doors late at night for her lessons. In 1868, after she accepted a Gallatin, Tennessee, teaching position, Ella set her sights on Fisk University. Again she taught music to pay her way, until Fisk could offer a permanent staff position. Ella first entered the university as a student. She had six dollars in her pocket and a desire to advance her already solid basic education. The pocket money was gone in three weeks, but Ella was willing to work for her tuition and board. She continued for two years, at the end of which Fisk finally made her a music teacher.

During the school's fund-raising period between 1871 and 1878, Ella helped the Jubilee Singers raise $150,000, enough money to insure their school's future as a major black educational institution. The money was used to replace campus buildings, which were abandoned Civil War army barracks. The funds also built Jubilee Hall, the first permanent building in the United States designated solely for the education of blacks (eventually a national historic landmark).

In 1882, after the most successful years of the Jubilee Singers, Ella Sheppard married George W. Moore. She helped him in missionary work and organized Jubilee choirs wherever that work led her. During these missionary journeys through Mississippi, Ella came upon her mother and a sister, neither of whom she had seen since childhood. She immediately brought them to Nashville to live.

Ella Sheppard Moore's undated autobiography, *Before Emancipation*, was published by the American Missionary Association sometime after 1882 (she died in 1914 at age sixty-three). In that work, she explained the magnitude of her reunion with her family—how her grandfather's prayers, from the time he and her mother had toiled on the Mississippi plantation, had been unrelenting:

> They knew only the severest form of farm life. . . . The few Christians among the house slaves began to pray, sometimes spending a whole night in prayer, telling it all to Jesus, often singing. . . .
>
> My grandfather was the leader of the Christians and often strengthened my mother's faith by telling her that the Lord had promised him that she would be free and that she would yet join her daughter, and spend her last days under her own vine and fig tree.

And indeed the grandfather's words came to pass.

115
William R. "Sawney" Webb

Reviving the Schoolhouse

Over the course of two decades beginning in 1870, William R. "Sawney" Webb lectured the students at Webb School nearly every morning and evening for ten minutes to two hours. Webb always read a Bible passage and led prayer. One day he exclaimed: "My son, your mother is your best friend. When you get back to your room I want you to write to her a letter that will make a bird sing in her heart. You may have the day!"

Webb's relationship with his own mother was best explained in his words:

My mother used to say to me with so much emphasis, "My son, if you are polite to the Queen and rude to the servant that blacks your boots, you are not a gentleman. You are a fraud and a sham." I was tied to my mother's apron strings. I hope to be tied to her apron strings throughout eternity.

So it was that duty to family, morality, and religion merged with a classical education as the hallmarks of Webb School in post-Civil War Middle Tennessee. Governors and farmers alike eagerly sent their children (including their daughters, who attended day school) to Webb for a quality education based on certain values. The student body averaged from 150 to 200 pupils. They generally boarded in nearby homes, including Sawney Webb's, and they spent their school days sitting on wooden benches or in cane-bottomed chairs, holding their books in their laps. Webb was a tough educator who emphasized the importance not only of scholarship but also of citizenship. Ten graduates became Rhodes scholars; three became governors of different states.

Webb School began in a Methodist church basement in the small community of Culleoka, located in Maury County. There, in 1870, Webb had settled from his native North Carolina, a state that was suffering immense economic and social problems during the Reconstruction era. A former Confederate officer and prisoner of war, Webb was searching for a peaceful hamlet that needed the services of a good teacher. The people of Culleoka encouraged him to stay, and Webb built a school that became an educational magnet for those living in the wake of school systems destroyed by the Civil War. During this time, he married Emma Clary of Unionville and built a large home which could double as a boarding house for students. His brother, John M. Webb, joined him as coprincipal in 1873.

Not all townspeople, however, were accommodating to Webb's principles. A dedicated Methodist, he determined to leave the town in 1886 after some local merchants refused to stop selling alcohol to his students. Webb examined the opportunities at Bell Buckle, forty miles east. It was a railroad boom town in need of a school, and in need of Webb's kind of education. According to historic lore, the place was named in the early nineteenth century when Indians killed a settler's cow, hanging the animal's bell and buckle from a tree as a warning to settlers to keep their animals off Indian lands. Now that the railroad

William R. "Sawney" Webb (left) and John Webb at Bell Buckle, Tennessee.

was bringing prosperity to Bell Buckle, residents offered Webb twelve thousand dollars to reestablish his school there. He accepted and used a portion of the money to build several clapboard structures.

But most of the endowment was spent on books. To his students, Webb declared that "bricks and mortar" do not an education make. Developing what would become a college-preparatory agenda, Webb emphasized Greek, Latin, and math. He also developed a game called "trapping," which rewarded his students for learning. When questions were asked, students at the front of the class had the first opportunity to answer. If they could not, others tried. The student with a correct response "trapped" his classmates by moving to the front seat. If that student was able to keep his lead position until the end of the class, he received an extra credit.

At the time that Webb was working out these ideas, another young man from Bedford County (and future United States commissioner of education), Philander P. Claxton, was beginning a career that would help reform education on a broader scale—in the South's public schools. With the chaos brought by war and Reconstruction, he would write: "Our money flows in a golden stream to the states to the north of us, whose skill enables them to make things that we need and cannot make." In the late nineteenth century, he saw education as the answer to such true economic advancement. To help develop public schools, Claxton, a leading educator at the University of Tennessee, used his oratory skills in a speech-making crusade which took him to every county in Tennessee. He followed this with a round of lobbying at the state legislature. Everywhere he went, he argued for basic reforms in Tennessee's public-education system. At the center of his proposals were the ideas of creating grade levels and using taxes to support schools.

While Claxton continued to lay the foundation for a standardized public-school system, Webb labored to send as many scholars as possible to colleges and universities by having one of the finest private-subscription schools in the South. In the 1890s, tuition was $37.50 a semester; room and board averaged $3.00 a week.

During his long life as an educator, Webb also involved himself in public affairs and championed temperance, one of the dominant social issues of the day. In the late 1890s, he became one of the Tennessee Anti-Saloon League's most popular speakers. In 1913, he was appointed to the United States Senate to fill the remaining months of the late Robert L. Taylor's term.

Prohibition remained a passionate principle throughout Webb's life, up to the very end. In the fall of 1926, a bronchial condition from which he suffered led to pneumonia and occasional periods of delusion. During a more lucid moment, he whispered into the ear of a son, Daniel Clary Webb: "Son, do you know what they [the doctors and nurses] tried to give me? It was whiskey. I have hated that stuff all my life, and wouldn't it make a fine story to be told down here in town that the 'old man' on his deathbed took whiskey, trying to save his life?"

Shortly before his death at eighty-four, Sawney Webb left a statement for his students, published by the school on December 19, 1926, of which the following is an excerpt:

> Give my boys my love and tell them to lead a large life. A large life is no mere piffle but one that makes the world better because you have lived. If the world is better because of you, you are a wonderful success. If it's worse because of you, you're a miserable failure.
>
> When you come to the end you will find that the only things that are worthwhile are character and the help you've given to other people. The first step in the development of character is loyalty and obedience to your parents, your teacher and to God. And don't forget, never do anything that you've got to hide.

In addition to the Bell Buckle campus, Webb's concept of education was applied at a Webb School in Claremont, California, founded in 1922 by Webb's youngest son, Thompson Webb. In the 1950s, Webb School of Knoxville was founded by a nephew, William R. Webb III.

116
Lewis Shepherd

The Melungeons:
Unraveling a Mystery—Or Not?

Of the many ways to build a thriving law practice, defending a dark-skinned Melungeon in the post-Civil War South seemed one of the least promising options.

The Melungeons, a people of unknown origin, lived an isolated life primarily in the remote hill country of several East Tennessee counties. Identified by their dark skin, blue eyes, and straight blond or black hair, the racially mixed Melungeons were often ostracized by the mainstream population that surrounded them. Many theories abound as to their beginnings in the eighteenth century, including the suggestion that they might be part of the "lost colony" of Sir Walter Raleigh. Other theories maintain that Melungeons come from a mixture of cultures: European, Anglo-Saxon, Indian, and Negro.

In 1872, Lewis Shepherd, twenty-six, was the youngest attorney in Chattanooga when he argued the case of a Melungeon girl struggling to claim her inheritance. Shepherd was also serving as newly elected attorney general of the Hamilton County Criminal Court. A native of the area, he was descended from South Carolina planters. His great-grandfather was a Revolutionary War veteran who fought with Tennesseans at the Battle of Kings Mountain. Lewis Shepherd's father later migrated to East Tennessee as a planter. At the age of fifteen, young Shepherd joined the Confederate army and fought his way into popularity among Tennesseans, who knew about his war service and imprisonment by the Union. When the war ended, he became an attorney—and a convincing one in the courtroom.

Shepherd had his own theory about the origin of the Melungeons. Using the argument that they were of Carthaginian origin, therefore legally white, he prevailed in a chancery court trial on behalf of his client. Shepherd's later memoirs detailed the case (although he avoided mentioning most names for reasons he did not explain). The memoirs were first published in serial form for the *Chattanooga Times*, which headlined what it called a "Romantic Account of the Celebrated 'Melungeon' Case."

The story began with the marriage between a young Chattanooga man, Jerome Simmerman, who had inherited several large farms in Moccasin Bend, and a Melungeon woman, Jemima Bolton. Due to Simmerman family attempts to block the marriage, the couple wed in Dade County, Georgia. When his wife died a week after the 1858 birth of a daughter, Martha, the grief-stricken husband fell into such a severe emotional state that a guardian had to be appointed to manage his affairs.

Simmerman's widowed (and remarried) mother and his half sisters took up a new battle: fighting his efforts to leave the entire estate to his child. The women devised a scheme, enticing the child's maternal aunt to relocate with the baby in Illinois, where her identity and claim to the estate could be forgotten.

Fifteen years later, Simmerman's surviving half sisters, assuming that the rightful heir was a faded memory, filed a lawsuit to replace the guardian as overseers of the estate. Their ploy might have worked if not for Simmerman's friend Samuel Williams, a pioneer merchant in Hamilton County sometimes called "the Father of Chattanooga" (Chief John Ross also shared the honor). He had monitored the child's whereabouts and had been in touch with the maternal aunt. On the girl's behalf, Williams hired attorney Lewis Shepherd.

The trial hinged principally on the contention made by Simmerman's relatives that his marriage was illegal, the father being white, the mother black. (In Tennessee, marriages were illegal between a white person and another with "Negro blood to the sixth degree.")

When Shepherd argued that Melungeons were dark-skinned descendants of the Carthaginians, the prosecution countered with black witnesses who testified that the heir's mother had considerable Negro blood and features. Little did the prosecution know that Samuel Williams had brought the child from Illinois to be available for trial. Asked to include a sample of her hair along with a deposition, Martha unveiled a four-foot length of flowing locks. Her attorney also revealed that the child's Melungeon grandfather (a tenant farmer on the Simmerman estate) had fought in the War of 1812 and had been allowed to vote during an era in which black citizens were denied that privilege. The court had no more questions about Martha's bloodline and ruled in favor of her rightful inheritance, a ruling upheld by the Tennessee Supreme Court.

Because she had been raised in poverty along the banks of the Mississippi River, Martha used the proceeds of her father's estate to obtain an education. She quickly advanced through all grades and eventually married her teacher, J. M. Carter, described by Shepherd as "a splendid young man" whose own brilliance added considerably to her wealth. Her father, Jerome, however, was unable to enjoy his daughter's return and her victorious new life, as he remained mentally ill.

One later writer about the Melungeons, Jean Patterson Bible, claims that this case "furnished a legal guidepost which affected decisions concerning Melungeons for many years afterward." Four years after the trial, Lewis Shepherd entered the state legislature and also married Lilah Pope, the daughter of a wealthy Sequatchie County landowner. He afterwards became a chancery court judge and a longtime general counsel in Tennessee for two major railroads. In 1891, Shepherd received a certificate from the United States Circuit Court of Appeals for presenting "the first case ever taken before that body anywhere in the country."

His book *Memoirs of Judge Lewis Shepherd*, which also featured other Chattanooga general history and biographies, was published privately for friends and relatives after its appearance in the newspaper. Before his death in 1917 at the age of seventy-one, Shepherd wrote as much as he could about his varied career and his knowledge of the area's history. But his theory about the origin of the Melungeons found its way into a *Saturday Evening Post* article in 1947 which stated:

> Like so many of the people who have written and spoken on the subject of the Melungeon mystery, Shepherd nowhere quoted his authorities. . . . There was nobody then, and there is nobody now, to support in any way his theory or to argue with him on any basis except improbability. But he did win the court case.

117
Napoleon Hill

Cotton Is King in Memphis Again

Although Mary Wood Hill's parents did not realize it back in 1858, her impetuous and seemingly reckless husband, Napoleon Hill, *did* have good sense. He was proving it each day in the Memphis cotton industry. He was, in fact, becoming one of the richest men in the South.

But on the couple's 1858 wedding day, the bride's anxious mother could only watch in dismay when a team of six white horses thundered into the yard of her Bolivar home, stirring up a whirlwind of dirt before halting suddenly at her door. The carriage driver, Hill himself, stood up, his body taut as he strained (three reins in each hand) to control his animals. He was dressed in a stovepipe hat, a "monstrous collar and ascot," and garish gloves. As the dust cleared, Mary's mother sobbed over the thought of her daughter's imminent wedding to this twenty-seven-year-old Memphis businessman with a flair for risk and speed.

The son of a doctor, Hill was a former neighbor of the Woods family who had spent his early childhood in Hardeman County. His parents then relocated to Mississippi, where his father died, leaving fourteen-year-old Napoleon as head of the family. After moving back to West Tennessee, the boy got a job in his uncle's general store at Bolivar. At nineteen, Hill and his best friend ventured west during the 1849 California Gold Rush and established a successful grocery and liquor business. When Hill sensed that Indians in California were growing restless, he and his partner sold the business and returned to Tennessee (the new owners were massacred). Hill, meanwhile, landed in Memphis with ten thousand dollars in his pocket and began a solid business supplying goods to the cotton brokers.

His intended, Mary Wood, a descendant of the late President James K. Polk, had wealth and breeding. The father of the bride was not to be outdone by the flamboyant groom: Wood had planned a grand gesture of his own. When Hill approached the family's front door on the day of the wedding, two slaves presented him with trays stacked high in half dollars, as many as they could carry. The wedding gift totaled twenty-five thousand dollars.

The couple settled in Memphis until the Civil War destroyed the cotton business. Hill, who was sympathetic to the Union, eluded the war altogether by moving his family back to their Hardeman County farm and awaiting the end of hostilities. Memphis citizens did not criticize him for his Civil War stand or his avoidance of the battlefront; after the war, they gladly welcomed back such a savvy business leader who could help the local economy. Hill became Memphis's "Merchant Prince," the city's first major cotton operator. He knew how to help cotton growers, and himself as well. Hill made money from the planters in numerous ways. They depended on him for loans (at his interest rates), for supplies from his store (obtained on credit at higher prices), and for his ability to sell their cotton (for a commission).

Hill's fortune was based as much on luck as on his business sense. Years later, in 1879, he made a small fortune due to an argument with one of his business partners. Their disagreement came about when Hill referred a nail salesman to his partner, who bought five thousand kegs of nails at $1.60 per keg. Recog-

nizing a bargain, Hill believed that more nails should have been purchased. The partner refused and accused Hill of overstepping the bounds of his authority within their partnership. Rebuked, Hill made his own deal and bought fifty thousand kegs with his own money. Soon, the price of nails rose to $7.00 per keg, netting him a quick personal profit of $270,000.

By 1888, Hill owned the third-largest cotton supply business in the world, handling one hundred thousand bales and earning $5.5 million annually. In addition to his cotton interests, he dabbled in numerous other business pursuits, including the formation of Union Planters Bank.

As with many other men who became rich in the cotton industry, Hill displayed his wealth publicly, and usually with an opulent mansion. His "French Renaissance" manor house was so luxurious that it became a Memphis landmark. Twelve-foot-high mirrors abounded, as did Oriental rugs and prized paintings. The house also featured an extravagant bedroom suite with a ten-foot-tall headboard, which had won a first prize during Philadelphia's 1876 Centennial Exposition.

Most Memphians, however, came to know Hill through a daily downtown ritual that involved him and three distinguished friends, who met on the same Memphis street corner precisely at ten o'clock each morning during the 1870s and early 1880s. The other three also were riveting post-Civil War figures: Judge D. P. "Pappy" Hadden, a dapper Kentucky native credited with helping restore Memphis after the yellow fever epidemics, when he became president of an emergency three-man commission to run the city; Archibald Wright, a native of Giles County and former Tennessee Supreme Court judge instrumental in fashioning Tennessee law; and Henry Montgomery, an Irish immigrant who parlayed a cotton-press device into riches and built the city's nationally famous harness horse-racing track. The four discussed issues of the day and shared a few laughs. Their daily routine not only caught the fancy of the citizenry but also that of a local artist, who painted what became a popular portrayal of the quartet, called appropriately, *The Four Men on a Corner*. The painting was later displayed in the Memphis library.

Hill's activities came to a sudden halt in 1894 when a stroke left him paralyzed at the age of sixty-four and confined to his home. He died several years later.

118
Annanias Honeycutt
A Hanging Offense No More

Even after the rope around his neck rendered him speechless, East Tennessee farmer Annanias Honeycutt continued to protest his innocence.

In 1875, Honeycutt and his prominent Claiborne County neighbor Thomas Ausmus had become embroiled in a dispute over a hog. Honeycutt admitted hitting Ausmus with a rock in self-defense but denied inflicting fatal injuries. As he was leaving the fight scene, Honeycutt claimed, another man was present and probably killed Ausmus. The court disagreed and sentenced the Powell Valley prisoner to hang.

The hanging became a public spectacle with a reported five to six thousand people attending, many arriving in wagons full of picnic supplies. Legend claims that one witness to the event was notorious outlaw Frank James, likely visiting his grandparents who lived nearby along the Powell River. Many Claiborne Countians, however, believed that Jesse James, and not his brother Frank, was actually the one who attended, and did so because Honeycutt was a member of his gang. Little did the attending crowd know that this execution would someday be considered "the most outstanding public hanging in Tennessee."

One of the preachers comforting Honeycutt gave him a handkerchief, asking that he show his innocence by switching it from hand to hand in his dying moments. The rope tightened around Honeycutt's neck, and he swung violently in the afternoon air . . . all the while "shifting the handkerchief from hand to hand."

Many dismayed onlookers were so upset at the proceedings that no capital punishment was carried out in Claiborne County after that day in 1875.

But the life of Annanias Honeycutt may not have ended that day. Perhaps he somehow survived his hanging, only to be hanged again several years later in Kansas for yet another crime. Claiborne Countian Dave Ellison was in Kansas at the time and reported seeing such a hanging. The man on the gallows admitted to having been hanged in Tennessee for the killing of Ausmus.

Such accounts added fuel to other rumors, some of which were told to Ausmus's granddaughter, Mrs. Rosalee Ausmus Keever of Knoxville. In a 1984 newspaper interview, Mrs. Keever said that Ku Klux Klan riders disrupted the Honeycutt hanging. The crowd dispersed, and in the confusion, Jesse James and his companion Bob Ford took Honeycutt away. The coffin itself held nothing more than a large rock.

119
James Jackson Pennington
Aviation Pioneer: Propelling Mankind

When two strangers mysteriously visited Middle Tennessean James Jackson Pennington about 1883, their quick and silent departure from Lawrence County created decades of rumor, conjecture, and suspicion. Why the sudden unannounced visit and the secretive air regarding Henryville's popular and controversial inventor and local newspaper correspondent?

The story behind James Jackson Pennington began in 1872, when at fifty-three he designed an early flying machine which he called the "Aerial Bird." Since gasoline was not yet an everyday fuel, Pennington used a clock spring to power the small device, which was able to carry the weight of a four-pound book. He flew it in front of several curious Henryville neighbors that same year. Pennington acquired a United States patent on September 4, 1877, adding a Canadian patent seven months later. His patent described an invention for the propulsion and guiding of air machines. The hand-held model he created featured a balloon from which Pennington "suspended a fan that would draw air into a chamber and expel it," causing an air thrust to launch the balloon. Describing the maneuverability of his device, he later wrote to a fellow inventor and engineer, Eugene F. Falconnett, who lived in Davidson County, saying that the Aerial Bird had "the power to go & to guide right & left and up and down & thats all a Buzzard has or any other fowel[.]"

Another Tennessean, Melville Milton Murrell, was also building a successful flying machine near Morristown, but one that desperately needed a propulsion device. A frustrated Murrell had to rely instead on manpower. Despite the lack of an engine, he was able to lift and transport a hired hand in a wood-and-canvas plane, or ornithopter, which stayed aloft for several-hundred yards. It was flown down a hill with the aid of three hundred feet of guide wire. To keep the plane in the air, "the operator pushed on a crossbar with his feet to make the wings flap." Murrell too received a patent in 1877, the fourth patent given an ornithopter. He and his life-sized model provided the "first recorded man-carrying glides in a heavier-than-air machine in the United States." Dispirited that he could not sustain a lengthy flight without a motor, Murrell soon gave up his aviation experiments and became a Methodist circuit rider. Before his death in 1932, he was able to realize his life's desire by riding in an airplane over his Hamblen County home in Panther Springs.

The several years following Pennington's patent, meanwhile, were filled with excited and frustrated attempts to obtain financial support for the Aerial Bird's propulsion concept. He ran into negative opinions and ridicule, which he fought at every turn. Because he was a regular contributor to the *Lawrenceburg Press* with local town happenings, Pennington also fought the local editor just as regularly when references to the plane were cut from his copy. The editor, who often scoffed at Pennington, whom he described as a "quack" for inventing a flying machine, admitted in print: "We confess we have, on numerous occasions, made free use of friend Pennington's articles, remodeling them, and using only such portions as we think best suited to our readers." Pennington grumbled (in print) that people in the 1880s were not ready for a radical innovation like air travel. But he never lost faith in his belief that humans could actually travel by air and do so safely.

When Pennington in the summer of 1883 took a working model of his patented Bird to the Columbian Exposition in Louisville, Kentucky, he hoped to find financial backing. Two men offered to buy all rights to the invention. He declined to sell. According to one story, the same two strangers whom Pennington had rebuffed in Louisville later visited him at Henryville in a lengthy and secret meeting, during which they purchased rights and the working model to the Aerial Bird.

The subsequent rumors, conjectures, and suspicions about the identity of these strangers were fueled by a flying exhibition December 17, 1903, at Kitty Hawk, North Carolina, more than thirty years after Pennington's flying feat in front of his neighbors. For decades after Kitty Hawk, the people of Henryville and family members wondered: Could the two strangers have been Wilbur and Orville Wright?

Since the Wright brothers were teenagers during Pennington's last days, the real truth may have been revealed by a neighbor, W. P. Oliver, a Lawrence County historian who wrote under the pen name "Fleetwood." Oliver remembered when the two strangers came to town. After Pennington demonstrated his Aerial Bird, the two men decided to conclude a deal. "I never knew what amount they offered," wrote Oliver, "but the offer was accepted and they put it under the seat of their buggy and after that there came a rumor that those men were from Paris, France, and that this model was improved until it became an air-ship that could haul passengers."

Pennington himself wrote to the *Lawrenceburg Press* on October 2, 1884, explaining that France had his model. Here is his statement (exactly as written), expressing his lament that he never obtained financial support for his experiments:

> France has my aerial bird flying. I sent it first to President Grevy and in December of 1883 to the Aeronautic Society. I offered to sell it to France for ten millions of dollars. I told them it was not feathered but how to equip it for flying. In place of buying it, they have taken my bird, winged it with my cigar shaped balloon with car and rudder underneath and have electric that I ordered Edison to make for me. If I could have commanded $2,000, this air ship would have first sailed over American soil and the honor have come to Lawrence County.

Three months later in January 1885, Pennington died of pneumonia; he was sixty-four. He never witnessed the advance of aviation, but future Lawrence Countians showed their appreciation of his efforts. In honor of his achievements and his clear vision, they named their modern airport Pennington Field, for "a man who had a dream and a revolutionary invention that would allow men to soar through the atmosphere like an eagle."

120
Jesse James
The Neighborly Mr. Howard of Tennessee

In September 1876, Jesse James was fleeing the law and thinking about changing professions. His latest effort as an outlaw was a foiled bank robbery in Minnesota with brother Frank and the Younger brothers.

In the manhunt that followed, the Youngers were captured. Having escaped, the James brothers were being sought by angry vigilantes and law officers throughout the Midwest. Jesse James, who was tending his wounded brother, was nowhere to be found. The nation's most famous outlaw was headed south to Tennessee, and farming looked more attractive by the mile.

Jesse and Frank James resisted heading for their grandparents' East Tennessee farm, which was located along the Powell River in Claiborne County. They also decided against nearby Huntsville, where the brothers reportedly operated a small grocery store years earlier. They chose, instead, to start life anew in a place where no one knew them.

Jesse found his refuge on land between Middle and West Tennessee and adopted the alias J. D. Howard, a simple farmer, family man, and horse-racing addict. He settled temporarily on a rented farm near Waverly in Humphreys County. Frank relocated about seventy miles away in Nashville and became equally "respectable" under the alias Frank Woodson. The respectability lasted four years.

Jesse James's residency in Humphreys County was better documented than most of his other Tennessee activities. While living near Waverly, Jesse's wife, Zee, gave birth to twins who lived only a week. Their burial spot was well known by citizens of the day. As J. D. Howard, he also raced his own steed, a prized racehorse named Red Fox, which once stumbled and fell near the finish line, causing its owner to come in last. Insulted, James stood up, dusted himself off, stormed up to the judges, and demanded a rematch. He got it, and won the race. James's love of fast horses and fast tracks became well known. So did an episode one day at the local voting place when he fainted from heat exhaustion, revealing under his coat guns that no average farmer would possess.

James also had a strange attitude toward debts. Some he deemed worthy of repayment as a matter of principle; to others he did not give a second thought. He once borrowed sixty dollars from Postmaster William Jackson of present-day Denver, which he repaid; he also obtained nine hundred dollars' worth of cattle on credit from Mark Cooley, which he did not repay.

Facing the prospect of bleak times as a farmer and disagreement with Cooley, Jesse James suddenly left Humphreys County. He packed his family and his belongings into a covered wagon and moved to Nash-ville, near his brother's place; there he remained for the next two years. Cooley tracked his whereabouts, then filed and won a Nashville lawsuit. James appealed to the Tennessee Supreme Court, which dropped the appeal when J. D. Howard did not pursue the matter in person.

James, in a spirit of friendship, kept in touch with some citizens of Humphreys County. He sent letters to such Denver friends as H. E. Warren and often itemized various debts incurred while living in the county. The letters also explained the manner in which he desired to pay off these debts, preferably through his favorite sport: horse racing. One sample is as follows (with original spelling):

May 18, 1879

Dear Sir

I felt very bad all day yesterday after drinking so much beer, but I am OK today. I expect to attend the faul races at Nashville this week and invest on the Louisville events and hope you will attend. If we will be prudent I think we can win some money. If you come up bring up those claims you had at the races against me and the first winnings I make I will pay you. . . . . Your friend, J. D. Howard.

While living near Nashville, Jesse James chucked his identity as farmer Howard and temporarily assumed a new role, traveling preacher. Legend claims that he preached a sermon in the Hermitage Church. Rejoining brother Frank in Nashville, he reportedly became a member of a local Methodist church, where he could sing "his well-loved hymns."

Frank, meanwhile, was a popular figure in Davidson County and gained such esteem that national law enforcement never thought to track him down at his principle haunts: the race track (where he rode his own horse and often won); the Nashville Fair (where his prize hogs routinely won first place); the voting booth on election day (where he never failed to appear); or the offices of the mayor and the sheriff (his good friends).

When they feared their true identities might be revealed by a former gang member who was arrested in Tennessee, the James brothers departed Nashville. In early 1881, they left Tennessee altogether and moved to the West.

Some accounts claim that the brothers never committed a crime while in Tennessee. Other stories point with pride to colorful occasions when Jesse James bent the law, appearing more like Robin Hood than the nation's most hunted fugitive.

According to one bit of Middle Tennessee folklore revealed by writer William Lynnwood Montell, the James brothers boarded one night in Gainesboro with a fellow called "Old Man Williams," who, it was told, made no secret of his wealth or the fact that he accumulated it by charging exorbitant interest rates on loans he made to poor farmers. He revealed that he would soon foreclose on one black man who had fallen behind in his payments. Williams also made the mistake of telling the two guests where he kept his money.

"So the James brothers stayed up all night with him," recalled a farm tenant in later years. "He [one of the brothers] got up during the night and got the money that the man owed him [Williams]. He went down and give it to this [black] man. Says, 'you go pay this place off.'"

Another legendary tale places Jesse James in a Knoxville jail for reasons unknown or untold. He escaped and walked to Kingston along Kingston Pike, which travels west from the city. Neither his date of incarceration nor his offense was recorded. In Kingston, James spent the night at the home of Jesse Richard Love, whose wife, Louisa, feared the stranger, who *seemed* like a fugitive. While Louisa lay awake, unable to calm her fears, her husband sat up with his houseguest, engaged in a lively conversation. As Love's descendants recalled, "James was the most intelligent, most entertaining man he [Love] had ever met." When a posse arrived the next morning looking for the escaped prisoner, farmer Love reported he had never seen Jesse James.

James was shot to death April 3, 1882, while living as Tom Howard in St. Joseph, Missouri (his wife, Zee, lived until 1900). Six months after the reported death of his brother, Frank James surrendered to authorities and discovered that his legendary stature as an outlaw had made him a folk hero no jury would convict. Thereafter appearing as himself in Wild West shows across America, he often returned to Tennessee, especially to visit his relatives in East Tennessee. He died of natural causes in 1915 at age seventy-two.

121
Father D. A. Quinn
Yellow Terror: The Destruction of Memphis

Father D. A. Quinn experienced firsthand the horrors of yellow fever when it hit Memphis in the 1870s.

A ravaged, lifeless, and bankrupt Memphis could barely get to its feet in 1878. Most of its citizens were running for their lives, leaving behind them six thousand dead. Those who could not or would not leave had to fight against an unseen, but not unfamiliar, assailant called "yellow fever." The enemy had been there before, in 1873, and left twenty-five hundred dead; a series of smaller outbreaks also claimed lives in the 1850s and 1860s.

One man witnessed yellow fever's horror during its worst epidemics, watching from a vantage point close enough to feel the pain and smell the stench of death. He was Father D. A. Quinn, a Catholic priest from Ireland who wrote a wrenching historical account of the plagues: *Heroes and Heroines of Memphis*. A former Catholic circuit rider in Tennessee and two other states, Quinn had settled in Memphis, where he remained for a decade.

Of the city's fifty-six thousand inhabitants in 1878, most fled on foot, by trains, boats, mules, horses, and any other means of transportation, leaving death, their belongings, and often their loved ones behind them. Some people, thinking only of their own lives, simply abandoned their families and took flight. More than thirty thousand people escaped the city as the plague of 1878 brought Memphis to its knees and the rest of the nation to its doorstep. America mobilized to save Memphis with a relief campaign that made headlines throughout the world. Some writers speculated that the worst wounds of the Civil War were finally put to rest by the North's willingness to help one of the South's major cities.

The 1878 relief was massive for the times. Employees of the Singer Sewing Machine Company in New Jersey contributed $4,000. New York City alone sent $266,167, raised in one week. New York City's Medical Society doctors, after attending a speech by a bishop from the Episcopal Diocese of Tennessee, contributed thousands of dollars on the spot, many of them handing over blank checks. A group in St. Louis raised $25,000 for a relief boat to dispense medical aid and food up and down the Mississippi River wherever yellow fever touched. Memphis, with a daily death toll that often topped all other cities combined, was the principal target of this noble gesture.

Speaking in Minneapolis, President Rutherford B. Hayes auctioned a tattered Bible given to him by an ex-Union soldier, who donated it (his only possession) so that proceeds from its sale might benefit an ex-Confederate in the South. The Reverend R. N. Countee, a leading Memphis black minister, was moved to write his clerical colleagues in Atlanta to plead for aid. "Dear Brothers," his letter began, "Our distress beggars description. We are often at the graveyard until 10 at night burying the dead. The white people are doing all they can, but we are compelled to call on our brothers. I have 300 of my flock of 2,907 left. For God's sake, help us."

Although Memphis had been known as an "unhealthy place" since the early 1830s, and several cleanup campaigns had been proposed but never carried out, no one was prepared for the lethal effects of such a disease. Neither did anyone know (until 1900) that yellow fever is caused by the bite of infected "domestic" mosquitoes that breed prolifically in unsanitary human habitats. Quinn shared the belief held by some Memphians that the nearness of the Arkansas swamps might have something to do with the fever outbreak, as well as with the cholera epidemic that preceded it. But most people believed the fever was spread by contact with other infected persons.

The epidemics in Memphis were likely caused by the transportation of infected mosquitoes in cargo from New Orleans, where ships made port from the yellow fever-infested West Indies. Increasing numbers of mosquitoes created by the squalid living conditions in the Memphis slums elevated the outbreak to an epidemic ravaging every neighborhood.

Most of those left behind to fight the disease were unable to afford an exodus, primarily poor Irish or poor blacks. Because the fever struck down whites at a significantly higher rate (70 percent) than it did blacks (8 percent), the remaining white population was overwhelmed. More than one-third of the dead were Catholic, and Father Quinn, when he was not giving the last rites, was trying to get help for those who managed to survive.

The first major fever in 1873 provided Quinn with many tales and observations. He related one account of a dying Irish servant girl who had been abandoned by her fleeing employers. Father Quinn agreed to compose a will for her. The girl willed the few dollars she had saved to her mother in Ireland, her chain and locket to one friend, and her little gold ring to another. She asked to be buried with her prayer book and her rosary beads. Quinn observed:

> It was the poorest will I ever indited—and yet I felt it all the more sacred to execute. A strange feeling crept over me as I noted these trifles . . . this young maiden's inventory revealed a heart full of faith, friendship and love. Before she felt herself worthy to face God, she wished to divest herself of the few baubles poverty had thrown in her way; and taking only the two emblems of her religion, she felt as though she was fully equipped for the journey of eternity.

Quinn discovered one child stricken with the fever, whom he identified only as Mollie; she was lying beside her already dead mother when he entered their home on Main Street. Although the family was wealthy, no one else remained to care for the child or to bury the mother. Quinn said he experienced difficulty finding anyone willing to help. The next day, he visited the little girl. She told him that she hated to die, but she must: "mamma appeared to me last night at the window and told me I should go with her." The girl died shortly thereafter, and her last words greatly affected the priest: "Oh, Father, it is a hard thing to die and appear before God."

Doctors were working in all directions to ward off such tragedies. Quinn described a malodorous substance, assafoetida, which doctors prescribed to be worn around the neck to repel yellow fever. One young priest of Quinn's acquaintance found its smell so disgusting, however, that he removed the substance, threw it into the fire, and grumbled: "Here, let me die if I will, but I shall never be brought to my grave with such a detestable odor." Quinn agreed.

The more overpowering and deadlier plague of 1878 left even survivors of the previous epidemic shocked by the devastation. According to the priest's continuing journal and other reports of the day, coffins were piled three deep at cemeteries because burials had fallen behind the death rate. Many parents, unable to find help, dug their children's graves with their own hands.

"A city of horrors" was the description given by Dr. William T. Ramsey after arriving with a group of Howard Association nurses. (The Howard Association was activated to provide medical services and other needs for yellow fever victims.) Ramsey wrote:

> The stench of Memphis sickened me before I got within 5 miles of the city. No words can describe the filth I saw, the rotten wooden pavements, the dead animals, putrifying human bodies and the half-buried dead combining to make the atmosphere something fearful. I took 30 grains of quinine and 120 drops of tincture of iron every day and wore a thick veil soaked with carbolic acid over my face.
>
> Many of the nurses, both men and women, smoke cigars constantly while attending patients to ward off the stench. In the Peabody Hotel where I stayed, pans of sulphur were kept burning in the halls.

Among the untold number of clergy in all denominations who battled the disease and tried to help victims, was the Reverend Dr. Sylvanus Landrum of Central Baptist Church, a member of the Citizens Relief Committee and one of the city's senior clergymen. Described as "unflagging in his efforts to serve those in need" during the plague, Reverend Landrum and his wife were also stricken. He was forced to leave his sick bed on September 12 to bury his son Herbert, who was city editor of the *Avalanche*. Within fourteen days, the still-afflicted pastor was digging another grave, this time for his son George, who also worked on the newspaper.

One of the stories that suggested faith as an antidote to yellow fever involved Father William Walsh's church camp, established outside of Memphis to feed and house the poor. He isolated his camp with strict rules regarding the comings and goings of all persons, and he celebrated mass each morning. Of an estimated four hundred inhabitants, only ten died.

As the disease kept spreading, the citizens of Somerville in adjacent Fayette County regretted an advertisement previously placed in the *Memphis Appeal* portraying their town as a haven for Memphians. "Escape the mosquitoes and the summer heat of the city," the ad read. "The Memphis & Charleston Railroad has lowered its rates to Somerville."

Somerville and most of the surrounding towns, however, began instituting quarantines against Memphis's deserters, enforcing these quarantines at gunpoint. Humboldt, located in Gibson County on the rail line through the interior of West Tennessee, did not allow bundles of the Memphis newspaper to be tossed from trains passing through town. Union City, at the western tip of the state in Obion County, escaped contamination by paying two men, who had visited sick friends in Memphis, ten dollars per day not to return home.

J. M. Keating, editor of the *Memphis Appeal,* tirelessly continued printing the newspaper, even though he was forced to run it virtually by himself when seventy-three of his seventy-five employees were stricken by the fever. The *Atlanta Constitution* reportedly said of him: "On more than one occasion Col. Keating did all the editorial work, the reporter's work, set the type and made up the forms. It is the moral heroism of such men that evokes our greatest admiration."

Father Quinn recalled an ironic conversation he overheard between two priests standing at a cemetery shortly after the 1878 fever had subsided. One of them, pointing to a pair of gravesites, said, "Doctor, *there* is your place next year, and *here* is mine." When the less-severe 1879 plague hit, they were the first two of five hundred total casualties.

In his role as a journalist, Keating saw much that hardened his heart. A reunion he witnessed in 1879, however, warmed his very soul. Two young boys, who had only each other on whom to depend, were stricken. One friend left his own sickbed to help the other. Despite a valiant attempt to endure together, the boys were separated during the epidemic. Authorities later mistakenly told one of them that the friend he previously nursed had died. Days later, Keating recalled:

> The two met unexpectedly near Court Square. A thrill of sentiment, almost to the verge of weeping, went through the dozen spectators who had their attention drawn to the two little fellows, who despite the crowd, despite the dust of the street, the jingle of the street-car bells, the hum and confusion incident to reviving Memphis, embraced each other, their joy finding utterance in the shedding of copious tears.

Throughout the epidemics, one woman, from the "wrong" side of town, became a heroine who inspired eulogies nationwide. Thousands who came to know her considered bordello manager Annie Cook a nineteenth-century Mary Magdalene, which is how history recorded her.

Annie had just moved from Louisville, Kentucky, when the first epidemic hit between September 14 and November 9, 1873, claiming the first two thousand lives. According to the *Louisville Courier-Journal*, she opened her "house" for the care of fever patients and "watched over the dead and dying like a ministering angel." By 1876, she had moved her business into the lush "Brick Mansion" located at 34 Gayoso Street. When yellow fever returned in 1878, this time claiming 5,100 victims in four months, Annie again closed her business and opened her quarters to the sick.

Keating, her great admirer, gave his personal accolade in written editorials. Most Memphians acknowledged her unselfishness silently, but the Christian Women of Louisville (Kentucky) applauded Annie publicly in a letter which concluded:

> History may not record this good deed, for the good deeds of women seldom live after them; but every heart in the whole country responds with affectionate gratitude to the noble example you have set for Christian men and women. God speed you, dear madam, and, when the end comes, may the light of a better world guide you to a home beyond.

Six days after contracting yellow fever, Annie died at thirty-eight. She was buried in the Howard Nursing Association Lot at Elmwood Cemetery, reserved for those who nursed during the yellow fever epidemic. Mere yards away were the graves of two ministers who were also martyrs of the disease.

Annie, called the fallen/risen angel, was the subject of such glowing tributes as this one from the *Chicago Tribune*:

> The *Tribune* readers are familiar with the facts concerning Annie Cook, whose grave, strewn with flowers, is among the prominent features of the Howards' lot in Elmwood. She did the best she could, and, after a troubled life, the prayers of hundreds throughout this broad land go up this bright morning to the Throne, that she sleeps in peace. . . .

"Reviving Memphis" had many lessons to learn, and the city finally took steps to protect itself from future catastrophe. So did the nation, as Congress appointed a Yellow Fever Commission to study every community affected by the disease. At Memphis, which had lost its city charter, sanitation became the priority. Therefore, George Waring of the National Board of Health designed and built the most advanced city sewer system ever created, attracting nationwide attention. Years later, in a speech before the Scientific Institute of Great Britain, Waring said that Memphis "has put its house into more nearly perfect order than any other city in the country."

In the 1880s, Memphis also established systems to eliminate garbage and standing water, although it was not yet known that these were breeding grounds for mosquitoes. To further insure their chances of survival, Memphians finally agreed to "elaborate" quarantines against all ships from the West Indies whenever yellow fever was reported in that part of the world.

Father D. A. Quinn continued to help the city in its recovery, but he ultimately returned to his native Ireland, where he died in 1911.

122
Robert R. Church Sr.

From Slave to Millionaire

The son of a slave woman and a white steamboat captain who owned a Mississippi plantation, Robert R. Church had spent most of his life on his father's steamers. Having experienced numerous terrifying river accidents, he simply had grown tired of life on the Mississippi River. When invading Union troops, therefore, boarded the steamboat *Victoria* during a wartime takeover of Memphis, the young Church made his escape. Bidding good-bye to the river as well as to slavery, he simply swam to shore, climbed the riverbank, walked into the city, and got a job.

Church's industriousness was soon rewarded by ownership of a Memphis saloon. He eventually built a real estate empire which included a restaurant and hotel. The key to his rapid wealth, however, was the perseverance to stay in Memphis through three devastating yellow fever epidemics while most residents of the city fled. In the aftermath of the disease, Church was able to purchase abandoned city tracts when property taxes went unpaid. He parlayed these parcels into future investments and larger riches, making him America's first black millionaire.

Although he and his father, Charles Church, never publicly acknowledged their biological relationship, the two men clearly loved each other. After he was established in Memphis, the younger Church made frequent visits to the Mississippi plantation where he was born in 1839 (his mother died in 1851).

On these trips, Church generally brought along his small daughter Mollie, and the old captain always greeted her with gifts and affection. However, the truth did not remain hidden from her for long. After one such visit, little Mollie commented on the captain's generosity toward them. Then she dropped a disconcerting observation: "And don't you know, Papa, you look just like Captain Church." The younger Church took Mollie aside and confided that the captain was more than a friend.

Neither his riches, his brilliance as a real estate investor, or his generosity as an entrepreneur could earn Robert Church total acceptance in the white community of nineteenth-century Memphis. During a trip to the North in the 1870s, Church spotted a beautiful sleigh. Acting on a whim, he bought and shipped it to Memphis, despite the fact that the city rarely got snow. Friends laughed, but Church vowed that one day he would use this colorful carriage, which indeed he did. Triumphantly one winter, he rode up and down Main Street in his sleigh, drawn by a high-stepping horse. A few fellow Memphians gleefully engaged in snowball fights along the roadside and launched a handful at Church. He accepted this pummeling with a good-natured laugh until he realized that many were filled with rocks. After one of these struck him in the face, Church pulled out his revolver and fired a shot into the direction of the ruckus. As Mollie Church Terrell would later recall: "It was a desperate thing for a colored man to do anywhere, particularly in the South, and it is a great wonder he was not torn limb from limb, even though he was shooting in self-defense."

This was not Mollie's only brush with bigotry in her childhood. She had experienced a train ride and a degradation that she never forgot. While her father had stepped temporarily to another compartment, the conductor, spotting Mollie in the first-class area, began pulling her from the seat, demanding, "Whose little nigger is this?" When Church returned, he found his daughter standing in the aisle, utterly humiliated. He boldly told the conductor that neither he nor his daughter would be leaving the first-class car, and the conductor relented under the commanding voice of an outraged father.

Despite such treatment, Church never allowed racial hatred to alter his views toward his adopted city or his fellow citizens. When the yellow fever epidemics of 1878-79 left Memphis in financial ruin and forced the loss of its charter, the city issued bonds to fund its large municipal debt. The value of these bonds was questionable, but Church stepped forward and purchased the first one. The impact was tremendous. As one magazine article reportedly noted: "With this example before them, capitalists of the Caucasian race could not afford to be shy, so they followed his example and all the bonds were sold."

Church proved his generosity again in 1901, donating one thousand dollars to help promote a Confederate reunion in Memphis. When questioned by members of his own race, Church explained that the war was over and that all people should work together to heal the city's wounds and promote harmony among the races. A. B. Pickett, editor of the *Evening Scimitar*, applauded the deed:

Whereas Robert R. Church, a colored citizen of Memphis, has contributed the sum of $1000 to the reunion fund, therefore be it resolved that the thanks of the Committee be extended to the generous donor, who on this, as on all other occasions, when aid was sought for a worthy public purpose, has given an example of that liberal spirit which should animate all citizens of Memphis.

In 1906, Church marked one of his lifetime achievements: the organization of the Solvent Savings Bank and Trust Company, a bank that actually withstood the money panic of a year later. About the same time, he bought six acres on Beale Street, then built and donated to the black community Church's Park and Auditorium, billed as the "largest black-owned theater in the world," to be used for vaudeville, concerts, conventions, and commencements. At his death in 1912, the seventy-three-year-old Memphis philanthropist was worth more than one million dollars.

Although Church tried to overlook bigotry, his daughter became more interested in trying to overcome it. The highly educated Mollie grew up to become the renowned activist/lecturer/author Mary Church Terrell, a charter member of the National Association for the Advancement of Colored People (NAACP) and a pioneer in the women's rights movement. She was three-time president and a founder of the National Association of Colored Women. One of her most notable accomplishments occurred around 1904 when she addressed the International Congress of Women in Berlin, Germany. Mollie surprised the assembled multitude by being the only English-speaking delegate of any nation to deliver her speech entirely in German, and then she delivered it in French as well.

Church's son, Robert Church Jr., also bore a strong allegiance to his race and worked to overcome prejudice. While his father concentrated on economic power, the younger Church utilized political muscle. He became a political power broker with the formation of the Lincoln League, an organization of black Republican voters in Shelby County. Through control of black votes, Church gained clout with men like Memphis Mayor Edward Hull "Boss" Crump and other leading white politicians. Many presidents, especially Herbert Hoover, considered him an important ally. Robert Church Jr.'s downfall came when he finally refused to support Crump. City tax collectors during

the Great Depression descended on Church's properties. Unable to pay Crump's tally of past-due debts, Church had to leave town, and the family fortunes came to an end.

123
Adolph S. Ochs
A Voice for the New South

When eleven-year-old Adolph S. Ochs took a cleaning job at the *Knoxville Chronicle* in 1869, his only aim was to provide financial help to his parents and five brothers and sisters. He swept the floor so well that the editor, Captain William Rule, promoted him to delivery boy and gave him the sum of $1.50 a week.

By the age of twenty, Ochs was so steeped in the world of newspapers that he was prepared to take advantage of a major business opportunity (others thought it a major business liability) and borrowed $250 to purchase one-half interest in the *Chattanooga Times*. The paper's owners, only too glad to rid themselves of this speculative venture, also turned over full control and title of the debt-ridden *Times*. In June 1878, the paper announced that it had a new publisher. But few citizens realized that Ochs's father had to travel from Knoxville to sign the deal since his son was still a legal minor. The youth represented, however, the new blood needed to save the Chattanooga newspaper—and his skills would eventually save another big-city newspaper, the *New York Times*.

Adolph S. Ochs was born in Cincinnati in 1858 to German-Jewish immigrants. His parents moved to Knoxville toward the end of the Civil War and suffered the same financial strains as other postwar families. When he began his boyhood janitorial work at the Knoxville paper, Adolph immediately showed an unlimited enthusiasm and energy despite his meager earnings. In 1870, hoping to improve family finances even further, his father sent him to an uncle in Rhode Island to work in a general store. Adolph, although only twelve years old, attended business school at night. A year later, he returned home to Knoxville where he apprenticed in a drugstore and entered East Tennessee University (forerunner of the University of Tennessee).

By the age of fifteen, Adolph was again at the newspaper—this time cleaning the presses as a printer's devil. But the employees at the *Chronicle* saw something else in him; they referred to Adolph as a "human interrogation point." The teenager wanted to know everything about the newspaper business.

In 1875, a new Knoxville paper opened its doors and hired the young man. At the *Knoxville Daily Tribune*, the seventeen-year-old rose from the composing room to reporter. But he found his stepping-stone to opportunity as an assistant to business manager Franc M. Paul, who gained fame during the Civil War as publisher of the Confederacy's propaganda paper, the *Rebel*. Paul, responding to the lure of the postwar's many upstart newspapers, followed the print trail to Chattanooga and became publisher of the new *Chattanooga Daily Dispatch*. He took Ochs with him. He also took respected editorial writer J. E. MacGowan, a former Union colonel.

The three found 1878 Chattanooga to be a frontier town where "Nothing but the most miserable dirt roads was at the command of the farmers . . . and only a crude ferry operated by an old mule on a treadmill bridged the river." Within the year, Ochs, a victim of the paper's financial problems, was scurrying to make ends meet. Since Ochs liked Chattanooga, he found a way to make money without leaving: by preparing a city directory. This venture gave him contact with prominent community leaders and insight into the makeup of the city. (One of the directory's most revealing statistics was that of Chattanooga's 11,488 citizens, only 773 were native Tennesseans. The rest of the adult male population came from all but four of the states and nineteen foreign countries.)

Since Ochs soon had more knowledge about Chattanooga than most residents, people gave him more than passing notice when he later became their newspaper publisher. To that end, Ochs faced the difficult task of borrowing $250 to take over the *Chattanooga Times*, which he characterized as "utterly dilapidated, demoralized and publicly and privately anathematized." Circulation had dropped to about 250 daily. Press room, composing room, and business office were all housed in a space of twenty by forty feet. In buying the paper, Ochs also agreed to assume a fifteen-hundred-dollar debt. At the end of his first week, he had to borrow extra money to meet the payroll.

However, Ochs had good business sense and an able editor in MacGowan. In addition to a dedication to responsible journalism, Ochs was determined to "put his subscribers and advertising patrons on a purely business relationship." If necessary, he would barter. It was not unusual to swap farm produce for a newspaper subscription.

Within months of Ochs's purchase, yellow fever reached epidemic proportions and hit East Tennessee, where a frenzy for news of the fever's spread and its death list helped escalate circulation to fifteen hundred copies per day. But the fever brought no profits, since all business was nearly at a standstill. With the help of printers in other cities, Ochs was able to publish. He also rallied Chattanoogans to a sense of optimism and hope for the future, which made him the city's biggest cheerleader, a role he would never forsake.

In March 1879, with endless months of hard labor behind him, Ochs celebrated his twenty-first birthday. On the pages of the paper, he revealed his true age to readers and admitted that he had been a minor when he became publisher. One Chattanooga businessman, H. S. Thacher, responded by sending Ochs several bottles of fine wine and liquor along with a note which read: "if the *Times* has been published by a 'boy' since you became the purchaser until now, then I wish there were more 'boys.'"

In less than ten years, Ochs built the *Chattanooga Times* into one of Tennessee's "most aggressive and progressive papers," according to some of his fellow Southern editors, who also agreed that the newspaper helped Chattanooga develop into one of the South's most thriving cities.

While Ochs proved to be an able publisher, he was a poor investor. By 1893, his real-estate ventures created such a personal crisis that he needed bank loans to pay the interest on his debt. Rather than file bankruptcy or cause injury to the *Times*, Ochs decided simply to seek another investment: what was for him a sure investment—another newspaper. At the suggestion of an associate, he investigated struggling newspapers in New York City.

Now thirty-eight, Ochs—having worked from the bottom to the top of the business as a printer's devil, reporter, editor, business manager, advertising solicitor, and publisher—was ready to jump into his next biggest challenge as publisher of another nearly bankrupt paper, the *New York Times*. Other New York newspaper executives did not believe the paper could be saved. Losses totaled a thousand dollars per day. Under the deal he negotiated in 1896, Ochs obtained full control with a promise of becoming major stock-holder if he made the paper solvent within three years.

Under Ochs's leadership, the *New York Times* became one of the world's most successful and recognizable newspapers by covering major social and political changes in the United States. Its success was accomplished with Ochs's independent editorial voice: a guarantee that no advertiser or politician could influence what his presses printed.

For more than forty years after leaving Chattanooga, Ochs made New York City his home and the *New York Times* his publishing haven. Despite the distance, Ochs always thought of himself as a citizen of Chattanooga and often returned. Recognized as one of the pioneers of modern journalism, Ochs made his last visit in April 1935 at the age of seventy-six. While sitting in a local coffee shop, he died suddenly, and as he might have hoped, within a block of the *Chattanooga Times* building.

124
Joseph Alexander Mabry/ Thomas O'Conner

Deadly Duels—Alive and Well

Knoxvillians marked October 19, 1882, as the day two of their most prominent businessmen took their feud to the street and died in a shootout. More newspapers were sold in Knoxville the following day than ever before. That the two would taunt and kill each other was somewhat ironic since Joseph Alexander Mabry and Thomas O'Conner were once close friends. Mabry, in fact, was a former associate who had helped establish O'Conner in business.

Mabry, born in 1826 outside of Knoxville, came from a pioneer landowning family and loved thoroughbred racing. Among his ancestors was an English baron who helped force the king of England to sign the Magna Carta in 1215. During the 1850s and 1860s, Mabry built his wealth both as an investor in businesses and as the king of railroad lobbyists. (He was adept at manipulating politicians to his benefit.) His investments ranged from the temporary ownership in 1869 of the *Knoxville Whig* to stock purchases in the Knoxville and Kentucky Railroad, which he also served as president. The railroad profited from Mabry's shrewd

lobbying at a time when barrels of brandy could assure hefty state loans. His killer, O'Conner, a Georgia native, was described as one of the wealthiest men in Tennessee. The president of Mechanics' National Bank, O'Conner was able to add consistently to his wealth in real-estate deals.

Mabry himself had been involved in two previous shootings. One ongoing battle with John Baxter over railroad dealings (and perhaps a large debt owed Mabry) culminated in Mabry confronting Baxter on a Knoxville street in 1870. "Business is business," Mabry was quoted as having said. Then he shot at Baxter, wounding him in the hand. Baxter's life was spared only because he ran away before Mabry could take aim at a more vital part.

When Mabry's youngest son, Will, was shot to death by Constable Don Lusby in a barroom brawl in 1881, another shooting lay ahead. Mabry saw his son's death as part of a greater conspiracy concocted by his old friend O'Conner, with whom he and Will were involved in a real-estate deal. According to some accounts, Mabry believed that O'Conner ordered (or at least influenced) Will's killing in order to secure the land for himself.

In August 1882, Mabry and another son, Joseph Jr., received threats from Constable Lusby and a brother. The Mabrys summoned police to arrest the brothers and accompanied the group to the police station. When they arrived, a brawl erupted. In the struggle, the Mabrys shot and killed both Lusbys, later arguing in court that they were simply helping police disarm the prisoners. The judge cleared them of all charges.

Two months later, Mabry and O'Conner came face to face at the fairgrounds in Knoxville. A dispute took place, and O'Conner threatened Mabry's life. Mabry retaliated by issuing a challenge to settle the score that day. O'Conner declined, adding that the timing was not right.

Just two days later, the timing must have been right for O'Conner. He stood in the door of his bank building, holding a loaded double-barreled shotgun in his arms, with another shotgun resting just inside the bank. Mabry and his friend Robert Steele turned the corner at Clinch Avenue onto the main business thoroughfare of Gay Street and headed for the Lamar House bar. As the two approached Mechanics' National Bank, O'Conner stepped out and fired at Mabry, who pitched forward, dead. O'Conner then waved aside onlookers who had gathered and leveled another blast into the body. Taking up the other shotgun, O'Conner shouted for Steele, who had found refuge in a nearby store.

Attending to some business nearby was Joseph Mabry Jr., who heard the shots. Running into the street, he drew his gun and fired a fatal shot at O'Conner. Just as he was falling, O'Conner managed to discharge the second shotgun, killing young Mabry as well.

In addition to the three fatalities, seven bystanders were wounded during the brief but bloody battle. The incident fascinated all who read about it, far beyond Knoxville. The Associated Press telegraphed at least ten thousand words to its member newspapers, many of which deemed it the worst outbreak of violence since the Civil War eighteen years earlier. When press accounts of the shooting also found their way to Mark Twain, he used the Mabry-O'Conner shootout in *Life on the Mississippi* to illustrate that life in the South was not always as genteel as advertised.

125
Samuel A. McElwee

Fighting the Color Line in Tennessee Politics

During the 1880s, when black state legislator Samuel A. McElwee pressed his colleagues for increased funding for the education of black teachers in Tennessee, he was not just paying lip service to a political theme. McElwee was speaking from a wealth of experience. Born into slavery in 1858, he had learned to read with the help of his master's children. Attending school sporadically during the Reconstruction era while working on a farm, McElwee covered all grades in six years, studying until midnight. At the age of sixteen, he took charge of his own school in Haywood County.

While continuing to help his father on their farm near Brownsville, he taught for a year at the school. Then McElwee went to college in Ohio, hoping to advance his knowledge. He earned expenses by doing whatever chores were available, generally cleaning windows or waiting tables. More than a year later, he was back in Tennessee, penniless and with no prospects for continuing his education.

McElwee wandered the Tennessee backroads selling Bibles and historical charts and occasionally peddling medicines. Eventually, another teaching job came his way. But the need to upgrade his education was foremost in McElwee's mind. Toward that end, he hired a white Vanderbilt University student to tutor him, and plodded ten miles two nights every week to get help in the classics, foreign languages, and algebra. Admiring McElwee's devotion, the tutor informed Nashville's Fisk University about him.

Fisk immediately enrolled McElwee, who continued to sell Bibles and historical charts to pay expenses. He excelled both as a student and as a popular political figure. Before his graduation in 1883, he had already served his first term in the Tennessee House of Representatives.

In the same year, McElwee introduced legislation to increase appropriations for educating black teachers. He sought an increase from twenty-five hundred dollars to five thousand dollars, arguing that blacks in Tennessee deserved a good education for their "patient, unrequited toil, and industry." But the legislature, dominated by his opposition Democratic Party, tabled the request; later it gave only a fraction of what McElwee sought.

The local and national press, however, were impressed by McElwee and began to write about him. The *Nashville Daily American* reprinted his entire speech for black education, calling him "a magnetic speaker, forcible debator and indefatigable worker" and pronouncing him "the recognized political leader of his race." He began to accept speaking engagements nationwide and represented Tennessee as commissioner of the Colored Department of the New Orleans Exposition. He also suffered the loss of his first wife, who died in 1885. Leaving his children with their grandparents, McElwee pursued the cause of justice and equality for blacks. The *New York Globe*, during its coverage of McElwee, asked for an autobiographical sketch, which it printed in 1884.

When his first legislative session ended, McElwee returned home to Haywood County, opened a grocery, sold cotton on the side, and began to study law. He would pursue a law degree at Central Tennessee College, Nashville, just as his second legislative term began.

McElwee became known as one of the Tennessee legislature's most active members during his tenure (1883-89), once nominated by his party to be Speaker of the House. He was among twelve black citizens who served in the legislature during the 1880s, able to access the political system after their Republican Party put its candidate in the governor's chair. The black lawmakers introduced a wide range of legislation trying to curb the system of racial discrimination that was emerging. Lynching, election fraud, and a bias against black laborers led a list of issues. They fought also for penitentiary reform and an end to discrimination in public facilities. Historian Joseph H. Cartwright, noting that these men would be the last blacks in the Tennessee legislature until the 1960s, writes of this period:

> The black men who served in the Tennessee legislature during the 1880's by and large proved to be very capable representatives. Several were men of superior education, energy and talent. The measures they introduced, the protests they registered . . . indicate that they attempted to represent the interests of their constituents by working to improve educational opportunities, labor conditions, and respect for civil rights.

McElwee also led the triumphant effort to create an asylum for the mentally ill in West Tennessee. But his political success story would soon come to a close.

Times were continuing to change throughout the South and in Tennessee. Radical Reconstruction had ended, and black citizens no longer had federal protection at voting places. When McElwee ran for re-election in 1888, a new climate of white political dominance prevailed. Armed guards within the opposition party roamed parts of West Tennessee to keep black voters at home, and McElwee lost the election by a considerable margin. His life was also threatened, and he was compelled to leave the region.

First he moved to Nashville and practiced law. Years later, he would settle in Chicago, where his Tennessee friend Ida B. Wells, a national figure for civil rights, was also living. McElwee's presence in Chicago predated by only a few years a mass migration of black citizens from the rural South to northern cities to seek new opportunities. While McElwee (until his 1914 death) occasionally revisited Tennessee and sometimes made special appearances at black-sponsored events, he now spent his time and energy as a family man and as one of Chicago's forty-six black attorneys.

126
Robert Love Taylor/ Alfred Alexander Taylor

The Governor's Chair:
A Family's "War of the Roses"

Nearly twenty-five years after the Civil War turned brother against brother, Tennessee's 1886 gubernatorial race did the same. The Republican state convention nominated Alfred Alexander "Alf" Taylor; a month later, Democrats nominated Robert Love "Bob" Taylor, Alf's younger brother. Their sibling rivalry became known as the "War of the Roses" after the English struggle between the houses of York and Lancaster, and the Taylors played along—generally on the fiddle. Alf wore a red rose, Bob a white one, and they enjoyed entertaining the public. Their mother, pestered by reporters to reveal which one she supported, indicated simply that she was behind "Taylor" all the way. Even the national press, which became engrossed in this election, sent reporters to cover the Taylors, who scheduled forty-one joint debates across Tennessee. The peculiarity of two brothers running against each other prompted the eastern papers to give them front-page coverage.

The Taylors, raised in Carter County's Happy Valley region near Elizabethton, were born into one of the most prominent families in upper East Tennessee. They were direct descendants of Revolutionary War soldiers and original Carter County settlers, including politicians and orators. Family notables included their father, Congressman Nathaniel Green Taylor, a Princeton graduate and Methodist minister; grandfather James P. Taylor, first attorney general in Tennessee's first judicial circuit; great-grandfather Nathaniel Taylor, who fought with Andrew Jackson in various military campaigns and rose to the rank of general; and a maternal uncle, Landon Carter Haynes, one of Tennessee's two representatives in the Confederate Congress (the family also was divided in Civil War loyalties).

Alf and Bob came to their divergent political views through their father, who was a Whig leader in Congress, and through their uncle, Colonel Robert Love, an opposing Jacksonian Democrat, for whom Bob

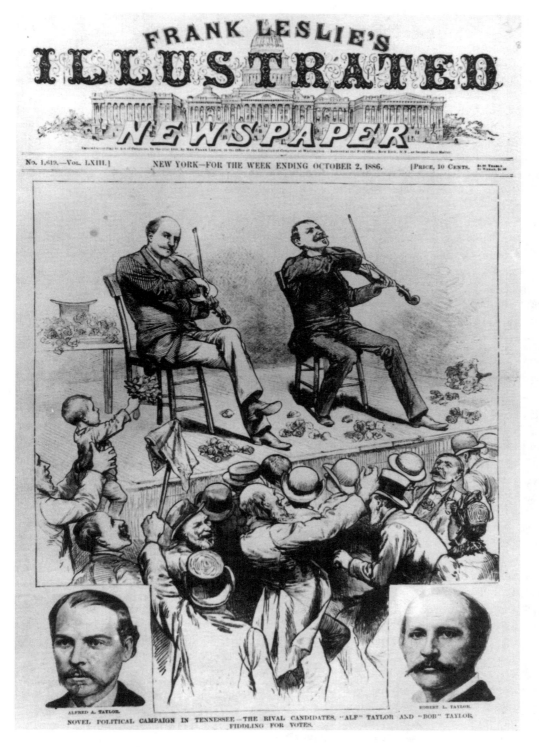

The Taylor brothers fiddled their way through campaign debates in the 1886 race for governor.

Taylor was named. Despite their political differences, Bob and Alf canvassed the state together, sharing the same hotel rooms, and speaking from the same platforms. This arrangement, on at least one occasion, produced comical results. During a campaign stop at Chattanooga, Alf worked diligently on his speech, then left it in the hotel room while he greeted friends. Moments later, he was taken aback to hear his arduously prepared speech being given by his brother. When Bob finished, Alf could only follow with a spontaneous talk. It was apparently quite convincing, because Alf carried Chattanooga. Bob, however, carried Tennessee, preceding his brother to the governor's office by thirty-four years. This election was the first display of political muscle by the rising farmers' movement that chose to organize behind Bob Taylor. Two years later, the new Agricultural Wheel registered more farmers in Tennessee (seventy-eight thousand) than any other state.

When the Taylor brothers were not running against each other, they were trying to win converts to their respective political parties—again in good-natured fun. This was always the case in their native Carter County, where, at the turn of the twentieth century, the two were prominent fixtures on Court Day. Considered one of the more important days in the life of a small town, Court Day offered citizens entertainment or politicking, both of which were favorite Taylor pastimes. Neither man missed a chance to advance his case. On one occasion, Bob played his fiddle (as usual) before "a gang of young Democrats," while Alf called forth some other youngsters for horseshoes "and 'told 'em how it'd be good if they growed up to be Republicans." In the background, the remaining citizenry was trading, conversing, or appearing before the court on personal matters. While able-bodied men did their share of building roads and digging ditches by promising two or three days in service to the county, the old or disabled might petition the court for an exemption; others might petition to be exempt from a poll tax.

Regarded as one of the most beloved politicians in state history, Bob (or "Our Bob" as many referred to him) continued to find success in running for governor. He was reelected twice more, in 1889 and in 1897. In his last term, he hosted the state's Centennial Exposition in Nashville and welcomed President Grover Cleveland to celebrate one hundred years of

Tennessee. The electorate then sent Taylor to the United States Senate, where he served until his 1912 death at the age of sixty-two.

Alf, who served in the United States House of Representatives, finally realized his greatest political dream when he became Tennessee's governor in 1921. During that election, Alf generally took the podium with his foxhound, Old Limber, and broke into a few songs with a singing group that included his sons. Along with family and friends, the candidate entertained the crowds with religious music and songs of the mountains.

When his own governorship was over, however, Alf often said he would rather talk about his brother's career than almost any other subject. Alf lived until the age of eighty-three, dying in 1931.

127
Thomas Hughes
One Last British Colony in America

The prospect of establishing a settlement in frontier Tennessee, and fashioning it after England's Rugby School so excited novelist Thomas Hughes that he called his 1880 brainchild "the New Jerusalem."

The *London Punch* called it a pipe dream:

'Tis a scheme that is truly gigantic.
Tom Hughes has just started, for he
Is taking across the Atlantic
To settle in far Tennessee

A new colony; peopled by dozens,
Male settlers, the young and the old
With their wives, and their sisters, and cousins
Are all gathered into the fold.

They're to sow on the far mountain ranges,
They're to reap and to trade in the mart;
And through all Fortune's troublesome changes
They're still to be English at heart.

Quoth the wily American, "Thank'ee
Though now of Old England you're types.
In a very few years you'll be Yankee
and swear by the Stars and the Stripes.

Stung by this criticism, the *Rugby Social Club Paper* reciprocated in kind:

This scheme that was truly gigantic
Will succeed with the aid of the vine,
For those that have crossed the Atlantic
A fortune will make out of wine.

The new colony, peopled by dozens
Of hard workers, the young and the old,
Are learning the arts of their cousins
And are gradually piling up gold.

We have sown on the far mountain ranges
And have kept up our end at the mart;
And though Fortune has given us changes
We are beginning to think ourselves smart.

To America we kindly say Thank'ee,
Though no longer of old English types,
We cannot yet swear like a Yankee
But will guess by the Stars and the Stripes.

The British-born settlers of Rugby, Tennessee, located in the mountains of Morgan County, proved far better at clever retorts than at manual labor. One young Briton hired himself out, worked all day for a dollar, and then framed his wage. "It is the first and last," he proclaimed, "that I will ever earn in that manner." Many Rugby inhabitants shared his sentiment. They had been born into privileged families but were victims of a caste system which blessed eldest sons with inheritance and cursed later-born offspring with the task of finding work in medicine, law, or the priesthood—three already crowded fields.

Hughes, author of *Tom Brown's Schooldays*, hoped to populate the East Tennessee Rugby with these gifted "second sons." Many accepted the chance to travel abroad and build the unique town. And build they did, starting with something they felt no rugged frontier town should be without: a tennis court. This was, perhaps, the first indication that naive young Englishmen would have difficulty adapting to their new surroundings.

They also had some difficulty adapting to their new neighbors. As historians Gilbert E. Govan and James W. Livingood noted: "A great gulf existed between the natives and the settlers, who held themselves aloof from the mountain people. The colonists persistently clung to the manners and speech of the homeland, which caused their new neighbors to think of them as peculiar."

Occasionally this reliance on the king's English produced comical results. When one of the com-

munity's oldest natives died and there was no native preacher to deliver the funeral service, the rector of Rugby was pressed into action. The service progressed smoothly until the rector made a reference to passing the bier (pronounced *beer*, for the stand on which a coffin rests before burial). The rector's suggestion enraged the deceased's eldest son, who leaped to his feet and shouted, "I know Pa was a drinkin' man, but I'll be danged if yer serve drinks at his funeral."

Despite such growing pains, the so-called Rugby experiment seemed to thrive. It eventually boasted a guest house (the Newbury), a church (Christ Episcopal), a hotel (the Tabard Inn), a newspaper (*The Rugbeian*) and a schoolhouse (the Arnold School). The town's crowning achievement, however, was the Thomas Hughes Library, a facility with seven thousand books, which one day would comprise America's foremost collection of Victorian literature. By 1884, the settlement had nearly 450 inhabitants plus sixty-five buildings. The town captured the imagination of those in England, and visits to the American Rugby became "the thing to do."

Problems began to mount, however. Litigation over land titles, absentee corporation rule, and the settlers' difficulties adapting to the harsh Tennessee climate began to stunt the settlement's growth. When a typhoid epidemic claimed seven victims, many residents left and many would-be immigrants changed their minds.

Hughes, who never resided in Rugby but visited often, paid his last visit in 1887. The occasion was the burial of his mother at the town cemetery. Having lost $250,000 on the Rugby experiment, he returned forever to England, where he and his wife had to sell their home and move to less expensive quarters. By 1892, Rugby was a virtual ghost town, eventually known as "the last organized, chartered English colonization effort in the United States." Hughes apparently felt no regret about the failed "noble experiment." Before his death at seventy-four in 1896, he penned a final letter to the colony, addressed to the children of the Rugby school. The letter closed with the assurance that "the memories of my visits will always remain amongst the evergreen spots of my life."

128
Bob Riley

Rafting the Logs to Market—With a Tale to Tell

Bob Riley could steal someone's shirt with the greatest of ease—and generally with the victim's full cooperation. No one else could have pulled quite as many pranks and remained as welcome in so many homes on the Upper Cumberland Plateau. He was one of the first rafting pilots between Celina and Nashville and "one of the finest raft pilots to run the Cumberland."

Few Middle Tennesseans in the late nineteenth century who knew the mischievous Cumberland River raftsman could resist telling stories of Bob Riley—the con artist with a heart. He was considered a master trickster at pilfering from nearby farms when his raft floated downriver. Riley's talent did not lie in his stealth, however, since he was frequently caught. Rather, his unique talent was in talking his way around and out of trouble.

Beginning in the 1880s, when the timber industry was the area's principal source of income, many families built their homes along the Cumberland River. A tale frequently repeated by his family and neighbors focused on one excursion down the Cumberland, when Riley, who was lovingly called "Uncle Bob," was interested in getting a turkey from a flock on shore. His men were hungry, and so was he. Quite the showman, he announced to his crew that the owner would give him one of those turkeys, most likely the best of the bunch. Riley stopped his raft and canoed ashore. He knocked on the cabin door, told the farmer's wife how his turkey had flown away from his raft and landed in her flock. Could she assist him? She agreed, called forth her son to help, and asked which one might be the turkey in question. Riley pointed to a big, fat one, perhaps the biggest he could spot, and, within moments, he happily returned to his astonished crew members. On his next trip down river, Uncle Bob apparently felt pangs of guilt. He stopped by the farm, told his victim the truth, and paid the woman for her turkey.

On yet another voyage to Nashville, said Riley's daughter, Rachel Langford, he spotted a calf on shore. Riley knew that the local farmer might not be sympa-

thetic to hungry river men. After shooting and dragging the animal aboard his raft, Riley prepared an elaborate disguise and tale of woe (again postponing payment for another day). He placed rubber boots on the animal's hind legs and wrapped a quilt over the rest. Momentarily, the suspicious farmer, who had heard a gunshot, canoed toward the raft and inquired about his missing calf. Tearfully, of course, Riley invited the farmer aboard, explaining a terrible incident: "Oh, my man just died of the smallpox. There he lays now," Riley sobbed, pointing toward the listless quilt and continuing his crying. Out of the corner of his eye he caught sight of the fleeing farmer, canoeing away as quickly as possible from Riley's fictitious disease.

For all of his theatrics and nuisance, Robert Robinson Riley was an upstanding resident of Clay County. The Rileys were among the area's original land-grant settlers after Riley's grandfather, Isaac Riley, a former soldier in George Washington's army, made his way from Virginia to Tennessee. Riley's maternal grandparents were General Joseph Martin, a United States Indian agent who had fought at the Battle of Kings Mountain, and a Cherokee woman whose mother was Nancy Ward, the famous Beloved Woman of the Cherokee.

One of Riley's first cousins was Cordell Hull, who became a United States secretary of state, the "Father of the United Nations," and a recipient of the Nobel Peace Prize. It was Cordell's father, William Hull, who invited young Riley to join him in the lumber business. The elder Hull has been credited with discovering the novel idea of rafting logs out of the 120,000 acres of timberland that now make up the counties of Clay, Overton, Pickett, and Fentress, and floating them to Nashville. As a partner in the business, Riley spent much of his time on a Cumberland River raft and made a small fortune doing so.

The log-rafting business became one of the biggest money-making pursuits between the 1880s and 1930s "in the entire Upper Cumberland region." A typical raft was manned by five men and a cook who ate and slept in a shanty built in the raft's center. Composed of "three tiers of logs bound together by strong, pliable hickory waling, it usually contained about 300,000-500,000 board feet of timber and was more than 100 feet long."

Because of his travels, Riley (born in 1856) would remain a bachelor until the age of fifty, when a young widow he had known became his wife. But he never really settled down, according to his daughter, and he still loved pranks, especially toward his children. They learned to chuckle and ignore him.

As a buyer and seller of land, Riley was often involved in disputes over titles and deeds during an era when the strength of such documents was highly questionable, especially among the mountain people to whom he sold the deforested land. After one such dispute in 1903, Riley was ambushed near one of his sawmills. His stature in the community was such that medical aid, in the form of renowned surgeon Dr. Paul Eve Jr., was summoned by train from Nashville. Upon examination, Eve discovered that several shotgun pellets had penetrated Riley's intestines. He declared that the wound would be fatal. Riley disagreed. He told Dr. Eve: "I've got the greatest faith in your skill and ability; but, even you do not know it all. I'll live to be a pallbearer at your funeral, if you want me to serve."

Although he lapsed into a coma, Riley began to recover after about three weeks of care, and within three months was able to travel. A few years later, he made his way to Nashville to fulfill a promise: serving as a pallbearer in Dr. Eve's funeral.

By 1919, Riley moved his family from the farm into Celina, where his children could be near a good school. As the years progressed, Rachel Langford recalled, his hearing deteriorated. At their home near the town square, he often sat on the porch reading. "He was an avid reader; he would read anything, from one meal to the next meal," she said. As the result, Riley could also quote any passage from the Bible with very little prompting. Guests were always welcome in his home, and they were always visiting, perhaps to hear the latest Bob Riley tale.

One particular day, Rachel recounted, her father and local banker Ed Fowler were in deep discussion when they were interrupted by a commotion. "My daddy said it sounded like someone driving cattle." The two men jumped up from their chairs to investigate. As they walked along the town square, Riley discovered that his "commotion" was coming from the Methodist church, where numerous women were praying loudly—yelling, in fact.

"Ed got tickled cause my daddy was such a big Methodist," Rachel explained. "When he got home, my mother asked, 'Bob, what was all that noise?'"

"Well, he was just as serious as he could be," she related. "He said, 'I've read the Bible from cover to cover, and this is the first time I ever realized the Lord God was deaf.'"

Bob Riley continued to amuse the local populace until his death in 1938; he was eighty-two.

129
Ida B. Wells

The "Princess of the Press"
Demanding Civil Rights

In 1883, Ida B. Wells, a petite black schoolteacher, was leaving Memphis for her regular ten-mile train ride to a teaching job in the small town of Woodstock. She was stunned when the conductor ordered her to move from her accustomed seat in the first-class coach. When Ida refused to surrender her seat, the conductor tried forcibly to remove her. She bit his hand and braced her feet against the seat in front of her. The conductor returned moments later with reinforcements. Three men were required to pry Ida from her seat and push her out of the coach at the next station. Some passengers cheered when she stumbled down the stairs and fell to the ground, her body bruised and her clothes tattered.

Ida B. Wells had just begun to fight back. She would, in fact, dedicate the rest of her life to the struggle against racial discrimination, and predate modern civil-rights movements by at least seventy years.

This initial battle on the train to Woodstock came soon after the United States Supreme Court repealed the Civil Rights Act of 1875 forbidding discrimination in public places. In response to the law's disappearance, prominent black journalist T. Thomas Fortune of the *New York Age* was quoted: "The colored people of the United States feel as if they had been baptized in ice water." He went on to suggest that blacks refuse to move from first-class seating on trains, even if such acts of defiance resulted in their deaths. "One or two murders growing from this intolerable nuisance," he surmised, "would break it up."

Because the new Supreme Court ruling said that black citizens could file claims in a state court for wrongdoings, Ida hired an attorney and sued the railroad. It was the first such court case in the South following

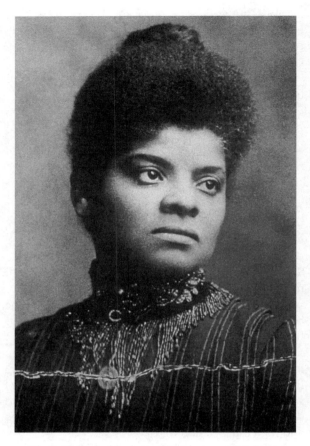

Ida B. Wells declared an editorial war on lynching.

Born during the Civil War in Holly Springs, Mississippi, Ida was sixteen when both parents died from yellow fever, leaving her responsible for her many brothers and sisters, one of whom was disabled. Their father had been a "literate carpenter" and trustee of a freedmen's school. Despite her young age, Ida was able to pass a teacher's examination and earn money for the family's basic needs. When one of her father's sisters invited her to Memphis, she took along two younger sisters and began a new life there. One of their mother's sisters took the remaining children, and all depended upon the income that Ida would always send.

After the train incident of 1883 insured that her path would veer permanently into civil-rights issues, Ida wrote often about the guiding principles that ruled her life: "self-help and thrift." She was clear-headed about the best interests of her readers and had no problem attacking black institutions as well as white establishments if injustices or unfair practices existed.

Ida lost her teaching job after attacking the poor quality of black schools in Memphis, forcing her to earn a living entirely from her newly purchased weekly. By soliciting subscriptions and advertising at black public gatherings throughout Tennessee, Mississippi, and Arkansas, she was able to put the paper on a solid financial footing.

When the Tennessee Supreme Court subsequently overturned her five-hundred-dollar judgment against the Chesapeake & Ohio Railroad, Ida was astonished and heartbroken. In her diary, she wrote: "God, is there no redress, no peace, no justice in this land for us? Thou hast always fought the battles of the weak & oppressed. Come to my aid & teach me what to do, for I am sorely, bitterly disappointed."

In 1892, after a vigilante group killed her good friend, community leader Tom Moss, and his business partners, Ida B. Wells used her newspaper to mount a spirited attack against racism and lynchings. Moss had been the community postmaster, a neighborhood grocer, and Sunday school teacher. As a grocer, he always attracted more customers than his white counterpart across the street, who became so resentful that he sent armed men to run Moss out of business. During the attack, three white men were wounded in an exchange of fire. Moss was arrested (along with thirty other black men who were accused of conspiracy) and his grocery store destroyed by looters. In a later prison raid, masked men kidnapped and lynched

the repeal of the Civil Rights Act, and she was awarded five hundred dollars. A *Memphis Daily Appeal* headline nonetheless reported her victory in disparaging terms: "A DARKY DAMSEL OBTAINS VERDICT FOR DAMAGES AGAINST CHESAPEAKE & OHIO RAILROAD."

In passionate tones, Ida wrote an account of her case for *The Living Way*, a black church weekly. Readers loved what she had to say, and she became a regular contributor. She had a pen name, "Iola," and a new profession, journalism. With both came national fame.

Ida B. Wells's articles began to appear in other black publications across the country, including Fortune's *New Age*. Then she purchased a one-third interest in the *Memphis Free Speech and Headlight*, a small weekly. With bold words about justice and humanity, the fighting schoolteacher of Memphis—who stood only four and a half feet tall—began to ignite a generation with the written word. She was known as the "Princess of the Press."

Moss and his partners. Ida's despair was deepened by her attachment to the Moss family, as she was godmother to one of the children.

Ida demanded the arrest and conviction of those killers who were known. When that did not happen, she wrote: "There is only one thing left that we can do—leave a town which will neither protect our lives and property, nor give us a fair trial, but takes us out and murders us in cold blood."

When Ida's presses rolled, more than six thousand of Memphis's most-respected black citizens—whole congregations of churches, entire black neighborhoods, and numerous black leaders—fled the city in just two months. Among the prominent black pastors who led their congregations out of Memphis were R. N. Countee and W. A. Brinkley. White Memphians, meanwhile, begged Ida to stop the "black exodus." Businesses that depended on black customers were "practically at a standstill."

In her crusade, Ida B. Wells helped organize boycotts of white-owned businesses, notably the streetcars. Six weeks into the boycott, representatives of the local transportation company asked her to use her influence to get blacks riding the streetcars again. They argued that the streetcar company had no part in any lynching and, in fact, was "owned by northern capitalists."

"And run by southern lynchers," she snapped.

Ida suggested in print that most lynchings were the result of trumped-up charges against black men (and some women) in order to establish white supremacy. She conducted an extensive investigation into the lynchings of more than seven hundred blacks and introduced new findings. Although charges of rape were behind one-third of the lynchings, Ida found either no evidence to suggest rape or simply, in some cases, that two consenting adults were involved in an affair.

Ida was in New York when this editorial ran. In her absence, her presses were destroyed and her life was threatened. She remained in New York, where her good friend, T. Thomas Fortune, gave her a job writing for the *New Age*. Persisting in her cause to denounce lynchings, she now signed her columns "EXILED."

Quickly becoming one of the nation's most influential writers for civil rights, Ida B. Wells had a power that reached an international scale. Her pamphlet *The Red Record: Tabulated Statistics and Alleged Cases of Lynching in the United States, 1892-1894* led to speeches in London, England, where an Anti-Lynching Society

was soon founded. In America, Ida and other black leaders put forth the idea of the National Association for the Advancement of Colored People (NAACP). She also organized, in 1913, the first black women's political group, the Alpha Suffrage Club.

Several years later, Ida moved permanently to Chicago, where she died in 1931 at the age of sixty-nine. When the United States government later built the city's first federal housing project, it was named in honor of Ida B. Wells, the woman who had devoted nearly a half century to the struggle against racial discrimination in jobs and in public places, against the disfranchisement of blacks and women, and against the legal persecution of minorities.

130
Walter C. Harriman

Inspiring the "Town That Temperance Built"

In 1889, temperance advocate Walter C. Harriman, a former New Hampshire official, was on horseback headed through the East Tennessee mountains of Roane County. He was accompanied by several wealthy and nationally prominent Boston, New York, and Philadelphia businessmen. The men made up the board of directors in the East Tennessee Land Company, and they were en route to inspect ten thousand newly purchased acres; many of their investors were along for the ride. Their collective goal was to build a model town built not only upon their own sound financial backing but also upon the moral principles of prohibition then sweeping the nation. The group stopped to give their horses a rest at the home of Benjamin P. Margrave.

In the ensuing conversation, Margrave remembered that another Yankee once liked the financial prospects of the area. He was referring to a Union colonel whose troops and wagon train had camped at nearby Byrd's Ferry before joining General Ambrose Burnside in Knoxville. The colonel often carried spring water from behind the Margrave house. "The Colonel used to come up on the porch and talk with me," related Margrave, who was a child at the time. "I remember he said once that this would make a fine place for a town."

Asked if he knew the name of the colonel, Margrave answered, "Yes, Colonel Harriman. He was a very friendly man."

This news at first startled the younger Harriman, whose father, Union General Walter Harriman, did indeed pass through these very mountains during the war, in the winter of 1864 when the officer camped on the banks of the Emory River.

As a result of Margrave's comments, the northern investors changed their plans for the town's name, now wanting to call the place Harriman instead of Fiskville, which would have honored Union General Clinton B. Fisk, a fellow investor serving as the land-company president. Fisk was also founder of Fisk University in Nashville and a former Prohibitionist candidate for president of the United States.

What the elder Harriman had found so appealing during the Civil War was the area's plentiful water supply, as well as the railroad lines and Roane County's coal and iron deposits. These assets were ideal ingredients for industrial development. Instead of pursuing his hunch about Roane County, however, General Harriman returned to his native New Hampshire, where he was twice elected governor. He died in 1884. About this time, his son was already spending winters in East Tennessee to restore his health, then returning to New Hampshire to practice law.

Also during the 1880s, ardent prohibitionist Frederick Gates was conceiving what would be known as "the town that temperance built." He was a businessman (a native New Yorker) who made money in Chattanooga real estate, then founded the East Tennessee Land Company and helped accumulate three hundred thousand acres across several Cumberland Plateau and East Tennessee counties. Gates often retreated to his Roane County summer home, Deermont. Here he drafted plans for the new town and chose a team of investors and front men to bring it to life. In addition to Fisk, they included northern textile giants; the publishers of Funk and Wagnalls dictionary (A. W. Wagnalls eventually would be president of the land company); the former postmaster general of the United States; and the "oatmeal king" of America (cereal icon Ferdinand Schumacher was the first man to manufacture oatmeal). While young Walter C. Harriman was vacationing in East Tennessee, he met these promoters and decided to cast his lot with them, beginning to live year-round in the mountains.

The prohibitionists chose a town site that once was the plantation of a Union officer, the late Colonel Robert K. Byrd. They paid the widow Mary Lea Byrd ten thousand dollars for most of the estate, then purchased nearby Tandy Farm's 310 acres for the center of town. When the widow Byrd later decided not to remain in her plantation house, she sold the balance of her property for another sixteen thousand dollars.

The town of Harriman was staked out by Christmas Day, 1889, and heavily publicized in northern newspapers "extolling the virtues of a new community with the highest of moral standards and the abhorrence of vice and especially of 'Demon Rum.'" So many buyers appeared at the February 1890 sale of town lots that investors like Gates and the younger Harriman were amazed. Bidding was furious, and by day's end, more than six hundred thousand dollars had transferred hands. Mary Lea Byrd, however, was not as happy. Having profited only thirty-six thousand dollars from the original sale, she was so upset that she left the area, never to return.

Town leaders, serious about establishing a new utopia—based on industry rather than agriculture—poured three million dollars into roads, housing, stores, and factories. All real-estate transactions within Harriman's city limits featured deeds prohibiting the sale, purchase, or storage of alcohol. Even the Women's Christian Temperance Union in Tennessee centered its headquarters in Harriman, which soon carried the nickname "Happy Harriman."

A year later, in 1893, an institution for higher learning was founded. The catalog of the American Temperance University reportedly declared: "We are up in arms against smoking, gambling, theft, lying, profanity, obscenity and drunkenness. . . . These vices, separately or collectively, ought to have no place in college life. We give none." Nor did the university give grades, because students were expected to have a perfect score each day.

Before the school closed its doors in 1908, it had gone through a change in name to American University and a horrible 1905 football season, in which the team lost to the University of Tennessee 140-0, reportedly the largest number of points the state university ever scored in one game.

Although the temperance school did not survive, "Happy Harriman" did, outlasting economic changes with its base of twenty-nine manufacturing companies. Because of the varied interests of its companies, Harriman prospered when other single-economy manufacturing towns died. Among those business leaders who paved the way to success was Walter C. Harriman, who resigned from the land company to be president of the First National Bank of Harriman and treasurer of a leading lumber and manufacturing company.

A nearby town, meanwhile, was the brainchild of yet another Yankee visitor during the Civil War who had stopped at the Margrave home. Unlike General Harriman, General John T. Wilder did return after the war to take advantage of local mineral deposits. Wilder purchased land, formed the Roane Iron Company, and established the company town of Rockwood.

The city of Harriman continued as a dry town until August 1993. After a century of temperance, the sale of liquor was finally allowed.

131
Joel Owsley Cheek

Brewing the President's Coffee

When President Theodore Roosevelt dined in Nashville in 1907 and declared, according to the legendary story, that the Maxwell House Hotel coffee was "good to the last drop," Joel Owsley Cheek repeated the president's remark and held it up as a testament for coffee drinkers.

Cheek was a genius at promotion. He had perfected his coffee blend in 1892. It became the world's first blended coffee and transformed Nashville into the nation's center for coffee manufacturing. The famous Maxwell House Hotel was responsible for helping him. Ever since the hotel had agreed to make his the house coffee, Cheek had been on a path toward fame and the wealth that accompanied it.

Cheek's merchandising career began on horseback, however, riding along a lonesome 1870s route in the backcountry of Tennessee and Kentucky. The son of a rural Kentucky doctor, Cheek originally planned a career in teaching. That dream ended when he realized that a teacher's salary could not prevent foreclosure on his father's farm. Seeking more money, Cheek became a horseback salesman (or drummer) for a Nashville wholesale grocer.

As a twenty-year-old grocery salesman, Cheek observed that people everywhere seemed to like coffee. What the public did not have was a good coffee, because local grocers who purchased his wares selected only the cheapest beans. Cheek became part owner of the grocery company in 1882 and moved to Nashville.

In 1892, Cheek began blending several types of coffee beans, hoping to produce one quality offering in contrast to the typically bitter brew that came from a single variety. Confident that the public would pay higher prices for a good coffee, he sought help from Nashville coffee broker Roger Nolley Smith, an Englishman. Smith, who had once operated a coffee plantation in Brazil, could identify the origin of various beans quickly and suggest the best, which Cheek then purchased for his blend.

When Cheek managed to convince the Maxwell House Hotel to offer his coffee on Sundays, customers raved. Furthering his marketing schemes, Cheek advertised in *Life* magazine and maintained close contact with major national advertisers. He was reportedly one of the first to order a full-page newspaper ad. According to family history, Cheek's artistic son, Robert, designed a trademark for the blend: a tipped coffee cup spilling the last drop, thus enhancing what had become their slogan after the president's remark, "good to the last drop."

In 1902, Cheek broke with the wholesale grocery business and focused all of his attention on *Maxwell House Coffee*. In 1928, he sold the company to General Foods for forty-two million dollars, half in cash and half in General Foods stock.

Asked what had inspired him to make his fortune in coffee, Cheek traced the answer to his father's farm mortgage. It was the "burden that was laid on my shoulders when I was young," he explained.

In 1935 when Cheek died at eighty-three, General Foods compiled newspaper clippings showing that his obituary had appeared in every state of the union. He was remembered for his many generosities often given without fanfare or notice, his kindly manner to all people, and his devotion to family (every one of his eight adult sons took daily lunch at the Cheek home, often accompanied by their own families).

132
Opie Read

Traveling Laughter on the Side Shows

One night in the 1870s Gallatin student Opie Read, who was putting himself through the Neophogen Male and Female College by setting type for the college magazine, opened his door to one of the most famous men in American letters. Mark Twain, who was visiting the Middle Tennessee campus to meet with students, spent the greater part of the evening with Read. The two smoked corncob pipes while Twain philosophized.

Read later said of this encounter, "Oh, how wiser was he than our book-foundered president," which was a strange statement from a youth who spent most of his life indulging in books. But the meeting with Twain apparently confirmed a bit of advice that Read had heard from a friend: "A man without experience is but a dog with no tricks."

Read's decision to end his formal education set him on the path of his idol Twain. As Read's biographer, Robert L. Morris, put it: "Possessing the skilled fingers of a printer for a sword, he could duel honorably with the world. . . . To follow Mark Twain's example was the proper course. To be a wandering printer and hopeful writer of sketches . . . was his chosen destiny."

Read's ability to tell a tale and his insight into the tastes of the reading public eventually led to a literary career. If not as enduring as Twain's, the career was equally profitable in terms of popular acclaim during his lifetime. Read became "the Dean of American Newspapermen," the author of more than fifty novels (one sold more than a million copies in the late nineteenth century), and a touring humorist who was cheered for more than forty years in small towns and larger cities across America. One contemporary journalist claimed "Few men in America have written more books"; another said he "has lectured to a clientele that numbers millions"; and Read declared that he had visited "every county seat in the United States." The reason for his popularity was no mystery. Read always laughed *with* people "out of common kinship," explains his biographer, and not *at* people and their frailties as human beings.

Opie Read was born in Nashville in 1852, but his parents moved to Gallatin soon after his birth to escape the stiff competition of the carriage-making industry in which his father, Guilford Read, was engaged. The elder Read, remembering his alcoholic father, was determined to set a better example for his own children and became religious, temperate, and strict.

When Opie's older sister brought home from boarding school a copy of *Robinson Crusoe* and read the story aloud for her family, Guilford Read thought the book was an autobiography. When he discovered it was fiction, he was shocked: "And I have been kept up here night after night listening to a lie? Throw that book behind the fire." A hard-working man, Opie's father considered fiction an indulgence in idleness. Opie recorded in his memoirs, "His order was imperative, and I sat there looking tearfully upon the martyr (Crusoe), burned at the stake."

Opie, however, was already addicted to storytelling. Fulfilling his father's worst nightmare, Opie became known for his fictional tales. He spent his childhood entertaining Sumner County neighbors (first at Gallatin and then Portland) with Bre'er Rabbit stories. The more he read, the more his imagination and tale-spinning ability grew.

When he left college, Read traveled the South, picking up work as a printer and newspaperman wherever he could, eventually settling in Little Rock, Arkansas. In his freelance coverage of the 1878 Memphis yellow fever epidemic, Read reported the tragedy so well that he was named city editor for the *Arkansas Gazette*, the oldest paper west of the Mississippi River.

Soon he was interviewing such national figures as former President Ulysses S. Grant and Grant's Civil War comrade General William Tecumseh Sherman. Read thought that Grant "had peculiarities. With him laughter was exceedingly rare. In his eyes there was more of a censure than a welcome." Sherman, Read believed, was even colder. He said of him: "Looking into his eyes, I felt for the first time in my life that I had met a human being created by satan."

Read lasted only a year as city editor because the position limited the time he could spend writing humorous character sketches of southerners. Such stories became increasingly popular in northern newspapers and Read was soon working in Cleveland, Ohio. Deciding that Cleveland "was somewhere near the North Pole" and the job was a grind, he returned to Arkansas. Read joined his brother-in-law Philo Benham in founding a "humorous and literary" weekly newspaper, *The Arkansaw Traveler*, a title which played off the spelling of the state. Gaining a national following, the *Traveler* was in touch with the average reader, thanks to Read. In 1887, Read and Benham moved the paper to Chicago, and there it became "a national institution," sealing Read's reputation as the dean of American newspapermen.

When his first humorous novel *Len Gansett* was well received in 1888, Read left the newspaper business. By the mid-1890s, he was nationally famous as "a romancer of the South," and his 1896 novel, *The Jucklins*, sold more than one million copies. Most of Read's fifty novels dealt with "customs and manners of earlier Tennessee in an easy conversational style."

His national celebrity hit a new plateau with his platform performances on the Chautauqua circuit (begun in Chautauqua, New York, as a religiously influenced movement which later consisted of traveling fairs offering music, educational lectures on various subjects of public concern, and pithy commentary by wiseacres such as Read). When Opie Read appeared, audiences went wild with delight.

The Chautauqua tent fairs reached their peak of popularity in rural America before the World War I era. Read's fellow tour lecturers included presidents-to-be and former presidents: Warren G. Harding, William McKinley, William Howard Taft, Grover Cleveland, and Read's favorite, Theodore Roosevelt. Roosevelt once phoned him spontaneously, asking that he come immediately to the White House "and break bread with me." (Other guests breaking bread that day included the western gambler and law officer, Bat Masterson.)

Also a star on other lecture tours, Opie Read was a permanent traveler on the Chautauqua circuit from 1908 until the age of eighty-one in 1933 (he died in Nashville in 1939). His biographer Morris, who was acquainted with Read and often attended the tent fairs, remembered:

Every year we counted on that week in July when actors and opera singers, Swiss bell ringers and magicians, inventors, practical philosophers, travelers, and humorists—strange people all—would come before us on the unpainted boards of the temporary platform that we had set up in the brown tent on the school yard.

When Read came on stage, one of his trademark lines was to ask the audience, "Well now, is life worth living?" His reply: "It depends on the liver!"

133
James Carroll Napier

A Brotherly Barrier to Tennessee's Black Exodus

In becoming a national black leader, Nashville's James Carroll Napier believed in choosing his battles. During the late nineteenth and early twentieth centuries, some blacks accused him of accommodating Jim Crow laws which promoted racism, but Napier believed he could guarantee equal rights through black education and black jobs, and do so within the black community.

When the Tennessee legislature enacted the first Jim Crow law in 1881, hard-won rights for Tennessee blacks were legally dissolved. The bill required "railroad companies to provide separate first-class facilities for black passengers," establishing a precedent for segregation. Napier's philosophy was to fight for black rights within the framework of the law. Years later, when Governor James B. Frazier persuaded the Tennessee state railroad commission to "interpret the existing 1881 statute broadly enough to cover all forms of railroad travel," the nation's leading black leaders, Booker T. Washington and W. E. B. DuBois, asked Nashville friends to take action in the courts.

For Napier, a close friend of Washington's, the more natural course of action was to turn to Todd Lincoln, president of the railroad's powerful Pullman Company and son of the late President Abraham Lincoln, the signer of 1863's Emancipation Proclamation. In a telegram, Napier urged young Lincoln "in the name of your revered father . . . [to] use your great influence to avert this calamity and prevent additional oppression." The appeal had little effect, and Napier, a follower of Booker T. Washington's famous "accommodation policies," was forced to accept yet another restriction upon black freedom until he could draft a better plan of action.

Born in Nashville in 1845, James Carroll Napier was the son of a livery stable operator, William Carroll Napier. The elder Napier had been freed in 1848 on the Dickson County plantation where he was born as the son of plantation owner Dr. Elias Napier, a physician and local iron manufacturer. The doctor died that year, and, in his will, ordered the freedom of his black seamstress and his four sons and daughter by her. The slaves also received, according to his dictates, a sum of money, "food, furniture, transportation, and shelter." The will advised that the seamstress and children leave the area for their own safety.

While most of the family resettled in Ohio, William Napier chose to live in Nashville, where he married, entered business, and began his own family. With the help of other free blacks in Nashville, he tried to found a school for their children's education. The school was closed shortly after its 1859 opening because of the legal battles necessary in trying to provide black education. His son James Carroll Napier, therefore, received his education at Ohio's Wilberforce University and Oberlin College prior to the Civil War. James then accepted a federal clerkship in Washington, D.C., during the Lincoln administration.

The youth returned to Nashville and became one of the city's most powerful citizens after the war: a lawyer, city councilman, and Republican Party leader. The first black to preside over the Nashville city council, he was instrumental in hiring the first black teachers for black schools, in building Nashville's first modern black schools, and in organizing the city's first black fire engine company in 1885.

Within the limits set in the 1880s by Jim Crow laws, Napier hoped to promote black schools to create steady economic improvement among Tennessee blacks. As with his lifelong friend Booker T. Washington, Napier argued that if blacks worked to succeed in their trades and professions, they could use this economic uplift to acquire equal rights. In 1902, Napier helped charter the black-owned One-Cent Savings Bank and Trust Company in Nashville and encouraged the black citizenry to save money. Napier's bank was later distinguished as the second-oldest minority-owned bank in America and the oldest in Tennessee.

In 1909, Napier began work toward the founding of Tennessee Agricultural and Industrial Normal School, which would provide college degrees for black students in accordance with the separate-but-equal doctrine endorsed by the Supreme Court. The college granted its first degree in 1924. (It merged in 1979 with the University of Tennessee at Nashville to become Tennessee State University.) Napier later worked on the Integrated Commission on Interracial Cooperation, which sought to prevent a repeat of the bloody Knoxville race riot of 1919. He also served on the board of trustees for both Fisk University in Nash-

ville and Meharry Medical College, and then Howard University in Washington, D.C., where he had earned his law degree.

When Presidents Theodore Roosevelt and William H. Taft offered him foreign posts, Napier declined. What he wanted was to work with the United States Treasury, and that opportunity came in 1911 when President Taft chose Napier to become register of the treasury, a post he held for two years. In 1916, he succeeded Booker T. Washington as president of the National Negro Business League. Napier then began giving speeches encouraging the black citizenry to stay in the South at a time when some black leaders were urging them to seek better opportunities elsewhere.

The "father of the Black Exodus" was fellow Nashvillian Benjamin "Pap" Singleton, who in 1873 led his first group of black emigrants (three hundred in all) aboard Cumberland River steamboats, then by train, and finally by wagon to other areas of the nation. One favorite relocation area was Kansas, where a section of Topeka was known as "Tennessee Town." Helping to form a homestead association, Singleton kept up the steady emigration well into the 1880s, leading as many as eight thousand people from southern states and founding a dozen towns. A coffin maker by trade, Singleton apparently was driven to promote these migrations after years of burying lynching victims in the black community. Convinced that he and his brethren would have a better life elsewhere in the nation, Singleton became one of the chief players in the movement westward. The thousands who were involved became known as Exodusters.

Not only did Napier want black citizens to remain in the South and to go into business, but he also prodded them to seek more political rights. In 1919, Napier was named honorary president of the National Negro Business League, and he never relinquished that title. At his death in 1940 at the age of ninety-four, Napier was eulogized for creating remarkable business and educational opportunities in an era of growing repression for black citizens.

134
Lena Angevine

Breaking Yellow Fever's Mystery

In 1878, a house servant pried open a shutter of the boarded-up Mississippi plantation house of his former master, Saxton Smith Angevine, a prominent Memphis attorney. The Angevine family and many friends had sealed themselves in the house in a futile effort to keep out yellow fever. Raging up and down the Mississippi River, the fever had previously claimed the lives of Angevine's wife, a descendant of prominent New Englanders, and his father, a physician.

When the servant peered into the house, he saw nine-year-old Lena Angevine surrounded by the fly-covered bodies of her five brothers and sisters, her father, the farm's houseguests, and other servants. Although the child appeared to be dead, the servant broke into the house and carried her to his own home. He placed a piece of raw bacon across her lips. When she began to suck at the meat, her body involuntarily responding to nourishment, the servant sought medical help. This was to be the first standoff in Lena's many confrontations with death. By the end of her long life in 1948, death would find in her a formidable adversary.

When the girl recovered, her grandmother sent her to boarding school in Memphis. Here, due in large part to the family tragedies of her youth, she determined to become a nurse. Memphis had only recently opened a facility for training student nurses at Maury Infirmary, and Lena Angevine would become Memphis's first graduate nurse. She was believed to be Tennessee's, and perhaps the South's, first graduate nurse. In 1897, after a decade at Maury Clinic, she organized Tennessee's first accredited school of nursing in the new City Hospital.

Lena soon found herself as leader of four volunteers, supplied by Memphis's Daughters of the American Revolution chapter, who were sent to Cuba during the Spanish-American War. In Cuba, her leadership abilities and medical knowledge were called into question. When one soldier appeared to be dying of appendicitis, the doctor in charge insisted the problem was Lena's old nemesis, yellow fever, which was nearing epidemic status. The physician ordered the camp quarantined and curtly dismissed Lena's pleas that the man could be saved with an appendectomy. "We'll confirm your diagnosis," the doctor declared, "at the autopsy." Lena persisted and, after several failures, finally located a doctor willing to operate, although he had never performed surgery. The operation was a success; the patient recovered; and Lena Angevine's medical reputation soared.

Typically, Lena would continue to disregard her own safety. When cholera struck Cuba, she was exposed to the deadly disease in a hospital tent while trying to give medical care to army deserters. Afterwards, the afflicted nurse was consigned to a special camp and left for dead. Cholera, however, failed to defeat her, just as yellow fever had failed years earlier. Regaining her strength, Lena astounded fellow nurses and doctors by walking out of her death tent and into their gathering one day. Becoming chief nurse of the island, she was promoted to the officer corps and was given permission to design uniforms for army nurses.

Returning home a heroine, Lena Angevine did not linger in the States but returned to Cuba with Dr. Walter Reed's Army Medical Corps unit. As the nurse in charge of Reed's search for the source of yellow fever, she was instrumental in discovering the *Aedes aegypti* mosquito, which had brought so much death to her family and to the city of Memphis.

More personal tragedy, however, awaited her in Cuba. Lena fell in love with one of the doctors on Reed's staff, Edward D. Warner, and soon married him. Three months later, Warner died. Some said he was another victim of yellow fever. Lena's sorrow once again spirited a determined woman to new levels of greatness. She returned to the United States to further her education, and in 1904 earned a doctorate in bacteriology from the University of Chicago. Returning to Memphis, she helped form Red Cross chapters.

When the nation entered World War I, Lena was medically ready once more. University of Tennessee cadets training for military service were struck down by the deadly worldwide influenza epidemic of 1918. Off to Knoxville Lena went, helping student soldiers through their illness. There she would remain, a member of the university's extension service, teaching better health for rural areas until her retirement in 1945.

When Lena Angevine Warner died in 1948, a plot was reserved for her in Arlington National Cemetery.

But she always considered Memphis her only home. There she was buried in the city that yellow fever had nearly destroyed in the 1870s—a city that had given the nation and the world a woman who helped defeat a disease which nineteenth-century sailors had nicknamed "yellow jack."

135
Benjamin Franklin Thomas

Deal of the Century: A One-Dollar Handshake

Benjamin Franklin Thomas was a United States soldier stationed at Cuba in 1898 when he purchased a Cuban-bottled soft drink, *Piña Fría,* and hit upon an idea that would make him a fortune. The *Piña Fría* ("cold pineapple") was carbonated and served in a bottle, and the combination reminded him of the Coca-Cola he once drank at Chattanooga soda fountains.

Thomas, originally from Ohio, had made Chattanooga his home after visiting the city during his college days (a classmate was a native). In 1899, when Thomas returned from Cuba, he explored with good friend and fellow attorney Joseph Brown Whitehead the possibility of bottling Coca-Cola. Having already pondered the need for liquid refreshment at baseball parks, Whitehead agreed that a carbonated drink would be the perfect solution.

The two lawyers contacted mutual friend Sam Erwin, a cousin to Coca-Cola executive Asa Candler; a meeting was arranged in Atlanta. But Candler, who had already discouraged a similar offer, took a dim view of the bottling idea. The Chattanoogans persisted until Candler finally agreed to their exclusive rights to bottle Coca-Cola throughout most of the United States. The deal, made on July 21, 1899, was short and uncomplicated; to make it legally binding, Candler was to receive one dollar for the bottling rights. Oddly enough, he never sought the one-dollar payment for what turned out to be, according to Coca-Cola tradition, one of the most lucrative contracts in American history.

Thomas and Whitehead set up a corporate office at 17 Market Square in Chattanooga. By dividing the nation into two territories, each man controlled his own region and subsequently built his own bottling plant.

Thomas scraped together the five thousand dollars necessary to open a factory in a three-story build-

ing at 23 Patten Parkway. (He soon sold it, marking the first Coca-Cola bottling franchise handed out.) In order to build his own plant, Whitehead, lacking sufficient funds, sold half of his shares to successful Chattanooga businessman and attorney John Thomas Lupton, who became a partner in the parent company. Lupton's ties in the community were numerous. He had been working with his father-in-law, a former Union soldier named Z. Carter Patten, who moved to Chattanooga after the Civil War and started various citywide companies, among them Chattanooga Medicine Company. With Lupton's money added to his own, Whitehead opened a plant in Atlanta in 1900.

Of these original partners, Lupton lived the longest to witness the magnitude of Coca-Cola's growth; Whitehead died in 1906 at the age of forty-two and Thomas in 1914 at the age of fifty-two. Although he remained active in his other Chattanooga businesses, Lupton was part of the proliferation of Coca-Cola bottling franchises throughout the nation and eventually the world—an idea that began with Benjamin Franklin Thomas's guzzling a bottle of fizzy *Piña Fría* on a hot day in Cuba.

136
Casey Jones

An Engineer's Legend—
In Locomotive No. 382 with Sim at His Side

When Jonathan Luther Jones of Jackson, Tennessee, slammed locomotive No. 382 into the stalled caboose and cars on the main track at Vaughan, Mississippi, in the morning darkness of April 30, 1900, he was thrown to his death, and into American legend.

The wreck first became the talk of the roundhouse at nearby Canton, where black engine-wiper Wallace Saunders, who knew "Casey" Jones, began to sing some stanzas of a song that would make Jones a true folk hero:

Come all you rounders, if you want to hear,
A story about a brave Engineer.
Casey Jones was the rounder's name,
On a big eight-wheeler, boys, he won his fame.

The caller called Casey at a-half-past-four,
He kissed his wife at the station door,
He mounted to the cabin with his orders in hand,
And he took his farewell trip to the promised land.

Contrary to some legend, Casey Jones, who took his nickname from Cayce, Kentucky, where he grew up, was not known for his heroics or bravery as an engineer. Although the Illinois Central blamed him for the accident in which he was the only casualty, "he was proud of a record which had never seen a passenger or crew member seriously injured or killed," said writer James W. Moody Jr. In an industry with spirited competition, Casey Jones was a "fastroller" but not careless. Because advertisements billed railroad travel according to time schedules, every engineer "had to be a bit of a daredevil" to make trips in the time promised. Moody wrote that Jones, one of the better engineers, "was doing just that when he was killed."

Jones's father was a Kentucky schoolteacher, and as a boy Casey spent time at the Cayce water tank admiring the engines and engineers of the M & O (Mobile and Ohio) Railroad. At the age of fifteen, he went to work for the company as a telegrapher. Three years later, he became a locomotive fireman.

When the yellow fever epidemic of the late 1870s struck down many train crews of the Illinois Central, Jones applied for a job with the hope that he would soon earn a promotion to engineer. It came two years later. In 1886, he married Janie Brady of Jackson and ran a train from Jackson to Water Valley, Mississippi. By January 1900, Jones's reputation for speed and safety earned him an assignment to a fast passenger train on the line between Canton and Memphis. With three children to support, Jones welcomed the extra pay and prestige.

On the night of April 29, when he pulled into the station at Memphis, Jones learned that the engineer on the New Orleans Special was sick. Jones agreed to a double shift but insisted on using No. 382, a speedy engine with a distinctive whippoorwill whistle. He also insisted on the services of his favorite fireman, a black man named Sim Webb from McComb, Tennessee.

They left Memphis after midnight with "95 minutes to make up on the 190-mile run. The normal speed was 35 mph, but Casey would have to average 50 mph." He knew that he would have to pass several trains at Vaughan. He did not know that an air hose on one of those trains had broken and a caboose and several cars with locked brakes were stuck on the main line.

When they sped around a curve at seventy-five miles per hour heading into north Vaughan, Webb spotted the lights of the caboose ahead. Jones shut the throttle, applied the brakes, and threw back the reverse lever. He ordered Webb to jump for his life. No. 382 rammed the caboose at twenty-five miles per hour, but the collision was enough to kill Casey Jones.

Webb maintained for the rest of his life that he and Casey "saw no flagman or fusees, we heard no torpedoes . . . without any warning we plowed into that caboose. They should have put warning signals against us." The other train crew had, in fact, put out flares, but something had gone wrong, and they were not lit when No. 382 rounded the curve.

Jones's family in Madison County received three thousand dollars in insurance from the railroad. Webb, who got five dollars for injuries sustained in the jump, eventually returned to the railroad, often working the same run.

After Wallace Saunders's song about engineer Jones became a favorite in roundhouses up and down the line, it found its way into the vaudeville act of performers Bert and Frank Leighton. The modern version with some new lyrics was copyrighted and published by T. Lawrence Seibert, who "claimed the words, and Eddie Newton, who acknowledged the music." The song became a hit in the early years of the century. "By 1913, they were singing a calypso version in Trinidad, and the song went to Europe with the Doughboys," noted historian Moody.

Soon, stories about Casey Jones's bravery began to circulate. One tale had him walking along his train's running boards when he caught sight of several small children dashing across the tracks. One little girl got halfway across, then froze. Seeing that the train was going too fast to stop and the girl was not responding to his shouts, Jones dashed to the front of the engine. Poised on the tip of the cowcatcher, he scooped the little girl into his arms, held her until her fears subsided, then sent her home with the other children, warning her to be careful of trains.

Sim Webb lived until 1957. He helped to perpetuate the legend of Casey Jones and always insisted that his friend did nothing wrong that day. Toward that goal, Webb had been a guest in Jackson for Casey Jones Day, proclaimed across the state of Tennessee in 1950 and marked with a commemorative stamp from the United States Post Office.

Jones's wife, who generally wore black in his memory, reached the age of ninety-two before she died

211

in 1958. Janie Brady Jones participated in the making of her husband's legend by appearing in such radio and television shows as *Ripley's Believe It or Not, We the People*, and *I've Got a Secret*. She also appeared at many fairs and expositions and allowed her name to be used in patriotic appeals. Janie, however, never received money (other than expenses) for her appearances or for the sheet music to the ballad "Casey Jones, The Brave Engineer."

After the television series *Casey Jones* appeared in 1958, the city of Jackson purchased exclusive rights to the use of the engineer's name. The Casey Jones home and railroad museum afterwards became a tourist mecca in Jackson.

137
Elizabeth "Miss Lizzie" Freeman
Growing Succeeding Generations on the Farm

When Squire Jim Freeman died in 1899, his wife, Elizabeth, found herself with ten children to raise and the Woodley Farm to oversee. After assessing her situation, the Weakley County widow adopted a simple plan for survival: Grow it, use it, and sell what is left.

A grandson, journalist Holland McCombs, who became a writer for *Time* magazine, recalled in 1972: "her policy made of Woodley an almost self-sufficient world within itself. . . . She reasoned that if the people of Woodley produced all they needed for themselves of a product and sold the surplus, that there was no way to go broke."

That philosophy worked especially well for the enterprising "Miss Lizzie" Freeman, whose farm population was immense. In addition to her own brood, she provided and cared for other relatives and several black families who lived on the farm, while also keeping an open door for company. "We seemed to always have 'company' and loved it that way," said McCombs.

The former Elizabeth Rast of Charleston, South Carolina, had married widower Squire Jim in December 1875. When her husband died, she donned mourning garb, which she wore throughout the remaining sixteen years of her life. Her explanation: "I think Mr. Freeman would've wanted it this way."

She spent her widowhood running the thirteen-room house and the 482-acre Woodley Farm with a firm resolve—and a firmer hand. "There was rarely any mistaking as to who was the boss of Woodley," McCombs continued. "If things went too far out of line, this erudite, cultured and classic five-foot-two little lady in black satin and lace would pick up a buggy whip and painfully instill a proper remembrance."

McCombs, who was born in 1901, also recalled his grandmother's compassionate side, noting, "If a young black or white was orphaned or left without sufficient care and guidance she took over completely and raised the child."

At any given time there were forty to fifty people living at Woodley Farm (six children, four stepchildren, numerous grandchildren and hired hands), all under Miss Lizzie's total care.

"She doctored people all over the place, day or night," McCombs wrote. "Dr. Sebastian [perhaps C. M. Sebastian] would come if the case was serious. Otherwise she cured us herself. She had her own Nature's remedy concoctions. Dr. Sebastian would laugh and say, 'She's the best doctor west of Town.'"

With a love for education, Lizzie Freeman sent each of her children (and a few others) to school; most of them continued through college. Besides a good education, family members also had good social skills. McCombs was specific:

In wintertime there would be song fests, plays and recitations in the Parlor. Some of those in the family of that generation could do Shakespeare for hours—without any books! Our Aunt Polly . . . could and would recite pages of Virgil in Latin. "Uncle Price" (Professor R. N. Price) read the Bible in Latin and Greek. "Sis Nola" (Lucy Nola Freeman, our aunt) played the piano. Bubber (our uncle Otis Freeman) and our aunt Johnnie Freeman Bratton would lead the song fest.

McCombs underscored: "It was a wonderful way, a wonderful and wholesome world. I have worked and traveled the world over, but have never found a better one."

The nearest town was Martin, the thriving railroad junction which was settled in part by McCombs's ancestors. Despite the entertainment that Martin provided (including an opera house, which the family sometimes attended), McCombs said "we didn't go to town much. Too much excitement and things going on at Woodley." His greatest pleasure as a child in the early twentieth century, however, had little to do with entertainment:

But with all of the fun things and more going on I believe the most exciting times on old Woodley in the early century had to do with the works! The works-life of the Farm was divided into times: Hog Killing Time, Hay Saving Time, Wheat Threshing Time, Tobacco Curing Time, Horse Breaking Time, Cotton Picking Time, Pea Picking Time, Canning Time, and so on. These were hard working times but to us they were more like hard playing games or competitive socials. Big tables were spread out under the trees to feed the "hands." Threshing was done by traveling troups of colorful characters, who sometimes camped out in the fields and woods at night—and we'd go visiting. Haytime was joined in by everybody at once—and tall tales were told as the wagons were heaped high. Cotton chopping was like a gossip and sing song fest in the fields—along with pain and sunburn. . . . Strawberry time brought in pickers and packers from all over. It was probably the most fun of all. Mrs. Ed Lovelace and other ladies from town came out to help pack the crates. We hauled wagon loads to the iced fruit express cars. . . .

The farm, said McCombs, had a remarkable diversity:

We produced enough pork, beef, fowl, corn, wheat, hay, syrup, tomatoes, potatoes, beans, peas, fruits, vegetables, grapes, strawberries, nuts, game, timber, etc., etc., for "the place"—and sold the surplus. No matter how low the market . . . for a particular product, there was always some profit in producing it.

Woodley, named for the surrounding trees, remained a model farm and family center until 1915 when its matriarch died at the age of sixty-five. In the following ten years, Miss Lizzie Freeman's place became a part of the educational world—a junior-college campus, and eventually the University of Tennessee at Martin.

138
James Brantley/Albert Dement
Those Great Tennessee Walking Horses

When Tennessee horse breeders consider the rags-to-riches story of the founding sire of the Tennessee Walking Horse, they also think of the man who nurtured an aging throwaway named Black Allan into one of the finest breeding horses in American history.

Coffee County's James Brantley was prominent in Middle Tennessee horse circles at the turn of the twentieth century for his fine stable and its breeding program. Black Allan was a reject, nearing old age unappreciated, unloved, and unrecognized as an animal with royal bloodlines (and a perfectly gaited pace that future equestrians would covet). The horse and the man came together in 1903.

Brantley accepted Black Allan as a bargain in the purchase of another animal. In fact, Brantley eagerly accepted Black Allan. A student of good bloodlines, Brantley knew beforehand from a relative that this old black horse descended from one of the American Trotting Register's greatest stallions. Not a fast or talented horse in his own right, Black Allan had to endure a seventeen-year odyssey of bargain resales from dissatisfied customers who wanted a trotter and not this horse with a penchant for pacing. Thus, he once was traded, one on one, for a black-jack (jackass) and a work mule; and once for a cow, a yearling filly, and twenty dollars. That he would become the highest-ranking horse in the registry of Tennessee Walking Horses was unimaginable—not at his age and not with his history of rejection.

When Brantley purchased Black Allan, the horse was being used for breeding mules, an indication of his lowly status in the stable. Because mules are sterile crossbreeds of male jacks and female horses, a stallion is needed to encourage a mating mood from the mare. In this role, Black Allan had been given the nickname "The Old Teaser."

Brantley, unlike many fellow horse traders, believed that good bloodlines show. He began to breed Black Allan to walking-horse mares for six dollars per living foal. As these foals grew and began to display their exceptional qualities, Black Allan's stud fee began to rise.

In 1909, the horse was sold one last time when Brantley's friend, Albert Dement (the other finest horse

James R. Brantley (left) and Albert Dement with an early Tennessee Walking Horse.

breeder in Middle Tennessee), added Black Allan to his stock at Wartrace. Dement had been instrumental in creating the horse country that existed in adjacent Bedford County. A native of the region (Cannon County), he had been selling superb horses since the late nineteenth century, when horse buyers from the North journeyed into the area asking for those "Tennessee walking horses." In these early days of trying to produce the perfect walking horse, Dement needed cash but he refused to sell an animal that he thought was necessary to his success as a breeder. Dement's persistence resulted in the best walkers Tennesseans had ever seen. His triumph came in 1892 when "walking horse" became part of the official name of the once-renowned plantation saddle horse, which had been transformed into a true-gaited walker.

After Black Allan arrived at the Dement stables in 1909, the stallion serviced 111 mares in the seven months that remained in his life, a considerable feat

for a twenty-four-year-old (perhaps older) stallion. Not undeservedly, Black Allan was described by one trainer as "the gamest horse I ever saw."

When the Tennessee Walking Horse Breeders and Exhibitors Association of America was founded at Lewisburg in 1935, Black Allan's bloodline was confirmed in the pedigree of 10,000 of the first 11,800 horses registered. Of that number, nearly 3,000 incorporated his name, Allan. Officially, the designation "F-1" was appended to Black Allan's name to identify him as the single horse most influential in the development of the modern Tennessee Walking Horse.

Dement's other popular horse, Merry Legs, foaled by Black Allan, became what many believe was the most influential *mother* of the breed. She was the most recognizable horse on the show circuit during her day. Merry Legs possessed one flaw that added to her uniqueness: her rear end. Once, as a pony, she was allowed to graze with calves on Dement's farm.

Apparently the grass was not as appetizing to the calves as was Merry Legs's long, flowing tail. The horse could be identified in the show ring by the tail which failed to reach her hocks.

At the time of Dement's death in 1940, he was serving as president of the Tennessee Walking Horse Breeders' Association of America. Brantley, his friend who discovered the great Black Allan, lived until 1945 and, prior to his death at eighty-three, always regretted selling The Old Teaser.

139
"Aunt Polly" Williams

Only Hotel for Miles Around

The colorful "Aunt Polly" Williams with her hard-to-miss accessories.

When "Aunt Polly" Williams spoke, people jumped, whether they were common folks, judges, or governors. Dressed in her over-the-shoulder shawl, her trademark man's hat tilted back from her forehead,

her wire-rimmed eyeglasses—and sometimes puffing from her long-stemmed pipe—Aunt Polly became one of the most memorable, outspoken, and beloved figures to stand her ground in Jackson County during the late nineteenth and early twentieth centuries.

She was born Mary Ann Christian Lock in 1839 near Gainesboro, but few Middle Tennesseans in the Upper Cumberland Plateau knew her as anyone other than Aunt Polly, the thrice-married manager of Gainesboro's only hotel and one of the best cooks around. Polly came from sturdy stock. As a child, she helped her father operate the local ferry that crossed the Cumberland River. By the age of ten, she "could pull the [ferry] boat across both Cumberland and Roaring Rivers, as quick as any man."

By the time she had her own business, the Gainesboro Hotel, Aunt Polly also meant business; anyone late for the dinner bell simply could not eat. She fed as many as two hundred hungry mouths each day when the Jackson County court was in session.

On one occasion, she became irritated after she rang the dinner bell for court to adjourn, and no one responded. She rang her bell again. When the presiding judge did not quickly end the court session, she kept ringing her bell and ranting against the judge by name: "Court or no court, Cordell Hull or no Cordell Hull, you better git here in a hurry and eat my food while it's hot or you won't eat at all." Every man in the courtroom jumped to his feet; proceedings came to an abrupt halt, and Circuit Judge Hull, the future United States secretary of state and "Father of the United Nations," had "met his match." (Hull's early law days were spent in Gainesboro sharing an office with Judge John Gore.)

Aunt Polly was no less blunt in her manner toward her three husbands, the first of whom, James Eaton, she married in 1852 when she was thirteen; she bore nine children by him. While her husband was away during the Civil War, Polly faced down Union soldiers attempting to get into her whiskey supply. Pulling her gun, she warned them: "The first one to touch that whiskey is my man."

The Yankees retorted, "Why we could shoot you."

Aunt Polly's reply: "You'd better be damned quick about it!"

The liquor supply went undisturbed.

Eaton survived the war but died soon thereafter. The story goes that the morning he died, he remembered a dream and kidded his wife that he might drown crossing the nearby Caney Fork River. Polly joked back that if he did, she would not come looking for him. Two weeks later when the dream proved to be a premonition, Eaton's body went undiscovered for several weeks, and it was the grieving widow who found the body.

Polly's second marriage was to Norman Frost, who died by gunshot; and her last marriage was to a local barber and Confederate veteran Thomas Jefferson Williams, who survived her. Polly confessed to both that she could never love another man the way she had loved Eaton.

Sometime after 1908, Aunt Polly rode a steamboat to Nashville and made a foot-stomping call on Governor Malcolm Patterson. She planned to seek clemency for a black employee in her livery stable who had been arrested by the local sheriff. When informed that a woman smoking a pipe and wearing a man's hat waited in his outer office, the governor immediately told his secretary to "Send Aunt Polly."

According to the story told, Polly was straightforward with the governor, whom she addressed by his nickname: "Ham, they've got my negro, Andy, in jail and I want to get him out."

Governor Patterson asked what the charges were; Aunt Polly readily replied that Andy was charged with selling whiskey.

"Is he guilty?" asked Patterson.

"Why yes, he's guilty as hell, but that's not the question," she shot back. "I can't run my business without him." Aunt Polly returned to Gainesboro with a pardon from the governor in her possession.

Revered for charity toward others, she made certain that the poor and hungry, the sick or the hurt, were never turned away from her dinner table or her lodging. All were treated like paying customers.

When she neared her eightieth birthday in 1919, Aunt Polly Williams suffered a stroke that rendered her unable to speak. Days later, still conscious, she signaled her last communication, when, according to relatives, she "raised her right hand gently, though weak, and pointed toward Heaven and her spirit returned to God . . . with a smile on her palid face."

140
Zack Bragg
A Lumber-Camp Point of View

At the turn of the twentieth century, sawmill owner Zack Bragg sometimes oversaw a motley bunch of backwoods creatures, including two of the four-legged variety.

Like so many other sawmills and lumber camps, Bragg's camp could provide extra pay for area farmers, many of them black sharecroppers. But his camp also featured a cast of misfits and convicts, along with a bear cub and young raccoon that served as pets to the rugged loggers. "They worry you to death, though," Bragg once noted, "can't put nothin' to eat where them little devils can't git it. And play! They never got done playin'. That's why we had 'em."

The highlight of the camp's routine was bathing day for the pets. The animals did not need washing (in general, their smell was no worse than that of many loggers). But the men enjoyed seeing the cub and coon growl, claw, and struggle whenever they were immersed in soapy water.

After the turn of the twentieth century, lumber camps were set up to cut the tremendous tracts of virgin timber surrounding Memphis. The region was a sudden mecca for lumber companies, which had exhausted the virgin timber of the northeastern United States and the Midwest. At Memphis and beyond in the riverbottom lands along the Mississippi River, these men were ready to profit from the nation's biggest supply of hardwood timber (80 percent of the nation's total). A timber rush not unlike the gold rush of an earlier period was underway. Memphis historian Shields McIlwaine writes:

> Before the early 1880's, if one stood on the roof of a tall building in Memphis and looked west across Arkansas, east toward Middle Tennessee, north into Kentucky, and south across Mississippi, everywhere summer seas of green treetops stretched away to dark expanses on the horizon. . . . Trees under whose dripping leaves DeSoto in the sixteenth century floundered in a flooded river bottom of Arkansas; trees that now were ready for axes.

By the time of Bragg's arrival in 1905 (nearly twenty years after heavy logging had begun), there was still so much virgin land around Memphis that timbermen reported killing a seven-foot black wolf only eight miles from downtown Memphis. Riverbottom land was cheap, because plantation owners were more interested in clearing other property to grow cotton. Bragg, just fourteen years old at the time, had come from Utica, Mississippi, crossed the Mississippi River at Memphis, and set up a sawmill on the opposite bank in the bottomland of Arkansas. As late as 1912, Bragg observed that the forested region around Memphis "was full of gray wolves, black deer, coons, turkeys, and other game. 'We'd go out a little ways from camp and shoot a deer, like in your back yard. . . . One day I shot sixteen coons in a few hours."

Bragg had big plans for his sawmill, hoping for a windfall of profits if it could be incorporated into a town. In a later newspaper interview, he explained: "There wasn't anything but timber over here. . . . In those days Memphis was known everywhere for its good lumber. If the inspectors saw it was stamped from Memphis, they didn't even look at it a lot of times.

"So, I thought," he added, "if I could get my sawmill place incorporated as a town, my lumber would be stamped from West Memphis and that would be a big help." The sawmill, however, simply remained known by its nickname, "Bragg City."

Like so many turn-of-the-century camps, Bragg's was a world apart from civilization. The men who worked in these camps clearly had to be as tough and sometimes as primitive as the woods in which they worked.

The black loggers, called "flatheads," took pride in facing the harsh conditions, engaging in hard labor under conditions that felled many white loggers like the ancient trees they cut. McIlwaine notes:

The flatheads, stripped to the waist in the hot summer woods, laughed at the normal supply of mosquitoes. . . . As flatheads were paid a dollar a thousand feet and could quit anytime they liked after a fair number of hours, they had a lot of satisfaction. Usually they cut until 5:30 P.M., made around five dollars, and went back to camp. . . .

According to an account by another regional lumberman, Richard Douglas, many sawmill hands in West Tennessee also were black and "were by far the best workers and the most reliable. The white men were drifters, some fugitives from the law." Douglas, originally from Nashville and a Princeton graduate, entered the sawmill business about the same time as

Bragg, in 1907. Douglas, however, located at the Big Hatchie River bottoms, where three counties (Madison, Haywood, and Hardeman) came together. He would later write:

There were no roads. I had to learn directions, using a tall cypress tree as my guide. I always carried a gun in my saddle holster. I was not afraid of anybody; there was not anybody within miles of me. I was not afraid of any animal; the biggest I ever saw were wildcats, quite numerous, but they would always run away.

In his newspaper interview, Bragg noted that "those first days of logging were the roughest." He said they purchased "mosquito nets by the gross instead of by the dozen. Had malaria twice a year—the first winter day and the first spring day." But with a humorous inflection, he added: "We just drank a teacup of quinine and went on."

Soon it was obvious that many of the black loggers would not remain in the backwoods without a domestic life, "So cottages were furnished for every couple that applied." But not all of the men wanted to settle down, so the lumber barons provided money to build "honkey-tonks," which were a combination dancehall and gambling den to entice the men to stay near the camps. White loggers, however, preferred the weekend city life, and thousands of them from the logging camps that formed a radius around Memphis converged on the city.

As tough as the workers were, Bragg was even tougher. Discipline in the camps was extremely harsh. Lumber camps made their own laws, since no logging supervisor in the forests around Memphis had time to retrieve a distant law officer, leave work, and testify in a courtroom. Due to this distance from proper society, the backwoods camps were ideal for escaped convicts or renegades fleeing criminal prosecution (especially when campsites were near the state border). They were hired—no questions asked, no information volunteered. Once, when Bragg found that a new worker had stolen some of his equipment, he called the crew together, tied the man to a tree, and used his bullwhip as punishment. Bragg lost very little equipment after this episode.

From 1880 until 1910, Memphis was a boom town, thanks to the loggers who filled its streets. Their money filled city banks and flowed freely through businesses and small industries. Lumber operators built fine homes, and, in 1898, founded the Lumbermen's Club "to prove that cotton was not the only king in town." Some people claimed that Memphis was "the largest hardwood market on earth."

By World War I, the boom was over. Where once there were big trees, only clear-cut land remained. Many of the lumber companies moved on, while others decided to chart a new course, planting trees and fabricating lumber. A new process for curing gum trees without warping the wood helped the Memphis area to continue its lumber business on a smaller scale, using vast quantities of what had once been called "the junk of the woods"—red gum trees, persimmon, and hickory. Gum was found to be perfect for veneer; the hardness of the persimmon was perfect for golf-club heads; hickory was perfect for skis to send to Minnesota and New England and for handles of axes, hoes, and shovels for most of the nation. The twenty-million-dollar wood-products business remained a part of Memphis life even throughout the Great Depression of the 1930s.

Gone were the lumber barons and the daily sound of the sawmill—at least the sound of most sawmills. Zack Bragg was not gone at all. Both Bragg and his sawmill could still be found in the river bottomland across the Mississippi (until the Depression forced him to sell), but more than that, Bragg's place had become a real town after all. In 1928, its seventy or so residents, most of them employees of the sawmill, elected Bragg as first mayor of the little town which, true to his dream, he had finally named "West Memphis" (Arkansas). Until his death in 1967, Bragg was West Memphis's most prominent citizen and one of the Memphis area's most compelling storytellers about its once-vibrant logging history.

141
Ben Walter Hooper

Illegitimate Boy to Liquor-Bashing Governor

After learning in 1870 that she was pregnant, seventeen-year-old Cocke County resident Sarah Wade asked Dr. L. W. Hooper, a young Newport physician, to legitimize their child through marriage. He declined, explaining that he was engaged to someone else. "Well, then," she continued after a moment's reflection, "if that is true, the birth of my child will be a disgrace to you and me and a shame to your wife. And worse than all, it will be like a millstone around the neck of the child itself." So Sarah, admitting to pressures from her family, asked Hooper to abort their child. He declined again. "There is a chance that its illegitimacy might not be such a handicap as you now think. That child may be a son," he theorized, "and, for all we know, he might some day be Governor of Tennessee."

Both of Dr. Hooper's conjectures would come to pass. Their illegitimate child was a son, Ben Walter Hooper, and that son served as governor of Tennessee from 1911 to 1915. What Dr. Hooper could not have predicted was his son's major role in bringing long-lasting liquor prohibition to Tennessee.

The doctor offered to help Sarah as much as he could. She was the daughter of an Italian immigrant and Irish mother and one of many siblings. But an interfering sister of Sarah's "stirred up such animosities between Dr. Hooper and the Wade family that friendly relations were entirely broken off," according to Ben Walter Hooper's later writings.

Beginning life as Ben Walter Wade, the boy spent his earliest years in poverty wandering the East Tennessee roadsides. With his mother and grandfather (the latter soon died on the road), he moved from town to town living the life of a vagabond. The family journeyed to Dandridge, to Jefferson City, to New Market. In 1875, the boy and his mother finally settled in the poorest section of Knoxville, where Ben played in the streets and had local ruffians as playmates. Sarah found a job and tried to keep him in a private school, which he hated and often left.

Without help to watch her son during the day, Sarah acted on a suggestion to enter him into St. John's Orphanage. Ben remembered the day his mother gave him "an unusually thorough scrubbing and put on me the best clothing available, which was doubtless none too good at that. I wondered where I was going, for I had never been to Sunday school, and it wasn't Sunday, anyway."

Although he no longer lived with his mother, Ben adjusted quickly to his new surroundings and lived there for two years. Dr. Hooper and his wife, unable to have children, then learned of his whereabouts. Working out a plan for adoption, the couple changed his name to Ben Walter Hooper and returned the child to Newport. In his autobiography, *The Unwanted Boy,*

Hooper never mentions his mother again, although he is aware that she lived to an old age.

For the first time, Ben learned that he had a father: "My astonishment can be imagined, for it had never occurred to me before that I had a father. I had noticed that many other boys had fathers, but if I had ever asked any questions about the matter, they had been evaded."

In Newport, Ben discovered also that he was illegitimate. When new friends taunted him on the matter, he ignored them. "Instead of my supposed handicap generating an inferiority complex, it motivated a spirit of ambition and determination that furnished the impetus to carry me over many a hill in my young days," Hooper recalled. "I immediately endeavored to take my place at the head of my classes in the public school of the little town."

At home, his life revolved around farm work: "I fed, watered, and curried a horse, fed and milked a cow, raised and attended to hundreds of chickens, cultivated a big garden, cared for a lawn, and for flowers, washed dishes and churned, and soon became able to cut and carry in all the wood for a stove and fireplace."

Ben's father, who vehemently opposed alcohol, occasionally became extremely drunk, usually with disastrous results, and always with a stern lecture to his son about the evils of drinking. Hooper recalls the doctor's drunken binges:

> When my father was thoroughly inebriated, his legs were still trustworthy, but his reason had abdicated its throne. He went completely berserk, filled all his pockets with an assortment of the deadliest weapons obtainable—Bowie knives, dirks, stilettos, pistols and whatnot—and went forth looking for trouble. . . .
>
> Such occurrences happened only a few times, perhaps a year or two apart, but I lived in constant dread of them. . . . So, taking his good precepts and his bad example both together, I had a hatred of intoxicants ground into my very being.

Ben Walter Hooper supported prohibition his entire life, beginning his crusade against liquor by joining prohibition clubs when he was sixteen. This hatred became evident during Hooper's later political career.

His move into politics began shortly after his graduation from Carson-Newman College in Jefferson City. Dismissing his father's request that he study medicine, Hooper instead began practicing law.

Elected a Republican state representative in 1892, the twenty-two-year-old Hooper served in the same legislature with another young man, Democrat Cordell Hull (the future United States secretary of state and "Father of the United Nations"), whom he described as "cold-blooded and admirable." The two men, the youngest representatives in the house, rarely saw eye to eye on anything, as one of Hooper's recollections suggested:

> [Cordell] Hull's name on the alphabetical roll-call followed immediately after mine, and Hull frequently made the jocose remark that, if he happened to be out of the hall when the call of the roll began and did not know what the question was, it was not necessary to make any inquiry; he just voted contrary to Hooper and felt safe.
>
> I countered with the observation that I was sure Hull wanted to vote wrong.

There was a twist of fate for Hooper's life which did not reach its conclusion until his marriage in 1901. His adoption by his biological father had been accomplished only after some soul-searching by his stepmother, who initially opposed the move. The friend who helped convince her to adopt the boy was her Newport neighbor, Ella Randolph Jones, whose daughter, Anna B. Jones, became Mrs. Ben Walter Hooper.

By 1910, prohibition was gaining support in the populace and dividing the Democratic Party, leaving the governor's chair open for the prohibitionist Hooper, the first Republican to be governor in thirty years. In pushing prohibition as state law, Hooper helped to extend Tennessee's four-mile law (banning the sale of liquor within four miles of churches or schools) to include the entire state, not just small towns.

"I wish my father could have lived to see how loyally I have stood by his counsel and how many hard punches I have given King Alcohol on many a hard-fought field," Hooper wrote. "When incapacitated by ill health, I have fought it, lying on my back in bed."

Hooper, who became a national figure in 1921 when President Warren G. Harding named him to the United States Railroad Labor Board, lived to the age of eighty-seven, dying in 1957. His autobiography, which had been written as a Christmas gift to his family two decades earlier, finally surfaced in the family home, after which University of Tennessee professors urged its publication.

142
John Walter Oliver

*Vigil over a Century-Old Community
in the Smoky Mountains*

Neither snow, nor rain, nor heat, nor gloom of night could stay John Walter Oliver from the swift completion of his appointed rounds. But ministering could.

Oliver performed the dual role of postman/preacher in Cades Cove after the turn of the twentieth century, proving equally adept at delivering mail and delivering sermons. The two roles occasionally proved incompatible. Oliver often interrupted his mail route to perform ministerial functions: visiting the sick, comforting the bereaved, or performing a marriage. He recalled several occasions when he had "gone so far as to leave my route and hold funeral services with my mail bags hanging on the pulpit beside me."

Oliver, whose great-grandfather (also named John) was the first resident of Cades Cove in 1821, proved his physical mettle as a young man of twenty. In 1899, he hiked more than thirty miles from Cades Cove to attend classes at Maryville College, then worked for the college to pay his tuition, earning a little more than seven cents per hour. He later attended a business college in Louisville, Kentucky, graduating with such impressive credentials that he was offered employment by Louisville-area banks. Determined to improve standards in his home community, however, Oliver returned to Cades Cove and took a civil-service exam to become a rural mail carrier, beginning a career that would last thirty-two years.

Affectionately dubbed "Cousin Johnny," he knew every Cove resident and helped most of them. Oliver provided assistance to farmers by giving them new varieties of seed, bringing eggs of thoroughbred chickens to hatch, and teaching the latest farming techniques. "Many of his initial ideas came from farm journals, but by 1910 he turned increasingly to the College of Agriculture at the University of Tennessee for advice on an amazing variety of horticultural problems," relates grandson Durwood Dunn. A Cove resident noted in 1914 that Oliver provided proof that "an educated farmer can enjoy life to a greater extent than the one who does not keep up with the times."

One of Oliver's greatest contributions to Cove life involved Black Joe, a thoroughbred Angus bull he bred with his neighbors' cows. The stud fee was one dollar, but only if the union proved successful. Oliver's meticulous records showed that virtually every farmer in the Cove took advantage of the bargain. He later upgraded the Cove's hog, sheep, and poultry populations by purchasing first-class stock and allowing his neighbors to breed their animals with his. He also brought the Italian honey bee to the Cove and built an apiary with more than one hundred hives.

Oliver simultaneously introduced the latest farm machinery, including tractors and threshing machines. Following his lead, Cades Cove resident A. W. Shields in 1911 purchased a gasoline engine, thrasher box, and feed crusher and operated these machines on behalf of his neighbors every Saturday.

Oliver's contributions made their way into other arenas. A staunch naturalist, he organized an agricultural club for boys and spearheaded many conservation efforts, including the stocking of Abrams Creek with rainbow trout. Stressing the conservation of mountain forests, he backed the creation of a national park in the Smoky Mountains to prevent forest fires.

Ever the progressive thinker, Oliver also affected his neighbors' views on womanhood. He sent both of his daughters to junior college, effectively combating the popular idea that higher education was inappropriate for females. He backed educational reform by helping to open a model consolidated school, the first in Blount County, prompting a local newspaper to proclaim, "the people of Cades Cove are among the most progressive in the county."

Oliver then became involved in two major battles identified with the Progressive era. Witnessing numerous tragedies associated with moonshining (among them increased murders), he became a supporter of prohibition and helped law enforcement rid the Cove area of illegal moonshine stills. The price Oliver paid for his beliefs was immense. His barn and that of his parents were set on fire by unknown arsonists (believed to be moonshiners) in the middle of the night in 1921. Barn burning, in fact, was a common means of vigilante justice. Though he lost a favorite plow horse, Oliver and his neighbors were able to save most of his livestock, a corncrib containing a season's harvest, and his farm machinery. But his parents lost everything on which their farm depended, an estimated twenty-five years of work. They lost "all their livestock—cattle, milk cows, horses, mules—in addition to plows, mowing machine, hay rake, harnesses, bridles, saddles, and a barn full of hay." Oliver attributed his mother's death four years later to the shock of that night's tragedy.

Oliver's final battle, a losing fight, was against the efforts of the state and federal government to carry Cades Cove into the Smoky Mountain National Park and to relocate the Cove population. Ironically, park boosters were trying to displace one of their original and strongest supporters, Oliver himself.

Because he had an understanding from Knoxville park promoters and leading politicians, including Governor Austin Peay, that the Cove settlement would never be destroyed, Oliver was lulled into a sense of security. After years of false promises, the real truth surfaced in 1927 when the Tennessee General Assembly approved a bill to seize homes and farms within the park boundaries. The targeted land included Cades Cove, the community that had existed since the state's pioneering days. Feeling betrayed at the hollow promises made to him and to the entire area, Oliver went on the offensive.

In 1929, after condemnation began on Oliver's land, he filed a lawsuit to obtain a better price than the ten thousand dollars offered. His case was in litigation from 1929 until 1935 and involved three appeals made in vain to the Tennessee Supreme Court. Most of the Cove's 120 families were removed by early 1937 and their homes demolished, including Oliver's. Thus ended a community that had flourished for 116 years in a mountain valley "cleared and under cultivation since the 1820's." With the original inhabitants gone, another irony surfaced: Officials artificially created a community of small cabins as an example of living history, to show what mountain communities were supposedly really like, although Oliver and his neighbors actually lived in clapboard farmhouses.

As his great-grandfather had been the first to settle the Cove, Oliver was one of the last to leave. He was evicted on Christmas Day 1937. Oliver resettled near Townsend, where he spent the remainder of his life. And until his 1939 retirement, he returned to the Cove area every day to carry the mail. Oliver continued his religious work until his death in 1966 at the age of eighty-eight.

According to his son, Hugh R. Oliver:

A deeply religious man, he harbored no animosity toward the State or the Park and in 1948, while discussing the research I was to continue on our Oliver family genealogy, he instructed me to omit anything which he may have written which was offensive to the Park. In fact, in later life in keeping with his strong conservation principles, he took considerable satisfaction in the permanent preservation of the Great Smoky Mountains.

143
Frances "Fannie" Elliott Davis
The Value of a Freedmen's Education:
A Nurse for America

In 1899, Frances "Fannie" Elliott fled a cruel foster home in Pittsburgh, Pennsylvania, and ran away to the place of her birth, Knoxville, Tennessee. She knew no one there; she had no family.

The irony was that her natural mother had once escaped to Knoxville also. Seventeen years earlier, she had gone there to give birth to Fannie. The mother, Emma Elliott, was the daughter of a white plantation owner in Asheville, North Carolina, and had been involved with a plantation sharecropper who was half Cherokee and half black. Emma fled to Knoxville after becoming pregnant, and the sharecropper disappeared to parts unknown; both feared the attitudes of prejudice around Asheville. The plantation owner, fearing for his daughter's well-being, made arrangements for monthly payments to her and the child. He died shortly thereafter. Five years later, Emma died of tuberculosis, and the child, Fannie, began her life in foster homes chosen by a black ministerial college in North Carolina. Her grandfather's monthly stipend continued to help her, and now gave assistance also to the families with whom Fannie lived.

The child's early years went well, until the age of twelve. In her final placement with a black minister who transferred to Pittsburgh, Fannie learned that he was keeping her grandfather's payments entirely for his own use. Buying expensive clothes for himself and his family, he reduced Fannie to rags and shoes with holes while she labored daily in the household. To have her own money, she decided to find a job. Answering a want ad placed by a jewelry store owner,

Fannie was hired immediately, becoming the popular housekeeper in a Pittsburgh mansion. Demanding this money also, her foster father twisted her arm, forcibly grabbing her wages.

Fifteen at the time, Fannie Elliott discovered that she could tell her troubles to her new employers, the Reeds. They were a kindly couple who became her best friends and discussed ways to help her. Two years later, they would pay for her return to Knoxville and guarantee her education at Knoxville College. Founded in 1875 by the United Presbyterian Church, the college offered black citizens a grade school and normal school in addition to college courses.

On the train to Knoxville, Fannie reached in her pocket and retrieved a note that Mrs. Reed had given her:

Dear Fannie,
Use the money for some new shoes and whatever else you need. We shall send more later. We know that you will do well in school and make us proud of you. Miss Mary and little Katharine will miss you— we all shall. Please write as soon as you are settled so we will know how things are going for you.

In her loneliness at Knoxville, she wrote them every day. She also adopted their surname, Reed, as her middle name.

Enrolling in fifth-grade studies, Fannie began an accelerated pace, advancing through all grade levels and graduating from high school (or normal school) in 1907 at the age of twenty-five. Although she planned for a curriculum in teaching to please the Reeds, she longed to be a nurse. After much agonizing about the decision, Fannie took a job at Knoxville College's new hospital, the only one within two hundred miles providing total care for black citizens. She began by handling menial tasks: changing beds, scouring bed pains, and the like.

But Fannie had her heart set on the Freedmen's Hospital Nursing School in Washington, D.C. To get there, she decided to break her engagement to a suitor who insisted she give up nursing; then she worked as a teacher to pay for her tuition. Fannie went on to fulfill her goal, graduating in 1913. All the while, she kept in touch with the Reeds and made periodic visits to them. In 1914, she returned again to Pittsburgh after learning that the youngest Reed daughter, Katharine, had health problems. The dedicated

Fannie remained several months to nurse her, despite the family's objections that she was jeopardizing her new career.

Fannie Elliott, however, soon became successful in nursing, holding an administrative position in a Baltimore hospital. Then she read about the Red Cross and its work in rural areas of America; she wanted to join the ranks, hoping to become a nurse in the South. In 1916, she was accepted into the Red Cross training program at Columbia University Teachers College. A year later, Frances "Fannie" Elliott stepped forward to receive historic badge Number *1A*—designating her as America's first black nurse to wear a Red Cross pin.

Her opportunity to go South came quickly. In the summer of 1917, she transferred to Jackson, Tennessee. Fannie was a member of the Red Cross's visiting nurse program for rural areas and small towns, a program soon to be called Public Health Nursing. At Jackson, she endured a few problems with a prejudiced supervisor, but Fannie loved the town, which reminded her of the kind of southern town she had known in her childhood. In the spring of 1918, she also spent a month in Chattanooga tending to the needs of military families and those servicemen at Chickamauga Base who were preparing for World War I and the European battlefront.

Later that summer, a deadly influenza epidemic sweeping across America hit Jackson. Tent hospitals went up and other emergency measures were put into place: Public buildings closed their doors, and public servants wore masks. But nothing seemed to control the outbreak and the number of victims. People often died within twenty-four hours of contacting the virus. There were only two public-health nurses in Jackson, and when her colleague fell ill, Fannie Elliott alone took care of the town's nursing needs.

Her biographer, Jean Maddern Pitrone, relates: "To Fannie, the town had turned into an inferno of hundreds of clamoring hands . . . hundreds of sunken, pleading eyes . . . hundreds of mouths, parched with fever and gasping for breath." So desperate was the town that white citizens who formerly used only white nurses were grateful for Fannie's service to them. She worked by day and into the night, until the epidemic in Jackson subsided. Only then did the fever make Fannie one of its victims. She would be quoted as saying, "God kept me well and strong as long as I was needed."

Battling a severe case of the influenza, Fannie Elliott had to seek rest in Washington, D.C., as a patient of the Freedmen's Hospital. While she did not become one of the nation's more than 540,000 dead, she did suffer permanent heart damage.

In 1920, Fannie was assigned to a hospital in Detroit and remained in that city the rest of her life. She married piano teacher Will Davis a year later. In making their home in Detroit's once-proud black suburb of Inkster, where the Great Depression left most of its men unemployed, Fannie Elliott Davis began to campaign for the destitute and hungry there. Automobile mogul Henry Ford agreed to help her. He set up a commissary to distribute food, then began a community project in which he accepted responsibility for all personal debts in exchange for Inkster's able-bodied men as employees at the Ford plant and as workers in rebuilding Inskter (part of their wages would repay any remaining debt).

Years later, a nursing friend of Fannie's who also lived at Inkster would recall those days:

> There were very few of us out there in Inkster in the thirties who didn't have a chance to shake Mr. Ford's hand. He would come out to the commissary in an ordinary Ford car . . . and he would ask Mrs. Davis what was most needed in the community. She would speak right up and tell him what the people were most in need of, and he would see that quick action was taken.

After her daily work in the commissary, Fannie continued as a nurse visiting the homes of the infirm, the aged, and ill children. She also conducted classes in nutrition for the residents of Inkster and became a member of the school board. Throughout the passing decades, the Reed family remained in close communication. In 1960, Fannie received a surprise visitor, the daughter Katharine, who would later write: "I . . . visited with Fannie for a few days because I knew she wasn't well and I thought the visit would please her. . . . Fannie always used to say that my folks were the only family she ever had, and now there were only Fannie and myself left."

Despite continuing ill health, Fannie Elliott Davis persevered in some form of nursing until her death at the age of eighty-two, which came in 1964 only months before the Red Cross planned to honor her at its national convention. She was placed in her coffin wearing the new Red Cross uniform and cap that she had purchased for the occasion.

144
Cordell Hull
A River-Rafter's Journey to the World Stage

United States Representative Cordell Hull at his desk, circa 1926.

During the late 1880s, a teenaged Cordell Hull worked diligently on his English diction, trying to develop a sophisticated accent which might not belong to a river man. He was a raftsman on the Cumberland River, helping his father support the family. But Cordell had greater ambitions. When the rafts landed in Nashville, he usually headed for the nearest bookstore and doled out his small wages on law books.

Most of the loggers and farmers of his region along the Upper Cumberland Plateau spoke "King Alfred language, as I call it," he later explained, "meaning the early Anglo-Saxon or Saxon tongue. It was a sort of home-grown English." In regard to his own language skills, Hull admitted: "I recognized good English in print, but had few occasions to use it in speech, for to do so gave a stilted impression and was quick to draw ridicule. This was a tremendous drawback in my learning to deliver stump speeches. . . ."

After graduating from Lebanon's Cumberland Law School and fulfilling a dream to be an attorney, Hull began a campaign for public office. At the age of twenty-one, he won election to the state legislature. Rafting experiences, however, were so much a part of his life that Hull's river excursions continued throughout his early political success. They ended when he had no free time after becoming a state circuit judge, who imposed exacting justice upon ten counties of the Upper Cumberland.

Hull did develop a forcefulness with the spoken word. His great oratorical skills and his passion for politics became the springboard for a future as one of the world's leading speakers and peacemakers. He would become President Franklin D. Roosevelt's secretary of state from 1933 to 1944 and the recipient of the Nobel Peace Prize for helping to create the United Nations. But Cordell Hull, it happens, would never have been born if his father, William "Billy" Hull, had been anything less than a sturdy, resilient frontiersman who could take a bullet between the eyes, and live to tell the story.

On the Cumberland Plateau, where Civil War loyalties continued to divide Tennesseans after the war, the elder Hull was a Confederate shot by guerrillas (men who used their wartime allegiances as an excuse to rob and threaten civilians). The bullet, from the gun of a Union guerrilla, destroyed Hull's right eye and exited the back of his skull, leaving him in continual misery for the rest of his life. Had a neighbor, a Mrs. Loveless, not rushed to his side, thrown her apron over his head, and pronounced him dead, the Yankee irregulars would have finished him off. Billy Hull never forgot Mrs. Loveless, whom he later assisted financially many times. Nor did he forget his assailant, a man named Stepp. After a long period of recovering from his wound, Hull tracked Stepp across two states and into Kentucky. "Father went straight to him without ceremony," Cordell Hull would later write, "and shot him dead."

The younger Hull always remembered his upbringing on the Upper Cumberland Plateau. Against the backdrop of this rugged Middle Tennessee region, Hull had been born in 1871 in a rented log cabin. His parents, hard working and poor, were from Overton (later Pickett) County near the county seat of Byrdstown. Farming, which was his father's chosen work, was equally tough on the Plateau. While farming profits

were elusive, logging income was not. His father moved the family to the Obed River bottom and became the area's first major logger in the late 1870s, discovering that log rafts could float to Nashville, be disassembled, and sold. Billy Hull bought his own farm, built a small store (where Cordell clerked at the age of eleven) and undertook years of successful rafting.

The country store and the people who filled it each day were later credited in the autobiography of Cordell Hull with shaping his early thinking. As a boy, he was fascinated with the wisdom of Civil War veterans who gathered there for lengthy conversations, which he explained:

Many of these old soldiers knew as much about government as high government officials and college instructors.

They infused the whole doctrine and spirit of individual liberty and freedom in the young people who were fortunate enough to listen to them and I was one. Partly as a result of absorbing the talk of these veterans, a few of us could answer virtually any question to be found in our political histories, and we knew the names and political records and doctrines of most of the Senators and leading Congressmen, the Cabinet and members of the state and county governments.

In these discussions, we boys learned to thrill to the military achievements of our State of Tennessee, to its constant readiness to respond to our country's call for whatsoever purpose, right from the very beginning.

Always a bright student, Cordell spent 1885 shuttling between schools at the family's new Clay County home of Willow Grove (where his father bought a farm on credit) and their old territory, Byrdstown, where he and his brother Ress divided their time lodging between a local hotel and a private home. The boys attended a Byrdstown subscription school. Hull relates, "Our crude homemade clothes, including heavy white wool socks knitted by Mother, marked our origin, and some of the wealthier students held aloof from us. The same reception was to occur at later schools as well."

Transferring to a free school in Willow Grove, Cordell learned how to debate his way to respect and attention. The families of these students were mostly farmers of limited financial means, and parents founded a debating society to give their children experience in speaking publicly. Parents closely followed these debates. Hull wrote:

> They would not stand for levity. I remember that at one debate various parents rose and protested that some of us had not fully prepared our arguments. In my first effort to speak before this society I was so excited that I remained completely speechless and sat down without having uttered a word.

In a subsequent debate, Hull performed very well. "I not only made what was thought to be a really good showing, but started my career on its way." The debate went so well that Cordell's father was determined to send him to the best schools possible, including Montvale Institute at the Clay County seat of Celina. Hull continued attending court, a practice that he started in Byrdstown. "Here," he revealed, "I finally developed the definite purpose to become a lawyer. I was then fourteen."

First, however, Cordell played an important role in his father's log-rafting business, a hard life which took special skills. When the crops were planted, Billy Hull and his five sons entered logging season. They cut the logs, lifted them aboard his wagon, and pulled them toward the Obed River, where logs were made into rafts and floated to Nashville's sawmills. (The Upper Cumberland's varied hardwoods and virgin forests were among the finest in the United States.) Since logging provided the best, and perhaps the only, living for many Tennesseans, tales of their adventures, trials, and tribulations became part of the Upper Cumberland's folklore. River stories claim that so many rafts filled the Cumberland River tributaries that a person could walk "six miles up the river by jumping from one raft to another." Cordell made his first journey at sixteen. The fifty-yard-long but fragile rafts negotiated a treacherously cramped Cumberland River to reach Nashville. These homemade structures gingerly took river turns and passed around islands and towheads (sandbars), while also dodging the wakes left by huge steamboats that could destroy the entire craft.

Like most post-Civil War Middle Tennesseans, including his father, Cordell Hull was a Democrat. "Those of the Confederate persuasion adhered to a man to the Democratic Party," he wrote. "In Pickett County it was possible for a candidate for county of-

fice to forecast within two or three votes the vote he would receive in a forthcoming election. . . . Each person stood solidly by his politics and religion."

Hull also stood by the rigid rules of the law, often appearing to have a "glacial" demeanor and refusing to put up with nonsense. While presiding over court in the early years of the twentieth century (perhaps 1905), Judge Cordell Hull became irritated with a disruptive conversation in back of the Smith County courtroom. He ordered the offender brought forward and solemnly stared into the face of a familiar Upper Cumberland character who had taught him to be impartial in such moments as these, no matter the circumstance. The judge thus fined his own father, the old Confederate log-rafter Billy Hull, for contempt of court.

Cordell Hull's eventual worldwide fame followed a lengthy career of nearly twenty-five years in both houses of Congress. While serving in the United States House of Representatives in 1917, he met and married Rose Frances Witz Whitney. Hull was elected to the Senate in 1930 but resigned in 1933 to become the United States secretary of state. He served in that position longer than any predecessor and despite some disagreements with President Roosevelt. Hull's tenure through World War II resulted in his attempts at global peace by helping to form the United Nations. He was awarded the Nobel Peace Prize in 1945 for his efforts, thereafter carrying the name "Father of the United Nations."

Within a year of his wife's death in 1954, Hull also died after years of declining health. He was eighty-four.

145
John T. Wilder

The Friendly Carpetbagger

A visitor to the top of Roan Mountain in the late nineteenth and early twentieth centuries could stand with one foot in Tennessee and the other in North Carolina—and never touch the ground. Such a feat was easy for guests at the Cloudland Hotel, which happened to straddle the state border. To emphasize the point, hotel owner John T. Wilder, a former Union general and Civil War hero, had a two-inch-wide line painted down the middle of the dining room.

Jeeter Gouge, who grew up in the Cloudland, where his father, John, was the caretaker (and later manager), said in subsequent interviews that people often rushed to write letters to family and friends after standing in both states at the same time. Hotel guests also slept in one state and dined in the other, lucrative gimmicks that lured thousands of visitors annually to the upper East Tennessee mountains of Carter County.

Wilder, who made his money as a major industrialist in the Reconstruction era, decided to build the Cloudland just below the highest point of Roan Mountain, where he had purchased seven thousand acres in 1870. The mountaintop was home to the world's largest display of natural rhododendron and other mountain flora, which made it a mecca for tourists. One Harvard professor called it "the most beautiful mountain east of the Rockies," and promotions noted that the Roan plateau was "free from the thunderbolts" (being above the clouds) and just as free from poisonous snakes and insects. When nearing the mountain, visitors traveled along a twelve-mile-long road of balsam wood. Built by a logging company at Wilder's request, the wooden roadway ran from Roan Mountain Station to the hotel.

Aside from his role as a hotel owner, Wilder's other business life was in the iron-works industry. What he accomplished in this undertaking was critical to the rebuilding of East Tennessee after the Civil War and gained him recognition throughout the South.

A native New Yorker whose ancestors fought in the Revolutionary War, Wilder operated his own small foundry and millwright business in Indiana when the Civil War began. Converting his foundry to the casting of six-pound cannon, Wilder then organized a light-artillery company and finally a light-horse brigade whose expeditions became famous, known by both sides as "Wilder's Lightning Brigade." Wilder equipped his troops with the newly developed Spencer repeating rifles. To the enemy under fire from these weapons, the brigade appeared to be twice its size. He also invented a "rail twister" that made enemy repair of railroad track nearly impossible, thus destroying major transportation routes. After Wilder's Lightning Brigade successfully covered defeated Union troops at the Battle of Chickamauga and helped them retreat to Chattanooga, Wilder was compared to the Confederacy's Nathan Bedford Forrest, whom he respected and befriended after the war.

Suffering frequently with complications from a bout of typhoid fever, General Wilder was forced to retire from the war in 1864. He decided to move to Chattanooga, hoping the milder climate would allow him a full recovery. Since he had noticed Tennessee's abundant natural resources, notably iron ore, Wilder wanted to continue his career in the iron ore and foundry business. In 1867, he established the Roane Iron Company and founded the small East Tennessee company town of Rockwood, named for a business associate, Major W. A. Rockwood. Here, the South's first coke-blast furnace was put into operation.

In rapid moves, Wilder also founded the Roane Rolling Mills in Chattanooga and organized the Carnegie Land Company in Johnson City. Then he eyed the Cumberland Plateau and established the mining town of Wilder to supply coal for another of his enterprises, the Fentress (County) Coal Company. (Contrary to local lore, Wilder, Tennessee, did not earn its name for being wilder than any neighboring town.) He lived in both Chattanooga, where he was elected mayor in 1871, and in Johnson City, where he took an active role in railroading and helped to organize a power company. During the 1880s, Wilder built yet another home and another hotel, both at the base of Roan Mountain. This smaller hotel along the Doe River was a "one-night stopover for people en route to the Cloudland Hotel" which allowed visitors to fish from the back porch.

Even in his later years (he lived to be eighty-seven), Wilder, who was six feet, two inches tall, was described by his friend and biographer Samuel C. Williams as moving "with ease and a degree of grace. His eyes were particularly penetrating and bright; they were readily kindled by merriment. . . . He was a total abstainer from intoxicants and made no use of tobacco." Wilder's abstention was in contrast to the bootleggers who were attracted to the Cloudland Hotel. Because alcohol was legal in Tennessee but illegal in North Carolina, guests could only drink on one side of the hotel. North Carolina bootleggers found staying at the Cloudland quite convenient to their business, and a North Carolina sheriff loved to be on hand in case someone crossed the line. The guest register was more refined, often including society's most elite names: European royalty and noted Americans of the day. Most guests, however, remembered the Cloudland as a refuge for hayfever sufferers or anyone with respiratory problems.

In 1917, the year of Wilder's death, the Cloudland Hotel (or what was left of it since being abandoned in 1910) was sold to a man in Burbank, Tennessee. He promptly began selling pieces of the building to local people. As a result, the rich balsam wood, which comprised most of the hotel's construction, and its hard-maple floors were used to build many entire houses and businesses in the area.

Perhaps Wilder's greatest legacy was not only helping to bring the industrial age to East Tennessee (he is credited with making Chattanooga one of the mid-South's premier industrial centers), but also helping to bring peace between former Confederates and Unionists. Both sides considered him a friend. Wilder, in fact, was made an honorary member of the United Confederate Veterans by the Nathan Bedford Forrest Post in Chattanooga. He claimed that the reason for this honor being given to a Yankee veteran and carpetbagger was that he had some mysterious form of affinity with the Confederates. Indeed, when he was buried in Chattanooga, a former Confederate soldier delivered the sermon.

146
Jacob L. Vowell

A Page from a Coal Mine Disaster— Voices from the Grave

Absenteeism was generally rampant on Mondays following payday at the Fraterville Mine near Coal Creek (present-day Lake City) in Anderson County. But that was not the case on May 19, 1902. Jacob L. Vowell and his teenage son, Elbert, were among the unusually large number of miners who reported that day. Both were also among the more than 180 men killed in an explosion that ranked as one of the worst mining catastrophes in American history. "Not one man who entered the mine escaped with his life," reported one Lake City historian. According to reports, the explosion left only three adult males living in the East Tennessee village of Fraterville. Many women lost every male family member: husband, sons, father, and brothers.

The catastrophe began when weekend workers tapped into a nearby mine that had been closed for several years. When its combustible gases began leaking into the Fraterville mine, a Monday morning spark triggered an enormous explosion. The mine shaft collapsed, killing many instantly. Those who survived the initial crash were trapped without fresh air; they died over the next eight hours. Rescuers, hundreds of whom gathered from all parts of Tennessee and surrounding states, could hardly get past fallen rock and poisonous fumes.

Some of the trapped miners survived long enough to write good-bye notes to their families. Jacob Vowell penned two of these. One, written to his wife, contained this message:

> We are shut up in the head of the entry with a little of air and the bad air is closing in on us fast. Dear Ellen, I have to leave you in a bad condition. But dear wife set your trust in the Lord to help you raise my little children. Ellen take care of my little darling Lily. Ellen, little Elbert said that he had trusted in the Lord. Chas. Wood says that he was safe if he never lives to see the outside again he would meet his mother in heaven. . . . Elbert said for you all to meet him in heaven. . . .

Mine superintendent George M. Camp, giving his account of the tragedy and the slow rescue to the *Knoxville Journal and Tribune*, said at least two thousand people quickly gathered at the mine's entry. "Women were frantically trying to force their way into the mine," he reported, "and strong men were groaning in agony in fear that perhaps brother, father, or child were lying dead within." Wooden coffins were ordered and unloaded from train cars; and undertakers waited in their oilcloth aprons at the mine's opening for the dead to be brought out. It took nearly four days for all bodies to be recovered.

Mining accidents became common at the turn of the twentieth century. Besides major catastrophes, mining presented daily hazards. Hancock County native Alex Stewart recalled one incident involving a foreigner hired early in the century:

> Then there was a hunk come in up there at Stonega and went to work. He'd never been in the mines before. Back then you had to buy your own tools—a shovel, pick, crowbar, and lights. He bought him an outfit and went in there to work, and worked about a week. He was going in at night and had his pick on his shoulder. The pick hit that electric wire and it killed him. Yes sir, I was there and I helped take him out.

Coal Creek had another mine tragedy only nine years later, in 1911, when a blast at Cross Mountain Mine killed eighty-four more miners. In this disaster, survivors William Henderson and his son, Milton, surfaced from the Briceville mine after a two-day rescue to find their graves had been ordered for them. Only three others were also found alive: Dore Irish, Irwin Smith, and Arthur Scott, who had walled themselves into an area to keep out the deadly black-damp fumes.

Hugh LeRue would have suffered a similar fate had it not been for his wife's premonition. LeRue scoffed when she pleaded with him to stay home that morning. He wavered when she vividly described a dream of "headless and mangled forms" being carried from the mine. He stayed home—and stayed alive.

In the end, 53 women and 146 children joined the ranks of the widows and orphans of the region's coal mines.

147
Edward W. Carmack

A Smoking Gun—And a Martyr for Prohibition

Edward W. Carmack's crusading days were numbered.

On a November afternoon in 1908, when a Nashville police officer investigated what sounded like gunshots coming from Seventh Avenue, he found the body of former United States Congressman and Senator Edward W. Carmack, shot twice through the heart, a smoking cigar still clutched in his left hand.

Called "one of the most controversial personalities in the story of Tennessee," Carmack always loved a good political fight. His last great battle, which caused his death, also turned him into a martyr, and made prohibition the law in Tennessee for nearly a quarter-century.

Born in 1858 near Castalian Springs, Edward W. Carmack was the son of a poor preacher who died when Edward was still a child. The boy's teen years were spent as a farm hand until friends helped him obtain a classical education at Webb School, then located at Culleoka in Maury County. Later becoming a Columbia attorney, Carmack developed a taste for politics, which took him to Nashville in 1884 as a state legislator. His way with words became apparent when he entered the world of journalism and indulged in political bouts: first at the *Columbia Herald* and then the powerful *Nashville American* in 1886. By the time he reached Memphis to become editor of the *Memphis Daily Commercial*, Carmack was gaining a statewide reputation as a crusader, equally persuasive with either the written or the spoken word.

In 1896, Memphians were torn by a bitter national debate as to whether silver should be part of the monetary standard. Carmack believed that a silver standard could rid the nation of economic panic and depression. He even accompanied prosilver United States presidential candidate William Jennings Bryan on a local speaking tour. The tour caused a fight within Carmack's own newspaper, where most of the owners promoted gold. In 1896, after a fiery April board meeting, the publishers told Carmack that the only thing keeping him from being fired immediately was his five-year contract. Whereupon the editor pulled out his contract, dramatically tore it up, and shouted, "I have resigned!"

The real fight was just beginning, because Carmack immediately set out to take the United States congressional nomination from incumbent Josiah Patterson, who had converted from silver to become a "gold bug." Bad feelings developed between the two men and involved Patterson's son and campaign manager,

Malcolm. This bitter 1896 campaign resulted in Carmack's victory, and he remained in the United States House of Representatives for two terms. In 1900, he won election to the United States Senate but was defeated in 1906.

When he returned to his Nashville law practice, Edward W. Carmack found a new crusade: to end liquor sales in Tennessee. Prohibition was a key ingredient in the reform movement sweeping the nation, and Carmack rallied behind the issue. Because he also had a passion to unseat now-Governor Malcolm Patterson, Carmack entered the race for governor and took Prohibition into open debate. In Memphis, eight thousand people gathered to hear the two old enemies. In the end, Carmack lost. Although he was mentioned for the United States presidency in 1907, Carmack returned to the one career he seemed to enjoy the most, that of a newspaper editor.

At the *Nashville Tennessean*, he gave readers a steady dose of his sarcasm against any enemy of prohibition. His principal target was the governor of Tennessee. His barrage of words also attacked Governor Patterson's closest advisor and friend, Duncan Cooper, a former Confederate colonel from Maury County, a onetime state legislator, a railroad man, and one of the most powerful men in Tennessee politics. During 1908, the *Nashville Tennessean*'s blistering editorials against Cooper finally drove him to threaten editor Carmack's life. Cooper was overheard to say that if his name appeared in the *Tennessean* again, "he or Senator Carmack must die." Cooper also wrote a note to Carmack: "You have no more right to say those things in the newspaper than you do to my face, which so far you have not had the temerity to do."

Considering a duel, Cooper borrowed a gun. Carmack, too, borrowed a gun (although he knew nothing about pistols); Carmack also printed his last editorial attack against Cooper that fateful November 9, 1908. When Cooper saw the editorial, he rushed to his son's office in a fury. Robin Cooper tried to calm his father and, failing that, simply accompanied him for the rest of the day.

Edward W. Carmack later happened upon the two men along Seventh Avenue. According to one witness, insults filled the air, and Carmack drew his pistol, mistakenly believing the elder Cooper had also drawn his. Of the two shots that Carmack fired, one hit Robin Cooper in the shoulder. As quickly as the

shots rang out, Robin Cooper drew his own gun and killed Carmack, pumping three bullets into him.

The father and son faced public scorn from Carmack supporters, who branded them assassins. Both were convicted of second-degree murder and sentenced to twenty years in prison. But the elder Cooper was pardoned by his patron, Governor Patterson; Robin Cooper was set free after a Tennessee Supreme Court ruling declared a mistrial, and his case was never retried. (Robin Cooper was murdered in 1919, though no evidence tied his death to these events of 1908.)

A statewide furor over Carmack's killing and the handling of the Coopers was the decisive political factor in making Tennessee a prohibitionist state in 1910, nearly a decade before nationwide Prohibition. The death of Carmack also divided the Democratic Party between wet and dry factions, resulting in the 1910 gubernatorial victory for prohibitionist Ben Walter Hooper, the first Republican elected governor in three decades.

One of the great ironies of Carmack's death was that his beginning as an editor actually came from Duncan Cooper, who in 1886 had wanted to help the struggling country lawyer and state legislator. As president of the *Nashville American*, Cooper placed Carmack in charge of the paper's editorial page and gave him a boost up the political and professional ladder. When Carmack left the Nashville paper for Memphis, he credited Cooper with helping his journalism career, acknowledging "the debt I owe and the gratitude I feel toward Col. D. B. Cooper, under whose management I first became acquainted with the *American* and with journalism. . . . I cannot recall one word, act, or incident which has marred the harmony of our relations during the whole time of our intimate association."

148
Marion Scudder Griffin
Paving a Way in Law and Politics:
First Woman Attorney

In 1907, Marion Scudder Griffin sued over a dead calf. The calf's owner, who was her first client, watched her win a fifty-dollar judgment against the L & N Railroad, owner of the train that hit the animal. As part of this victory, Marion Scudder Griffin was also marking her place in history as the first woman to serve as legal counsel in Tennessee.

She had moved to Memphis in her teens to study law under Judge Thomas Scruggs. Born in 1881 in Georgia, Marion was the daughter of a Confederate veteran (who served at the age of fourteen), and grand-daughter of a wartime surgeon for the Confederacy. An ancestor, Colonel Nathaniel Scudder, served on General George Washington's staff and was reputed to be the only member of the Continental Congress to be killed during the Revolutionary War.

While studying law in Memphis, Marion passed the bar examination in 1901 but could not gain entry into the all-male Tennessee Bar Association. She then carried her struggle to the Tennessee Supreme Court, which ruled against her due to specific laws regarding the status of women. Since the law protected married women from being sued, a single female attorney, theoretically, could seek the refuge of marriage to avoid lawsuits brought against her and her clients.

Delayed but not deterred, Marion Scudder Griffin earned her law degree in 1906 from the University of Michigan. Returning to Tennessee, she began to lobby for legislation to permit women to become attorneys, and succeeded a year later. After her success against the L & N Railroad, the young attorney later tried her first criminal case by defending the son of her black cook. She convinced the court that the boy, charged with murder, was mentally deficient and needed an institution, not a jail.

She achieved another historic first in 1923 when she became the first woman elected to the Tennessee House of Representatives (two years earlier, Mrs. Anne Lee Worley served in the state senate, filling the unexpired term of her late husband, J. Parks Worley of Bluff City). As a representative from Shelby County, Marion Scudder Griffin opposed liberal divorce laws, arguing that easy divorce would allow men to abandon their wives and children. She fought equally hard for financial aid for destitute mothers.

Retiring in 1949 after a forty-two-year career, Marion lived until 1957. She had set the stage in the legal profession for other accomplished women, but the state supreme court did not have a woman on its bench during her lifetime. In 1990, eighty-eight years after the court denied Marion the right to practice law, Nashville's Martha Craig Daughtrey made the final breakthrough, becoming the first woman associate justice of the Tennessee Supreme Court.

149
T. S. Stribling
A Pulitzer Prize Awaits

As a baby only moments old, Thomas S. Stribling fulfilled the ritual of a baby's first touch, which, according to nineteenth-century Tennessee folklore, would give some clue of future endeavors. Someone produced a pen and laid it across the infant's fingers, probably because his parents ran a small Middle Tennessee newspaper at the time. T. S. Stribling's life as a writer seemed destined.

Born in 1881 to a Union father and Confederate mother in Clifton, along the Tennessee River in Wayne County, the child admittedly disappointed his father by favoring his mother's side of the family. His early childhood summers were spent at his maternal grandparents' plantation in Florence, Alabama. Disdaining hard work and social responsibilities, T. S. seemed to his father to be both lazy and reclusive. By the age of eight, however, the avid young reader had devoured almost all of Charles Dickens's writings.

As a child, T. S. set up a small writing table in his closet. Alongside his pencils, paper, and a lamp, he placed glasses of vinegar and watered-down baking soda. While jotting jokes and notes, T. S. mixed the vinegar and soda, watched it fizz, then drank the bitter concoction—in honor of all great writers who drank.

At the age of twelve and working in his parents' general store, the boy spent most of his time observing and listening to customers, reading pulp fiction, and hiding behind the counter, where he scribbled imitations of the kind of stories he had read. On numerous occasions, he was warned by his father, who had a practical view of life, to stop "fooling around." Young Stribling persisted, however, saying later that his father's insistence that writers lived in poverty had little effect on him. He had already observed, he said, that poor people in Clifton had just as much fun as the wealthy.

When he was fifteen, the boy volunteered to write articles for a local weekly newspaper. (His parents, realizing that a general store provided more security, had already sold their own newspaper.) The experience was short-lived because the paper was soon sold. When his father sent him to Florence Normal School, hoping that the boy would latch onto a practical way to make a living, T. S. came under the influence of his English teacher, who supported his efforts to be a writer. (He later dedicated his novel *Red Sands* to her.)

In his later youth, T. S. Stribling failed miserably as a teacher. He seemed more interested in observing the bizarre behavior of students than in teaching or disciplining his charges. His parents decided to mold their son into a lawyer, a more lucrative occupation for someone who fancied arguing and writing. After graduating from Alabama's law school, Stribling clerked in Florence, Alabama, in the law firm of the former Alabama governor, Emmett O'Neal. The governor was pleased to see the young man at a typewriter, hammering industriously every day, doubtlessly churning out legal notes. One day, the shocked governor sent a letter to Stribling's Uncle Lee, who had arranged the job: "I glanced over some of his notes, and it's some sort of tomfoolery about how a boy loved a girl, and that's what he's been sweating over for months."

Having failed now as a teacher and a law clerk and later as a newspaper reporter for the *Chattanooga News* (not creative enough, he said of the job), Stribling finally broke free to pursue his favorite pastime: writing fiction. Stribling initially achieved success as a pulp writer; formula writing paid the bills and allowed him to travel. He then advanced to novels in the late 1910s and became part of the literary movement, the Southern Renaissance. He published his first novel, *Birthright*, in 1922, and continued to write about the people and culture of the South. Unlike earlier writers who romanticized the Old South, Stribling took a more realistic view. His novels, like the later ones of William Faulkner in nearby Mississippi, outraged many readers but prompted others to examine southern social institutions.

In 1933, T. S. Stribling, whose parents used every effort to turn him away from writing, won the Pulitzer Prize for fiction with *The Store*, part of a trilogy based on his experiences in Clifton, Tennessee, and Florence, Alabama. Another novel in the trilogy, *The Forge*, made Stribling the first American to have a book chosen by the English Book League. He wrote more than twelve novels during the 1920s and 1930s, most of which achieved great popularity, and many of which were partially written in Clifton, where he often returned. In 1959, Stribling and his wife moved permanently to Clifton, where he lived until his death in 1965.

150
W. C. Handy
"Father of the Blues"—
From Beale Street to America

Blues master W. C. Handy actually wrote more spirituals than blues songs.

He was an obscure musician when he agreed to play on the bandwagon of mayoral candidate Edward Hull Crump during Memphis's 1909 election. Equally obscure at the time was the catchy tune he wrote that served as Crump's campaign theme. Neither the composer nor the song would remain obscure for long. The musician, W. C. Handy of Florence, Alabama, and his song, afterwards released in sheet music as "Memphis Blues," were destined for fame.

In 1912, Handy made arrangements with a white music-shop operator to publish one thousand copies of the song. After some time had passed, Handy became discouraged when the operator showed him a stack of nearly one thousand unsold pieces of sheet music. Believing the tune a failure, Handy sold his interest to the shop owner for a hundred dollars, without knowing that the man had actually printed two thousand copies, more than half of which had already sold. Years later, Handy won back his copyright (and generated a few more royalties), but by then the music store operator had become rich with "Memphis Blues."

The hit song created a considerable following for Handy, as did another upbeat tune and national hit, "St. Louis Blues," released in the late 1910s. At the request of Handy, an unknown nineteen-year-old blues singer from Memphis introduced the song in Chicago. As the result of her Chicago days and Handy's tune, Alberta Hunter also became famous. The tune was so powerful that many a listener became mesmerized by its seductive charm. One of these was a tall, shapely Memphis black woman known as Black Carrie. One evening at one of Memphis's glitzier nightclubs, the Monarch Club, Carrie was so moved by the piano strains of "St. Louis Blues" that she ran to the middle of the dance floor, lifted her skirt above her knees, and writhed to the sultry rhythm. She was exhorted by one onlooker: "Go on, Carrie, shake it! Ah, shucks, you ain't gwine tuh heben nohow!" Carrie obliged, whirling and dancing until she collapsed, totally exhausted, onto the floor. Handy's music routinely inspired such passion, eventually earning him the tribute, "Father of the Blues."

W. C. Handy's fascination with the blues, with Beale Street, and with such places as the Monarch Club, actually began in his Alabama hometown, where he was born in 1873. There, in 1888, a coincidence brought him into contact with Memphis musician Jim Turner. Handy, the son of a minister who deplored music as a sinful pursuit, was fifteen at the time. His new friend Turner had arrived in Florence by accident. Turner, it seems, had been so distraught by an ill-fated love affair that he drank heavily and showed up at the Memphis train depot, plunking down a handful of bills and requesting a hundred dollars' worth of tickets. Asked where he wanted to go, Turner answered: "Anywheres. Just anywheres."

"Anywheres" turned out to be Florence. When he met the teenaged Handy, Turner saw that the boy already had set his sights on a future in music. Accomplished on the cornet, Handy later explained in his autobiography that musicians were considered "idlers, dissipated characters, whisky drinkers and rounders." His father once told him, "I'd rather follow you to the graveyard than to hear that you had become a musician."

Turner, meanwhile, was organizing an orchestra and teaching dancing. He dazzled the youth with his stylized music and his tales of Beale Street, planting in the W. C. Handy's heart "a seed of discontent, a yearning for Beale Street and the gay universe that it typified," Handy would later recall.

Handy cut class one day for an out-of-town engagement with Turner's band. Inspired about the future of his own music, Handy later joined a minstrel show as a cornet player and wandered the nation learning about show business. He worked odd jobs to advance his musical training and settled down to become an instructor of music, spending more than ten years teaching band and voice at Alabama's Agricultural and Mechanical College.

In training dance bands, Handy again traveled extensively and saw firsthand that audiences wanted a different sound. When his own band played white clubs in Memphis in the early twentieth century, Handy provided the traditional symphony and orchestra music. But he noticed that audiences were even more thrilled when fill-in black bands played rhythmic, soulful, mournful tunes long associated with black laborers who worked in the fields or along the river wharves. Handy began penning those tunes at every opportunity.

"His great accomplishment," wrote historian Paul R. Coppock, "was writing in the notes of the scale the weary tones of Negroes building levees and hoeing cotton. He made the translation into a written music that was admired by the dancing public." According to popular accounts, Handy wrote "Memphis Blues" on the cigar counter of a Memphis neighborhood bar, Peewee's, where a telephone was always accessible for the poor blues musicians and singers who gathered there; they could count on Peewee to take their messages and to schedule their bookings.

W. C. Handy's bands (he had more than seventy musicians on call) were a hit throughout the South and especially in Memphis, where Handy made his home for fifteen years. On many Sunday nights after church services, Handy worked late with Memphis lyricist Harry Pace, who wrote stirring lyrics for many Handy tunes. When Pace and his music-publishing house moved to New York City in 1917, Handy followed shortly thereafter. He and Pace then decided to release "St. Louis Blues," certain that it would become a hit.

The mammoth success of that song catapulted Handy into the forefront of a blues-music movement and stirred the masses into a desire for every Handy blues song. Parades and celebrations of every kind were given in his honor. In Memphis, a square at Beale and Third was renamed Handy Park, where a statue of W. C. Handy and his horn later dominated the landscape. Even the popular composer George Gershwin admitted to him: "Your work is the grandfather of mine."

Handy, however, never relinquished his religious upbringing; he spent even more years composing spirituals (he reportedly wrote five times as many spirituals as blues songs). He generally "dressed like a deacon" and said that the strongest memory of his first trip to Memphis was "the figure of John the Baptist on the cupola of Beale Street Baptist Church, pointing to heaven."

Because of his love for Memphis, Handy returned for regular visits over the decades. His last visit was in 1958. Eighty-five years old and blind, W. C. Handy died in the city that he had helped to make famous.

151
Emma Bell Miles

A Mountain Woman's Struggle with Herself

Like a meteor, Emma Bell Miles's journalistic career flashed for one brief moment, then it was gone. She could turn a phrase, but she could not turn down a no-account suitor. Despite the choice she made to live as a mountain woman married into hopeless poverty near Chattanooga, Emma had a genius for literature and art, and they made her "a legend up in the hills of Tennessee."

Emma Bell first arrived in East Tennessee in 1892 at the age of twelve. Her schoolteacher parents had left Indiana seeking a mild climate, primarily for Emma. Her father cultivated in her a love for books and urged her early in life to keep a diary, and so she did throughout her short life. Artistically inclined, Emma left home at eighteen and spent two years attending an art school in St. Louis, where the city's art community was so impressed that it was willing to finance her advanced training in Europe. But the young woman was homesick for the East Tennessee mountains and a handsome young mountain man, Frank Miles. She came home instead.

Despite parental protests, Emma, now a teacher in her parents' log-cabin school, married the illiterate Miles, a carriage driver between Chattanooga and Walden's Ridge. He quit his full-time job after their marriage in 1904 and never took another. Each year in her fifteen-year marriage, Emma had either a baby or a miscarriage; she bore five children (one would die of scarlet fever) and worked to produce the family's main income. Miles, meanwhile, bounced from one day job to another. Emma's displeasure with this arrangement was evident from an entry in her diary: "The pinch of utter abject poverty became harder and harder until, as the children's demands grew with their growth, its misery and shame grew insupportable."

Emma Bell Miles did, however, author a book within a year after her marriage. She had carved out enough time to write *The Spirit of the Mountains*, which Chattanooga librarian Adelaide Rowell described as being "as good as the best that has ever been written about the mountain people." Although Emma needed the money for her family's livelihood, the book brought her little more than recognition. She supplemented the family resources somewhat by selling occasional poems to magazines and finding willing buyers for her drawings of mountain scenes. Between 1908 and 1912, Emma also developed a national audience when her stories (all containing mountain themes and ample doses of nature) were published in such periodicals as *Harper's*, *Putnam's*, and *Lippincott's*.

Her stature as an artist, a writer of books, and a contributor to national magazines was more than enough in April 1914 for her to be offered a job as a featured columnist in the society department of the *Chattanooga News*. "Now," she wrote in her diary, "I behold new and wider fields in beauty opening before me in larger relationships and limitless hunting grounds."

While her husband took care of the children during the week (coming after her on weekends), Emma discovered a less difficult lifestyle in her Chattanooga boarding house. Here she could converse with people knowledgeable about current affairs and take hot baths without hauling the water from a nearby creek. Despite her mere nine-dollar-per-week salary, she felt her life had attained emotional, if not financial, fulfillment. "My position on the *News* enables me to come in touch with large and vital issues," she stated. "This position is one which to others seems underpaid and insignificant; but it allows me to express myself, and with some hours of extra outside work which I do as I can, the pay of $9 a week permits us to live."

Emma Bell Miles wrote thirty-four columns between April 3 and June 30, 1914, showcasing a rare humor, subtlety, and creativity that attracted and riveted readers regionwide. She showed an interest in every aspect of life and in all living things. Her columns featured make-believe conversations through the eyes of animals and birds gathered around Fountain Square in Chattanooga and its large lawn dotted with trees. In the center of the square was a fountain, topped by a statue of a fireman (a memorial to two firemen killed in the line of duty in 1887), which she described at the beginning of her first column:

> One may think of him as harsh and stern, but the birds know better. For them he always has a drink and a bath ready, and rest, and sanctuary from cats and popguns. And in return for his unfailing hospitality they bring him the news, straight and sure from its sources of all that goes on within the city limits and even from far beyond.

The statue, in moderating discussions, explained the point of view of humans to the animals, a forum actually for Emma Bell Miles's own beliefs and observations, which were many. One of her strongest beliefs, and that of the newspaper for which she worked, was in support of women's suffrage, which was just gaining a toehold in the South. Her character, the White Pigeon, conveyed these thoughts succinctly in her April 15, 1914, column: "I wasn't raised in a house, and I can't see anything particularly sacred in man's established order of things. Nature's order stands infinitely above it; and Nature's order is what women are trying to rise to."

Emma also cautioned against overwork:

> It is often a woman's own fault that she falls by the wayside, or grows hard and bitter, with no song in her heart. Many a woman grows prematurely old because she does not know when to stop. . . . Some who ought to be in bed will still stand at the ironing board, doing up milkcloths and bath towels that would be quite as clean and comfortable without ironing. . . .

Nonetheless, Emma praised the typical mountain woman who spent endless hours making quilts, seeking extra family money by selling her handiwork, sometimes to entrepreneurs who would pay "one-

third of what a man would have earned for a task requiring the same time and skill." At dinnertime, she wrote, the typical mountain woman would eat the least-desirable portion of a chicken "not because nobody else would eat this piece so much as because she could not bear that anyone else should have to."

Emma Bell Miles's writings also touched on topics such as peace, the environment, and animal rights. For example, her character the Gray Pigeon questioned humankind's priorities when he saw a bronze cannon from the Spanish-American War:

> What a strange thing to see. . . . Yonder is a group of buildings representing some of the greatest activities of civilization—the library, three churches in view, and the *Times* building, not to speak of the shops; and in the foreground, half hid among the greenery, this archaic survival of the age of brute force.

Readers found such philosophies and observations exciting, and Emma's career was flourishing when she learned she was pregnant for the sixth time. Too ill to write, she set aside her newfound career, which had lasted a little more than two months. Then she miscarried.

Still weakened by the ill-fated pregnancy, Emma was forbidden by her possessive husband to return to writing. In February 1915, she entered the Pine Breeze Sanitorium, suffering from tuberculosis. She stayed for a year before Frank Miles took her home, where her improved condition deteriorated rapidly in their drafty shack. Emma had considered leaving Miles and had even made plans to divorce him, but he charmed her once again. Emma relented, but she recorded this lament: "All is lost now; my hope, my health, all sacrificed to a man's pleasure. . . . God deliver my daughters from such love as has ruined me. Since I left town about a month ago I have been too ill to earn a cent."

During the last four years of her life, Emma contributed occasional poems to the *News*. Aware of her destitute existence, newspaper officials often sent her various food items along with advances on her writings. She continued to make money for her family by painting watercolors and postcards, which she sold to the summer people living on Walden's Ridge, and offering booklets of her poetry. Maintaining her kinship with nature, Emma Bell Miles wrote her last book, *Our Southern Birds,* before her death in March 1919. She was thirty-nine.

152
Samuel Jones

Health Seekers and the Mineral Springs Resort

In 1819 along the Upper Cumberland Plateau, settler Samuel Jones observed a deer drinking from a particular spring rather than from the creek that ran by it. Believing this place special, he decided to move his family there—to the place called "the little red ."

Jones did not have to travel farther than an adjacent county to get his family. He purchased the springs (popularly known as Jones Springs for some time thereafter) and at least 350 acres that lay around it. More than twenty years later, another man noticed something special about "the little red." Legend has it that in the 1840s a settler by the name of Shepherd Kirby visited the springs and splashed some water on his ailing eye. He later claimed that the water cured it. When the news spread, health seekers flocked to Red Boiling Springs with its bountiful mineral-water springs and salt licks. In a later resort boom on the Plateau, townspeople would call their Macon County haven "the South's Greatest Health Resort."

Other than the tale of his healed eye, little is known of Kirby. But much is known about this small Middle Tennessee town, which, after 1900, hosted so many summertime vacationers from all parts of Tennessee and Kentucky that a hotel-building boom could not keep pace. At its resort peak in the 1920s and 1930s, Red Boiling Springs boasted nine downtown hotels, lining the banks of Salt Lick Creek where pioneer Samuel Jones had seen the deer drinking.

Jones never knew about health seekers and health resorts. These were developments that came after his death in 1842. In his will, Jones left "the little red" to his youngest son, Jesse, and a life estate to his widow, Elizabeth. For Jesse, however, the inheritance had one stipulation: that he take care of his mother for the rest of her life.

Two years later, Jesse and Elizabeth sold the sulphur springs and surrounding land (which also included several fresh-water springs) to Gainesboro businessman Samuel E. Hare. Realizing the potential of the sulphur springs, Hare began to sell parcels to investors, and in 1849, helped build the first inn, or "house of entertainment." Rows of cabins also began to appear. As a resort, Red Boiling Springs started as the "poor relation"

of other Tennessee resorts. Its first boom days were in the 1850s, only to be interrupted by the Civil War.

While many people were investing in Red Boiling Springs, a legal problem was brewing. It seems the land's previous owner, Jesse Jones, was not taking care of his mother. Jesse, in fact, had abandoned her altogether and left Macon County. On her behalf, other family members filed a series of lawsuits to retrieve the property, arguing that the terms of Samuel Jones's will had been broken. The courts finally agreed with them in 1871, long after the widow Jones's death. However, the late Samuel Jones had had the last word about "the little red," and all land reverted to the original family, who began reselling it (most likely back to those who had parcels repossessed).

Because Red Boiling Springs was the health spa farthest from any train station, vacationers visiting during the late nineteenth century first had to endure a day-long coach ride from the depot (either Carthage or Huntsville). When paved roads came to the Cumberland Plateau in the twentieth century, the springs became far more accessible. Investors replaced the one or two rows of log cabins with an array of two-story hotels, each with a long veranda upstairs and down, as well as bath-houses and cafés. Although vacationing at most mineral-springs resorts declined after 1900, Red Boiling Springs remained an attraction for another three decades.

There were different-colored waters which supposedly had various curative effects upon the human body. The colors assigned to these waters were designated either by the color of its precipitate or by the color changes of silver coins tossed in the water. Brochures in the 1920s proclaimed:

The red is recommended for treatment of Bright's disease, diabetes, hemorrhages, cystitis, and rheumatism.

The BLACK water is an alternative and laxative. It is a sulphur-magnesia water of desired medicinal properties. The combination of magnesia with hydrogen sulphide present is recommended for treatment of gallstones, catarrhal conditions of the gall bladders, many forms of stomach trouble and constipation.

Also included was the "double and twist" water, so packed with minerals that it made a fine bath but was unsafe to drink.

Vacationers could drink the waters, bathe in the waters, receive "body shampoos" using the waters, or merely enjoy any one of a selection of massages. By day, guests rested, received treatments, or exercised; by night, they took part in festivities which included dining, dancing, bowling, canoeing, gambling, and consuming bootleg liquor. One resident claimed that alcohol was so accessible during Prohibition that all a person had to do was give a whistle.

Such amusements became nearly as important to visitors as the sulphur waters. An important part of the entertainment was the music provided by bands and orchestras at local pavilions for dancing or (as in the case of the Palace Hotel) provided by a house band, which added flavorful sounds to the main meals. If visitors did not want to retire early, Red Boiling Springs was more than accommodating with cafés that often stayed open all night.

Home cooking was perhaps one of the biggest draws in town. Every hotel specialized in southern fried chicken, biscuits, gravy, garden vegetables, and the like, and offered three family meals daily as part of the room price. Two of the hotels had their own gardens, and one, the Cloyd, had its own hogs in the back to consume table scraps or provide an occasional cured ham.

If there were no available rooms in town, which was often the case in the 1920s and 1930s, few guests worried about the inconvenience. One hotel operator rented the same room to thirteen people, who in turn used it only as a dressing room and slept in their cars. Extra cots also were generally available in a hotel corridor. When daybreak came, many guests simply strolled in their robes to the nearest bath-house.

In the summer of 1936, more than fourteen thousand people checked into Red Boiling Springs' hotels. Most of the visitors were of the middle-class: doctors, lawyers, and owners of small-town businesses in the region. Those vacationers who could afford it tended to congregate at the Palace, the largest hotel, which "dominated" the business district. So overcrowded was the Palace that its owners built the adjacent Farmers' Hotel for the overflow. When the hotels were full, town residents often made extra money by renting rooms in their homes.

Outlasting the Great Depression, Red Boiling Springs prospered until after the 1930s, when improved roads eventually took the touring public to other points of interest in the nation. But the Springs managed to revive itself after a major flood in 1969, offering several large hotels and guest houses for the tourists who continued to come.

153
Robert Z. Taylor
A Battleground at Reelfoot Lake

In 1908, the Reelfoot Lake Night Riders hanged Quentin Rankin and shot into the night hoping to hit his business partner, Robert Z. Taylor. But Rankin's death, and the disappearance of Taylor, essentially killed the Night Riders. Front-page headlines called for justice. The whole nation now knew about the violence that had torn apart upper West Tennessee. The fight was centered at Reelfoot Lake, the state's largest natural body of water, which straddles Obion and Lake counties.

Journalists nationwide hastened to the scene to write their stories and tell about the two men, both of whom were reported dead. Rankin, thirty-nine years old, was one of Tennessee's "most promising" attorneys. A graduate of Vanderbilt University, he once readied a company of men for duty in the Spanish-American War, although the troops were never needed in action. He enjoyed statewide popularity, as did his good friend Taylor, who was sixty-three. Called "Colonel," Taylor was remembered as a teenaged Confederate soldier in the cavalry of General Nathan Bedford Forrest. A Trenton attorney who had spent his life in adjacent Gibson County, Taylor became a West Tennessee leader in the Democratic Party after the Civil War, dabbled in local politics, and helped to build the Gibson County Courthouse. Both men were leading officials of the West Tennessee Land Company.

The violence began as a dispute over fishing and hunting rights. In order to support their families, many area homesteaders depended upon the fish and game they were able to catch at Reelfoot. This dependence on the lake had existed since its formation during the New Madrid earthquake of 1812, at which time the Mississippi River flowed backwards and filled nearly thirty thousand sunken acres in the northwest corner of the state. Hunters, fishermen, and trappers then came in great numbers (among them David Crockett) to settle the area. Eventually, they "came to look upon the lake as their rightful domain . . . and the feeling was passed on to succeeding generations."

But at the turn of the twentieth century, land speculators (especially those in the West Tennessee Land Company) began to acquire property at the lake and deprive the squatters and others of their freedom to hunt and fish. The problem came to a head after a 1908 local court ruling upheld the developers' exclusive ownership and fishing monopoly.

Unable to get help either from petitioning the land company or from the courts, local men formed the Night Riders. Among their number were a few fishermen whose livelihood was at stake and others sympathetic to them, including an occasional law officer. In order to dissuade future land buyers, the Riders began a scare campaign. They resorted to seven months of intimidation which evolved into arson, whippings, and killings, actually extending across the Kentucky border. One of their first acts of violence was to burn the fishing docks of J. C. Burdick, a wholesaler who profited at their expense from his contract with the land company. Burdick paid the company an annual fee to control the fishing and passed along that fee to the fishermen already burdened with low prices for their catch.

Attorneys Rankin and Taylor came to the area to finalize the purchase of even more land, "preliminary to draining Reelfoot into the Mississippi." The appearance of the two on the scene was a display of courage, because other company officials were too frightened to come.

In the middle of the night on December 19, 1908, the Night Riders roused each man from his bed at Ward's Hotel, a sportsman's lodge at Walnut Log, very near the waters of Reelfoot. The Riders walked Rankin and Taylor toward the swamps a quarter-mile away and demanded that they reopen the lake to free public fishing.

"I couldn't possibly do that," Rankin insisted.

"Get the rope," one of the Night Riders ordered.

As the noose was being fitted around Rankin's neck, one of the Riders suggested he be given time to pray. "Gentlemen," Rankin declared, "I've already attended to that." Hoisted for the hanging, Rankin struggled: "Gentlemen, don't do that; you're killing me!"

"Damn you," one of the Riders shouted. "That's what we intended to do."

The night got out of hand. The Riders continued to hoist Rankin up and down and tried to get him to relent. One or more of them finally took aim and shot him. Whether or not murder was intended, Rankin was dead. Taylor bolted for freedom by jumping into a nearby slough and swimming underwater for his life. Bullets flew again. Taylor disappeared.

When news spread the next day that Taylor, too, was dead, more than one hundred wreaths decorated his home in Trenton. Meanwhile, the leader of the Night Riders told his men to go home and to burn their disguises.

Thirty hours later, a stranger staggered from the swamp to the door of a farmer. His name, he said in a weak voice, was Robert Z. Taylor. When he told his story to the governor and to the press, a public outcry ensued, prompting Governor Malcolm Patterson to lead the investigation into Rankin's murder and to interrogate suspects personally.

The governor was not new to the problems of Reelfoot Lake. West Tennesseans had sent him numerous appeals to put a stop to the terrorism. Hoping for a politically safe solution to the fishing issue, Patterson had considered retrieving the land for the state of Tennessee. But the violence became widespread, and law officers were scared away. With Rankin's death, there was no alternative but to order the state militia into the area and to begin a massive search. During a sweep of houses, eighty citizens were arrested and questioned. Devoting himself to this cause now gave Patterson's reelection campaign a boost; he was later victorious at the polls.

Several Night Riders were arrested and held for a lengthy trial. Six were convicted of first-degree murder and sentenced to hang. Two more were found guilty of second-degree murder and sentenced to twenty years. The Tennessee Supreme Court overturned the case a year later and remanded it for a new trial. The case was delayed indefinitely and eventually thrown out. The defendants were released from jail.

Robert Z. Taylor, reputed to be one of the best land attorneys in the state, returned to Trenton after the events of Reelfoot and continued his law practice until his death in 1922 at the age of seventy-six.

The state legislature soon made Reelfoot Lake a public domain "to the low water mark." More than a decade later in 1925, the state of Tennessee, upon the urging of Governor Austin Peay, purchased the surrounding land and created the Reelfoot Lake State Fish and Game Preserve, assuring six thousand acres as protected public lands. This was one of the first attempts by the state to set apart its natural resources for the public. In 1937, the Tennessee Department of Conservation created a state-park division; and, in 1956, Reelfoot Lake State Park came into existence.

154
Carroll Gideon Bull

A Country Scientist:
His Cure for Tomorrow's Wars

In 1901, after spending the day behind the family's old plow mule, twenty-year-old Carroll Gideon Bull and his brother, Jacob, stopped plowing and began to walk toward the shade of the nearby trees. The two lived on their parents' Jefferson County farm located at Dumplin. During the break, Gideon initiated a major life change. He had decided to follow his sister's repeated advice to advance his education and make something of himself. Asking Jacob to return the mule to the barn, Gideon walked to the house and prepared to leave home.

When he enrolled at nearby Carson-Newman College in Jefferson City, Gideon Bull took his first step in a career that would make American medical history—a history that would unfold during World War I and save the lives of countless soldiers on European battlefields. Bull would discover the toxin for gas gangrene, one of the greatest horrors on the Western Front, and then create a cure with its antitoxin. He would become, in fact, the first American to discover an antitoxin of any kind.

Behind these discoveries was knowledge that Bull had gleaned from his tireless climb up a varied educational ladder, beginning in Tennessee. He studied at such places as Nashville's George Peabody College and Lincoln Memorial University's Medical Department in Knoxville, where he was a professor and resident pathologist until 1912. According to a later medical journal, Bull "paid his own way by doing odd jobs—he sold books, collected laundry, made fires, waited on table[s], worked as a carpenter—and still found time in between to play on the baseball team" during his college studies. He also attended the University of Chicago and Harvard University. In 1913, Bull accepted a position with the Rockefeller Institute for Medical Research in New York City to concentrate on the study of gas gangrene.

He knew that gas gangrene was an infection which spread from soil bacteria into the wounds of soldiers and released a deadly gas that bubbled under the skin, often causing the loss of a limb, if not a life. Because the European front involved trench warfare, soldiers sat, slept, and fought in dirt or mud throughout their days and nights. Before Bull's historic breakthrough in 1917, amputations were commonplace. His new antitoxin increased victims' survival chances; and, if given early, it eliminated the need for amputation.

When Bull reported his findings, a group of scientific directors at the Rockefeller Institute faced a dilemma: whether or not to publish Bull's discoveries or classify them as a military secret, thereby preventing details of the antitoxin from reaching enemy hands. The question came before the United States secretary of war.

Dr. William H. Welch, liaison officer between the nation's scientists and the United States Army, was pleased with the secretary's immediate decision. Welch later wrote: "The Secretary took at once the humane view and said we should not consider for a moment holding back such a life-saving discovery on the ground that the enemy could also make use of it." Welch, who had encouraged Bull's research to find a treatment, had himself laid the groundwork for the breakthrough by isolating the infection's causative agent, which was known as *bacillus welchii*. In his own laboratory experiments, Bull was able to isolate the poisons that the bacteria produced.

Immediately commissioned a major in the Army Medical Corps, Bull was sent to Europe to demonstrate the antitoxin before the world's leading scientists and doctors. He also spent time on the British front at Flanders, France. Armed with his discovery, Bull and other Allied doctors began to save limbs and lives. In 1919, France awarded Bull the *Silver Medaille de Reconnaissance Francaise* for his lifesaving discoveries.

In addition to solving the mystery of the disease, Bull's work laid the foundation for modern immunological theory and practice. He came to be recognized as one of the world's leading immunologists.

After the war, Bull helped develop the curriculum for a department of immunology at the Johns Hopkins Medical School in Baltimore and its new School of Hygiene and Public Health. In 1922, he was named the "first professor in America to head his own separate department of immunology," serving in that position until his death in 1931 at the age of fifty-one.

Section Four
The Twentieth Century

Historical Background
The Twentieth Century

During the harrowing time from the Reconstruction period that followed the drums of war at home to the specter of war abroad in 1914, Tennessee grew apart from the more urban and industrial sections of the nation. After World War I, while other regions were rapidly industrializing, small-scale farming and traditional rural folkways continued to dominate the state.

In the first two decades of the twentieth century, issues such as liquor prohibition and women's suffrage pitted the traditional values of the countryside against the city-centered forces of modernism. Tennessee's position as a cultural battleground became evident when the state enacted Prohibition years before the nation. In 1920, when Governor Albert H. Roberts called a special legislative session to consider the constitutional amendment giving women the right to vote, national supporters on both sides of the issue converged on Nashville to lobby the General Assembly. Tennessee became the deciding thirty-sixth state to ratify the Nineteenth Amendment—making women's voting rights the law of the land. Women promptly made their presence felt in the 1920 presidential election by swinging Tennessee to Warren Harding, marking the first time the state had voted for a Republican presidential candidate since 1868.

The famous 1925 Scopes trial at Dayton brought Tennessee center stage on a national issue. Although the case involved the teaching of Darwin's theory of evolution in the schools (illegal under a new Tennessee law), in a larger sense the state and the rural South were on trial. Some northern writers, like H. L. Mencken, accused Tennesseans of wearing blinders to the progress of modern science. But the trial revealed the divided nature of America itself in the young twentieth century. Of all the nationally publicized events of the Roaring Twenties, the circus-like Scopes trial symbolized the clash of the nation's traditional religious values versus newer intellectual values. Although the country had become involved in these heated exchanges, the Scopes trial began as a scheme by a few Dayton businessmen, who recognized that agriculture could no longer serve as the foundation for the state's growth. Encouraging such a trial was their way of developing publicity, and, in turn, tourism for the town.

The average Tennessee farmer had already realized what these Dayton boosters knew. As in other states, North and South, many Tennessee families left farms that would no longer support them and sought work in the cities. As a consequence, Memphis, Chattanooga, Knoxville, and the Tri-Cities of Bristol, Kingsport, and Johnson City all experienced population surges and a new cultural mix. The Tennessee countryside had become an exporter of people to other regions and cities.

Already considered a paragon of rustic life, Tennessee became even more of an icon during the 1920s, when its music spread to the rest of the nation. The musical phenomenon called "the blues" began in the cotton fields and Delta towns like Ripley and Brownsville, as well as the lower Mississippi Delta. Railroads which linked most Delta towns carried former sharecroppers into the cities, especially into Memphis where the Beale Street clubs offered a stylish setting for the music patronized by middle-class black society. Memphis, in turn, became a pipeline for this new music genre to cities as distant as Chicago and New York, where blues personalities from Tennessee found national acclaim. The state's black population, in general, decreased after 1920, as farm prospects worsened, driving many ex-tenants out of the region altogether.

Bluegrass and old-time country music (much of it steeped in religion) also had their origins in rural communities, in this case the mountains of East Tennessee. The radio, more than any population movement, developed a wide audience for country music. Rural musicians from throughout Tennessee became instant celebrities on the airwaves of Nashville's WSM radio and its hit show, the *Grand Ole Opry*. This radio program helped Americans felt connected to a tradition of values and cultural folksiness that often seemed missing in urban life.

Ironically, the Great Depression of the 1930s forced many city dwellers to return to the farms to survive. Tennessee was still overwhelmingly a state of small farmers, but signs of a major change were at hand. The creation in 1933 of the Tennessee Valley Authority (TVA) made life on the farm and elsewhere a little easier by providing electricity to rural households. By building power-generating dams, TVA laid the groundwork for industrial growth. Its early dam projects provided nonfarm employment and supplied cheap power to attract new industries.

Like the rest of the nation, Tennessee did not snap out of the Great Depression until World War II, which brought the most far-reaching social changes. The military struggle from 1941 to 1945 had a decisive impact, with 308,000 Tennesseans serving in the Armed Forces, and hundreds of thousands more working in war-related industries or on farms. In the East Tennessee farm country of Anderson and Roane counties, a top-secret United States government operation called the "Manhattan Project" was born in 1942. Along with the Manhattan Project, the military created Oak Ridge, which grew into Tennessee's fifth-largest city in just three years and at a cost nearing one hundred million dollars. Unknown to those involved, the secret work being done at Oak Ridge helped to end the war entirely. The truth became known in August 1945 when the United States dropped two atomic bombs on Japan and forced an unconditional surrender.

Among other things, World War II transformed traditional gender roles. Women entered the work force (33 percent of the work force was female by war's end), earned wages, and achieved a measure of economic independence. The war afforded the first opportunity for thousands of ordinary Tennesseans to see other parts of the world, to collect a regular paycheck, and to save some money. These savings provided seed money for many to make a fresh start after the war. Few people were willing to go back to the old mule-powered, back-breaking regime of farm labor. While some Tennesseans did return to farms, most migrated to the cities. Once the traditional farm economy began to disintegrate, the changeover was rapid. One measure of this changeover was the near-total replacement of mules by tractors in a few short years after the war.

Between 1955 and 1965, more industry located in Tennessee than in any other state. By 1960, the census found that for the first time more Tennesseans dwelled in towns and cities than on farms. By 1963, Tennessee had become the sixteenth-largest industrial state in the nation, an amazing transformation for a state which not so long before had been predominantly agricultural. This basic shift in the way people made a living and where they lived, after long decades of stable continuity, altered Tennessee and ushered it into the late twentieth century.

One direct outcome of military service and the urbanization that World War II brought was a restlessness on the part of black Tennesseans who had served during the war and had grown less tolerant of Jim Crow discrimination back home. They were more inclined to defend themselves and their communities against the lynchings and attacks that had taken place in the past. Moreover, the growing density of blacks in the cities generated the numbers and strength necessary for collective action. A preview of the civil rights struggle to come occurred in Columbia in 1946 when black ex-servicemen confronted local whites and state troopers who tried to enforce the old racial norms. The legal aftermath of this showdown, called the Columbia "riot" (which actually stopped short of being a riot), constituted an important step in building a commitment from the federal government to protect all southerners from racial violence.

Returning GIs also helped change the old political order in Tennessee. In the 1946 "Battle of Athens," reform-minded veterans challenged the entrenched McMinn County political machine tied loosely to the statewide power of Memphis's Edward H. Crump. By showing that the machine system could be defeated at the ballot box, victorious GIs and the Battle of Athens proved to be the opening gun of statewide political reform. In 1948, reform candidates from within Crump's own Democrat Party, among them Estes Kefauver and Gordon Browning, rode the tide of antiboss sentiment to victory and spelled the end of Crump's control over Tennessee. With the repeal of the voters' poll tax in 1953, the power of local machines to control elections was finally curtailed.

At the midway point of the twentieth century, Tennessee again occupied the national spotlight, as it had in the 1920s with ratification of the Nineteenth Amendment and with the Scopes trial, in the 1930s with the creation of TVA, and in the 1940s with the Manhattan Project. This time, the focus was on the Civil Rights movement among black Americans. Four years before the United States Supreme Court's landmark *Brown v. Board of Education* decision in 1954, black parents in Clinton, Tennessee, filed a lawsuit seeking to desegregate local schools. The courageous efforts of these East Tennessee parents and their children to break the color barrier found support from a new generation of Tennessee politicians—they were moderate on the race question and avoided the hardline segregationist tactics adopted in other states.

Some of these politicians became key players in Congress and contenders for national office, helping return Tennessee to political center stage in the nation.

In 1960, black students in Nashville began sit-in demonstrations at downtown lunch counters in a bid to break down another form of racial discrimination. These young men and women from local black colleges were highly disciplined, yet dogged in their confrontation of the Jim Crow system in restaurants, hotels, and bus terminals. Their nonviolent tactics were widely admired and copied, and several of these student activists went on to become national leaders in the Civil Rights movement. By the 1960s, the struggle broadened to include West Tennessee tenant farmers demanding the right to vote and Memphis sanitation workers striking for comparable pay and an end to workplace discrimination. In support of the sanitation workers' cause, the Reverend Martin Luther King Jr., the most respected Civil Rights leader, came to Memphis. Here, on the balcony of the Lorraine Motel, King was shot to death by an assassin on April 4, 1968. But the legacy of his cause for nonviolence lived after him.

Communities statewide continued to emphasize hard work and self-reliance, tempered by a commitment to family, neighbors, and church. Leaders and innovators in chosen fields drew strength from having been nurtured in such stable, deeply rooted communities. A stream of diverse individuals who shared a common Tennessee heritage reached national heights in business, entertainment, politics, science, and the arts. Among them were the founder of Federal Express; the founder of Piggly Wiggly grocery stores; the founder of Holiday Inn; a film director who helped shape the motion-picture industry during Hollywood's "golden age"; a columnist who helped mold the American sports industry's own golden age; those who influenced one of the most important American literary movements in the twentieth century; the first American woman to win three gold medals in the Olympics; and a vice president of the United States.

Tennessee's economic success and population growth during the 1970s and 1980s were due in part to its appealing blend of the traditional and the high tech. Following a period of rapid industrial growth, Tennessee became home to a number of advanced, science-based companies. Nissan Motor Corporation in 1980 built the world's largest truck-assembly plant near Smyrna, starting a trend that made Tennessee one of the chief markets for direct foreign investment (by 1994, Tennessee had garnered six billion dollars' worth of Japanese investment alone). The state emerged as a center of health care and medical research in the South and augmented its strong agribusiness and manufacturing base with a booming tourism industry, drawing people from around the world. The diversity of Tennessee's economy reduced its vulnerability to recession, and the state enjoyed the lowest unemployment and highest per capita income in its history.

Side by side with state-of-the-art manufacturing and innovative service facilities was the Tennessee landscape, still predominately rural and still majestic. The beauty that had lured the pioneers of the frontier continued to entice people. And a quality once derided as a liability by critics such as Mencken (the persistence of old-fashioned, rural folkways in Tennessee) had become a great asset. Tennessee's tradition of tightly knit communities and the rich physical legacy of its past became the state's greatest attraction in the latter twentieth century. A variety of people helped Tennessee and the nation to forge ahead with a new array of talents, accomplishments, a sense of duty and purpose, and often soul-searching debates on the century's major national issues. Here, then, are some of their stories.

Historical background essay written in collaboration with Dr. Wayne Moore, archivist, Tennessee State Library and Archives.

155
Alvin York

*From Turkey-Shoot Marksman
to World War I's Most Decorated Soldier*

Alvin C. York upon his return from Europe, 1919.

Through the love of a woman, Alvin York learned there was more to life than cards, whiskey, and firearms.

The tall farm boy from Pall Mall, whom Fentress Countians had nicknamed "the Big-Un," came from a long line of mountain dwellers who depended on their weapons for survival. The son of a blacksmith, York was descended from Conrad (nicknamed "Coonrod") Pile, an early settler who had discovered and named the Valley of the Three Forks of the Wolf and other regional spots. Another ancestor, Preston Brooks, had fought for the Union in the Civil War and had battled afterwards with Southern terrorist Tinker Dave Beaty and his gang. Brooks met a violent death at their hands.

For York, gun play was both a source of food and daily recreation. At Cumberland Plateau turkey shoots, marksmen shot the heads off turkeys when the birds peeked from behind trees. Riflemen also shot for "beeves"—a kind of wager in which five shooters would pool their resources to purchase a steer and then shoot targets for the privilege of claiming the best cuts. On occasion, York had all five best shots, walking away with the entire steer on the hoof. People around Pall Mall claimed that York could "put ten rifle bullets into a space no larger than a thumbnail."

Trips to the nearest saloon became another favorite pastime. York and his friends loved to frequent "blind tiger" saloons, which straddled the state line between Kentucky and Tennessee. Drinkers from Tennessee, a dry state, would drink on the Kentucky side. By doing so, they could claim that they had not broken Tennessee law. Drinkers from equally dry Kentucky likewise drank on the Tennessee side. But York's activities frequently meant trouble for him. When his local drunken shooting sprees resulted in arrest warrants, he took a quick escape route to Kentucky to avoid local law enforcement.

Because of his friend, Gracie Williams, Alvin York changed his life. For her, York gave up drinking forever. Through her gentle religious persuasion, he also became a Christian and renounced the vices he once so happily cultivated. While Gracie trusted her reformed beau, her parents did not. The young couple were forced to meet at a discreet forest rendezvous, while he supposedly hunted and she ostensibly fetched the cows for milking. They carved the dates of their meetings in the trees.

York's newfound religious faith changed his life permanently in many ways. Ultimately, he broke only one tenet of his religion. The denomination that York joined, the Church of Christ in Christian Union, took literally the commandment against killing. When he was drafted for World War I, York made repeated attempts to be classified as a conscientious objector. The small sect to which he belonged, however, had no written creed to present to the draft board. York searched his soul and came uneasily to the conclusion that perhaps by fighting Germans he could prevent more deaths. His decision would make him famous.

At the European battlefront with the Eighty-seventh Division on October 8, 1918, York headed out with a patrol in a critical area of the Argonne Forest.

Making its way through thick brush and along an old trench, the patrol surprised and captured a group of Germans in camp. Suddenly, York looked toward a nearby hill and noticed that German machine-gunners were aiming their weapons on his comrades. When the guns opened fire, six United States soldiers were killed and three wounded. Everyone else, including the prisoners, hit the ground.

Although pinned down, York was the only soldier with a clear view of the machine-gun nest, which happened to be forty yards away—the same firing distance that he had mastered during his hometown turkey shoots. Each time an enemy soldier popped up his head from a hiding place in an effort to spot him, York picked him off easily. With every German that fell, York yelled up the hill, "Well! Come on down!"

They did not understand his call for a surrender. Instead, they sent seven men with fixed bayonets to flush York from the bushes. He calmly drew his pistol and shot each man, the last one first so as not to "panic" the men in front into firing at him. When the seventh German fell, the bodies were said to have "formed a line down the hillside."

A previously captured German officer soon signaled for a surrender of the nearest machine-gunners, and ninety Germans loped down the hill. But York was not finished; he wanted the entire German machine-gun battalion. Positioning his surviving comrades strategically within two columns of prisoners, he set out to clear the hill of the remaining enemy. York walked at the front of the column, using his pistol to prod one German officer ahead of him, securing additional protection by positioning a German officer on either side.

At one gun entrenchment after another, York ordered enemy troops to surrender. When the entire area was cleared, York had captured 132 prisoners and destroyed 35 machine-gun nests, in addition to the 25 Germans he had previously killed.

News that one American soldier had captured an entire German machine-gun battalion was broadcast around the world, and military experts were astounded. Despite the accolades of the United States Army and testimonies of his heroism from comrades, York preferred not to discuss the details of that day, not even with his own mother. In a diary he kept during the war, York placed the credit elsewhere:

So you can see here in this case of mine where God helped me out. I had been living for God and working in church work sometime before I came to the army. I am a witness to the fact that God did help me out of that hard battle for the bushes were shot off all around me and I never got a scrach [sic].

York's heroics earned him the United States Congressional Medal of Honor as well as nearly fifty other decorations. In May 1919, he returned to the United States as the most acclaimed American soldier of World War I. After York's arrival in New York City, the New York Stock Exchange suspended business "as the members rode him upon their shoulders over the floor of the Exchange where visitors are not allowed." Later, in Washington, D.C., York was honored with a standing ovation in Congress. "The people saw in this simple, earnest mountaineer the type of American that had made America," wrote York's later biographer, Sam K. Cowan, who spent time in Tennessee interviewing the war hero.

When offers of money came pouring in, York never seriously considered taking them; he believed such rewards had "unworthy" motivations. To him, the duties of citizenship were sacred, a subject he had addressed before going to war: "Liberty and freedom and democracy are so very precious that you do not fight to win them once and stop," he had declared. "You do not do that. Liberty and freedom and democracy are prizes awarded only to those peoples who fight to win them and then keep fighting eternally to hold them!"

Since he had not fought for personal profit, York turned down, by some estimates, nearly five hundred thousand dollars in promotions, screen rights offers, and acting offers. But Tennesseans had their own welcome-home surprise. Through the *Nashville Banner,* a fund-raising campaign made a down payment on a several-hundred-acre farm and animal stock for York's homecoming. In June 1919, when he traveled from Pall Mall to Nashville to receive a medal from the state of Tennessee, York discovered that the farm was also his. His widowed mother, to whom he had assigned nearly all of his army paycheck, accompanied him on what was her first railroad ride. The trip turned out to be York's honeymoon as well. Two days earlier, the governor of Tennessee, Albert H. Roberts, had performed the hero's marriage. It was an outdoor ceremony with the folks in and around Pall Mall invited . . . to a rock ledge where York and Gracie Williams once had met in secret.

The couple settled on the farm that Tennesseans had provided for them, but times were hard, as crop prices crashed in the postwar economy. Keeping the farm proved to be a challenge, but York persevered.

He also attempted to turn his national stature to the benefit of Fentress County, raising funds for public schools, an industrial institute, and a Bible school. While he had never completed high school, York nevertheless valued education and became a leader in bringing educational opportunity to his corner of the Cumberlands. York also became the subject of Hollywood's 1941 version of his life, *Sergeant York*, starring Gary Cooper. Some of the proceeds from the film helped to fund the Alvin York Agricultural Institute in Jamestown. York remained active in community service until the day of his death in 1964. Gracie York lived another twenty years.

156
Lawrence D. Tyson

A Grieving General's Assault on the Hindenburg Line

His boat was small. The water was choppy, icy, and treacherous. The odds, according to his World War I superiors, were as bleak as the gray October sky in 1918. Hour after hour, day after day, mile after mile, a solitary figure patrolled the coastline of the North Sea. General Lawrence D. Tyson was searching for more than his son's remains; he was searching for peace of mind. He could not—and would not—go home without recovering his son's body from a downed aircraft.

Two years earlier in Knoxville, father and son had joined the war effort just months apart. General Tyson, then a prominent Knoxville attorney and a businessman, was retired from the army. His earlier military career had begun with graduation from West Point and duty in the West pursuing Apaches and their great war leader, Geronimo. He left that life to become commandant of the University of Tennessee's military science program. Tyson also engaged in politics, having risen to Speaker of the Tennessee House of Representatives. He was married to Knoxville's

Bettie McGhee, the daughter of retired railroad president Colonel Charles McClung McGhee. Despite his military retirement, Tyson reentered the service as an officer in the Spanish-American War, helping to recruit and train the Sixth United States Volunteer Infantry; he became the military governor of northern Puerto Rico for several months after that war.

With America's sudden entry into World War I, Tyson again volunteered his extensive military experience, and President Woodrow Wilson appointed him a United States Army brigadier general, the only one from Tennessee. Tyson immediately trained and commanded the Fifty-ninth Brigade, part of the soon-to-be famous Thirtieth (or "Old Hickory") Division, comprised of national guard units from Tennessee and the Carolinas and named in honor of Andrew Jackson. Many of the Old Hickory units and regiments descended from frontier militias, some dating to the Revolutionary War and also including some which fought with Jackson at the Battle of New Orleans.

General Tyson's son, McGhee Tyson, a Princeton graduate and manager of his father's Knoxville Spinning Company, was among the first to volunteer for the newly formed Navy Air Corps, becoming "Knoxville's first flying officer." He was quickly sent to England, leaving behind his wife of two months.

General Tyson's Fifty-ninth Brigade, meanwhile, was among the first group of Americans to enter wartime Belgium. The night of September 28, 1918, Tyson told his eight-thousand-man brigade of mostly Tennesseans that they were on the verge of fighting one of history's most important battles—the assault on the seemingly "impregnable" Hindenburg Line, key to Germany's defense. The battle would be fought in dense fog and under heavy rain clouds. Their entire Old Hickory Division would attack in conjunction with the Twenty-seventh Division, receiving additional help from British and the Australian units. During the fight, General Tyson received the news that his son had been shot down over the North Sea. Because of the strategic importance of the battle his division was engaged in, the grief-stricken father continued to lead his men against the Hindenburg front.

Tyson's Fifty-ninth, charging with the Sixtieth Brigade, took heavy losses while overwhelming German trenches and barbed wire and sealing a major entrance to the enemy's underground tunnel system.

Because there were also other enemy exits from the tunnel, Germans "oozed up from the ground behind them to shoot them in the back." A major Australian division, coming behind the Americans, managed to wipe out these enemy gunners in a mopping-up campaign. A Tennessee Memorial, honoring Tennesseans from the Fifty-ninth and Sixtieth Brigades who lost their lives breaking through the Hindenburg Line, was later erected in France at the main-tunnel entrance.

The battle sealed the doom of Germany, its surrender coming six weeks later. Tyson swiftly requested a leave of absence to locate his son. Although assured by others that this quest would prove futile, the general persisted. In his search, which lasted for several days, he tirelessly traveled up and down the North Sea coast in a small boat, doggedly probing the unforgiving waters. Miraculously, he found the body of his son. Then Tyson prepared for the long trip home to Knoxville where a hero's welcome awaited him. Among the 4.5 million men in the American army during the war, Tyson's Fifty-ninth Brigade received nine of the war's seventy-eight Congressional Medals of Honor, reportedly the most of any brigade in the army.

Because postwar transportation for American soldiers in Europe was delayed for months, the body of the younger Tyson would not be brought home soon. Several months later, a newly discharged soldier, James M. Meek, was finally on his way home when he noticed a flag-draped coffin being lifted aboard his train. Meek's journey ended when he reached his hometown, Knoxville; the coffin's journey ended there also, met by an honor guard, family, and friends. Meek soon discovered that he had accompanied home the body of McGhee Tyson, his best friend.

The twenty-nine-year-old Tyson's funeral was one of the more notable in Knoxville's history, attracting the governor, his entire staff, and other state officials who came to honor one of the city's leading families. The youth's parents later donated land for downtown Tyson Park in memory of their deceased son, in whose honor McGhee Tyson Airport in Knoxville is also named.

General Lawrence Tyson, who purchased the *Knoxville News-Sentinel* after returning from the war, utilized his popularity to be elected to the United States Senate in 1924. He was still a senator at the time of his own death in 1929 at the age of sixty-eight.

157
Luke Lea

Attempting to Capture the Kaiser—
And Political Power at Home

On January 5, 1919, headlights lit the entrance to a darkened chalet in Holland, and a Tennessean emerged from his car to approach a German guard. Luke Lea, who had studied German as a student in Sewanee, Tennessee, was fluent enough for the moment. He issued a command in his most guttural tones, pointed to the castle, then aimed a flashlight toward his officer's belt. The guard did not question the man's authoritative presence and agreed to escort him toward the chalet. Accompanying the stranger were seven fellow soldiers. These men were mostly Tennesseans hand-picked for this expedition; none of them had advance knowledge of their assignment or destination. Showing incredible nerve, Colonel Lea, commander of the 114th Field Artillery, recipient of a Distinguished Service medal, a former Tennessee United States senator, and founder and publisher of the *Nashville Tennessean,* was in the process of trying to abduct Germany's Kaiser Wilhelm II.

The kaiser had fled his homeland at the end of World War I and had successfully escaped every Allied attempt to take him prisoner. That the kaiser was enjoying political asylum in this fortified castle in Holland infuriated Lea, who planned to use his newspaper credentials to arrange a bogus interview with him. Once inside the castle, Lea hoped to kidnap Wilhelm and transport him to Paris for a war-crimes trial. First the kaiser would be delivered to President Woodrow Wilson, who was in peace-treaty negotiations at Versailles.

Lea knew the president well. Having previously served in the United States Senate, where he was one of the South's leading reformers (notably as a prohibitionist), Lea had been an early Wilson advocate. He supported the president's election, was a champion of Wilson's policies in the United States Congress, and served on the Senate Military Affairs Committee. When the war erupted, Lea helped organize the 114th Field Artillery.

In Holland, many reputations were at stake. Lea carefully avoided breaking any laws in his pursuit of the kaiser. He had talked his way into special leave papers allowing him unrestricted travel, and his prestige as a former United States senator secured special passports into neutral Holland. He claimed he was conducting "Journalistic Investigations."

The kaiser's host, Count Bentinck, met the Tennesseans in the chateau library. The moment proved the undoing of a Dutch interpreter whom Lea had hired for the occasion. Lea wrote later:

Our interpreter had evidently often day dreamed of rubbing elbows with royalty. When the Count entered with great gusto, the Dutch boy apparently thought his day dreams had come true all at once. He was prostrated with excitement and overcome with joy. Then he fell on the floor in a dead faint. Mr. Brown, our communication officer, at a signal from me, dragged the interpreter from the scene and took him to our cars after he had only had a whiff of near royalty.

Rising to this new challenge, Lea thought he might make an impression with his own fluent German. He requested an audience with the kaiser. Count Bentinck left the room for a few minutes and returned. Lea wrote that "his 'August Majesty' had considered our request for an audience and could not grant it unless we stated the object of our interview." Suddenly, a Dutch official from a nearby town entered the library, and the ruse began to unravel. Lea continued to speak in German, but the Dutch official interrupted him in perfect Bostonian English: "Ah, Colonel Lea, I am sure we will progress more rapidly speaking in English. I am a graduate of Harvard University."

The three of them, said Lea, "fenced in English for several minutes." He was told that unless he represented President Wilson or the Peace Commission he needed an appointment. Unwilling to lie or force his way for fear of violating international law, Lea simply repeated his wish to see Kaiser Wilhelm.

The delay worked against Lea, who realized that his host had purposely lengthened their conversation until reinforcements could arrive. Lea and his men quickly excused themselves, returned to their vehicles (which were by now surrounded), and departed gingerly through a knot of Dutch troops.

The American high command soon learned of Lea's adventure and investigated the incident. The kaiser, meanwhile, filed a complaint against Lea for making him "nervous."

Lea wrote:

I finally stated I would serve any sentence a court martial might impose for the crime of making the Kaiser "nervous," and that after the sentence was completed I would go on the Vaudeville stage at $1,000.00 a week, as the only soldier who had been proved to have made the Kaiser "nervous." . . .

Kaiser Wilhelm could not travel to France to press charges without being arrested for war crimes; Lea could not be reprimanded for more than being "amazingly indiscreet." American Commanding General John Pershing reportedly remarked of the whole affair to a fellow general: "I'd have given a year's pay to have been able to have taken Lea's trip into Holland, and to have entered the castle of Count Bentinck without invitation."

Cleared of his trespasses, Lea was soon adding to his luster. In another postwar pursuit, he volunteered to help his friend Lieutenant Colonel Theodore Roosevelt (a son of the former president) to form the American Legion. The idea took shape after the war's armistice when American officers met in Paris to discuss morale problems among the more than two million idle American soldiers awaiting transportation home. Along with establishing temporary sports leagues and other activities, Roosevelt proposed an organization of American veterans of war, and Lea helped organize the American Legion on both the national and state level upon his return to America.

After resuming his publishing duties at the *Nashville Tennessean,* which he had founded in 1907 as a prohibitionist newspaper, Lea surfaced as a major Tennessee political force throughout the 1920s. Politics came naturally to members of his family. One grandfather, East Tennessean William Cocke, had been Tennessee's first United States senator, and the other grandfather, John M. Lea, had been a Reconstruction-era judge. Despite his own love of politics, Lea turned down a 1929 appointment to the United States Senate after the death of Senator Lawrence D. Tyson. Instead, Lea chose to be a behind-the-scenes power broker: a consultant to governors Austin Peay and Henry H. Horton and a business partner to investment banker Rogers Caldwell. This latter association was Lea's undoing.

Caldwell and Lea controlled two major newspapers, the Memphis *Commercial Appeal* and the *Knoxville*

Journal, and ruled a financial empire with banks in Tennessee and surrounding states. Lea's power rivaled that of Memphis's political boss, Edward Hull "Boss" Crump, and Lea's competition with Crump became ruthless. When the Great Depression toppled the business community, Lea's fortunes sank, along with the banks in which he was a major stockholder. In 1931, the state of North Carolina responded to the failure of one of its banks by indicting bank leaders, including Lea. The resulting scandal toppled Lea from power, allowing Crump to consolidate control over a statewide political machine.

While Rogers Caldwell (considered by some people the chief schemer in the bank's business) avoided prosecution by refusing extradition, Lea voluntarily crossed state lines to confront the North Carolina courts. In 1934, his political career officially ended with a two-year imprisonment based upon accusations of bank fraud. He was paroled in 1936 and pardoned a year later. But the colorful Lea could never regain his previous stature or power. Until his death in 1945, he tried to repay personal and business debts rather than assume bankruptcy, according to his daughter Mary Louise Lea Tidwell.

The saga of Luke Lea did not end, however, because his daughter and other family members continued for decades to maintain his innocence in the bank affair. In a 1993 biography of her father, in which she tried to clear his name, Mary Louise wrote:

> While he was in prison the highly respected A.M. Pullen & Company, certified public accountants with which he had had no previous connection, made an audit of all Lea interests' transactions with the Central Bank. That audit cleared him of any wrongdoing on the charges on which he was convicted. Thereby is strengthened his often repeated assertion that his imprisonment was a miscarriage of justice instigated by his political enemies in Tennessee to strip him of his influence.

158
Harry T. Burn

Running To and Fro—A Woman's Right to Vote

In the summer of 1920, Mrs. J. L. Burn of Niota could not yet vote, but she had power over someone who could.

Her son, twenty-four-year-old Harry T. Burn, was the youngest representative in the Tennessee legislature, a body which was about to make national history. The legislature convened to consider the Nineteenth Amendment, a measure to give women the right to vote. Since thirty-five states had approved the amendment, passage in Tennessee would be the final link to guarantee women's voting rights across the nation.

Although the Tennessee State Senate had approved the measure by a huge margin five days earlier, on August 13, 1920, passage in the House was far from assured. The political climate in Tennessee was charged on both sides. Leading statewide suffragists, such as Nashville's Anne Dallas Dudley and Knoxville's Lizzie Crozier French, had worked hard in organizing their supporters, in speech making, and in lobbying their politicians. Mrs. French, a widow who was raising a young son, said: "Nobody can revere and respect people who have no power . . . and by power I do not mean force, but I mean there must be some way to compel." There were also nationally known suffrage leaders, like Henderson's Sue Shelton White, who had been willing to be arrested as part of a demonstration in Washington, D.C. When anti-suffragists argued that only those who bear arms should vote, Anne Dallas Dudley countered with the slogan "Women bear armies."

Suffragists wore a yellow rose pinned to their clothes; antisuffragists wore a red rose, and the East Tennessean Harry T. Burn wore his red rose proudly. After heated debate, Speaker of the House Seth Walker moved that the amendment be tabled, essentially burying it. Forty-eight representatives, including Burn, voted in favor of tabling. There was a tie. In view of this deadlock, Walker had no choice but to call the measure to a ratification vote. No doubt he presumed that the forty-eight representatives who had voted to table the amendment moments earlier would now vote to defeat it.

All of them did, too—until Burn's turn arrived. Reversing his earlier stand, he voted in favor of the amendment and thus assured its passage. After realizing Burn had changed his mind, Walker also changed his vote to "aye," producing a final tally of fifty in favor of and forty-six against.

Burn had been warned earlier by his McMinn County constituents that there might be a revolt if the suffrage amendment passed, and what followed in that special session of the General Assembly nearly constituted an uprising. Antisuffragist forces converged on Burn, who had to escape through an office window onto a third-floor ledge. He then made his way to the Capitol attic, where he hid until his new enemies gave up the hunt.

In the house chamber the next day, Burn dismissed charges that he had been bribed. The change of heart, he said, was his mother's telegram:

Dear son:
Hurrah, and vote for suffrage. Don't keep them in doubt. I noticed some of the speeches against. They were bitter. I have been watching to see how you voted, but have not noticed anything yet. Don't forget to be a good boy and help (Mrs. Catt) put the "Rat" in ratification.
Your mother.
(Mrs. J. L. Burn, Niota)

(Mrs. Catt was Carrie Chapman Catt, president of the National American Woman's Suffrage Association. During the legislature's special session, she gave speeches in Tennessee's major cities and then settled into Nashville's Hermitage Hotel to await the bill's outcome.)

"I know that a mother's advice is always best for her boy to follow," Burn told his colleagues, "and my mother wanted me to vote for ratification."

Harry T. Burn pleased his mother, but he did not please many others statewide. A newspaper clipping in Burn's scrapbook, believed to be an editorial from the *Chattanooga Times* or *Cleveland Herald,* noted:

Coincident with the Knoxville suffragist entertainment for Representative Burn, who made the lightning change from "anti" to "pro" in the period of five minutes, comes the news from that city that because of the lawlessness and crimes of violence in that city, the attorney-general of the criminal court has advised the people to keep firearms in their homes in readiness to "shoot and shoot to kill". . . there is no telling what the balance of us may have to do before the effect of the example of young Burn and other nullifiers runs its course.

"Young Burn" still had his supporters, and they outnumbered his detractors, but only barely. Less than three months after his controversial vote, Burn managed to retain his seat in the state house of repre-

sentatives. He defeated J. H. Jones by fewer than two hundred votes in what the *New York Times* called a harsh campaign.

When his second two-year term came to end, however, Burn left the political arena temporarily and returned to Niota to practice law. After running unsuccessfully for the governor's office in 1930, Burn again returned home. He served the state in various capacities, including fifteen years on the planning commission and as a delegate to the Tennessee Constitutional Convention. Burn moved for a while to Rockwood and became president and chairman of the board of the First National Bank of Rockwood. He lived to be eighty-one and died in 1977.

159
"Sleepy John" Estes/ Hammie Nixon

Singing the Blues:
The West Tennessee Musical Circuit

John Estes fashioned a homemade guitar in 1914 from a cigar box and a broom, then strummed the first notes of a blues career that would span sixty-three years.

Born in Ripley, John was eleven years old in 1914, the year his sharecropping parents packed up their sixteen children and crossed from Lauderdale County to neighboring Haywood County, settling in Brownsville. Shortly thereafter, John's passion for music took flight when he constructed the makeshift instrument, which he recalled years later for writers of Beale Street blues history:

I got me a broom handle, took the wire off of it, and made me a guitar out of an old cigar box. Started playing on that one finger there, I'd catch the sound from that one finger. And finally I playing. My daddy told mother, said, "That boy's going to make music. You live to see it."

She did. When his father bought him a real guitar, "Sleepy John" Estes began joining other musicians on "cotton pickings" in West Tennessee. The laborers worked the fields all day, then played their music at night. Sometimes Sleepy John's music brought him a dollar in pay and a free meal.

Next came medicine shows and, by the 1920s, Sleepy John and his friends had carved out a blues circuit in Lauderdale, Haywood, and Madison counties. Appearing constantly in Ripley, Brownsville, and Jackson, these musicians honed the skills that would take most of them to the blues capital—Memphis's famous Beale Street, the stepping stone to future recording careers that nearly all of them had. The names of other West Tennesseans on this celebrated 1920s blues circuit also became known to a nation of blues lovers: Brownsville guitarists Willie Newbern and Son Bonds; Jackson harmonica player Sonny Boy Williamson; pianist Jab Jones; Brownsville mandolin player Yank Rachel; and Ripley harmonica player Noah Lewis.

The youngest of these local musicians was eleven-year-old Hammie Nixon, a harmonica player whom Sleepy John met in 1918 at a Haywood County picnic. Hammie recalled that day in Union when their famous musical partnership began, a lifelong association punctuated by more than twenty years together as hobos:

> he had heard me playing that harmonica . . . and John said, "Come on, help me," said "We'll just rack the money." I think they was paying him about six dollars. That was big money. He asked my mother, said, "How about letting him go to town with me? I bring him back tomorrow." 'Course, John was always a big liar, you know. And he kept me about six months, all in Memphis, Arkansas and Missouri.

During their jaunts, Hammie taught his friend how to save travel expenses by hopping a freight train. Sleepy John marveled at his knack for such dangerous activity:

> He'd take my guitar and his jug, which he played the jug, too, and he'd take all that stuff and swing onto the train with one arm. I couldn't even catch it with not anything. I be holding onto that train with mouth, teeth, knee, and everything. And sometimes when I finally catch ahold and climb on, we get throwed right off.

The two got "throwed right off" so often trying to hop a freight in Bowling Green, Kentucky, that Sleepy John Estes penned a song to mark such occasions. He called it "Railroad Police Blues." Hammie, meanwhile, had wanderlust in his heart and broke away for a solo musical venture in Chicago. He, of course, hopped a freight to get there.

Despite its big-city crime and famous gangsters such as Al Capone, Chicago seemed tame to those who lived there, as Hammie Nixon would learn. Memphis, in fact, had a worse reputation, as he also would discover: "And finally someone told me, said, 'What you say you from Memphis for? Don't tell nobody you from Memphis, man, you never do no good here.'"

His earliest Chicago fans were Capone and his entire gang, who often listened to his Tennessee harmonica and vocals at various dens across the city. "And he'd [Capone] come in there and drop money on you, maybe twenty dollars at a time. As he was coming back, he liable to throw another twenty at you. Oh, he was crazy about that music."

In 1934, Hammie teamed with fellow Haywood Countian Son Bonds for three Decca recording sessions. But he soon returned to Tennessee to renew his partnership with Sleepy John Estes, who had a recording career of his own which began with Victor Records in Memphis. At that time, big music companies had enough money to make "field trips" to the South and record on site. Among the more noted Sleepy John Estes songs were "Someday Baby Blues," "I Ain't Gonna Be Worried No More," "Corinna, Corinna," "Broken-Hearted, Ragged and Dirty Too," and "Diving Duck Blues." He loved to sing about everyday people—generally the people he had known in Brownsville.

The Depression era sent both men to the streets again—as hoboes. But Hammie talked Sleepy John into a trip to Chicago, where their luck shifted into high gear with recording sessions. After their blues careers peaked in the late 1930s and early 1940s recording for Decca in New York, both men became victims of union battles in the music industry that canceled many recording sessions, and entire recording careers.

Life on the road ended in 1949 when Sleepy John Estes got married and settled in Memphis with his family; Hammie Nixon settled nearby and took jobs as a chauffeur and cook. But Sleepy John could never shake his yearning for Brownsville. Around 1951, he decided to move his family back home. Both he and Hammie carried their talents back to Brownsville and there spent the rest of their lives finding whatever work they could. Few, if any, royalties from old records were forthcoming (Hammie claimed that he never did receive a royalty check), and the men spent more than a decade barely making ends meet.

In the early 1960s, when interest in the blues and blues musicians stirred American music fans, the two finally gained widespread recognition and some measure of profit for their music. They dusted off their musical instruments and their voices for a 1964 tour of Europe, part of the American Folk Festival, followed with a tour appearance in Japan.

The last note of Sleepy John's life was played June 5, 1977, the same day he was scheduled to leave for another European tour. Hammie Nixon lived until 1984.

160
Bessie Smith

Made, Not Born—A Depression-Era
"Empress of the Blues"

Before she sang the blues, Bessie Smith lived them. By the age of nine her father was dead, and her mother, a domestic worker, was too sick to provide much financial support. As a result, Bessie and her brother Clarence sang and danced for pennies on a downtown street corner in their native Chattanooga, where Bessie was born about 1894.

They were heading home one day when, overcome by hunger, the children decided to steal some potatoes a local grocer had left in a bin outside his store. In an attempt to prevent the theft, the grocer reached out and knocked the two into the mud. Minus their potatoes and their dignity, Bessie and Clarence bolted for home. The children were greeted by a big sister, who announced that a white man was waiting to see them. Bessie assumed the visitor was a policeman who would arrest her for stealing, and she prepared to run. Instead, the visitor was an agent for Chattanooga's Ivory Theater. Having heard her win a talent contest, he hoped she would sing at his club.

Bessie agreed, then sang her nine-year-old heart out the next week, and spent the eight dollars she earned on a pair of roller skates. Although this purchase led to a roller skating championship, the extravagance sent her mother into such a tirade that Bessie ran away in tears and spent the night at the base of Lookout Mountain, hiding in a farmer's outhouse. In this manner, the career of "one of the greatest of all 'blues' singers" had begun.

Shortly afterwards, Bessie's mother died, leaving her an orphan living with an older sister. Bessie found herself at the mercy of other relatives who took her wages and occasionally whipped her. But the noted blues singer Gertrude "Ma" Rainey, while performing in Chattanooga, spotted the child wandering the streets late at night. Bessie was "nobody's child," and Ma Rainey, worried that a street child would get into trouble without guidance, decided to become her protector.

Ma Rainey, whom some music historians credit with being the first blues singer, was the star of one of the most popular traveling minstrel-tent shows, the *Rabbit Foot,* managed by her husband. The two agreed to help Bessie Smith. The child was literally kidnapped by two of the show's employees. Tossed into a sack (kicking and cursing), Bessie was taken to Ma, who was known on the road as the "Mother of the Blues." When the wagons began to roll away from Chattanooga toward Georgia, Ma Rainey declared to her new protégé: "No turning around now, Bessie Smith. . . . We'll do our talking in the morning. I'm going to teach you the blues, gal."

Bessie had heard of Ma Rainey, who had been touring the minstrel-show circuit for three years. Ma, in fact, was famous in all the towns and cities where she had toured throughout the South. Backed by a piano and full band, she delivered a powerful and glittering show, for she realized "what her audiences after a hard day's work would most need to hear would be the blues."

During the next six or seven years in the 1910s, the teenaged Bessie Smith lived along the minstrel road and learned from her mentor the "right way to sing the blues." Practicing daily with the help of the piano, Ma Rainey instructed her. Author Carman Moore described Ma's approach: "Let the instruments or the piano do what they're going to do, just as long as that beat is firm; slide that note; let that last note be full and strong, but let it also cry; let that piano work all through your melody."

At night, Bessie watched and listened as Ma, decked in showy costumes and jewelry, dazzled her audiences and regularly brought them to their feet with her booming voice. Importantly, Bessie learned that the blues without an audience was incomplete, as was a church sermon without its congregation. One later historian, Berkley Kalin, even claimed that Bessie Smith's singing seemed to "'preach' the blues" and "had the powers of an old-time revivalist."

This was an era in which many black Americans could only make good money by performing in touring medicine shows, minstrel shows, tent shows, or in vaudeville acts. Bessie sent home as much money as she could, and, at the age of nineteen, she revisited her family in Chattanooga. In time, she sought her own spotlight. Signing independently with the Theater Owner's and Booker's Association, Bessie left Ma Rainey behind and traveled another road. (Ma would spend twenty years touring the South with the minstrel shows, and she even recorded a few records.) Some black entertainers grumbled that the booking agency's initials, TOBA, stood for "Tough On Black Artists" because of the pitiful pay they received. Bessie received a mere $2.50 per week, in contrast to the $2,000-plus weekly salary she would command after making her first New York City record in 1923.

At the time of her recording deal, Bessie was performing and living in Philadelphia, Pennsylvania, where she met and married policeman Jack Gee. Once her records hit the marketplace, Bessie Smith was famous overnight. Tall, polished, and elegantly dressed, she became the undisputed "Empress of the Blues"—a musical legend.

Bessie had followed the same well-traveled road of other blues greats, a path from the South (often the rural South) into large, northern cities where even more fame and money awaited. Her popular voice sold nearly ten million records during the 1920s and made more than seven million dollars for Columbia Records with such hits as "Baby Doll," "Nobody Knows You When You're Down and Out," "There'll Be a Hot Time in the Old Town Tonight," and "Muddy Water."

As an example of her nationwide popularity, every time a Bessie Smith record hit the stores on Chicago's south side, a line formed a city block long with customers eager to buy a copy. Many of the major blues songs of the 1920s and 1930s were composed by Bessie in collaboration with fellow Chattanoogan Lovie Austin and Memphis's Alberta Hunter. (Lovie Austin became a noted pianist and band director at Paramount Records, and Alberta Hunter, who had been born on Beale Street, had her own recording and stage career.) Some of the era's greatest jazz musicians, including Louis Armstrong, accompanied Bessie in her recording sessions. She was reportedly the outstanding blues singer in the mainstream of jazz and probably influenced all that was to come.

Bessie Smith made so much money from recordings and touring that, in 1926, she could afford to move her entire family from Chattanooga to Philadelphia and to buy several homes near her own. During her glory years just before the Great Depression, she spent most of the money that she made, perhaps as much as one million dollars, often in good-hearted generosity to others, many of whom were strangers. When the Depression hit, Bessie found herself once again in poverty.

The public then rediscovered her in the same place where audiences had been introduced to her voice the first time: along the touring minstrel circuit. At the age of thirty-nine, Bessie Smith was making a comeback. But in 1937 during one of these tours, the Empress of the Blues was killed in a car accident in Mississippi. Her mentor, Ma Rainey, who, at fifty-one, was already retired from the business, died two years later in her native Georgia.

161
Edward Hull "Boss" Crump
The Power of a Political Machine

Smiling broadly as the photographers' bulbs popped around him, Edward Hull Crump emerged from a Memphis saloon in 1908 with the two things he had gone after: a covey of gamblers and free publicity. A man who loved theatrics and was determined to build a political arena for himself in Memphis, Crump staged these sudden raids with care. The raids were a fitting opening act for the long and colorful political career of a man who created one of the most extensive political machines in Tennessee and who would become one of the nation's most powerful political bosses.

Crump, a native Mississippian, had joined the ranks of respectable Memphis society in 1902 by marrying socially prominent Bessie Byrd McLean. He made his first entrance into local politics that same year when he became a ward representative for the Democratic Party. While Crump was primarily interested in using his new political connections to benefit his carriage and harness business, he soon realized he had a flair for politics and an appealing message for a city riddled with corruption and criminal infiltration.

He was elected to the Memphis City Council in 1905 as a reform candidate. Intent on cleaning up the city

Edward Hull "Boss" Crump became a household name
in Tennessee politics.

erage by launching a bid for mayor in 1909—and won. While creating some reform measures, he also wanted to keep the saloon keepers happy. As a result, liquor and gambling continued to flourish in Memphis saloons. Bar owners, in turn, helped finance Crump's political machine and organized voters with meetings at their saloons. The meetings were run by ward captains who handed out literature and built the nucleus of the vast Crump political network.

Ruling Memphis with a fearless and a feisty nature, Boss Crump did whatever was needed, inside or outside of the law, to maintain control of the city. Many historians admitted that he established an efficiency in city government, bringing order out of chaos. For instance, he improved the city's health system and traffic safety, brought down fire insurance rates and crime rates. Memphians celebrated the man every year with "Crump Day" at the local fairgrounds, an extravaganza financed by Crump himself.

Critics accused him of ballot stealing and false voter registrations. Citizens complained that they were not able to vote freely and without fear, nor were they able to select their candidates for office. Public officials who refused to work within the Crump machine were either fired or driven out of office. While Crump decided which careers to help and which ones to destroy, his influence gradually spread beyond Shelby County. By keeping United States Senator Kenneth D. McKellar in office for thirty-six years, Crump exerted force over federal patronage jobs—thus entrenching his political machine across the state.

Crump was easily reelected mayor in 1911, thanks in large part to his popularity among black voters who accepted his candidates. Crump undeniably improved life for many Memphis blacks, but many detractors suggested that Crump's affection for black citizens was a ruse; once he got their votes, his compassion ebbed. Others thought he did care, but in a paternalistic manner reminiscent of the Old South; in their view, Crump saw blacks as unequal and in need of fatherly care.

Crump's formula for creating support at the grassroots level was simple: pay the poll tax (generally two dollars) for tens of thousands of the poorer voters, many of whom were black, and they would vote for Crump candidates. Outside of Memphis, the turnout of voters was small because poor citizens unable to pay the tax stayed away from the polls. In

and its government, he fumed during a 1908 council meeting when he heard the mayor and two other city council members insist that gambling did not exist in Memphis. Crump, who knew better, decided to prove them wrong.

First, he sought out eighteen of his boyhood friends from Holly Springs, Mississippi, and had them deputized by a cooperative justice of the peace. Then he tipped off the press so that the media would be handy when the action began. Leading his self-appointed posse, Crump descended on three black-owned saloons where dozens of men and women were shooting craps. Crump's men began making arrests, and, according to newspaper accounts of the day, for two hours the paddy wagons rolled into the police station carrying load after load of gamblers. Crump was on hand to greet them with his engaging grin.

Such grandstanding earned considerable ink in Memphis area newspapers. Crump exploited the cov-

his prime, Crump could deliver a bloc of sixty thousand Memphis votes to the candidate of his choice. That number was massive in a statewide election that generally had no more than two hundred thousand voters. As a result, Crump often controlled who was governor of Tennessee.

Crump's exploitation of the black vote can best be illustrated by his saturation of the black community in 1914 with the name of a candidate for sheriff. Through a legal technicality, John Riechman's name had been omitted from the ballot. Crump promptly flooded Beale Street with workers campaigning with blackboards and chalk, banners and trucks bearing signs, all intent on teaching potential voters how to spell the tricky name for a write-in campaign. Memphis newspapers decried the tactic, but Riechman was elected by a large majority.

Crump seemed invincible. When the state legislature outlawed open saloons (because they defied existing prohibition laws), he thumbed his nose at the law. Memphis had not voted for the measure, he argued, and would not abide by it. A lower court in 1915 ordered Crump to face ouster charges for this bit of insubordination, an order he fought before the Tennessee Supreme Court. Yet, he continued to enjoy enormous popularity in Memphis and was reelected mayor in 1915. When the state supreme court ruled against him, Crump realized his best course of action was to resign, but only after picking his successor.

Later that year, Crump began his political comeback by making a successful bid for county trustee. He also widened his business interests, adding a soft-drink bottling plant in New York state and the E. H. Crump Company, which became one of the South's largest insurance-writing firms.

One key to the insurance company's growth was Crump's penchant for political maneuvering. When, for example, a Michigan merchant tried to open a jewelry store in Memphis, the city inspector announced that the building did not meet codes and a portion would have to be rebuilt. The merchant's contractor informed him the problem was political, not structural. If the merchant would purchase his insurance from E. H. Crump Company, the structural problems would disappear. The merchant did. . . and the problems did.

A legacy of nineteenth-century yellow fever epidemics (caused by the city's filth and decay) had inspired in Memphis a strong tradition of public sanitation and beautification. Believing that "good housekeeping" was good politics, Crump also conjured up a city-beautiful campaign involving women across Memphis who policed every street, alley, building, and yard looking for violators of Crump's definition of beauty. In or out of the mayor's chair, Crump kept his power base. In 1927 (a year when he was not mayor), Crump's chauffeur toured him once a week along city streets while a secretary took notes on Crump's list of eyesores. Since newly elected Mayor Watkins Overton owed his election to the Boss, he made a visit to Crump's insurance office for instructions on city business; he walked away with a list of physical blemishes as top priority. In return for Crump's obsessive crusade, the city annually won an award as "Cleanest Town in Tennessee," and the Boss annually proved who really ruled every inch of Memphis. He was its political power broker for nearly a half a century.

Crump's years in the political wilderness did not diminish his role as a kingpin of politics. Ironically, his own Democratic Party helped in ways it had not intended. In 1930, thanks to ineptitude from party rivals who caused a scandal in the administration of their own governor, Henry Horton, Crump was able to grab the reins of the party's power. He also was elected to the United States House of Representatives.

With his political reputation again on the rise, Crump took aim at Memphis utility companies, which he blamed for his ouster as mayor in 1916. He gained his revenge as a congressman by helping to create the Tennessee Valley Authority (TVA), which would drive private power companies from the city. On November 6, 1934, Crump purchased a huge advertisement in the Memphis *Commercial Appeal* asking voters to approve a nine-million-dollar bond issue to obtain a lighting plant. He admitted that "when the TVA wires come in, loaded with electricity, there should be an all-day celebration and rejoicing, a thrill I have been waiting for."

Memphis voters did not disappoint the Boss. They voted a resounding seventeen to one in favor of the bond issue, ridding the city of private utility companies. To celebrate, Crump reacted in typical grand style. He "arranged" the name change of a street running in front of his investment-banking building. Memphians frequently talked about the origin of "November 6th Street."

Boss Crump's power continued for years, but he was finally toppled by veterans returning from World War II who wanted and demanded real reform in state politics. By 1948, Crump's rule was threatened from within his own party by Estes Kefauver and the former governor (and war hero), Gordon Browning. Crump's high-profile attacks on Kefauver were particularly damaging to the old boss's powers. When Crump accused Kefauver of the kind of deceit characteristic of a raccoon, Kefauver turned the insult to his own advantage. He poked fun by donning a coonskin cap, to the delight of the voters.

Overcoming Crump's opposition, both Kefauver and Browning won their elections: Estes Kefauver as a United States senator and Gordon Browning again as governor. (Browning had served a term in 1937 with Crump's blessing, but had lost reelection when Crump removed his bloc of sixty thousand Shelby County votes). When he died in 1954, Edward Hull Crump was still recognized as a politician without equal in Memphis—or in Tennessee.

162
Sidney Hirsch

Defending the South—
A New Literary Movement

When Nashville's Sidney Hirsch began hosting a group from Vanderbilt University in 1914 for the purpose of encouraging intellectual conversations, he did not realize that he was fostering a new literary movement in America.

Though not connected with the university, Hirsch enjoyed the lively dialogue found in academic circles. His half-brother, Nat, was a Vanderbilt student who began inviting home some fellow students, among them Alec B. Stevenson, Stanley Johnson, William Yandell Elliott from Murfreesboro, and Donald Davidson from Campbellsville. Soon, they would be joined by such faculty members as John Crowe Ransom of Pulaski, a young member of the Vanderbilt English Department who became "firmly fixed as the intellectual leader of the group," and Walter Clyde Curry, a young South Carolina doctor of philosophy who had just joined the faculty. Eventually, their number would include Robert Penn Warren. A Kentucky native who had moved to Nashville during high

school, Warren would join the group while pursuing a Vanderbilt undergraduate degree and go on to win three Pulitzer Prizes, including one in 1946 for his novel *All the King's Men*.

Initiating one of twentieth-century America's most important literary groups, these men called themselves "the Fugitives." They came to represent the new poetry and criticism of modern literature's Southern Renaissance period. Hirsch remained a key player in their midst—not a writer of their magnitude, but a spellbinding force who guided many of the group's greatest days.

A native Nashvillian, Hirsch had been born in 1885 and in his youth temporarily attended William R. ("Sawney") Webb's prestigious Webb Academy at Bell Buckle as well as several colleges. But he also traveled the world and augmented his education with a personal tutor because his parents felt he was such a genius that any one school could not meet his educational needs. During those travels, Hirsch lived among fashionable writers and artists in New York City's Greenwich Village, developing notoriety as a poet and mystic. Upon returning to Nashville in 1913, he focused his artistic ambitions on writing and producing a "Greek pageant" that *Collier's Weekly* called "the most artistic and ambitious spectacle ever given in the South."

Hirsch's reputation as a "poet, journalist, orientalist and linguist" impressed Nat and his friends. Although Hirsch was frequently out of town, the group met regularly at the family's Twentieth Avenue apartment two blocks from campus. The meetings continued until World War I.

Sessions were said to have been demanding yet easy-going. Author Louise Cowan claimed that Hirsch encouraged "enthusiastic but somewhat undisciplined largeness of thought," sometimes drifting into meditations on mysticism that his associates soon learned they had to rein in. Ransom, the son of a Middle Tennessee Methodist minister, was noted for his "fine discrimination between ideas." Students Stevenson and Johnson soon brought to the group a new kind of poetry, its most notable characteristic being free (generally unrhymed) verse.

By the time of the war, the group's focus had shifted to the writing and discussion of their own original works. The intensity of their forums was so great that they returned after the war to resume their regular meetings, now at the home on Whitland Avenue of new member James M. Frank. Soon, William Frierson, Allen Tate, and Middle Tennessee's Merrill Moore (from Columbia) joined their ranks.

Discussions now focused firmly on poetry as a craft. In 1922, Hirsch suggested that they publish a literary journal to spotlight their original works. In April, the first issue of *The Fugitive* was published. Its writers announced their break with the traditions of the Old South and the establishment of a new kind of southern writer. They and their friends (including Robert Penn Warren in 1924) who began to write for the magazine had an impact upon all poets who followed them.

The Fugitive published only nineteen issues before folding in December 1925, primarily because no member of the circle was willing to edit the periodical full-time. Especially noteworthy was the journal's defense of the South and southern culture after uncomplimentary national coverage surfaced during the 1925 Scopes trial in Dayton, Tennessee. The quality of Fugitive poetry also contradicted the anti-South bias of northern critics such as H. L. Mencken, who was in Dayton to cover the trial and ridiculed the South's intellectual values.

The Fugitives eventually disbanded, but most all of the group's members enjoyed notable academic and literary careers. Several members became part of yet another Nashville literary circle of national significance, the Agrarians. In 1930, a collection of Agrarian essays, *I'll Take My Stand,* not only defended the southern way of life but also promoted it as a better choice than an industrialized America. Finally, some members added to their luster by establishing the twentieth century's third major literary movement, the New Critics.

When a reunion of the original surviving Fugitives was held at Vanderbilt in 1956, one of the participants was seventy-one-year-old Sidney Hirsch (he lived until 1962). The highly publicized reunion was organized by Louis Rubin Jr., of the American Studies Foundation. He said of the founding members: "The Nashville Fugitives were not simply an array of promising young poets; they were a *group,* a functioning organization, a dynamic unit of young men who performed their literary labors in common and who cooperated with each other in the perfecting of their art."

Rubin believed that the later individual achievement of these men was "related in a certain important

way to their having lived in Nashville at a particular time, having been associated with Vanderbilt University, and having taken part in the regular meetings of the Fugitives."

Rubin helped define their place in history: "Here, then, was something rare in American letters, something one tends to associate with European literature rather than our own—a collective outcropping of poetry, an organic society of poets, a community-wide literary endeavor, a Movement."

163
Clarence Saunders
The Self-Service Grocery—
A National Phenomenon

Small-town grocery clerk Clarence Saunders left his poor Montgomery County background in 1904 and headed for Memphis, where, a little more than a decade later, he opened his own national chain of stores and became so wealthy that he began construction on the most palatial mansion Memphians had ever seen. Ironically, he would never live there.

Saunders, a native Virginian, had moved to Middle Tennessee in 1896 to escape the poverty of his family's tobacco farm. Before trying his luck in Memphis, the virtually self-educated fifteen-year-old was a general store clerk in Palmyra and then a horse-and-buggy traveler for a wholesale grocer in nearby Clarksville. Motivated by strong ambitions, the high school dropout worked hard to build a life at Memphis. By 1922, his fortunes were immense—thanks to his concept of the self-service grocery store.

Traditionally, customers presented their shopping list to a clerk, who obtained their items behind the counter and often made home deliveries. Saunders saw immediately that high labor costs were a problem with this system. Showing rare marketing genius, he bought billboards and full-page newspaper ads with the message, "PIGGLY WIGGLY IS COMING!" fueling speculation as to what a Piggly Wiggly was.

When his first Piggly Wiggly grocery store opened in 1916, it became an immediate success. Besides a self-service approach, the store also undersold competitors by doing business on a cash-only basis. By not dealing in credit, Saunders could offer cheaper prices. The concept caught on quickly, and Piggly

Wiggly in the early 1920s expanded with 2,500 locations in the United States and Canada. Clarence Saunders was flamboyant, but the critical key to his success was that he paid attention to details. Among those details was to patent the concept of a self-service grocery store. He then wrote pamphlets detailing his concept and explaining exactly how he set up his store.

Saunders used some of his profits to invest in Cla-Le-Clare, a 160-acre estate with a twenty-two-room mansion named for his children—Clay, Lee, and Amy Clare. "If I never do anything else," he once said, "I'll give Memphis a landmark, a real Showplace of the South." He hired southerners and used southern products to make the dream come true.

In 1922, he had millions. A year later, he had nothing. Before his million-dollar house, nicknamed the "Pink Palace," was finally completed in 1923, Saunders suffered setbacks on Wall Street in one of the era's great financial battles: a power play between Saunders and numerous New York City stockbrokers. Saunders lost the fight, and Piggly Wiggly stock hit bottom. Its founder, unable to continue his fight against the muscle of big business in the East, went bankrupt, selling his mansion before ever occupying it. The new owners were developers who turned the Pink Palace into Chickasaw Gardens (later a natural resources museum).

Clarence Saunders never again wielded the power he did when Piggly Wiggly first caught the public's imagination, but he did not fade into the background. In the mid-1920s, he seemed on the verge of a major comeback with a new grocery chain under his own name. The Piggly Wiggly Corporation tried to stop him from using his name, as well as the self-service concept he had pioneered. But Saunders won a court battle and continued with his new stores, which were called "Clarence Saunders, Sole Owner of My Name Stores, Inc." This chain collapsed during the Depression, however, and Saunders again lost what money he had. He remained a boom-and-bust entrepreneur in what was a boom-and-bust era.

Undaunted, Saunders found financial backing for "Keydoozle" (Key Does All), a grocery concept that would allow the customer to insert a key beside selected items in a glass display case. The chosen items would be automatically conveyed to the checkout counter. Keydoozle was ahead of its time (actually ahead of the technology then available) and never quite caught the public's fancy. During this time, Saunders revealed his grand visions:

> I've been "broke" since 1931. I've been asked to take part in many propositions that would bring me from $50,000 to $100,000 a year. But I wasn't interested in them.
>
> I either made a lot of money in a business or I quit it. I'm not interested in a local business. I can't be confined to one city. Not even big cities like New York or Chicago. I want my business to expand—out over the country, over the world.

Clarence Saunders was preparing to launch one final creative fling—an even more intricate automated store called "Foodelectric"—at the time of his death in 1953 at the age of seventy-two.

164
Moses McKissack III/ Leatrice McKissack

To Build a Nation—A Family Tradition

Kidnapped in West Africa and sold into slavery in the early nineteenth century, the first Moses McKissack was shackled and carried toward the coast of North Carolina. Throughout his bondage, he always remembered how he and his kinsmen sought symbolic protection against rain, sun, and nature through a primitive figure that resembled an umbrella, which was also a symbol of leadership. The tradition would continue on another continent.

Two generations later in Nashville, his grandson and namesake, Moses McKissack III, used the umbrella as a company symbol when he founded the nation's "oldest continually operated" minority-owned architectural firm. But neither man could imagine the extent to which one woman, in 1983, would expand their heritage as builders and designers. More than 150 years after Moses McKissack I landed in America, Nashvillian Leatrice McKissack would create even more acclaim for the McKissack name.

Moses McKissack I, who had been abducted from the Ashanti tribe of Ghana, developed his artistic talents with a chisel when he became a slave and master builder to one of America's first contractors, William McKissack of Charlotte, North Carolina. Given as a

259

wedding gift when William Jr. married into the Max-well family of Tennessee, Moses relocated with his wife and their children to Spring Hill. It is believed that he became the head-slave foreman on brick and mortar construction projects in and around Maury County for the McKissack family.

Before his death in 1865, Moses McKissack taught the trade to his own sons and helped build many of Middle Tennessee's most noted structures. Among these were the famous Maxwell House Hotel in Nash-ville and the Giles County Courthouse.

His grandson, Moses McKissack III, learned the building trade as a child in Giles County, where his parents moved after the Civil War and emancipation. Settling in Pulaski, the family began a construction business and established a good reputation during an era in which builders were responsible for both design-ing and building their structures. Working alongside his father, the child quickly advanced his skills.

In 1890, at age eleven, he was employed by a white Pulaski architect. By sixteen years of age, he was a construction supervisor building homes in Pulaski, Mount Pleasant, and Columbia.

In what would be a historic move, Moses McKissack III left for Nashville in 1905 and built a home for Vanderbilt University's dean of architecture and engi-neering, earning the attention of other faculty mem-bers who also requested his services. That same year, he opened an office at the Napier Court Building and completed correspondence courses in architecture and engineering. With his reputation and his business skyrocketing, McKissack received the commission in 1908 to build one of the first major structures in America designed by a black professional, the Carnegie Library at Fisk University. He also constructed churches throughout the South, numerous buildings for other college campuses, and many of Middle Tennessee's finer homes. These included the mansion of Gover-nor Albert H. Roberts and many private Nashville resi-dences in the Vanderbilt and Belle Meade areas.

Joined in 1922 by younger brother Calvin, McKissack formed the architectural firm McKissack & McKissack. The brothers were among the first registered archi-tects in the state of Tennessee, having qualified al-most immediately under Tennessee's new architec-tural licensing law.

The McKissack brothers achieved national atten-tion in 1942 when they were awarded a $5.7 million government contract to build an air base at Tuskegee, Alabama—the largest United States contract ever given a black firm until that time. That same year, the McKissacks received a Spaulding Medal for operating the most outstanding black business firm in the United States. The honors continued when Moses McKissack III was invited to the White House by President Franklin D. Roosevelt for a conference on urban housing problems.

After Moses McKissack III died in 1952, followed by his brother sixteen years later, the family business continued into the fourth generation with Moses's ar-chitect son, William DeBerry McKissack. In 1983, William had a debilitating stroke. But two days later, his wife, retired teacher Leatrice McKissack, stepped into the company's leadership. Although she had been in retirement for fifteen years, Leatrice geared up to the task by learning what she had to know. By now, the business had built more than four thousand structures nationwide.

"I went from doing almost nothing to being presi-dent of a company. And I mean overnight. I didn't sleep for three months," she said during one inter-view shortly after becoming chairman and chief ex-ecutive officer.

To insure that McKissack & McKissack would sur-vive into a fifth generation of the family, Leatrice McKissack invited her three daughters to join the firm soon after their father's death in 1988. Andrea, Cheryl, and Deryl brought distinguished credentials. Follow-ing the tradition begun by Moses McKissack I, the three during their youth had accompanied their father ev-ery Saturday to his building sites. In high school, each young woman had been accomplished at architec-tural drawing and had excelled in industrial arts. In college, all had earned engineering degrees. When called upon to begin a new era of the nearly century-old McKissack & McKissack, the daughters opened satellite offices in New York City, Washington, D.C., and Philadelphia—quickly transforming the firm into one of the nation's leading mother-daughter busi-nesses. Fisk University historians wrote in the "Fisk News": "What started and continued as a firm for al-most a century of McKissack male architects is today a firm of McKissack female architects."

In addition to keeping the company together, Leatrice McKissack generated hundreds of millions of dollars in contracts during her first years. She soon added to the family's business reputation with one of her own. In 1990, she was named the National Female Entrepreneur of the Year by the United States Department of Commerce, receiving the award from President George Bush at the White House.

165
May Cravath Wharton

"Doctor Woman of the Cumberlands":
A New Brand of Medicine

Dr. May Cravath Wharton loved, and was loved by, the people she served along the Cumberland Plateau.

One evening in the early twentieth century, May Cravath Wharton looked out the window of her simple home at Pleasant Hill Academy on the Cumberland Plateau and "saw a light bobbing up the hill," coming toward the house. A few minutes later, a man approached the door and called, "Hello, hello the house. Whar's the doctor woman at?" The man had come in search of the only doctor in the vicinity.

She had arrived in 1917 from New Hampshire as a missionary with her husband, Edwin Wharton. He was fifty-one and she was forty-five at the time. They had come to Cumberland County to operate the missionary school. But May discovered how medical care was also needed in this isolated and inaccessible portion of Middle Tennessee.

The academy, fifteen rugged miles from Crossville, was a boarding school that offered high school, some college courses, and a "normal" school to train teachers. Dr. May Cravath Wharton began her life there by teaching math and science and tending to the various ailments of students and fellow teachers.

A woman doctor was a novelty, and area citizens were skeptical of her at first. Among the skeptics was a man who met May at the Crossville train station and transported her to Pleasant Hill to join her husband. While the two rode along a treacherous mountain pass in the icy cold of winter, he said to her: "Miz' Wharton, they tell me you do some doctoring. Now, I ain't never heerd of a woman being a doctor, so I reckon they got it mixed up a little."

"Well, they didn't. I am a doctor," she responded.

The man was still doubtful. "Mostly for women-folks and children, I reckon?"

"No, for anyone," she replied.

"Well, well," he pondered, scratching behind his ear. "Well, well . . ."

It was actually the worldwide killer-flu epidemic of 1918 that sent Dr. May Cravath Wharton into the surrounding hills and valleys to help the populace, and she was able to save the lives of untold numbers. Within a year, everyone in the region knew about the woman doctor of the Cumberland, about her skills, and about her concern for their lives. People came from miles around to ask for her help. Invariably, she gave it to them, usually at no cost.

During the first years of her practice, May walked everywhere she went. When people came to her door at all hours of the day and night begging for help, she picked up her bag and set out with them on foot unless the petitioner brought along a mule or horse for her to ride.

One night, a man appeared at her door and asked her to visit his small daughter. He wore his coal miner's hat and apologized to her for his dirty appearance. He had just gotten home from work when his wife sent him in search of the doctor woman. May and the man set out together, he carrying her medical bag and she struggling to keep pace on the three-mile walk up and down mountain terrain to his cabin. "I squared my shoulders, reminding myself that mountain women stride along behind their men Indian fashion, stolidly keeping pace. I determined to do as well," she later wrote in her 1953 autobiography, *Doctor Woman of the Cumberlands*.

The family's cabin was neat and clean. An oil lamp lit the room. Ruffled curtains made from tobacco cloth were draped at the windows. Rough floors had been scrubbed white and clean quilts covered the beds. When she entered May saw a young mother bending over the child. "Do ye feel better, honey?"

May examined the girl and discovered that the child had diphtheria. The disease's antitoxin was eighteen miles away, but an exhausted father borrowed a mule and rode for the medicine while May did what she could to ease the girl's suffering. May was surprised and pleased to learn that the couple had attended Pleasant Hill Academy, met there, and married after graduation. They had learned about "nice things" and had tried to make the most of their home. The wife was the teacher for the settlement's three-month-long winter school.

May was gratified to see how the academy influenced lives. When the medicine arrived, the group prayed over the child and then the husband picked up the doctor's medical bag and walked her home.

Several nights later, he returned to her door and said that he needed advice. May wondered, however, what the man's real purpose had been in coming into town. "Well, you see, Doc, the little chap said she wanted a pair of shoes."

He held a package under his arms. May remarked, "But she can't wear shoes for a long while yet."

"No, ma'am, but just seeing 'em on the bed might make her get well faster."

May Wharton never forgot that visit: "He had routed out the storekeeper, who, after the kindly manner of the mountain people, was glad to open up the store to supply the shoes." She also remembered the lesson that she learned: "More than likely the father was right about their importance, for the lovely little girl got well in record time."

Such people as these were also concerned about Dr. May Wharton's well-being. They paid what they could for her services. Sometimes it was a dollar or two, but more often than not it was a sack of beans or a piece of pork from their hog-killing. "We aim to make it right with ye," they would say.

May often skipped meals and ate nothing but fruit while en route to see a patient. She remembered one woman's comment, "Shore is hard on ye, Dr. May, to walk ever'where. Couldn't you git you a horse to ride?"

May told her that the mission certainly did not have money for something as extravagant as a horse. But the need for an animal was soon passed along the missionary grapevine. One day, a check appeared from a supporter in the East, and May purchased the horse that she named "Missionary Billy." Together they rode up and down mountain paths in good weather and bad. Because she could not find a side-saddle, May concocted an outfit that would work with the saddle she had. "Much of the time in winter," she explained, "I wore a heavy flannel shirt, corduroy riding breeches, sheepskin-lined footwear inside of large, high boots, and over all this a very long heavy coat split so that it hung on both sides of my feet."

When the mission needed money, May traveled to New Hampshire to raise the funds from friends and churches. While she was there in 1920, she received a telegram that her husband had become critically ill. She rushed back to Tennessee but discovered there was no hope for Edwin.

In their last few hours together, just three years after coming to the Plateau, May tried to make her husband comfortable. "Maynie," he said, "have Miss Flora come over and sing for me, please." She did, and as Edwin's life was drawing nearer its end, he uttered his final words: "Maynie, don't leave the Mountain. They need you. Lift up your head and the King of Glory will come in."

May Wharton had grown to love the Cumberland Plateau and its people. She did not want to leave. But a new director for Pleasant Hill Academy would soon arrive, and she would have no place to live nor the basic financial support of her husband's salary. When she began packing her belongings to consider medical opportunities in other parts of the nation, May wondered what to do. She and her friend Elizabeth Fletcher, the academy's art teacher, considered the options.

During the packing process, a delegation of neighbors appeared. "We come to tell you how sorry we

262

are, Dr. May," one of them told her. "We'd all be proud to he'p you with your movin'. We brung you this paper to read."

When she opened it, the paper turned out to be a written plea from members of fifty families. It read:

Dr. May Wharton
In behalf of the town and surrounding community we wish to express our sympathy for you in your trouble and we feel we have suffered a great loss in the death of professor Wharton. The people here wants you to stay here as their Dr. and pay you monthly and also help you with your hospital. We feel that we cannot do without you.

May Cravath Wharton decided to remain on the Plateau and resolved to bring medical aid within the reach of "their homes and their thin pocketbooks." Along with Elizabeth Fletcher and a nurse from Canada, Alice Adshead, she worked out of a makeshift medical office: a two-story frame house that cost four dollars a month. Within a year, a small annex there was turned into a two-bed hospital, which soon received a charter as the first hospital in Cumberland County. The small hospital expanded its number of beds through the years, and, in 1937, a building was added to care for tuberculosis patients.

The three women also taught nursing and held health clinics throughout the region. May's idea of a community-health program was revolutionary in rural America, bringing with it suggestions about nutrition and hygiene that were not well known or practiced during this era. She and her helpers frequently took off into the nearby wilderness to see a patient who was too sick to travel and too poor to pay for transportation into major towns. When critical cases surfaced, May brought in surgeons from the neighboring areas to perform simple surgical procedures.

Vowing that she would somehow build a small hospital to care for the most serious cases, she often went on speaking tours. Her intention was to build this new hospital in a more accessible place for the local populace. To raise funds, she and her associates kept up a correspondence of requests to the American Missionary Association as well as to friends, relatives, and churches in all parts of the country. The efforts were relentless; and the responses were favorable and steady. In 1950, May Wharton, along with Elizabeth Fletcher and Alice Adshead, founded the

modern and well-equipped Cumberland Medical Center at Crossville, the county seat.

Although she was seventy-seven years old at the time, May immediately embarked on yet another major project: a retirement community at Pleasant Hill (the academy had closed in 1947). The result of her new campaign was the founding of Uplands, Inc., retirement center; at the heart of the retirement community was the May Cravath Wharton Nursing Home, dedicated in 1957. The woman who inspired it remained involved with this project and the lives of Cumberland Plateau citizens until her death in 1959 at the age of eighty-six.

166
"Shufflin' Phil" Douglas
Pitching Away Baseball's Hall of Fame

In the 1921 World Series, Phil Douglas started three games, won two, and struck out Babe Ruth four times when his New York Giants defeated Ruth's New York Yankees.

A year later, Douglas, the pride of Grundy County (and of its equally proud neighbor, Marion County), was out of baseball, banned for life, all the result of a one-paragraph note he wrote after being abducted and abused by club officials.

"Shufflin' Phil," so named because of an unorthodox gate resulting from polio, became one of the most tragic stories in the game's history. The story was told many times in the *Chattanooga Times* and other area newspapers.

A native of Tracy City in the Sequatchie Valley, Douglas had a 15-10 record in 1921 and led the National League in shutouts. In August 1922, he was 11-4 and at the peak of his career. A week later, his career was finished.

He had failed to show for a game he was scheduled to pitch, earning a severe reprimand from Giants manager John "Little Napoleon" McGraw. The tirade so upset Douglas that he decided to go drinking, a habit that had caused him problems previously in his career.

Although Douglas was clever enough to escape a man McGraw had hired to follow him, McGraw promptly hired other detectives to hunt down the pitcher, who was sleeping off his binge at the apartment of a friend. Rousing Douglas with night sticks, detectives literally kidnapped him, taking him against his will and without the knowledge of his wife, to a sanitarium. There he was forced to undergo a brutal withdrawal treatment known as the "Keely Cure," which consisted of stomach pumping, "boiling out" hot baths, and huge doses of sedatives.

On a Saturday, after five days, Douglas was released. On Monday, when he reported to the baseball park, his speech was still slurred and his feet unsteady, effects of the drugs administered without his consent. McGraw accused Douglas of being drunk again and humiliated him in front of his teammates. Douglas also learned that the Giants were sending him a bill for the sanitarium stay and fining him $100.00 plus five days' pay. The total was $512.15, a sizable amount to a man whose annual salary was $6,500.

That day's game was rained out, but Douglas, who was angry, confused, and still reeling from drugs, remained at the clubhouse after other players had gone. He then made the biggest mistake of his life. Locating a piece of team stationary, he wrote one paragraph, a request for money, to Leslie Mann, an outfielder for the other team in the pennant race, the St. Louis Cardinals.

"I want to leave here but I want some inducement," wrote Douglas. Referring to McGraw, he said: "I don't want this guy to win the pennant and I feel if I stay here I will win it for him. You know I can pitch and win."

The embittered pitcher promised to be "on the next train" after money was in his hands. Later, when confronted, Douglas explained: "I decided that I just couldn't pitch for McGraw. He was running me crazy. . . . He rode me every minute. He called me vile names. Everything I did seemed to be wrong. . . . I did my share of drinking, but I was charged with plenty I didn't do."

When Shufflin' Phil's anger subsided, he had second thoughts about the note he had mailed. That night, he reportedly telephoned Mann and asked him to destroy the letter when it arrived. Mann, who denied receiving such a call, immediately took the letter to Cardinal manager Branch Rickey. Rickey advised Mann to present the letter to commissioner Kenesaw Mountain Landis.

A hard-nosed dictator entrusted with restoring baseball's integrity following the notorious "Black Sox Scandal" of 1919, Landis decided to make an example of Douglas. The commissioner paid a visit to Douglas's hotel, where he and McGraw met with the pitcher. After Douglas admitted writing the letter, Landis asked him why he had done so. Scared and a bit confused, Douglas replied: "A man has to live. I guess I figured I was out of a job if Mac let me go. I reckoned with this letter I might pick up some money and get along for a time."

Landis stuck his finger in the ballplayer's face and vowed: "Douglas, you are through with organized baseball."

Shufflin' Phil, virtually in shock, wandered back to his hotel room and told a reporter: "I'm just waiting for someone to loan me enough jack to get out of town. I'm ashamed to wire my wife." Then he cried.

Douglas returned to the South, where he worked at odd jobs as a truck driver and coal miner. Two years after he was banished from baseball, he was back in Tracy City working at a sawmill for $1.50 per day. His only contact with baseball was coaching youth teams and occasionally pitching for semiprofessional clubs, sometimes with pay. He pitched well into his forties and, according to local lore, occasionally struck out every man he faced during an entire game.

In 1935, the manager of the Giants, Bill Terry, described Douglas as one of the finest pitchers in club history. There were only three others on his list: Christy Mathewson, Rube Marquard, and Joe McGinnity. All but Shufflin' Phil Douglas made the baseball Hall of Fame.

By the age of forty-six, Douglas was penniless and desperate. He convinced a sportswriter to contact Landis about lifting the ban so that he could return to professional ball as a coach or a scout. Landis declined, but sent him a small check. A year later in 1937, Shufflin' Phil Douglas was on welfare.

He died in 1952, destitute and bitter, and was buried in an unmarked grave along Highway 56 in Tracy City. In 1971, residents of his hometown staged a benefit baseball game on his behalf, buying a tombstone for the man whose ten-year, big-league career and chance at baseball's Hall of Fame was cut short by one involuntary drug-induced act of defiance.

167
John Thomas Scopes

National Debate over a "Monkey Trial"

In the summer of 1925, teacher John Thomas Scopes sat in Robinson's Drug Store in downtown Dayton, Tennessee, and agreed to be arrested. A trial, he was told, would attract considerable publicity, and this was just what the town needed. Seated at the table with Scopes were prominent businessmen in this East Tennessee community who hoped for so much public notice that tourism dollars were bound to follow. When Scopes said yes to the suggestion that he test a new state law, drug store owner F. E. Robinson rushed to phone the *Chattanooga News:* "This is F. E. Robinson in Dayton. I'm chairman of the school board here. We've just arrested a man for teaching evolution."

Twenty-four-year-old Scopes was a newcomer to Tennessee, having lived in Dayton no more than a year. But his name would become one of the state's most famous—and Dayton would host the nation's most sensational trial, dubbed by nationally known journalist H. L. Mencken as "the Monkey Trial."

The series of events began when Scopes, a substitute science teacher and football coach at Rhea County Central High School, finished the school year. Planning to spend the summer with his family in Kentucky, he decided to remain in Dayton a few days so that he could make a date with a young woman he had met. While Scopes tarried in town, a few civic leaders were meeting at Robinson's Drug, where most issues of town importance were best discussed. They argued the pros and cons of the new Tennessee law forbidding the teaching in public schools of evolution, a theory that ran counter to the Biblical story of Creation

John Thomas Scopes (left) shakes hands with nationally renowned Clarence Darrow, the newest member of the Scopes defense team headed by Rhea County's John R. Neal (standing between them).

by claiming that all forms of life gradually evolved over millions of years from lower life forms. Many state lawmakers had held reservations about the law, the Butler Act, but rural representatives who were in favor had managed to get it passed in the legislature; Governor Austin Peay had signed it but never believed it would be enforced. George W. Rappelyea, a New Yorker who had married a Rhea County native, introduced the grand scheme to "put Dayton on the map." Other town leaders, who held varying opinions on the subject of evolution, agreed that a good trial would be good for business. They sent for Scopes.

Rappelyea told him: "John, we've been arguing, and I said that nobody could teach biology without teaching evolution." Scopes agreed, but he was reluctant to become the test case against the new law. Rappelyea, who had read that the American Civil Liberties Union (ACLU) would pay the costs of a test case in Tennessee, eventually talked him into it. After all, Scopes had been using a textbook that included evolution, and he believed in the freedom to teach from such a book.

Dayton's leading citizens were not the only ones to scurry into action to make the news: so did the ACLU, which planned to appeal any conviction to the United States Supreme Court, hoping the law would be ruled unconstitutional. Three days after that phone call to the press from Robinson's Drug Store, Scopes's arrest was known around the globe.

The ensuing trial brought the country's top journalists to camp on Dayton's doorstep, and it brought two of the nation's top attorneys: former presidential candidate William Jennings Bryan, who would give the fundamentalist view for the prosecution, and colorful Clarence Darrow, who would hammer away for the defense. Scopes especially wanted Darrow as his attorney, reasoning that only a "slugger" like Darrow could give him a fighting chance of making his view understood by the public. Former Tennessee law professor John Randolph Neal was named chief defense counsel.

In a small irony, prosecutor Bryan was already acquainted with the accused; six years earlier, Scopes had laughed out loud during a commencement address Bryan had given at their shared high school alma mater in Salem, Illinois.

During his stay in Dayton, Bryan spoke to the Rhea County School Board, and, according to *Knoxville Journal* reporter W. C. "Cary" Ross, "He believed there is no conflict between education and religion, but if

there be . . . religion must be first, for what we learn in school is useful for but three score years and ten, but what we learn in the Bible is for eternity."

During the media frenzy, loudspeakers trumpeted the proceedings to the masses assembled outside the courthouse. The *Baltimore Sun's* famous H. L. Mencken, who sided with Darrow and Scopes on the issue, said the state belonged to that portion of the nation that he coined "the Bible Belt." Generally in his writings, he was critical of the South's lifestyle. Such relentless outpourings spawned a response from Tennessee writers centered at Vanderbilt University who called themselves "the Fugitives" and whose works were creating a major literary movement in America. Many of these Tennessee writers regrouped into yet another outstanding literary movement, the Agrarians, which frequently defended the South's culture and put Tennessee in a good light.

Judge John Tate Raulston, explaining that the case hinged not on whether evolution was a valid theory but on whether Scopes had violated the Butler Act by teaching it, refused to allow Darrow's expert witnesses on evolution. Darrow, enraged because Bryan had been able to freely discuss religion, approached the bench: "I do not understand why every request of the state and every suggestion of the prosecution should meet with an endless amount of time, and a bare suggestion of anything that is perfectly competent on our part should be immediately overruled."

Judge Raulston, visibly upset, responded: "I hope you do not mean to reflect upon the court?"

Darrow replied: "Well, your Honor has the right to hope."

Darrow was cited for contempt with bail posted at five thousand dollars. But the trial's highest drama actually came near its conclusion when Bryan agreed to take the stand as an expert witness on the Bible. Darrow jumped into an intense cross-examination. His relentless approach, combined with the equally intense summer heat, forced Bryan's responses to reveal anger and confusion.

Despite the prosecution's weak case, John Scopes was convicted of violating Tennessee law and fined one hundred dollars. Within hours, he made a startling revelation to a reporter by admitting that he had never taught evolution to his class. Scopes said he had skipped the chapter in question and had consented to be tried for an offense he had not committed.

The effect of the trial's intensity upon the health of William Jennings Bryan became apparent one week after the trial's conclusion. After finishing a large Sunday dinner, he returned to his rented Dayton cottage, made a phone call to Knoxville's David C. Chapman to confirm a planned visit to the Smoky Mountains, then took a nap; he died in his sleep.

The conviction that Bryan had worked so hard to obtain failed in an appeal to the Tennessee Supreme Court, which overturned the decision on a technicality. The Butler Act, however, was not repealed until 1967.

Scopes was given the opportunity to remain in the Dayton school system but chose to leave and attend graduate school in Chicago (defense witnesses raised the money to extend his education). After two years at the University of Chicago, Scopes was about to accept a fellowship to a technical school. But when school officials at his new destination learned about his role in the Dayton trial, he received a terse note telling him to "take your atheistic marbles and play elsewhere."

Scopes finished his master's degree and spent the next forty years as a geologist, working for oil companies in Texas, Louisiana, and South America before his death in 1970.

The quotable Grantland Rice.

168
Grantland Rice

*Igniting the Golden Age of Sports
with Poetic Prose*

The epic heroes and wars of Greek and Latin literature so captured the imagination of Middle Tennessee's Grantland Rice that he transposed them to the playing fields of America in the 1920s. He immortalized sports players with his own classic language and became the first famous sportswriter in America. With his writing, he fashioned America's Golden Age of Sports.

Rice was immersed in classical literature as a student at Vanderbilt University about 1900. In his first sports-writing job in 1901 with the newly formed *Nashville Daily News,* he began introducing verse into his sports columns. Rice's poetic lines eventually captured the essence of America's feeling for sports during the 1920s. Perhaps his most famous and enduring verses conclude his poem, "Alumnus Football," which he composed and read for a Vanderbilt alumni reunion in the summer of 1908:

> For when the One Great Scorer comes to mark
> against your name.
> He writes—not that you won or lost—but how
> you played the Game.

Rice would later explain in his autobiography, "How or why . . . I don't know, but rhythm and rhyme seemed to come naturally." He said that scanning Latin poetry had perhaps given him an ear and an eye for adding verse to his writing. Numerous literary allusions and images were then incorporated into his descriptions of sporting events and players.

In one of his more widely recognized pieces of prose, Rice wrote of the 1924 Notre Dame backfield: "Outlined against a blue-gray October sky, the Four Horsemen rode again." Although the term "Four Horsemen" had been previously coined, it was Rice's dramatic touch that converted the players into mythical levelers of opposing teams.

He also first characterized Illinois running back and later professional player Red Grange as "The Galloping Ghost" and first called baseball pitcher Walter

Johnson "Big Train" because of his speedy fastball (Johnson was one of the first five players elected to baseball's Hall of Fame).

Born in Murfreesboro in 1880, Rice was named for his maternal grandfather, former Confederate Major Henry Grantland, an English immigrant who made a fortune in the cotton trade after the Civil War. In 1884, the Rice family moved to Nashville. A few years later, the boy received a football, baseball, and bat for Christmas. "Those three presents were the sounding instruments that directed my life," Rice wrote. He said that it was while attending Tennessee Military Institute and the Nashville Military Institute that he "learned a lot of football and eventually got my biggest thrill out of a game for which I was totally unfitted, physically."

Rice participated on both Vanderbilt football and baseball teams. Undersized for football, he suffered numerous gridiron injuries. Following his graduation in 1901, he briefly toured Tennessee as a member of a minor-league baseball team before being summoned by his father to seek more steady employment at home. Rice first tried his hand as a store clerk but found more suitable work as a journalist when he was named sports editor of the *Daily News.*

Because the managing editor felt that sports coverage was not a full-time job, he assigned Rice to politics and social events as well. Rice frequently (and secretly) traded his political assignments for sports assignments belonging to Louis Brownlow, a rival reporter at the *Nashville Banner.* Each man covered the other's story, and their respective bosses were none the wiser. (Rice's passion for sports was equaled by Brownlow's passion for politics; Brownlow would someday be the city manager of Knoxville.)

In 1902, Rice left the *News.* Before establishing himself in New York City as America's first premiere sportswriter, he honed his skills in Atlanta; there he met his future wife and became a major southern celebrity via his sports articles. Then he moved to Cleveland, Ohio. He returned home in 1907 to write for the newly founded *Nashville Tennessean.* During his next three years at the *Tennessean,* Rice helped make the paper one of the region's most widely read. But the newspaper was forced to share him with Vanderbilt University. Rice served simultaneously as a Vanderbilt baseball coach and scout for the football team under Coach Dan McGugin, one of the legends of southern

sports with whom he became close friends. During the football season, Rice often refereed collegiate games nationwide (even Vanderbilt's on occasion). His popular columns in the *Tennessean* led one later sports historian to call him a "poet laureate of sorts for Nashville and especially for Vanderbilt."

Rice's regional fame expanded considerably when he went to the *New York Herald-Tribune* in 1914. His syndicated column appeared in at least 250 newspapers, and his prestige grew even more with a weekly article for *Collier's* magazine, his freelance material to other national magazines, and his role as producer of monthly ten-minute newsreels. During the second radio broadcast of a World Series in 1922, Rice captivated an audience of more than one million people within three hundred miles of New York City alone. It was the largest audience ever to hear a human voice.

One of his trademarks was to develop the heroes of the sports era into mythological figures, not unlike those he had studied as a student of ancient poets. Rice's sports giants were baseball's Babe Ruth, boxing's Jack Dempsey, golf's Bobby Jones, football's Knute Rockne. Although Rice became close friends with many of the sports figures about whom he wrote, he preferred to focus on their game performances rather than on their personal lives and problems. It was his tendency towards optimism that prompted him to portray only the best in each individual. He also fed the optimism of the nation after World War I during the Roaring Twenties. "No one has ever accused your humble but cheerful correspondent of being a calamity howler," Rice wrote. "He has always preferred looking on the sunny side of things; and he hasn't spent much time peering into the shadows searching for ghosts of trouble and phantoms of sorrow."

According to those who knew him, Rice believed in what he wrote. As he said more than once: "Almost every one of these heroes of sport taught me something, gave me some insight into how to live and added to my philosophy of life."

Rice, whose talents earned him more than one hundred thousand dollars a year during the 1920s, was elected to the National Sportswriters and Sportscasters Hall of Fame. Through his friendship with McGugin and others from years past, Rice remained in contact with Nashville. His reputation as America's best-known sportswriter endured even after his death in 1954.

169
David C. Chapman

*Fathering the Great Smoky Mountains
National Park*

In the early 1920s when a campaign for a national park in the Great Smoky Mountains was little more than a fanciful notion among a few Knoxvillians, wholesale druggist David C. Chapman transformed the notion into a reality. In 1923, he decided to push aside his family business, his social life, and his favorite pastimes of hunting and fishing and make the park his consuming life work. Later newspaper articles described him as a man who "gave a sizeable chunk of his life to preserve for all of the people of this nation and the world the scenic heart of the Smokies." Chapman, by rallying the forces, piloted a hard-fought crusade that devoured more than a decade and sometimes threatened his well-being and his reputation. But he persevered, gaining recognition as the "father of the Great Smoky Mountains National Park."

Chapman, a former gridiron hero, military leader, entrepreneur, and civic organizer, was a natural leader in undertaking this mission. He was quite well known throughout East Tennessee where early fund drives for the park would be concentrated. Born in Knoxville in 1876, Chapman had been the University of Tennessee's star quarterback and sometime coach between 1894 and 1897, doggedly playing every minute of every quarter of every game. The *Knoxville Journal and Tribune* claimed a quarter-century later that Chapman's playing time was "a record not equaled since." His 1894 and 1895 teams competed unofficially as the Knoxville Athletic Club and included both student players and Knoxville residents. A year later, as the university became a member of the Southern Inter-Collegiate Athletic Association, Chapman quarterbacked the University of Tennessee's first undefeated season and at a time when the team was without a coach. When the football program was suspended in 1898 during the Spanish-American War, Chapman stepped from the university cadet corps into the Third Tennessee Infantry and went to Cuba. After the war, he helped reorganize the Third Tennessee as a national guard unit, serving as adjutant before resigning his post.

He began working in his father's business, the Chapman, White, Lyons Company, which produced some of the South's most recognizable drugstore products stamped with its trademark white lion. Eventually taking over the business and creating the Chapman Drug Company, thirty-one-year-old David C. Chapman became a major civic leader, also helping transform the Knoxville Board of Trade into the city's chamber of commerce. He was married to Knoxville socialite Sue Ayres Johnston, the daughter of one of the area's major capitalists, John Yates Johnston. With the outbreak of World War I, now-Colonel Chapman busily organized the Fourth Tennessee at the request of Governor Thomas C. Rye, raising sixteen hundred men in three weeks.

But Chapman's later job of creating a national park was more difficult than he could have imagined. While other national parks were carved out of federal land, the Smokies would have to be purchased entirely from private land owners, among them powerful and resistant lumber companies. Remarking on his chance at success, Chapman later revealed: "They say you can't do anything unless you think you can. Well, that's not so. I didn't think we could."

His initial inspiration came from his friend Willis P. Davis, whose wife had suggested the Smokies national park campaign. Having just vacationed in the West, the couple believed that the scenery of the Appalachians was as beautiful as any they had seen. Davis, who was the manager of the Knoxville Iron Company, immediately organized the Great Smoky Mountains Conservation Association; Chapman attended a meeting merely out of curiosity. "I was born here, raised here and went to U-T, and I had hunted and fished in the Smokies, but I never had heard anybody say there was anything superlative about the Smokies. I had no means of comparison," Chapman told a local newspaper. His obsession with the national park idea ignited after he read President Theodore Roosevelt's glowing descriptions of the Appalachians in a library book.

One of the best and earliest decisions made by Chapman and Davis was to hire Knoxville photographer James E. Thompson, whose photographs of the Smokies revealed the splendor of the mountains in all four seasons. The majestic beauty portrayed in such pictures became one of the more successful tools used by park supporters to convince the United States Congress's Southern Appalachian Park Committee to visit the area. That visit set up a chain reaction of pivotal moments.

All the while, Knoxville boosters visualized tourism dollars pouring into their city and the surrounding area. Some critics accused them of being motivated by profit only.

Chapman, meanwhile, continued to rise in power. He was named chairman of the Tennessee State Parks and Forestry Commission and talked the state into contributing money for the first major land purchase: 76,500 acres from Little River Lumber Company. He also talked the city of Knoxville into donating one-third of the cost (Knoxville was the only city to give any money for the Smoky Mountain campaign). Still millions of dollars away from a national park, Chapman took his own financial risk. He borrowed five thousand dollars so that he could make a personal donation, hoping to jump start a public fund drive. Its most attention-getting phase involved pledges of pennies, nickels, and dimes from forty-five hundred East Tennessee schoolchildren from Knox, Blount, Cocke, and Sevier counties. The children's hard-earned $1,391 hardly made a dent in the amount needed, but their money inspired a stream of donations throughout East Tennessee and North Carolina that would bring in one million dollars. (David C. Chapman's gift would be the largest amount given by a private source.)

Later in the park's publicity push, Chapman invited the famous participants in the Scopes "Monkey Trial," then being held in Dayton, to visit the Smoky Mountains. Newsmen from across the nation, already in Tennessee to report on the 1925 trial, followed the caravan of personalities, which included defense attorney Clarence Darrow and Scopes himself. Prosecuting counsel William Jennings Bryan called to confirm his intention to make the trip, but died the same day.

At the same time that Knoxvillians were working on the park project from the Tennessee side, North Carolinians were engaged in the campaign also. One of the most famous was Horace Kephart, a former midwestern librarian who had left behind his family and friends to live a solitary wilderness life near Bryson City. His book *Our Southern Highlanders,* written after two years of wandering through Tennessee and other states in the Appalachian chain, was widely read. (He later helped chart the route of the Appalachian Trail across the Smokies into northern Georgia.)

David Chapman soon had five million dollars from fund-raising and congressional approval to go with it. But all of this was not enough. The difference would come from an unexpected source: a surprise gift from one of the nation's wealthiest men, John D. Rockefeller Jr., who used a family trust to donate another five million dollars. Now the purchase of small mountain farms could proceed swiftly. One later newspaper reporter observed: "Some of the deeds should be in museums. One specified a boundary marker as the 'point where the old sow swam the river.' Several referred to certain rows in hillside cornfields."

Despair, however, came with this sudden buying frenzy in Cades Cove, which was subjected without warning to what Tennessee author Durwood Dunn called "death by eminent domain." A proud community for more than a century, the Cove was not supposed to be uprooted. A decade of promises by the Knoxville boosters and state politicians, including the governor himself, had assured Cove inhabitants that their homes would never be "molested."

One day near Missionary Ridge Baptist Church, Chapman came upon a handmade sign posted during one of his attempts to buy land: "Col. Chapman. You and Hoast are notify. Let the Cove People Alone. Get Out. Get Gone. 40 m. Limit." The forty miles reference was the distance to Knoxville, where Cove residents felt that Chapman should stay, if he knew what was good for him. But Ben A. Morton, a former Knoxville mayor and a member of the park commission, was able to smooth the way. He was the son of a Maryville physician who often treated Cove residents. While visiting each Cove family which had not sold out, Morton helped negotiate successful contracts.

Within other nearby communities, a few homesteaders reacted with similar resentment. Some agreed to lifetime lease agreements with the purchase of their lands. Among them were the Walker Sisters (Hettie, Margaret Jane, Polly, Louisa Susan, and Martha Ann), who inspired the naming of Five Sisters Cove (the Greenbrier Cove area of adjacent Sevier County). Louisa Susan was so disturbed by the government's intrusion that she wrote a poem about it. Key verses (original grammar, spelling, and punctuation intact) are as follows:

But now the park commesser
Comes all dressed up so gay
Saying this old house of yours
We must now take away

They coax they wheedle
They fret they bark
Saying we have to have this place
For a National park

For us poor mountain people
They dont have a care
But must a home for
The wolf the lion and the bear. . . .

The Walker Sisters relented in 1941, however, and sold their fifty acres to the government for $4,750 and a lifetime lease. When the *Saturday Evening Post* heard about the sisters in 1946, the magazine profiled them in an article that turned their home into a tourist attraction.

Of the remaining 80 percent of mountain land targeted for the national park, Chapman faced logging companies that made his efforts especially lengthy and even more bitter, especially Champion Fiber Company. Finally, on March 30, 1931, Champion agreed to Chapman's terms to sell its entire 92,814 acres, what would be the heart of the park on both the Tennessee and North Carolina sides and well-known sites to future travelers: Mount Le Conte, Chimney Tops, Greenbrier Wilderness, part of Clingman's Dome, and part of Mount Guyot.

Chapman's long fight, nearing its end, still was not completed officially until September 2, 1940, at Newfound Gap. Standing practically at the border of Tennessee and North Carolina, President Franklin D. Roosevelt formally dedicated that day what was already reputed to be the most popular national park in the country. Its fourth-highest peak carried the name "Mt. Chapman."

When the father of the park died four years later, his Chapman Drug Company continued on, eventually becoming "one of the largest independently owned pharmaceutical distributors in the nation." But before his death, David C. Chapman was able to travel along another namesake, Chapman Highway, a major roadway leading from his hometown of Knoxville to his greatest triumph, the Great Smoky Mountains National Park.

170
Mordecai Johnson

*Civil Rights—and an Inspiring Voice
for Nonviolence*

Carolyn Johnson had always focused her attention on her only child, Mordecai, born in 1890 at Paris, Tennessee. Instilling in him a love of books and education, she read him poetry and stories from the Bible, many of which had to do with enslaved peoples seeking and achieving their freedom. A later historian was quoted as saying: "Most often she told him the story of Mordecai (for whom he was named), member of a race despised and enslaved by the Medes and the Persians . . . who by his cleverness and the charm of his beautiful niece, Queen Esther, . . . raised his own people to leadership."

The boy's father was the Reverend Wyatt Johnson, a former slave. The elder Johnson earned his living by operating a stationary engine at a Paris mill. But he also had a calling to preach the gospel and founded Mount Zion Baptist Church of Paris, where he pastored.

In pursuit of the strong education and religious training that his parents encouraged, Mordecai attended Howe Institute in Memphis. At the age of sixteen, he gained admission to Atlanta Baptist College (which became Morehouse College). Upon graduating in 1911, he earned a series of degrees that concluded in 1922 with a master's in theology from Harvard University.

Carrying these heavy educational credentials, Mordecai Johnson taught English for two years at Atlanta Baptist Seminary and then became a pastor. He was assigned to Charleston, West Virginia, where his work as a church leader came to a sudden halt in 1926. The field of education beckoned once more, as administrators at Howard University in Washington, D.C., asked him to serve as its first black president.

In the 1920s, Howard University was a mere collection of "unaccredited academic departments surrounding a dental, medical and law school," said the *Washington Star*. "Its finances depended on the whim of Congress, some of whose members were frankly hostile to Howard's purpose." The college had been founded soon after the Civil War by Union General Oliver O. Howard, once the commander of Union forces in Tennessee, who was interested in promoting the education of blacks and poor whites. He also was the first commissioner of the Freedmen's Bureau, designed to help destitute blacks make their way in life after war's end. Howard University, according to its founder's desires, promoted an open admissions policy for black and white, male and female—an uncommon practice in the late nineteenth and early twentieth centuries.

During the course of what would be a thirty-four-year tenure as Howard University's president, Mordecai Johnson led the school into national prominence as an institution of higher learning. The full-time Howard Law School (attracting leading attorneys as faculty) eventually paced the United States in the area of civil rights. Howard graduates became leaders in major legal battles against racial discrimination. Most of the legal team for the National Association for the Advancement of Colored People (NAACP) that successfully fought segregation before the United States Supreme Court were Howard-trained lawyers. They included Thurgood Marshall, who would himself become a Supreme Court justice. Among the famous Howard Law School tutors was Knoxvillian William Hastie, a Harvard University graduate who became the first black federal judge, the first black federal appeals judge, and the first black governor of the Virgin Islands. While Mordecai Johnson also generated accreditation of Howard University's dental and medical schools and strengthened or opened many other schools on campus, it was the Law School that became one of his most celebrated achievements.

When, however, he gave a sermon to a group of Atlanta college students on the nonviolent principles of Mahatma Ghandi, Johnson had no idea of the impact he was having on one student—and again upon the future of the United States. Absorbed in the flow of Johnson's words, Martin Luther King Jr. was so impressed with the concept of nonviolence that he adopted the philosophy as his own. King, in fact, would receive a Nobel Peace Prize in 1964 because of his nonviolent leadership of America's Civil Rights movement.

Johnson's hometown, Paris, was proud of its native son's increasing accomplishments and influence. A *Paris Post-Intelligencer* editorial would recall: "Henry County has more than ordinary interest in this philosophy of selflessness. We take quiet pride in knowing that it was a native Henry Countian, Dr.

Mordecai Johnson, who laid in King's soul the cornerstone of what became the moral foundation of the civil rights movement."

By the time of his retirement in 1960, Johnson had become the embodiment of his parents' educational and religious dreams. In these pursuits, he had developed friendships with United States presidents and received more than ten honorary degrees, as well as a multitude of awards and honors from American civil rights organizations and several foreign countries. In 1960, President John F. Kennedy wired him: "You have truly been one of the outstanding leaders in American education in this century."

Mordecai Johnson, who returned many times to be honored in his West Tennessee hometown, lived until 1976, when he died at the age of eighty-six.

171
"Uncle Dave" Macon
Backcountry Music Resounding over National Airwaves

"People always liked him," fiddler Sid Harkreader said of his friend and fellow musician "Uncle Dave" Macon. "He made people laugh."

If those around him felt good, so did Macon, who was fourteen in 1884 when he saw a banjo player at a Nashville circus and realized that performing could be a lifelong passion and career. As Macon later recalled, "There was a feller . . . played the banjo like the very mischief and I was just plum fascinated with it and when I went home I urged my mother to get me a banjo so I could learn and the upshot was that she did."

The ultimate result was the creation of a part of country music history, because Macon went from playing "in the light of kerosene lamps and unshaded electric light bulbs in country stores and schoolhouses" to making people "feel good" for thirty years on the stage of the *Grand Ole Opry* and across the airwaves of WSM radio. He was the "Dixie Dew Drop"—a showman, storyteller, supreme banjo picker, and one of the personalities who helped create country music. "More than anyone else," wrote music historian Charles K. Wolfe, "Uncle Dave took the nineteenth-century folk music and turned it into twentieth-century country music."

Born in 1870 in Warren County, Dave Macon developed his love of the banjo at about the same time that his father was killed. In 1886, the elder Macon was actively supporting the Democratic gubernatorial candidate, Robert Love Taylor, who was running against his brother, Alfred "Alf" Taylor. At a wild political celebration after his candidate won, Dave's father was knifed to death by a fanatical supporter of the opposition. Several months later, Dave and his mother moved to Readyville and purchased a farm along the Cannon County-Rutherford County line. They also built a roadside platform upon which Dave entertained travelers who rode their horses or drove their wagons and buggies along the dusty turnpike.

After he married in 1898 and settled nearby in Rutherford County's community of Kittrell, Dave Macon abandoned his stationary platform for a mobile one. Beginning in 1901 (and continuing for the next twenty years), he captivated farmers with his tunes while he guided a mule-driven freight wagon along a route between Murfreesboro and Woodbury. "Uncle Dave," as he came to be known, played and sang loud enough for people to gather at the roadside as he passed. Some days, he even gave an impromptu concert in a local town square.

When the gas-powered trucking industry finally put an end to his wagon-freight business in 1921, Macon did not mourn its passing. "All I want is my banjo," he said, and Middle Tennessee had enough schoolhouses and picnics to provide an audience. In 1924, Uncle Dave was discovered by the rest of the country. A Loew's Theater manager heard him play in a Nashville barber shop, and, wanting to hear more, encouraged a duet with "Fiddlin Sid" Harkreader, who was from Gladeville. Hired immediately, they were soon joined by another Middle Tennessean, guitarist Sam McGee from Franklin. Playing to packed theater crowds and then to audiences on the Loew's national vaudeville circuit, Uncle Dave perfected his homey combination of storytelling, singing, and banjo picking.

A talent scout for Vocalion Records liked the performance so much that he sent Macon (joined by Harkreader) to New York City for recording sessions. Undaunted by the big city and its presumed sophistication, Uncle Dave Macon kept his foot-stomping style, which he claimed helped his rhythm. His motions shook the floor, and along with it the record stylus, causing great difficulty in making what would

become one of the nation's first records of traditional country music by a Tennessean.

When Macon approached the microphone in the same way he performed in vaudeville, a recording supervisor tried to coach him on his singing. Uncle Dave shot back:

> Now Cap, I can sing any way I want to and still be heard. I've got a smokehouse full of country hams and all kinds of meat to eat up there in Readyville. I've got plenty of wood hauled up, and I don't have to be bossed around by some New York sharpshooter just to make a few records, 'cause I've done my part on the record-making anyway.

Although he made 175 recordings, Macon was more at home on the radio. In December 1925, he became one of the regulars on the new Nashville-based WSM *Barn Dance*—which would be the beginning of the *Grand Ole Opry*. Among his fellow performers on the show were seventy-seven-year-old "Uncle Jimmy" Thompson from LaGuardo in Wilson County and Dr. Humphrey Bate and "his friends and neighbors from Castalian Springs" (which is how they were advertised). Bate, a physician, had also been a traveling musician in Tennessee, playing all types of southern music on steamboats, in movie houses, and at Middle Tennessee "socials." He was perhaps the first to recognize and use radio as an outlet for country music in Nashville.

Guiding these early performers into entertainment history was well-known announcer George D. Hay, who came from Chicago to begin the *Barn Dance*. Nearly all of his entertainers were Tennesseans from within a hundred miles of Nashville. The show grew so steadily in popularity that even after WSM became an NBC affiliate in 1927, the station manager preempted network programming each Saturday night to broadcast the *Barn Dance*. It followed the NBC *Music Appreciation Hour,* a rather highbrow offering where the conductor reportedly once said "there is no place in the classics for realism."

Amused by the comment, announcer Hay came back with a rejoinder on the air in December 1927. He opened the *Barn Dance* with a parody of the conductor's remark. Said Hay to his listeners: "For the past hour we have been listening to music taken largely from Grand Opera, but from now on we will present the 'Grand Ole Opry.'"

Hay then introduced Deford Bailey, a popular black harmonica player who broke into a train song, "Pan American Blues," with its true-to-life imitation of a train whistle. He was so good at reproducing these sounds even train engineers had difficulty making a distinction. Dubbed the "Harmonica Wizard," Bailey developed this talent as a young boy sitting under train tracks near his Carthage home, listening to train sounds and duplicating them on his harmonica. His radio performance that December 1927 would go down in music history.

By 1932, WSM earned clearance to broadcast with enough power to reach the entire South and Midwest, carrying Uncle Dave Macon and his fellow country-music performers to stardom. Macon's own promotion included a touring wagon not unlike the one he once used to haul freight. On its side he painted: "Banjoist and Songster, Uncle Dave Macon, Slowing Down but Still Moving. Old Time Religion, Old Reliable Way. My Gasoline Consists of Corn, Oats, Whip, and Hay."

He and Deford Bailey toured together for a while. Music fans seemed oblivious to Bailey's race, but hotel owners were not. Whenever Bailey was refused lodging, Macon resolved the problem by insisting that Bailey was his valet with whom he needed to share a room.

At the age of seventy, Uncle Dave Macon joined Opry newcomer Roy Acuff in Acuff's station wagon for a cross-country trip to Hollywood. The two were among the featured performers in the 1939 movie *Grand Ole Opry,* a production that caused confusion for Macon every time someone yelled "cut." When the crew placed a microphone in front of him, he was equally frustrated and gave orders to "take that thing out of the way."

Uncle Dave Macon lived to be eighty-two. He performed on the *Opry* for the last time in March 1952 and died a few days later. In Rutherford County in 1978, the town of Murfreesboro began to celebrate Uncle Dave Macon Day each July in honor of a man who had helped preserve and popularize the musical heritage of Tennessee.

172
J. Fred Johnson

*Enticing Northern Money
to Create a Southern City*

Each time that George Eastman, the inventor of the Kodak camera, arrived in Kingsport during the early twentieth century, he brought with him a passion for hunting wild birds. Keeping a powerful northern industrialist like Eastman happy was a top priority among city promoters, who gladly planned hunting excursions for him. Local jokes abounded that these hunts were so well planned that scores of ducks and other fowl could be found scattered on the ground with just one shot from Eastman's gun.

Such social catering was part of a larger master plan so often used by J. Fred Johnson, the undisputed "father of Kingsport." He laid the economic foundation of twentieth-century America's first city to be financed privately, planned professionally, and diversified in business. Eastman, one of the nation's leading manufacturers, was a man who could provide jobs for Tennesseans in this northeast corner of the state, and Johnson needed the man and his money.

While in Kingsport, Eastman also dined in the J. Fred Johnson home, and the conversation generally turned to the future of the city. At the time, Eastman owned a small local wood-distillation plant. Johnson, whose persuasive powers were legendary, urged him to expand his operations for the sake of hardworking local people, who were dependable, honorable, and devoted—and certainly not likely to join labor unions.

Listening intently around 1930 to some of the spirited dialogue between these two men was the teenage son of Johnson's neighbor. Then in high school, John Shelton Reed was invited to the Johnson house and soon found himself the focus of attention. He later explained: "Mr. Johnson would introduce me as 'one of our fine young men' and tell Eastman 'we need your industry here because lads like this need the good schools and their families need jobs'; he nearly cried when he talked. He was a very emotional man . . . and an unselfish man when it came to the needs of other people."

Eastman was affected. So was John Shelton Reed. The youth, along with several of his friends, soon received a college scholarship to the University of Rochester in upstate New York, near Eastman's company headquarters. To welcome the students there, the benefactor dispatched his vice presidents to meet the arriving train and later hosted a dinner party at his mansion. (These Eastman scholars would go on to outstanding professional achievements. Reed would become a physician like his father and eventually return home to practice medicine, while one of his best friends, Robert Shetterly, would become vice president of Procter & Gamble Company and then president of the Clorox Company.)

To reward the people of Kingsport, Eastman expanded coveted job opportunities. He enlarged the local plant into what would become Tennessee Eastman. The eventual result was the nation's largest manufacturing site for Eastman Chemical Company, supplying chemicals for Kodak's photographic business.

The lure of Kingsport was more than a dependable work force. Located on the Holston River in the shadow of the Appalachian Mountains, Kingsport began as a railroad junction. That railroad, the Carolina, Clinchfield and Ohio, was founded by J. Fred Johnson's brother-in-law, George L. Carter. It was Carter who originally envisioned a model industrial city in the Tennessee mountains, a place where logging and fur trapping were the main trades. Both men came from Hillsville, Virginia, not far from the Tennessee border.

Because of his own mountain background, J. Fred Johnson felt that he had a special kinship with the people of upper East Tennessee. In 1902 at the age of twenty-eight, he moved to Bristol and settled in as the Clinchfield Railroad's general agent, acquiring rights of way and developing trade along the rail route being constructed. He shared his brother-in-law's vision for a model city built with northern industrial dollars. George L. Carter, meanwhile, also donated land in nearby Johnson City for what would become East Tennessee State University.

In 1914, however, Carter sold his holdings (sixty-three hundred acres spread across Sullivan and Hawkins County), enabling a man with even more money, New York City financier John B. Dennis, to build modern Kingsport. The railroad town (thanks to J. Fred Johnson) was already home to a cement plant, a brick plant, and a plant which produced explosives during World War I. After moving to the area, Dennis enlisted his newfound friend Johnson to be the guiding light of the city's construction.

Johnson dictated a massive building plan: a system of government and education, sanitation, water supply, housing, tree-lined boulevards, and parks. From across the nation came city planners, architects, and landscape artists to provide the details. But it was Johnson who controlled the details, large and small. When he stressed the importance of religion and the building of churches, designers answered by putting churches at the very center of town and creating Kingsport's famous Church Circle, which became a landmark.

When dealing with major industries locating in Kingsport during the early twentieth century, Johnson could get visibly upset if they did not provide health insurance and other benefits much like the ones he had designed for city employees. He once refused to dine with Borden Mills' owners because they planned worker bungalows without indoor plumbing. As a result of his social boycott, workers received better housing.

Kingsport remained under Johnson's total control until it was incorporated in 1917. In the years leading up to the Great Depression, the Kingsport Press joined Tennessee Eastman in putting food on the tables of East Tennesseans who could now earn a steady paycheck (the Kingsport Press eventually evolved into the largest book-manufacturing plant in the United States). When the Great Depression dealt the country its worst economic crisis of the twentieth century, Kingsport was poised to survive, and to rescue others. Its windfall of employment also provided jobs for hardworking people in its sister cities, Johnson City and Bristol.

The man who set the stage for this Depression-era survival had become an employer himself. J. Fred Johnson was the president of local banks, an electrical parts company, and the Kingsport Brick Company, as well as owner of a department store that carried his name. After the death of his wife in 1933, Johnson married Elizabeth Doggett of Kingsport. Because he never had his own children, he often provided generous gifts to the children of others (some of them received entire wardrobes on their way to college). Just before his death in 1944, Johnson was well aware that the "model city" he had helped to build was successful. Kingsport was still leaping forward with economic good fortune and playing its part in yet another world war. The Holston Army Ammunition Plant was assisting America's World War II efforts, and Johnson could still be found rallying the region's people. This time he was boosting morale by writing letters to Kingsport's servicemen throughout the world. Johnson was seventy when he died in October 1944 near the war's end.

173
Clarence Brown

Defining the Golden Age of Hollywood

When Knoxville's Clarence Brown decided in 1915 to launch a career in the silent film industry, he ignored the infant town of Hollywood. Brown instead headed for Fort Lee, New Jersey, the home of Peerless Studios, making what Brown considered the finest films of the era.

When he arrived that day, he found French director Maurice Tourneur arguing with a production assistant. Though not involved in the initial dispute, Brown surfaced as the ultimate winner in the argument. Armed with two engineering degrees from the University of Tennessee, he inquired about replacing the production assistant. Tourneur was not impressed by the young man, particularly when he learned that Brown had no film experience.

"Why don't you try an experiment?" Brown challenged brashly. "Take a young, fresh mind that knows nothing about the film business and bring him up the way you want him."

The idea intrigued Tourneur. Becoming the youth's mentor, he ignited a film career that spanned decades and engineering capabilities that brought technical innovations to the emerging motion-picture industry. Brown made his first silent movie in 1920. He remained with Tourneur several years, then eventually accepted in 1926 a contract at Metro-Goldwyn-Mayer Studios in Hollywood, where he spent the remaining twenty-six years of his career. In helping to shape the youngest days of the cinema, Brown directed—and molded—the nation's most notable screen stars, among them Greta Garbo, whose legendary stature began in the several films (including her first talkie, *Anna Christie* in 1930) in which Brown was her director and friend. "She was a shy person; her lack of English gave her a slight inferiority complex," he once explained the Swedish actress who was one of the most popular movie stars of Hollywood's most glamorous period. "I used to direct her quietly. I never

Clarence Brown directing actress Greta Garbo.

gave her a direction above a whisper. . . . She hated to rehearse. . . . She took her work seriously, though."

Brown considered Garbo and Rudolph Valentino "the greatest personalities of the screen . . . the two who are going down through posterity." The growing personality parade under his direction also included Jean Harlow, Clark Gable, Spencer Tracy, Myrna Loy, Hedy Lamarr, Gary Cooper, Irene Dunn, Tyrone Power, Katharine Hepburn, Joan Crawford, James Stewart, and Elizabeth Taylor (Brown directed her first important film, *National Velvet*).

Born in Massachusetts in 1890, Clarence Brown moved in his childhood to Knoxville, where his father became supervisor of a cotton mill; his mother was a weaver. After graduating from Knoxville High School at fifteen, Clarence received special permission in 1905 to enter the University of Tennessee, where his interest in engineering drove him to obtain two degrees in that field by the age of nineteen.

Initially, he went to work as a mechanic and auto dealer in Birmingham, Alabama, but he found himself attracted to the point of obsession by silent movies being shown on machines in the penny arcades. Aware that he had to make a decision about the course of his life, Brown followed his instincts to New Jersey. From Tourneur, he learned to appreciate the values of composition and the use of light. During the 1930s and 1940s, Brown's own "imaginative visual values" began to distinguish his many movies. His films won eight Academy Awards from a total of thirty-eight nominations, including six "best director" nominations. He helped create a movie classic, *The Yearling,* starring a Nashville child, Claude Jarman Jr., whom Brown had discovered after a search through the South. Wanting no publicity as he sought his "star," Brown received permission from Nashville school officials to pose as a maintenance man. He studied hundreds of faces until the search stopped with the fifth-grader whom Brown directed in an Academy Award-winning performance. Jarman won a special Oscar for outstanding child actor in 1946 and gave Clarence Brown the credit.

Brown's technical innovations in motion pictures were perhaps equal to his contributions as a director. In addition to using dollies, cranes, and hydraulic lifts in order to film scenes, Brown employed multiple cameras to capture a given scene from as many as eight angles in one take, thereby avoiding the noise of stopping and starting the primitive soundtrack equipment of the time. In 1922, he worked with Kodak to develop a new color system for motion pictures.

Brown also became noted in Hollywood for his loyalty to his alma mater, the University of Tennessee. When the football team traveled to California to play in the 1940 Rose Bowl, he gave team members a tour of MGM Studios, then entertained the players at his ranch, introducing them to the leading film stars of the day. When the previously undefeated Volunteers were unable to score during their losing effort, sportswriters jokingly speculated that perhaps Brown had entertained the team too well prior to the game.

After retiring from filmmaking in 1952, Brown remained in contact with the university. In 1970, he saw the dedication of a lasting tribute to his name, the Clarence Brown Theater for the Performing Arts on the university's Knoxville campus; the professional Clarence Brown Theater Company simultaneously was formed.

Author Kevin Brownlow claimed in *The Parade's Gone By* that "Clarence Brown is one of the great names of American motion pictures—one of the few whose mastery was undiminished by the arrival of sound. . . . He is unlikely to become a neglected master." When the director died in 1987, he was ninety-seven years old, leaving behind a historic entertainment legacy both through his sensitive and unusual camera techniques that others adopted and through his power to direct great acting performances during Hollywood's Golden Era.

174
Robert R. "The General" Neyland
Transforming Collegiate Football

Robert R. Neyland was hired in 1926 as the University of Tennessee football coach with the understanding that his main task was to defeat powerful archrival Vanderbilt. But he failed in his first attempt; his team lost to the Commodores by a 20-3 score. Then he nearly lost his calm demeanor.

"I remember when I was walking into the Vanderbilt clubhouse after the game to congratulate [Coach] Dan McGugin and his men, I thought to myself that I would much prefer engaging Dan in physical combat," Neyland afterward told *Atlanta Journal* columnist Morgan Blake. "I was that sick over it."

McGugin, who had been Vanderbilt's head coach for more than twenty years, enjoyed a national football reputation, having won ten southern championships with his Vanderbilt teams while also doubling as a corporate attorney. Vanderbilt simply overwhelmed opponents, generally averaging at least four times as many points. Since 1904, McGugin had built one of the highest winning percentages in college football.

Reminded that he had displayed sportsmanship when he congratulated McGugin, Neyland grumbled: "That just shows that we are all more or less hypocrites. No coach, who has just lost a game to his main rival, ever feels in the humor to make a sportsmanlike statement."

Neyland, a native of Greenville, Texas, was hired from his alma mater, West Point, where he was an aide to the school's superintendent general, Douglas MacArthur, in addition to being an assistant coach in numerous sports. The University of Tennessee in Knoxville wanted Neyland to lead its ROTC program as well as its football team. Following his initial setback to Vanderbilt, Neyland did not have to indulge in mild-mannered hypocrisy with other coaches for quite some time. He would guide Tennessee through its next thirty-three games without a loss. In addition to stifling the mighty Commodores during that winning streak, Neyland marked another triumph on October 20, 1928. On that day, he had his first encounter with another titan, Alabama, considered the South's new powerhouse and a certain bet for the Rose Bowl. The night before the game, Tennessee's star tailback, Gene McEver, whom newspapers nicknamed the "Bristol Blizzard," bragged to quarterback Bobby Dodd: "If they kick that ball to ol' Gene . . . he's gonna run it back for a touchdown."

McEver made good on his boast the next afternoon, returning the opening kickoff for a score and spurring Tennessee to a stirring 15-13 upset victory when the oddsmakers did not believe the University of Tennessee would even score. Sports historians believe that game, more than any other, vaulted the Tennessee Volunteers to the nation's attention and, thanks to Neyland's command of football, into major sports circles. The coach brought military-science precision and discipline to the game.

In the winning years that followed, Neyland sought even more powerful nationwide opponents on his schedule, but he was unsuccessful in getting Georgia Tech, Army, Ohio State, Pittsburgh, Southern Cal, or Michigan to play his teams. He said he always took two things into consideration in scheduling: first, he wanted to protect his players from "overwork and injuries," and second, he wanted to "make a financial success of the football team because it pays the way for other sports at the university."

While he was teaching military law, Neyland had a spirited conversation with a dean who questioned why military law students consistently received good grades. In his retort, Neyland blasted back, in part: "I have a good class, and I'll tell you why I have a good class. In my first lecture, I told this class that it would learn military law, that I would teach it to them." Neyland was just as adamant with his students, to whom he declared: "If there is anyone here that I find isn't studying, that man and I will then retire behind this building to settle a question of disobedience, man to man."

During World War II, Neyland utilized his leadership and aggressiveness while serving as a brigadier general in the China-Burma-India campaign. Although his Knoxville gridiron career was twice interrupted by wartime service (he also missed the 1935 season while on duty in Panama), Neyland guided the Volunteers to 173 victories, 31 losses, and 12 ties. His 1939 team was the last in the nation to be unbeaten, untied, and unscored-upon during the regular season. Ironically, the result of the 1940 Rose Bowl against Southern Cal found this same team in the position it had placed all of its regular-season foes—the Vols were unable to score. The final score was 14-0.

Before the game, University of Tennessee alumnus and Hollywood film director Clarence Brown had hosted the team at his ranch, where players mingled with celebrities of the day, among them Lana Turner, Esther Williams, Roy Rogers, Gene Autry, Tom Mix, Robert Montgomery, June Allyson, and Florence Rice, who was the actress-daughter of Tennessee's famous sportswriter, Grantland Rice. Many University of Tennessee fans light-heartedly blamed the loss on Hollywood, where the glitz and glamour of being entertained by movie stars was perhaps too distracting and tiring for the team. At the game itself, movie stars such as Clark Gable, Robert Taylor, and Jack Benny were so prominent that even Tennessee fans were distracted from the playing field. Coach Neyland, however, held a different view of the Volunteer loss. He stated simply: "We got beat by a better football team. The Trojans were hot. They took advantage of our mistakes, and they didn't make any themselves. They had a tremendous line and more hard-running backs than the world ever saw before."

The Volunteers and Neyland, who was now nicknamed "the General," remained in the national spotlight, earning even more prominence. Neyland's 1951 team captured the national championship, and his 1952 team, despite a regular-season loss to Duke and a Cotton Bowl loss to Texas, is said by seasoned observers to have been the best Tennessee football team ever to take the field. Neyland retired from coaching at the end of the season with five SEC championships to his credit. His accomplishments and his contributions to collegiate football became the topic of football analysts, and according to his biographer Bob Gilbert:

> he was a great innovator—the first coach in the South to use press box telephones to the field, and the first coach to use: game films for evaluation; light-weight jerseys that would tear away in an opponent's grasp; low-top shoes and light-weight hip pads to enhance speed; and canvas coverings to protect football fields.

Neyland won 82.9 percent of the time—a national record among coaches who spent twenty or more years at major colleges. Retiring in 1953, he became the University of Tennessee athletic director and helped plan stadium expansions to accommodate ninety-two thousand people. On his seventieth birthday in 1962, the coach was lying in a New Orleans hospital bed suffering from cancer when he learned that the facility would be called Neyland Stadium. He died shortly thereafter. Neyland's wife and two sons brought him back to Knoxville, where he was buried in the United States military cemetery.

175
Joseph Wellington Byrns
Speaker of the House Delivers a New Deal

Joseph Wellington Byrns was not certain what he wanted to do with a law degree after his graduation in 1890, but the Middle Tennessee farm boy was emphatic about one specific: "There's one thing I won't do, and that's be a politician."

Byrns, however, would become one of the longest-serving Tennessee congressmen in the United States House of Representatives. In 1934, he became Speaker of the House, and from this pinnacle he guided passage of President Franklin D. Roosevelt's revolutionary New Deal legislation.

Born in 1869, Byrns was a Scots-Irish descendant of Robertson County pioneers who came through North Carolina. He was educated both in his hometown of Cedar Hill and at Nashville, where his parents moved so that he could attend high school in the city. His former one-room schoolteacher knew him as "Joe Wellie" and recalled the youth's intense interest in reading. Byrns studied literature at Vanderbilt University but later switched his major to law. After practicing his profession for five years, Byrns finally buckled under the pressure of friends who insisted that he run for the state legislature. He was elected from Davidson County in 1895 and ultimately became Speaker of the Tennessee House of Representatives. During this time, he married Julia Woodward, the daughter of Nashville's Judge John Woodward, also from Robertson County.

Having caught the political fever, Byrns next won election to the state senate before seeking national office in 1908—the beginning of a twenty-seven-year career in Congress that made Byrns one of the nation's leading Democrats when Roosevelt began his presidency in 1933.

Early in Roosevelt's first term, Congress assumed its shape largely from an arrangement engineered by the Memphis political boss, Congressman Edward Hull Crump. The deal allowed Byrns, a candidate for House Speaker, to step aside and become House majority leader while an Illinois congressman became the Speaker. This deal was supported by Congressmen from Tennessee, Texas, and New York's "Tammany" delegation. While Byrns was majority leader, Roosevelt's First Hundred Days of New Deal legislation received easy House passage. The House Speaker, however, died between sessions of Congress in 1934, and Byrns ascended to the post, becoming the third Tennessean to be Speaker of the United States House of Representatives (the other two were Williamson County's John Bell in 1834 and Maury County's James K. Polk in 1835).

President Roosevelt's upcoming Second Hundred Days would aim at adjusting how the American government worked and expand federal relief, a move that led later historians to describe Roosevelt as having "veered sharply leftward." *Newsweek* magazine, which described Byrns as an "ultra" conservative throughout his career, observed: "but his unfailing loyalty to the President leaves no doubt that he will champion any and all New Deal policies." Despite any misgivings about the liberal legislation being proposed, Byrns succeeded in pushing through the Second New Deal, which included the Social Security Act of 1935. He repeatedly reminded his fellow congressmen of the size of their agenda, urging extra sessions and long hours.

Several New Deal programs assisted Tennessee more than most states in getting people back to work. Dozens of statewide work programs, for instance, began under the Works Progress Administration (WPA); more than seventy thousand of Tennessee's Depression-era farmers began receiving paychecks from the Civilian Conservation Corps (CCC) to build state parks and roadways; and the Tennessee Valley Authority (TVA) put thousands more to work building dams. Those farmers who continued to labor on their land could now receive a direct subsidy under the Agricultural Adjustment Act.

As it turned out, Byrns's tenure as House Speaker was short. In June 1936, when the congressional session was winding down, he suffered a heart attack and then a cerebral hemorrhage that resulted in his death. While at the peak of his political power, Byrns became the first Speaker of the United States House of Representatives to die while Congress was in session.

His later funeral procession through the streets of Nashville, with more than sixty congressmen and the president of the United States in attendance, ended at Mount Olivet Cemetery.

176
Erastus R. "Ras" Lindamood
TVA—Disrupting and Dislocating Tennesseans

Because the tale grew and grew about a perpetual fire that existed in his family hearth, Union County's Erastus R. "Ras" Lindamood became a bigger and bigger concern to the newly created Tennessee Valley Authority (TVA).

In 1934, when TVA began efforts to convert valleys into lakes, Union County was in its path. The federal government's plan was to control the Tennessee River and its tributaries with a system of dams bringing widespread flood control, cheaper power, and recreation to the area. Like his East Tennessee neighbors, Lindamood had to give up his ancestral homestead to make way for the first major TVA project, Norris Dam. Norris Lake was also being created, a plan which would submerge thousands of farms. The story circulated that TVA was threatening to extinguish a flame which had burned more than seventy-six years. Suddenly, a confrontation between the longstanding traditions of East Tennessee and the modern forces which TVA represented took shape. The fact that TVA surveyors trampled Lindamood's crops and left open his gates did not help matters.

TVA took the case seriously, and, in the fall of 1934, a Knoxville businessman presented a TVA official with a "chunk box," used to transport burning coal from one location to another. When TVA gave the box to Lindamood at his log-cabin home and birthplace, he was more irritated than grateful but expressed his thanks anyway. At the time, he was living with a sister and with his son and family (Mrs. Lindamood had left years earlier, leaving Ras to raise their son alone).

With TVA's help, Lindamood moved to a farm on Chestnut Ridge along the border of Anderson and Knox counties. According to traditional accounts, embers from his old fireplace went with him. A TVA official, Marshall A. Wilson, wrote: "Whether he ever used the chunk box or any other device to take his fire to his new home, I do not know." Wilson, who was TVA's chief social worker in the Norris area, remembered Lindamood and other displaced families in his book *Tales from the Grass Roots of TVA, 1933-1952*. In all, TVA forced nearly three thousand families (or fourteen thousand people) to leave their homes and farms.

The site of the new dam was below the confluence of the Powell River and Clinch River. Construction required housing for thousands of workers, and TVA built the town of Norris to meet those needs. The town was also designed to be a permanent community served by nearby Knoxville; newly built homes became a test site for new ideas and innovations. Norris houses, for instance, featured all-encompassing electric heat—the nation's first household use of ceiling heat.

The town, the dam, and the lake were named for the Nebraska congressman, George Norris, who had been instrumental in TVA's creation. In 1946, TVA held a public auction to sell the town, which had fallen into the hands of Philadelphia, Pennsylvania, investors. Norris tenants ultimately were able to lease and then buy their homes.

In 1956, CBS decided to do a story on Lindamood's perpetual fire, finding the tale believable enough to broadcast a story on May 10, 1956. Lindamood had his doubts about how perpetual the fire was, but he had no problem admitting that the embers were always warm. His father, Isaac Lindamood, had started the fire nearly a century before in Wythe County, Virginia. The family brought the fire with them in 1859 to Union County and Long Hollow, located about twenty-five miles north of present-day Maynardville. Erastus, the youngest of ten children, was born in 1864. He explained that cooking so much food for so many children may have forced his parents to keep the blaze going year-round between 1859 and 1879.

The arrival of the family's first stove at Christmas of 1879 may (or may not) have caused the fire to die that summer. The saga of the perpetual flame, however, did not die. It was maintained (some say revived) around 1930 when Lindamood's sister came down with "consumption." To drive away a heavy fog, he revived the fire and kept it going more or less continuously. Lindamood himself lived to be seventy-eight. He died in 1942 at LaFollette, Tennessee.

177
George Washington Lee

Carrying Black Pride to America

In 1933, Memphis insurance executive George Washington Lee rushed out of his office every morning to get the mail—hoping to intercept it before his secretaries could get there. A would-be author, Lee knew that he was likely to find another publisher's rejection slip and his returned manuscript, which painted what he believed to be an irresistible portrait of black Americans on Beale Street—told by one of their own. The book was about black pride, and Lee was a proud man. He did not want his secretaries to witness his daily defeat.

Lee had spent years collecting his material, then assembling and writing it. He sought professional opinions over the years, but one friend, George Schuyler, an editorial writer in Pittsburgh, Pennsylvania, told him it would never get beyond a local publisher. Schuyler's best suggestion was "Get drunk, and then rewrite, playing up the old music, how the musicians were trained, and how the Blues were born."

Lee's persistence, and a little rewriting, paid him historic dividends. Consulting with noted black author James Weldon Johnson, Lee reworked his manuscript and found a national publisher. The new author became involved in promoting the book nationwide, by now renamed *Beale Street: Where the Blues Began.* Lee spoke on NBC Radio and attended New York City cocktail parties where guests delighted in hearing his colorful stories about "honky tonks." For George Washington Lee, however, the more important feature of the book was highlighting the success of many Beale Street blacks and the describing how they were helping one another in Memphis.

Sales were slow at first because stores did not stock the book, until a review in the *New Yorker* magazine said that *Beale Street* provided "the authentic color of good crackerbox gossip." Sales then soared, and the publisher hired a clipping service to collect the reviews. Lee's pride soared too, and he hired another clipping service to make certain no review went unnoticed. He was soon chosen as the first black writer to be advertised by the Book-of-the-Month Club. Informally, Lee was called the "Boswell of Beale Street."

His advisor Schuyler, now among the nation's best-known reviewers, wrote: "George W. Lee, well-known Memphis businessman and politician, has moved up to the front rank of Negro authors, and produced a work of real historical merit of which any American writer might be proud."

Lee's biographer Tucker also noted that the Book-of-the-Month Club review was equally glowing:

W. C. Handy set the country to singing its "blues" and now George W. Lee has told its story, a story of booze and dope, of bad men and smart men, of politics, of schools and churches, of poverty and easy money, of little thrifty black grocers, of gamblers and bright-skinned women. It is a story rich in material for both the romanticist and the sociologist. He presents all the material, the stirring beside the commonplace, the story of universal appeal beside the cataloguing of prominent shopkeepers who pay their rent on Tennessee's most famous street.

"Tennessee's most famous street" became even more so. Americans everywhere were dazzled by the glitter and charm of Beale Street that flowed from Lee's pages. He followed this success with a 1937 Book-of-the-Month Club alternate selection, *River George.*

The author was rapidly adding to his growing lifetime accomplishments, all of which revolved around black pride, and generally around Beale Street, a place where black success could be measured not only in music but also in business and in politics. George Washington Lee distinguished himself in each.

Since first arriving in Memphis from Mississippi poverty in 1912, Lee had captured attention. He obtained the most prestigious and lucrative occupation then available for a black man by becoming a bellhop. At the city's finest hotel, the Gayoso, Lee made good money and even better connections within the white community, setting the stage for his future as a Memphis black leader. While working at the Gayoso, Lee also attended college, traveling across the state border to take classes at Mississippi's Alcorn College.

With the coming of World War I, Lee made American military history as one of the nation's few black United States Army officers. After training at Fort Des Moines, Iowa, the country's first officer-training camp for black men, Lee was shipped out to France. He reported there in June 1918 as a member of the all-black

Ninety-second Division. Lee was promoted on the battlefield for his bravery, and the French awarded him their greatest honor, the *Croix de Guerre*.

When the war ended, Lee was convinced he could do more for his fellow blacks as a businessman than as a peacetime soldier. He began selling life insurance for black-owned Mississippi Life in 1919. Within weeks, he rose to manager; within the year, he was vice president. When the company came under white ownership, Lee resigned, took most of its black agents with him, and became local manager of the newly organized, black-owned Atlanta Life Insurance Company. Convinced that black business could help "make the South blossom like a rose," Lee became one of Memphis's rising young businessmen.

Black business, however, was wilting in Memphis. The failure of Roddy's Citizen's Cooperative Store in 1922 set off a chain of events that left the city's black banking empire in shambles. Numerous black bank officials had been jailed on fraud and embezzlement charges, heaping embarrassment on the city's entire black population. Lee chose to rally the black community, believing that black business was the key to a better future. "We must step forward and build upon the ashes of the ruins," he wrote. "To turn back means disintegration and economic slavery. Crookedness is not a racial trait. Main Street has been sending her white crooks to the penitentiary for years. Beale Street must do the same and then march on with confidence in our race and in our God." It would take many years, but Memphis's black citizenry eventually had another successful major bank—and one of its directors would be George Washington Lee.

When he selected politics to advance himself further, Lee, a Republican, was jumping into "one of the few opportunities of integration in the South" at the time, because white politicians often teamed with their black counterparts to win elections and hold patronage jobs. After 1920, Lee was the virtual spokesman for Robert Church Jr., the most powerful black political leader in Memphis and eventually in the nation. While Church organized behind the scenes to control local and national black voting blocs (his famous Lincoln League), George Washington Lee was in the foreground as Church's chief "lieutenant," giving platform speeches. His gifts as an orator made Lee one of the most popular black speakers of his day.

Lee also became adept at obtaining federal patron-age jobs from Republican presidents. But he found that he had to align himself with Democratic Memphis Mayor Edward Hull "Boss" Crump in order to obtain other patronage for blacks. Such association with local white leaders often placed Lee in jeopardy with his brethren, many of whom began to believe that he was little more than a "brown screw in the Crump machine."

In 1952, Lee's political power was strong enough for national viewing. Following two decades of Democratic Party rule, Republicans saw 1952's presidential election as an opportunity to return to national prominence. Lee's fervent support of Robert Taft for the Republican nomination earned him two appearances on national television during the 1952 GOP convention; one appearance was a seconding speech for Taft. Lee broke into the national spotlight with the help of upper East Tennessee Congressman B. Carroll Reece, former Republican national chairman. Although Taft lost the nomination to Dwight D. Eisenhower, Lee was still powerful. Eisenhower conferred with him and called Lee's speech for Taft "brilliant." When Lee returned to Memphis, the black citizenry proclaimed George W. Lee Day.

In 1956, Lee's political career peaked when he helped to carry Tennessee for Eisenhower. With the victory came more federal patronage jobs in Memphis for his friends. But Lee's influence began to wane thereafter. Democrats were gaining increasing control of Memphis black politics by appearing more sympathetic to black needs than Republicans. Protest, and not accommodation to whites, was the new theme. George Washington Lee, nonetheless, was still an institution in black Memphis. When popular singer Mahalia Jackson and Civil Rights leader Martin Luther King Jr. came to the city in 1959 to rally black voters for a local election, the "lieutenant" was asked to deliver opening remarks. Lee used the occasion to deliver one of his most inspiring addresses, proving that while he might be politically weakened, he was still an orator of the first degree: "The major issue," he told the crowd in his thundering voice, "is whether a Negro can live as a man and not as a boy in Memphis, and walk the streets in dignity and self-respect."

George Washington Lee, a descendant of black political power brokers from days gone by, had watched as his brand of politics disappeared. But he adamantly remained a staunch Republican until his death at the age of eighty-two. A 1976 automobile accident took the life of the man who was an acclaimed orator, writer, frequent guest at the White House, one of the South's leading black businessmen, and a political force over the course of four decades.

178
Laura Cook
Women Taking Charge on the Homefront

Along the Cumberland Plateau in 1940, women decided to take over the town of Spencer. The town had undergone a period without government, and this state of affairs was particularly hard on all of Van Buren County, since Spencer was the county seat. Helping to resurrect the town was sixty-five-year-old Laura Cook; she faced the task in her wire-rimmed glasses and with her hair pulled into a bun behind her head. Laura was the new police chief.

The new city government was behind her—and there was no problem that she was a woman and that she was of retirement age. No problem at all—not to the mayor, Mrs. J. M. "Mother" Gordon, who was most likely in her seventies, nor to the city recorder, Mrs. Ella B. Powers, who had that same wise bearing that only years of living provided. A poll of the city aldermen would have yielded unanimous approval, too. To a woman, they agreed. Mrs. Osma Lewis (Womack), Mrs. Edgar Rascoe, Mrs. D. L. Bouldin, Mrs. T. F. Page, and Mrs. J. L. Graham were all happy to see their friend as police chief. As it so happened, every officeholder was a member of the Better Homes and Gardens Garden Club. The women had drawn straws to determine who would hold which office.

Police Chief Cook had lived in Spencer for nearly twenty years, since leaving her native Bedford County farm so that some of her children could attend Burritt College. A widow at the time, she was accustomed to raising cotton and other crops. In Spencer, she kept a boarding house on Breezy Hill for nearby college students, making enough money to help her through the Great Depression. Having made her own way since her husband's death thirty-two years earlier, Laura Cook was not reluctant to become the town's chief law enforcement officer.

The city administration had been defunct since the previous mayor's death. Because Spencer had con-

tinued to run smoothly, most voters (mostly men) did not seem to think they needed a new mayor. Since they disagreed about the need for government, garden club members had decided to elect themselves. After all, Spencer was losing its portion of state tax money without a government in place. No one else had considered that fact or that little Spencer was bankrupt.

When the election campaign began, the women's platform was catchy: "No taxes, no salaries, a Community House, and more fun for all!" Donations poured in from the garden club (three hundred dollars in all) to get the government back on its feet. To raise more money for beautification projects in Spencer, the candidates held a pie supper, a fiddling contest, and a contest at ten cents per vote to determine the prettiest girl in town and the ugliest man. More money was raised with a "Fat Hen Drive" (every family but two donated their biggest hens), quiltings, and concerts featuring regulars from the *Grand Ole Opry*. The victorious garden club followed 1940's election with six years of a female-only government.

Generally, serious trouble never visited Spencer. In 1941, however, Police Chief Cook and Mayor Gordon (better known as Mother Gordon) had to make an official visit to a local restaurant owner and reprimand the fellow for selling beer. The moment was described in *Collier's* magazine:

Chief of Police Cook hasn't had much to do. Of course the men would help if anything right bad happened. About a year ago, R. D. Hutchenson who runs a café on Main Street started selling beer. Chief Cook and Mayor Mother Gordon went down to see him. Nobody was going to sell beer in Spencer they said. At first, Hutch got sore, threatened to get into politics himself, run for mayor maybe.

But Hutch calmed down, said he'd quit selling beer. Hutch had tears in his eyes too. Said he guessed it wasn't right to have little Sammie, his baby, growing up where beer was sold.

Garden club members counted other small triumphs. They ran the town through World War II, and, by the end of their third term in 1946, these officeholders had unveiled new sidewalks, a new American Legion Hall, upscaled landscaping, and a city treasury balance of $1,050. Deciding not to seek reelection, the women finally stepped aside, allowing men to return to office when many returned from wartime duty. But Spencer Garden Club members, without previous experience, had already shown they were capable of bringing a town back to life.

Their able chief of police became ill about this time. Doctors offered to treat Laura Cook's unidentified illness with radium, which they said might soften her bones. The options were "take the treatments, or, go home and die," remembered her grandson, Thomas Hoyte Cook Sr. "Laura elected to go home and die."

Instead, she lived on and on, and doted on her many grandchildren to the age of eighty-four. She died in 1960 at her old boarding home atop Breezy Hill.

179
Roy Acuff

The King of Country Music—A Soldier's Choice

Roy Acuff preserved the traditional sounds of country music.

During World War II, a story circulated in the United States that Japanese soldiers on Okinawa, trying to demoralize American Marines, led their attack with the cry "To hell with Roosevelt; To hell with Babe Ruth; To hell with Roy Acuff!"

Roy Acuff never actually intended to devote his life to music, which had made him something of a national hero. Born in Maynardville in 1903, he had set his sights on becoming more like Babe Ruth—a professional baseball player. As a teenager in Knoxville, Acuff pursued this goal for five years with some success, but after suffering a severe sunstroke in 1929, Acuff was forced to relinquish his dream. While recuperating, he reacquainted himself with the fiddle he had learned to play as a child from listening to his father, who was a Baptist preacher. Acuff also worked on his singing style, using his experience from church singing and getting help from his sister, who had been given voice lessons. He then listened to records of the day, which included those of the Carter Family from Virginia. Some of these records had been produced at the famous 1927 Bristol sessions, during a time when companies traveled to East Tennessee and recorded local musicians in their own settings. The record companies moved from Bristol to Johnson City to Knoxville, creating a national audience for mountain-style music.

Developing a singing style influenced by the sacred music of the Tennessee mountains, Acuff decided to become an entertainer. He joined a traveling medicine show and then worked at Knoxville radio stations WNOX and WROL. During the Great Depression, the pride of Union County became a household name among East Tennesseans who spent time listening to WNOX and its popular country-music radio show, Lowell Blanchard's *Mid-Day Merry-Go-Round*.

Acuff even recorded a few songs, which were sold in 1936 through the Sears, Roebuck and Company Catalog. The most famous of these were "The Great Speckled Bird" and "The Wabash Cannonball." But Acuff was not content simply with the popularity he was building in the Knoxville market. What he really wanted was to perform on the emerging *Grand Ole Opry* being broadcast over WSM Radio. Acuff sent letter after letter to the show's manager and announcer, George D. Hay, but the efforts were in vain. Hay feared that Acuff's music might be perceived as too old-fashioned.

Not until 1938, when popular fiddler Arthur Smith left the show, did Roy Acuff get his chance. After playing some competent fiddle pieces that failed to ignite the audience, Acuff launched into his rendition of "The Great Speckled Bird," a performance that made him an *Opry* celebrity almost overnight. A year later, he was the show's first great singing star. That same year, NBC agreed to broadcast a portion of the *Grand Ole Opry* on its network, giving the Opry its first coast-to-coast exposure. Almost immediately, Hollywood produced the movie *The Grand Ole Opry,* and the starring role went to Acuff, who would soon be known as "the king of country music."

At a time when country music was becoming more sophisticated and influenced by "western swing," Roy Acuff and his Smoky Mountain Boys helped preserve the more traditional acoustic sound of mountain music and the spiritual depth of the old mountain singing tradition. He sang with such intensity that he often broke down and cried during his own performances. Audiences responded to his sincerity, and sold-out concerts accompanied him throughout the United States.

In 1942, Acuff began another music-related venture in Nashville. With his composer-friend Fred Rose, he created Acuff-Rose Publications, the nation's "first exclusive country music publishing house."

During World War II, Acuff's music was broadcast across the world wherever United States armed forces were stationed. In Germany, servicemen answered an informal poll conducted by Armed Forces Network and voted Roy Acuff their favorite singer over the big-band crooning of Frank Sinatra.

Acuff's popularity also brought him into the political arena in Tennessee. In 1948, the Republican Party's attempt to find a popular candidate to break the political machine of Memphis-based Democrat Edward Hull "Boss" Crump resulted in Acuff's name being placed on the primary gubernatorial ballot. Much to Acuff's surprise, he won the nomination. Hoping to defeat the Crump machine, Acuff campaigned in earnest. He conducted a statewide effort which, with his musical approach to electioneering, resembled a concert tour. Acuff lost to Democrat Gordon Browning, a former governor from Carroll County who also was anti-Crump. Browning capitalized on the postwar mood of voters demanding that the democratic process (not machine politics) and military heroes (such as himself) should provide new political leadership. As for Acuff, he was only too glad that he had played a part in the downfall of the Crump machine, even if he had not won the political race.

Politics aside, Acuff continued to be a performer, becoming a mainstay and goodwill ambassador of the

Grand Ole Opry. Country music historian Bill C. Malone noted that Roy Acuff's name and that of the *Opry* "became almost synonymous." Acuff was a regular performer there for fifty-four years until his death in 1992.

180
Minnie Pearl
(Sarah Ophelia Colley Cannon)
Grand Ole Opry Smiles and Laughter for a Nation

Minnie Pearl (Sarah Ophelia Colley Cannon) with her trademark hat and dangling price tag.

As a child, Sarah Ophelia Colley could play the piano beautifully—a talent that made her mother very happy. Ophelia (as she was known) could also play the "clown"—a talent that did not make her mother quite as happy but that would make Ophelia famous. "Someone has said that each time a baby is born on earth, the angels in Heaven smile," she wrote years later in her autobiography. "When I was born they must have laughed right out loud. I'm sure they felt they had played some wonderful joke on my proud, conventional Southern parents."

Her father, Tom Colley, was a lumberman. While living in Franklin, he met Fannie Tate House, whom he married in 1897 and took to Centerville, the Hickman County seat. Still a frontier town, Centerville was a good place for Middle Tennessee lumbermen to prosper at the turn of the twentieth century. There, Colley built a house for his refined wife who had a finishing school background, elegant manners, and a knowledge of good music.

Sarah Ophelia, born in 1912, was the youngest of five daughters and the center of attention. "While Daddy was making me into a tomboy and my sisters were encouraging me to be a show-off, my poor mother was trying to raise a little lady," she said. "The fact that my natural inclinations leaned more toward Daddy's and the girls' influences didn't make her job any easier."

Sarah Ophelia's older sisters called her "Ophie" and taught her to recite poems, sing, dance, and perform in front of audiences, prompting her to love the spotlight and to entertain thoughts of a show business career. In general, Ophie was brought up to enjoy the classics, both in literature and in music. If a stage career was in her future, she was certain that it would involve drama.

After graduating from Ward-Belmont Academy of Nashville where she majored in stage technique, Ophelia taught dance. But she soon found a niche with the Sewell Production Company of Atlanta. Traveling the South for six years, she brought dramatic productions to small towns and used locals as actors. She also developed a country-girl comedy routine inspired by her years of directing plays in rural communities. "To help publicize the show in each town, I would appear before the Lion's Club and other groups," she explained. "In return for them letting me announce my show, I'd do a couple of minutes entertainment for them. I'd do an interpretation of a country girl, Minnie Pearl." Shortly before her father died in the late 1930s, he told her: "You'll make a fortune off that some day, Phel, if you keep it kind."

Despite her own refined upbringing, Ophelia developed her country-bumpkin act to such an extent that it became her second self. When the Sewell com-

pany hit hard times because the populace was staying home to enjoy recordings and radio, Ophelia headed back to Centerville. To earn a living, she took a job in the Works Progress Administration (WPA) supervising a local recreation center and earned extra money teaching drama and dance to children.

One night in 1939, she entertained for a bankers' convention. As usual, she charmed the group with her homespun humor and country tales. "I had been collecting country stories and anecdotes from the time I'd begun on the road, and it was fun to repeat them in dialect," Ophelia would write. This time, she was recommended to a WSM radio executive in Nashville. What followed was an audition with the *Grand Ole Opry*, followed by an invitation in 1940 to become a member of the *Opry* family. To her own family and friends, she remained Sarah Ophelia Colley. To country music fans, she would always be her make-believe character, "Cousin Minnie Pearl."

Like many country stars of the 1940s, Minnie Pearl kept her act before the public by performing in as many places as she could during the week before returning to the *Grand Ole Opry* on Saturday night. Often, a group of entertainers traveled in a caravan organized by a major sponsor and a business manager. Life on the road, especially during the war years when rationing made gasoline and tires hard to come by, tested the endurance of these performers. Minnie Pearl remembered riding through winding two-lane roads in an old hearse the business manager had purchased so that he could cluster as many performers and as much equipment as possible:

> so eight or nine of us crowded in a space that would have been uncomfortable even for six on long distances. There was absolutely no way to get comfortable. You couldn't stretch out. You could barely move. There were no headrests on the backs of the seats, so you sat straight up with your hands in your lap, stuffed in like sardines.

During the Second World War, Minnie Pearl became even more famous when she took her act to United States military bases, joining a number of *Opry* stars who entertained American troops. In 1947, she married former United States Air Corps pilot Henry Cannon, who became her business manager and frequently flew his wife and other performers to their destinations. Under his guidance, Minnie Pearl's career continued to flourish, making her the one woman "most closely identified with the Opry" during this time.

She continued decade after decade to bring kind-hearted humor to the lives of audiences everywhere, and Minnie Pearl received a plaque in 1975 from Nashville's Country Music Hall of Fame saluting her as "the first country humorist to be known and loved worldwide." The tribute further stated: "Humor is the least recorded, but certainly one of the most important aspects of live country music. No one exemplified the values of pure country comedy more than Minnie Pearl." Years later, she would be the first woman chosen for the National Comedian Hall of Fame, which was established in Florida.

Cousin Minnie's shrill "How-dee!" as she greeted audiences had become a famous trademark. So had her straw hat, with its dangling price tag ($1.98 to be exact), which was originally not a planned part of her costume. It occurred quite by accident one night during an *Opry* appearance, as she explained in her autobiography:

"Everything happens to me. Nothing comes off without some flaw. Buy a suit with two pair of pants, you burn a hole in the coat"—the hillbillies' comment on luck. (That's why I wear a price tag on my hat—another accident. I put some dime-store flowers on my hat for the Opry one night and mistakenly left the price tag on them. As I moved my head around during my act, the tag dangled down off the brim. Someone laughed at it, so I left it there, and Minnie has worn a price tag on her hat ever since. Anything for a laugh, I always say.)

Sarah Ophelia Colley, born to refinement, education, and southern manners, had scaled the heights of country music stardom by portraying a slapstick, back-country comedienne. The laughter did not end until Minnie Pearl's death in 1996.

181
Cornelia Fort

A Woman Pilot—
Dodging the Attack at Pearl Harbor

Cornelia Fort, a WASP on World War II duty.

She had spotted something headed her way—another airplane, clearly on a collision path, and mysteriously aimed at her own craft. Grabbing the controls away from her startled student, Cornelia Fort barely averted a midair collision that would have killed both of them and the careless military pilot in the other plane.

When she caught sight of the other plane's identification, she was shocked to see that it was the characteristic red ball of a Japanese fighter. Glancing toward Pearl Harbor, Cornelia also saw an ominous cloud of black smoke rising. Responding to her oblivious student's petition to fly solo, she declared, "Not today, brother!" and quickly returned to their landing field.

While Cornelia taxied in, machine-gun bullets sprayed the runway ahead of her. She jumped out of the cockpit and ran toward the hangar, warning fellow civilian pilots that Pearl Harbor was being attacked. They laughed at her, but the truth lay only seconds away on this December 7, 1941. A mechanic then dashed pell-mell into the hangar and announced that the airport manager had been killed by bullets from an overhead plane.

Cornelia Fort, twenty-two, was the daughter of prominent Nashvillians, and a debutante who had chosen to abandon fox hunts, social clubs, and high-society dances to pursue her real love—aviation. Raised on a large farm in Davidson County and taught a spirit of independence, she attended exclusive Ward-Belmont School for girls, then entered Sarah Lawrence College in New York.

Soon, she was in Hawaii giving flight lessons to the many government employees working in the islands before the war. Cornelia was a flight instructor for Andrew Flying Service in Honolulu. This uncommon occupation for a woman in the 1930s and early 1940s had become the love of her life.

With the outbreak of hostilities against America, Cornelia Fort's new ambition was to get home and contribute to the war effort. After making promotional appearances and starring in a war-bond movie about her well-publicized encounter over Oahu, she became a Woman Air Force Service Pilot (WASP), hoping to perform special aviation duties in order to free the men for war. Women pilots shuttled planes from the factories to military bases and, in time, also tested new aircraft or new aircraft equipment in special flying missions.

Although issued uniforms and subject to military discipline, these women were not considered members of the armed forces. Frequently, they were resented and harassed by their male counterparts in the aviation community. In the air, some male pilots often tried to buzz or dogfight flying women, who were under strict orders to stay five hundred feet away from other planes at all times.

When one airman in 1943 swooped close over Cornelia Fort's aircraft, he either lost control or merely assumed she would dodge out of the way. Instead, his landing gear smashed her canopy and she was killed in the crash that followed.

In 1979, Congress finally recognized WASPs as members of the armed forces between 1942 and 1944 and accorded them all distinctions and privileges associated with military service. Nashville's Cornelia Fort, thirty-six years after her death, was honored as the first woman killed in the line of duty in the United States Air Force.

182
Austin Shofner
Surviving in the Jungle as a World War II Prison Camp Escapee

Escaped World War II prisoner of war Austin Shofner described himself as the "bull moose" of his band of escapees in April 1943. After enduring ten months and twenty-eight days as a Japanese prisoner in the Philippines, Shofner was the only man in his crew who weighed more than 100 pounds, and he topped out at 120.

Born in 1916 and raised in Bedford County, Shofner relied on an athletic background and natural leadership skills to overcome his ordeal. During his college days at the University of Tennessee, he had held varsity letters in football and wrestling and won an award as the athlete with the highest grades. In 1937, due to his scholarship and leadership, Shofner was the only university graduate to receive an appointment to the United States Marine Corps that year.

In early 1941, Shofner was on duty in Shanghai, China, as a company commander in the Fourth Marine Regiment. In November, the regiment was transferred to the Philippine Islands. Shortly after the war began, Shofner participated in the defense of Bataan and Corregidor in action that won him the Silver Star with Oak Leaf Cluster and a promotion to captain. Upon the surrender of Corregidor, he was captured by the Japanese and imprisoned.

In Shofner's battalion, only one other officer survived the rigors of prison camp. It claimed the lives of many friends who could not endure near-starvation and disease. Five groups had tried unsuccessfully to escape their imprisonment on the island of Mindanao, but they had been unable to pass the main fence. Shofner had a different line of attack. He and nine fellow prisoners walked out the front gate with forged passes, saluted the Japanese, then ran for their lives.

Moving deep into a hostile jungle, the escapees encountered tribes that had never seen white men. Using a cache of goods he had pilfered at the camp, Shofner was able to placate tribal chiefs and gain safe passage in the jungle. The men wandered thirty-five days before they found another group of Americans, who had not surrendered to the Japanese but instead joined a Filipino guerrilla unit in the wilderness. Shofner became the guerrillas' deputy chief of staff and operations officer. United, the men printed their own money and built a telephone "with a generator powered by a little boy on a bicycle" as well as a radio "made with parts from an old movie projector and copper coiled around some bamboo."

In November 1943, an American submarine bringing supplies to the guerrillas rescued Shofner and his men. "It was the first time in the history of warfare that a ship came in and docked in enemy territory," Shofner said. "The USS *Narwhal* tied up alongside the pier in a harbor on the northern coast of Mindanao, in broad daylight, while the guerrilla band played 'Anchors Aweigh.'"

After returning to the United States, Shofner was anxious for new assignments. Promoted to major, he received from General Douglas MacArthur the nation's second-highest military decoration, the Distinguished Service Cross. Shofner's diary of the dramatic prison escape and the jungle experiences that followed made *Life* magazine in February 1944. Plans for a motion picture were underway until President Franklin D. Roosevelt intervened to prevent a breach in national security. Three books, however, were later written on the exploits of Shofner and his companions.

Austin Shofner was back in the Pacific theater within five months. Joining the First Marine Division, he was an assault battalion commander on Peleliu, where he was wounded on D-Day in 1944 and received a Purple Heart. Now a lieutenant colonel, Shofner was then assigned to the United States Army for the landing at Luzon, Philippines, serving as an advisor on guerrilla warfare. In April 1945, he was again with the First Marine Division, for the lead assault on Okinawa, remaining on the front lines in this last major landing in the Pacific. Shofner was honored as "one of the leading Marines in number of days of combat and one of the most decorated for combat during World War II."

In a subsequent tour of duty, Shofner was stationed at the Marine Corps Base in Quantico, Virginia, continuing as battalion commander and becoming head

football coach of the Quantico Marines. In 1947, he married Kathleen King of Knoxville. The couple, who would become parents to five sons, relocated to Lima, Peru. There, Shofner served as naval attaché at the American Embassy under Ambassador Prentice Cooper, a former governor of Tennessee. Shofner was decorated by that nation's president for fostering good relations between Peru and the United States

With the outbreak of the Korean War in 1950, Shofner reported to Camp Lejeune, North Carolina, as executive officer of the Second Marine Regiment to train replacements for the war effort. Four years later, he was assigned to the chief of Naval Operations in Washington, D.C., as planning officer for Latin America.

Late in his career, Shofner served as commanding officer of the famous Sixth Marines and on the staff of the commanding general of the Second Marine Division. While attending the Army War College, Austin Shofner was promoted to brigadier general. He retired in 1959 and returned home to Shelbyville to become a businessman.

183
R. Ernest Frankland
On the German Battlefront with the Best Shot in Jackson

Besides being a popular battalion commander in 1940 and possessing a distinguished twenty-year career with the Tennessee National Guard, R. Ernest Frankland was known around his hometown of Jackson as a dead shot with a pistol.

When the United States entered World War II, Frankland was a first lieutenant with the guard, but was soon promoted to lieutenant colonel. His was the highest wartime rank generally handed out to guardsmen after guard units were federalized to join the regular army.

Described by his hometown friend Ben Emerson as a fun-loving man, Frankland was also a swing-band drummer who had a favorite saying, "I believe in working hard, then playing hard." During the war, his work ethic was never questioned. He doggedly led his men from Omaha Beach to Germany's Elbe River. Frankland's command was the First Battalion, 117th Infantry, part of the acclaimed "Old Hickory" (or Thirtieth) Division,

R. Ernest Frankland (left) and Walter L. Frankland, brothers on the European front during World War II.

which landed in Normandy, France, immediately after D-Day in June 1944. His brother Walter Frankland happened to be another twenty-year guardsman and a fellow lieutenant colonel. Walter served as Old Hickory's supply officer with the complicated duty of stocking an infantry that was moving rapidly inland (all American and British forces were supplied from the invasion beaches).

The Old Hickory Division, named for Andrew Jackson, was heir to many old-time militias from Tennessee and the Carolinas which had carried a proud tradition of bravery and tenacity since before the Revolutionary War. It was organized as the Thirtieth Division before World War I and played a stellar role in that war. During World War II, the Thirtieth's deeds helped break the back of Germany, giving the Allies a victory in the European theater of the war.

According to one later chronicler, R. Ernest Frankland did not just command the First Battalion, the battalion "*belonged* to Ernest Frankland, much

like the medieval military formations that were the personal property of the barons who raised, trained, and commanded them."

After the D-Day invasion, the Allies remained bottled-up for weeks in the hedgerow country. As part of the massive breakout from the beachhead, the Old Hickory Division was assigned to hold open the breach in German lines in the vicinity of Mortain. The situation became critical. American bombers, impeded by weather and other factors, hit Old Hickory troops as well as the enemy. Then the infantrymen became a primary target for Germany's counterattack, spearheaded by two German panzer (tank) divisions, including Adolph Hitler's legendary and feared First SS Panzer Division.

Setting up a defense to protect the French village of St.-Barthelmy, R. Ernest Frankland received a report that the only Germans were northeast of town. Hitler's First SS Panzer Division, however, made a surprise assault along the southern approach in addition to attacking from the north. Frankland's First Battalion faced annihilation. Two platoons in the surrounding hillsides were nearly wiped out, leaving Company A with only one officer and twenty-seven men. Frankland's command post in St.-Barthelmy was also in trouble. While trying to reestablish radio contact with his units, Frankland heard a tank pull up outside the two-story headquarters. He grabbed his .45 automatic pistol and ran to the back of the house. Two of his radiomen were heading out the door with their hands up and German soldiers prodding them at rifle point.

Accounts differ about what happened next. According to Frankland, he shot the two German riflemen and escaped with his soldiers to help rally the remains of the battalion. According to his men, Frankland not only shot the German riflemen, but also killed the tank commander atop the panzer, then leaped on the tank, threw open the hatch, and killed the entire enemy crew. "If it had been written up, he'd have gotten the Congressional Medal of Honor," claimed Sergeant James Waldrop, also from Jackson. "But the colonel never reported it. He wouldn't brag on himself. No way, no shape, no form or fashion."

The headquarters group headed for the hills to join forces with Company B, while Colonel Frankland made his way alone to find what was left of Company A. He gathered his surviving men, met up with Company B (mostly men from Athens, Tennessee, and the adjacent East Tennessee area) and ordered a quick withdrawal of all jeeps and trucks in the region "just in time for all but two of the vehicles to escape safely." The badly decimated Company C continued to fight off the Germans' southern attack. In all, the First Battalion delayed the Germans for six hours, assuring the Allied victory at nearby Mortain.

Partly because of the heroic stand of R. Ernest Frankland's battalion, along with equally tough defenses around Mortain by other elements of Old Hickory, the two German divisions were driven off, and the breakout was saved. Postwar interrogations of three enemy generals revealed that the Germans considered Mortain to be an astonishing failure on their part and one of Germany's decisive losses in France. A later United States military historian said that Frankland's First Battalion, despite its heavy losses, "inflicted far heavier casualties on the two attacking panzer divisions." Added Alwyn Featherston:

"Surprised, outnumbered, and largely unsupported, the defenders of St.-Barthelmy turned the tide of the Battle of Mortain in a forgotten struggle that ranks as one of the epic engagements in World War II."

Now the Allied liberation of France was rapid. Old Hickory, described on Nazi radio as "Roosevelt's SS," fought its way across France with the Germans in retreat toward their own border. Given very little rest during the entire campaign to free France, Old Hickory's 117th Infantry was the first Allied unit to push beyond the border of Holland, another German-occupied country waiting for the Allies to bring freedom. At the forefront was Frankland's First Battalion, "which was engaged in a fierce firefight soon after it crossed the border." Company B captured the automobile of a leading German general's aide. Documents were seized that detailed the entire German defense, including that of the famous Siegfried Line within Germany's borders—the next and greatest obstacle to complete victory on the European front. Nazi propaganda called this line impenetrable; the Germans had prepared a front of pillboxes, minefields, and dugouts.

The southern end of this line, near the German city of Aachen, was already under siege by the regular United States Army's First Infantry Division, which gained fame as the Big Red One. The northern end, even more terrifying with a major river and steep banks, was assigned to the Old Hickory Division. Frankland's First Battalion made intensive study on paper of the German defense system and did reconnaissance on the river to determine the best places to cross. Old Hickory launched an attack on October 2, 1944. After five days of heavy fighting, General S. Leland Hobbs, commander of the division, reported that Old Hickory had blown a hole in the Siegfried Line "big enough to drive two divisions through; I have no doubts this line is cracked wide open."

Trying to establish contact with the Big Red One, Old Hickory ran into a massive German counterattack. "Once again," wrote historian Featherston, "Old Hickory held its ground and beat off everything the Germans could throw at them." Then the division helped capture Aachen. The Big Red One sent a formal letter of thanks. A week later, its commander, Major General Clarence Huebner, walked into an Old Hickory regimental camp to make an announcement: "I wish you'd get it around to your people that we never could have taken Aachen without your help."

The upcoming, decisive conflict, the Battle of the Bulge, was a replay of all previous victories. Old Hickory set up a major frontal line and once again faced Hitler's famous First Panzer SS Division. During the Bulge, Old Hickory held on tenaciously to its position in the Ardennes, maintaining a northern location and joining the Eighty-second Airborne to retake the town of St.-Vith. "Still, by Christmas Day of 1944, it was clear that Roosevelt's SS had won its third major battle with Hitler's lifeguards," stated Featherston.

Assigned to the Ninth Army in January 1945, Old Hickory now prepared to spearhead the critical crossing of Germany's Rhine River. Generals Dwight D. Eisenhower and William Simpson visited the troops to explain the importance of the Rhine and to determine the odds for a successful crossing. An East Tennessee sergeant from R. Ernest Frankland's Company B, Leroy Sumner, assured both leaders that he and his Old Hickory comrades from Company B would cross the Rhine or "you can give up hope for the whole Ninth Army."

The troops crossed with the greatest of ease, marched steadily through Germany (collecting prisoners as they went), and earned another nickname (given by an Associated Press correspondent) as "the American Army's work horse division." On a steady path toward the grand prize of Berlin, Old Hickory took the city of Magdeburg on the Elbe River.

But the capture of Berlin was canceled. The infantry was forced to stop after the American high command decided to wait on the Russians, who were promised the privilege of being the first to enter Germany's capital and to secure the end of the European conflict. The wait took three weeks, and the German surrender came on May 8, 1945.

Most of the Old Hickory Division returned to the United States aboard the ocean-liner *Queen Mary,* arriving in New York City to an uproarious welcome on August 21. On October 30, Old Hickory Day was proclaimed in the four states that contributed the most manpower to the division: Tennessee, the Carolinas, and Georgia. When United States Army historian S. L. A. Marshall made a special report for General Eisenhower, the Thirtieth ("Old Hickory") Division was ranked as "the finest infantry division in the European theater of operations." The book *Work Horse of the Western Front* came out in 1946 to detail the Thirtieth's exploits. Even decades later, publications were still offering a replay of its heroics. To follow Old Hickory's success was to tell the story of wartime America's victory in Europe.

R. Ernest Frankland returned home to his father's auto-supply shop, which he and his brother Walter helped manage. The brothers eventually divided the business, expanding into other fields as well. Their father, who had migrated from Canada in 1904, founded the business as Frankland Carriage Company and also owned a hotel, furniture store, and other Madison County ventures. The Frankland brothers continued to operate their own businesses until Ernest died in 1986 and Walter in 1987.

184
Margaret Polk
The Real "Memphis Belle"

Margaret Polk became famous during World War II, although most Americans knew her only by her nickname, "Memphis Belle"—a name that proved lucky for an airplane but unlucky for love.

Margaret, a college student, was visiting a sister in Seattle when she met an Asheville, North Carolina, military pilot, Robert Morgan. The two began dating, fell in love, and continued their relationship after her return home to Memphis. Exchanging continuous letters, they became engaged shortly before Morgan's overseas assignment to England. He placed a photo of his fiancée on his B-17's instrument panel and painted "Memphis Belle" on its fuselage in her honor.

Wartime American casualties, meanwhile, were astronomical during B-17 bombing missions. While the *Memphis Belle* took several hits from enemy fire, the plane and its crew continued to survive. Morgan and his men were one of the first American crews to complete a required twenty-five missions. The *Memphis Belle* stayed in combat so long that she went through seven new engines.

The United States War Department, sensing an opportunity to boost morale and sell war bonds, decided to exploit the romance by sending the plane's crew on an American publicity tour. While Robert Morgan and Margaret Polk wanted to get married immediately, the army preferred to promote their unmarried status and kept them apart. They became the nation's top wartime love story during a tour that made them celebrities. But it also destroyed their relationship. After extensive time apart, the two decided to break their engagement.

As for the *Memphis Belle,* an aviation junkyard awaited in Oklahoma, where the plane was held until it was sold in 1946 to Memphis Mayor Walter Chandler and the city of Memphis for $350. Attempts by Margaret Polk and fellow Memphians to fund restoration efforts continually failed until 1985, when the United States Air Force threatened to reclaim the neglected B-17. The people of Memphis took immediate action and managed to raise enough money to restore the plane.

Two years later, in May 1987, the two former sweethearts joined hands once again. They cut a ceremonial ribbon for the Memphis Belle Pavilion at Mud Island in tribute to the four thousand B-17 crew members who did not return from their missions. Margaret Polk and Robert Morgan, who had married others but remained friends and corresponded for decades (he and his wife also visited with Margaret in her home), saw each other for the last time. Margaret died three years later from a brain tumor.

185
John Hendrix

A Vision of War Coming Full Circle: The Manhattan Project

Oak Ridge was not created by Anderson Countian John Hendrix, but it was a perfect vision in his mind. In 1900, he prophesied that the future city would exist, where it would be built, and the role it would play in a major world war.

Hendrix was able to see forty-three years into the future after making a trek one day through the forests near his East Tennessee home. He claimed that he heard a voice "as loud and as sharp as thunder." The voice instructed him to spend forty nights sleeping in the woods, during which time he would receive visions of the area's future. He did as he was told. On the forty-first day, Hendrix emerged from the woods and headed for a nearby crossroads store where he often visited. He shared his many visions with anyone who would listen. Hendrix confounded bystanders with seemingly ridiculous ramblings, but he bravely proceeded with the details of his prophesy anyway.

"Big engines will dig big ditches and thousands of people will be running to and fro," Hendrix revealed. "They will be building things and there will be great noise and confusion and the earth will shake. . . .

"I tell you, Bear Creek Valley some day will be filled with great buildings and factories," he claimed, "and they will help toward winning the greatest war that ever will be . . . I've seen it, it's coming."

Bear Creek Valley eventually became Oak Ridge—home of the massive United States atomic energy complex. The efforts there became an integral part of the Manhattan Project, which constructed the atomic bomb. This weapon of mass destruction would bring an abrupt end to World War II.

Although Hendrix (who died in 1903) foresaw the so-called Atomic City, he perhaps did not foresee the impact it would have on the lives of future generations of Tennesseans. Tennessee author-historians such as Charles W. Johnson, Charles O. Jackson, and George O. Robinson Jr. pieced together stories and facts behind the total disruption of East Tennessee lives and the colossal United States commitment to science's then unfamiliar world of atoms.

In 1942, Hendrix's vision began to unfold when the governor of Tennessee, Prentice Cooper, received a visit from a United States Army official. The governor flew into a rage when Captain G. B. Leonard informed him that the United States government had annexed part of Anderson County and planned a "total exclusion area." Governor Cooper, who had no prior knowledge about this invasion into his state, shredded the documents Leonard handed him and deposited them in a wastebasket, signaling an end to the meeting. Anderson Countians were just as chagrined by the intrusion of the federal government as was Governor Cooper.

One ex-resident noted:

All the folks in these parts were farmers. They worked the ground and minded their own business, peaceful folks living a simple life. We didn't pay much attention to the outside world and they didn't bother with us. That was up to 1942, anyway, when one day a man came to our house and said he was from the Government. "We're going to buy up your land," he said to me. "All of it?" I asked. "Yes, sir," he said, "we're going to buy all the land in this section. Everyone has to go."

Being uprooted was not a new experience for some Anderson Countians. The most unlucky ones were being displaced for the third time in three decades, having previously fallen victim to the establishment of the Great Smoky Mountains National Park in the 1920s and then to the construction of the Tennessee Valley Authority's Norris Dam in the 1930s. One riled resident probably summed up the feelings of many when he said of the invaders: "The only difference is when the Yankees came before, we could shoot at them."

More than one thousand families had to leave. Arriving behind them quickly was the federal government and its high-security area that would house the top-secret Manhattan Project. Oak Ridge began overnight. It was located on more than fifty thousand acres in Anderson and Roane counties along the Clinch River, and its mission was to process raw uranium into uranium 235, the substance that would power the first atomic bombs. Peak employment on the project came to about eighty-two thousand people in May 1945, which included forty-two thousand construction workers and forty thousand defense-project workers. To house and support everyone, construction workers built ten thousand family houses, thirteen thousand dormitory units, sixteen thousand barrack units, and three defense plants, along with two hundred miles of streets, a drug store, grocery store, hospital, and several churches, schools, and other facilities. The total cost of Oak Ridge was ninety-six million dollars.

The area had been chosen for the Manhattan Project because of the availability of TVA's government-produced power, combined with a mountain seclusion that seemed unlikely to stir much curiosity among outsiders. Nonetheless, curiosity surfaced. A later writer quoted *Oak Ridge Journal* columnist Mrs. Stafford Warren, who said the span of 1943-45 represented "a two-and-a-half year period of a concentration of curiosity."

One scientist, weary of repeated questions from his wife, offered a deal: "I'll give you a choice," he finally said. "I'll tell you exactly what I'm doing, but then you can't breathe a word of it to a soul. Or I'll continue to keep you in the dark and you can make up all the stories you want to tell your friends." She chose the latter.

The mother of another employee wrote to say: "It's all right, son, if you can't tell me what you're doing in Oak Ridge, but I do hope it's honorable."

In addition to creating curiosity, the Manhattan Project also created confusion in the newly built Oak Ridge. One worker, after quitting his job, returned home and explained his departure to friends in the following manner:

There they were, all those thousands of people. They were all getting good money, same as I was. And there were more buildings than you can imagine, and a lot of new roads and a lot of other new things, and they were costing a heap of money. I thought it all over, thought it over long and hard. And to tell you the truth, I had in mind that whatever it was the Government was making over there, it would be cheaper if they went out and bought it.

In the fall of 1945, Oak Ridge had a population that averaged seventy-five thousand people. Although the government completed a new house every thirty minutes, accommodations were still lacking. Many newcomers lived in whatever shelter they could obtain: prefabricated huts, railroad cars, barracks, dormitories, and government trailers. Grocer Horace Sherrod related the nightmare of providing food for the masses and dealing with distributors who simply could not find Oak Ridge:

I started filling my shelves in 1943 and didn't manage to get them completely filled until 1946. When I asked the big shippers to send me food, they'd say "We never heard of Oak Ridge, it can't be a priority city." A carload of merchandise I ordered hadn't arrived in four weeks and I inquired about it. The shipper wrote back and said nobody could tell him where Oak Ridge was; he said he didn't believe there was such a place.

Chaos existed with every other service, from undelivered coal to lost laundry, and in living quarters where power and water outages were frequent. Captain P. E. O'Meara, town manager of the Manhattan District, had tried to restore calm with an open letter to residents that was printed September 25, 1943, in the local paper. After listing all typical complaints, O'Meara added some hope for improvements in living conditions and offered a dose of realism. Among them:

A third shift will be started in the laundry as soon as we can get help. . . . Milk WILL be imported, maybe butter. . . . The townsite WILL be restricted. . . . An officer is in Washington now arranging for the change from a fourth to second rate post office. . . .

More bowling alleys WILL be built. . . . Workmen WILL come by and ask where your house leaks. . . .

Town Management personnel has been instructed that YOU are always right. . . . Personnel estimates increased faster than dorms could be built, more WILL be built. . . . They ran out of beer in Knoxville and "back home" the same night it ran out here. . . . More telephones are coming. . . . Meat is rationed. . . . 3,000 people cannot be fed in two hours and not have confusion.

Every effort is being made to get your houses ready. . . . Construction must go on, even when you are asleep. . . . More dance space WILL be made available. . . . The guest house will be full for months. . . . Soda fountain equipment is almost unobtainable, but we WILL have one. . . .

Some employees will ALWAYS be inefficient. . . .

Were you ever ANYWHERE that you liked everyone? . . . Things WEREN'T different back home. . . . Everything can't be done at once, because we need more help. We would have planned it differently too if we had thought of it in '33.

Because the Anderson County landscape had to be heavily graded to accommodate the glut of new buildings, mud became a perpetual nightmare for Oak Ridge newcomers. Guests routinely removed their shoes before entering a friend's home. Mud was so bad that women attending formal dances had to wear hip-boots to the front door, where they changed into their high heels. One budding poet captured the soggy situation in verse:

In order not to check in late,
I've had to lose a lot of weight,
From swimming through a fair-sized flood
And wading through the [expletive deleted] mud;
I've lost my rubbers and my shoes
Perpetually I have the blues
My spirits tumble with a thud
Because of all this [expletive deleted] mud.
It's in my system so that when
I cut my finger now and then
Instead of bleeding just plain blood
Out pours a stream of [expletive deleted] mud!

Along with mass curiosity and confusion, the Manhattan Project created considerable paranoia. Outsiders soon learned that what went on inside the fence (which surrounded the entire town of Oak Ridge) was definitely none of their business.

After reading a speculative article on atomic energy in an old magazine, a Maryville minister in nearby Blount County referred to the atom in his sermon that Sunday. Shortly thereafter, he received a visit from a government agent who convinced him to resist mentioning atoms again.

The work that was finally accomplished at Oak Ridge and at another site, the Hanford Works in Washington state (which produced plutonium), finally came together at Los Alamos, New Mexico, where the assembly and testing of a new bomb took place. In August 1945, the atomic bomb was dropped on the Japanese cities of Hiroshima and Nagasaki, and World War II soon came to a close. In 1947, after the Atomic Energy Commission assumed control of the United States Army facilities in Oak Ridge, the defense plants became less of a nuisance to native Anderson Countians. One native summed up the situation by noting that it "was kind of like a headache. . . . You know it's there, and you don't stop to think just when it went away, but it's gone."

The city that was left behind, however, had become the fifth-largest in Tennessee, a government creation that had grown from non-existence on East Tennessee farmland in a period of three years. John Hendrix's naive vision had come to pass in a way that he had not imagined: taking shape far beyond the great war as one of the nation's major high-technology centers.

186
Ralph Duggan

Back Home Again:
The GI Party and the Battle of Athens

At the close of World War II, Navy Lieutenant Ralph Duggan rushed home to East Tennessee obsessed with one thought—to help save McMinn County from a corrupt and brutal political machine run by the sheriff. Machine cronies had tormented every law-abiding citizen, sometimes killing those who raised an opposing voice against the gambling joints, the bootlegging operations, the fee-grabbing, the beatings, and the crooked elections. Even during his wartime duties, Duggan admitted, he had worried as much about McMinn County as he had about the Japanese he was fighting.

From an office in downtown Athens in February 1946, Duggan pored through his law books and set up a plan of action for hundreds of returning veterans. Spurred by letters from their loved ones and neighbors detailing the corruption at home and the dangers to their lives, the fighting men were still in a fighting mood. Their goal was simple: recapture McMinn County, and do it with the ballot box.

The story of what came to be known as the Battle of Athens was one of the nation's leading headlines a year after the war ended. While the confrontation occurred in 1946, the trouble began ten years earlier when Paul Cantrell became state senator from the McMinn County area and boss of local politics. He was tied to the statewide political machine of Memphis's Democrat Edward Hull "Boss" Crump, who exerted control over Tennessee elections and everyday state politics. Cantrell created an East Tennessee "outpost" of corruption with his own sheriff, the transplanted Georgian Pat Mansfield, and sixteen regular deputies (some with prison backgrounds). All answered only to Cantrell. The local machine also had twenty or thirty others (mostly Georgians) available to deputize in "emergencies."

The out-of-state deputies frequently used strong-arm tactics (fists and blackjacks) on those they arrested and routinely threatened to kill citizens they did not like. One GI, home on leave during the war, was shot to death by a deputy at an Athens night club. A sailor met a similar fate at the other end of the county.

Cantrell, meanwhile, lived an extravagant lifestyle on his humble five thousand dollar annual salary bolstered by his expense money, which was based on the number of persons jailed. Between 1936 and 1946, Cantrell pocketed three hundred thousand dollars in this manner, while also allowing gambling dens and bootlegging to flourish in McMinn County. The citizenry was wise to Cantrell's ways but unable to overcome his most powerful tool: control over ballot boxes. "Names from graveyards throughout the county were often prominent among those who had voted," claimed later McMinn County historian C. Stephen Byrum. Members of the Cantrell machine also were the only ones allowed to count the ballots (which they altered) and to release the results to the public.

Angry returning veterans quickly formed the GI Party and put together a slate of candidates—three Democrats and two Republicans—for the August elec-

tions of 1946. Cantrell had decided to run for sheriff this time. Attorney Duggan counseled his fellow GIs to make certain they complied with Tennessee election laws. Their platform was a promise to the voters: "Your Vote Will Be Counted As Cast!"

The GIs asked for help from the governor, but he was a Crump man himself. Help did not come. Veterans then turned to the United States attorney general's office and the Knoxville FBI, but with no luck.

The GIs spread out over the countryside trying to get out the vote and promising citizens that this would be an honest election. Secret meetings were held in homes, in churches, in school houses. Secret donations were given to the GI Party by area businessmen who feared retaliation from the machine. Trucks traveled country roads with a loudspeaker urging citizens to stand behind the new slate of candidates for county office.

When election day dawned on August 1, 1946, voters found the polling places manned by two hundred armed deputies, most of them strangers. Since Tennessee law required that each polling place have watchers from both parties, the GIs were ably represented at each station—at least for a while. One GI was removed from his post for asking to see the ballot box opened and demonstrated empty as required by law. Another GI was whisked away to jail for an unspecified offense. When Tom Gillespie, a black man, tried to vote at the 11th precinct, a member of Cantrell's force told him he could not vote there. The GI watcher contradicted the order, prompting one deputy to yell, "Get him!" as Gillespie tried to run. Someone slugged Gillespie, who was shot in the back by a deputy. At the 12th precinct, GI watcher Bob Hairell was rushed to the hospital after an opponent split open Hairell's forehead with a blackjack.

The GIs now resolved to declare open warfare. At 8 P.M., they gathered at the National Guard Armory outside of Athens, armed themselves with rifles and machine-guns, and marched on the jail to retrieve the ballot boxes and two of their comrades. From within the jail, a voice rang out: "Are you the law?"

A GI replied: "There isn't any law in McMinn County!"

The answer to that was gunfire from the jail. Soon, firepower from the hilltops and surrounding streets rained on the jail building. Hundreds of war veterans were firing everything they had. At their side were hundreds of civilians shooting also, using hunting guns, bird guns, shotguns, and any other type of gun or rifle they happened to own. The local radio station broadcast a live report from the scene, describing every detail, with shots audible in the background. From the distant countryside, farmers left their radios and picked up their own hunting rifles, headed for town, and joined the shootout. Five hours and thousands of bullets later, the GIs had accomplished little, since their bullets could not penetrate the jail's brick walls. They brought in dynamite, and when the smoke cleared, portions of the jail lay scattered on the front lawn.

Deputies surrendered, four of whom were injured. The servicemen marched the rest into the courtyard, their hands held aloft. The GIs now found themselves protecting their prisoners from enraged civilians. Onlookers yelled, cursed, and booed the captives. Some people attacked deputies' automobiles, either smashing windows or burning the entire vehicle. One person in the crowd reached out with a razor and slashed the throat of a deputy. Duggan subdued the assailant, who told him that the deputy had once arrested and beaten him. Despite Duggan's pleas for sanity, the assailant tried to strike again. "Then Duggan slugged him into obedience and led the deputy off to the hospital," according to *Harper's Magazine* writer Theodore White in his own report, published several months later.

When calm finally returned to the streets of Athens that night, a three-man volunteer committee was formed to conduct the county's affairs for several days until county court could untangle the election confusion. The final results showed that the GI Party had been duly elected and that the new sheriff was Knox Henry, a war hero who had been decorated in the North Africa campaign. Henry, who owned a local gas station, immediately named eight former GIs as his deputies.

The GIs then disbanded their political party, turning over local power to the Good Government League, which formed "branches" in various communities throughout McMinn County and became "the public whip." *Harper's Magazine* reported: "Many were thinking as Ralph did—that if democracy was good enough to put on the Germans and Japs, it was good enough for McMinn County, too."

Ralph Duggan resumed his life as an Athens attorney, and he continued in that pursuit until his 1960 death. But the opening gun had sounded for an end to Boss Crump's statewide political machine—and the concept of any kind of bossism over the lives of Tennessee citizens.

187
Kemmons Wilson

*Accommodating a Mobile Society—
A New Way to Travel*

In 1951, Kemmons Wilson and his family left their home in Memphis for a leisurely trip to Washington, D.C., which proved to be, in Wilson's words, "the most miserable vacation I ever had." The problems they encountered were familiar ones nationwide for any traveler who journeyed by car: rustic and cramped motel accommodations, few conveniences, and extra charges for each child (the Wilsons had five children). A homebuilder, Wilson knew what needed to be done: "I decided to build a motel that had all the things we missed," he told *Time* magazine years later. Soon after returning to Memphis, he began construction of a 120-room inn that offered free parking, free television and telephone, free ice, and free lodging for children under twelve accompanied by a parent; he also added a swimming pool, restaurant, and air conditioning. The motel was so popular with travelers that Wilson opened three more in the Memphis area.

His next step revolutionized the motel industry. With his partner, Wallace E. Johnson, he began to sell franchises nationally and then internationally. Wilson's brainchild—Holiday Inn—would become the leading motel chain in the world.

Born in Osceola, Arkansas, Wilson lost his father when he was nine months old. Newly widowed Ruby Wilson moved with her infant son to Memphis. When she lost her job during the Depression, her son quit school, purchased a fifty-dollar popcorn machine and set up a concession in a Memphis theater. "I was soon making more than the theater manager," Wilson recalled, "so he threw me out and took over the popcorn concession himself."

Selling the manager his popcorn machine for his fifty-dollar investment, Wilson then bought five pinball machines. Two years later, in 1933, he cashed in his pinball business for seventeen hundred dollars and constructed a house, and then another. Leaping into the house-building business, Wilson became wealthy.

His decision in 1951 to build a high-service motel led Wilson into an association with designer Eddie Bluestein, who penned "Holiday Inn" across the bottom of the architectural drawings, borrowing the name from a Bing Crosby movie, *White Christmas,* which he had watched the previous night.

By 1979, Kemmons Wilson had accumulated a personal fortune estimated in excess of two hundred million dollars with 1,752 inns around the world. He retired that year as board chairman of Holiday Inns, having seen the time when a new Holiday Inn room opened every thirty-six minutes. He had made the cover of *Time* under the heading, "The Man with 300,000 Beds," and the *Sunday Times* of London, which ranked him among the one thousand most important men of the twentieth century along with Winston Churchill.

The Depression-era high-school dropout who wanted to make a living for his family had soared to the top of the motel industry. "When you get an idea," he explained, "you've got to think of a reason for doing it, not of a reason for not doing it."

188
Elvis Presley

Rewriting American Musical History

In 1956, residents along Memphis's Audubon Drive appeared en masse at the house of their new neighbor and planned to make him an offer they thought he could not refuse. They wanted to buy his house.

"It's not for sale," Elvis Presley told them. "But I tell you what I'll do. You all get together on how much you want for your places, and I'll just buy them all."

Presley was joking. But he was not unsympathetic to their plight. Since his purchase of a three-bedroom home for his parents in a fashionable Shelby County neighborhood earlier that year, devoted fans and curiosity seekers had turned the once-quiet street into chaos. Cars had created such traffic jams that Presley's neighbors no longer had access to their own driveways. Each night, a crowd of at least fifty fans sat in vigil until 5 A.M., hoping to catch a glimpse of the popularly known "King of Rock 'n' Roll."

When his neighbors offered to buy him out, Presley knew it was time to find a more secluded family dwelling. His parents, Vernon and Gladys, his uncle Vester and Aunt Clettes soon toured Memphis in the family's pink Cadillac, hoping to find a new home. The perfect solution would be a place of peace and

Elvis Presley at the beginning of his career.

quiet where a teen idol, whose first name was a household word, could be shielded from the adoring legions and the glare of the media. They found such a place at the edge of Memphis in a southern mansion called "Graceland." Church services were underway inside the house when Presley's parents paid their first visit one Sunday morning, and they had to wait until midafternoon to see the house. In a later telephone call from his father, Presley, who was out of town, agreed to purchase the eighteen-room retreat for one hundred thousand dollars.

Presley's life in Memphis did not begin with this sudden stardom as a rock-and-roll vocalist in the mid 1950s. He was thirteen when his parents left Tupelo, Mississippi, and made their way to Tennessee. Author Dave Marsh described the future superstar:

Set down in the poorest part of Memphis at the crucial age of thirteen, he moved from a world of fewer than 10,000 people, where everyone at least knew *about* everyone else, to a world of more than 300,000 that couldn't have cared less about a poor cracker kid—that gaped at his hick idea of what was suave when it paid attention at all. So there he was. Gawky, acned, extraordinarily sheltered even in his poverty; peculiarly shy and polite, hypersensitive to any slight; neither tough nor articulate but inwardly *seething*.

During his teen years, Elvis spent much of his time along Beale Street where he absorbed the sound of the blues. He graduated from L. C. Humes High School and then took a job at Precision Tool Company. After a few weeks, he left to drive trucks for Crown Electric Company at $1.25 an hour.

On a chance, he visited Sam Phillips's Memphis Recording Service where the motto was, "WE RECORD ANYTHING—ANYTIME—ANYWHERE, $3 One Side, $4 Two Sides." Marion Keisker was overseeing the shop that day, and she struck up a conversation with the youth. "What do you sing?" she asked.

"I sing all kinds."

"Who do you sound like?" she asked.

"I don't sound like nobody."

Recognizing the truth, according to one account, Marion Keisker secretly recorded a second version of two Ink Spots tunes Presley sang that day, "My Happiness" and "That's When Your Heartaches Begin." While she clearly was impressed, Presley clearly was not. Hearing his demonstration tape, he grumbled that it was "terrible . . . sounded like someone beating on a bucket lid."

Phillips had long maintained that if he could find a white youth who sang with the feel of a black singer "he could make a billion dollars." Though only slightly impressed with the sound of young Elvis Presley, the recording executive ultimately signed the new singer and released one of his songs, "That's All Right," on July 5, 1954.

While he did not succeed in his first appearance at Nashville's *Grand Ole Opry* (*Opry* manager Jim Denny told him to go back to driving trucks), nor in his first engagement at Las Vegas (the stint scheduled for two weeks was canceled after one), Elvis Presley would persevere to become one of the most influential vocalists in the history of American music.

Historically, Presley helped define the relatively new music form rock and roll (from a phrase coined in 1951), which traced its heritage to the southern Delta and the blues. When rural black performers made their way to large cities, they altered many of their blues sounds to appeal to the wider audiences. They created rhythm and blues—an urban sound for blacks and whites alike, especially for the younger members of each audience. Musical pop charts of the early 1950s began to show rhythm-and-blues hits, but major commercial success was still out of reach.

Then Presley combined the blues and bluegrass on his first record for Phillips. "Never before had the musical culture of blacks and lower-class whites been so closely conjoined as they were in the early stylings of Presley," wrote southern culture expert James C. Cobb. "This remarkable synthesis was apparent on Presley's first single."

The phenomenon of Elvis Presley, whose recordings eventually sold more than "any individual or group in the history of recorded voice," ended at age forty-two. He died at Graceland in 1977. In the years following Presley's death, the list of accomplishments became legendary: more than one billion records sold worldwide, and, in 1992, a presentation to the Presley estate of 110 gold and platinum record awards, the "largest presentation" of its kind in musical history (the numbers would have been even higher, said Graceland officials, except that the music industry did not keep exact documentation in Presley's early career). The awards were given by his label RCA and the Recording Industry Association of America.

As for Phillips, he had sold Elvis's contract in November 1955 for thirty-five thousand dollars, well shy of the billion he said he would make. Although he probably lost millions of dollars by selling, Phillips had little reason to regret the move. He invested the money in the fledgling Memphis-based hotel chain, Holiday Inn.

189
William R. Anderson

For Mankind and America—The Nautilus

In his childhood during the 1920s, William R. Anderson loved to join his friend James Beckham in launching rowboats on a small river near their Waynesboro home. The boys occasionally made crude submarines from these homemade crafts and practiced underwater breathing techniques. Thirty years later, United States Navy Captain William R. Anderson's underwater pursuits would carry his name into world history. As commander of the first atomic-powered submarine, USS *Nautilus,* he made the first voyage by ship to the North Pole—by journeying under the polar ice cap—and then completed the first Pacific-Atlantic crossing that, in Anderson's words, blazed "a new northwest passage."

Born in 1921 into a Humphreys County farm family at Bakerville, William Anderson moved frequently around Middle Tennessee when his family's fortunes declined during the Great Depression. After recovering from the bad economic times, his father, David H. Anderson, operated a lumber mill. Having access to wood products, the boy was able to build his various river crafts, and in the process, also develop a passion for the navy.

After attending public schools in Waynesboro, young Anderson then pursued his fascination with sea vessels by attending Columbia Military Academy in Maury County and afterwards the United States Naval Academy. During World War II, he took part in eleven submarine combat patrols in the Pacific.

In January 1956, Anderson was supervising submarine combat training at the United States Submarine School in New London, Connecticut, when Admiral Hyman G. Rickover—the "father of the atomic submarine"—called him into his office. Rickover conducted an interview regarding a special assignment aboard the superadvanced *Nautilus.* Anderson wrote later: "Her performance and reliability had electrified submariners the world over. . . . But, I thought, what kind of job could I do for Admiral Rickover?"

After the lengthy interview process, which delved into Anderson's entire Tennessee life history and required a list of recently read books, Rickover chose him as the new commander of the *Nautilus.* In 1958, Anderson guided the vessel into its historic accomplishments as the first ship to the North Pole and the first to travel from the Pacific to the Atlantic Ocean (or the famous Northwest Passage).

Sonar equipment traced "the contour of the underside of the ice," collecting more data on both the ice and the arctic floor than mankind had ever assembled. In his later book, *Nautilus-90-North,* Anderson wrote, "I saw incredibly steep clifts—undersea ranges—rise

thousands of feet above the ocean floor. . . . The shape of these undersea mountains appeared phenomenally rugged, and as grotesque as the craters of the moon."

When he approached the North Pole, he knew that "no bells would ring, nor would we feel a bump. Only our instruments could tell us how close we had come." Anderson reached for the ship's intercom and announced the moment to his entire crew. In his book, he recalls his exact words:

"All hands—This is the Captain speaking. . . . In a few moments Nautilus will realize a goal long a dream of mankind—the attainment by ship of the North Geographic Pole. With continued Godspeed, in less than two days we will record an even more significant historic first: the completion of a rapid transpolar voyage from the Pacific to the Atlantic Ocean."

Asking the crew for a moment of silence "dedicated with our thanks for the blessings that have been ours during this remarkable voyage," Anderson remembered that only the sonar's pinging sound could then be heard.

I glanced again at the distance indicator, and gave a brief countdown to the crew. 'Stand by, 10 . . . 8 . . . 6 . . . 4 . . . 3 . . . 2 . . . 1. MARK! August 3, 1958. Time, 2315 (11:15 P.M. Eastern Daylight Saving Time). For the United States and the United States Navy, the North Pole.' I could hear cheers in the Crew's Mess.

Anderson's navigator looked at the instruments and reported to him: "Captain, you might say we came so close we pierced the Pole." Anderson remembered his own private silence, "awe-struck at what *Nautilus* had achieved." When the submarine finally surfaced in the open sea, a military helicopter picked up Anderson and flew him immediately to the White House to make his report to an anxious President Dwight D. Eisenhower, who had been one of the chief supporters of the voyage. After joining the president for a news conference, Anderson returned to the *Nautilus,* journeying with his ship and crew into New York harbor—and preparing for a New York City ticker-tape parade.

Retiring from the navy in 1962, William B. Anderson set his sights on Congress and, representing the huge Tennessee Sixth District, became a member of the United States House of Representatives from 1965 to 1973. He afterwards settled into a private business life in Washington, D.C.

190
Estes Kefauver

A Maverick Senator: Taking on Corporations,
Crime, Even Truman

The brothers—Carey, eleven, and Robert, thirteen—were so close that, as one elderly Madisonville resident recalled in later years of the mayor's sons: when calling both of them, all a person had to do was yell out for one of them.

Yet there was a difference. Robert was the elder son, said to have been more aggressive, brighter, and quicker than Carey. After Robert died from a swimming accident in the Tellico River in 1914, Carey isolated himself in his room, grieving for his brother and escaping into books. He emerged from the experience with a new resolve. "I felt," he said, "that I had to do better to make up to my parents for his loss."

This determination helped Carey Estes Kefauver of Monroe County to become a successful attorney, a United States senator, United States presidential candidate, and a vice presidential nominee. Kefauver, who was born in 1903, had been raised in a political family. His father was not only a farmer involved in the hardware and farm-equipment business, but he was also the unpaid five-time mayor of Madisonville. His mother's uncle was Judge Joe Estes of Memphis, and a cousin was a Missouri governor who fought corruption in his state.

In Republican-dominated Monroe County, young Kefauver became fascinated with politics when he accompanied his father in campaigning during the 1916 presidential election. The youth also became enthralled with becoming an attorney when he attended legal proceedings at the Madisonville Courthouse. He joined a high school debating team and wrote in a classmate's annual: "Ambition—To be President."

Known for his size—he reached the height of six feet, three inches—and modesty, Kefauver decided to pursue his education at the University of Tennessee. Hoping to make a good impression upon his arrival in Knoxville, he donned "a new iridescent suit, . . . a small cap, two stickpins, and his Sunday school buttons." A cousin, Thomas Walker, met him at the train. Embarrassed, Walker sneaked him into the Kappa Sigma fraternity house. One fraternity member wondered of Walker: "Where did you find that rube?"

Kefauver added to his embarrassment by trying out for the football team, although he had never played the game (Madisonville High School only had basketball and baseball teams, and Kefauver excelled in both). Soon he realized that he did not have the football skills of other players, and, when he returned to Madisonville several weeks later, Kefauver was visibly upset. His mother gave him what he called "the best advice I ever received." She told him to turn his stumbling blocks into stepping stones. Later, she encouraged him with letters from home, filled with such inspirational messages as "Leave no tender word unsaid" and "Do good while life shall last."

Kefauver's work in football earned him a place on the team; his work after classes stoking furnaces earned him room and board in the fraternity house. He also became editor of the college newspaper and student body president. After graduation, Kefauver continued in this vein, working for money to enter law school. He worked his way through Yale University by tutoring other students, clerking in a bookstore, and waiting on tables. He spent his summers as a Bible salesman throughout Tennessee.

Upon graduating from Yale, Kefauver tried to jump-start his legal career in various cities, including Knoxville, but with no luck. Then he passed through Chattanooga, where he visited some cousins. Collectively, they made up the law firm of Cooke, Swaney and Cooke. In exchange for running errands, Kefauver received a desk in the firm's library.

After admission to the Chattanooga Bar Association in 1926, Kefauver tried and lost his first case—not from a shortage of experience but from an abundance of compassion. His client was a grocer attempting to collect a delinquent account of eighteen dollars. Advised by his cousins to conduct the case "as if you were trying to collect $18,000 for United States Steel," Kefauver went into court with fire in his eyes.

Discovering that the defendant was a shabbily dressed woman of considerable age, crying softly as she awaited her hearing, Kefauver was quickly filled with remorse. He called a meeting and convinced his client to drop the suit, promising that the woman would pay her debt.

For the next two years, Kefauver devoted much of his practice to defending the rights of those who were poor and the powerless (at first the only clients he could get), and most were black citizens. As his biographer

Harvey Swados explained: "But if he was not getting rich he was learning a lot about the poor who are supposedly protected by the law, but are all too often its victims."

During his years in Chattanooga, Kefauver also did legal scholarship from the stacks of books surrounding him in his cousins' library. One of his papers, published in the *Tennessee Law Review,* was on a subject that he would revisit as a United States senator: the development of the law on corporation practices. The paper also helped him toward a partnership in a prestigious law firm, setting the stage for his becoming prominent in the Tennessee legal profession. While still in his twenties, Kefauver was elected an officer in the city bar association and named East Tennessee vice president of the Tennessee Bar Association. Working with the new law firm, Sizer, Chambliss and Sizer, he was an investigator and adjuster on insurance cases. Such investigative skills would also serve him well in the United States Senate.

In 1936, Kefauver married Scottish-born Nancy Pigott, whom he met while she was visiting her aunt in Chattanooga. The couple afterwards kept their permanent home in Chattanooga as Kefauver rose through the political ranks, beginning in 1939 when he was appointed state commissioner of finance and taxation. Months later, he resigned to run for the United States House of Representatives and remained there for the next nine years.

With experience under his belt and ambition tugging at his sleeve, Kefauver ran for the Senate in 1948, campaigning against a Democratic-machine candidate hand-picked by Edward Hull "Boss" Crump of Memphis. Crump likened Kefauver to a pet coon "that puts its foot in an open drawer in your room, but invariably turns its head while its foot is feeling around in the drawer—hoping that through its cunning in turning its head, it will deceive any onlookers as to where its foot is and what it is into."

Kefauver, deciding that humor was the best way to fight Crump, turned the insult to political advantage by donning a coonskin cap and taking to the stump. In one of his more successful volleys, Kefauver charged that while he might have rings on his tail, he had no rings in his nose. "The coon is an easy animal to domesticate, but a mighty hard little critter to put a collar on," retorted Kefauver, whose subsequent victory

helped signal an end to Crump's power within the Democratic Party. Kefauver kept the coonskin cap as his campaign symbol for years.

As a United States senator, Kefauver quickly gained national attention chairing the Crime Investigation Committee. He was one of the first politicians to use television to his advantage. Broadcasts of his committee hearings on underworld crime and corruption of public officials made Kefauver famous. But gaining the national spotlight and also discovering corruption in President Harry S. Truman's administration did little to endear him to many fellow Democrats when he ran for president in 1952.

Kefauver entered sixteen state primaries. He won fourteen. Democratic Party leaders, however, refused to follow the public mandate. Kefauver failed to get the nomination in part because he had entered the race without seeking approval from the party leader, President Truman, as well as from other top Democrats. The nomination went to Adlai Stevenson, who lost the election to Dwight D. Eisenhower.

Democrats, however, began to acknowledge Kefauver's growing popularity as a "maverick" among southern senators. He backed the 1954 Supreme Court ruling that supported school integration; two years later, he was one of only three southern senators who refused to sign a Senate resolution called the "Southern Manifesto," which censored the Supreme Court ruling and promoted the concept of "separate but equal public facilities." (Joining Kefauver in his defiance of the Southern Manifesto was his fellow Tennessee senator, Albert Gore Sr.) In an open convention in 1956, Democrats nominated Kefauver for vice president in Stevenson's ultimately unsuccessful campaign against the incumbent, Eisenhower.

Returning to the Senate, Kefauver continued his high profile role on investigative committees. Among his well-publicized activities was his Subcommittee on Juvenile Delinquency, where he spearheaded investigations into the violence and sex that existed in television, motion pictures, and publications.

Despite his inability to reach the nation's top political posts, Estes Kefauver ranked among America's most prominent congressional politicians of the 1950s. He was remembered from his earliest Senate days for probing relentlessly into any important public issue; *Time* magazine named Kefauver one of the United

States Senate's ten most valuable members and the Washington press corps pointed to him as second in importance among senators, primarily because of his work on the Crime Investigation Committee.

In 1963, forty-nine years after his brother's death, Kefauver had a prophetic conversation in his Washington office. While he had rarely spoken of his brother following the summer of 1914, he made an exception now. "If there is anything to religion," he told staff member Jowanda Shelton, "I ought to see my brother Robert again. I suppose it's odd, but I wonder to myself, if we'd meet, would he be a grown man?"

Afterwards, during a speech in the Senate, Kefauver felt a stabbing pain in his chest. Rather than surrender the floor, he whispered to a colleague that a roll call might be in order to determine if a quorum was present. Kefauver regained his composure but died thirty-six hours later of a ruptured artery. He was sixty. At the time of his death, Estes Kefauver was still battling on behalf of the powerless: this time investigating monopolies and price fixing in major American industries.

191
Bobby Cain

The First Black Graduate of an All-White High School

The distance from his home on Foley Hill to Clinton High School was two-tenths of a mile, but on August 27, 1956, it seemed the longest walk sixteen-year-old Bobby Cain had ever undertaken.

After a night of prayer and his mother's encouragement, Bobby was among a dozen black youngsters enrolling in the previously all-white East Tennessee school. Although Clinton black parents had filed a lawsuit six years earlier to allow their children into local white schools, the United States Supreme Court had only recently allowed it, by virtue of its ruling in the famous *Brown v. Topeka Board of Education* case. Bobby and his friends would no longer attend the all-black Austin High of Knoxville, where Anderson County had been paying their tuition and transportation. Due to a federal court order to integrate Clinton High School, sending local black students to Austin High was no longer an option, although Bobby would rather have stayed there.

After Sunday evening church services on August 26, Bobby Cain knelt by his bed and prayed, asking "The Lord to watch over me during the day." He then spent a sleepless night tossing and turning, fearing the events that lay ahead.

The next day began smoothly enough. Bobby, as the oldest and the only male, led eleven other black students down the hill to the school entrance. There, they met only token resistance from a small group of picketers. For the most part, blacks and whites in Clinton had always had good relations.

On the second day, however, Bobby and the eleven girls were met after school by an angry mob shouting racial epithets and profanity. Apparently led by a self-styled "rabble rouser" from New Jersey named John Kasper, the number of segregationists increased with each passing day. Kasper was going door-to-door stirring up trouble. Eventually, the protests began to affect the black students' classmates, a few of whom harassed Bobby and his friends and vandalized their lockers. Most of the time, the school was relatively safe compared to what waited on the streets. Protests grew to such an extent that Governor Frank Clement sent in the Tennessee National Guard. Bobby Cain, meanwhile, kept leading the girls—day after day, week after week—and received the brunt of the verbal and physical abuse.

As soon as the national guard was withdrawn, white supremacists began bomb attacks on both black neighborhoods and on those with integration sympathizers, creating such tension that the Anderson County sheriff withdrew all twelve black students from Clinton High. *Collier's* magazine later interviewed Bobby Cain. He admitted that, upon arriving at his family home, he "sat and trembled for a long time . . . I decided I wasn't going back."

He did, though, thanks to an inspirational talk from his mother. "I had to scuffle to get what little education I got," she told her son. "I'm as worried about that mob as you are. But what about the others in there asleep? Where are your brothers and sisters going to school if you don't stick?"

When Bobby and his female classmates returned to school on December 4, they were accompanied by the Reverend Paul Turner, the white pastor of First Baptist Church in Clinton. Turner's support ignited additional racially motivated incidents, and he was beaten as he left the school grounds. Turner might have been killed had not a CBS correspondent called the police.

That afternoon, principal David James Brittain closed Clinton High School. It remained shut down for six days, as Anderson County's Board of Education and law enforcement officials, plus several high school teachers and students, joined forces in hopes of preventing and/or combating future incidents.

Once classes resumed on December 10, the black students found able allies in their white classmates. One show of unity was recalled years later by faculty member Margaret Anderson:

> strong white boys moved near the doorways, and edged over and managed "conveniently" to find seats in front of, to the side of and behind the Negroes. It was the most spontaneous, undirected gesture of true brotherhood, from the hearts of children, I have ever seen in my whole life.

Further evidence that many students supported their black classmates was made apparent when a former Clinton High student and some followers accosted a group of black students on the streets one day. Several of the high school's football players came to the rescue—snatching the black students from the angry mob, then escorting them to the protective custody of the principal's office. One of the rescued was Bobby Cain.

The turning point in Bobby's battle against bigotry actually came en route to a local black diner to have lunch. When an angry group of white adults followed and surrounded him, Bobby tried to defend himself with a pen knife. He was rescued this time by the police, who took him into custody. He thought it strange that he, rather than the ones who had threatened him, was being led away to jail. "After that day . . . I found a little courage of my own," he recalled in the interview with *Collier's*. "I won't say I wasn't afraid after that. But it came to me for the first time that I had a right to go to school. I realized that it was those other people who were breaking the law, not me. That night I determined to stick it out for Bobby Cain, and not for anybody else."

In the spring of 1957, and enduring the glare of the national news media, Bobby Cain became the first black student in the South to graduate from a state-supported, previously all-white high school. But the day of graduation was not without further trauma for

him and his family. After the ceremonies, graduates went to the basement to take off their caps and gowns. Someone turned out the lights and hit Bobby in the face. When leaving the building, Bobby and his family spotted someone walking away from the vicinity of their parked car. Their minds filled with fear about vandalism or even worse, dynamite.

White supremacists had no plans for explosives that night, but they did remain unrelenting. Five months later, during the early hours of an October Sunday morning, they detonated three bombs that partly destroyed Clinton High School. The incident prompted an immediate national fund-raising crusade, endorsed by syndicated columnist Drew Pearson, to rebuild the school. It reopened in 1960.

John Kasper was among seven segregationists convicted in federal court in 1957 for interfering with integration; Clinton High's principal, David James Brittain, later detailed the Anderson County desegregation struggle in his doctoral dissertation at New York University; and Bobby Cain, who "never saw himself as a hero," became a social worker, preferring never to discuss the intimate details of his crisis between the autumn of 1956 and the spring of 1957.

192
James Agee

A Posthumous Pulitzer—
Another Death in the Family

At his Knoxville home on May 17, 1916, Hugh "Jay" Agee received a phone call from his brother, urging him to come immediately to the family farm near LaFollette because their father was dying. Agee drove most of the night to reach nearby Campbell County, only to discover that his father's condition had been exaggerated. On the return to Knoxville near dawn, Agee's car hit an embankment and overturned, killing him instantly.

Jay Agee left behind a six-year-old son who would turn this personal tragedy and its impact on his family into a novel. *A Death in the Family* became a twenty-three-year project and masterpiece for its author, James Agee, resulting in a posthumous Pulitzer Prize in 1958.

His father's death threw the family into confusion. Not the least of their concerns was that Jay Agee had never been baptized and, according to the family's religious beliefs, was no doubt bound for hell. But something happened at the funeral as the coffin was being put into the ground, which the family embraced as a sign of grace: "A perfectly magnificent butterfly alighted on it and just stood there for several seconds while they kept on lowering the coffin." Since the butterfly was seen as a symbol of resurrection, many onlookers were swayed. James Agee was not at the burial, but his Uncle Hugh Tyler related the story and said, "If I ever believe in God, it will be because I remember what I saw today."

After the death of his father, young Agee (known then by his middle name, Rufus) spent most of his youth visiting relatives. He pursued his education first at St. Andrew's, a boys' school at Sewanee, where his mother rented a cottage in 1919. During his many years there, he made a lifetime friend in Father James H. Flye, the Episcopal priest who also became his mentor and friend. For Agee, Father Flye's home and family possessed what one historian believes was "the familial love he had lost through the death of his father."

In 1924, Agee's education continued at Knoxville High School. A year later, he moved to New Hampshire's Phillips Exeter Academy, where he developed an interest in poetry, and then entered Harvard University, where he graduated in 1932. He soon married for the first time.

Agee kept in constant touch with Father Flye, usually by letter and once by visiting Sewanee. Between 1941 and 1954, Father Flye conducted annual summer parish duty in New York City, where Agee worked and visited him frequently.

By the time he began work on *A Death in the Family,* Agee was an accomplished journalist who had achieved considerable respect as a feature writer for both *Time* and *Fortune* magazines, as well as a writer of film reviews and screenplays. His first book, *Let Us Now Praise Famous Men,* represented a pioneering form of documentary journalism. Combining Walker Evans's photographs with a description of the lives of southern tenant farmers, Agee produced a powerful poetic prose. This style would be an Agee hallmark. Author Kenneth Seib's description of *A Death in the Family* states emphatically: "The novel has an almost symphonic arrangement, and anyone who has listened to Samuel Barber's *Knoxville: Summer of 1915* knows how readily Agee's prose can be set to music."

In writing *A Death in the Family,* Agee had in mind the image of the butterfly on his father's coffin. It became a crucial part of the largely autobiographical novel that he did not live to see published. By the time he got around to devoting his attention to the book, his heavy smoking, regular drinking, and chronic insomnia had taken a toll on his body. In 1951, Agee was paralyzed by pain in his arms, chest, and teeth. Doctors and friends urged him to take better care of himself, but he was unwilling to change the way he lived. When film director John Huston, for whom he had written the script for *The African Queen,* cautioned him to change his habits, Agee pondered a moment, then reportedly said rather simply: "Well, I wouldn't want to change my way of life."

When he died in New York City of a heart attack in 1955, Agee was forty-five, married to his third wife, and the father of three children. He was also in the prime of his career. His body was taken to St. Luke's in Greenwich Village. By a coincidence, Father Flye happened to be in the parish that day. At the funeral service he conducted (recalled by an Agee friend, Robert Saudeck), Father Flye stepped up to the coffin, saying: "It is not the custom of this church to eulogize its departed. I want to say only that anyone who ever met Rufus Agee will never forget him."

Agee's final work, *A Death in the Family,* owed its publication to another longtime Tennessee friend, David McDowell. When they first met, McDowell was an eighteen-year-old senior at Agee's alma mater, St. Andrew's School in Sewanee. Agee, then twenty-six, was on leave from *Fortune* magazine, visiting the school and Father Flye. McDowell, struggling with the introduction of his commencement speech, asked Father Flye for input. Because he always liked to help others, Agee asked if he could read it, scanned the material, and said he had an idea. He left the room and did not reappear for an hour and a half, at which time he presented McDowell with a simple but splendid introduction.

McDowell returned the favor more than twenty years later when he edited the unfinished manuscript of *A Death in the Family* and published it, winning for Agee a posthumous Pulitzer Prize for fiction. Renamed *All the Way Home* for the Broadway stage in 1960, the work won another Pulitzer, and then became a motion picture three years later.

Several Agee associates noted that if he had taken better care of himself, he would have enjoyed a longer life and produced a greater body of work. Director John Huston dismissed such an idea: "But we who [knew] him recognize the fact that his body's destruction was implicit in his makeup, and we thank heaven that it was strong enough to withstand for so many years the constant assaults he leveled on it."

193
Wilma Rudolph

*The Most Golden Olympics
for American Women*

At age four, she could not walk. But by age nineteen, she could run faster than any woman in the world.

Overcoming childhood bouts of scarlet fever, polio, and double pneumonia that left her near death and then partially paralyzed, Wilma Rudolph of Clarksville became the "girl who wouldn't give up." Behind the magazines and newspapers in 1960 which headlined the Tennessee State University track star was a mother who also never gave up. Although hers was a poor black family, Blanche Rudolph was tireless in her efforts to create a better day for each person in it. She had a job as a domestic worker, and her husband, Ed, was a local dry goods clerk. Blanche was devoted to her many children, especially her seventeenth, Wilma, born in 1940, weighing little more than four pounds and ill more often than not. When four-year-old Wilma Rudolph became paralyzed in her left leg as a result of scarlet fever and pneumonia, her mother wrapped her in blankets for a ninety-mile round trip to Nashville's Meharry Medical Center.

Doctors could only make recommendations for daily therapeutic massage. Unable to make the long trip more than once a week for therapy, Blanche Rudolph asked to be taught the procedure. For the next two years, she came home from her job, cooked for her family, and toiled diligently on her daughter's left leg. On her only day off, she made the ninety-mile trip to the medical center in Nashville. During those two years, doctors could detect only slight improvement.

Declaring that her daughter *would* walk, Blanche turned for help within the family, teaching the procedure to her three oldest children. "Rubbing Wilma" became the family ritual. The recovery was painfully slow. But, by the age of eight, Wilma's strengthen-

ing muscle reflexes enabled her to walk with a brace, replaced soon by a specially designed high-top orthopedic shoe. One day in 1951, Blanche Rudolph looked out her window to see eleven-year-old Wilma shed her corrective shoe and, in her bare feet, begin to play basketball with her brothers.

When Wilma Rudolph entered Clarksville's Burt High School, she became a basketball star, playing with such intensity that her coach, Clinton C. Gray, nicknamed her "Skeeter." Wilma, in fact, was so fast that Gray created a track program to showcase her talents. At a state high school track meet, a visiting track coach eyed those talents also. He was Tennessee State University's Edward S. Temple, who would become Wilma Rudolph's mentor and friend. Temple's own determination and grueling track camps, which Wilma attended in her high school summers, led to her first Olympic appearance in 1956 in Melbourne, Australia. Barely five years after discarding the shoe brace, she was a seasoned athlete. At Melbourne, Wilma won a bronze medal running the third leg of the United States 4 x 100-meter relay team. On the same day that she returned home to Clarksville, Wilma also played a high school basketball game.

Coach Temple soon offered a scholarship and the chance to be a Tennessee State University Tigerbelle. Elated at the news, Blanche Rudolph reminded her daughter: "You're the first one in this house that ever had the chance to go to college. If running's going to do that, I want you to set your mind to be the best! Never give up."

As a Tigerbelle for Tennessee State, Wilma Rudolph made a return trip to the Olympics in 1960, this time in Rome. She quickly became the toast of international sports by winning three gold medals in women's track and field—an achievement unprecedented for an American woman. While Wilma was racing to her third gold medal, the Olympic audience chanted *"Gazella Nera,"* meaning "Black Gazelle."

In Europe, she was the first American woman named Sportsman of the Year. On her return to the United States, which named her Woman Athlete of the Year, Wilma attended celebrations nationwide for ten days before she was able to get back home. In Clarksville, Tennessee, she was the pride and joy of a hometown that held its first racially integrated event in her honor. While giving Wilma an Olympic homecoming, teary-eyed County Judge William Hudson was so overcome with emotion during a speech in Montgomery County that he could hardly talk. Every Clarksville school and every business was closed, and the streets were lined for the biggest parade the town had ever seen.

When the tumultuous ovations and congratulatory speeches finally subsided, Wilma finished her degree in elementary education and devoted the rest of her life to amateur athletics. After marrying Robert Eldridge, she also became the mother of four. Her athletic work culminated in 1982 with the Wilma Rudolph Foundation, organized in Indianapolis to help disadvantaged youths with education and sports. She continued to be a goodwill ambassador, lecturer, and author, as well as a women's track coach at DePauw University. In 1994, Wilma Rudolph was unable to overcome a malignant brain tumor which doctors had discovered. She died in Nashville at the age of fifty-four.

194
Frederick Wallace Smith

"Absolutely, Positively Overnight"—
Very Big Business

In the mid-1960s, Yale University student Frederick Wallace Smith sat down to a term paper that absolutely, positively had to be done overnight.

A Memphian whose late father had been founder of Dixie Greyhound Bus Lines as well as chairman and president of Toddle House Restaurants, Smith theorized in his paper that an air express company could deliver mail and packages with remarkable speed and efficiency anywhere in the nation, if they could be routed independently of passenger air lines. While the concept seemed brilliant, the term paper received only an average grade. But Smith would not forget the idea.

Born in 1944 and with a birth defect that kept him in braces and on crutches throughout grammar school, Smith barely knew his father (also named Frederick), who died when he was four. Raising her child in Memphis, Sally Wallace Smith encouraged him to become active in physical pursuits, which he did. The elder Smith, who was the son of a Mississippi River steamboat captain, had built his first bus from the body of a truck. While developing one of

the South's largest bus lines, he drove the bus himself until he started adding new routes. He wrote a letter to be read on his son's twenty-first birthday, which came shortly after the youth's graduation from Yale in 1966. The letter included advice that the son put his inheritance money to work. "My father didn't want me to be a fop," Smith later said.

Returning home a few years later from United States Marine Corps duty in Vietnam, Smith decided to enter the business world, bravely delving into his term paper's theory. Using his ample inheritance, he purchased an Arkansas airplane company and converted it into an air express service, which began operations in 1973 as Federal Express Corporation. On its first night, the company served 25 cities and delivered 186 packages.

Within a decade, thanks to his perseverance and the relaxed aviation regulations regarding independent air routes, Smith had a thriving business. He made Memphis his hub and contributed mightily to the city's economic rebirth. By the mid-1990s, Federal Express was generating more than two billion dollars annually to the state of Tennessee through various taxes and its purchase of goods and services. It was delivering more than 2.5 million articles daily in 210 countries. Smith's slogan, "When it absolutely, positively has to be there overnight," became recognized around the world.

195
Rhea Seddon

First Women Astronauts:
Outer Space for Cosmic Rhea

Her coworkers in 1978 called her "Cosmic Rhea."

A surgeon at Veterans Hospital in Memphis, Dr. Rhea Seddon was a recent graduate from the University of Tennessee School of Medicine. But now, she was also among the nation's first women to be accepted for training as an astronaut by the National Aeronautics and Space Administration (NASA). Within the year, she would be a member of the pioneering space shuttle program.

Born in 1947 at Murfreesboro, Margaret Rhea Seddon had wanted to be an astronaut since the age of ten. Growing up in the 1960s during America's focus on

Astronaut Rhea Seddon in a 1980 NASA portrait.

Seddon also knew that other factors were in her favor. She was unmarried ("not that I planned it that way") and a pilot in her spare time. "Everything that I had done happened to be the proper preparation," she said. Her interest in prescribed nutrition for surgical patients also aided her application. "We know a great deal about human physiology on earth and very little about it in outer space. I'm interested in the differences between the two," she explained at the time. She also began to perform clinical research into the effects of radiation therapy on nutrition in cancer patients. After her NASA selection, Rhea told the press how it was "hard to believe how perfectly the timing in my life has worked out."

Her marital status also soon changed. She met and married fellow astronaut Robert "Hoot" Gibson and, in 1982, became the first pregnant American astronaut. That same year, Rhea gave a newspaper interview about the space shuttle program (the first shuttle had gone into space a year earlier):

I think we're trying, . . . with the space shuttle, . . . to make access to space very routine. Perhaps that detracts a little bit from the excitement of it, but I liken it to Orville and Wilbur Wright's first flight. At that time it was very exciting to even go up in an airplane, but now we don't think too much of it. . . . I think the space program is going to become the same way eventually.

outer space, Rhea looked skyward but was restrained by gender from pursuing her dream.

Encouraged by her mother to seek "some sort of career," the fifth-generation Tennessean set her sights high by choosing medicine. After completing a bachelor's degree in physiology from the University of California at Berkeley in 1970, she returned to Tennessee and prepared to be a surgeon. She rotated her residency between the University of Tennessee College of Health Sciences and Veterans Hospital in Memphis. It was then that a series of coincidences, and the general realization that women could endure space flight just as well as men, led to the fulfillment of her childhood dream.

She heard that NASA was seeking new astronauts. "I thought, 'Shoot, that's when I'm going to be finished with my surgery residency. That's when I'll be looking for a job,'" she told a magazine interviewer.

Realizing that she fit the age category, Rhea

Rhea Seddon made her own first space shuttle expedition in 1985, helping conduct several medical experiments aboard *Discovery's* 109 orbits of the earth. Soon, she was assigned as a crew member on the first Spacelab flights dedicated to space and life sciences missions. The second of these, aboard the shuttle *Columbia* in 1993, became the "most successful and efficient Spacelab flight" that NASA had flown. Serving as *Columbia's* payload commander, she supervised numerous "neurovestibular, cardiovascular, cardiopulmonary, metabolic, and musculoskeletal medical experiments," reported NASA.

Her expanded duties with NASA included being a member of the Aerospace Medical Advisory Committee as well as a technical assistant to the director of flight crew operations and spacecraft communicator in the Mission Control Center at Houston, Texas. On free days, she became an emergency department physician in Houston area hospitals.

196
William P. Lawrence

A Vietnam Prisoner—And His Tennessee Poem

Hopelessly trapped for two months within a seven-foot-square cell in solitary confinement—no ventilation, no light, only bits of food, and temperatures topping 120 degrees—the navy pilot and captain, William P. Lawrence, reached out for sanity. Trying to endure this agony of his six years as a prisoner of war in Vietnam, his thoughts settled on home, and he relentlessly kept repeating: "Oh Tennessee, My Tennessee."

While attending high school in his native Nashville, Lawrence had been one of the shining academic, athletic, and ROTC stars—he graduated first in his class. At the United States Naval Academy, he was one of the top graduates, a brigade commander, member of three varsity sports teams, and class president. At the United States Naval Test Pilot School, he excelled yet again—number one in his class. Years of distinguished military flying and prestige followed, inspiring author James Michener in the novel *Space* to claim William P. Lawrence as "perhaps the ablest flier, all things considered" who had come from the naval test pilot school. In 1958, Lawrence was the first navy pilot to double the speed of sound in a navy plane.

Now as a prisoner of war who was gasping for air, Lawrence considered survival and self-respect to be a form of triumph. His body was so sore that he could not move. A heat rash had broken out in welts over his entire body. Unable to change his position without agonizing pain, Lawrence relied upon mental discipline. To merely hang on, he began to meditate on poetry.

Composing a poem entirely in his mind, Lawrence tried to seize a particular poetic rhythm that he remembered from his early schooling. A favorite that came to mind was Sir Walter Scott's "Lady of the Lake." Reflecting on his own inadequacies in relation to Scott's brilliance, Lawrence later admitted that his poem was not in the same league with Scott, but he was proud of it nonetheless: "I knew that he had genius, but I had time; and I was determined to stay with the task until I completed it." Lawrence kept the results in his mind for years:

Oh Tennessee, my Tennessee
What love and pride I feel for thee,
You proud old state, the Volunteer,
Your fine traditions I hold dear.

I revere your many heroes
Who bravely fought our country's foes,
Renowned statesmen, so wise and strong,
Who served our country well and long.

I thrill at thought of mountains grand,
Rolling green hills and fertile farm land,
Earth rich with stone, mineral and ore,
Forests dense and wild flowers galore,
Powerful rivers that bring us light,
Deep lakes with fish and fowl in flight,
Thriving cities and industries,
Fine schools and universities,
Strong folks of pioneer descent,
Simple, honest, and reverent.

Beauty and hospitality
Are the hallmarks of Tennessee.

And o'er the world as I may roam,
No place exceeds my boyhood home.
And oh how much I long to see
My native land, my Tennessee.

Lawrence's chances of seeing Tennessee ever again diminished daily. A prisoner since his fighter plane was shot down over the Red River Delta in June 1967, he was kept at a POW complex near Hanoi that Americans had nicknamed "Camp Vegas." It was notorious for its starvation diet and the torture which provided propaganda for the Communists. Usually kept in individual cells, prisoners were punished for communicating with one another.

William P. Lawrence landed in a brutal solitary confinement when his captors caught him trying to send a note to a fellow officer. Generally, the prisoners communicated by various ingenious means, using a simple letter code they had devised. They tapped messages through the walls of their cells, through the sounds made by sweeping their brooms, and by coughing, hacking, and sneezing in code. A chain of command was agreed upon during these communications, and Lawrence was made a senior officer. His job was to encourage the morale and military backbone they would need to endure. Through this elaborate communication system—with no words exchanged—they maintained their unity, their morale, and their identity as American fighting men.

Lawrence later reported in an article he wrote that their captors "for many years tried to prevent us from engaging in religious activity because they were aware of the strength and comfort we would derive. . . . Some POWs suffered cruel punishment at the hands of our enemy because of their participation in religious services." When several leading American officers were punished for holding these services, prisoners responded by singing "The Star-Spangled Banner" at the top of their voices. After the protest resulted in some form of religious liberty, Lawrence said, "We considered this one of our great victories as POWs."

In his article, Lawrence summarized his feelings: "I have come to realize that the qualities and values which enabled us to endure . . . are the very same qualities and values of the American national character that have made our country so great. . . . The spiritual faith of the POWs was an important influence in our lives."

During the last years of captivity, prisoners who were not in solitary confinement managed to converse with one another when guards were not present. Prisoners used these opportunities to great advantage: conducting classes in which each man would teach the others his area of expertise. "We all gained considerable knowledge in such diverse fields as mathematics, history, photography, and automobile mechanics," Lawrence noted.

After the United States ended its direct military involvement in Vietnam, Lawrence was finally released in March 1973. At a welcome-home ceremony in Nashville, he presented a copy of the POW poem he had composed by memory to the Tennessee General Assembly. One month later, the legislature adopted "Oh Tennessee, My Tennessee" as the state's official poem.

Five years and numerous nationwide honors later, Rear Admiral (and then Vice Admiral) William P. Lawrence became the head of the United States Naval Academy between 1978 and 1981. One of his children, Lieutenant Commander Wendy Lawrence, a naval academy graduate, would become the first woman naval aviator selected for the nation's space program. After retiring from the navy in 1986, William P. Lawrence held the Chair of Naval Leadership at the naval academy and taught midshipmen the vital link between leadership, personal discipline, and the preservation of freedom.

Two fellow Vietnam prisoners also became prominent after their release: Jeremiah Denton, with whom Lawrence was communicating when he was caught and thrown into solitary confinement, became a United States senator from Alabama, and James Stockdale ran for vice president of the United States in 1992 on an unsuccessful ticket with Ross Perot.

Stockdale said that Lawrence—awarded the United States Distinguished Service Medal for "inspirational leadership of fellow POWs as senior ranking officer of Camp Vegas"—was "resilient" under torture. "He repeatedly paid the price of being perceived by the enemy as a source of their troubles," noted Stockdale. "He could not be intimidated and never gave up the ship."

197
Ron Emery/Ray Hester
Life on the Line: A Marine and His Battlefield Surgeon

After a wait of thirteen years, a journey from Vietnam to Vanderbilt, and a coincidence that would stretch the imagination, former United States Marine Ron Emery of Knoxville was able to say "thank you" to the former army surgeon whose newly devised methods for brain surgery saved Emery's life on the battlefield.

Emery was descended from the family that built Emery's 5 & 10, a multistate dimestore chain begun in 1927 by his grandfather E. L. Emery and great-uncle R. V. Emery. In high school, the youngest Emery developed a romanticized view of war after reading, he said, "too many Ernest Hemingway books." In 1969, a month before graduating from Knoxville's Webb School, he enlisted in the Marine Corps. After graduation, while every other Webb graduate went straight into college, Emery headed straight for basic training.

The chance to partake of war came immediately. Landing in the Southeast Asian country of South Vietnam on April 6, 1970, Emery was now surrounded by the Vietnam War, fighting with United States forces against communist North Vietnam. He learned that the most dangerous times of a soldier's tour of duty were his first two months and his last two. "Our routine at night was to set up an ambush. We would arrive at a position and dig our foxholes. Everyone would stay awake until 12 or 1 o'clock and then we would take turns on guard duty."

On the night of June 6, Emery lay in the foxhole he and his comrades had dug. He said his prayers and went to sleep with a sense of relief that he had safely passed through his first two months of duty. But by morning, a deadly skirmish broke out, and Emery awoke to the sounds of the attack. Sitting up in the foxhole, he took a blow to the back of his head which destroyed a critical part of his brain.

"I don't remember the battle," he later said. A United States Navy corpsman, exposed to enemy fire, came to his rescue. Cradling Emery's head in his lap, the corpsman waited for reinforcements. Emery could hear the overhead sound of rotors from a helicopter, "probably the prettiest sound I ever heard." When the craft quickly set down, Emery was tossed on board. He soon realized that he was grievously wounded. Battlefield surgeons confirmed the worst prognosis: little if any chance of survival.

Rushed to the nearest field hospital, which happened to be a United States Army facility, Emery could feel his life slipping away. In tormenting pain, he tried to crawl off the operating table at the Ninety-fifth Evacuation Hospital, Da Nang. Chief of neurosurgery Ray Hester, having already lost a soldier with similar head wounds, decided that the only way to save his patient was to dispense with conventional operating methods. Dr. Hester immediately implemented a technique he had devised which controlled head trauma, giving enough time for extensive surgery. He grabbed an instrument he had invented to control the bleeding, then began to operate.

Awakening from a coma four days after the surgery, Emery was paralyzed on one side and suffering from amnesia. But he was still alive, and Dr. Hester sensed that a recovery was likely. Emery later recalled: "I remember all of the other doctors standing around, studying me. They couldn't believe it. I knew something was unique but had no idea what had happened; I was unable to speak for some time."

Through a strenuous two-week physical and mental rehabilitation in Japan, Emery grew healthy enough to travel. Sent next to a Memphis military hospital, he worked to regain his coordination over the next four months, and did so with help from family members who rallied around him there. His sister Susie continually massaged his arm and leg to get blood flowing, and his brother Roy lifted him from bed one day to help him walk.

Finally released from the hospital, Ron Emery arrived home in Knoxville with most of his memory and mobility intact. Finishing his college education, he became a successful businessman. But he never forgot the man who saved his life.

Emery made countless attempts trying to find the surgeon, Ray Hester. Impossible, claimed officials of the American Red Cross, who reported that a man could not be tracked through a complex military system without more information. Years went by, and Emery reluctantly abandoned his quest.

More than a decade had passed when, in 1983, a lunchtime conversation at Knoxville Rotary Club spurred Ron Emery to complete his search. A discussion about Vietnam and war injuries led to his own story about his wartime surgeon and the desire to find this man. The dialogue lit up a face across the table and provoked a question: "His name isn't Ray Hester, is it?"

Thunderstruck, Emery nodded yes to Dr. Robert Finelli, himself a neurosurgeon.

"Well," Dr. Finelli announced, "he's a good friend of mine at Vanderbilt Hospital," further explaining that he had trained under Hester and often heard the neurosurgeon mention a "very special surgery during the Vietnam War."

In a matter of minutes, a phone call across Tennessee ended a pursuit begun thirteen years and thousands of miles earlier. Battlefield patient and doctor made arrangements to meet in Nashville. They came together over dinner, where Emery's long-awaited thank you was given.

Dr. Hester had been a longtime resident of Nashville, where he had obtained both his undergraduate and medical degrees from Vanderbilt University. He would return to his private practice and to his work with the clinical staff at Vanderbilt. Emery would return to Knoxville, where he would soon realize another long-lasting goal. Although Emery's 5 & 10 was obliterated by the advent of national discount chains, he managed to reopen the Knoxville store and reestablish a part of the family legacy.

198
Alex Stewart

Honoring a Tennessee Craftsman

When ninety-two-year-old East Tennessean Alex Stewart stood on a Washington, D.C., stage in 1983 to accept the Heritage Fellowship Award from the National Endowment for the Arts, his bib overalls and plow shoes spoke before he did.

At the sight of the master craftsman from Hancock County, the crowd rose to show its appreciation of a man described as a "national treasure." Many wept openly during the standing ovation. Stewart was humble and concise in his response: "I think I've about done my part, and now I'm aiming to turn it over to someone else and go home and rest for a while."

A virtual encyclopedia of century-old folkways, Alex Stewart became the first Tennessean to receive the award, and, in doing so, represented thousands of other Appalachian craftsmen and women who were discovered anew by historians and artists during the 1970s.

Stewart's life began in the previous century, in 1891, a time when survival in rural areas meant being a jack of all trades. He learned to dig for ginseng on the forested East Tennessee hillsides (for eventual export to China); he hunted freshwater pearls in the Clinch River (bringing in three to four dollars on average per pearl, although he heard of one fellow at Sneedville who got one thousand dollars for a single pearl); he rafted logs down the same river to nearby Anderson County and Clinton; he drove steel for railroads; and he dug mine shafts for coal companies. Also a tenant farmer, Stewart could make almost anything needed with his hands, including a moonshine still he once used to produce homemade whiskey, thus continuing a mountain heritage derived from a Scots-Irish ancestry.

Alex Stewart's cedar buckets, along with his other crafts, became sought-after treasures.

Although he knew the pioneering ways, Stewart kept up with the twentieth century, displaying a thorough knowledge of current topics and issues. An avid reader of newspapers and books, he could discuss everything from the latest medicines to a public referendum.

He lived a rather quiet life until 1962 when John Rice Irwin, founder of the Museum of Appalachia at Norris, heard of Alex Stewart's wealth of experience and knowledge. Irwin was looking for someone to produce a typical pioneer craft for his museum collection of mountain artifacts and thought Stewart might be the man to do it. Their initial meeting blossomed into a twenty-five-year friendship, ultimately resulting in Irwin's 1985 book *Alex Stewart, Portrait of a Pioneer* and in Stewart's rise to national attention.

"What I most remember about that meeting was his response to my question about making a piggin," Irwin wrote. "I remember his amused laugh. 'Why son, I've been out of that business for 40 years. These here store-bought buckets, plastic containers, and such put me out of commission. Anyhow I don't have no timber. It takes good cedar timber to make vessels.'"

Irwin soon provided the proper cedar log, which Stewart examined with the greatest of care. "Then he threw in a little philosophy," remembered Irwin, "the likes of which I was to hear so often as we spent more time together."

On this particular day, Alex Stewart impressed upon Irwin how timber and people were often alike.

> You can go out here in the woods and find you the purtiest looking tree. You cut it down and when you get inside you may find rotten places, and doty places and it's no account. Then you can get an old knotty, scubby looking tree and it'll make the best lumber ever you seen. And that's just the way of people too. I've thought a lot about that.

When Irwin asked him if he would fashion a traditional butter churn from the cedar log, Stewart agreed to undertake the task. Three weeks later, and to Irwin's amazement, Stewart had produced nearly two dozen churns, tubs, buckets, and other pioneer implements. "A year's work, I thought," Irwin claimed, "and yet this fragile little man had done all this in three weeks."

Stewart's work soon gained the attention of another man: Oak Ridge whittler and craftsman Bill Henry, who secured a grant from the Tennessee Craft Council to serve an apprenticeship with Alex Stewart.

By 1976, when Stewart turned eighty-five, he was surprised at the fame he had gained. Letters and telegrams arrived from the governor as well as from state and congressional representatives and senators.

Accompanied by Henry, Stewart went to Washington in 1976 to participate in the Festival of American Folklore. Although he said he "always wanted to go to Washington and see 'all them foreigners,'" Stewart also wanted to avoid meeting the United States president, who might ask him all kinds of questions and "see that big badge I had on that said I was a cooper, and he'd come down home aggravating me to death, wanting to learn that trade."

Stewart next found himself the subject of a documentary film, *Alex Stewart: Cooper,* produced by East Tennessee State University's Dr. Thomas Burton, as well as the focus of a nationwide documentary produced by Westinghouse Corporation about Tennessee and Kentucky. In 1975, Stewart's celebrated name led *National Geographic* to place him on the cover of its book *Craftsmen of the World.* The tributes seemed endless. Alex Stewart was also given a section in *Foxfire 3,* inspiring that book's editor to proclaim him the greatest of all old-time craftspeople of his day: "I'd put Alex at the very top of the list—hands down."

When such honors began, Irwin wrote, they came every few weeks. In 1979, the city of Oak Ridge designated Alex Stewart Day, a recognition also duplicated in his native Hancock County. His crafts were displayed throughout the United States, including at the Smithsonian Institution in Washington, D.C.; his words filled magazines and newspapers throughout the world (as far away as Japan). In 1982, when the city of Knoxville hosted the World's Fair, Stewart's crafts became one of the fair's permanent displays for international travelers to view.

When he received his heritage award from the National Endowment for the Arts, Stewart had reached a pinnacle. "There he sat, 92 years old and only 94 pounds, the sole person on the stage of one of Washington's largest convention halls," wrote Irwin. "He was but a tiny speck on the grand stage, which he later described as being bigger than one of his corn fields."

Returning home to Hancock County, Alex Stewart lived to the age of ninety-four. His old log cabin, where he had raised many children, was relocated to the Museum of Appalachia. Irwin made a lasting tribute to one of the nation's leading craftsmen by building a permanent exhibit at the museum's Hall of Fame, showcasing the life and times of Alex Stewart and featuring hundreds of his crafts.

199
William Jarnagin

*Working His Way through
the Twentieth Century*

Still on the job at the age of 102, which he surpassed in 1996, William "Bill" Jarnagin persevered through the twentieth century because of his willingness to go an extra mile, and then some. As the world's oldest living Ford dealer, Jarnagin believed in being consistent about hard work. He also believed in being the first one to open his business in the mornings. Even at 102, Jarnagin continued to arrive at work before other employees and to open the doors of his Rutledge dealership six days a week. To get there, he drove (cautiously) along the back roads of Grainger County.

For those who were interested in the dawn of modern times after the invention of the automobile, Jarnagin held court and gave a few history lessons. During the 1910s, he recalled, selling cars was made more challenging by two simple facts: people did not know how to drive and cars arrived unassembled.

After his cousin, John R. Jarnagin, opened the dealership in 1916 and hired him as mechanic, salesman, and part owner, Bill Jarnagin assembled his first car, delivered it, and taught his customer how to drive in an open field. The training sometimes became involved. He once spent hours teaching driving to a would-be buyer from Bean Station. By dusk, the customer felt comfortable behind the wheel but was too timid to drive into Rutledge. Determined to seal the deal, Jarnagin left the car behind and began walking the moonless night sixteen miles home.

Since few of his neighbors in and around Grainger County had ever driven a car, Jarnagin eventually taught most of them. But the general public's demand for cars soon exceeded his supply. When a train shipment finally arrived at the railhead in Knoxville, the unloading task was monumental—requiring six- to eight-man crews to lift but one unassembled auto.

Sometimes there were not six men available. Jarnagin eventually designed and patented a dolly for the task, winning national notoriety for his device that could do "the work of six men," he proclaimed. With the device, two mechanics could put together twelve Model T's in a single day.

Once the vehicle was in an owner's hands back in Rutledge, car repair was relatively simple and most always done by the owner. According to Jarnagin, "Anybody could fix it [a car] with bailing wire."

When his business career was interrupted by World War I, he volunteered to instruct United States Army motor-transport specialists. From a training ground in Knoxville, Jarnagin taught soldiers both how to drive and do car repairs. "I trained them up and shipped them to Georgia," he said. "Then they went on [to the war]." While Jarnagin held no rank, he did receive a sergeant's pay and privileges.

In addition to Grainger County's first automobile dealership, Jarnagin also started its first electric company. He and his cousin John R. bought a power system in 1919 to light their garage and start the engines. "We had the first lights in Rutledge," Bill Jarnagin said. "We got a Delco light plant," referring to the Delco 110-volt electrical system that ran on fifty-six brass batteries. Townspeople were so intrigued by the lights that they encouraged the Jarnagins to run lines to their houses. The Jarnagin light plant soon was helping illuminate most of Rutledge.

The system became overloaded, however, causing brownouts and surges. The Jarnagins increased their capacity, but their small electric company lost both power and money. They held on for nearly a decade before selling their enterprise to a Morristown investor for the token price of $150. He, too, failed in the venture, leaving Rutledge literally in the dark for some time to come (until TVA eventually brought reliable electrical service to the region).

During the 1920s, Jarnagin began traveling to Ford's plant in Cincinnati to obtain fully assembled cars. Collecting his shipment, Jarnagin and his drivers formed a caravan back to Tennessee. Each trip always included a stop at an inn and restaurant near Lexington, Kentucky. The fried chicken was especially tasty there, and the inn's proprietor was courteous enough to provide tarpaulins for Jarnagin's vehicles. The innkeeper, Colonel Harland Sanders, eventually started a chain of restaurants to market his kitchen specialty under the name "Kentucky Fried Chicken."

As Jarnagin's business grew, the Ford Motor Company in 1937 sent representatives to Rutledge, hoping to discover how Jarnagin was outselling most of the nation's dealers. What they learned was that he often devoted twenty hours any given day to his work.

By the 1990s, Jarnagin Ford had become one of the oldest dealerships in Ford history. As to his own longevity, Jarnagin had a simple philosophy: "hard work and clean living." His grandson and the dealership's general manager, John Jarnagin, affirmed that Jarnagin "can't stand for anyone to beat him to work." But if what the younger Jarnagin said is true, there may be even more to it: "He also eats food smothered in onions!"

200
Al Gore

His Earth in Balance—
A Vice President's Agenda

On a warm spring afternoon in 1989, the six-year-old son of United States Senator Al Gore, filled with the excitement of just having seen a baseball game, broke from his father's grasp and dashed into the street in Baltimore, Maryland.

In frozen disbelief, Gore watched his youngest of four children, Albert, "get hit by a car, fly thirty feet through the air and scrape along the pavement another twenty feet until he came to rest in a gutter." When Gore rushed to his son's side, the boy was, in Gore's words, "limp and still, without breath or pulse. His eyes were open with the nothingness of death."

Despite the obvious signs that he was about to lose his son, Gore held the boy and began to pray. His son's injuries were so severe that both Gore and his wife, Tipper, lived at the hospital for the first month of the many that would mark young Albert's long recovery.

The trauma of this episode was pivotal, sending Senator Gore into a reflection on his life. He had just turned forty, and only a year before in 1988 had lost the Democratic bid for the presidency after winning primary contests in seven states. As he wrote later, he was "vulnerable to the change that sought me out in the middle of my life." Gore said he had "a new sense of urgency about those things I value the most" and

that he became "increasingly impatient with the status quo, with conventional wisdom, with the lazy assumption that we can always muddle through."

Caution, Gore believed, contributed to his lack of success as a presidential candidate when he began to doubt whether the issues he cared about, especially the environmental crisis he believed was rapidly assuming worldwide proportions, could form the basis of a major campaign. Terms like "global warming" and "nuclear arms control" were not political catchphrases at the time. "As a result, for much of the campaign I discussed what everybody else discussed."

Gore's belief that he could help combat some of the world's problems, most notably devastating assaults on the earth's atmosphere and habitats, led to his research and writing of the 1992 book *Earth in the Balance: Ecology of the Human Spirit.* He summarized his reflections on life in the book's introduction.

Gore's interest in environmental issues came somewhat naturally. He was born in 1948 to parents from Tennessee farm families. His father was United States Senator Albert Gore Sr., and young Gore divided his time between his native Washington, D.C., and his parents' 250-acre farm near Carthage. While attending school in Carthage, Gore also became active in the local 4-H Club. "My earliest lessons on environmental protection were about the prevention of soil erosion on our family farm," he explained, "and I still remember clearly how important it is to stop up the smallest gully 'before it gets started good.'" Conversations at the family dinner table with his parents reinforced these lessons. Gore's mother, Pauline, who also happened to be one of the first women to receive a law degree from Vanderbilt University, was instrumental in such dialogue. She once directed her children's attention to a classic book about DDT and pesticide abuse, what Al Gore would later call "nearly invisible" poisons.

It was a life lived close to the soil and close to politics from the beginning for Gore, who labored each childhood summer in farm work and eventually had his own Smith County farm. He would come to believe that in his political career, the two lives finally merged. But the connections would evolve gradually over the passing years.

The summer of 1969 was a time of decision for the twenty-one-year-old from Harvard University who had just graduated with honors and gained a degree in

Al Gore taking the oath of office in January 1993 as vice president of the United States.

government. His father, now a thirty-year veteran of Congress, was a towering force in the United States Senate. The nation was gripped by one of the defining debates of the century, a furor over the morality of using American military power in the tiny southeastern Asian nation of Vietnam. The military draft had become a focal point of the protests against the war—protests that spilled into the streets, pitting the young against the established order. Such was the case at Harvard, where Gore's father was revered for his politically outspoken views against the war, voiced almost daily in the Senate Committee on Foreign Relations.

Although he was against the war, young Gore refused to join radical protest movements, believing instead that he had to enlist in the armed forces. He knew that if he signed up in Carthage, cynics might link the act to his father's reelection campaign, an uphill battle due to the Vietnam issue. Seeking ano-

nymity, Gore walked into a recruiting office in Newark, New Jersey, and became a private in the United States Army. He also soon married Boston University graduate Mary Elizabeth "Tipper" Aitcheson from Arlington, Virginia, whom he had dated throughout their collegiate days.

Gore, who trained as an army journalist, eventually saw combat in Vietnam during his coverage of firebases and learned about another atmospheric poison, Agent Orange, a herbicide that cleared jungle hiding places used by the enemy. Returning from Vietnam in 1971, not long after his father lost his campaign for reelection, Gore tried to sort out the moral questions of such wars. For a time, he attended the Vanderbilt University School of Divinity.

Having been trained as a journalist, he also became a reporter at the *Nashville Tennessean* and eventually wrote about local political corruption. Life became filled with other pursuits as well: partnership in a small homebuilding business and enrollment in Vanderbilt Law School.

Gore remained three years at the *Tennessean* and might have stayed longer had not a congressional seat come open. When Joe Evins, the representative from Gore's district in Carthage for thirty years, decided to retire, Gore felt an immediate urge to campaign for the seat, also once held by his father. He called the elder Gore to ask what he thought of a possible campaign.

"Well, son," his father reportedly told him. "I'll vote for you."

The successful election that followed in 1976 for twenty-eight-year-old Al Gore made him one of the youngest congressmen to be elected from Tennessee in the twentieth century. During his first years in Congress, he organized the first congressional hearings on toxic waste after receiving a letter from a farm family in Toone, Tennessee, about hazardous pesticide waste being dumped on neighboring land and causing the family's illness. In 1981-82, Gore also became educated on the nuclear arms race, studying on the subject weekly for thirteen months.

He held on to his congressional seat through 1984, and then he decided to run for the United States Senate. After winning that election, he was reelected in 1990, becoming the first candidate in modern history to win all ninety-five of Tennessee's counties. A nationally recognized leader on technology issues, Gore soon introduced and steered Senate passage of the High Performance Computing Act to create a national, high-speed computer network and increase research and development of high-performance technologies. The act was later signed into law.

In July 1992, Democratic presidential candidate Bill Clinton chose Gore to be his running mate. A few months later, United States Senator Al Gore took the oath of office as the forty-fifth vice president of the United States.

Although he became active in a wide range of initiatives, Gore continued to be an advocate of environmental issues that he had begun discussing at his mother's dinner table in Carthage. As his parents had involved him, he also found a way to involve children in protecting the earth. Among an array of environmental programs and recommendations, Vice President Gore introduced GLOBE (Global Learning and Observations to Benefit the Environment), bringing the world's children together with educators and scientists to monitor the global environment.

In 1996, President Bill Clinton and Vice President Al Gore were elected to a second term of office, as Tennessee and the nation approached the twenty-first century.

Notes

These citations are keyed to the sources in the selected bibliography.

Acklen, Adelicia Hayes
"some of the": Culpepper, 383.
"It don't make": Graham, 349.
"I like this": ibid.
"My mother always": Kiser, 42.

Acuff, Roy
"To hell with": Malone, 193.
"the king of": Wolfe, 72.
"first exclusive country": Malone, 193.
"became almost synonymous": ibid., 190.

Agee, James
"A perfectly magnificent": Bergreen, 19.
"the familial love": Seib, 4.
"The novel has": ibid., 78.
"Well, I wouldn't": ibid., 14.
"It is not": Madden, 23.
"But we who": ibid., 146.

Anderson, William R.
"a new northwest": Anderson and Blair, 213.
"Her performance and": ibid., 19.
"the contour of": ibid., 213.
"I saw incredibly": ibid., 214.
"no bells would": ibid., 221.
"All hands—This": ibid., 222-23.

"dedicated with our": ibid., 223.
"I glanced again": ibid.
"Captain, you might": ibid.
"awe-struck at": ibid., 223-24.

Angevine, Lena
"We'll confirm your": Coppock, 176.

Barnes, John C.
"General Tipton's celebrated": Williams, 68.

Bell, John
"I am a": Bell, 96.
"a dark bottle": ibid., 187.
"He will never": ibid., 188.
"the driver could": ibid., 65.
"It is the": ibid., 65.
"suddenly the braggart": ibid., 66-67.
"There is another": ibid., 67.

Bell, Montgomery
"Do write a": Corlew, "Some Aspects," 359.

Blount, William
"the Indians looked": Blount Mansion Assn., 10.
"the door stood": ibid., 11.
"We beg to": Bond, 179.
"This goes to": ibid.

Bowie, Elve
"Mr. Sheriff, I": Douglas, 3.

Bragg, Zack
"They worry you": McIlwaine, 249.
"Before the early": ibid., 247.
"was full of": ibid., 249.
"There wasn't anything": Crawford.
"The flatheads, stripped": McIlwaine, 251-52.
"were by far": Douglas, 44.
"There were no": ibid., 40.
"those first days": Crawford.
"so cottages were": McIlwaine, 253.
"to prove that": ibid., 256.
"the largest hardwood": ibid.
"the junk of": ibid., 257.

Brantley, James/Albert Dement
"gamest horse I": Green, 28.

Brown, Clarence
"Why don't you": Brown, n.p. "Recollections of Early Days."
"She was a": Brownlow, 146-47.
"the greatest personalities": ibid., 146.
"imaginative visual values": ibid., 139.
"Clarence Brown is": ibid.

Brown, Joseph
"I fell on": Brown, 211.
"I was within": ibid., 210.
"I saw that": ibid.
"nor on the": ibid.

Brownlow, William G. "Parson"
"exuberance and redundancy": Kelly, 28.
"I was influenced": Walker, 165.
"I never courted": ibid., 163.
"This is the": Fink, 29.
"into high gear": ibid., 31.
"wrestling matches or": Kelly, 33.
"If you will": Creekmore, *Arrows to Atoms,* 83.
"Glory to God": Coulter, 5.
"I therefore pronounce": Kelly, 34.
"rushed into each": ibid., 156.
"The Parson Brownlow": ibid., 157.
"Anna, is that": Mackin, 414.
"had I my": Kelly, 172.

Buchanan, Daniel
"thrust it down": McClain, 9.
"In the struggle": ibid.
"no match in": ibid.

Bull, Carroll Gideon
"paid his own": Bates, "The Life and Work," 141.
"The Secretary took": ibid., 144.
"first professor in": ibid., 145.

Burn, Harry T.
"Nobody can revere": Dykeman, 26.
"Dear son: Hurrah": McKinney, 85.
"I know that": ibid.
"Coincident with the": Burn scrapbook.

Burnett, John G.
"[I] remained so": Burnett, 180.
"the blackest chapter": Higgs and Manning, 51.
"In the year": Burnett, 183.
"Future generations will": ibid., 184.
"In another home": Higgs and Manning, 52.
"I made the": Burnett, 181.
"was carried unconscious": ibid., 182.

Byrns, Joseph Wellington
"There's one thing": Coode, 132.
"veered sharply leftward": Boyer et al, 884.
"but his unfailing": Galloway, 71.

Cain, Bobby
"the Lord to": McMillan, 69.
"rabble rouser": Brittain, 101.
"sat and trembled": McMillan, 69.
"I had to": ibid.
"strong white boys": Brittain, 187.
"After that day": McMillan, 69.
"never saw himself": Adamson, 40.

Campbell, Francis Joseph
"the first blind": McRaven, 3.
"Skating, swimming, rowing": ibid.
"I took my": ibid., 4.
"almost two columns": ibid., 8.

Carmack, Edward W.
"one of the": Coppock, 49.
"I have resigned": ibid., 52.
"he or Senator": Summerville, 11.
"You have no": ibid., 10.
"The debt I": ibid.

Caruthers, Hanson
"Marster would shake": Egypt, 261.
"This was the": Watson, 179.
"I was hungry": ibid., 181.
"I was in": Egypt, 253.
"the troops exhibited": Civil War Centennial Commission, 1: 398.
"I went to": Egypt, 253.

Chapman, David C.
"gave a sizeable": Robinson.
"a record not": "Men of Affairs."
"They say you": "Col. D. C. Chapman."
"I was born": Robinson.
"Some of the": ibid.

"death by eminent": Dunn, 241.
"Col. Chapman. You": Dykeman and Stokely, 142.
"But now the": ibid., 155.
"one of the": Cardinal Health, Inc.

Chavannes, Anna
"Everybody goes on": Babelay, 69.
"which pleased us": ibid., 70.
"The director of": ibid., 70-72.
"As we are": ibid., 71.
"to congratulate myself": ibid.
"animals could be": ibid., 8.
"largest European ethnic": East Tennessee Historical
   Society.
"In a very": Babelay, 220.
"When any of": ibid.
"Brother, be sure": ibid.
"Her whole life": ibid.

Cheairs, Nathaniel
"Surrender? After whipping": McBride, 121.
"General, you have": ibid., 122.
"the most disgraceful": ibid.
"Colonel Hurst, I": ibid., 131-32.
"pardon for all": ibid., 135.

Cheatham, Benjamin Franklin
"back upriver.": Losson, 37.
"There was no": Evans, 302.

Cheek, Joel Owsley
"good to the": Cheek biographical file, "Maxwell House
   Messenger," 19.
"burden that was": Davis.

Church, Robert, Sr.
"And don't you": Terrell, 2.
"It was a": ibid., 8.
"Whose little nigger": Sterling, 123.
"With this example": Hutchins, 101.
"Whereas Robert R.": ibid., 103.
"largest black-owned": Pink Palace, 7.

Clemens, John
"But may God": *The Commercial Appeal.*

Cocke, William
"I don't reckon": Gerson, 11.
"the Daniel Boone": ibid., 10.
"the King did": Moore and Foster, 99.
"No one wrote": Gerson, 16.
"Senator Cocke's record": McBride and Robison, 153.
"the defense of": Gerson, 11.

Cockrill, Mark Robertson
"Some of the": Ewing, 8-9.
"feeds the soil": ibid., 51.

"good shepherd": ibid., 10-11.
"as fine as": ibid., 40.
"Is there going": Cockrill, 52.

Cook, Laura
"No taxes, no": Van Ark, 59.
"Chief of Police": ibid.
"take the treatments": Cook letter.

Crockett, David
"a pretty good": Crockett, 234.
"the gentleman from:" Lofaro, *Davy Crockett: The Man,* 5.
"I understand the": Rourke, 117.
"Sometimes they get": ibid.
"My little boy": ibid., 118.
"I like hunting": ibid.
"might swallow us": Marshall, 9.
"rocked about like": ibid.
"took a notion": ibid.
"knocked down and": Crockett, 239.
"Since you have": Lofaro, "Why Davy Won't Die," 17.
"Be always sure": Lofaro, *Davy Crockett: The Man,* 104.

Crump, Edward Hull "Boss"
"good housekeeping": Tucker, 26.
"Cleanest Town in": ibid., 27.
"when the TVA": Popham, 12.
"November 6th Street": ibid.

Daniel, Jack
"Old Lincoln County": Bigger, 7.
"foot washin'": ibid., 5.
"One of your": Green, 38.
"I've heard that": ibid., 111.
"Gentlemen, the judges": ibid., 113.
"Hey Elder Webster": ibid., 119-20.
"Square Shooter": Bigger, 7.

Davis, Frances "Fanny"
"Dear Fannie, Use": Pitrone, 48.
"To Fannie, the": ibid., 99.
"God kept me": ibid., 101.
"There were very": ibid., 141-42.
"I . . . visited with": ibid., 184.

Davis, Sam
"I pleaded with": Walker, 47-48.
"Do you suppose": Meredith, 315.
"Oh how painful": ibid., 313-14.
"He displayed great": ibid., 315.
"the person who": ibid.
"given to Sam": Smith, 1973.
"plowing and hoeing": ibid., 1974.
"My young master": ibid.

Dickinson, Perez
"in the sight": Creekmore, 145.

Doak, Samuel
"Help us as": Dixon, 59.
"they unavoidably came": Kilgo, 27.
"flea-bitten grey": Foster, 244.
"first real institution": ibid., 243.
"Often it would": Fink, 27.
"Give me the": Bond, 81.
"Here is a": ibid., 82.
"the Apostle of": Foster, 252.

Douglas, "Shufflin' Phil"
"I want to": Johnson.
"I decided that": ibid.
"A man has": ibid.

Downing, Henry
"may you and": Curtis.
"Good luck, Captain": ibid.

Driver, William
"Old Glory Driver": Davis, 118.

Duggan, Ralph
"Names from graveyards": Byrum, 116.
"Your Vote Will": ibid., 117.
"Are you the": White, 59.
"Then Duggan slugged": ibid.
"the public whip": ibid., 60.
"Many were thinking": ibid., 56.

Effler, Lawrence
"After the fight": Masters, 28.

Ellis, Daniel
"As a general": Ellis, 33.
"Orders had been": ibid., 27.
"This was sad": ibid., 29.
"A more bloodthirsty": ibid.
"Entertaining as I": ibid., 30.
"You shall not": ibid., 31.
"I became frightened": ibid., 34.
"Some bawled out": ibid., 31.
"Surely at this": ibid., 33.
"I must here": ibid., 33-34.
"saved one poor": ibid., 34.
"taken thousands of": Hesseltine, 38.

Embree, Elihu
"a gradual abolition": White, v.
"to trample on": ibid., vii.

Emery, Ron/Ray Hester
"too many Ernest": Emery interview.
"Our routine": ibid.
"I don't remember": ibid.
"probably the prettiest": ibid.
"I remember all": ibid.
"His name isn't": ibid.

Estes, "Sleepy John"/Hammie Nixon
"I got me": McKee and Chisenhall, 158.
"he had heard": ibid., 159.
"He'd take my": ibid.
"And finally someone": ibid., 161.
"And he'd [Capone]": ibid., 162.

Farragut, David Glasgow
"A prize! Ho": *Under Both Flags,* 3-4.
"I, being inspired": Williams, 87.
"a series of": ibid.
"I give the": ibid., 94.

Ferguson, Champ
"They said that": Montell, 66.
"marauding band": Civil War Centennial Commission, 1:15.
"Ferguson was described": Montell, 65.

Fisher, Thomas Burr
"Reason dictates and": *War of the Rebellion,* 49, Part 2: 1289-90.
"Our hearts were": J. E. Fisher, 318.
"Here my life": T. B. Fisher, 21.
"always loved books": J. E. Fisher, 318.
"The first time": T. B. Fisher, 3.
"work harder than": J. E. Fisher, 319.
"there were many": ibid.
"was standing with": T. B. Fisher, 77.
"I venture to": ibid.
"I found them": ibid., 76.

Ford, Loyd, Sr.
"black children": Howington, 252.
"an old school": ibid., 254.
"put it in": ibid.
"proper parties": ibid., 256.
"A slave is:" ibid., 249.

Foreman, Stephen
"He Labored with": Evans, 237-38.
"Four miles the": ibid., 234.
"Get a good:" Ibid., 237.

Forrest, Nathan Bedford
"greatest general": Henry, 462.
"the most remarkable": Crawford, 35.
"Officers of our": Henry, 464.
"the incalculable value": ibid.
"keep Forrest occupied": Duke, 37.
"General, now I": Henry, 441.
"John, I hear": Morton, 344.

Fort, Cornelia
"Not today, brother!": Tanner, 89.

Frankland, R. Ernest
"I believe in": Featherston, 98.
"belonged to Ernest": ibid., 97.

"if it had": ibid., 105-6.
"just in time": ibid., 106.
"inflicted far heavier": ibid., 110.
"which was engaged": ibid., 225-26.
"big enough to": ibid., 227.
"Once again, Old": ibid., 228.
"I wish you'd": ibid., 229.
"Still, by Christmas": ibid., 235.
"you can give": ibid., 237.
"the finest infantry": ibid., 240.

Freeman, Elizabeth "Miss Lizzie"
"Her policy made": McCombs, "As It Was," 19.
"We seemed to": ibid., 17.
"I think Mr.": McCombs, "Freemans of Woodley."
"There was rarely": McCombs, "As It Was," 18.
"If a young": ibid.
"She doctored people": ibid., 18-19.
"In wintertime there": ibid., 17-18.
"It was a": ibid., 18.
"we didn't go": ibid., 21.
"But with all": ibid., 23-24.
"We produced enough": ibid., 19.

French, Lucy Virginia
"queen of the": Shirley, 44.
"seeing that the": Gower, 92.
"one of the": ibid., 91.
"We had been": ibid., 94.
"Letha, one of": ibid., 94-95.
"On Sunday last": ibid., 98.
"While the Capt.": ibid., 99.
"scarlet fever and": ibid., 101.

Furber, George C.
"to take up": Furber, 45.
"noise made upon": ibid., 47.
"joined in the": ibid., 48.
"the rusty head": ibid., 60-61.
"all were so": ibid., 76.
"adventurers, without valor": ibid., 96.
"pouring over its": ibid.
"dizzy and bewildered": ibid., 499.
"found themselves on": ibid., 504.
"impregnable fortress": ibid., 521.
"The enemy retreated": ibid., 543.
"vomito": ibid., 613.
"the War Horse": Crutchfield, 81.
"each experienced a": ibid., 614.

Gailor, Charlotte
"The doctor was": Gailor, 7.
"The most important": ibid., 8.
"My word is": ibid., 9.
"We met General": ibid., 11.
"Maj. Martin Walt": ibid., 14.

"I will never": ibid., 15.
"You have taken": ibid., 16.
"Don't be afraid": Davies-Rodgers, 44.

Gardner, John A.
"the fundamental principles": Corlew, 261.
"Jacksoniana": Gardner, 68.

Gloster, Mary Hayes
"The granchild's presence": Davies-Rodgers, "Mrs. Gloster," 95.

Gordon, George W.
"The famous snowball": Vaughan, 89.
"as high as": ibid., 90-91.
"With a shout": ibid., 92-93.

Gore, Al
"get hit by": Gore, 13.
"vulnerable to the": ibid., 14.
"a new sense of": ibid.
"As a result": ibid., 8.
"My earliest lessons": ibid., 2.
"nearly invisible": ibid., 3.
"Well, son, I'll": Hillin, 101.

Grayson, James W. M./Tom Dula
"This time tomorrow": Warner, 59.
"Hang down your": ibid.

Handy, W. C.
"Go on, Carrie": Lee, 83.
"Anywheres. Just anywheres": Handy, 15.
"idlers, dissipated characters": ibid., 11.
"I'd rather follow": ibid.
"a seed of": ibid., 16.
"His great accomplishment": Coppock, 254.
"Your work is": ibid.
"dressed like a": ibid., 259.
"the figure of": ibid.

Harding, William Giles
"if this is": Wills, "Black-White Relationships," 21.
"consideration of certain": Miller, 89-90.
"You said in": ibid., 89.
"fly to me": Wills, "Black-White Relationships," 23.
"without the least": ibid.
"had won more": Wills, "Home of the Race Horse," 163.
"You have been": Wills, "Black-White Relationships," 28.

Harpe Brothers
"The whole community": Breazeale, 139.
"You're a": ibid., 147.

Harriman, Walter C.
"The Colonel used": Shelley and Hall, 69.
"extolling the virtues": ibid.
"Happy Harriman": Davis.
"We are up": ibid.

Hendrix, John
"as loud and": Robinson, 18.
"Big engines will": ibid., 19.
"I tell you": ibid., 18-19.
"total exclusion area": Johnson and Jackson, 49.
"All the folks": ibid., 41.
"The only difference": Robinson, 30.
"a two-and-a": ibid., 57-58.
"I'll give you": ibid., 58.
"It's all right": ibid.
"There they were": Johnson and Jackson, 51-52.
"I started filling": Robinson, 52.
"A third shift": ibid., 54-55.
"In order not": Johnson and Jackson, 19.
"was kind of": ibid., 209.

Higgason, Amy Elizabeth
"I guess you": Claxton interviews.
"Does this mean": ibid.
"after all, a": ibid.

Hill, Elizabeth "Bettsey"
"Bettsey Mamie": Peterson and Rankin, 6.
"most significant ancestors": ibid.
"She's the mother": ibid.
"out of bondage": Webb, n.p.
"It's practically an": Peterson and Rankin, 6.
"I'll come back": de la Cruz.

Hill, Napoleon
"monstrous collar and": McIlwaine, 224.
"Merchant Prince": ibid., 221.

Hirsch, Sidney
"firmly fixed as": Young, 21.
"the most artistic": Cowan, 18.
"poet, journalist, orientalist": ibid., 17.
"enthusiastic but somewhat": ibid., 18.
"fine discrimination between": ibid., 19.
"The Nashville Fugitives": Rubin, 16.
"related in a": ibid., 16-17.

Honeycutt, Annanias
"the most outstanding": Holt, 39.
"shifting the handkerchief": ibid., 41.

Hooper, Ben Walter
"Well, then, if": Hooper, 5.
"There is a": ibid., 6.
"stirred up such": ibid.,
"an unusually thorough": ibid., 10.
"My astonishment can": ibid., 12.
"Instead of my": ibid., 13-14.
"I immediately endeavored": ibid., 14.
"I fed, watered and": ibid., 15.
"When my father": ibid., 23-24.
"cold-blooded and": ibid., 19.
"[Cordell] Hull's name:" Ibid.
"I wish my": ibid., 24.

Hopkins, Montgomery "Gum"
"Fighting Hopkins Brothers": O'Dell, 98.

Houston, Sam
"liked the wild": Wiltshire, 249.
"Tell him I": Baggett, 158.
"plum-colored coat": Davis, 10.
"a demented man": ibid., 21.
"He knelt before": ibid., 17.

Hughes, Thomas
"the new Jerusalem": Egerton, 44.
"'Tis a scheme": Stagg, 219.
"This scheme that": ibid., 220.
"It is the": Walker, 24.
"A great gulf": Govan and Livingood, 342.
"I know Pa": ibid., 343.
"the last organized": Stagg, 209.
"noble experiment": Walker, 23.
"the memories of": Stagg, 222.

Hull, Cordell
"King Alfred language": Hull, 6.
"I recognized good": ibid., 16.
"Father went straight": ibid., 4.
"Many of these": ibid., 16-17.
"Our crude homemade": ibid., 14.
"They would not": ibid.
"I not only": ibid.
"Here I finally": ibid., 17.
"six miles up": DeLozier, 66.
"Those of the": Hull, 7.

Hurst, Fielding
"laid on the": Blankinship, 74.
"every pig path": ibid., 80.
"Lincoln Black Republicans": Stewart, 50.
"If I got": Blankinship, 76.
"meanest and cruelest": ibid., 78.
"played the role": ibid., 82.
"and the officers": ibid., 83-84.
"a disgrace to": ibid., 85.
"as mile posts": ibid., 83.

Isler, William B./Margaret Clark Griffis
"We began our": Carroll, 299.
"The river is": ibid., 298.
"On Monday which": ibid., 300.
"The singing was": ibid., 302.
"I just wish": ibid.
"The Southerners seem": ibid., 300.
"I feel an": ibid., 301.

Jackson, Andrew
"Great God! Have": Walker, 105.
"We shot them": Remini, *Andrew Jackson*, 1: 193.
"No, all his": ibid., 194.
"he may have": ibid.

"To see these": ibid., 316-17.
"a great General": Wassam, 163.
"and now I": ibid.
"Justice to them": A. Walker, 24.
"rather be a": Remini, *Andrew Jackson,* 2: 149.
"monied aristocracy": ibid., 34.

James, Jesse
"Dear Sir, I:" Garrett, 164.
"So the James": Montell, 81.
"James was the": Morris.

Jarnagin, William
"the work of": Jarnagin interview.
"Anybody can fix": ibid.
"I trained them": ibid.
"We had the": ibid.
"hard work and": ibid.
"He also eats": interview, J. Jarnagin.

Jobe, Abraham
"There goes Dr.": Jobe, 48.
"fully half as": ibid., 47.
"I never suffered": ibid., 47.
"difficult, dangerous, and": ibid., 48.

Johnson, Andrew
"you never saw": Templeton, 32.
"I voted against": Milton, 30.
"I intend to": ibid.
"He's all right": Thomas, 21.
"a man of": ibid., 85.
"shot on sight": Milton, 28.
"I will suffer": ibid., 34.
"the gravel": ibid., 24.
"dazzling, tender, beautiful": ibid., 25.
"his face beamed": ibid.
"left behind a": Bassett, 166.

Johnson, J. Fred
"Mr. Johnson would": Reed interview.

Johnson, Mordecai
"Most often she": Mathews, C1.
"unaccredited academic departments": ibid.
"Henry County has": Editorial, "World's Ignorance," A2.
"You have truly": Hailey, B6.

Jones, Casey
"Come all you": Moody, 110.
"he was proud": ibid., 112.
"had to be": ibid.
"was doing just": ibid.
"95 minutes to": ibid., 113-14.
"saw no flagman": Shaw, 69.
"claimed the words": Moody, 115.
"By 1913, they": ibid.

Jones, Samuel
"the little red": Roddy, 21.
"the South's Greatest": Denning, 224.
"house of entertainment": ibid.
"the red is": ibid., 228-29.

Kefauver, Estes
"I felt that": Swados, 2.
"Ambition—To Be": ibid., 4.
"a new iridescent": ibid., 5.
"Where did you": ibid.
"the best advice": ibid., 6.
"Leave no tender": ibid.
"as if you": Anderson, 39-40.
"But if he": Swados, 10.
"that puts its": Carter, 12.
"The coon is": Swados, 37.
"If there is": ibid., 3.

King, George
"I told her": King, 8.
"write for the": ibid., 7.
"I told him": ibid., 4.
"hollared with joy": ibid., 11.
"After I had": Culp, 75.
"(Because) the company": ibid.

Knox, George L.
"the Negro-traders": Knox, *Slave and Freeman,* 43.
"Our masters had": ibid., 57.
"cook, nurse, servant": ibid., 9.
"preeminent black Republican": ibid., 23.
"Do you remember": ibid., 7.
"dean of Negro": ibid., 40.
"If a newspaper": ibid.

Lawrence, William P.
"perhaps the ablest": Lawrence, biographical sketch.
"I knew that": Lawrence, "Our Foundation," 77.
"Camp Vegas": ibid., 76.
"for many years": ibid., 76.
"We considered this": ibid.
"I have come": ibid., 80.
"We all gained": ibid., 78.
"inspirational leadership": Lawrence, biographical sketch.

Lea, Luke
"Journalistic Investigations": Lea, 229.
"Our interpreter had": ibid., 235.
"his 'August Majesty'": Ibid., 236.
"Ah, Colonel Lea": ibid., 237.
"fenced in English": ibid.
"I finally stated": ibid., 255.
"amazingly indiscreet": ibid., 261.
"I'd have given": ibid.
"While he was": M. L. L. Tidwell, 3.

Lee, George Washington
"Get drunk, and": Tucker, 108.
"the authentic color": ibid., 111.
"Boswell of Beale": ibid., 105.
"George W. Lee": ibid., 112.
"W. C. Handy": ibid.
"make the South": ibid., 64.
"We must step": ibid., 65.
"one of the": ibid., 81.
"brown screw in": ibid., 133.
"brilliant": ibid., 161.
"The major issue": ibid., 171.

Lewis, Meriwether
"I am no": Daniels, 175.
"He lies buried": ibid., 183.
"spoiled by 'elegant'": ibid., 169.
"extra twists": ibid., 170.
"like a lawyer": ibid., 175.
"O Lord!": ibid.
"It seems more": ibid., 182.

Lindamood, Erastus "Ras"
"Whether he ever": Wilson, 80.

Little Carpenter (Attakullakulla)
"he could make": Satz, 60.
"remarkably small": Kelly, 2.
"They are welcome": ibid., 4.
"took . . . the last": ibid.

Louis Philippe
"Do you still": Parker, 749.
"that earnest tourist": Bishop, 90.
"house of entertainment": *Knoxville Gazette*.
"more than that": Parker, 753.

Mabry, Joseph Alexander/Thomas O'Conner
"Business is business": Taylor, 63.

Macon, "Uncle Dave"
"People always liked": Mason, 220.
"There was a": ibid., 221.
"in the light": ibid., 220.
"More than anyone": Wolfe, 40.
"All I want": Mason, 222.
"Now Cap, I": ibid., 223.
"For the past hour": ibid.
"Banjoist and Songster": ibid., 224.
"take that thing": ibid., 225.

Mallicoat, Milton
"scoffed": Ridenour, 63.
"a faraway look": ibid.
"It was the": ibid.

Marcum, Julia
"highest proportionate vote": Sanderson, 25.
"If the": ibid., 26.

"plenty to live": ibid., 28.
"men without a": ibid., 26.

Massengale, Solomon
"Jordon Roach made": Fink, 23.

Maury, Matthew Fontaine
"My earliest recollections": Davis, 83.
"The sea is": ibid., 89.
"It is another": ibid., 90.
"I set out": ibid., 99.

Mayberry, Lu
"She stayed with": Egypt, 274.
"I'm going to": ibid., 268.
"You just let": ibid., 267.

McConnico, Garner
"like a trumpet": Burnett, 364.
"raised his voice": ibid.
"father of camp": Norton, 26.
"In the name": Burnett, 364.

McDonald, Mary Elizabeth
"Confederate Memorial Association": Armstrong, 55.

McElwee, Samuel
"patient, unrequited toil": Cartwright, "Black Legislators," 276.
"a magnetic speaker": "A Remarkable Negro."
"The black men": Cartwright, "Black Legislators," 283-84.

McGavock, "Carrie"
"the amputated limbs": Aiken, 24.
"Every room was": Carnton Assn.
"cool porches of": Aiken, 20.

McKissack, Moses/Leatrice McKissack
"oldest continually operated": Wynn, "McKissack and McKissack."
"I went from": "Leatrice McKissack: Enterprising Entrepreneur," 63.

McLemore, John Christmas
"at great expense": Howard, 58.
"nearly all the": ibid., 57.
"it leaked too": ibid., 64-65.

Meigs, Return, Jonathan
"Nay, Jonathan, I": Wooten, 184-85.
"useful implements of": Malone, 4.
"Fine muslin, Tamboured": ibid., 12.
"that are really": ibid.
"1 Gross of": ibid.
"Under some pretext": ibid., 7.

Meriwether, Elizabeth Avery
"To the Provost": Meriwether, 75.
"I learned to": ibid., 80.
"General Sherman, I": ibid., 81.

"I am not": ibid., 87.
"Gov. Harris had": ibid., 196.
"the chief representative": Scott, 173.
"when the Yankees": ibid., 195.
"During the first": ibid., 197.
"the chief representative": Scott, 173.
"In 1916 both": Meriwether, vi.

Miles, Emma Bell
"a legend up": Rowell, 77.
"The pinch of": Gaston, "Miles and the 'Fountain
    Square' Conversations," 416.
"as good as": Rowell, 81.
"Now I behold": Gaston, "Miles and the 'Fountain
    Square' Conversations," 416.
"My position on": ibid., 420.
"One may think": ibid., 419.
"I wasn't raised": ibid., 421.
"It is often": ibid., 427-28.
"one-third of": ibid., 426.
"not because nobody": ibid.
"What a strange": ibid., 422.
"All is lost": ibid., 428-29.

Moon, Virginia "Miss Ginger"
"Hurrah for Jeff": Smith, 101.
"Buttons": ibid., 104.
"My child, why": ibid., 107.
"You may have": ibid., 108.
"galloping through Union": ibid., 113.
"I am seventy-five": ibid., 115.

Moore, Ella Sheppard
"They knew only": Moore, 4.

Morgan, John Hunt
"Thunderbolt of the": Conklin, 377.
"Tell Mattie that": Ramage, *Rebel Raider*, 58.
"a scene from": ibid., 134.
"their state": ibid., 137.
"Where are they": ibid., 237.
"It's no use": ibid.
"pierced Morgan's heart": Conklin, 383.
"interment in the": ibid., 388.

Murrell, John A.
"Great Western Land": Penick, 175.
"stately old time": ibid., 174.
"genteel manners": Davidson, 221.
"Mystic Clan of": Penick, 175.

Napier, James Carroll
"railroad companies to": Lamon, *Blacks in Tennessee*, 59.
"interpret the existing": Lamon, *Black Tennesseans*, 6.
"in the name": ibid., 7.
"food, furniture, transportation": Clark, "Napier: Na-
    tional Negro Leader," 243.
"father of the": Lovett.

Neyland, Robert R. "The General"
"I remember when": B. Gilbert, 68.
"That just shows": ibid.
"Bristol Blizzard": ibid., 72.
"If they kick": ibid., 73.
"overwork and injuries": ibid., 129.
"I have a": ibid., Ibid., 71.
"We got beat": ibid., 141.
"he was a": ibid., 6.

Ochs, Adolph
"human interrogation point": Govan and Livingood,
    "Adolph S. Ochs," 86
"Nothing but the": ibid., 88.
"utterly dilapidated, demoralized": ibid., 94.
"put his subscribers": ibid., 97.
"if the Times": ibid., 104.
"most aggressive and": Govan and Livingood, "A New
    Spokesman," 336.

Offield Brothers
"June the 28": Aiken, 117.
"August 25, 1861": ibid., 118.
"you no [know]": ibid., n. 3.
"Apr 21st 1862": ibid., 119-20.
"the Rheumatism": ibid., 119.
"June the 4th": ibid., 120.
"Aug 19th '64": ibid., 123.
"I was truly": ibid., 124-25.
"August 23rd '64": ibid., 124.

Oliver, John Walter
"gone so far": Dunn, 224.
"Many of his": ibid., 227.
"an educated farmer": ibid.
"the people of": ibid., 231.
"all their livestock": ibid., 236.
"cleared and under": Oliver and Oliver, 10.
"A deeply religious": ibid.

Overton, John/John Overton Jr.
"Father of Memphis": Moore and Foster, 1: 376.
"one of the": ibid., 2: 201.
"the President went": McNeilly, 46-47.

Pearl, Minnie
"clown": Pearl and Dew, 11.
"Someone has said": ibid.
"While Daddy was": ibid., 18.
"To help publicize": Stambler and Landon, 559.
"You'll make a": Pearl and Dew, 122.
"I had been": ibid., 121.
"so eight or": ibid., 175.
"most closely identified": Wolfe, 103.
"the first country": Stambler and Landon, 560.
"Everything happens to": Pearl and Dew, 170.

Pennington, James Jackson
"suspended a fan": Swint and Mohler, 228.
"the power to": ibid.
"the operator pushed": Dwiggins, 170.
"first recorded man-carrying": ibid., 172.
"We confess we": Pennington biographical file, Murray Company newsletter, 23.
"I never knew": ibid., *Lawrence County Historical Society Bulletin* no. 44.
"France has my": ibid., Niedergeses, 1.
"a man who": ibid., Murray Company newsletter, 24.

Pickens, Lucy Holcombe
"Queen of the": De Berry, 135.
"widely known and": Fuller, 49.

Polk, James K.
"He can foresee": Sellers, *James K. Polk, Jacksonian,* 65.
"The one who": West, 363.
"Don't you see": Nelson and Nelson, 39.
"Who is James": McCoy, 30.
"Young Hickory": Washburn, 60.
"undoubtedly the nation's": West, 357.
"religion's answer to": ibid.
"It awakened the": ibid., 369.
"but in the": ibid., 371.

Polk, Leonidas
"Follow Your Granny": Walker, 47.
"suddenly there came": ibid.
"The spirit of": Parks, 164.
"arms folded": Catton, 382.

Presley, Elvis
"It's not for": Presley, 52.
"Set down in": Marsh, 15.
"WE RECORD ANYTHING": ibid., 16.
"What do you": ibid., 19.
"terrible . . . sounded like": ibid., 22.
"he could make": ibid.
"Never before had": Cobb, 300.
"any individual or": Elvis Presley Enterprises, Inc. (*Graceland Express*).

Quinn, Father D. A.
"Dear Brothers, Our": White.
"It was the": Quinn, *Heroes and Heroines,* 98.
"mamma appeared to": ibid., 79-80.
"Here, let me": ibid., 90.
"A city of": White.
"The stench of Memphis": ibid.
"unflagging in his": *Church News,* LaPointe, 6.
"Escape the mosquitoes": White.
"On more than": ibid.
"Doctor, there is": Quinn, *Heroes and Heroines,* 168.
"The two met": Keating, 191.

"watched over the": Wright, 46.
"History may not": ibid., 52.
"The Tribune readers": ibid., 53.
"has put its": White.

Raht, Julius Eckhardt
"I couldn't help": Barclay, 227.

Ramsey, J. G. M.
"I had the": Ramsey, 55.
"in the western": ibid., 56.
"low revenge and": ibid., 173.
"more than forty-two": Moore and Foster, 2:218.
"Some of the": Ramsey, 252.

Read, Opie
"Oh, how wiser": Morris, 41.
"A man without": ibid.
"Possessing the skilled": ibid., 41-42.
"the Dean of": "Sumner County Sesqui-Centennial."
"few men in": Morris, 196.
"has lectured to": ibid.
"every county seat": ibid.
"out of common": ibid., 197.
"And I have": Read, 6.
"had peculiarities": Morris, 74.
"Looking into his": ibid.
"was somewhere near": Morris, 77.
"humorous and literary": ibid., 87.
"a national institution": ibid., 117.
"customs and manners": Federal Writers' Project, 147.
"and break bread": Morris, 194.
"Every year we": ibid., introduction.
"Well now, is": ibid.

Reed (a Slave)
"God lived close": Egypt, 47.
"A Negro has": ibid., 46.
"but God Almighty": ibid., 44.
"pot-likker": ibid., 43.
"come out and": ibid., 45.

Rees, David Nelson
"a beautiful young": Reynolds, Rees family memoirs, 5.
"Gen. Bee had": ibid., 4-5.
"I hitched my": ibid., 6.
"She was bright": ibid.
"I expect I": ibid., 5.

Rice, Grantland
"How or why": Rice, 9.
"Those three presents": ibid., 5.
"learned a lot": ibid., 6.
"poet laureate of": Fountain, 93.
"No one has": Inabinett, 3-4.
"Almost every one": ibid., 6.

Riley, Bob
"one of the": Montell, 109.
"Oh, my man": Langford, tape recording.
"in the entire": Overstreet.
"three tiers of": ibid.
"I've got the": ibid.
"He was an": Langford, tape recording.
"My daddy said": ibid.

Robertson, James
"fight it out": Moore and Foster, 1: 116.
"He had an": ibid., 1: 74.
"Father of Tennessee": ibid., 2: 223.
"After scalping him": ibid., 1: 172.
"first white child": ibid., 1: 116.
"Not dead yet": ibid., 1: 173.

Robertson, Sterling C.
"We are the": McLean, 2: 59.
"the successive peals": ibid., 8: 68.
"Have mercy upon": ibid., 3: 64.
"young ladies of": ibid., 6: 42-43.
"that if he": ibid., 8: 80.

Rogan, Hugh
"an affinity for": Walker, 163.
"Deliver to your": ibid., 166.
"What does he": ibid.

Ross, Chief John
"Father of Chattanooga": Moore and Foster, 2: 225.
"A traitor in": Brown, 488.
"It has become": ibid.
"poked cutting sarcasm": Byrum, 17.
"John Marshall has": Brown, 493.

Rucker, Edmund W.
"You are my": Horn, 151.

Rudolph, Wilma
"girl who wouldn't": Haley, 140.
"Rubbing Wilma": ibid., 142.
"You're the first": ibid., 144.
"Gazella Nera": ibid., 147.

Ryan, Father Abram
"General, you have": Mackin, 410.
"Take that banner": Painter, 108.

Saunders, Clarence
"PIGGLY WIGGLY IS": Weeks, 176.
"If I never": ibid., 178.
"I've been broke": Chumney, 7.

Scopes, John Thomas
"This is F. E.": Settle, 44.
"put Dayton on": ibid., 39.
"John, we've been": ibid., 43.
"He believed there": Ross, A1.

"I do not": Settle, 95.
"take your atheistic": Scopes and Presley, 240.

Seddon, Rhea
"Cosmic Rhea": "From Surgery to Outer Space," 102.
"some sort of": ibid.
"I thought, 'Shoot'": ibid.
"not that I": ibid.
"Everything that I": ibid.
"We know a": ibid.
"hard to believe": ibid.
"I think we're": Klebenow.
"the most successful": Seddon.

Sequoyah
"talking leaves": Satz, 74.
"Young Cherokees travel": ibid., 76.

Sevier, John
"Jump, my Bonnie": Walker, 35.
"I would gladly": Stephens interview.
"the first men": Moore and Foster, 69.
"greatest Indian fighter": Stephens, materials sent.
"a poor pitifull": Remini, 101.
"Services? I know": ibid., 121.
"Great God! do": ibid.
"the sacred soil": ibid.
"a curious dream": Walker, 37.
"descending in the": ibid.
"act a prudent": ibid., 38.

Shepherd, Lewis
"the father of": Wilson, *Chattanooga's Story,* 31.
"a splendid young": Bible, 66.
"furnished a legal": ibid.
"the first case": Moore and Foster, 2:179.
"Like so many": Worden, 130.

Shofner, Austin
"with a generator": James, 44.
"It was the": ibid.
"one of the": Shofner biographical sketch.

Smith, Bessie
"one of the": Oliver, 12.
"nobody's child": Moore, 13.
"No turning around": ibid., 20.
"what her audiences": ibid., 16-17.
"right way to": ibid., 22.
"Let the instruments": ibid.
"'preach the blues'": Kalin, 51.
"Tough on Black": Oliver, 7.

Smith, Daniel
"with girls of": Burke, 24.
"all the education": ibid., 25.
"Tell her to": ibid., 26.
"For intelligence, well": ibid., 22.

Smith, Frederick Wallace
"My father didn't": Sigafoos and Easson, 26.

Spencer, Thomas Sharpe
"Mr. Spencer, if": Durham, "Thomas Sharp Spencer," 248.
"Spencer told me": ibid., 254.
"a respectful distance": ibid., 245.

Stewart, Alex
"national treasure": Irwin, *Alex Stewart,* 12.
"I think I've": ibid., 11.
"What I most": ibid., 13.
"Then he threw": ibid.
"You can go": ibid., 13-14.
"A year's work": ibid., 15.
"always wanted to": ibid., 276-77.
"I'd put Alex": ibid., 280.
"There he sat": ibid., 11.

Stokes, William B.
"Bald Eagle of": Darrah, 25.
"gentleman gambler": ibid., 13.
"Ariel": ibid., 6.
"[the] right of": ibid., 65-66.
"Officers and men": Civil War Centennial Commission, 1:332.
"the dung-hill": Darrah, 203-4.
"gallant and meritorious": ibid., 86.

Stowers, Thomas
"You can stay": Wells, 17-18.
"the sole survivor": ibid., 17.

Stribling, T. S.
"fooling around": Eckley, 14.
"I glanced over": ibid., 16.

Talley, Spencer
"Hell's Half Acre": McDonough, "Cold Days in Hell," 29.
"a goodly supply": ibid., 193.
"After our bands": Womack, 202.
"Who knows what": Worsham, 69.
"tell whether the": Womack, 214.
"When his body": ibid., 215.

Taylor, Robert Love/Alfred Alexander Taylor
"a gang of": Crowe, 52.

Taylor, Robert Z.
"most promising": Vanderwood, 43.
"came to look": Bell, 7.
"preliminary to draining": ibid., 9.
"I couldn't possibly": Vanderwood, 45.
"Get the rope": ibid., 46.
"to the low": Bell, 11.

Tecumseh
"When the white": Daniels, 192.

Turney, Peter
"Peter—march your": Walker, 225.
"Peter, you had": ibid.
"Hail Columbia, happy": ibid., 226.
"passed through his": ibid.
"Mountain Boys": Civil War Centennial Commission, 1:170.
"Who lives here?": Walker, 227.

Tyson, Lawrence
"Knoxville's first flying": Creekmore, 160.
"oozed up from": Essame, 188.

Van Dyke, Thomas Nixon
"If these are": *War of the Rebellion,* 6: 891.
"Unpleasant as the": ibid., 8: 273.

Vaughan, A. J.
"a shell from": Vaughan, 86.
"I then began": ibid., 87-88.
"These few men": ibid., 84-85.
"a magnificent Gray": ibid., 84.
"favorite son": "Bivouac 18, A.C.S. and Camp 28, U.C.V.," 567.

Vowell, Jacob
"Not one man": Rogers, 58.
"We are shut": ibid., 61.
"Women were frantically": ibid., 60.
"Then there was": Irwin, 93.
"headless and mangled": "Saved by Dream."

Walker, Thomas Jefferson, "T. J."
"our side shirt": Walker, 67.
"You have been": ibid.
"Confound the luck": ibid.
"many comforts in": ibid., 42.
"My son, I": ibid., 43.
"The Lightning Bug": ibid., 64.
"Often times a": ibid., 49.
"Oh, how my": ibid., 46.
"While water was": ibid.

Walker, William
"On entering a": Carr, 5.
"Missy": Bell, 1.
"get rid of:" ibid., 8.
"In the name": McPherson, 113.

Ward, Nancy (Nan-ye-hi)
"behind a log": Cornwell, 34.
"You know that": Alderman, 65.
"When she died": Cornwell, 42.

Watkins, Sam R.
"as hard as": Watkins, 62.
"I cannot tell": ibid.
"I helped bring": ibid., 83.

"We supposed our": ibid., 85.
"a big, fat": ibid., 65.
"My son, I": ibid.
"Just look at": ibid., 67.
"The soldier may": ibid., 114.
"No . . . Boys, my": ibid., 114-15.
"the very incarnation": ibid., 116.
"Bob, you wern't": ibid.
"Ten of them": ibid., 136.
"some popinjay of": ibid., 207.
"What is this": ibid., 207.
"He started toward": ibid., 208.

Webb, William R. "Sawney"
"My son, your": Stokes, 421.
"My mother used": ibid., 419-20.
"bricks and mortar": Holliman, 290.
"Our money flows": Lewis, 100.
"Son, do you": Holliman, 297.
"Give my boys": ibid.

Wells, Ida B.
"The colored people": Sterling, 71.
"One or two": ibid., 72.
"A DARKY DAMSEL": ibid., 72-73.
"self-help and": ibid., 75.
"God, is there": ibid., 77.
"There is only": ibid., 79.
"practically at a": Wells, 53.
"owned by Northern": ibid., 54.
"EXILED": Sterling, 83.

Wharton, May Cravath
"saw a light": Wharton, 55.
"Miz' Wharton, they": ibid., 14-15.
"I squared my": ibid., 56.
"Do ye feel": ibid., 57.
"Well, you see": ibid., 59.
"We aim to": ibid., 55.
"Shore is hard": ibid., 69.
"Much of the": ibid., 70.
"Maynie, have Miss": ibid., 87.
"We come to": ibid., 94.
"Dr. May Wharton": ibid., 95.
"their homes and": ibid., 96.

White, "Granny"
"the best brandy": Walker, 134.

White, Hugh Lawson
"all the financial": Moore and Foster, 2: 255.
"first machinery of": Scott, 28.

Whiteside, Harriet Leonora Straw
"She brought to": "Harriet Leonora Whiteside," 130.
"bawdy house": Gaston, 342.
"extortion": ibid., 343.
"The fight in": "Harriet Leonora Whiteside," 130.
"Harriet Whiteside breathed": Gaston, 345.

Wilder, John T.
"the most beautiful": Kozsuch, 67.
"rail-twister": Williams, 13.
"one-night stopover": Wilson, 79.
"with ease and": Williams, 46, 48.

Williams, "Aunt Polly"
"could pull the": Young, 77.
"Court or no": Douglas, 239.
"met his match": ibid., 240.
"The first one": Young, 79.
"Send Aunt Polly": ibid.
"Ham, they've got": ibid.
"raised her right": ibid., 78.

Wilson, Kemmons
"the most miserable": Harkins, 191.
"I decided to": Grant, 79.
"I was soon": ibid.
"When you get": ibid., 78.

Winchester, Marcus Brutus
"honey-skinned": Weeks, 27.
"homemade money": ibid., 29.
"I must have": ibid., 33.
"I never can": ibid., 31.

Wright, Frances "Fanny"
"the most interesting": Egerton, 17.
"coarse": ibid.

York, Alvin
"put ten rifle": Cowan, 30.
"Well! Come on": ibid., 31.
"formed a line": ibid., 33.
"So you can": ibid., 248-49.
"as the members": ibid., 271.
"The people saw": ibid., 269.
"liberty and freedom": Lee, 109.

Selected Bibliography and Suggested Readings

Information for historical background essays which introduce each time frame was prepared by state archivist Dr. Wayne Moore, Tennessee State Library and Archives, Nashville.

Readers interested in general works of state history should consult John Trotwood Moore and Austin P. Foster, *Tennessee: The Volunteer State, 1769-1923*, vol. 1, 1923; Gentry R. McGee, *A History of Tennessee from 1663 to 1930*, 1930; Robert E. Corlew, *Tennessee: A Short History*, 2nd ed., 1981; Wilma Dykeman, *Tennessee: A History*, 1975; and Paul H. Bergeron, *Paths of the Past: Tennessee 1779-1970*, 1979. The Office of the Tennessee State Library and Archives, 403 Seventh Avenue North, Nashville, 37243-0312, also has a wealth of information available to the general public and can provide personal assistance to guide the amateur historian.

Acklen, Adelicia Hayes

Brackett, Carolyn. "Civil War Mistress Saved Her Cotton to Make a Million." *Knoxville News-Sentinel*, 13 January 1991.

Culpepper, Marilyn Mayer. *Trials and Triumphs: Women of the American Civil War*. East Lansing: Michigan State University Press, 1991.

Daniels, Jonathan. *The Devil's Backbone: The Story of the Natchez Trace*. New York: McGraw-Hill, 1962.

Graham, Eleanor. "Belmont I: Nashville Home of Adelicia Acklen." *Tennessee Historical Quarterly* 30, no. 4 (Winter 1971): 345-68.

Hudson, Patricia L., and Sandra L. Ballard, "Belmont Mansion." In *The Smithsonian Guide to Historic America: The Carolinas and the Appalachian States*, 316-19. New York: Stewart, Tabori & Chang, 1989.

Kiser, John W. "Scion of Belmont." Part 1. *Tennessee Historical Quarterly* 38, no. 1 (Spring 1979): 34-61.

Acuff, Roy

Bledsoe, Wayne. "A Memory Revisited: Old Time Radio Stars Recall Their Heyday." *Knoxville News-Sentinel*, 18 April 1991.

Majors, William R. "The Restoration." In *The End of Arcadia: Gordon Browning and Tennessee Politics*, 159-79. Memphis: Memphis State University Press, 1982.

Malone, Bill C. *Country Music, U.S.A*. Rev. ed. Austin, Tex.: University of Texas Press, 1985.

Wolfe, Charles K. *Tennessee Strings: The Story of Country Music in Tennessee*. Knoxville: University of Tennessee Press, 1981.

Agee, James

Bergreen, Laurence. *James Agee: A Life*. New York: E. P. Dutton, 1984.

Madden, David, ed. *Remembering James Agee*. Baton Rouge: Louisiana State University Press, 1974.

Seib, Kenneth. *James Agee, Promise and Fulfillment*. Pittsburgh, Pa.: University of Pittsburgh Press, 1968.

Anderson, William R.

"Anderson, William A." U.S. Navy biographical sketch dated 11 April 1967 and newspaper clippings. U.S. Naval Academy. William W. Jeffries Archives, file no. 15612.

Anderson, William R. (Great Falls, Va.). Biographical materials provided to Tennessee Folk History Project Archives, University of Tennessee, March 1995.

———. Telephone interviews with University of Tennessee graduate assistant John Walter for the Tennessee Folk History Project, 29 February and 8 May 1995.

Anderson, William R., with Clay Blair Jr. *Nautilus 90 North*. Cleveland, Ohio: World, 1959.

Harte, Barbara, and Carolyn Riley, eds. "Anderson, William Robert." In *Contemporary Authors: A Bio-Bibliographical Guide to Current Authors and Their Works*, rev. ed. Vols. 5-8. Detroit: Gale Research Co., 1989.

U.S. Congress. "Anderson, William Robert." In *Biographical Directory of the United States Congress 1774-1989*. Bicentennial Edition. Washington, D.C.: U.S. Government Printing Office, 1989.

Angevine, Lena

Coppock, Paul R. "Hospital Heroes: First Nurse." In *Memphis Memoirs*, 173-77. Memphis: Memphis State University Press, 1980.

Greenhill, E. Dianne. "Nursing License #000001." *Tennessee Nurse* (Spring 1993): 26-27.

Barnes, John C.

McGee, Gentry R. *A History of Tennessee: From 1663-1930*. Revised and enlarged by C. B. Ijams. New York: American Book, 1930.

Williams, Joseph S. *Old Times in West Tennessee*. Memphis: W. G. Cheeney, 1873.

Bell, John

Bell, Charles Bailey. *A Mysterious Spirit: The Bell Witch of Tennessee*. 1934. Facsimile reproduction, which also includes reprint of *The Bell Witch of Middle Tennessee*, 1930. Nashville: Charles Elder, 1972.

Brehm, H. C. *Echoes of the Bell Witch in the Twentieth Century*. Nashville: Author, 1979.

Federal Writers' Project of the Works Projects Administration. "Tour 8: The Bell Witch Farm." In *The WPA Guide to Tennessee*, 92-93. 1939. Reprint, Knoxville: University of Tennessee Press, 1986.

Ingram, M. V. *An Authenticated History of the Famous Bell Witch*. 1894. Reprint, Nashville: Rare Book Reprints, 1961.

Lockhart, Teresa Ann Bell. "Twentieth Century Aspects of the Bell Witch." *Tennessee Folklore Society Bulletin* 50, no. 1 (Spring 1984): 18-24.

McFadden, Sharon. "The Bell Witch." Research paper. University of Tennessee Library Special Collections, 4 June 1984.

Walker, Hugh. "Tracking the Bell Witch." In *Tennessee Tales*, 39-40. Nashville: Aurora, 1970.

Windham, Kathryn Tucker. "The Witch Who Tormented the Bell Family." In *Thirteen Tennessee Ghosts and Jeffrey*, 150-59. Huntsville, Ala.: Strode, 1977.

Winters, Ralph L. "Red River Baptist Church." In *Hospitality Homes and Historic Sites in Western Robertson County, Tennessee*. Ralph L. Winters. Clarksville, Tenn.: Author, 1971.

Bell, Montgomery

Brehm, H. C., and Cindy Curtis. *The Narrows of the Harpeth and Montgomery Bell*. Nashville: Authors, 1981.

Corlew, Robert Ewing. *A History of Dickson County Tennessee*. Nashville: Tennessee Historical Commission and Dickson County Historical Society, 1956.

———. "Some Aspects of Slavery in Dickson County." *Tennessee Historical Quarterly* 10, no. 3 (September 1951): 224-48; 10, no. 4 (December 1951): 344-65.

Walker, Hugh. "Bell's Tunnel: A Visit to the Narrows of the Harpeth." In *Tennessee Tales*, 1-3. Nashville: Aurora, 1970.

Blount, William

Blount Mansion Association. *William Blount: The Man and His Mansion*. Pamphlet. Knoxville: Blount Mansion Association, 1977.

Bond, Octavia Zollicoffer. "The Sovereign's Will." In *Old Tales Retold Or, Perils and Adventures of Tennessee Pioneers*, 176-79. 1907. Reprint, Nashville: Charles and Randy Elder, 1973.

Corlew, Robert E. "The Young State, 1796-1821." In *Tennessee: A Short History*. 2nd ed., 126-44. Knoxville: University of Tennessee Press, 1981.

Gray, Carolyn. "A Reason for Treason?" *Tennessee Illustrated* 2, no. 4 (July-August 1989): 40.

Moore, John Trotwood, and Austin P. Foster, eds. "The Admission of Tennessee as a State and the First Series of Administrations of John Sevier." In *Tennessee: The Volunteer State, 1769-1923*, 1: 271-95. Nashville: S. J. Clarke, 1923.

Thompson, Isabel. "The Blount Conspiracy." *The East Tennessee Historical Society's Publications* 2 (1930): 3-21.

Bowie, Elve

Douglas, C. L. *James Bowie: The Life of a Bravo*. Dallas: Banks Upshaw, 1944.

Bragg, Zack

Bragg, Zack T. Biographical file including newspaper clippings regarding his life in lumber camps and the founding of West Memphis. Memphis and Shelby County Room, Memphis Shelby County Public Library and Information Center.

Crawford, Carl. "West Memphis Founder Reminisces." *Memphis Commercial Appeal*, 9 April 1962.

Douglas, Richard. "Logging in the Big Hatchie Bottoms." *Tennessee Historical Quarterly* 25 (1966): 32-49.

"Founder of West Memphis, Zack T. Bragg, Dies at 76." *Memphis Commercial Appeal*, 24 July 1967.

Maum, Emmet. "Death Claims Two Experts in Varied Fields of Lumber." *Memphis Commercial Appeal*, 31 July 1967.

McIlwaine, Shields. "Big Money Gilds the Town: Bonanza from the Big Woods." In *Memphis: Down in Dixie*, 247-59. New York: E. P. Dutton, 1948.

Brantley, James/Albert Dement

Brantley, Charles Emmett. "James Robertson Brantley." Unpublished sketch submitted to the Tennessee state legislature. N. d.

Green, Ben A. *Biography of the Tennessee Walking Horse*. Nashville: Parthenon Press, 1960.

Tennessee Walking Horse Breeders and Exhibitors Association. "There Is Only One Tennessee Walking Horse." Brochure. Lewisburg, Tenn.: Author.

Brown, Clarence

Brown, Clarence. Biographical file including newspaper clippings, theater pamphlets, and printed theater programs regarding Brown and his motion pictures. University of Tennessee Theater Department, Knoxville.

———. "Recollections of Early Days." Transcript of address given by Clarence Brown as part of "A Tribute to Clarence Brown," hosted by the Directors Guild of America, 16 July 1977. Held by Special Collections, University of Tennessee Library, Knoxville.

Brownlow, Kevin. "Clarence Brown." In *The Parade's Gone By. . .,* 139-53. New York: Alfred A. Knopf, 1968.

Estrin, Allen. *The Hollywood Professionals*. Vol. 6, *Capra, Cukor, Brown*. South Brunswick, N.Y.: A. S. Barnes, 1980.

Brown, Joseph

Brown, Joseph. "Captivity Narrative." *Journal of Cherokee Studies* 2, no. 2 (Spring 1977): 208-18.

King, Duane H. "Lessons in Cherokee Ethnology from the Captivity of Joseph Brown, 1788-1789." *Journal of Cherokee Studies* 2, no. 2 (Spring 1977): 219-29.

Kirke, Edmund. "The Southern Gateway of the Alleghanies." *Harper's New Monthly Magazine*, 74, no. 443 (April 1887): 659-76.

MacKellar, W. H. *Chuwalee*. Originally published in serial form for the *Winchester Chronicle*, 1937-1938. Reprint, Winchester, Tenn.: Franklin County Publishing Co., 1973.

Miller, C. Somers. "The Joseph Brown Story: Pioneer and Indian Fighter in Tennessee History." *Tennessee Historical Quarterly* 32, no. 1 (Spring 1973): 22-41.

Moore, John Trotwood, and Austin P. Foster, eds. "Indian Wars and Warriors in Tennessee. In *Tennessee: The Volunteer State, 1769-1923*, 1: 157-250. Nashville: S. J. Clarke, 1923.

Brownlow, William G. "Parson"

Coulter, E. Merton. "Parson Brownlow's Tour of the North during the Civil War." *The East Tennessee Historical Society's Publications,* no. 7 (1935): 3-27.

Creekmore, Betsey Beeler. *Knox County Tennessee: A History in Pictures*. Norfolk: Donning, 1988.

———. "The War between the States" and "William G. Brownlow." In *Arrows to Atoms: The Story of East Tennessee*, 59-94. Knoxville: University of Tennessee Press, 1959.

Fink, Paul M. "The Lighter Side of History." *The East Tennessee Historical Society's Publications,* no. 39 (1967): 26-41.

Govan, Gilbert E., and James W. Livingood. "Road to Reunion." In *The Chattanooga Country, 1540-1962: From Tomahawks to TVA*, 281-311. Chapel Hill: University of North Carolina Press, 1963.

Kelly, James C. "William Gannaway Brownlow." Parts 1-2. *Tennessee Historical Quarterly* 43, no. 1 (Spring 1984): 25-43; 43, no. 2 (Summer 1984): 155-72.

Mackin, Sister Aloysius, O.P. "Wartime Scenes from Convent Windows: St. Cecilia, 1860 through 1865." *Tennessee Historical Quarterly* 39, no. 4 (Winter 1980): 401-22.

Moore, John Trotwood, and Austin P. Foster, eds. "William Gannaway Brownlow." In *Tennessee: The Volunteer State, 1769-1923*, 2: 74-75. Nashville: S. J. Clarke, 1923.

Queener, Verton M. "William G. Brownlow as an Editor." *The East Tennessee Historical Society's Publications,* no. 4 (January 1932): 67-82.

Seymour, Digby Gordon. "Now I Can Have a Good Snooze." In *Divided Loyalties: Fort Sanders and the Civil War in East Tennessee,* 205-12. Dayton, Ohio: Morningside House, 1963.

Walker, Nancy Wooten. "Eliza Ann O'Brien Brownlow." In *Out of a Clear Blue Sky: Tennessee's First Ladies and Their Husbands*, 163-69. Cleveland, Tenn.: Author, 1971.

Buchanan, Daniel

Greene, Lee Seifert. *Lead Me On: Frank Goad Clement and Tennessee Politics*. Knoxville: University of Tennessee Press, 1982.

McClain, Iris Hopkins. *A History of Houston County*. Columbia, Tenn.: Author.

Bull, Carroll Gideon

Bates, Walter Lynn (descendent of C. G. Bull). Biographical materials, personal notes, and general family information provided to Tennessee Folk History Project Archives, University of Tennessee.

———. "The Life and Work of Dr. Carroll Gideon Bull, Pioneer in Medicine." *Tennessee Historical Quarterly* 46, no. 3 (Fall 1987): 141-47.

Burn, Harry T.

Burn, Harry T. "Harry T. Burn Scrapbook on Woman Suffrage, 1920." University of Tennessee Library Special Collections.

Cornwell, Ilene J. "Burn, Harry Thomas." In *Biographical Directory of the Tennessee General Assembly.* Vol. 3, *1901-1931.* Nashville: Tennessee State Library and Archives and the Tennessee Historical Commission, 1988.

Dykeman, Wilma. *Tennessee Women, Past and Present.* Edited by Carol Lynn Yellin. Memphis: Tennessee Committee for the Humanities and Tennessee International Women's Decade Coordinating Committee, 1977.

Ferrar, Rebecca. "Suffrage Victory: 75 Years Ago, Tennessee Made the 19th Amendment a Permanent Part of the Constitution." *Knoxville News-Sentinel,* 13 August 1995.

McKinney, R. Frank, comp. "Harry Put a New Dress on Women." In *Tall Tales and Unusual Happenings of McMinn County, Tennessee,* edited by Bill Akins, 84-85. Etowah, Tenn.: McMinn County Historical Society, 1988.

Obituary of H. T. Burn, Athens (Tenn.) *Daily Post-Athenian,* 21 February 1977.

Taylor, Elizabeth A. *The Suffrage Movement in Tennessee.* New York: Bookman Assoc., 1957.

Burnett, John G.

Burnett, John G. "The Cherokee Removal through the Eyes of a Private Soldier." *Journal of Cherokee Studies* 3, no. 3 (Summer 1978): 180-85.

Corlew, Robert E. "The Indians' Expulsion and Public Lands." In *Tennessee: A Short History.* 2nd ed., 145-58. Knoxville: University of Tennessee Press, 1981.

Crum, Mason. *The Story of Lake Junaluska.* Greensboro, N.C.: Piedmont Press, 1950.

Finger, John R. *The Eastern Band of Cherokees 1819-1900.* Knoxville: University of Tennessee Press, 1984.

Higgs, Robert J., and Ambrose N. Manning, eds. "John G. Burnett." In *Voices from the Hills—Selected Readings of Southern Appalachia,* 47-54. New York: Frederick Ungar, copublished with Appalachian Consortium Press, 1975.

Junaluska, Chief. File including biographical information and general North Carolina Cherokee history. Qualla Boundary Public Library, Cherokee, N.C.

Spoden, Muriel M. C. "Cherokee Removal West, 1838." In *Kingsport Heritage: The Early Years, 1700 to 1900,* 223-24. Johnson City, Tenn.: Overmountain Press, 1991.

Byrns, Joseph Wellington

Boyer, Paul S., et al. "The New Deal Takes Shape." In *The Enduring Vision: A History of the American People,* 2: 876-93. Lexington, Mass.: D. C. Heath, 1990.

Byrns, Joseph W. Biographical file including newspaper clippings. Gorham-MacBane Public Library, Springfield, Tenn.

Coode, Thomas H. "Tennessee Congressmen and the New Deal, 1933-1938." *The West Tennessee Historical Society Papers* 31 (October 1977): 132-58.

Galloway, J. M. "Speaker Joseph W. Byrns: Party Leader in the New Deal." *Tennessee Historical Quarterly* 25, no. 1 (Spring 1966): 63-76.

McBride, Robert M., and Dan M. Robison. "Byrns, Joseph Wellington." In *Biographical Directory of the Tennessee General Assembly.* Vol. 2, *1861-1901,* edited by Robert M. McBride. Nashville: Tennessee State Library and Archives and the Tennessee Historical Commission, 1979.

Cain, Bobby

Adamson, June N. "Few Black Voices Heard: The Black Community and the Desegregation Crisis in Clinton, Tennessee, 1956." *Tennessee Historical Quarterly* 53, no. 1 (Spring 1994): 30-41.

Anderson, Margaret, and Robert Marlowe, eds. *Clinton— An Identity Rediscovered.* Clinton, Tenn.: *Clinton Courier-News,* 1985.

Brittain, David James. "A Case Study of the Problems of Racial Integration in the Clinton, Tennessee, High School." Ph.D. diss., New York University, 1959.

"Clinton and the Law." Videotape of a 1957 episode of *See it Now.* 54 min. New York: McGraw-Hill, N. d.

Lamon, Lester C. *Blacks in Tennessee, 1791-1970.* Knoxville: University of Tennessee Press, 1981.

McMillan, George. "The Ordeal of Bobby Cain." *Collier's* 138, no. 11 (23 November 1956): 68-69.

Campbell, Francis Joseph

Beard, William E. "Sir Francis Joseph Campbell." In *Nashville: The Home of History Makers,* 82-83. Nashville: Civitan Club, 1929.

"Dark Path." WPA Project. Stories of Tennessee. MS div., ac. no. 1776, box 23 of 33, VI-b-4. Tennessee State Library and Archives, Nashville.

McRaven, William Henry. "Sir Francis Joseph Campbell: Knighted Blind Educator Who Climbed Mont Blanc." In Tennessee Prodigies. 1966 unpublished papers. MS div., ac. no. 67-30. Tennessee State Library and Archives, Nashville.

Carmack, Edward W.

Coppock, Paul R. "As It Was: Editor, Senator, Martyr." In *Memphis Memoirs,* 49-54. Memphis: Memphis State University Press, 1980.

Crutchfield, James A., comp. "Edward Ward Carmack." In *Footprints across the Pages of Tennessee History.* Nashville: Williams Press, 1976.

Faries, Clyde J. "*Carmack vs. Patterson:* The Genesis of a Political Feud." *Tennessee Historical Quarterly* 38, no. 3 (Fall 1979): 332-47.

Summerville, James. *The Carmack-Cooper Shooting: Tennessee Politics Turns Violent, November 9, 1908.* Jefferson, N.C.: McFarland, 1994.

Caruthers, Hanson

Civil War Centennial Commission of Tennessee. "12th U.S. Colored Infantry Regiment." In *Tennesseans in the Civil War: A Military History of Confederate and Union Units with Available Rosters of Personnel,* part 1: 397-98. Nashville: Author, 1964.

Egypt, Ophelia Settle, comp. "All My Bosses Were Nigger Traders." In *The American Slave: A Composite Autobiography*. Vol. 18, *Unwritten History of Slavery (Fisk University)*, 253-61. 1941. Reprint, edited by George P. Rawick, Westport, Conn.: Greenwood, 1972.

Horn, Stanley F. *The Decisive Battle of Nashville*. Baton Rouge: Louisiana State University Press, 1991.

Watson, A. P., comp., and Paul Radin, ed. "Times Got Worse after the War." In *The American Slave: A Composite Autobiography*. Vol. 19, *God Struck Me Dead (Fisk University)*, 176-84. 1941. Reprint, edited by George P. Rawick, Westport, Conn.: Greenwood, 1972.

Chapman, David C.

Campbell, Carlos C. *Birth of a National Park in the Great Smoky Mountains*, 1969. Rev. ed. with preface by Horace Albright. Knoxville: University of Tennessee Press, 1984.

Cardinal Health, Inc. General informational file including letter from director of human resources regarding Chapman Drug Company history and booklet, "A Century of Service: 1880-1980," provided to Tennessee Folk History Project Archives, University of Tennessee.

"Col. D. C. Chapman, Great Smoky Park 'Creator,' Dies at 67." *Knoxville News-Sentinel*, 27 July 1944.

"Col. Chapman's Widow Dies at Topside Home." *Knoxville Journal*, 24 May 1966.

Dunn, Durwood. *Cades Cove: The Life and Death of a Southern Appalachian Community, 1818-1937*. Knoxville: University of Tennessee Press, 1988.

Dykeman, Wilma, and Jim Stokely. *Highland Homeland: The People of the Great Smokies*. Washington, D.C.: National Park Service, 1978.

Ellison, George. Introduction to *Our Southern Highlanders: A Narrative of Adventure in the Southern Appalachians and a Study of Life among the Mountaineers*, by Horace Kephart. Rev. ed., ix-xlvi. 1922. Knoxville: University of Tennessee Press, 1987.

"Even a Schoolroom Caricaturist Would Find Chapman a 'Natural,'" *Knoxville Journal*, 22 November 1935.

"Men of Affairs in Knoxville; D. C. Chapman." *Knoxville Journal and Tribune*, 5 April 1921.

Moore, John Trotwood, and Austin P. Foster, eds. "David C. Chapman." In *Tennessee: The Volunteer State, 1769-1923*, 2: 871-72. Nashville: S. J. Clarke, 1923.

"Mrs. Sue Chapman, Ex-Gibson Girl, Dies." *Knoxville News-Sentinel*, 23 May 1966.

O'Steen, Neal. "The Lost Years: UT Football, 1894-1895." *Tennessee Alumnus* 63, no. 3 (Summer 1983): 24-26.

"Park Will Get Chapman Picture." *Knoxville News-Sentinel*, 6 May 1945.

Robinson, Donnie Tom. "Man behind the Park." *Knoxville News-Sentinel*, 1 September 1940.

"Rockefeller Pays Chapman Tribute." *Knoxville News-Sentinel*, 29 July 1944.

University of Tennessee Sports Information Office. Magazine and journal clippings regarding university football teams.

Chavannes, Anna

Babelay, David. *They Trusted and Were Delivered: The French-Swiss of Knoxville, Tennessee*. Vol. 1. Knoxville: Vaude-Tennessee, 1988.

East Tennessee Historical Society. *Swiss Faces in East Tennessee*. Brochure for Knoxville historical exhibit, 28 June-31 October 1991.

Cheairs, Nathaniel

Corlew, Robert E. "The Civil War in Tennessee." In *Tennessee: A Short History*. 2nd ed, 302-27. Knoxville: University of Tennessee Press, 1981.

Little, Thomas Vance. "A Short History of Williamson County." In *Historic Williamson County, Tennessee, Established 1799*. Brochure. Franklin, Tenn.: Williamson County Tourism Committee, n.d.

McBride, Robert M. "The 'Confederate Sins' of Major Cheairs." *Tennessee Historical Quarterly* 23, no. 2 (March-December 1964): 121-35.

McPherson, James M. "The River War in 1862." In *Battle Cry of Freedom: The Civil War Era*, 392-427. New York: Oxford University Press, 1988.

Smith, Reid. "Rippavilla." In *Majestic Middle Tennessee*, 59. Prattville, Ala.: Paddle Wheel, 1975.

Cheatham, Benjamin Franklin

Dictionary of American Biography. S.v. "Cheatham, Benjamin Franklin."

Evans, Clement A., ed. "General Benjamin Franklin Cheatham." In *Confederate Military History*. Vol. 8, *Tennessee*, 302-4. Atlanta: Confederate Publishing Co., 1899.

Losson, Christopher. "One of the Wickedest Men I Ever Heard Speak: The 1850s and the Onset of the Civil War." In *Tennessee's Forgotten Warriors: Frank Cheatham and His Confederate Division*, 20-39. Knoxville: University of Tennessee Press, 1989.

McPherson, James M. *Battle Cry of Freedom: The Civil War Era*. New York: Oxford University Press, 1988.

Moore, John Trotwood, and Austin P. Foster, eds. "Gen. B. F. Cheatham." In *Tennessee: The Volunteer State, 1769-1923*, 2: 98. Nashville: S. J. Clarke, 1923.

Cheek, Joel Owsley

Cheek, Joel Owsley. Biographical file: Materials include newspaper and magazine clippings, including "Business Career of J. O. Cheek Nothing Short of Romance." *Nashville Banner*, February 1924, reprinted in the "Maxwell House Messenger" (copy from General Foods Public Relations Library); and death notice in *Nashville Tennessean*, 14 December 1935. Nashville Room, Ben West Library, Nashville and Davidson County Public Library.

Davis, Louise. "Good since the First Drop." *Nashville Tennessean*, 4 January 1976.

Force, William W. "The Cheeks of Nashville." In *Nashville: A Family Town*, 145-63. 1975-76, Number 5. Nashville: Nashville Room, Public Library of Nashville and Davidson County, 1978.

Regal Maxwell House. Informational flyer, public relations department. Nashville: Regal Maxwell House, Nashville, 1993.

Church, Robert R., Sr.

Biles, Roger. "Robert R. Church Jr. of Memphis: Black Republican Leader in the Age of Democratic Ascendancy, 1928-1940." *Tennessee Historical Quarterly* 42 (1983): 362-82.

Church, Annette E., and Roberta Church. *The Robert R. Churches of Memphis: A Father and Son Who Achieved in Spite of Race.* Ann Arbor, Mich.: Edwards Bros., 1974.

Crawford, Charles W. "Decades of Disaster: War, Reconstruction, and Plague." In *Yesterday's Memphis*, 29-52. Seemann's Historic Cities Series, no. 25. Miami: E. A. Seemann, 1976.

Harkins, John E. *Metropolis of the American Nile: An Illustrated History of Memphis and Shelby County.* Edited by Charles W. Crawford. Woodland Hills, Calif.: Windsor, 1982.

Hutchins, Fred L. "Beale Street." In *What Happened in Memphis*, 94-103. Kingsport, Tenn.: Kingsport Press, 1965.

McKee, Margaret, and Fred Chisenhall. *Beale Black and Blue: Life and Music on Black America's Main Street.* Baton Rouge: Louisiana State University Press, 1981.

Pink Palace Museum. "Robert R. Church." In *Historic Black Memphians.* Exhibit material. Memphis State University Archives.

Sterling, Dorothy. *Black Foremothers: Three Lives.* Old Westbury, N.Y.: Feminist Press and McGraw-Hill, 1979.

Terrell, Mary Church. *A Colored Woman in a White World.* Signal Lives: Autobiographies of American Women Series. New York: Arno Press, 1980.

Clemens, John

"Beyond the Five Senses." In *Psychic Powers*, Mysteries of the Unknown Series, 14-15. Alexandria, Va.: Time-Life Books, 1987.

The Commercial Appeal. "'God Bless Memphis!' Wept Mark Twain." In *The Commercial Appeal, 1840-1965: The Story of a Great Institution Dedicated to the People's Right to Know*, Appendix II. Memphis: Memphis Publishing Co., 1965.

Ensor, Allison. "The 'Tennessee Land' of the Gilded Age: Fiction and Reality." In *Tennessee Studies in Literature,* edited by Richard Beale Davis and Kenneth L. Knickerbocker, 15: 15-23. Knoxville: University of Tennessee Press, 1970.

Hogue, Albert R. *Mark Twain's Obedstown and Knobs of Tennessee (A History of Jamestown and Fentress County, Tennessee).* Jamestown, Tenn.: Cumberland, 1950.

Cocke, William

"The Cocke Family: Gen. William Cocke." *The Virginia Magazine of History and Biography* 4, no. 4 (April 1897): 442-44.

Corlew, Robert E. "The State of Franklin." In *Tennessee: A Short History.* 2nd ed., 72-84. Knoxville: University of Tennessee Press, 1981.

Dictionary of American Biography. S.v. "Cocke, William."

Gerson, Noel B. *Franklin: America's "Lost State."* New York: Macmillan, 1968.

McBride, Robert M., and Dan M. Robison. "Cocke, William." In *Biographical Directory of the Tennessee General Assembly.* Vol. 1, *1796-1861*, edited by Robert M. McBride. Nashville: Tennessee State Library and Archives and the Tennessee Historical Commission, 1975.

Moore, John Trotwood, and Austin P. Foster, eds. "William Cocke." In *Tennessee: The Volunteer State, 1769-1923*, 2: 99-100. Nashville: S. J. Clarke, 1923.

U.S. Congress. "Cocke, William." In *Biographical Directory of the United States Congress, 1774-1989.* Bicentennial Edition. Washington, D.C.: U.S. Government Printing Office, 1989.

Cockrill, Anne Robertson

Cockrill, Mary Harris. "The Cockrill Family." In *Nashville: A Family Town*, 43-68. Nashville: The Nashville Room, The Public Library of Nashville and Davidson County, 1978.

Moore, John Trotwood, and Austin P. Foster, eds. "The Cumberland Settlement." In *Tennessee: The Volunteer State, 1769-1923*, 1: 102-17. Nashville: S. J. Clarke, 1923.

Williams, Samuel C. *Ann Robertson: An Unsung Tennessee Heroine.* Nashville: Tennessee Historical Commission, 1944.

Cockrill, Mark Robertson

Cockrill, Mary Harris. "The Cockrill Family." In *Nashville: A Family Town*, 43-68. Nashville: Nashville Room, Public Library of Nashville and Davidson County, 1978.

Ewing, Mrs. Albert III. "The Story of Mark Robertson Cockrill: 'Wool Champion of the World.'" In *Makers of Millions, Not for Themselves—But for You*, edited by Louis D. Wallace, 1-65. Nashville: Tennessee Department of Agriculture, December 1951.

Cook, Laura

Cook, Thomas Hoyte, Sr. (grandson of L. Cook), Matthews, N.C. Biographical information and newspaper clipping provided to Tennessee Folk History Project Archives, University of Tennessee, Knoxville, 2 June 1995.

Van Ark, Carroll. "Women Rule a Cumberland Town." *Collier's* 110, no. 19 (7 November 1942): 58-59.

"Women and the Law-Spencer 1940." *Van Buren County Historical Journal* 3 (1984): 55-58.

Zechman, Patricia. "Women United for the Betterment." *Warren County (Tenn.) News*, 13 October 1977.

Crockett, David

Bell, Ed. "Reelfoot Waters." WPA Project. Tennessee Stories. MS div., ac. no. 1776, VI-b-4, box 23 of 23. Tennessee State Library and Archives, Nashville.

Bruns, Roger. "Assassination Attempt of President Andrew Jackson." *The West Tennessee Historical Society Papers* 31 (October 1977): 33-43.

Burke, James Wakefield. "Off to Congress." In *David Crockett: Man behind the Myth*, 160-79. Austin, Tex.: Eakin Press, 1984.

Byrum, C. Stephen. "The Cherokee Removal." In *McMinn County*, edited by Frank B. Williams Jr., 16-19. Tennessee County History Series. Memphis: Memphis State University Press, 1984.

Crockett, David. *Davy Crockett's Own Story as Written by Himself*. New York: Citadel Press, 1955.

Downing, Marvin. "Notes and Documents: Memorial Tributes to David ("Davy") Crockett in Trenton." *The West Tennessee Historical Society Papers* 33 (October 1979): 81-94.

Garland, Hamlin, ed. *The Autobiography of David Crockett*. New York: Charles Scribner's Sons, 1923.

Lofaro, Michael A., ed. "Preface" and "A Crockett Chronology." In *Davy Crockett: The Man, the Legend, the Legacy, 1786-1986*, xiii-xxiii. Knoxville: University of Tennessee Press, 1985.

———. "Why Davy Won't Die." *Tennessee Illustrated* 1, no. 2 (July-August 1988): 12-18.

Marshall, E. H., ed. "Davy Crockett." In *History of Obion County*, 7-10. Union City, Tenn.: *The Daily Messenger*, 1941.

McBride, Robert M. "David Crockett and His Memorials in Tennessee." *Tennessee Historical Quarterly* 26, no. 3 (Fall 1967): 219-39.

McBride, Robert M., and Dan M. Robison. "Crockett, David." In *Biographical Directory of the Tennessee General Assembly*. Vol. 1, *1796-1986*, edited by Robert M. McBride. Nashville: Tennessee State Library and Archives and the Tennessee Historical Commission, 1975.

Moore, John Trotwood, and Austin P. Foster, eds. "David Crockett." In *Tennessee: The Volunteer State, 1769-1923*, 2: 108-9. Nashville: S. J. Clarke, 1923.

Morris, Doug. "Justice Rarely So Swift Today." *Knoxville Journal*, 24 July 1979.

Parsons, Stanley B., William W. Beach, and Dan Hermann. *United States Congressional Districts, 1788-1841*. Westport, Conn.: Greenwood, 1978.

Rourke, Constance. *Davy Crockett*. New York: Harcourt, Brace & World, 1934.

Shackford, James Atkins. *David Crockett: The Man and the Legend*. Chapel Hill: University of North Carolina Press, 1956.

U.S. Congress. *Congressional Quarterly's Guide to U.S. Elections*. 2nd ed. Washington, D.C.: Congressional Quarterly, 1985, 712-20.

Williams, Emma Inman. *Historic Madison: The Story of Jackson and Madison County Tennessee From the Prehistoric Moundbuilders to 1917*. Jackson, Tenn.: Madison County Historical Society, 1946.

Crump, Edward Hull "Boss"

Coppock, Paul R. "Red-Headed Reformer." In *Memphis Sketches*, 186-88. Memphis: Friends of Memphis and Shelby County Libraries, 1976.

Corlew, Robert E. "Reform and War, 1911-1923." In *Tennessee: A Short History*. 2nd ed., 433-53. Knoxville: University of Tennessee Press, 1981.

Dictionary of American Biography. S.v. "Crump, Edward Hull."

Lee, David L. "The Attempt to Impeach Governor Horton." *Tennessee Historical Quarterly* 34, no. 2 (Summer 1975): 188-201.

Miller, William D. *Mr. Crump of Memphis*. Baton Rouge: Louisiana State University Press, 1964.

Popham, John N. "Dixon-Yates Runs Afoul of Crump's Machine and Public Power Stand." *New York Times*, 18 February 1955.

"Ring-Tailed Tooter." *Time*, 27 May 1946, 20-23.

Tucker, David M. "Mister Crump." In *Memphis Since Crump: Bossism, Blacks, and Civic Reformers 1948-1968*, 22-39. Knoxville: University of Tennessee Press, 1980.

Daniel, Jack

Bigger, Jeanne Ridgway. "Jack Daniel Distillery and Lynchburg: A Visit to Moore County, Tennessee." *Tennessee Historical Quarterly* 31, no. 1 (Spring 1972): 3-21.

"Jack Daniel Dies at his Home in County of Moore." *Nashville Tennessean*, 10 October 1911.

Jack Daniel Distillery. Corporate and product history, public relations department. Lynchburg, Tenn.: Jack Daniel Distillery. N.d.

Green, Ben A. *Jack Daniel's Legacy*. Nashville: Rich Printing Co., 1967.

Davis, Frances "Fannie" Elliott

Pitrone, Jean Maddern. *Trailblazer: Negro Nurse in the American Red Cross*. New York: Harcourt, Brace & World, 1969.

Davis, Sam

Meredith, Owen Nichols. "The Sam Davis Home." *Tennessee Historical Quarterly* 24, no. 4 (Winter 1965): 303-20.

Smith, Coleman Davis. *The Tennessee Civil War Veterans Questionnaires*. Vol. 5, *Confederate Soldiers*. Compiled by Gustavus W. Dyer and John Trotmore Moore. Edited by Colleen Morse Elliott and Louise Armstrong Moxley. Easley, S.C.: Southern Historical Press, 1985.

Walker, Hugh. "Sam Davis and David Crockett." In *Tennessee Tales*, 45-52. Nashville: Aurora, 1970.

Dickinson, Perez

"Col. Dickinson Dead: Breathed His Last at 2:18, Pioneer Merchant Gone." *The Knoxville Sentinel*, 17 July 1901.

Creekmore, Betsey Beeler. "Perez Dickinson." In *Knoxville*, 131-47. Knoxville: University of Tennessee Press, 1958.

Herndon, Mary. "Cousins of New England Poetess Had Active Part in History of Knoxville." *Knoxville Journal*, 16 September 1971.

Patton, Charles V. "Dickinson's 'Cowdog' Collie Had Daily Task in Cattle Roundup." *Knoxville Journal*, 1 February 1948.

———. "Fame of Record-Breaking Hog Drew Visitors to Knox Farm." *Knoxville Journal*, 22 February 1948.

Doak, Samuel

Bond, Octavia Zollicoffer. "Incidents of Early Times." In *Old Tales Retold; Or, Perils and Adventures of Tennessee Pioneers*, 74-85. 1907. Reprint, Nashville: Charles and Randy Elder, 1973.

Burnett, J. J. *Sketches of Tennessee's Pioneer Baptist Preachers*. Nashville: Marshall and Bruce, 1919, 1: 320-21.

Dixon, Max. *The Wataugans*. Johnson City, Tenn.: Overmountain Press, 1989.

Fink, Paul M. "The Lighter Side of History." *The East Tennessee Historical Society's Publications,* no. 39 (1967): 26-41.

Foster, Isabelle. "Washington College and Washington College Academy." *Tennessee Historical Quarterly* 30, no. 3 (Fall 1971): 241-58.

Kilgo, John Wesley. "Politics and Love of East Tennessee." In *Campaigning in Dixie: With Some Reflections on Two-Party Government*, 16-30. New York: Hobson Book Press, 1945.

Moore, John Trotwood, and Austin P. Foster, eds. "Triangular Controversy over the Public Lands—Early Customs—Establishment of Religious Denominations." In *Tennessee: The Volunteer State, 1769-1923*, 1: 313-33. Nashville: S. J. Clarke, 1923.

Norton, Herman A. *Religion in Tennessee, 1777-1945*. Knoxville: University of Tennessee Press, 1981.

Ramsey, Dr. J. G. M. *The Annals of Tennessee to the End of the Eighteenth Century*. 1853. Rev. ed. with biographical introduction by W. H. Masterson for the East Tennessee Historical Society. Kingsport, Tenn.: Kingsport Press, 1967.

Douglas, "Shufflin' Phil"

Douglas, "Shufflin' Phil." Biographical file including newspaper and magazine clippings. Jasper Public Library, Jasper, Tenn.

"Fans Defend Shufflin' Phil." *Dunlap (Tenn.) Tribune*, 5 April 1990.

Johnson, Buck. "This Story Needs Told Once More." *Chattanooga Times*, 20 February 1990.

Patton, Dave. "A Remembrance: Phil Douglas, World Series Champion." *Grundy County (Tenn.) Post*, 7 October 1987.

Thompson, Reba (granddaughter of P. Douglas), Dunlap, Tenn. Newspaper clippings provided to Tennessee Folk History Project Archives, University of Tennessee.

Downing, Henry

Curtis, Joe. "In the Pilothouse-Christmas Day, 1843, Marred by Tragedy." *Memphis Commercial Appeal*, 19 June 1942.

Driver, William

Davis, Louise Littleton. "Capt. William Driver and the Flag." In *Frontier Tales of Tennessee*, 105-18. Gretna, La.: Pelican. 1976.

Durham, Walter T. "Commerce and Civilian Control." In *Reluctant Partners: Nashville and the Union, July 1, 1863, to June 30, 1865*, 63-79. Nashville: Tennessee Historical Society, 1987.

———. "Living with the Yankees." In *Nashville: The Occupied City, The First Seventeen Months—February 16, 1862, to June 30, 1863*, 232-51. Nashville: Tennessee Historical Society, 1985.

Duggan, Ralph

Byrum, C. Stephen. "The Battle of Athens." In *McMinn County*, edited by Frank B. Williams Jr., 112-24. Tennessee County History Series. Memphis: Memphis State University Press, 1984.

Ensminger, Neal (former ed., *Athens [Tenn.] Daily Athenian*). Telephone interview with University of Tennessee graduate assistant John Walter for the Tennessee Folk History Project, May 1994.

"GIs May Ask Special Session." *Knoxville Journal*, 7 August 1946.

McKinney, R. Frank. "A Miracle No One Was Killed." In *Tall Tales and Unusual Happenings of McMinn County, Tennessee,* edited by Bill Akins, 53-56. Athens, Tenn.: McMinn County Historical Society, 1988.

White, Theodore H. "The Battle of Athens, Tennessee." *Harper's Magazine*, January 1947, 54-61.

Wilson, Amy Lyles. "1946—The Battle of Athens." *Tennessee Illustrated* 1, no. 3 (September-October 1988): 39.

Effler, Lawrence

Cemeteries of Unicoi County Tennessee. Erwin, Tenn.: Unicoi County Historical Society, 1989.

Masters, Roxie A. "Social, Economic, and Cultural Activities: Musters." In *The Valley of the Long Hunters*, 23-28. Parsons, W.Va.: McClain, 1969.

Siler, Tom. "Erwin." In *Tennessee Towns: From Adams to Yorkville*. Knoxville: East Tennessee Historical Society, 1985.

Ellis, Daniel

Brown, Campbell H. "Carter's East Tennessee Raid: The Sailor on Horseback Who Raided His Own Backyard." *Tennessee Historical Quarterly* 22, no. 1 (March 1963): 66-82.

Civil War Centennial Commission of Tennessee. *Guide to the Civil War in Tennessee*. 3rd rev. ed. Nashville: Author, 1977.

Ellis, Daniel. *Thrilling Adventures of Daniel Ellis, the Great Union Guide of East Tennessee for a Period of Nearly Four Years During the Great Southern Rebellion, Written by Himself, Containing a Short Biography of the Author*. 1867. Reprint, Johnson City, Tenn.: Don & Mignon, 1974.

Hesseltine, W. B. "The Underground Railroad From Confederate Prisons to East Tennessee." *The East Tennessee Historical Society's Publications,* no. 2 (1930): 55-69.

Kozsuch, Mildred, ed. *Historical Reminiscences of Carter County Tennessee.* Johnson City, Tenn.: Overmountain Press, 1985.

Madden, David. "Unionist Resistance to Confederate Occupation: The Bridge Burners of East Tennessee." *The East Tennessee Historical Society's Publications,* nos. 52, 53 (1981, 1982): 22-39.

Sharp, Arthur G. "Daniel Ellis." In *An Encyclopedia of East Tennessee,* edited by Jim Stokely and Jeff D. Johnson. Oak Ridge, Tenn.: Children's Museum of Oak Ridge, 1981.

Ellis, Josey Towson

Death notice, Capt. H. C. Ellis. *Confederate Veteran* 2, no. 12 (December 1903): 565.

Death notice, Mrs. Josephine E. Ellis. *Confederate Veteran* 20, no. 8 (August 1912): 390.

McMurtry, J. C. *History of Trousdale County.* N.p.: Vidette Publishing Co., [1970].

Embree, Elihu

Hoss, Rev. E. E. *Elihu Embree, Abolitionist.* Publications of the Vanderbilt Southern History Society, no. 2. Nashville: University Press Co., 1897.

White, Robert H. "Sketch of the Author." In *The Emancipator (Complete),* by Elihu Embree, 1820. Reprint, Nashville: B. H. Murphy, 1932.

Emery, Ron/Ray Hester

Emery, Ron. Tape-recorded interview by University of Tennessee graduate assistant Louis Burklow for the Tennessee Folk History Project, 10 February 1992.

Hester, Dr. Ray, Nashville, Tenn. Telephone interview with author Anne Klebenow, Tennessee Folk History Project, 6 June 1995.

Estes, "Sleepy John"/Hammie Nixon

Barlow, William. "Chocolate to the Bone: Urban Blues in the South." In *"Looking Up at Down": The Emergence of Blues Culture,* 182-229. Philadelphia, Pa.: Temple University Press, 1989.

Evans, David. "The Blues Singer." In *Big Road Blues: Tradition and Creativity in the Folk Blues,* 106-66. Berkeley: University of California Press, 1982.

McKee, Margaret, and Fred Chisenhall. "Sleepy John and Hammie." In *Beale Black and Blue: Life and Music on Black's America's Main Street,* 155-65. Baton Rouge: Louisiana State University Press, 1981.

Farragut, David Glasgow

Dictionary of American Biography. S.v. "Farragut, David Glasgow."

Under Both Flags: A Panorama of the Great Civil War as Presented in Story, Anecdote, Adventure and the Romance of Reality, Written by Celebrities on Both Sides; the Men and Women Who Created the Greatest Epoch of Our Nation's History. Philadelphia, Pa.: People's Publishing Co., 1896.

Williams, Samuel C. "George Farragut." *The East Tennessee Historical Society's Publications,* no. 1 (1929): 77-94.

Ferguson, Champ

Beard, William E. "Execution of Champ Ferguson." In *Nashville: The Home of History Makers,* 79-80. Nashville: Civitan Club, 1929.

Civil War Centennial Commission of Tennessee. "Captain Champ Ferguson's Cavalry Company." In *Tennesseans in the Civil War: A Military History of Confederate and Union Units with Available Rosters of Personnel,* part 1: 15-16. Nashville: Author, 1964.

Hogue, Albert R. "Champ Ferguson." In *Mark Twain's Obedstown and Knobs of Tennessee (A History of Jamestown and Fentress County, Tennessee),* 58-63. Jamestown, Tenn.: Cumberland, 1950.

Martin, James. "Ferguson, Champ." In *The Kentucky Encyclopedia,* edited by John E. Kleber. Lexington: University Press of Kentucky, 1992.

Montell, William Lynwood. "A Region Divided." In *Don't Go Up Kettle Creek: Verbal Legacy of the Upper Cumberland,* 52-82. Knoxville: University of Tennessee Press, 1983.

Sanderson, Esther Sharp. "Guerrilla Warfare during the Civil War." *The Tennessee Valley Historical Review* 1, no. 3 (Fall 1972): 25-33.

Fisher, Thomas Burr

"Correspondence, Etc.—Confederate. " In *The War of the Rebellion: A Compilation of the Official Records of the Union and Confederate Armies.* Series 1, vol. 49, part 2, 1289-90. 1897. Reprint, n.p.: Historical Times, 1985.

Fisher, John E. "Life on the Common Level: Inheritance, Conflict, and Instruction." *Tennessee Historical Quarterly* 26 (Spring-Winter 1967): 304-22.

Fisher, Thomas Burr. "Life on the Common Level." Manuscript, transcribed by William L. Jones (family genealogist; Milan, Tenn.) and provided to Tennessee Folk History Project Archives, University of Tennessee, n.d.

Jones, William L., comp. *The Fisher Scrap Book 1730-1972.* Milan, Tenn.: Author, n.d.

Ford, Loyd, Sr.

Howington, Arthur F. "'Not in the Condition of a Horse or an Ox,' Ford vs. Ford, the Law of Testamentary Manumission and the Tennessee Court's Recognition of Slave Humanity." *Tennessee Historical Quarterly* 34, no. 3 (Fall 1975): 249-63.

Mooney, Chase C. *Slavery in Tennessee.* 1957. Reprint, Westport, Conn.: Greenwood, 1971.

Foreman, Stephen

Corn, James Franklin. "Stephen Foreman." In *Red Clay and Rattlesnake Springs: A History of the Cherokee Indians of Bradley County, Tennessee,* 52-58. Cleveland, Tenn.: Author, 1959.

Evans, E. Raymond. "Notable Persons in Cherokee History: Stephen Foreman." *Journal of Cherokee Studies* 2, no. 2 (Spring 1977): 230-39.

Foreman, Minta Ross. "Reverend Stephen Foreman, Cherokee Missionary." *The Chronicles of Oklahoma* 18, no. 3 (September 1940): 229-42.

Walker, Robert Sparks. *Torchlights to the Cherokees: The Brainerd Mission.* New York: Macmillan, 1931.

Forrest, Nathan Bedford

Bowman, John S., ed. "12 April 1864." In *The Civil War Almanac.* New York: World Almanac, 1983.

Connelly, Thomas L. *Civil War Tennessee: Battles and Leaders.* Knoxville: University of Tennessee Press, 1979.

Crawford, Charles W. "Decades of Disaster: War, Reconstruction, and Plague." In *Yesterday's Memphis*, 29-52. Seemann's Historic Cities Series, no. 25. Miami: E. A. Seemann, 1976.

Duke, Kevin. *Why Brice's Crossroads? A Study of Tactical Victory and Strategic Defeat.* Memphis: WordMagic, 1984.

Gower, Herschel. "Beersheba Springs and L. Virginia French: The Novelist as Historian." *Tennessee Historical Quarterly* 42, no. 2 (Summer 1983): 115-37.

Henry, Robert Selph. *"First with the Most:" Forrest.* Indianapolis: Bobbs-Merrill, 1944.

McDonough, James L. "Glory Can Not Atone: Shiloh—April 6,7, 1862." *Tennessee Historical Quarterly* 35, no. 3 (Fall 1976): 279-95.

McPherson, James M. "The River War in 1862." In *Battle Cry of Freedom: The Civil War Era*, 392-427. New York: Oxford University Press, 1988.

Moore, John Trotwood, and Austin P. Foster, eds. "General N. B. Forrest." In *Tennessee: The Volunteer State, 1769-1923*, 2: 121-22. Nashville: S. J. Clarke, 1923.

Morton, John Watson. *The Artillery of Nathan Bedford Forrest's Cavalry.* 1909. Reprint, Paris, Tenn.: Guild Bindery Press, 1988.

Richardson, W. T. *Historic Pulaski: Birthplace of the Ku Klux Klan, Scene of Execution of Sam Davis.* Nashville: Methodist Publishing House, 1913.

"The Surviving Members of Forrest's Staff." *Memphis Commercial Appeal*, 9 June 1901, magazine sec.

Wills, Brian Steel. *A Battle from the Start: The Life of Nathan Bedford Forrest.* New York: HarperCollins, 1992.

Wyeth, John Allan. "The Ancestry and Earlier Life of N. B. Forrest." In *That Devil Forrest: Life of General Nathan Bedford Forrest*, 1-20. Baton Rouge: Louisiana State University Press, 1959.

Young, Bennett H. "Forrest's Raid Into Memphis, August 21, 1864." In *Confederate Wizards of the Saddle: Being Reminiscences and Observations of One Who Rode with Morgan*, 601-25. 1914. Reprint, Dayton, Ohio: Morningside Bookshop, 1979.

Fort, Cornelia

Tanner, Doris Brinker. "Cornelia Fort: A WASP in World War II." *Tennessee Historical Quarterly* 40, no. 4 (Winter 1981): 381-94; and 41, no. 1 (Spring 1982): 67-80.

Frankland, R. Ernest

Featherston, Alwyn. *Saving the Breakout: The 30th Division's Heroic Stand at Mortain, August 7-12, 1944.* Novato, Calif.: Presidio Press, 1993.

Fitts, Stella (daughter-in-law of R. E. Frankland), Jackson, Tenn. Frankland family information provided to Tennessee Folk History Project Archives, University of Tennessee, 8 October 1995.

Frankland, Hays (nephew of R. E. Frankland), Jackson, Tenn. Telephone interview with University of Tennessee graduate assistant John Walter for the Tennessee Folk History Project, 20 September 1995.

Frankland, Robert Ernest III (grandson of R. E. Frankland), Jackson, Tenn. Telephone interview with University of Tennessee graduate assistant John Walter for the Tennessee Folk History Project, 20 September 1995.

Giles, Warren. *Company B, 117th Infantry, 30th Infantry Division, Tennessee National Guard.* Athens, Tenn.: Author, n.d.

Hewitt, Robert L. *Work Horse of the Western Front: The Story of the 30th Infantry Division.* Washington, D.C.: Infantry Journal Press, 1946.

Freeman, Elizabeth "Miss Lizzie"

McCombs, Holland. "As It Was on a Martin Farm in the Early Century: The Place—The Economy—Work and Play." In *The West Tennessee Farm*, edited by Marvin Downing, 15-25. Martin: University of Tennessee-Martin, 1979.

———. "Freemans of Woodley; More Great Pioneers." *Martin (Tenn.) Weakley County Press*, Tennessee Centennial Edition, 28 June 1973.

French, Lucy Virginia

Gower, Herschel, ed. "The Beersheba Diary of L. Virginia French, Part I, Summer and Fall, 1863." *The East Tennessee Historical Society's Publications*, nos. 52, 53 (1980, 1981): 89-107.

Shirley, Patricia A. "Beersheba Springs." In *An Encyclopedia of East Tennessee*, edited by Jim Stokely and Jeff D. Johnson. Oak Ridge, Tenn.: Children's Museum of Oak Ridge, 1981.

Walker, Hugh. "Monteagle and Beersheba Springs." In *Tennessee Tales*, 83-85. Nashville: Aurora, 1970.

Furber, George C.

Brock, Reid, Sr., Thomas O. Brock, and Tony Hays, comp. *Volunteers: Tennesseans in the War with Mexico.* Vol. 1. Chattanooga: Kitchen Table Press, 1986.

Crutchfield, James A. *Tennesseans at War: Volunteers and Patriots in Defense of Liberty.* Nashville: Rutledge Hill Press, 1987.

Furber, George C. *The Twelve Months Volunteer; or, Journal of a Private, in the Tennessee Regiment of Cavalry, in the Campaign, in Mexico, 1846-7.* Cincinnati: J. A. and U. P. James, 1848.

Hamilton, Sinclair. "George C. Furber." In *Early American Book Illustrators and Wood Engravers, 1670-1870: A Catalogue of a Collection of American Books Illustrated for the most part with Woodcuts and Wood Engravings in the Princeton University Library*, 132. Princeton, N.J.: Princeton University Library, 1958.

Gailor, Charlotte

Davies-Rodgers, Ellen. "The Right Reverend Thomas Frank Gailor." In *Heirs through Hope: The Episcopal Diocese of West Tennessee*, 42-47. Memphis: Plantation Press, 1983.

Gailor, Thomas Frank. "The Civil War." In *Some Memories*, 1-17. Kingsport, Tenn.: Southern Publishers, 1937.

Gardner, John A.

Corlew, Robert E. "Party Politics, 1839-1859." In *Tennessee: A Short History*. 2nd ed., 254-83. Knoxville: University of Tennessee Press, 1981.

Gardner, John A. "Early Times in Weakley County: An Address." *The West Tennessee Historical Society Papers*, no. 17 (1963): 68-84.

Goodpasture, A. V. and W. H. Goodpasture. "Sam Turney." In *Life of Jefferson Dillard Goodpasture*, 68-72. Nashville: Cumberland Presbyterian Publishing House, 1897.

Moore, John Trotwood, and Austin P. Foster, eds. "John A. Gardner." In *Tennessee: The Volunteer State, 1769-1923*, 2: 129. Nashville: S. J. Clarke, 1923.

Seals, Rev. Monroe. *History of White County, Tennessee*. 1935. Reprint, Spartanburg, S.C.: Reprint Co., 1974.

McBride, Robert M., and Don M. Robison. "Gardner, John A." In *Biographical Directory of the Tennessee General Assembly*. Vol. 1, *1796-1861*, edited by Robert M. McBride. Nashville: Tennessee State Library and Archives and the Tennessee Historical Commission, 1979.

Vaughan, Virginia Clark (descendant of J. A. Gardner), Martin, Tenn. Family historical materials, including newspaper clippings and Martin centennial publication, 1993, provided to Tennessee Folk History Project Archives, University of Tennessee.

———. "John A. Gardner Left His Mark on Weakley County." *Martin (Tenn.) Weakley County Press*, 14 April 1992.

Gatlin, Radford

Creekmore, Betsey Beeler. "The Great Smoky Mountains National Park." In *Arrows to Atoms: The Story of East Tennessee*, 95-113. Knoxville: University of Tennessee Press, 1959.

Greve, Jeanette S. *The Story of Gatlinburg (White Oak Flats)*. 1931. Reprint, Gatlinburg, Tenn.: Marion R. Mangrum, Brazos Printing Co., 1964.

———. "Traditions of Gatlinburg." *The East Tennessee Historical Society's Publications*, no. 3 (January 1931): 62-77.

Trout, Ed. *Gatlinburg: Cinderella City*. Pigeon Forge, Tenn.: Griffin Graphics, 1984.

Gloster, Mary Hayes

Davies-Rodgers, Ellen. *Heirs through Hope: The Episcopal Diocese of West Tennessee*. Memphis: Privately published through Plantation Press, 1983.

———. "Mrs. Gloster and Her Horse-Ride." In *The Romance of the Episcopal Church in West Tennessee, 1832-1964*, 93-96. Memphis: Privately published through Plantation Press, 1964.

De Berry, John H. "La Grange—La Belle Village." *Tennessee Historical Quarterly* 30, no. 2 (Summer 1971): 133-53.

Gordon, George W.

"Bivouac 18, A.C.S., and Camp 28, U.C.V.: Gen. George W. Gordon." *Confederate Veteran* 5, no. 11 (November 1897): 566-67.

Moore, John Trotwood, and Austin P. Foster, eds. "Gen. A. J. Vaughn." In *Tennessee: The Volunteer State, 1769-1923*, 2: 245. Nashville: S. J. Clarke, 1923.

Porter, James Davis. "Biographical: Brigadier-General George W. Gordon," and "Additional Biographical Sketches: Brigadier-General George Washington Gordon." In *Confederate Military History*. Vol. 8, *Tennessee*, edited by Clement A. Evans, 309-10, 507-8. Atlanta: Confederate Publishing Co., 1899.

Vaughan, A. J. *Personal Record of the Thirteenth Regiment, Tennessee Infantry*. Memphis, 1897.

Gore, Al

Biographical information. Provided by the Washington, D.C., office of Vice President Al Gore.

Bradley, Carol. "Gores Thank Well-Wishers Praying for Injured Son." *Nashville Tennessean*, 5 April 1989.

Gore, Al. "Introduction." In *Earth in the Balance: Ecology and the Human Spirit*. Boston: Houghton Mifflin, 1992.

"Gore Son Struck by Car; Serious." *Nashville Tennessean*, 4 April 1989.

Hillin, Hank. *Al Gore, Jr.: Born to Lead*. Nashville: Pine Hall Press, 1988.

Grayson, James W. M. /Tom Dula

Baggelaar, Kristin, and Donald Milton. *Folk Music: More than a Song*. New York: Thomas Y. Crowell, 1976.

Johnson County Historical Society. *History of Johnson County, 1986, Sesquicentennial Edition*. Marceline, Mo.: Walsworth Press, 1985.

McBride, Robert M., and Dan M. Robison. "Grayson, James W. M." In *Biographical Directory of the Tennessee General Assembly*. Vol. 2, *1861-1901*, edited by Robert M. McBride. Nashville: Tennessee State Library and Archives and the Tennessee Historical Commission, 1979.

Warner, Frank M. *Folk Songs and Ballads of the Eastern Seaboard; From a Collector's Notebook*. Macon, Ga.: Southern Press, 1963.

———. "Frank Proffitt." *Sing Out*, 13, no. 4 (October-November 1963): 6-11.

Wolfe, Charles K. *Tennessee Strings: The Story of Country Music Tennessee*. Knoxville: University of Tennessee Press, 1977.

Griffin, Marion Scudder

Bridgforth, Lucie Robertson. "The 'New' Woman in an Old Role: Maternal-Child Care in Memphis." *The West Tennessee Historical Society Papers* 40 (December 1986): 45-54.

Cornwell, Ilene J. "Griffin, Marian [*sic*]." In *Biographical Directory of the Tennessee General Assembly.* Vol. 3, *1901-1931.* Nashville: Tennessee Historical Commission, 1988.

Griffin, Marion Scudder. Autobiographical sketch, 1922, for questionnaires about Tennesseans compiled by Tennessee state archivist. Tennessee Library and Archives, Nashville.

Lanier, Robert A. *The History of the Memphis & Shelby County Bar.* Memphis: Memphis and Shelby County Bar Assn., 1981.

"Women as Lawyers. They Are Barred from Practicing in Tennessee Courts." *Memphis Commercial Appeal,* 21 June 1901.

Handy, W. C.

Coppock, Paul R. "He Wrote in Blue." In *Memphis Sketches,* 254-59. Memphis: Friends of Memphis and Shelby County Libraries, 1976.

Handy, W. C. *Father of the Blues: An Autobiography.* London: Sidgwick & Jackson, 1957.

Lee, George W. *Beale Street: Where the Blues Began.* New York: Robert O. Ballou, 1934.

Pink Palace Museum. "William C. Handy, 1873-1958." In *Historic Black Memphians.* Exhibit material. Memphis: Pink Palace Museum. Memphis State University Archives.

Harding, William Giles

Horn, Stanley F. *The Decisive Battle of Nashville.* Baton Rouge: Louisiana State University Press, 1956.

Mackin, Sister Aloysius, O.P. "Wartime Scenes from Convent Windows: St. Cecilia, 1860 through 1865." *Tennessee Historical Quarterly* 39, no. 4 (Winter 1980): 401-22.

Miller, Randall M. "Letters from Nashville, 1862: Dear Master, II." *Tennessee Historical Quarterly* 33, no. 1 (Spring 1974): 85-92.

Wills, W. Ridley II. "Black-White Relationships on the Belle Meade Plantation." *Tennessee Historical Quarterly* 50, no. 1 (Spring 1991): 17-32.

————. "The Harding Family." In *Nashville: A Family Town,* 119-44. Nashville: Nashville Room, Public Library of Nashville and Davidson County, 1978.

————. "Home of the Race Horse." In *The History of Belle Meade: Mansion, Plantation, and Stud,* 163-80. Nashville: Vanderbilt University Press, 1991.

————. "Letters from Nashville, 1862: A Portrait of Belle Meade, I." *Tennessee Historical Quarterly* 33, no. 1 (Spring 1974): 70-84.

Young, Leona Pardue. "Elizabeth Irwin McGavock Harding, 1819-1867." In *Seven Women of Nashville: Nashville's Fine Flavor of Femininity,* 12-26. Nashville: Nashville Room, Public Library of Nashville and Davidson County, 1974.

Zibart, Carl F. *Yesterday's Nashville.* Seemann's Historic Cities Series, no. 16. Miami: E. A. Seemann, 1976.

Harpe Brothers

Breazeale, J. W. M. *Life as It Is: . . . Containing, amongst Other Things . . . [a] History of the Harpes (Two Noted Murderers). . .* 1842. Reprint, Nashville: Charles Elder, 1969.

Gooch, J. T. "Harpe Brothers." In *The Kentucky Encyclopedia,* edited by John E. Kleber. Lexington: University Press of Kentucky, 1992.

Hicks, Edward D. "Origin of the Name Harpeth." *The American Historical Magazine* 5, no. 2 (April 1900): 128-31.

Harriman, Walter C.

Beane, S. C. "General Walter Harriman." In *Successful New Hampshire Men.* Manchester, N.H.: John B. Clarke, 1882.

Davis, Louise. "Town Built for Teetotalers." *The Sunday Tennessean Magazine* (*Nashville Tennessean*), 19 November 1972.

Hadley, Amos. *Life of Walter Harriman with Selections from His Speeches and Writings.* Boston: Houghton Mifflin, 1888.

Metcalf, Henry Harrison, ed. "Walter C. Harriman." In *One Thousand New Hampshire Notables,* 193-94. Concord, N.H.: Rumford Printing Co., 1919.

Pulliam, Walter T. *Harriman: The Town That Temperance Built.* Maryville, Tenn.: Marion R. Mangrum, Brazos Press, 1978.

Shelley, Jack. Telephone interview with University of Tennessee graduate assistant John Walter for the Tennessee Folk History Project, 30 June 1995.

Shelley, Jack, and Jere Hall, eds. *Valley of Challenge and Change: The History of Roane County, Tennessee, 1860-1900.* Kingston, Tenn.: Roane County Heritage Commission, 1986.

Wroe, William Clarke, comp. *The Wroe and Chancellor Families.* Edgewater, Md.: Author, 1992.

Hendrix, John

Johnson, Charles W., and Charles O. Jackson. *City behind a Fence: Oak Ridge, Tennessee, 1942-1946.* Knoxville: University of Tennessee Press, 1981.

Robinson, George O., Jr. *The Oak Ridge Story: The Saga of a People Who Share in History.* Kingsport, Tenn.: Southern Publishers, 1950.

Higgason, Amy Elizabeth

Claxton, Lucy Anne, and Polly Claxton (great-granddaughters of A. E. Higgason). Interview with University of Tennessee graduate assistant William Todd Groce for the Tennessee Folk History Project, Somerville, Tenn., 23 July 1987.

————. Telephone interview with University of Tennessee graduate assistant John Walter for the Tennessee Folk History Project, 3 November 1995.

Claxton, Polly. (great-granddaughter of A. E. Higgason). Handwritten notes of an interview with University of Tennessee graduate assistant John Walter for the Tennessee Folk History Project, Somerville, Tenn., 20 October 1995.

"Memoirs from 'Frogmore.'" *The Fayette County Historical Society Bulletin* 1, no. 1 (April 1976).

Hill, Elizabeth "Bettsey"

de la Cruz, Bonna M. "Free Hills Alive in History," and "Stories Change, Names the Same." *Nashville Tennessean*, 3 October 1993.

Fitzgerald, Clyde V., comp. "Tombstone Inscriptions—Free Hills Cemetery." *Tennessee: Clay County Bible and Tombstone Records*. Works Projects Administration. Historical Records Project no. 465-44-3-115, December 15, 1937.

Peterson, Elizabeth, and Tom Rankin. "Free Hill: An Introduction." *Tennessee Folklore Society Bulletin* 50, no. 1 (Spring 1985): 1-9.

Webb, Walter E. "Sketches: Free Hills." In *Clay County Centennial, 1870-1970, Commemorative Brochure*. McClung Collection, Knox County Library System.

Hill, Napoleon

Crawford, Charles W. "Decades of Disaster: War, Reconstruction, and Plague." In *Yesterday's Memphis*, 29-52. Seemann's Historic Cities Series, no. 25. Miami: E. A. Seemann, 1976.

McIlwaine, Shields. "Big Money Gilds the Town: Napoleon Hill and the Cream Pitcher." In *Memphis: Down in Dixie*, 220-28. New York: E. P. Dutton, 1948.

Hirsch, Sidney M.

Corlew, Robert E. "Intellectual and Social Life." In *Tennessee: A Short History*. 2nd ed., 545-71. Knoxville: University of Tennessee Press, 1981.

Cowan, Louise. *The Fugitive Group: A Literary History*. Baton Rouge: Louisiana State University Press, 1959.

Rubin, Louis D. "Introduction." In *Fugitives' Reunion: Conversations at Vanderbilt, May 3-5, 1956*, edited by Rob Roy Purdy, 15-24. Nashville: Vanderbilt University Press, 1959, 11.

Stewart, John L. "John Crowe Ransom." In *American Writers: A Collection of Literary Biographies*, edited by Leonard Unger, 3: 480-502. New York: Charles Scribner's Sons, 1974.

Young, Thomas Daniel. *Tennessee Writers*. Knoxville: University of Tennessee Press, 1981.

Honeycutt, Annanias

Holt, Edgar A. "Annanias Honeycutt versus the State of Tennessee." In *Claiborne County*, edited by Joy Bailey Dunn, 39-41. Tennessee County History Series. Memphis: Memphis State University Press, 1981.

Morris, Doug. What Happened to Tom Ausmus' Murderer?" *Knoxville Journal*, 12 July 1984.

Hooper, Ben Walter

Corlew, Robert E. "Reform and War, 1911-1923." In *Tennessee: A Short History*. 2nd ed., 433-52. Knoxville: University of Tennessee Press, 1981.

Hooper, Ben W. *The Unwanted Boy: The Autobiography of Governor Ben W. Hooper*. Edited by Everett Robert Boyce. Knoxville: University of Tennessee Press, 1963.

Phillips, Margaret I. "Ben Walter Hooper." In *The Governors of Tennessee*, 127-30. Gretna, La.: Pelican, 1978.

Hopkins, Montgomery "Gum"

O'Dell, Ruth Webb. *Over the Misty Blue Hills: The Story of Cocke County, Tennessee*. N.p.: Author, 1950.

Houston, Sam

Back Home in Blount County: An Illustrated History of Its Communities. Maryville, Tenn.: Blount County Historic Trust, 1986.

Baggett, James Alex. "Sam Houston: Governor of Tennessee, 1827-1829." In *Governors of Tennessee*. Vol. 1, *1790-1835*, edited by Charles W. Crawford, 148-78. Memphis: Memphis State University Press, 1979.

Burns, Frank. "Sam Houston in Lebanon." In *Wilson County*, edited by Robert E. Corlew, 25-27. Tennessee County History Series. Memphis: Memphis State University Press, 1983.

Corlew, Robert E. "Governor William Carroll: A Harbinger of Jacksonian Democracy." In *Tennessee: A Short History*. 2nd ed., 159-77. Knoxville: University of Tennessee Press, 1981.

Davis, Louise Littleton. "Sam Houston and the Mystery of His Tragic Marriage." In *Frontier Tales of Tennessee*, 3-33. Gretna, La.: Pelican, 1976.

Tindell, Ted. "Maryville." In *Blount County: Communities We Live In*, 13-37. Maryville, Tenn.: Marion R. Mangrum, Brazos Press, 1973.

Walker, Nancy Wooten. "Eliza Allen Houston." In *Out of a Clear Blue Sky: Tennessee's First Ladies and Their Husbands*, 67-71. Cleveland, Tenn.: Author, 1971.

Wiltshire, Susan F. "Sam Houston and the *Iliad*." *Tennessee Historical Quarterly* 32, no. 3 (Fall 1973): 249-54.

Wiseheart, M. K. *Sam Houston: American Giant*. Washington, D.C.: Robert M. Luce, 1962.

Howard, Betsy Walker

Howard, Mrs. Benjamin Richard (Louise) III (family member of B. W. Howard), Perry County, Tenn. Telephone interview about the Howard family with author Anne Klebenow, Tennessee Folk History Project, 16 June 1994.

Lefler, Hugh T., and William S. Powell. "Establishing the Proprietary." In *Colonial North Carolina: A History*, edited by Milton M. Klein and Jacob E. Cooke, 29-55. New York: Charles Scribner's Sons, 1973.

Sisler, George. "They Still Hold the King's Land." *Memphis Commercial Appeal*, 25 November 1956.

Tennessee State Parks. *Mousetail Landing State Park*. Brochure. Tennessee Department of Environment and Conservation, 1992.

Hughes, Thomas

Armytage, W. H. G. "New Light on the English Background of Thomas Hughes' Rugby Colony in Tennessee." *The East Tennessee Historical Society's Publications,* no. 21 (1949): 69-84.

Egerton, John. *Visions of Utopia: Nashoba, Rugby, Ruskin, and the "New Communities" in Tennessee's Past.* Knoxville: University of Tennessee Press, 1977.

Govan, Gilbert E., and James W. Livingood. "Boom and Bust." In *The Chattanooga Country, 1540-1962: From Tomahawks to TVA,* 339-64. Chapel Hill: University of North Carolina Press, 1963.

Sanderson, Esther Sharp. "Cumberland Mountain Utopia." In *Scott County Gem of the Cumberlands,* 31-46. Huntsville, Tenn.: Author, 1974.

Stagg, Brian L. "Tennessee's Rugby Colony." *Tennessee Historical Quarterly* 27, no. 3 (Fall 1968): 209-24.

Walker, Hugh. "Rugby: A Noble Experiment." In *Tennessee Tales,* 23-26. Nashville: Aurora, 1970.

Hull, Cordell

DeLozier, Mary Jean. "The Good Old Days? Work and Play in the Upper Cumberland." In *Lend an Ear: Heritage of the Tennessee Upper Cumberland,* edited by Calvin Dickinson, et. al., 59-75. Lanham, Md.: University Press of America, 1983.

Dictionary of American Biography. S.v. "Hull, Cordell."

Douglas, Byrd. "Friction Dims the Golden Nineties: Period 1890-1900." In *Steamboatin' on the Cumberland,* 227-46. Nashville: Tennessee Book Co., 1961.

Hooper, Ben W. "Puppy Love, Education, and Politics." In *The Unwanted Boy: The Autobiography of Governor Ben W. Hooper,* edited by Everett Robert Boyce, 16-25. Knoxville: University of Tennessee Press, 1963.

Hull, Cordell. *The Memoirs of Cordell Hull.* 2 vols. New York: Macmillan, 1948.

Kilgo, John Wesley. "Diaper Jones the Voter." In *Campaigning in Dixie: With Some Reflections on Two-Party Government,* 128-39. New York: Hobson Book Press, 1945.

Knight, George Allen. "Illustrious Upper Cumberland Men." In *Our Wonderful Overton County Heritage,* 135-46. Knoxville: Southeastern Composition Services, 1975.

Pruden, Caroline. "Tennessee and the Formative Years of the United Nations: A Case Study of Southern Opinion." *Tennessee Historical Quarterly* 52, no. 1 (Spring 1993): 3-18.

Hurst, Fielding

Blankinship, Gary. "Colonel Fielding Hurst and the Hurst Nation." *The West Tennessee Historical Society Papers* 34 (October 1980): 71-87.

Civil War Centennial Commission of Tennessee. "7th Tennessee Cavalry Regiment, U.S. A." In *Tennesseans in the Civil War: A Military History of Confederate and Union Units with Available Rosters of Personnel,* part 1: 336-38. Nashville: Author, 1964.

Corlew, Robert E. "Storm Clouds." In *Tennessee: A Short History.* 2nd ed., 284-301. Knoxville: University of Tennessee Press, 1981.

Kozsuch, Mildred, ed. *Historical Reminiscences of Carter County Tennessee.* Johnson City, Tenn.: Overmountain Press, 1985.

Stewart, G. Tillman. "Lost Tranquility: 1861-1865." In *Henderson County,* edited by Joy Bailey Dunn, 47-55. Tennessee County History Series. Memphis: Memphis State University Press, 1979.

U.S. Congress. House of Representatives. Committee on Military Affairs. "Rebel Raid on Henderson, Tenn., in 1862." 44th Congress, 2nd Session, 2 March 1877, report no. 184.

Williams, James, and Lewis Jones, comps. *Reflections.* Henderson, Tenn.: First State Bank, 1979.

Younger, Lillye. *The History of Decatur County: Past and Present.* Southaven, Miss.: Carter, 1978.

Isler, William B. /Margaret Clark Griffis

Carroll, Rosemary F. "Margaret Clark Griffis, Plantation Teacher." *Tennessee Historical Quarterly* 26, no. 3 (Fall 1967): 295-303.

Civil War Centennial Commission of Tennessee. "15th Tennessee Infantry Regiment." In *Tennesseans in the Civil War: A Military History of Confederate and Union Units with Available Rosters of Personnel,* part 1: 205-8. Nashville: Author, 1964.

McPherson, James M. "The River War in 1862." In *Battle Cry of Freedom: The Civil War Era,* 392-427. New York: Oxford University Press, 1988.

Jackson, Andrew

Aiken, Leona Taylor. "Clover Bottom." In *Donelson, Tennessee: Its History and Landmarks,* 64-101. Kingsport, Tenn.: Kingsport Press, 1968.

Alderman, Pat. "Famous Greasy Cove Horse Race, 1788." In *Greasy Cove in Unicoi County: Authentic Folklore.* Johnson City, Tenn.: Overmountain Press, 1975.

———. "Greasy Cove Race." In *The Wonders of the Unakas in Unicoi County.* Erwin, Tenn.: Author and Erwin Business and Professional Women's Club, 1964.

Bond, Octavia Zollicoffer. "The Fiber of 'Old Hickory.'" In *Old Tales Retold; Or, Perils and Adventures of Tennessee Pioneers,* 198-213. 1907. Reprint, Nashville: Charles & Randy Elder, 1973.

Bruns, Roger. "Assassination Attempt of President Andrew Jackson." *The West Tennessee Historical Papers* 31 (October 1977): 33-43.

Burke, Pauline Wilcox. *Emily Donelson of Tennessee.* 2 vols. Richmond, Va.: Garrett & Massie, 1941, 1: 154-59, 173.

Byrum, C. Stephen. "The Cherokee Removal." In *McMinn County,* edited by Frank B. Williams Jr., 16-19. Tennessee County History Series. Memphis: Memphis State University Press, 1984.

Coke, Fletch, ed. *Dear Judge: Selected Letters of John Overton of Travellers' Rest.* Nashville: Travellers' Rest Historic Museum House, 1978.

Corlew, Robert E. "Social and Economic Life on the Frontier," and "The Young State, 1796-1821." In *Tennessee: A Short History.* 2nd ed., 106-44. Knoxville: University of Tennessee Press, 1981.

Daniels, Jonathan. "Jackson's Road." In *The Devil's Backbone: The Story of the Natchez Trace*, 200-219. New York: McGraw-Hill, 1962.

Davis, Louise Littleton. "Lincoya, Old Andy's Little Indian." In *Frontier Tales of Tennessee*, 54-58. Gretna, La.: Pelican, 1976.

———. "Politics and Pistols on the Frontier." In *More Tales of Tennessee*, 71-78. Gretna, La.: Pelican, 1978.

Dictionary of American Biography. S.v. "Blount, Willie."

Dictionary of American Biography. S.v. "Jackson, Andrew."

Ewing, James. "Sevier vs. Jackson: Tennessee's Greatest Nonduel." In *A Treasury of Tennessee Tales,* 50-52. Nashville: Rutledge Hill Press, 1985.

Galloway, Linda Bennett. "Andrew Jackson Junior." Parts 3-4. *Tennessee Historical Quarterly* 9, no. 3 (September 1950): 195-216; no. 4 (December 1950): 306-43.

Goff, Reda C. "A Physical Profile of Andrew Jackson." *Tennessee Historical Quarterly* 28 (Spring-Winter 1969): 297-309.

Goodpasture, A. V. "Genesis of the Jackson-Sevier Feud." In *Tennessee Old and New: Sesquicentenial Edition, 1796-1946*, 167-75. Nashville: Tennessee Historical Commission and Tennessee Historical Society, 1946.

Hill, George de Roulhac. "The Donelson Family." In *Nashville: A Family Town*, 1-22. Nashville: Nashville Room, Public Library of Nashville and Davidson County, 1978.

Jackson, Carlton. "Another Time, Another Place—The Attempted Assassination of President Andrew Jackson." *Tennessee Historical Quarterly* 26 (Summer 1967): 184-90.

James, Marquis. *Andrew Jackson: The Border Captain.* New York: Literary Guild, 1933.

Lawrence, Stephen S. "Tulip Grove: Neighbor to the Hermitage." *Tennessee Historical Quarterly* 26 (Spring-Winter 1967): 3-22.

Little, Thomas Vance. "A Short History of Williamson County." In *Historic Williamson County, Tennessee, Established 1799.* Brochure. Franklin, Tenn.: Williamson County Tourism Committee, n.d.

McGee, Gentry R. "Administrations of Willie Blount." In *History of Tennessee from 1663 to 1930*, revised and enlarged by C. B. Ijams, 122-30. New York: American Book, 1930.

Moore, John Trotwood, and Austin P. Foster, eds. "Administrations of Willie Blount, 1809-1815; The Creek War; and Battle of New Orleans." In *Tennessee: The Volunteer State, 1769-1923*, 1: 364-67. Nashville: S. J. Clarke, 1923.

Owsley, Harriet Chappell. "Andrew Jackson and His Ward, Andrew Jackson Donelson." *Tennessee Historical Quarterly* 41, no. 2 (Summer 1982): 124-39.

———. "The Marriages of Rachel Donelson." *Tennessee Historical Quarterly* 36, no. 4 (Winter 1977): 479-92.

Powelson, Richard. "Tennessee's 'Old Hickory' Is Subject of Smithsonian Exhibit." *Knoxville News-Sentinel*, 21 October 1990.

Remini, Robert V. *Andrew Jackson and the Course of American Empire, 1767-1821.* New York: Harper & Row, 1977.

———. *Andrew Jackson and the Course of American Freedom, 1822-1832.* New York: Harper & Row, 1981.

———. "The Final Days and Hours in the Life of General Andrew Jackson." *Tennessee Historical Quarterly* 39, no. 2 (Summer 1980): 167-77.

Rothrock, Mary U. "John Haywood, Historian of the Western Country." In *Natural and Aboriginal History of Tennessee*, by John Haywood, xi-xxvii. 1823. Reprint, Jackson, Tenn.: McCowat-Mercer Press, 1959.

Sanders, Michael O. "William Hall, Governor of Tennessee, 1829." In *Governors of Tennessee*, Vol. 1, *1790-1835*, edited by Charles W. Crawford, 179-204. Memphis: Memphis State University Press, 1979.

Smith, Reid. "Masonic Hall: Divine Words and Dying Men." In *Majestic Middle Tennessee,* 91. Prattville, Ala.: Paddle Wheel Publications, 1975.

Tennessee Presidents Trust, University of Tennessee, Knoxville. "Spotlight on Andrew Jackson." *The Legacy* 1, no. 3 (1990).

U.S. National Park Service. *Natchez Trace Parkway.* Brochure. Washington, D.C.: U.S. Department of the Interior, n.d.

Walker, Arda. "The Educational Training and Views of Andrew Jackson." *The East Tennessee Historical Society's Publications,* no. 16 (1944): 22-29.

Walker, Hugh. "The Dueling Ground." In *Tennessee Tales,* 105-7. Nashville: Aurora, 1970.

Wassam, Homer E. *The Avenging Angel of Nashville.* Philadelphia, Pa.: Dorrance, 1968.

James, Jesse

Croy, Homer. "Jesse Goes Farming in Tennessee." In *Jesse James Was My Neighbor*, 133-43. New York: Duell, Sloan & Pearce, 1949.

Garrett, Jill Knight. *A History of Humphreys County, Tennessee.* Columbia, Tenn.: Author, 1963.

Montell, William Lynwood. *Don't Go Up Kettle Creek: Verbal Legacy of the Upper Cumberland.* Knoxville: University of Tennessee Press, 1983.

Morris, Doug. "Jesse James Trip to ET Recalled." *Knoxville Journal*, 27 July 1976.

O'Steen, Neal. "The James Boys in Tennessee." *Tennessee Alumnus* 67, no. 3 (Summer 1987): 36-39.

Sanderson, Esther Sharp. "Robbery, Counterfeiting and Cheating." In *Scott County Gem of the Cumberlands*, 76-85. Huntsville, Tenn.: Author, 1974.

Jarnagin, William

Jarnagin, William. Tape-recorded interview by University of Tennessee graduate assistant John Walter for the Tennessee Folk History Project, Rutledge, Tenn., 17 August 1992.

Robinson, Jon G. "Bill Jarnagin Is Still Dealing Fords at Age 100." *Old Cars Weekly News & Marketplace*, 13 April 1995.

Jobe, Abraham

Jobe, Abraham. *Autobiography of Dr. Abraham Jobe of Elizabethton, Tennessee, Written between 1849 and 1902*. Original manuscript owned by Sophie Hunter Dixon of Durham, N.C.: Tennessee State Library and Archives, Nashville.

Street, Patty Greer. "Dr. Abraham Jobe." In *Carter County Tennessee and Its People, 1796-1993*, 176. Elizabethton, Tenn.: Carter County History Book Committee, 1993.

Johnson, Andrew

Basset, Margaret. *Profiles and Portraits of American Presidents and Their Wives*. Rev. ed. Freeport, Maine: Bond Wheelwright, 1969.

Cavender, Anthony, ed. *A Folk Medical Lexicon of South Central Appalachia*. Johnson City, Tenn.: History of Medicine Society of Appalachia, James H. Quillen College of Medicine, East Tennessee State University, 1990.

Goff, John S. "Colonel James P. T. Carter of Carter County." *Tennessee Historical Quarterly* 26, no. 4 (Winter 1967): 372-82.

Kramer, Constance. "Andrew Johnson: Private Sides of the Public Man." *Greene County (Tenn.) Bicentennial* (1983): 37-41.

Milton, George Fort. "Andrew Johnson—Man of Courage." *The East Tennessee Historical Society's Publications*, no. 3 (January 1931): 23-34.

Moore, John Trotwood, and Austin P. Foster, eds. "Thomas A. R. Nelson." In *Tennessee: The Volunteer State 1769-1923*, 2: 197-99. Nashville: S. J. Clarke, 1923.

Royall, Margaret Shaw. "The Battle of Nashville." In *Andrew Johnson—Presidential Scapegoat: A Biographical Re-Evaluation*, 44-47. New York: Exposition Press, 1958.

Templeton, Scott R. "Years of Conflict, 1860-1865." In *History of Washington County, Tennessee, 1988*, 32-40. Compiled by the Watagua Association of Genealogists—Upper East Tennessee. Johnson City, Tenn.: Watauga Association of Genealogists—Upper East Tennessee, 1988.

Thomas, Lately. *The First President Johnson: The Three Lives of the Seventeenth President of the United States of America*. New York: William Morrow, 1968.

"Thomas Nelson: Activist against Secession." *Jonesborough Herald and Tribune*, 24-26 May 1991, Special ed., 13-14.

Johnson, J. Fred

Eastman Chemical Co. *Eastman Chemical Company, 1920-1990: Years of Glory, Time of Change*. Kingsport, Tenn.: Author.

"J. Fred Johnson Dies." *Kingsport News*, 15 October 1944.

Johnson, J. Fred. Biographical file including newspaper clippings on Johnson's life and the city of Kingsport. Palmer Room, Kingsport Public Library.

Reed, John Shelton (neighbor and authority on the life of J. F. Johnson), Kingsport, Tenn. Telephone interview with author Anne Klebenow, Tennessee Folk History Project, March 1995.

Rotary Club of Kingsport. *Kingsport: City of Industries, Schools, Churches and Homes*. Kingsport, Tenn.: Author, 1937.

———. *Kingsport! Past, Present, and Future*. Kingsport, Tenn.: Author, 1977.

Wolfe, Margaret Ripley. "J. Fred Johnson, His Town, and His People: A Case Study of Class Values, the Work Ethic, and Technology in Southern Appalachia, 1916-1944." *Appalachian Journal* 7, no. 1-2 (Autumn/Winter 1979-80): 70-83.

———. "Kingsport." In *An Encyclopedia of East Tennessee*, edited by Jim Stokely and Jeff D. Johnson. Oak Ridge, Tenn.: Children's Museum of Oak Ridge, 1981.

———. *Kingsport, Tennessee: A Planned American City*. Lexington: University Press of Kentucky, 1987.

Johnson, Mordecai

Editorial. "World's Ignorance Can't Erase 'Dream,'" *Paris (Tenn.) Post-Intelligencer*, 18 January 1993.

Hailey, Jean R. "Dr. Mordecai Wyatt Johnson Dies." *Washington Post*, 11 September 1976.

Hastie, William. Biographical file, Beck Cultural Exchange Center, Knoxville.

Johnson, Mordecai. Biographical information and general-information file on Howard University. Howard University Archives, Moorland-Spingarn Research Center, Washington, D.C.

"Judge Hastie, Knox Native, Dies at 71." *Knoxville Journal*, 15 April 1976.

Mathews, John. "What an Impact One Man Made in 50 Years." *Washington Star*, 6 May 1976.

"University's President-Emeritus among Dignitaries Honored Here." *Paris (Tenn.) Post-Intelligencer*, 8 April 1972.

Ware, Gilbert. "The Signature of William Hastie." Paper presented at the Harvard Law School symposium, "William Henry Hastie: The High Mountain." 16 November 1984. Manuscript Division, Harvard Law School, Cambridge, Mass., 1989.

Weaver, Robert C. *The Crisis*, October 1976.

Jones, Casey

Hutchins, Fred L. *What Happened in Memphis*. Kingsport, Tenn.: Author, 1965.

Lee, Fred J. *Casey Jones: Epic of the American Railroad*. Kingsport, Tenn.: Southern Publishers, 1939.

Moody, James W., Jr. "Casey Jones." Edited by Robert McBride. In *Heroes of Tennessee*, edited by Billy M. Jones, 109-21. Memphis: Memphis State University Press, 1979.

Shaw, T. Clark. "The Legend of Casey Jones." *The West Tennessee Historical Society Papers* 36 (October 1982): 65-71.

Williams, Emma Inman. "The Railroads: Casey Jones in Song and Story." In *Historic Madison: The Story of Jackson and Madison County, Tennessee From the Prehistoric Moundbuilders to 1917*, 153-55. Jackson, Tenn.: Madison County Historical Society, 1946.

Jones, Samuel

Blankenship, Harold G. *History: Macon County, Tennessee*. Tompkinsville, Ky.: *Monroe County (Tenn.) Press,* 1986.

Denning, Jeanette Keith. "Good Times: Vacationing at Red Boiling Springs." *Tennessee Historical Quarterly* 42, no. 3 (Fall 1983): 223-42.

Macon County Historical Society, comp. *Macon County, Tennessee Cemeteries*. Vol. 2. Lafayette, Tenn.: Author, 1989.

Roddy, Vernon. *Thousands to Cure: On the Early Story of Red Boiling Springs, Tennessee, with Selected Supporting Materials*. Hartsville, Tenn.: Upper Country People Probe, 1991.

Walker, Hugh. "The Dueling Ground." In *Tennessee Tales*, 105-7. Nashville: Aurora, 1970.

Kefauver, Estes

Anderson, Jack, and Fred Blumenthal. *The Kefauver Story*. New York: Dial Press, 1956.

Carter, Hodding. "Hushpuppies, Stew—And Oratory: Southern Politicians Must Be Showmen, Too, but behind Their Act Is a Deadly Seriousness." *New York Times Magazine*, 18 June 1950.

Dictionary of American Biography. S.v. "Kefauver, (Carey) Estes."

Swados, Harvey. *Standing Up for the People: The Life and Work of Estes Kefauver*. New York: E. P. Dutton, 1972.

King, George W.

Culp, Frederick M. "Captain George King's Home Guard Company, CSA." *The West Tennessee Historical Society Papers* 15 (1961): 55-78.

[King, George W.] Gibson County, Tennessee. "Capt. King's Diary, 1865." Prepared by the Historical Records Survey Transcription Unit, Division of Women's and Professional Projects, Works Progress Administration in Memphis. Memphis: Historical Records Survey, 26 December 1938. Copy courtesy of Charlie King, Rutherford, Tenn.

Knox, George L.

Knox, George L. "The American Negro and His Possibilities." In *Twentieth Century Negro Literature, Or a Cyclopedia of Thought on the Vital Topics Relating to the American Negro*, edited by D. W. Culp, 454-63. 1902. Reprint, New York: Arno Press, 1969.

———. *Slave and Freeman: The Autobiography of George L. Knox*. Edited and introduction by Willard B. Gatewood Jr. Lexington: University Press of Kentucky, 1979.

Lawrence, William P.

Lawrence, William P. Biographical material from U.S. Naval Academy Public Affairs Office, Annapolis, Md.

———. Materials including biographical sketch provided by subject to Tennessee Folk History Project Archives, University of Tennessee.

———. "Our Foundation of Strength." *Foundation*, Spring 1991, 76-80.

Santoli, Al. "Operation New Wind: POW, William Lawrence." In *Everything We Had: An Oral History of the Vietnam War by Thirty-Three American Soldiers Who Fought It*, 229-46. New York: Random House, 1981.

State of Tennessee. Senate Bill No. 338. Act Designating Official State Poem. In *Public Acts of the State of Tennessee Passed by the Eighty-Eighth General Assembly, 1973*. Nashville: Curley Printing, 1973.

Lea, Luke

Dictionary of American Biography. S.v. "Lea, Luke."

Lea, Luke. "The Attempt to Capture the Kaiser." Edited by William T. Alderson. *Tennessee Historical Quarterly* 20 (1961): 222-61.

Majors, William R. "Gordon Browning and Tennessee Politics: 1937-1939." *Tennessee Historical Quarterly* 28 (Spring-Winter 1969): 57-69.

Moore, John Trotwood, and Austin P. Foster, eds. "Colonel Luke Lea." In *Tennessee: The Volunteer State, 1769-1923*, 4: 561-62. Nashville: S. J. Clarke, 1923.

Tidwell, Cromwell. "Luke Lea and the American Legion." *Tennessee Historical Quarterly* 28 (Spring-Winter 1969): 70-83.

Tidwell, Mary Louise Lea. "Preface." In *Luke Lea of Tennessee*, 1-5. Bowling Green, Ohio: Bowling Green State University Popular Press, 1993.

Lee, George Washington

"George W. Lee, 82; Was Leader of Memphis Republican Blacks." *Asheville (N.C.) Citizen-Times*, 3 August 1976.

Pink Palace Museum. "Lt. George W. Lee, 1894-1976." In *Historic Black Memphians*. Exhibit material. Memphis: Pink Palace Museum. Memphis State University Archives.

Tucker, David M. *Lieutenant Lee of Beale Street*. Nashville: Vanderbilt University Press, 1971.

Lewis, Meriwether

Bond, Octavia Zollicoffer. "On the Natchez Trace with Meriwether Lewis." In *Old Tales Retold Or, Perils and Adventures of Tennessee Pioneers*, 187-97. 1907. Reprint, Nashville: Charles & Randy Elder, 1973.

Chandler, David Leon. *The Jefferson Conspiracies: A President's Role in the Assassination of Meriwether Lewis*. New York: William Morrow, 1994.

Daniels, Jonathan. "So Strong to Die." In *The Devil's Backbone: The Story of the Natchez Trace*, 165-84. New York: McGraw-Hill, 1962.

Davidson, Donald. "Boatmen and Outlaws on the Natchez Trace." In *The Tennessee. Volume I—The Old River: Frontier to Secession,* 216-29. 1946. Reprint, with introduction by Thomas Daniel Young. Knoxville: University of Tennessee Press, 1978; Nashville: J. S. Sanders, 1991.

Moore, Frederick W. "The Death of Meriwether Lewis." *The American Historical Magazine* 9, no. 3 (July 1904): 218-30.

Riley, Michael. "Tales from the Crypt; To Solve History's Mysteries, Graveyard Sleuths Are Unearthing the Dead and Famous." *Time,* 14 September 1992, 64-65.

U.S. National Park Service. *Natchez Trace Parkway.* Brochure. Washington, D.C.: U.S. Department of the Interior, n.d.

Lindamood, Erastus R. "Ras"

Graves, Kathleen George, and Winnie Palmer McDonald, comp. and ed. *Our Union County Heritage.* 2 vols. Maynardville, Tenn.: Authors, 1981.

Wiersema, Harry. "TVA Dams." In *An Encyclopedia of East Tennessee,* edited by Jim Stokely and Jeff D. Johnson. Oak Ridge, Tenn.: Children's Museum of Oak Ridge, 1981.

Wilson, Marshall A. "Family Removals: Erastus R. Lindamood." In *Tales from the Grass Roots of TVA, 1933-1952,* 77-81. Knoxville: Author, 1982.

Little Carpenter (Attakullakulla)

Kelly, James C. "Notable Persons in Cherokee History: Attakullakulla." *Journal of Cherokee Studies* 3, no. 1 (Winter 1978): 2-34.

McGee, Gentry R. *A History of Tennessee: From 1663-1930,* revised and enlarged by C. B. Ijams. New York: American Book, 1930.

Moore, John Trotwood, and Austin P. Foster, eds. "Indian Wars and Warriors of Tennessee." In *Tennessee: The Volunteer State, 1769-1923,* 1: 157-250. Nashville: S. J. Clarke, 1923.

Satz, Ronald N. *Tennessee's Indian Peoples: From White Contact to Removal, 1540-1840.* Knoxville: University of Tennessee Press, 1979.

Stokely, Jim. "The Counsel of Caleb Starr." *Journal of Cherokee Studies* 3, no. 1 (Winter 1978): 54-56.

Louis Philippe

Beard, W. E. "French Royalty in Pioneer Nashville." In *It Happened In Nashville,* 5-6. 1912. Reprint, Nashville: Mini-Histories, 1988.

Bishop, Morris. "Louis Philippe in America." *American Heritage: The Magazine of History* 20, no. 3 (April 1969): 42-45, 90-97.

Federal Writers' Project of the Works Projects Administration. "Points of Interest: Chisholm's Tavern." In *The WPA Guide to Tennessee,* 242. 1939. Reprint, Knoxville: University of Tennessee Press, 1986.

Knoxville Gazette, 12 January 1793.

Parker, Jane Marsh. "Louis Philippe in the United States." *The Century Magazine* 62, New Series, vol. 40 (May 1901-October 1901): 746-57.

Mabry, Joseph Alexander/Thomas O'Conner

Morris, Doug. "Fusillade, 95 Years Ago, Left 3 Dead." *Knoxville Journal,* 11 October 1977.

Taylor, Jerome G., Jr. "The Extraordinary Life and Death of Joseph A. Mabry." *The East Tennessee Historical Society's Publications,* no. 44 (1972): 41-70.

Macon, "Uncle Dave"

Burns, Frank. "Depression and the Recovery: The Entertainers." In *Wilson County,* edited by Robert E. Corlew, 80-86. Tennessee County History Series. Memphis: Memphis State University Press, 1983.

Mason, Robert L. "Uncle Dave Macon." In *History of Cannon County, Tennessee,* 220-30. Murfreesboro, Tenn.: Cannon County Historical Society, 1984.

Wolfe, Charles K. *Tennessee Strings: The Story of Country Music in Tennessee.* Knoxville: University of Tennessee Press, 1981.

Wynn, Linda T. "Deford Bailey." Leaders of Afro-American Nashville Biographical Series. Edited by Tennessee State University Department of History and Geography for the Nashville Conference on Afro-American Culture and History, 1989.

Mallicoat, Milton

Cox, Connie White, ed. *Federal Census Schedule: Campbell County, Tennessee, 1900, Indexed.* Transcript. Knoxville: Author, 1984.

Gammell, Paula, and Edith W. Hutton. *Cemeteries and Tombstone Inscriptions from Campbell County, Tennessee.* 1: 32. Oak Ridge, Tenn.: Tennessee Valley Publications, 1987.

McPherson, James M. "We Are Going to be Wiped Off the Earth." In *Battle Cry of Freedom: The Civil War Era,* 774-806. New York: Oxford University Press, 1988.

Ridenour, G. L. *The Land of the Lake: A History of Campbell County, Tennessee.* LaFollette, Tenn.: LaFollette Publishing Co., 1941.

Sistler, Byron, and Barbara Sistler, ed. *1880 Census—Tennessee: Transcription for Campbell County.* Evanston, Ill.: Byron Sistler & Assoc., 1978.

———. *1890 Civil War Veterans Census—Tennessee.* Evanston, Ill.: Byron Sistler & Assoc., 1978.

Marcum, Julia

Bell, Mary Margaret. "Marcum, Julia Ann." In *The Kentucky Encyclopedia,* edited by John E. Kleber. Lexington: University Press of Kentucky, 1992.

Edwards, Joe. "Separate Peace? History Shows a Feisty Scott County." *Knoxville News-Sentinel,* 10 May 1994.

"Julia Ann Marcum." In *Whitley County, Kentucky: History and Families, 1818-1993,* 45-46. Paducah, Ky.: Turner Publishing, 1994.

Sanderson, Esther Sharp. "Guerrilla Warfare during The Civil War." *The Tennessee Valley Historical Review* 1, no. 3 (Fall 1972): 25-33.

Scott County Historical Society, eds. "William Marcum." In *Scott County Tennessee and Its Families,* 128. Huntsville, Tenn.: Author, 1988.

Massengale, Solomon

Cravens, Margaret. *The Massengales and the Pattersons.* N.p.: Humphrey Printing Co., 1975.

Fink, Paul M. *Jonesborough: The First Century of Tennessee's First Town.* Tennessee State Planning Commission. U.S. Department of Housing and Urban Development. Report no. TN-JONO-1-72-138-2, 1972.

Maury, Matthew Fontaine

Davis, Louise Littleton. "Matthew Fontaine Maury and the Seas." In *Frontier Tales of Tennessee,* 80-104. Gretna, La.: Pelican, 1976.

Dictionary of American Biography. S.v. "Maury, Matthew Fontaine."

Jahns, Patricia. "Young Mat Maury of Tennessee." In *Matthew Fontaine Maury and Joseph Henry: Scientists of the Civil War,* 11-26. New York: Hastings House, 1961.

Latham, Jean Lee. *Trail Blazer of the Seas.* Boston: Houghton Mifflin, 1956.

Moore, John Trotwood, and Austin P. Foster, eds. "Matthew Fontaine Maury." In *Tennessee: The Volunteer State, 1769-1923,* 2: 188-89. Nashville: S. J. Clarke, 1923.

Williams, Frances Leigh. *Matthew Fontaine Maury: Scientist of the Sea.* New Brunswick, N.J.: Rutgers University Press, 1963.

Mayberry, Lu

Egypt, Ophelia Settle, comp. "The Overseer Had a Bull Whip and Marster Had a Strap." In *The American Slave: A Composite Autobiography.* Vol. 18, *Unwritten History of Slavery (Fisk University),* 262-75. 1941. Reprint, edited by George P. Rawick, Westport, Conn.: Greenwood, 1972.

McConnico, Garner

Burnett, J. J. *Sketches of Tennessee's Pioneer Baptist Preachers, 1*: 359-64. 1919. Reprint with index, Johnson City: Overmountain Press, 1985.

Corlew, Robert E. "Some Aspects of Slavery in Dickson County." *Tennessee Historical Quarterly* 10, no. 4 (December 1951): 344-65.

Major, Lula Fain Moran. "Garner McConnico." Undated biographical sketch. Williamson County Historical Society, Franklin, Tenn.

Norton, Herman A. *Religion in Tennessee 1777-1945.* Knoxville: University of Tennessee Press, 1981.

McDonald, Mary Elizabeth

Armstrong, Zella. "War Sites and Scenes: A Company of Young Women." In *The History of Hamilton County and Chattanooga Tennessee,* 2: 54-55. Chattanooga: Lookout Publishing, 1940.

Brown, Fred. "Soldiers Aid Society Arrest Left History Questioning Who Were the Spartans?" *Knoxville News-Sentinel,* 30 October 1994.

Broyles, Bettye. *History of Rhea County.* N.p: Rhea County Historical Society, 1991. Photocopy supplied by Seth Tallent of the Rhea County Historical Society.

———. Private collection including "The W. G. Allen Scrapbook," unpublished manuscript which features miscellaneous Civil War correspondence; two undated photocopied clippings from the *Dayton Herald;* and miscellaneous stories from the *Athens Post* between 21 December 1860 and 22 August 1862; also undated letter from W. G. Allen to the *Dayton Herald.*

Campbell, Thomas Jefferson. "History at Haphazard." In *Records of Rhea: A Condensed County History,* 80-93. Dayton, Tenn.: Rhea Publishing Co., 1940.

———. "Steamboats in Wartime." In *The Upper Tennessee: Comprehending Desultory Records of River Operations in the Tennessee Valley, Covering a Period of One Hundred Fifty Years, Including Pen and Camera Pictures of the Hardy Craft and the Colorful Characters Who Navigated Them,* 49-56. Chattanooga: Author, 1932.

Corlew, Robert E. "The Civil War in Tennessee." In *Tennessee: A Short History.* 2nd ed., 302-27. Knoxville: University of Tennessee Press, 1981.

Govan, Gilbert E. and James W. Livingood. "Under Military Occupation." In *The Chattanooga Country, 1540-1962: From Tomahawks to TVA,* 253-80. Chapel Hill: University of North Carolina Press, 1963.

Tallent, Seth (a Rhea County historian), Spring City, Tenn. Letter to author Anne Klebenow, Tennessee Folk History Project, 27 October 1994.

McElwee, Samuel A.

Cartwright, Joseph H. "Black Legislators in Tennessee in the 1880's: A Case Study in Black Political Leadership." *Tennessee Historical Quarterly* 32, no. 3 (Fall 1973): 265-84.

———. *The Triumph of Jim Crow: Tennessee Race Relations in the 1880s.* Knoxville: University of Tennessee Press, 1976.

Couto, Richard A. *Lifting the Veil: A Political History of Struggles for Emancipation.* Knoxville: University of Tennessee Press, 1993.

McBride, Robert M., and Dan M. Robison. "McElwee, Samuel Allen." In *Biographical Directory of the Tennessee General Assembly.* Vol. 2, *1861-1901,* edited by Robert M. McBride. Nashville: Tennessee State Library and Archives and the Tennessee Historical Commission, 1979.

"A Remarkable Negro." *Nashville Daily American,* 9 June 1888.

McGavock, "Carrie"

Aiken, Leona Taylor. *The Descendants of James McGavock, Sr. and the McGavock Mansions: Fort Chiswell, Va. and Carnton, Franklin, Tenn.* Pamphlet. Rogersville, Tenn.: East Tennessee Printing Co., 1986.

Carnton Association, Inc. "Carnton Plantation Information." Typescript. Franklin, Tenn.: Author.

Carter, Rosalie. *Visit the Carter House.* Brochure. Franklin, Tenn.: Carter House Assn., 1961.

Clemmons, Ronald T. "The Death of General John Adams." *The Brigadier* 1, no. 1 (Winter 1991). Murfreesboro, Tenn.: Franklin Memorial Assn.

Faust, Patricia L., ed. "Quarles, William Andrew." In *Historical Times: Illustrated Encyclopedia of the Civil War.* New York: Harper & Row, 1986.

"Good Samaritan at Franklin." *Confederate Veteran* 30 (December 1922): 448.

Little, Thomas Vance. "A Short History of Williamson County." In *Historic Williamson County, Tennessee, Established 1799.* Brochure. Franklin, Tenn.: Williamson County Tourism Committee, n.d.

McBride, Robert M. "The 'Confederate Sins' of Major Cheairs." *Tennessee Historical Quarterly* 23 (March-December 1964): 121-35.

McDonough, James Lee, and Thomas L. Connelly. *Five Tragic Hours: The Battle of Franklin.* Knoxville: University of Tennessee Press, 1983.

McGavock, Carrie. Biographical file including newspaper death notice, "Beautiful Christian Character Called Home"; "The Good Samaritan of Williamson County," an undated transcript of articles in the *Williamson County News,* 12 January 1922; and "Mrs. McGavock," an undated biographical sketch by Mrs. S. E. F. Rose. Williamson County Historical Society, Franklin, Tenn.

Moore, John Trotwood, and Austin P. Foster, eds. "General John Adams." In *Tennessee: The Volunteer State 1769-1923,* 2: 9-10. Nashville: S. J. Clarke, 1923.

Riley, Harris D., Jr. "A Gallant Adopted Son of Tennessee—General John C. Carter, C. S. A." *Tennessee Historical Quarterly* 48, no. 4 (Winter 1989): 195-208.

Sifakis, Stewart. "Quintard, Charles Todd (1824-1898)." In *Who Was Who in the Civil War,* 527. New York: Facts on File, 1988.

Smith, Reid. "Rippavilla." In *Majestic Middle Tennessee.* 59. Prattville, Ala.: Paddle Wheel Publications, 1975.

McKissack, Moses III/Leatrice McKissack

Gite, Lloyd. "Like Mother, Like Daughter." *Black Enterprise,* August 1991, 93-96.

"Leatrice McKissack: Enterprising Entrepreneur." *Nashville Business and Lifestyles,* November 1990.

Peck, Jeanne. "Architecture Firm, CEO, Ex-Teacher, Began at Square 1." *Nashville Banner,* 7 December 1990.

Wynn, Linda T. "Building Tennessee: The Story of the McKissacks." *The Courier* [Tennessee Historical Commission], 16, no. 1 (October 1977): 4-6.

———. "McKissack and McKissack." Leaders of Afro-American Nashville Biographical Series. Edited by Tennessee State University Department of History and Geography for the Nashville Conference on Afro-American Culture and History, 1985.

McLemore, John Christmas

Coppock, Paul R. "The Fourth Founder." In *Memphis Sketches,* 91-95. Memphis: Friends of Memphis and Shelby County Libraries, 1976.

Downing, Marvin. "An Admiring Nephew-in-Law: John Christmas McLemore and His Relationship to 'Uncle' Andrew Jackson." *The West Tennessee Historical Society Papers* 44 (December 1990): 38-47.

Glasgow, Mary Ellen. "Christmasville." *The Tennessee Magazine* 30, no. 12 (December 1987): 16-21.

Howard, Memucan Hunt. "Recollections of Memucan Hunt Howard." *The American Historical Magazine* 7, no. 1 (January 1901): 55-68.

McLemore family Bible. General family information. Carroll County's Gordon Browning Museum and Library, McKenzie, Tenn.

Meigs, Return Jonathan

Campbell, T. J. "Hiwassee Garrison." In *Records of Rhea: A Condensed County History,* 41-50. Dayton, Tenn.: Rhea Publishing Co., 1940.

Malone, Henry T. "Return Jonathan Meigs: Indian Agent Extraordinary." *The East Tennessee Historical Society's Publications,* no. 28 (1956): 3-22.

Moore, John Trotwood, and Austin P. Foster, eds. "Return J. Meigs." In *Tennessee: The Volunteer State, 1769-1923,* 2: 189-90. Nashville: S. J. Clarke, 1923.

Wooten, John Morgan. "The Cherokee Indians in Bradley County History" and "War Record: Return Jonathan Meigs." In *A History of Bradley County,* 41-65, 184-85. Bradley County American Legion Post 81 in cooperation with the Tennessee Historical Commission, 1949.

Meriwether, Elizabeth Avery

Blain, Virginia, Patricia Clements, and Isobel Grundy. "Meriwether, Elizabeth (Avery)." In *The Feminist Companion to Literature in English: Women Writers from the Middle Ages to the Present,* 733-34. London: B. T. Batsford, 1990.

Bridges, Elinor B. "A Woman to Guide All of My Years." In *Tennessee Women, Past and Present,* narrative by Wilma Dykeman and edited by Carol Lynn Yellin, 27-28. Memphis: Tennessee Committee for the Humanities and Tennessee International Women's Decade Coordinating Committee, 1977.

Coppock, Paul R. "Mid-South Memoirs: A Fighting Daughter of the South." *Memphis Commercial-Appeal,* 7 June 1981.

Culpepper, Marilyn Mayer. *Trials and Triumphs: Women of the American Civil War.* East Lansing: Michigan State University Press, 1991.

Kaufman, Janet E. "Elizabeth Avery Meriwether." In *American Woman Writers,* edited by Langdon Lynne Faust, 2: 40-41. New York: Frederick Ungar, 1983.

Meriwether, Elizabeth Avery. *Recollections of 92 Years: 1824-1916.* Nashville: Tennessee Historical Commission, 1958.

Scott, Anne Firor. *The Southern Lady: From Pedestal to Politics, 1830-1930.* Chicago: University of Chicago Press, 1970.

Wedell, Marsha. *Elite Women and the Reform Impulse in Memphis, 1875-1915.* Knoxville: University of Tennessee Press, 1991.

Miles, Emma Bell

Gaston, Kay Baker. "Emma Bell Miles." In *An Encyclopedia of East Tennessee*, edited by Jim Stokely and Jeff D. Johnson. Oak Ridge, Tenn.: Children's Museum of Oak Ridge, 1981.

———. "Emma Bell Miles and the 'Fountain Square' Conversations." *Tennessee Historical Quarterly* 37, no. 4 (Winter 1978): 416-29.

Miles, Emma Bell. *The Spirit of the Mountains*. 1905. Reprint, Knoxville: University of Tennessee Press, 1988.

Rowell, Adelaide. "Emma Bell Miles, Artist, Author, and Poet of the Tennessee Mountains." *Tennessee Historical Quarterly* 25, no. 1 (Spring 1966): 77-89.

Moon, Virginia "Miss Ginger"

"A Confederate Woman Spy." *Confederate Veteran* 34 (1926): 45-46.

McIlwaine, Shields. "'Miss Ginny' Moon: Something Old, Something New." In *Memphis: Down in Dixie*, 260-65. New York: E. P Dutton, 1948.

McPherson, James M. "After Four Years of Failure." In *Battle Cry of Freedom: The Civil War Era*, 751-73. New York: Oxford University Press, 1988.

Smith, Ophia D. "The Incorrigible 'Miss Ginger.'" *The West Tennessee Historical Society Papers* 9 (1955): 93-118.

Moore, Ella Sheppard

Beasley, Kay. "Fisk Jubilee Singers." Leaders of Afro-American Nashville Biographical Series. Edited by Tennessee State University Department of History and Geography for the Nashville Conference on Afro-American Culture and History, 1990.

Bragg, Emma W. "Georgia Gordon Taylor." Leaders of Afro-American Nashville Biographical Series. Edited by Tennessee State University Department of History and Geography for the Nashville Conference on Afro-American Culture and History, 1991.

Howse, Beth. "Ella Sheppard (Moore), 1851-1914." Leaders of Afro-American Nashville Biographical Series. Edited by Tennessee State University Department of History and Geography for the Nashville Conference on Afro-American Culture and History, 1987.

Moore, Ella Sheppard. *Before Emancipation*. New York: American Missionary Association, n.d.

Pike, G. D. *The Jubilee Singers and their Campaign for Twenty Thousand Dollars*. Boston: Lee & Shepard Publishers, 1873.

Wynn, Linda T. "John W. Work III, 1901-1967." Leaders of Afro-American Nashville Biographical Series. Edited by Tennessee State University Department of History and Geography for the Nashville Conference on Afro-American Culture and History, 1990.

Morgan, John Hunt

Conklin, Forrest. "Footnotes on the Death of John Hunt Morgan." *Tennessee Historical Quarterly* 35, no. 4 (Winter 1976): 376-88.

Ramage, James A. "Morgan, John Hunt." In *The Kentucky Encyclopedia*, edited by John E. Kleber. Lexington: University Press of Kentucky, 1992.

———. *Rebel Raider: The Life of General John Hunt Morgan*. Lexington: University Press of Kentucky, 1986.

Scott, Samuel W., and Samuel P. Angel. *History of the Thirteenth Regiment, Tennessee Volunteer Cavalry, U.S.A.* Philadelphia, Pa.: P. W. Ziegler, n.d.

University of Tennessee. "Some Notable Acquisitions: The Colonel William W. Ward Diary." *Library Development Report, 1982-83*. Knoxville: University of Tennessee Library, 3-4.

Murrell, John A.

Davidson, Donald. "Boatmen and Outlaws on the Natchez Trace." In *The Tennessee. Volume I—The Old River: Frontier to Secession*, 216-29. 1946. Reprint with introduction by Thomas Daniel Young. Southern Classics Series. Knoxville: University of Tennessee Press, 1978; Nashville: J. S. Sanders, 1991.

Penick, James Lal, Jr. "John A. Murrell: A Legend of the Old Southwest." *Tennessee Historical Quarterly* 48, no. 3 (Fall 1989): 174-83.

Walton, Augustus Q. *A History of the Detection, Conviction, Life and Designs of John A. Murel, the Great Western Land Pirate*. Pamphlet. 1835.

Williams, Emma Inman. "John A. Murrell, the Outlaw." In *Historic Madison: The Story of Jackson and Madison County Tennessee from the Prehistoric Moundbuilders to 1917*, 237-44. Jackson, Tenn.: Madison County Historical Society, 1946.

Napier, James Carroll

Clark, Herbert L. "James C. Napier 1845-1940." Leaders of Afro-American Nashville Biographical Series. Compiled by Tennessee State University Department of History and Geography for the Nashville Conference on Afro-American Culture and History, 1983.

———. "James Carroll Napier: National Negro Leader." *Tennessee Historical Quarterly* 49, no. 4 (Winter 1990): 243-52.

Easley, Billy. "J. C. Napier Was Founder of Citizens Savings Bank." *Nashville Sunday Tennessean*, 2 March 1988.

Lamon, Lester C. *Black Tennesseans, 1900-1930*. Knoxville: University of Tennessee Press, 1977.

———. *Blacks in Tennessee, 1791-1970*. Knoxville: University of Tennessee Press, 1981.

Lovett, Bobby L. "Benjamin 'Pap' Singleton." Leaders of Afro-American Nashville Biographical Series. Compiled by Tennessee State University Department of History and Geography for the Nashville Conference on Afro-American Culture and History, 1990.

Low, W. Augustus, ed. "Washington, Booker Taliaferro." In *Encyclopedia of Black America*. New York: McGraw-Hill, 1981.

McDougald, Lois C., and Bobby L. Lovett. "Tennessee State University." Leaders of Afro-American Nashville Biographical Series. Compiled by Tennessee State University Department of History and Geography for the Nashville Conference on Afro-American Culture and History, 1984.

Wynn, Linda T. "Citizens Savings Bank and Trust Company." Leaders of Afro-American Nashville Biographical Series. Compiled by Tennessee State University Department of History and Geography for the Nashville Conference on Afro-American Culture and History, 1985.

Neyland, Robert R. "The General"

Conkin, Paul K. *Gone with the Ivy: A Biography of Vanderbilt University*. Knoxville: University of Tennessee Press, 1985.

Evers, John L. "McGugin, Daniel E. 'Dan.'" In *Biographical Dictionary of American Sports: Football*, edited by David L. Porter. Westport, Conn.: Greenwood, 1987.

Gilbert, Bob. *Neyland: The Gridiron General*. Savannah, Ga.: Golden Coast Publishing, 1990.

Gilbert, Daniel R. "Neyland, Robert Reese, Jr. 'Bob' 'The General.'" In *Biographical Dictionary of American Sports: Football*, edited by David L. Porter. Westport, Conn.: Greenwood, 1987.

Ochs, Adolph S.

Dictionary of American Biography. S.v. "Ochs, Adolph Simon."

Dictionary of American Biography. S.v. "Ochs, Julius."

Govan, Gilbert E., and James W. Livingood. "Adolph S. Ochs: The Boy Publisher." *The East Tennessee Historical Society's Publications*, no. 17 (1945): 84-104.

———. "A New Spokesman." In *The Chattanooga Country, 1540-1976: From Tomahawks to TVA*. 3rd ed., rev. and updated by James W. Livingood, 313-37. Knoxville: University of Tennessee Press, 1977.

Johnson, Gerald W. *An Honorable Titan: A Biographical Study of Adolph S. Ochs*. Westport, Conn.: Greenwood, 1970.

Livingood, James W. *Chattanooga: An Illustrated History*. Woodland Hills, Calif.: Windsor, 1980.

"Mr. Milton Ochs Buys Nashville American." *Confederate Veteran* 17 (1909): 158.

Offield Brothers

Aiken, Leona Taylor, ed. "Letters of the Offield Brothers, Confederate Soldiers from Upper East Tennessee." *The East Tennessee Historical Society's Publications*, no. 46 (1974): 116-25.

Holston Territory Genealogical Society. *Families and History of Sullivan County, Tennessee*. Vol. 1, *1779-1992*, 295. Kingsport, Tenn.: Author, 1992.

U.S. Census Bureau 1850. Sullivan County, Tenn.

Oliver, John Walter

Dunn, Durwood. *Cades Cove: The Life and Death of an Appalachian Community, 1818-1937*. Knoxville: University of Tennessee Press, 1988.

Oliver, Hugh R., and Margaret T. Oliver. *Sketches of the Olivers: A Family History, 1726-1966*. Pinehurst, N.C.: Authors, 1987.

Overton, John/John Overton Jr.

McNeilly, J. H. *Memorial: Colonel John Overton and Mrs. Harriet Maxwell Overton*. Privately published, N.p., n.d. Held by University of Tennessee Library, Knoxville.

Moore, John Trotwood, and Austin P. Foster, eds. "Administration of Joseph McMinn, 1815-1821" and "John Overton." In *Tennessee: The Volunteer State, 1769-1923*, 1: 368-94; 2: 201-2. Nashville: S. J. Clarke, 1923.

Roper, James. *The Founding of Memphis, 1818-1820*. Memphis: Author under the auspices of the Memphis Sesquicentennial, Inc., 1970.

Pearl, Minnie (Sarah Ophelia Colley Cannon)

Pearl, Minnie, with Joan Dew. *Minnie Pearl: An Autobiography*. New York: Simon & Schuster, 1980.

Stambler, Irwin, and Grelun Landon. "Pearl, Minnie." In *The Encyclopedia of Folk, Country & Western Music*. 2nd ed. New York: St. Martin's, 1983.

Wolfe, Charles K. *Tennessee Strings: The Story of Country Music Tennessee*. Knoxville: University of Tennessee Press, 1981.

Pennington, James Jackson

Anderson, William T., and Robert M. McBride, eds. "3 F 35—James J. Pennington." In *Tennessee Historical Markers Erected by the Tennessee Historical Commission*, 169. Nashville: Tennessee Historical Commission, 1962.

Brooks, Cora Davis. "Murrel." In *Tennessee Records of Hamblen County: History of Morristown, 1786-1936*. Prepared by the Historical Records Survey Unit, Division of Professional and Service Projects. Nashville: Works Projects Administration, 18 July 1940.

Carter, Judy. "Panther Springs: Beautiful Countryside Was Setting for Founding County and a Flying Machine." *Morristown (Tenn.) Citizens Tribune*, 29 June 1986.

Clarke, Basil. "The Siege of Paris Ushers in the Air Age." In *The History of Airships*, 31-36. New York: St. Martin's, 1961.

Combs, Harry. *Kill Devil Hill: Discovering the Secret of the Wright Brothers*. Boston: Houghton Mifflin, 1979.

Dwiggins, Don. "Yankee Doodlers." In *Man-Powered Aircraft*, 163-74. Modern Aircraft Series. Blue Ridge Summit, Pa.: TAB Books, 1979.

Hamblen County Centennial Celebration Committee. "Panther Springs: An Early Settlement." In *Historic Hamblen, 1870-1970*, 78-80. Morristown, Tenn.: Author, 1970.

Moles, Becky Jo Weesner. "Melville Milton Murrell." In *An Encyclopedia of East Tennessee*, edited by Jim Stokely and Jeff D. Johnson. Oak Ridge, Tenn.: Children's Museum of Oak Ridge, 1981.

"Murrell 'Flying Machine' Dedicated at Ohio Museum." Morristown (Tenn.) *Gazette Mail*, 13 October 1964.

Pennington, James Jackson. Biographical file including newspaper clippings; *Lawrence County Historical Society Bulletins*; general family history in "The Penningtons of Big Buffalo" by Ruth Dickey (which includes a drawing of Pennington's flying machine); and *Lawrence County, Tennessee: A Leader in Aviation* by Lawrence County historian Kathy Niedergeses, July 1995. Lawrence County Archives, Lawrenceburg, Tenn.

Swint, H. L., and D. E. Mohler. "Eugene F. Falconnett, Soldier, Engineer, Inventor." *Tennessee Historical Quarterly* 21, no. 3 (September 1962): 219-34.

Pickens, Lucy Holcombe

Burton, Orville Vernon. "The White Family and Antebellum Social Structure: Southern Womanhood." In *In My Father's House Are Many Mansions: Family and Community in Edgefield, South Carolina*, 123-36. Chapel Hill: University of North Carolina Press, 1985.

De Berry, John H. "La Grange—La Belle Village." *Tennessee Historical Quarterly* 30, no. 2 (Summer 1971): 133-53.

Dictionary of American Biography. S.v. "Pickens, Francis Wilkinson."

Fuller, Claud E. "Mrs. Lucy Holcombe Pickens." In *Confederate Currency and Stamps 1861-1865: Official Acts of Congress Authorizing Their Issue*, 48-49. Nashville: Parthenon Press, 1949.

Greer, Jack Thorndyke. *Leaves from a Family Album [Holcombe and Greer]*. Edited by Jane Judge Greer. Waco, Tex.: Texian Press, 1975.

Pickens family. Biographical file including newspaper clippings on Lucy Pickens and Francis W. Pickens. Old Edgefield District Archives, Edgefield, S. C.

Polk, James K.

Arnold, James R. *Presidents under Fire: Commanders in Chief in Victory and Defeat*. New York: Orion Books, 1994.

Clifft, Warner Wardell. "Early History of Hardeman County, Tennessee." Masters Thesis, George Peabody College for Teachers, Nashville, Tenn., 1930.

McCormac, Eugene Irving. *James K. Polk: A Political Biography*. 1922. Reprint, New York: Russell & Russell, 1965.

McCoy, Charles A. *Polk and the Presidency*. Austin: University of Texas Press, 1960.

Nelson, Anson, and Fanny Nelson. *Memorials of Sarah Childress Polk*. 1892. Reprint, Spartanburg, S. C.: The Reprint Co, 1974.

Sellers, Charles Grier, Jr. *James K. Polk, Continentalist, 1843-1846*. Princeton, N.J.: Princeton University Press, 1966.

———. *James K. Polk, Jacksonian, 1795-1843*. Princeton, N.J.: Princeton University Press, 1957.

Washburn, Clara Bracken. "Some Aspects of the 1844 Presidential Campaign in Tennessee." *Tennessee Historical Quarterly* 4 (March-December 1945): 58-74.

West, Earl Irvin. "Religion in the Life of James K. Polk." *Tennessee Historical Quarterly* 26, no. 4 (Winter 1967): 357-71.

Polk, Leonidas

Catton, Bruce. *Never Call Retreat: Centennial History of the Civil War*. Vol. 3. Garden City, N.Y.: Doubleday, 1965.

Dictionary of American Biography. S.v. "Polk, Leonidas."

Dosch, Donald F. "The Hornets' Nest at Shiloh." *Tennessee Historical Quarterly* 37, no. 2 (Summer 1978): 175-89.

Moore, John Trotwood, and Austin P. Foster, eds. "Bishop Leonidas Polk." In *Tennessee: The Volunteer State, 1769-1923*, 2: 215. Nashville: S. J. Clarke, 1923.

Parks, Joseph H. *General Leonidas Polk, C.S.A.: The Fighting Bishop*. Baton Rouge: Louisiana State University Press, 1962.

Sword, Wiley. *The Battle of Shiloh*. Harrisburg, Pa.: Historical Times, Eastern Acorn Press, 1987.

Walker, T. J. "Reminiscences of the Civil War." Edited by Russell B. Bailey. *Confederate Chronicles of Tennessee* 1 (June 1986): 37-74.

Yeatman, Trezevant Player, Jr. "St. John's—A Plantation Church of the Old South." *Tennessee Historical Quarterly* 10, no. 1 (March-December 1951): 334-43.

Polk, Margaret

Balloch, Jim. "Pilot Recalls Engaging 'Belle' Saga." *Knoxville News-Sentinel*, 21 October 1990.

Beifuss, John. "The Belle." *Memphis Commercial Appeal*, 15 May 1987.

Coppock, Paul R. "The Memphis Belle." In *Memphis Sketches*, 212-16. Memphis: Friends of Memphis and Shelby County Libraries, 1976.

Duerksen, Menno. "Memphis Belle Revisited—And Memories Are Stirred." *Memphis Press-Scimitar*, 27 July 1967.

Horne, Joan. "Time Dulls Sharp Edges of History." *Memphis Commercial Appeal*, 16 April 1977.

Porteous, Clark. "Repainting of Petty Girl Is First Business of Belle's Crew." *Memphis Commercial Appeal*, 8 September 1961.

Sorrells, John. "Crew of Belle Enjoys Bull Session—18 Years Old." *Memphis Commercial Appeal*, 9 September 1961.

Presley, Elvis

Cobb, James C. "The Blues Is a Lowdown Shakin' Chill." In *The Most Southern Place on Earth: The Mississippi Delta and the Roots of Regional Identity*, 277-305. New York: Oxford University Press, 1992.

Elvis Presley Enterprises, Inc. *Graceland Express* 7, no. 3 (1992). Memphis: Elvis Presley Enterprises, Inc.

Marsh, Dave. *Elvis*. New York: A Rolling Stone Press Book, 1982.

Presley, Vester. *A Presley Speaks*. Memphis: Wimmer Bros., 1978.

Quinn, Father D. A.

Church News: The Episcopal Church in West Tennessee 1, no. 6, (September 1986). Contains "Episcopal Laymen Also Served" and "Other Christians Who Served," by Patricia M. LaPointe; "Martyrdom Is upon Us," by Belinda Snyder; "The Martyrs of Memphis" and "Letter from an Episcopal Mother to Her Newborn Daughter," by Franklin N. Wright. Tennessee Folk History Project Archives, University of Tennessee. Courtesy of History Department, Memphis and Shelby County Public Library and Information Center.

Crawford, Charles W. "Decades of Disaster: War, Reconstruction and Plague." In *Yesterday's Memphis*, 29-52. Seemann's Historic Cities Series, no. 25. Miami: E. A. Seemann, 1976.

Keating, J. M. *A History of the Yellow Fever: The Yellow Fever Epidemic of 1878 in Memphis, Tenn.* Memphis: Howard Assn., 1879.

Quinn, D. A. *Autobiography.* Pamphlet. N.p.:Author, 1909. Tennessee Folk History Project Archives, University of Tennessee. Copy courtesy of the Diocese of Providence, R.I.

———. Biographical file including a biography of Quinn; a letter from Quinn to T. S. Byrne, 14 April 1894; and a letter from Rev. Bernard J. Canning, archivist of Diocese of Paisley, Scotland, to the Rev. Archivist, Diocese of Providence, R.I., 8 November 1985, regarding the activities of Rev. D. A. Quinn. Diocese of Nashville Archives, Catholic Center.

———. *Heroes and Heroines of Memphis, or Reminiscences of the Yellow Fever Epidemics That Afflicted the City of Memphis during the Autumn Months of 1873, 1878 and 1879.* Providence, R.I.: E. L. Freeman & Son, 1887.

White, Mimi. "Yellow Fever." *Memphis Commercial Appeal*, 31 October 1978. Special supplement.

Wright, Franklin. "Annie Cook: 'The Mary Magdalene of Memphis.'" *The West Tennessee Historical Society Papers*, no. 43 (December 1989): 44-54.

Raht, Julius Eckhardt

Barclay, R. E. *Ducktown, Back in Raht's Time.* Chapel Hill: University of North Carolina Press, 1946.

Lillard, Roy G. "The Copper Mines." In *An Encyclopedia of East Tennessee*, edited by Jim Stokely and Jeff D. Johnson. Oak Ridge, Tenn.: Children's Museum of Oak Ridge, 1981.

Ramsey, J. G. M.

Brown, Fred. "Scrapbook Tells the Story: J. G. M. Ramsey Was One of State's First Historians." *Knoxville News-Sentinel*, 18, January 1994.

Culpepper, Marilyn Mayer. *Trials and Triumphs: Women of the American Civil War.* East Lansing: Michigan State University Press, 1991.

Masterson, W. H. "Biographical Introduction." In *The Annals of Tennessee to the End of the Eighteenth Century* by Dr. J. G. M. Ramsey, xiii-xxix. 1853. Reprint., East Tennessee Historical Society, Kingsport, Tenn.: Kingsport Press, 1967.

Moore, John Trotwood, and Austin P. Foster, eds. "Dr. J. G. M. Ramsey." In *Tennessee: The Volunteer State, 1769-1923*, 2: 217-18. Nashville: S. J. Clarke, 1923.

Ramsey, J. G. M. *Dr. J. G. M. Ramsey: Autobiography and Letters.* Edited by William B. Hesseltine. Nashville: Tennessee Historical Commission, 1954.

Ramsey, Margaret Russell

Creekmore, Betsey Beeler. "The Distaff Side." In *Knoxville*, 178-203. Knoxville: University of Tennessee Press, 1958.

Harkness, David J. "Margaret Ramsey Was among Our Most Interesting People." *Knoxville News-Sentinel*, 2 November 1988.

———. "The Ramseys: First Family of Knoxville." *Old Knoxville* 1, no. 2 (1993): 10-12.

Herndon, Mary. "Margaret Ramsey Was Mother of ET Business Men, Cultural Leaders." *Knoxville Journal*, 12 May 1972.

Ramsey, Dr. J. G. M. *Dr. J. G. M. Ramsey: Autobiography and Letters.* Edited by William B. Hesseltine. Nashville: Tennessee Historical Commission, 1954.

Read, Opie

Durham, Walter T., and James W. Thomas. *A Pictorial History of Sumner County, Tennessee, 1786-1986.* Gallatin: Sumner County Historical Society, 1986.

Federal Writers' Project of the Works Projects Administration. "Writers of Tennessee." In *The WPA Guide to Tennessee*, 145-54. 1939. Reprint, Knoxville: University of Tennessee Press, 1986.

Harlow, Alvin F. "Chautauqua Movement." In *Dictionary of American History.* Rev. ed. Vol. 2. New York: Charles Scribner's Sons, 1976.

Morris, Robert L. *Opie Read: American Humorist.* New York: Helios Books, 1965.

Read, Opie. *I Remember.* New York: Richard R. Smith, 1930.

"Sumner County Sesqui-Centennial, 1787-1937." Souvenir book. N.p, 1937.

Reed (a Slave)

Egypt, Ophelia Settle, comp. "Slaves Have No Souls." In *The American Slave: A Composite Autobiography.* Vol. 18: *Unwritten History of Slavery (Fisk University)*, 43-52. 1941. Reprint, edited by George P. Rawick, Westport, Conn.: Greenwood, 1972.

Rees, David Nelson

"David Nelson Reese [*sic*]." *Confederate Veteran* 37, no. 4 (April 1931): 147.

Reynolds, Rose E. (granddaughter of D. N. Rees), Johnson City, Tenn. Rees family information, including "Family Memoirs" (unpublished autobiographical material by D. N. Rees) provided to Tennessee Folk History Project Archives, University of Tennessee.

Tipton, W. Hord, Sr. *The Tipton Family History.* Mt. Sterling, Ky.: Author, 1948. Held by McClung Collection, Knox County Library System.

Rice, Grantland

Brownlow, Louis. "Brief Returns to Nashville and Louisville." In *A Passion for Politics: The Autobiography of Louis Brownlow,* 312-28. Chicago: University of Chicago Press, 1955.

Fountain, Charles. *Sportswriter: The Life and Times of Grantland Rice.* New York: Oxford University Press, 1993.

Hickok, Ralph. "Rice, H. Grantland." In *The Encyclopedia of North American Sports History.* New York: Facts on File, 1992.

Inabinett, Mark. *Grantland Rice and His Heroes: The Sportswriter as Mythmaker in the 1920s.* Knoxville: University of Tennessee Press, 1994.

Rice, Grantland. *The Tumult and the Shouting: My Life in Sport.* 1954. New illus. ed., New York: A. S. Barnes, 1963.

Riley, Bob

Langford, Rachel Riley (daughter of B. Riley). Tape-recorded interview about family experiences, conducted by the Tennessee State Parks Folk Life Project for the Tennessee Department of Conservation, 1981. Tapes 81-SS-8 and 81-SS-23. Tennessee State Library and Archives, Nashville.

Montell, William Lynwood. "In the Woods and on the River." In *Don't Go Up Kettle Creek: Verbal Legacy of the Upper Cumberland,* 83-127. Knoxville: University of Tennessee Press, 1983.

Overstreet, Ken, as told to him by Charles P. Gray. "The Saga of Robert Robinson (Uncle Bob) Riley." *Celina (Tenn.) Clay Statesman,* 30 September 1971.

Teeples, Betty (descendant of Bob Riley) of Celina, Tenn. Newspaper clippings and biographical information sent to Tennessee Folk History Project Archives, University of Tennessee.

Robertson, James

Bond, Octavia Zollicoffer. "The Battle of the Bluffs." In *Old Tales Retold Or, Perils and Adventures of Tennessee Pioneers,* 123-33. 1907. Reprint, Nashville: Charles and Randy Elder, 1973.

Dixon, Max. *The Wataugans.* Johnson City, Tenn.: Overmountain Press, 1989.

History of Tennessee, Illustrated. 1887, Goodspeed Publishing. Reprint, with new material by S. Emmett Lucas Jr., Easley, S. C.: Southern Historical Press, 1979.

Kirke, Edmund. "On the Outposts—1780." *Harper's New Monthly Magazine* 76, no. 453 (February 1888): 420-26.

Moore, John Trotwood, and Austin P. Foster, eds. "The Cumberland Settlement," "Indian Wars and Warriors of Tennessee," and "Gen. James Robertson." In *Tennessee: The Volunteer State, 1769-1923,* 1: 102-17, 157-250; 2: 223-24. Nashville: S. J. Clarke, 1923.

Robertson, Sterling C.

Harllee, William Curry. *Kinfolks.* Vol. 3. New Orleans: Searcy & Pfaff, 1937.

McLean, Malcolm, comp. and ed. *Papers Concerning Robertson's Colony in Texas.* 18 vols. Vols. 1-3, Fort Worth: Texas Christian University Press, 1974-1976. Vols. 4-18, Arlington, Tex.: University of Texas at Arlington, 1977-1993.

Thrall, Rev. Homer S. *A Pictorial History of Texas.* St. Louis: N. D. Thompson, 1879.

Rogan, Hugh

Driver, Steve. "History of Sumner County." In *Sumner County Historic Homes.* Brochure. Gallatin, Tenn.: Sumner County Historical Society.

Walker, Hugh. "The Raw Irishman." In *Tennessee Tales,* 161-67. Nashville: Aurora, 1970.

Ross, Chief John

Anderson, Lee. *Chattanooga's Story.* Brochure. Chattanooga: Chattanooga Area Convention and Visitors Bureau.

Brown, John P. *Old Frontiers: The Story of the Cherokee Indians from Earliest Times to the Date of Their Removal to the West, 1838.* Kingsport, Tenn.: Southern Publishers, 1938.

Byrum, C. Stephen. "The Cherokee Removal." In *McMinn County,* edited by Frank B. Williams Jr., 16-19. Tennessee County History Series. Memphis: Memphis State University Press, 1984.

Foreman, Grant. *Indian Removal: The Emigration of the Five Civilized Tribes of Indians.* Norman: University of Oklahoma Press, 1953.

Govan, Gilbert E., and James W. Livingood. "The Trail Where They Cried." In *The Chattanooga Country, 1540-1962: From Tomahawks to TVA,* 75-98. Chapel Hill: University of North Carolina Press, 1963.

Moore, John Trotwood, and Austin P. Foster, eds. "John Ross." In *Tennessee: The Volunteer State, 1769-1923,* 2: 224-25. Nashville: S. J. Clarke, 1923.

Moulton, Gary E. "Cherokee Impasse." In *John Ross: Cherokee Chief,* 54-71. Athens: University of Georgia Press, 1978.

Satz, Ronald N. *Tennessee's Indian Peoples: From White Contact to Removal, 1540-1840.* Knoxville: University of Tennessee Press, 1979.

Wooten, John Morgan. *A History of Bradley County.* Bradley County Post 81 of the American Legion in cooperation with the Tennessee Historical Commission, 1949.

Rucker, Edmund W.

Catton, Bruce. "His Almost Chosen People." In *Never Call Retreat: Centennial History of the Civil War,* 3: 396-470. Garden City, N.Y.: Doubleday, 1965.

Evans, Clement A., ed. "Additional Biographical Sketches: Colonel Edmund W. Rucker." In *Confederate Military History.* Vol. 8, *Tennessee,* 691-92. Atlanta: Confederate Publishing Co., 1899.

"Gen. Edmund W. Rucker." *Confederate Veteran* 32, no. 5 (May 1924): 163-64.

Horn, Stanley F. *The Decisive Battle of Nashville*. Baton Rouge: Louisiana State University Press, 1991.

Sifakis, Stewart. "Rucker, Edmund Winchester." In *Who Was Who in the Civil War*. New York: Facts on File, 1988.

Sword, Wiley. *Embrace an Angry Wind—The Confederacy's Last Hurrah: Spring Hill, Franklin, and Nashville*. New York: HarperCollins, 1992.

U.S. Congress. "Spalding, George." *Biographical Directory of the United States Congress, 1774-1989*. Senate doc. 100-34. Washington, D.C.: U.S. Government Printing Office, 1989.

Wills, Brian Steel. *A Battle from the Start: The Life of Nathan Bedford Forrest*. New York: HarperCollins, 1992.

Rudolph, Wilma

Haley, Alex. "The Girl Who Wouldn't Give Up." *Readers Digest*, May 1961, 140-48.

Page, James A. "Rudolph, Wilma Glodean." In *Black Olympian Medalists*. Englewood, Colo.: Libraries Unlimited, 1991.

Porter, David L., ed. "Rudolph, Wilma Glodean." In *Biographical Dictionary of American Sports: Outdoor Sports*. Westport, Conn.: Greenwood, 1988.

"Requiem for a Tigerbelle." Editorial. *Knoxville News-Sentinel*, 15 November 1994.

"Storming the Citadel." *Time*, 10 February 1961, 57.

Wallechinsky, David. *The Complete Book of the Olympics*. Boston: Little, Brown, 1992.

"Wilma's Home Town Win: Returning Negro Olympic Star Gets a Rousing—and Integrated—Welcome." *Life*, 17 October 1960.

Ryan, Father Abram

Creekmore, Betsey Beeler. *Knox County Tennessee: A History in Pictures*. Norfolk, Va.: Donning, 1988.

Mackin, Sister Aloysius, O.P. "Wartime Scenes from Convent Windows: St. Cecilia, 1860 through 1865." *Tennessee Historical Quarterly* 39, no. 4 (Winter 1980): 401-22.

Painter, F. V. N. "Abram J. Ryan." In *Poets of the South: A Series of Biographical and Critical Studies with Typical Poems, Annotated*, 103-20. 1903. Reprint, Freeport, N.Y.: Books for Libraries Press, 1968.

Ryman, Thomas Green

Davis, Louise Littleton. "Steamboatin' Tom Ryman." In *Frontier Tales of Tennessee*, 119-42. Gretna, La.: Pelican, 1976.

Douglas, Byrd. "Reconstruction and Slow Poisoning." In *Steamboatin' on the Cumberland*, 180-206. Nashville: Tennessee Book, 1961.

Hudson, Patricia L., and Sandra L. Ballard. "Nashville." In *The Smithsonian Guide to Historic America: The Carolinas and the Appalachian States*, 309-14. New York: Stewart, Tabori & Chang, 1989.

Ryman Auditorium. *The Ryman Chronology*. Typescript. Nashville: Author, 1995.

Saunders, Clarence

Chumney, James R. "The Pink Palace: Clarence Saunders and the Memphis Museum." *Tennessee Historical Quarterly* 32 (Spring 1973): 3-21.

Coppock, Paul R. "Grocery Magic." In *Memphis Sketches*, 204-8. Memphis: Friends of Memphis and Shelby County Libraries, 1976.

Lanier, Robert A. "Clarence Saunders." In *Memphis in the Twenties: The Second Term of Mayor Rowlett Paine, 1924-1928*, 88-91. Memphis: Zenda Press, 1979.

Weeks, Linton. "Clarence Saunders: River City Visionary." In *Memphis: A Folk History*, 175-79. Little Rock, Ark.: Parkhurst, 1982.

Scopes, John Thomas

Campbell, Carlos C. "Wanted: Money and Publicity." In *Birth of a National Park in the Great Smoky Mountains*. Rev. ed. with a preface by Horace Albright, 37-43. Knoxville: University of Tennessee Press, 1969.

de Camp, L. Sprague. *The Great Monkey Trial*. Garden City, N.Y.: Doubleday, 1968.

Ross, W. C. "Cary," Jr. "Bryan, Noted Orator/In Favor at Dayton: Commoner Wins Board of Education by Speech before Body." *Knoxville Journal*, 10 July 1925. Transcript of newspaper clipping courtesy of Helen Ross McNabb's personal files, Knoxville.

Scopes, John T., and James Presley. *Center of the Storm: Memoirs of John T. Scopes*. New York: Holt, Rinehart & Winston, 1967.

Settle, Mary Lee. *The Scopes Trial: The State of Tennessee v. John Thomas Scopes*. New York: Franklin Watts, 1972.

Seddon, Rhea

"From Surgery to Outer Space." *Southern Living*, June 1978, 102.

Klebenow, Anne. "Bringing Space Down to Earth." *Knoxville Journal*, 1 April 1982.

Seddon, Rhea. Biography courtesy of National Aeronautics and Space Administration, Office of Public Affairs, Public Services Division, Houston, Tex.

Sequoyah

Begun, Eunice. "Sequoyah." In *An Encyclopedia of East Tennessee*, edited by Jim Stokely and Jeff D. Johnson. Oak Ridge, Tenn.: Children's Museum of Oak Ridge, 1981.

Foreman, Grant. *Sequoyah*. Norman: University of Oklahoma Press, 1938.

Moore, John Trotwood, and Austin P. Foster, eds. "Sequoia." In *Tennessee: The Volunteer State, 1769-1923*, 2: 225. Nashville: S. J. Clarke, 1923.

Satz, Ronald N. *Tennessee's Indian Peoples: From White Contact to Removal, 1540-1840*. Knoxville: University of Tennessee Press, 1979.

Williams, Samuel C. "Nathaniel Gist, Father of Sequoyah." *The East Tennessee Historical Society's Publications*, no. 5 (January 1933): 39-54.

Sevier, John

Corlew, Robert E. "Social and Economic Life on the Frontier." In *Tennessee: A Short History*, 2nd ed., 106-25. Knoxville: University of Tennessee Press, 1981.

Davis, Louise Littleton. "Politics and Pistols on the Frontier." In *More Tales of Tennessee*, 71-78. Gretna, La.: Pelican, 1978.

Dixon, Max. *The Wataugans*. Johnson City: Overmountain Press, 1989.

Ewing, James. "Sevier vs. Jackson: Tennessee's Greatest Nonduel." In *A Treasury of Tennessee Tales*, 50-52. Nashville: Rutledge Hill, 1985.

Goodpasture, A. V. "Genesis of the Jackson-Sevier Feud." In *Tennessee Old and New: Sesquicentennial Edition, 1796-1946*, 167-75. Nashville: Tennessee Historical Commission and Tennessee Historical Society.

Moore, John Trotwood, and Austin P. Foster, eds. "The Period of Pioneer Life—The First Settlers in Tennessee" and "Henderson's Purchase and Events Leading Up to the Battle of King's Mountain." In *Tennessee: The Volunteer State, 1769-1923*, 1: 63-95. Nashville: S. J. Clarke, 1923.

Remini, Robert V. "Land Speculator and Congressman" and "Mr. Justice Jackson." In *Andrew Jackson and the Course of American Empire, 1767-1821*, 86-124. New York: Harper & Row, 1977.

Stephens, Hal C. (descendant of John Sevier), Knoxville, Tenn. Biographical information sent to Tennessee Folk History Project Archives, University of Tennessee, and telephone interview April 1996.

Walker, Nancy Wooten. "Catherine Sherill Sevier." In *Out of a Clear Blue Sky, Tennessee's First Ladies and Their Husbands*, 35-39. Cleveland, Tenn.: Author, 1971.

Shepherd, Lewis

Bible, Jean Patterson. "The Celebrated Melungeon Case." In *Melungeons: Yesterday and Today*, 61-66. Rogersville, Tenn.: Author, 1975.

Evans, Clement A., ed. "Additional Biographical Sketches: Lewis Shepherd." In *Confederate Military History*. Vol. 8, *Tennessee*, 706-7. Atlanta: Confederate Publishing Co., 1899.

Moore, John Trotwood, and Austin P. Foster, eds. "Lewis Shepherd." In *Tennessee: The Volunteer State 1769-1923*, 2: 176-79. Nashville: S. J. Clarke, 1923.

Shepherd, Judge Lewis. "Romantic Account of the Celebrated 'Melungeon' Case." Chattanooga Times. 31 December 1911.

Wilson, John. *Chattanooga's Story*. Chattanooga: Author, 1980, 31.

———. "Simmerman Land, Melungeon Bride Figured in 1870s Case." *Chattanooga News-Free Press*, January 3, 1993.

Worden, William L. "Sons of the Legend." *The Saturday Evening Post*, October 18, 1947.

Shofner, Austin

James, Rebecca. "Escape from the Philippines." *Tennessee Alumnus* 67, no. 3 (Summer 1987): 42-44.

Shofner, Austin Conner. Diary, 1941-1943, and biographical sketch. Microfilm accession number 344. Tennessee State Library and Archives, Nashville.

Smith, Bessie

Dictionary of American Biography. S.v. "Smith, Bessie" and "Rainey, Gertrude Malissa Nix Pridgett."

Kalin, Berkley. "Ladies Sing the Blues." In *Tennessee Women, Past and Present*, narrative by Wilma Dykeman and edited by Carol Lynn Yellin, 50-51. Memphis: Tennessee Committee for the Humanities and Tennessee International Women's Decade Coordinating Committee, 1977.

Moore, Carman. *Somebody's Angel Child: The Story of Bessie Smith*. Women of America Series, edited by Milton Meltzer. New York: Thomas Y. Crowell, 1969.

Oliver, Paul. *Kings of Jazz: Bessie Smith*. South Brunswick, N.Y.: A. S. Barnes, 1971.

Smith, Daniel

Burke, Pauline Wilcox. "The Widow Donelson" and "Uncle and Aunt Jackson." In *Emily Donelson of Tennessee*, 1: 15-28, 29-41. Richmond, Va.: Garrett & Massie, 1941.

Driver, Steve. "History of Sumner County." In *Sumner County Historic Homes*. Brochure. Gallatin, Tenn.: Sumner County Historical Society.

"Incidents By the Way: Rock Castle and A Rock Castle Romance." In *The Historic Blue Grass Line*, 66-68. Nashville: Nashville-Gallatin Inter-Urban Railway, 1913.

Moore, John Trotwood, and Austin P. Foster, eds. "Major A. J. Donelson." In *Tennessee: The Volunteer State 1769-1923*, 2: 112-13. Nashville: S. J. Clarke, 1923.

Smith, Frederick Wallace

Federal Express Corporation. Public Relations Student Information Packet. Material includes biography of Frederick Wallace Smith, the FedEx Book, and basic historical information on Federal Express. Memphis: Federal Express Corporation. N. d.

Sigafoos, Robert A., with Roger R. Easson. *Absolutely Positively Overnight! The Unofficial Corporate History of Federal Express*. Memphis: St. Lukes Press, 1988.

Spencer, Thomas Sharpe

Driver, Steve. "History of Sumner County." In *Sumner County Historic Homes*. Brochure. Gallatin, Tenn.: Sumner County Historical Society.

Durham, Walter T. "Thomas Sharp Spencer, Man or Legend." *Tennessee Historical Quarterly* 31, no. 3 (Fall 1972): 240-55.

———. "Wynnewood." Parts 1-2. *Tennessee Historical Quarterly* 33, no. 2 (Summer 1974): 127-56; no. 3 (Fall 1974): 297-321.

Holladay, Alvis M., Robert B. Holladay, and Wendell G. Holladay. "Spencer's Companion: Who Was He?" *Tennessee Historical Quarterly* 39, no. 3 (Fall 1980): 282-91.

Moore, John Trotwood, and Austin P. Foster, eds. "The Cumberland Settlement." In *Tennessee: The Volunteer State, 1769-1923*, 1: 102-17. Nashville: S. J. Clarke, 1923.

Stewart, Alex

Irwin, John Rice. *Alex Stewart, Portrait of a Pioneer*. West Chester, Pa.: Schiffer, 1985.

———. Telephone interview with author Anne Klebenow, Tennessee Folk History Project, regarding A. Stewart and his crafts displayed at the Museum of Appalachia, Norris, Tenn., December 1995.

Stokes, William B.

Civil War Centennial Commission of Tennessee. "Captain Champ Ferguson's Cavalry Company" and "5th Tennessee Cavalry Regiment, U.S.A." In *Tennesseans in the Civil War: A Military History of Confederate and Union Units with Available Rosters of Personnel*, part 1: 15-16, 329-33. Nashville: Author, 1964.

Darrah, Marsha Young. *Political Career of Col. William B. Stokes of Tennessee*. Masters thesis, Tennessee Technological University, Cookeville, Tenn., August 1968.

DeLozier, Mary Jean. "Civil War and Reconstruction." In *Putnam County Tennessee, 1850-1970*, 32-53. Nashville: McQuiddy Printing Co., 1979.

"Gen. W. B. Stokes Passes Away." *Nashville American*, 15 March 1897.

Hale, Will T., and Dixon L. Merritt. "Champe Ferguson" and "The Reconstruction Blunder." In *A History of Tennessee and Tennesseans*, 3: 650-55, 692-701. Chicago: Lewis, 1913.

U.S. Congress. "Stokes, William Brickly." In *Biographical Directory of the United State Congress, 1774-1989: Bicentennial Edition*. Washington, D.C.: U.S. Government Printing Office, 1989.

Stowers, Thomas

DeLozier, Mary Jean. *Putnam County, Tennessee, 1850-1970*. Nashville: McQuiddy Printing Co., 1979.

Patton, Mrs. Maurine E. (Upper Cumberland Genealogical Association; Cookeville, Tenn.). Material regarding Stowers family genealogy provided to Tennessee Folk History Project Archives, University of Tennessee.

Wells, Wayne. "Echoes from the Little Big Horn." *Tennessee Conservationist*, 54, no. 1 (January-February 1988): 17-19.

Stribling, T. S.

Eckley, Wilton. *T. S. Stribling*. Boston: Twayne, 1975.

Kunitz, Stanley J. and Howard Haycraft, eds. "Stribling, Thomas Sigismund." In *Twentieth Century Authors: A Biographical Dictionary of Modern Literature*. New York: W. H. Wilson, 1942.

Stribling, T. S. *Laughing Stock: The Posthumous Autobiography of T. S. Stribling*. Edited by Randy K. Cross and John T. McMillan. Memphis: St. Luke's Press, 1982.

Talley, Spencer

Knoxville Business Directory. "Druggists (Ret.): Worsham, W. J." In *Johnson's Business Directory and Mercantile Register*, 307. Washington, D.C.: Johnson, 1903.

McDonough, James Lee. "Cold Days in Hell: The Battle of Stones River, Tennessee." *Civil War Times Illustrated* 25, no. 4 (June 1986): 12-51.

———. "Rosecrans Moves South." In *Stones River—Bloody Winter in Tennessee*, 64-80. Knoxville: University of Tennessee Press, 1980.

Womack, Bob. "What a Scene of Confusion, of Bloodshed, of War." In *Call Forth The Mighty Men*, 193-219. Bessemer, Ala.: Colonial Press, 1987.

Worsham, W. J. *The Old Nineteenth Tennessee Regiment, C.S.A.: June, 1861-April, 1865*. Knoxville: Paragon Printing, 1902. Copy held by Special Collections, University of Tennessee Library, Knoxville.

Taylor, Robert Love/Alfred Alexander Taylor

Corlew, Robert E. "A Troubled Decade, 1886-1896." In *Tennessee: A Short History*. 2nd ed., 372-93. Knoxville: University of Tennessee Press, 1981.

Crowe, Dan, with Harold Lingerfelt. "Court Day." In *Old Town and the Covered Bridge*, 52-54. Johnson City, Tenn.: Milligan Press, 1977.

Govan, Gilbert E., and James W. Livingood. "Issues and Controversies." In *The Chattanooga Country, 1540-1962: From Tomahawks to TVA*, 393-414. Chapel Hill: University of North Carolina Press, 1963.

Moore, John Trotwood, and Austin P. Foster, eds. "From John C. Brown to Robert L. Taylor." In *Tennessee: The Volunteer State 1769-1923*, 1: 551-73. Nashville: S. J. Clarke, 1923.

Robison, Daniel M. "The Political Background of Tennessee's War of the Roses." *The East Tennessee Historical Society Publications*, no. 5 (January 1933): 125-41.

Sims, Lydel. "1886—The Run for the Roses." *Tennessee Illustrated* 1, no. 1 (May-June, 1988): 40.

Taylor, Robert Z.

Association of Southeastern State Park Directors, comp. "History of the Tennessee State Park System." In *History of Southeastern State Park Systems*. Updated for Association of Southeastern State Park Directors Golden Anniversary Conference, Tallahassee, Fla., 1992.

Bell, Ed. "Reelfoot Waters." WPA Project. Tennessee Stories. MS div., ac. no. 1776, VI-b-4, box 23 of 23. Tennessee State Library and Archives, Nashville.

Corlew, Robert E. "Democrats and Prohibition, 1899-1911." In *Tennessee: A Short History*. 2nd ed., 415-32. Knoxville: University of Tennessee Press, 1981.

Culp, Frederick M., and Mrs. Robert E. Ross. "Bench and Bar." In *Gibson County: Past and Present*, 253-80. Trenton, Tenn.: Gibson County Historical Society, 1961.

Vanderwood, Paul J. *The Night Riders of Reelfoot Lake*. Memphis: Memphis State University Press, 1969.

Tecumseh

Daniels, Jonathan. "Annus Mirabilis." In *The Devil's Backbone: The Story of the Natchez Trace*, 185-99. New York: McGraw-Hill, 1962.

Gilbert, Bil [*sic*]. *God Gave Us This Country: Tekamthi and the First American Civil War.* New York: Macmillan, 1989.

Merrill, James M. ". . . Take Cump. He's the brightest." In *William Tecumseh Sherman,* 15-29. Chicago: Rand McNally, 1971.

Tucker, Glenn. "The Trail across the South." In *Tecumseh: Vision of Glory,* 195-217. Indianapolis: Bobbs-Merrill, 1956.

U.S. National Park Service. *Natchez Trace Parkway.* Brochure. Washington, D.C.: U.S. Department of the Interior, n.d.

Thomas, Benjamin Franklin

Coca-Cola Co. "Facts, Figures, and Features: The Coca-Cola Company." Brochure. Atlanta: Author, 1992.

Munsey, Cecil. "Thomas, Whitehead, and Lupton: Founders of the Coca-Cola Bottling Industry." In *The Illustrated Guide to the Collectibles of Coca-Cola,* 20-24. New York: Hawthorne Books, 1972.

Turney, Peter

Civil War Centennial Commission of Tennessee. "1st Confederate Infantry Regiment." In *Tennesseans in the Civil War: A Military History of Confederate and Union Units with Available Rosters of Personnel,* part 1: 170-71. Nashville: Author, 1964.

Corlew, Robert E. "Storm Clouds." In *Tennessee: A Short History,* 2nd ed., 281-301. Knoxville: University of Tennessee Press, 1981.

Evans, Clement A. "Additional Biographical Sketches: Colonel Peter Turney." In *Confederate Military History.* Vol. 8, *Tennessee,* 762-64. Atlanta: Confederate Publishing Co., 1899.

Moore, John Trotwood, and Austin P. Foster, eds. "Peter Turney." In *Tennessee: The Volunteer State 1769-1923,* 2: 241. Nashville: S. J. Clarke, 1923.

Walker, Nancy Wooten. "Casandra Garner Turney, Hanna Ferguson Graham Turney." In *Out of a Clear Blue Sky: Tennessee's First Ladies and their Husbands,* 224-28. Cleveland, Tenn.: Author, 1971.

Tyson, Lawrence D.

Creekmore, Betsey Beeler. "Lawrence D. Tyson." In *Knoxville,* 148-63. Knoxville: University of Tennessee Press, 1958.

Essame, H. "The Breaking of the Hindenburg Line." In *The Battle for Europe, 1918,* 178-93. New York: Charles Scribner's Sons, 1972.

Featherston, Alwyn. "Old Hickory." In *Saving the Breakout: The 30th Division's Heroic Stand at Mortain, August 7-12, 1944,* 1-17. Novato, Calif.: Presidio Press, 1993.

Holt, Tonie, and Valmai Holt. *Battlefields of the First World War: A Traveller's Guide.* London: Pavilion Books, 1993.

"Lawrence D. Tyson (1861-1929)." *Context* (a publication of the University of Tennessee), 16 January 1992.

Moore, John Trotwood, and Austin P. Foster, eds. "General Lawrence Davis Tyson" and "Lieutenant Charles McGhee Tyson." In *Tennessee: The Volunteer State, 1769-1923,* 2: 90-98. Nashville: S. J. Clarke, 1923.

Van Dyke, Thomas Nixon

Byrum, C. Stephen. "The Civil War." In *McMinn County,* edited by Frank B. Williams Jr., 28-40. Tennessee County History Series. Memphis: Memphis State University Press, 1984.

Lillard, Roy G. *Bradley County.* Edited by Joy Bailey Dunn. Tennessee County History Series. Memphis: Memphis State University Press, 1980.

"Mrs. Fannie Van Dyke Ochs." *Confederate Veteran* 17 (1909): 158.

"Prisoners of War and State, Etc.: Correspondence, Etc.—Union and Confederate." In *War of the Rebellion: A Compilation of Official Records of the Union and Confederate Armies.* Series 2, 6: 890-91; 8: 196-97, 272-75. Washington, D.C.: U.S. Government Printing Office, 1899.

Speer, William S. "Hon. Thomas Nixon Van Dyke." In *Sketches of Prominent Tennesseans,* 559-62. Nashville: A. B. Tavel, 1888.

Van Dyke, Thomas Nixon. Biographical file including magazine and journal clippings, plus transcript of 1939 notes on the Van Dyke graveyard and Cedar Grove Cemetery, Athens, Tenn., written by George Magruder Battey III, Washington, D.C. Edward Gauche Fisher Public Library, Athens, Tenn.

Vaughan, A. J.

"Bivouac 18, A.C.S. and Camp 28, U.C.V.: Gen. Alfred J. Vaughan." *Confederate Veteran* 5, no. 11 (November 1897): 566-67.

Death notice, A. J. Vaughan. *Confederate Veteran* 7, no. 11 (November 1899): 514.

Faust, Patricia L., ed. "Vaughan, Alfred Jefferson, Jr." In *Historical Times Illustrated Encyclopedia of the Civil War.* New York: Harper & Row, 1986.

Moore, John Trotwood, and Austin P. Foster, eds. "Gen. A. J. Vaughn [*sic*]." In *Tennessee: The Volunteer State 1769-1923,* 2: 245. Nashville: S. J. Clarke, 1923.

Sifakis, Stewart. "Vaughan, Alfred Jefferson, Jr. (1830-1899)." In *Who Was Who in the Civil War.* New York: Facts on File, 1988.

Vaughan, A. J. *Personal Record of the Thirteenth Regiment, Tennessee Infantry.* Memphis, 1897.

Vowell, Jacob L.

Gray Carolyn. "1902—The Fraterville Mine Disaster." *Tennessee Illustrated* 2, no. 2 (March-April 1989): 40.

Irwin, John Rice. *Alex Stewart: Portrait of a Pioneer.* West Chester, Pa: Schiffer, 1985.

Rogers, David, comp. *Reflection in the Water: Coal Creek to Lake City; A History of Lake City, Tennessee 1976.* Clinton, Tenn.: *Clinton Courier News,* 1976.

"Saved by Dream," *The Knoxville Daily Journal and Tribune,* 10 December 1911.

Walker, Thomas Jefferson "T. J."

Walker, T. J. "Reminiscences of the Civil War." Edited by Russell B. Bailey. *Confederate Chronicles of Tennessee* 1 (June 1986): 37-74.

Walker, William

Bell, Ed. "William Walker." Tennessee Stories. WPA Stories. MS div., ac. no. 1776, vi-b-4, box 23 of 31. Tennessee State Library and Archives, Nashville.

Carr, Albert Z. "The Galahad Complex." In *The World and William Walker,* 3-14. New York: Harper & Row, 1963.

Gerson, Noel B. *Sad Swashbuckler: The Life of William Walker.* Nashville: Thomas Nelson, 1976.

Kiser, John W. "Scion of Belmont." *Tennessee Historical Quarterly* 38, no. 1 (Spring 1979): 34-61.

McPherson, James M. "An Empire for Slavery." In *Battle Cry of Freedom: The Civil War Era,* 78-116. New York: Oxford University Press, 1988.

Ward, Nancy (Nan-ye-hi)

Alderman, Pat. *Nancy Ward, Cherokee Chieftainess—Her Cry Was All for Peace—and Dragging Canoe, Cherokee-Chickamauga War Chief—We Are Not Yet Conquered.* Johnson City, Tenn.: Overmountain Press, 1990.

Camp, Henry R. *Sequatchie County.* Edited by Robert B. Jones. Tennessee County History Series. Memphis: Memphis State University Press, 1984.

Cornwell, Ilene J. "Nancy Ward." In *Heroes of Tennessee,* edited by Billy M. Jones, 32-45. Memphis: Memphis State University Press, 1979.

History of Tennessee, Illustrated. 1887, Goodspeed Publishing. Reprint, with new material by S. Emmett Lucas Jr., Easley, S.C.: Southern Historical Press, 1979.

Moore, John Trotwood, and Austin P. Foster, eds. "William Been" [sic] and "Nancy Ward." In *Tennessee: The Volunteer State, 1769-1923,* 2: 35, 246-47. Nashville: S. J. Clarke, 1923.

Raulston, J. Leonard, and James W. Livingood. "New Fences and Old Faith" and "Appendix: Early Sequatchie Families—The Stewart Family." In *Sequatchie: A Story of the Southern Cumberlands,* 161-62, 253-54. Knoxville: University of Tennessee Press, 1974.

Watkins, Sam R.

"Samuel Rush Watkins." *Confederate Veteran* 9 (1901): 419.

Watkins, Sam R. *"Co. Aytch," Maury Grays, First Tennessee Regiment; Or, a Side Show of the Big Show.* 1882. Reprint with introduction by Bell Irvin Wiley, Wilmington, N.C.: Broadfoot, 1987.

Watterson, Henry

Beard, William E. "Feat of an Old Nashville Newspaper." In *Nashville: The Home of History Makers,* 80-82. Nashville: Civitan Club, 1929.

Marcosson, Isaac F. *"Marse Henry:" A Biography of Henry Watterson.* New York: Dodd, Mead, 1951.

Wall, Joseph Frazier. *Henry Watterson: Reconstructed Rebel.* New York: Oxford University Press, 1956.

———. "Watterson, Henry." In *The Kentucky Encyclopedia,* edited by John E. Kleber. Lexington: University Press of Kentucky, 1992.

Webb, William R. "Sawney"

Holliman, Glenn N. "The Webb School Junior Room, The Symbol of a School." *Tennessee Historical Quarterly* 36, no. 3 (Fall 1977): 287-304.

Lewis, Charles Lee. *Philander Priestley Claxton: Crusader for Public Education.* Knoxville: University of Tennessee Press, 1948.

Stokes, Walter, Jr. "'The Schoolmaker: Sawney Webb and the Bell Buckle Story', An Essay Review." *Tennessee Historical Quarterly* 30, no. 4 (Winter 1971): 419-22.

Wells, Ida B.

Page, James A., comp. "Wells (Barnett), Ida Bell." In *Selected Black American Authors: An Illustrated Bio-Bibliography.* Boston: G. K. Hall, 1977.

Pink Palace Museum. "Ida B. Wells, 1862-1931." In *Historic Black Memphians.* Exhibit material. Memphis: Author.

Sterling, Dorothy. *Black Foremothers: Three Lives.* Old Westbury, N.Y.: Feminist Press, 1979.

Wells, Ida B. *Crusade for Justice: The Autobiography of Ida B. Wells.* Edited by Alfreda M. Duster. Negro American Biographies and Autobiographies, ed. John Hope Franklin. Chicago: University of Chicago Press, 1970.

Wharton, May Cravath

Dougherty, John H., Sr. "May Cravath Wharton." In *An Encyclopedia of East Tennessee,* edited by Jim Stokely and Jeff D. Johnson. Oak Ridge, Tenn.: Children's Museum of Oak Ridge, 1981.

Tretter, Evelyn Kerr. "Doctor Woman." *The Tennessee Conservationist,* December 1988, 18-22.

Wharton, May Cravath. *Doctor Woman of the Cumberlands: The Autobiography of May Cravath Wharton, M. D.* Pleasant Hill, Tenn.: Uplands, 1953.

White, "Granny"

Loyd, A. Dennis. "The Legend of Granny White." *Tennessee Historical Quarterly* 27, no. 3 (Fall 1968): 257-61.

Smith, Jonathan K. T. "Political Heritage." In *Benton County,* edited by Joy Bailey Dunn, 27-47. Tennessee County History Series. Memphis: Memphis State University Press, 1979.

Towe, Emily. "A Pioneer in Family Rehabilitation." *The Sunday Tennessean Magazine (Nashville Tennessean),* 25 July 1937.

Walker, Hugh. "Granny White Pike." In *Tennessee Tales,* 131-38. Nashville: Aurora, 1970.

White, Lucinda (Granny). Biographical file. The Nashville Room, Ben West Library of the Nashville-Davidson County Public Library.

———. Last Will and Testament of Lucinda "Granny" White. Edited by Herschel G. Payne. Transcribed 6 December 1978 for the Nashville Room, Public Library of Nashville and Davidson County.

White, Hugh Lawson

Byas, Stephen D. "James Standifer, Sequatchie Valley Congressman." *Tennessee Historical Quarterly* 50, no. 2 (Summer 1991): 90-97.

Moore, John Trotwood, and Austin P. Foster, eds. "Territory of the United States South of the River Ohio," "Hugh Lawson White," and "Gen. James White." In *Tennessee: The Volunteer State 1769-1923*, 1: 144-56; 2: 248, 254-58. Nashville: S. J. Clarke, 1923.

Scott, Nancy N. *A Memoir of Hugh Lawson White*. Philadelphia, Pa.: J.B. Lippincot, 1856.

Whiteside, Harriet Leonora Straw

Gaston, Kay Barker. "The Remarkable Harriet Whiteside." *Tennessee Historical Quarterly* 40, no. 4 (Winter 1981): 333-47.

Govan, Gilbert E., and James W. Livingood. "New Hope." In *The Chattanooga Country 1540-1976: From Tomahawks to TVA*, 365-93. Knoxville: University of Tennessee Press, 1977.

Hale, Will T., and Dixon L. Merritt. "James Anderson Whiteside" and "Harriet Leonora Whiteside." In *A History of Tennessee and Tennesseans: The Leaders and Representative Men in Commerce, Industry and Modern Activities*, 6: 1739-49. Chicago: Lewis, 1913.

"Harriet Leonora Whiteside." *Confederate Veteran* 2, no. 3 (March 1903): 129-30.

"The Poisoning Sensation." *Chattanooga Times*, 25 January 1890.

Walker, Robert Sparks. *Lookout: The Story of a Mountain*. Kingsport, Tenn.: Southern Publishers, 1941, 194-200.

Wilson, John. "The Siege" and "Going through the Ruins." In *Chattanooga's Story*, 97-104, 115-29. Chattanooga: Author, 1980.

Wilder, John T.

Bledsoe, Wayne. "Roan Mountain Magic." *Knoxville News-Sentinel*. 18 June 1991.

Dictionary of American Biography. S.v. "Wilder, John Thomas."

Gouge, Jeeter. Tape-recorded interview about Roan Mountain experiences and the Cloudland Hotel, conducted in 1981 by the Tennessee State Parks Folk Life Project for the Department of Conservation. Tape 81-RM-1. Tennessee State Library and Archives, Nashville.

Kozsuch, Mildred, ed. *Historical Reminiscences of Carter County, Tennessee*. Johnson City, Tenn.: Overmountain Press, 1985.

Sifakis, Stewart. "Wilder, John Thomas." In *Who Was Who in the Civil War*. New York: Facts on File, 1988.

Williams, Samuel C. *General John T. Wilder: Commander of the Lightning Brigade*. Bloomington: Indiana University Press, 1936.

Wilson, Jennifer Bauer. *Roan Mountain: A Passage of Time*. Winston-Salem, N.C.: John F. Blair, 1991.

Williams, "Aunt Polly"

Brown, Joy Gailbreath (descendant of "Aunt Polly" Williams), of Gainesboro, Tenn. Newspaper clippings and biographical information sent to Tennessee Folk History Department Archives, University of Tennessee.

Douglas, Byrd. "Friction Dims the Golden Nineties: Period 1890-1900." In *Steamboatin' on the Cumberland*, 227-46. Nashville: Tennessee Book, 1961.

Knight, George Allen. "Illustrious Upper Cumberland Men." In *Our Wonderful Overton County Heritage*, 135-46. Knoxville: Southeastern Composition Services, 1975.

Young, Kim. "Family Record: Aunt Polly Was a Colorful Character" and "A Legend in Time." In *History of Jackson County*, 1: 77-86. Gainesboro, Tenn.: Author, n.d.

Wilson, Kemmons

Grant, James. "Rapid Rise of the Host with the Most." *Time*, 12 June 1972, 77-82.

Harkins, John E. *Metropolis of the American Nile: An Illustrated History of Memphis and Shelby County*. Edited by Charles W. Crawford. Woodland Hills, Calif.: Windsor, 1982.

Holiday Inn Worldwide. "Holiday Inn Worldwide—A Bass Company." Press release and biographical information on Kemmons Wilson. Atlanta: Holiday Inn Corp., 1995.

Winchester, Marcus Brutus

Capers, Gerald M., Jr. *The Biography of a River Town, Memphis: Its Heroic Age*. Chapel Hill: University of North Carolina Press, 1939.

Coke, Fletch, ed. *Dear Judge: Selected Letters of John Overton of Travelers' Rest*. Nashville: Travelers' Rest Historic Museum House, 1978.

Corlew, Robert E. "The Young State, 1796-1821." In *Tennessee: A Short History*. 2nd ed., 126-44. Knoxville: University of Tennessee Press, 1981.

Durham, Walter T. *James Winchester: Tennessee Pioneer*. Nashville: Parthenon Press, 1979.

Eckhardt, Celia Morris. "Nashoba and New Harmony." In *Fanny Wright: Rebel in America*, 108-40. Cambridge, Mass.: Harvard University Press, 1984.

Harkins, John E. *Metropolis of the American Nile: An Illustrated History of Memphis and Shelby County*. Edited by Charles W. Crawford. Woodland Hills, Calif.: Windsor, 1982.

McIlwaine, Shields. "The Major and Uncle Ike Build a River Town." In *Memphis: Down in Dixie*, 52-83. New York: E. P. Dutton, 1948.

Roper, James. *The Founding of Memphis, 1818-1820*. Memphis: Memphis Sesquicentennial, 1970.

Weeks, Linton. "The Tragedy of Marcus Brutus Winchester." In *Memphis: A Folk History*, 24-34. Little Rock, Ark.: Parkhurst, 1982.

Wright, Frances "Fanny"

Capers, Gerald M., Jr. *The Biography of a River Town, Memphis: Its Heroic Age.* Chapel Hill: University of North Carolina Press, 1939.

Coppock, Paul R. "Nashoba Utopia." In *Memphis Sketches*, 217-20. Memphis: Friends of Memphis and Shelby County Libraries, 1976.

Egerton, John. *Visions of Utopia: Nashoba, Rugby, Ruskin, and the "New Communities" in Tennessee's Past.* Knoxville: University of Tennessee Press, 1977.

Harkins, John E. *Metropolis of the American Nile: An Illustrated History of Memphis and Shelby County.* Edited by Charles W. Crawford. Woodland Hills, Calif.: Windsor, 1982.

Wells, Ann Harwell. "Lafayette in Nashville, 1825." *Tennessee Historical Quarterly* 34, no. 1 (Spring 1975): 19-31.

Williams, Samuel Cole. "The Nashoba Experiment." In *Beginnings of West Tennessee: In the Land of the Chickasaws, 1541-1841*, 239-43. Johnson City, Tenn.: Watauga Press, 1930.

York, Alvin

Brown, Fred. "The Home of the Hero; Questions Grow at Sgt. York Site: Funding? Ownership? Direction?" *Knoxville News-Sentinel*, 12 January 1992.

Cowan, Sam K. *Sergeant York and His People.* New York: Grossett & Dunlap, 1922.

Lee, David D. *Sergeant York: An American Hero.* Lexington: University Press of Kentucky, 1985.

McRaven, William Henry. "Alvin Cullom York: World War One Hero." In "Tennessee Prodigies." 1966. Unpublished papers, MS div., ac. no. 67-30. Tennessee State Library and Archives, Nashville.

Illustration Credits

Acuff, Roy. (Photograph courtesy of the Country Music Foundation)

Bell, John. (From M. V. Ingram, *An Authenticated History of the Famous Bell Witch,* 1894; courtesy of the Special Collections Library of the University of Tennessee, Knoxville)

Blount, William. (Tennessee Historical Society Collection, Tennessee State Museum)

Brantley, James/Albert Dement. (Courtesy of Charles E. Brantley, Wartrace, Tennessee)

Brown, Clarence. (Special Collections Library of the University of Tennessee, Knoxville; courtesy of the University of Tennessee Photography Center)

Brown, Joseph. (From *Harper's New Monthly Magazine,* April 1887.

Brownlow, William G. "Parson." (Painting by George Dury; courtesy of Tennessee State Museum Collection)

Campbell, Francis Joseph. (Tennessee School for the Blind; copy photography by June Dorman, Tennessee State Museum)

Carmack, Edward W. (From *Harper's Weekly,* June 29, 1907; courtesy of the Special Collections Library of the University of Tennessee, Knoxville)

Cheairs, Nathaniel. (Tennessee State Library and Archives)

Cheatham, Benjamin Franklin. (James A. Hoobler Collection, Tennessee Historical Society Collection, Tennessee State Library and Archives)

Crockett, David. (Charcoal sketch, artist unknown, circa 1835; courtesy of the Special Collections Library of the University of Tennessee, Knoxville)

Crump, Edward Hull "Boss." (Courtesy of the Tennessee State Museum; copy photography by June Dorman, Tennessee State Museum)

Daniel, Jack. (Courtesy of Jack Daniel Distillery, Lynchburg, Tennessee)

Davis, Sam. (Courtesy of Mike Miner, Sevierville, Tennessee)

Farragut, David Glasgow. (W. E. Beard Papers, Tennessee Historical Society, Tennessee State Library and Archives)

Forrest, Nathan Bedford. (Tennessee State Library and Archives)

Fort, Cornelia. (Courtesy of the Tennessee State Museum)

Frankland, R. Ernest. (Courtesy of Robert E. Frankland III, Jackson, Tennessee)

French, Lucy Virginia. (Tennessee State Library and Archives)

Gloster, Mary Hayes. (From the estate files of Ellen Davies-Rodgers, Brunswick, Tennessee; courtesy of Memphis/Shelby County Archives, Memphis/Shelby County Public Library and Information Center)

Gore, Al. (Courtesy of the White House)

Handy, W. C. (Courtesy of the Tennessee State Museum)

Houston, Sam. (Tennessee Historical Society Collection, Tennessee State Museum)

Hull, Cordell. (Courtesy of the Friends of Cordell Hull; copy photography by June Dorman, Tennessee State Museum)

Jackson, Andrew. (*General Andrew Jackson: The Hero, the Sage and the Patriot*, by N. Currier, New York, 1845; courtesy of the Special Collections Library of the University of Tennessee, Knoxville)

Johnson, Andrew. (Photogravure by Mathew Brady, circa 1876; courtesy of the Special Collections Library of the University of Tennessee, Knoxville)

King, George. (Courtesy of the Fred M. Culp Collection, Trenton, Tennessee)

Maury, Matthew Fontaine. (Tennessee Historical Society Collection, Tennessee State Library and Archives)

McConnico, Garner. (Big Harpeth Primitive Baptist Church and Williamson County Historical Society; courtesy of the Canaday Files, Franklin, Tennessee)

Meriwether, Elizabeth Avery. (Tennessee Historical Commission; courtesy of Memphis/Shelby County Archives, Memphis/Shelby County Public Library and Information Center)

Moore, Ella Sheppard. (Painting by Edmund Havel, 1873; courtesy of Fisk University Library Special Collections)

Morgan, John Hunt. (Courtesy of the Tennessee State Museum)

Pearl, Minnie (Sarah Ophelia Colley Cannon). (Photograph courtesy of the Country Music Foundation)

Pickens, Lucy Holcombe. (By permission of Gretta Greer Davis and Cherry Greer Little, Canton, Texas)

Polk, James K. (Tennessee Historical Society Collection, Tennessee State Library and Archives)

Presley, Elvis. (Elvis, Elvis Presley, and Graceland are registered trademarks of Elvis Presley Enterprises, Inc. All rights reserved. Image of Elvis used by permission)

Quinn, Father D. A. (Courtesy of the Diocese of Providence, Rhode Island)

Rice, Grantland. (Photographic Archives of Vanderbilt University)

Robertson, Sterling C. (Painting by William Henry Huddle; courtesy of the State Preservation Board, Austin, Texas)

Ross, Chief John. (From Thomas L. McKenney and James Hall, *The Indian Tribes of North America,* vol. 1, 1836; courtesy of the Museum of the Cherokee Indian, Cherokee, North Carolina)

Ryan, Father Abram. (McClung Historical Collection)

Scopes, John Thomas. Photograph by Underwood & Underwood, Chicago, 1925; *Looking Back at Tennessee, Photograph Collection,* Tennessee State Library and Archives

Seddon, Rhea. (Courtesy of the National Aeronautics and Space Administration)

Sequoyah. (From Thomas L. McKenney and James Hall, *The Indian Tribes of North America,* vol. 1, 1836; courtesy of the Museum of the Cherokee Indian, Cherokee, North Carolina)

Sevier, John. (Tennessee Historical Society Collection, Tennessee State Museum)

Spencer, Thomas Sharpe. (From Gentry R. McGee, *A History of Tennessee, From 1663 to 1930,* 1930; courtesy of the Special Collections Library of the University of Tennessee, Knoxville)

Stewart, Alex. (Photograph by Robin Hood, courtesy of John Rice Irwin, Museum of Appalachia, Norris, Tennessee)

Taylor, Robert Love/Alfred Alexander Taylor. (James A. Hoobler Collection, Tennessee Historical Society, Tennessee State Library and Archives)

Vaughan, A. J. (From *Confederate Military History,* vol. 8, 1899)

Walker, William. (From William Walker, *The War in Nicaragua,* 1860; courtesy of the Special Collections Library of the University of Tennessee, Knoxville)

Ward, Nancy (Nan-ye-hi). (Painting by Ben Hampton, 1976, Hampton House Studio, Chattanooga; courtesy of Tennessee Historical Society, Tennessee State Library and Archives)

Watkins, Sam R. (Courtesy of Franklin Fulton, grandson of Sam R. Watkins, Columbia, Tennessee)

Watterson, Henry. (*The Courier-Journal,* Louisville, Kentucky)

Webb, William R. "Sawney." (Courtesy of Robert Webb, Knoxville, and Webb School, Bell Buckle, Tennessee)

Wells, Ida B. (Tennessee State Library and Archives)

Wharton, May Cravath. (Courtesy of Uplands Retirement Village, Pleasant Hill, Tennessee)

Williams, "Aunt Polly." (Courtesy of Joy Gailbreath Brown, Gainesboro, Tennessee)

York, Alvin. (Courtesy of the Tennessee State Museum)

Index of People
and Tennessee Towns and Counties

(Boldface entries refer to a story's title and its page numbers)